JOURNAL FOR THE STUDY OF THE NEW TESTAMENT SUPPLEMENT SERIES
196

Executive Editor
Stanley E. Porter

STUDIES IN NEW TESTAMENT GREEK
7

Sheffield Academic Press

Text in a Whirlwind

A Critique of Four Exegetical Devices at 1 Timothy 2.9-15

J.M. Holmes

Journal for the Study of the New Testament
Supplement Series 196

Studies in New Testament Greek 7

May the words of my mouth
and the meditation of my heart
be pleasing in your sight,
O LORD, my Rock and my Redeemer.
Ps. 19.14, NIV

Copyright © 2000 Sheffield Academic Press

Published by
Sheffield Academic Press Ltd
Mansion House
19 Kingfield Road
Sheffield S11 9AS
England

Typeset by Sheffield Academic Press
and
Printed on acid-free paper in Great Britain
by Biddles Ltd
Guildford, Surrey

British Library Cataloguing in Publication Data

A catalogue record for this book is available
from the British Library

ISBN 1-84127-121-7

CONTENTS

Part III
1 CORINTHIANS 14.34-35: A PARALLEL?

Part IV
THE ROLE OF γάρ AT 1 TIMOTHY 2.13-15

This study was formerly a PhD thesis entitled '1 Timothy 2.9-15: A Reexamination of Four Exegetical Devices' submitted at La Trobe University in March 1995. Its publication has been delayed due to an extended illness in my immediate family. The research had its genesis in the painfully slow realization that my understanding of 1 Tim. 2.9-15 was more the result of supposition than of what the Greek text and context actually specify. As I explored the literature I gained many useful insights, but I also discovered that, generally speaking, the syntactical peculiarities and semantic ambiguities of the passage are not so much explained as explained *away*. That is to say that they are interpreted by some combination of: other problematic passages (themselves often interpreted by 1 Tim. 2.9-15, i.e. Genesis 2–3; Gal. 2.28; 1 Cor. 11.3-16; 14.34-35); not always convincing historical backgrounds; speculation; and unsubstantiated assertion. No interpretation I was able to find struck me as altogether compelling. Questions therefore arose. What if the difficulties of this passage were not moulded to fit what seems to be required, but were permitted to obstruct that supposition? What if one such difficulty were not eliminated before consideration of the next, allowing them to accumulate? Would some more satisfying reading emerge?

As I researched these ideas, I was assisted in many ways. I am pleased here to thank La Trobe University for my postgraduate scholarship, the cheerful staff of Inter-Library Loans in the Borchardt Library at La Trobe, and L. McIntosh and the staff at the Joint Theological Library, Ormond College, Melbourne University. I am also thankful to D. Sim, J. Painter, M. Harding, M. Lattke, S. Porter, R. Oster and D. Lee for criticisms; L. Dean-Jones, S. Dixon, C. Forbes and K. McKay for use of materials that have only since been published; C. Bloomfield and P. Rule for translation of some Latin passages; A. Murkies for some medical sources; H. Mees for solving some problems in German sources and, for this publication version, so generously translating at very short notice all the German passages; A. Vincent for computer assistance and for obtaining several additional works required for this publication version; A. Holmes for countless hours of discussion, assistance with proof-reading, and much, much else; and S. Porter and the staff at Sheffield Academic Press, particularly J. Willson, for their help and patience.

I especially thank my former supervisors, Dr A.E. Gardner and Professor G.H.R. Horsley, without whom the thesis would probably not have begun and would certainly have been far poorer. Anne from the beginning appreciated and facilitated what I was attempting to do, and to the end fought battles on my behalf. Greg constantly challenged me with his probing criticisms and eagle eye for detail, and eased the way by employing me from time to time. During the revision process Greg arranged a grant from the Greek Book Fund (Australia), and Anne provided the employment which has enabled access to sources and suitable computers. Each has remained throughout patiently and consistently available to help. Above all, the arguments which follow, although my own, owe whatever clarity they have to Anne and Greg. All remaining errors are mine.

I am particularly indebted to certain authors in my bibliography. Anyone with even a passing knowledge of the literature on 1 Tim. 2.9-15 will be aware that overall it is of an uneven standard. A closer examination reveals that at one end of a very broad spectrum some of the most profound or influential scholars themselves employ some weak arguments and, at the other end, some of those whose arguments are generally unconvincing make certain astute or influential observations. The 'liberal–conservative' division over the authorship of the Pastoral Epistles is a further complication—both sides being spread right across the spectrum. *It is a premise of this study that, with respect to this particular difficult passage, neither side in the authorship debate has the monopoly on excellence.* Regardless of their authorship preferences, during my research the generally careful work of some, right through to the clear, specific perceptions of some others, has earned my respect. Where I have disagreed with these it has often been because they enabled and stimulated further exploration.

During the revision process I have been privileged, within the categories of my already developed argument, to make use of additional literature. The thesis and its four conclusions here remain unchanged, but details have occasionally been simplified or modified. Confronted by the never-ending literature appearing on this passage, decisions about the nature and extent of inclusion of works that reached me late in the revision process have been finally settled by the need to draw a line after which substantial alteration became unrealistic. I regret that, due to the above-mentioned illness, Ulrike Wagener's detailed study *Die Ordnung des 'Hauses Gottes'* (Tübingen: J.C.B. Mohr [Paul Siebeck], 1994) came to hand too late for inclusion.

Most importantly, I gratefully acknowledge that, throughout this very long task, all three generations of my family have been wonderfully patient, understanding and helpful.

ABBREVIATIONS

A	Codex Alexandrinus
AB	Anchor Bible
AJP	*American Journal of Philology*
APOT	R.H. Charles (ed.), *Apocrypha and Pseudepigrapha of the Old Testament in English* (2 vols.; Oxford: Clarendon Press, 1913)
ATR	*Anglican Theological Review*
AusBR	*Australian Biblical Review*
AV	Authorised Version
B	Codex Vaticanus
BA	*Biblical Archaelogist*
B/A⁶	K. Aland and B. Aland (eds.), *Griechisch-Deutsches Wörterbuch zu den Schriften des Neuen Testaments und der frühchristlichen Literatur* (Berlin: de Gruyter, 6th edn, 1988)
BAGD	Walter Bauer, William F. Arndt, F. William Gingrich and Frederick W. Danker, *A Greek–English Lexicon of the New Testament and Other Early Christian Literature* (Chicago; University of Chicago Press, 2nd edn, 1958)
BARev	*Biblical Archaeology Review*
BDF	Friedrich Blass, A. Debrunner and Robert W. Funk, *A Greek Grammar of the New Testament and Other Early Christian Literature* (Cambridge: Cambridge University Press, 1961)
BGU	Staatliche Museen zu Berlin, *Aegyptische Urkunden aus den Königlichen Museen zu Berlin: Griechische Urkunden* (Berlin: Weidmannsche Buchhandlung, 1895–)
Bib.Pat.	*Biblia Patristica, Index des citations et allusions bibliques dans la littérature patristique* (5 vols.; Paris: Edit. du Centre National de la Recherche Scientifique, 1975–91)
BJRL	*Bulletin of the John Rylands University Library of Manchester*
BSac	*Bibliotheca Sacra*
BTB	*Biblical Theology Bulletin*
CBQ	*Catholic Biblical Quarterly*
CBQMS	*Catholic Biblical Quarterly*, Monograph Series
CChr	Corpus Christianorum, Series Latina (Brepols: Turnhout)
CH	*Church History*
CPR	*Corpus papyrorum Raineri archeducis Austriae* (Vienna: Verlag der Kaiserl. Konigl. Hof- und Staatsdruckerei, 1895–)

EncJud	*Encyclopaedia Judaica*
ETSJ	*Evangelical Theology Society (US) Journal*
EvQ	*Evangelical Quarterly*
ExpTim	*Expository Times*
FN	*Filología neotestamentaria*
GCS	Griechische christliche Schriftsteller
GTJ	*Grace Theological Journal*
HBT	*Horizons in Biblical Theology*
HR	*History of Religions*
HTR	*Harvard Theological Review*
HUCA	*Hebrew Union College Annual*
IBD	J.D. Douglas (ed.), *The Illustrated Bible Dictionary* (3 vols; Lane Cove, NSW: Hodder & Stoughton)
IBM	E.L. Hicks *et al.* (eds.), *Ancient Greek Inscriptions in the British Museum* (6 vols. in 4; Oxford: Oxford University Press, 1874–1916)
ICC	International Critical Commentary
IDB	George Arthur Buttrick (ed.), *The Interpreter's Dictionary of the Bible* (4 vols.; Nashville: Abingdon Press, 1962)
ILCV	E. Diel (ed.), *Inscriptiones latinae Christianae veteres* (4 vols.; Berlin: Berolini, apud Weidmannos, 1925–67)
JAAR	*Journal of the American Academy of Religion*
JB	*Jerusalem Bible*
JBL	*Journal of Biblical Literature*
JETS	*Journal of the Evangelical Theological Society*
JJS	*Journal of Jewish Studies*
JRH	*Journal of Religious History*
JRS	*Journal of Roman Studies*
JSJ	*Journal for the Study of Judaism in the Persian, Hellenistic and Roman Period*
JSNT	*Journal for the Study of the New Testament*
JSNTSup	*Journal for the Study of the New Testament*, Supplement Series
JSOTSup	*Journal for the Study of the Old Testament*, Supplement Series
JSPSup	*Journal for the Study of the Pseudepigrapha*, Supplement Series
JTS	*Journal of Theological Studies*
LCL	Loeb Classical Library
LPGL	G.W.H. Lampe, *A Patristic Greek Lexicon* (Oxford: Clarendon Press, 1961)
LSAM	F. Sokolowski (ed.), *Lois sacrées de l'Asie Mineure* (Paris: Ecole française d'Athènes, 1955)
LSCG	F. Sokolowski (ed.), *Lois sacrées des cités grecques* (Paris: Ecole française d'Athènes, 1962)

LSCGS	F. Sokolowski (ed.), *Lois sacrées des cités grecques.* *Supplément* (Paris: Ecole française d'Athènes, 1962)
LSJ	H.G. Liddell, Robert Scott and H. Stuart Jones, *Greek–English Lexicon* (Oxford: Clarendon Press, 9th edn, 1968)
LXX	*Septuaginta*, A. Rahlfs (ed.) (Stuttgart: Deutsche Bibelgesellschaft, 1979)
MAMA	B. Levick and S. Mitchell (eds.), *Monumenta Asiae Minoris Antiqua* 10 (*JRS* Monograph Series, 7; London: Society for the Promotion of Roman Studies, 1993)
MGM	W.F. Moulton, and A.S. Geden, *Concordance to the Greek Testament* (rev. H.K. Moulton; Edinburgh: T. & T. Clark, 5th edn, 1986)
MM	J.H. Moulton and G. Milligan, *The Vocabulary of the Greek Testament, Illustrated from the Papyri and Other Non-literary Sources* (Grand Rapids: Eerdmans, 1985)
N/A[27]	B. Aland, K. Aland, J. Karavidopoulos, C. Martini and B. Metzger (eds.), *Novum Testamentum Graece* (Stuttgart: Deutsche Bibelgesellshaft, 27th edn, 1993)
NASB	*New American Standard Bible*
NEB	*New English Bible*
Neot	*Neotestamentica*
NICNT	New International Commentary on the New Testament
NIDNTT	Colin Brown (ed.), *The New International Dictionary of New Testament Theology*, (3 vols.; Exeter: Paternoster Press, 1975)
NIV	New International Version
NovT	*Novum Testamentum*
NTS	*New Testament Studies*
OCD	*Oxford Classical Dictionary*
OLD	P.G.W. Glare (ed.), *Oxford Latin Dictionary*, I (Oxford: Clarendon Press, 1968)
OTP	James Charlesworth (ed.), *Old Testament Pseudepigrapha*
PG	J.-P. Migne (ed.), *Patrologia cursus completa...Series graeca* (166 vols.; Paris: Petit-Montrouge, 1857–83)
Phillips	Phillips Modern English Version
RB	*Revue biblique*
ResQ	*Restoration Quarterly*
RevExp	*Review and Expositor*
RevQ	*Revue de Qumran*
RSV	Revised Standard Version
RTR	*Reformed Theological Review*
RV	Revised Version
S	Codex Sinaiticus
SBL	Society of Biblical Literature
SBLDS	SBL Dissertation Series
SBLMS	SBL Monograph Series

SBLSP	SBL Seminar Papers
SC	Sources chrétiennes (Paris)
SEG	*Supplementum epigraphicum graecum* (Leiden: E.J. Brill; vols. 26–39, Alphen aan den Rijn: Sijthoff & Noordhoff; Amsterdam: Gieben)
SIG[3]	W. Dittenberger (ed.), *Sylloge inscriptionum Graecarum* (4 vols.; Leipzig: Teubner, 3rd edn, 1915–24)
SJT	*Scottish Journal of Theology*
SNTSMS	Society for New Testament Studies Monograph Series
ST	*Studia theologica*
Str–B	[Hermann L. Strack and] Paul Billerbeck, *Kommentar zum Neuen Testament aus Talmud und Midrasch* (7 vols.; Munich: Beck, 1922–61)
SVTP	Studia in Veteris Testamenti pseudepigrapha
TAPA	*Transactions of the American Philological Association*
TDNT	Gerhard Kittel and Gerhard Friedrich (eds.), *Theological Dictionary of the New Testament* (trans. Geoffrey W. Bromiley; 10 vols.; Grand Rapids: Eerdmans, 1964–)
TDOT	G.J. Botterweck and H. Ringgren (eds.), *Theological Dictionary of the Old Testament* (Grand Rapids: Eerdmans, 1979)
TEV	Today's English Version
TNTC	Tyndale New Testament Commentaries
TOTC	Tyndale Old Testament Commentaries
TrinJ	*Trinity Journal*
TS	*Theological Studies*
TSF Bulletin	*Theological Students' Fellowship Bulletin*
TTod	*Theology Today*
TWOT	R. Laird Harris, Gleason L. Archer, Jr and Bruce K. Waltke (eds.), *Theological Wordbook of the Old Testament* (2 vols.; Chicago: Moody Press, 1980)
TynBul	*Tyndale Bulletin*
UBSGNT	United Bible Societies' *Greek New Testament* (4th revised edn)
WTJ	*Westminster Theological Journal*
WUNT	Wissenschaftliche Untersuchungen zum Neuen Testament
ZPE	*Zeitschrift für Papyrologie und Epigraphik*

INTRODUCTION

Featuring prominently in any comprehensive consideration of the roles of women in the New Testament and in Christianity from the early patristic period until the present day is 1 Tim. 2.12:

> διδάσκειν δὲ γυναικὶ οὐκ ἐπιτρέπω οὐδὲ αὐθεντεῖν ἀνδρός, ἀλλ᾽ εἶναι ἐν ἡσυχίᾳ.
> I do not permit a woman to teach or to have authority over a man; she must be silent (NIV).

Historically this verse has constituted a major obstacle to egalitarian ecclesial practice based on the New Testament. It is frequently claimed today, however, that it affords no such obstacle. The passage is highly controversial, consensus existing about just one thing: women are here forbidden some kind of teaching role in the church. But is the 'teaching' of any kind at all, or only of a particular kind? If the latter, which? Is ecclesial authority-taking over men also forbidden, or only a particular type of authority, or is a woman in fact forbidden only a particular kind of authoritative ecclesial teaching? Is teaching (and authority-taking) over men in every sphere of life forbidden? Does the author intend the instruction to be normative?

1. *The Difficulties*

The above questions represent only the tip of an exegetical iceberg comprising three complex problems.

1. Since the early nineteenth century, when the debate over the authorship of the Pastoral Epistles began, many have interpreted 1 Tim. 2.12 as reflecting a conservative school of thought diverging from Paul and also in evidence in an interpolated 1 Cor. 14.34-35.

2. Those who maintain that Paul is the author are divided. Many believe the passage to be normative for Christians across time and culture, but as early as the seventeenth century it was argued that it addresses only certain women (Fell 1666–67: 10). This nowadays increasingly

popular view is buttressed by arguments constructed from the occasion of the letter and the ways both Jesus and Paul conduct their relationships with women. It is associated with the belief that 1 Cor. 14.34-35 is either an interpolation or forbids only speech of a specific kind. Alternatively, the Timothy passage is seen as a conservative modification in Paul's own thought. In either case the instruction is declared non-normative.

3. The verse and its immediate context are riddled with syntactic and semantic difficulties.

i. At v. 9, ὡσαύτως implies βούλομαι from v. 8, but is προσεύχεσθαι also implied, or is κοσμεῖν the only relevant infinitive?

ii. At v. 9, what is the meaning and extent of the instruction requiring καταστολῇ κοσμίῳ?

iii. At v. 10, is ἐπαγγελλομέναις to be understood as 'professing' or 'proclaiming'?

iv. At vv. 11 and 12, is ἡσυχίᾳ to be understood as 'quietness' or 'silence'?

v. At v. 12, to what do διδάσκειν and αὐθεντεῖν refer?

vi. At vv. 13-14, how are the selections from the Adam and Eve story to be interpreted?

vii. At v. 15, what does the number change between σωθήσεται and μείνωσιν signify?

viii. At v. 15, is σωτηρία spiritual, physical, or metaphorical?

ix. At v. 15, does τεκνογονία refer to general or specific childbirth, the bearing and rearing of children, or is it symbolic of woman's domestic role?

x. At v. 15, does διά mean 'by means of' or 'during/throughout'?

Not surprisingly, these three complex problems create vast diversity of opinion about both the author's general intention and the details of that intention.

2. The Thesis

It will be argued in the following study that, regardless of the identity of the author of the Pastorals, several contextual, linguistic, grammatical and literary components in 1 Tim. 2.9-15 have universally been either ignored or misunderstood.

3. *Approaches in the Literature*

Arguments about 1 Tim. 2.9-15 are based substantially upon prior decisions about authorship, but the nature of the evidence adduced for those decisions is such that what constitutes proof for some is simply rejected as unconvincing by others. In considerations of the letter as a whole, disproportionate attention is given to the authorship question, difficult passages often not receiving the care they deserve,[1] and little in the interpretations of opponents being found compatible. Reconstruction of an appropriate cultural–historical background further polarizes the situation. Even when opinions about authorship and general background coincide, the linguistic and exegetical difficulties alone lead to widely divergent interpretations. There are three main approaches (each with some variants) but, even granted its own presuppositions, each is problematic.

1. Those concluding that Paul here intends to prohibit women generally from teaching and taking authority over men in the church seek to reconcile this with other Pauline teaching and to resolve debates about women in ministry.[2] Circularity of argument is sometimes evident, with 1 Cor. 11.3-16; 14.34-35 and 1 Tim. 2.11-15 each being employed to interpret one another, when each has considerable difficulties of its own. The foundations upon which 1 Tim. 2.13-14 is interpreted (interpretations of Genesis 2–3) are often less than compelling. The roles of Paul's own female co-workers are inconclusively defined. The implications for total equality which others see in Gal. 3.28 are minimized or denied,[3] despite the fact that it is at best tenuous to claim that that passage is operative only *coram Deo*: see further below.

2. Those concluding that 1 Timothy is pseudepigraphic take the opposite approach, contrasting 2.9-15 with Pauline teaching, with Gal. 3.28 often prominent.[4] Parallels are commonly drawn between 1 Tim. 2.11-12 and (an interpolated) 1 Cor. 14.34-35 and appropriate contemporary literature. Feminist interpretations, their analyses grounded in the experience of women's oppression, are amongst those represented here. Those taking approach 2 maximize the potential harshness, conservatism or pragmatism in elements of 1 Tim. 2.9-15. Very often the

1. This is noted by A.T. Hanson 1968: 1; M.Y. MacDonald 1988: 3.
2. E.g. Knight 1980: 29-40 incl. n. 4.
3. E.g. Knight 1980: 14, 19-20, 39-40; Hurley 1981: 127.
4. E.g. Easton 1948: 127-28; Houlden 1976: 65.

exegetical difficulties are not even acknowledged.[5] Although Gal. 3.28 *is* potentially revolutionary, it in fact says nothing about a ministerial or ruling class to which men, slaves, Gentiles and women have/have not equal right.[6] Paul is concerned with *unity* (not equality) in Christ for existing social, racial and sexual divisions.[7] At 1 Cor. 7.17-24 he may sidestep any potentially revolutionary implications in the underlying formula by encouraging slaves to make use of their bondage, although this is uncertain.[8] The equality he outlines for men and women in that same chapter, however, is of the sexual, not the more generally marital, variety. Some Graeco-Roman and later rabbinic sources affirm a commonality similar to Gal. 3.28 and yet envisage role differences,[9] so Paul's goals should not be assumed to be identical with those of modern social egalitarianism (J. Davis 1976: 205). But even if the Galatians passage does, after all, envision total equality, the potential at 1 Tim. 2.11-15 for various interpretations undermines the claim that the two passages are utterly opposed.

3. Those who believe that at 1 Tim. 2.12 Paul limits his instruction to particular women or circumstances seek (like those in group 1) to reconcile Pauline thought and resolve debate on women's roles. These, however, minimize elements of vv. 11-12, seeking to demonstrate that the instruction is not, after all, in fundamental opposition to feminist egalitarian principles.[10] With Gal. 3.28, 1 Cor. 11.5 and Paul's relationships with various female co-workers in mind, 1 Cor. 14.34-35 and 1 Tim. 2.11-12 are 'disarmed, qualified and put in some historical context'.[11] But again, Gal. 3.28 is not necessarily a manifesto for totally

---

5.   See e.g. Kähler 1959: 10-11; A.T. Hanson 1966: 36, 38; Wendland 1970: 97; Ford 1971: 343-44; Swidler 1979: 336-37; Boucher *et al.* 1979: 612; R. Jewett 1979: 59-60; Walker 1983: 101; Schüssler Fiorenza 1983: 235; Brooten 1985: 85-87; Byrne 1988: 88; Dewey 1992: 353-56.

6.   For a useful survey of various approaches and a balanced interpretation see Snodgrass (1986: 161-81), who warns against overinterpretation. For additional useful comment see Porter (1989c: 85-97).

7.   Yoder 1982: 177 n. 23; Banks 1976: 82-83; 1981: 133-34; Fung 1987: 183. Cf. Byrne (1988: 4, 10-12), who notes the basic intention to emphasize oneness, but subsequently identifies an aspiration to equality.

8.   Cf. e.g. Kidd (1990: 161) with Llewelyn (1992: 67-70).

9.   Witherington 1981: 593-94; Snodgrass 1986: 170.

10.   E.g. Payne 1981: 169-81; Bilezikian 1987: 421-26; 1989: 178-84.

11.   From a paper (apparently unpublished) read by H. Washington at the International SBL Conference, Melbourne, July 1992.

equal opportunity. 1 Corinthians 11.5 does not mention teaching. Those accepting Pauline authorship for the Pastorals generally also accept it for Col. 3.18 and Eph. 5.21-33, where roles (even when seen as mutually submitted) are obviously to some extent viewed differently. The minimized words and expressions of 1 Tim. 2.11-12 may have stricter or broader applications, and no amount of assertion that they do not can be altogether satisfying.

Whether approach 1, 2, or 3 is taken, then, 1 Tim. 2.12 and its context remain a problem. The ripple effect is far-reaching. M.Y. MacDonald, for example, applies insights from the social sciences to trace the process of institutionalization in the Pauline tradition. The Pastorals, she believes, are pseudepigraphic, representing a third, that is 'community protecting' stage (cf. building, stabilizing). The beliefs and social structures she traces are therefore predicated partly upon foundations categorized above under 2. Since those foundations face some of the difficulties outlined for that approach,[12] the structures traced are correspondingly questionable. P.H. Towner explores the structure of theology and ethics in the Pastorals. His study is not based on an authorship preference, but the theology and ethics he finds at 1 Tim. 2.9-15 partly result from his application of implications perceived at Gal. 3.28,[13] and he faces some of the difficulties outlined under 3. 1 Timothy 2.12 and its context are clearly of fundamental importance for an adequate understanding of the nature of early and developing Christianity well beyond women's roles.

All three exegetical groups are included in the following study, but it should be noted at the outset that much recent literature emerges from the ongoing debate amongst those categorized above under 1 and 3, so some additional observations about those groups are called for here. Group 1 claims that the inspiration and authority of the scriptures are at stake,[14] and group 3 that circumstances at places of address must be distinguished from universally binding instruction.[15] This polarization has been the catalyst for some exploration of underlying hermeneutical and theological concepts.

---

12. M.Y. MacDonald 1988: 223. See further in this Introduction, below.

13. P.H. Towner 1989: 210-12. See further in subsequent chapters.

14. E.g. Lindsell 1976: 45-46.

15. E.g. Payne 1986: 101. Cf. Blomberg (1988: 403-21), who seeks 'a viable middle ground' but merely rearranges familiar arguments and fails to appreciate that the meaning may lie somewhere other than between two extant views.

Johnston has challenged the hermeneutical inadequacies of both sides, claiming that egalitarians dualistically isolate 'the time-bound from the universal, the human from the divine, the rabbinic from the Christian', and that traditionalists treat scripture ahistorically. Although both sides are convinced that the passages in question are clear, neither, he says, is willing to engage in fresh and exacting research, and discussion tends to be inconsistent, sometimes limited to selected proof-texts, and sometimes ignoring parts of even those selections. The claim that Gal. 3.28 constitutes an appropriate theological basis for the interpretation of other passages ignores the fact that theological texts have cultural components and that practical instruction has a theological dimension. Inconsistently, ecclesiastical instruction is sometimes said to be culturally determined but marital instruction timeless (Johnston 1978: 234-59). Johnston suggested 11 principles for a sound hermeneutic.[16] Since that time more rigorous research has certainly been attempted,[17] but without resolution of the problem. Johnston therefore probed even deeper, tracing studies which explore the human factors militating against agreement even by those subscribing to the same principles. The continuing debate on women's roles, he argued, could prove to be a hermeneutical test case for those espousing views 1 and 3.[18]

In regard to theology, Harris, for example, defines New Testament authority as being of various kinds and degrees, essentially charismatic, limited to the exercise of its particular ministry, and associated with mutual responsibility and self-submission.[19] Tucker and Liefeld explore ordination, concluding that no New Testament passage deals with it as it is usually conceived today (1987: 470-71). Liefeld with considerable force also establishes a New Testament theology of ministry, noting important differences from contemporary structures whose validity he therefore questions.[20] In interpreting 1 Tim. 2.12, however, each of

16. For critiques relevant to some aspects of his applications see below Parts II (re his iii. and iv.) and III (re his i.).

17. E.g. the debate between Moo (1980: 62-83; 1981: 198-222) and Payne (1981: 169-97; 1986: 96-115).

18. Johnston 1986: 30-41, citing various sources. See also Wiebe 1994: 54. For the continuing search for a soundly based hermeneutic see e.g. Köstenberger (1994: 259-83).

19. Harris 1987: 21-27. See also Howe 1979: 272-75; Tucker and Liefeld 1987: 466-68.

20. Liefeld 1987: 53-61. See also Foh 1979: 249.

these favours the perspective of category 3,[21] and fails to establish conclusively that its author deals only with a particular situation. They caution against the adoption of restrictive policies on the basis of this difficult verse. Their opponents resist the admission of egalitarian practice in the face of the same difficulties. The claims of both sides come down to questions of probability, often settled by personal preference. From group 1, Knight says

> [O]n the question of the possible role relationships in the teaching-ruling functions…1 Timothy 2:11-15…most clearly gives…Paul's verdict and his reasons… (1980: 29)

It is noteworthy, then, that Knight establishes its 'strong sense of absoluteness' by reference to what he himself sees as the less clear 1 Cor. 14.34-35, and that he can only guess at the reason for the 'basic, foundational' appeal to the Genesis record (1980: 31-32, incl. n. 4). From group 3, Scholer writes:

> It cannot be taken for granted that 1 Timothy 2:8-15 'controls' the evidence of other Pauline texts. It is just as defensible—for me, more defensible—to argue that the evidence of women's participation in authoritative teaching and leadership…[at e.g.] 1 Cor. 11:5, Phil. 4:2-3 and Rom. 16:1-18…'controls' 1 Timothy 2:8-15. (1983: 12)

Neither Knight nor Scholer is compelling. It is obvious that, even given a willingness to conform to the theological concepts which writers such as Harris and Liefeld outline, modern structures cannot be made biblical if the exegetical problems of texts such as 1 Tim. 2.12 have not been resolved. Dedication to the welfare of women may overcome obstacles to their emancipation, but it is no more effective than reworking the traditional reading (or, indeed, than group 2's rejection of Pauline authorship) in resolving the exegetical difficulties. Groups 1 and 3 both consider a primary goal of exegesis to be an appreciation of what the author intended to say.[22] Justifications of either existing or desired modern structures based to some extent upon this passage are effective only if that goal is convincingly reached. Satisfaction is found neither in adherence to tradition when there are alternatives, nor in the adoption of less onerous options which at best are only unproven possibilities.

21. Harris 1987: 32-33; Tucker and Liefeld 1987: e.g. 453, 460-62; Liefeld 1987: 50-53. Foh (see previous note) is an exception, taking a version of 1.

22. Others claim differently, but my focus here is upon Groups 1 and 3. See e.g. Köstenberger 1994: 268.

Never were the proverbial rock and hard place better exemplified than in this debate. Practice based on either view inevitably faces ongoing and painful controversy and division. Yet the practical ramifications of this passage are so important that few could agree simply to lay the debate aside.

At the beginning of a new millennium, then, at 1 Tim. 2.9-15 we are faced with an ever more diversifying literature from three general exegetical groups, increasingly finely nuanced in some of its detail. Although, when granted their own presuppositions, some arguments from each group make good sense of some aspects of the passage, all agree that it is problematic, and none is entirely convincing. The overall exegetical effect is that of a whirlwind beginning and proceeding in the direction chosen by the individual interpreter. A fresh approach is needed, yet after all that has been written on the subject it would appear reasonable to conclude that none could possibly be found.

4. *A Way Forward*

An alternative does, however, begin to emerge with recognition that decisions about authorship, dating, occasion of the letter, and social, cultural and historical backgrounds are valid interpretative devices *only* to the extent that linguistic, grammatical, literary and contextual components are adequately appreciated. I make no claim here that authorship, occasion and background are improper exegetical devices: each is clearly of major importance. Nor do I claim that more weight should be given to linguistic, grammatical, literary and contextual components than to other necessary hermeneutical elements.[23] The text, however, is the basic material from which the exegete must begin, and the limited purpose of this particular study is to focus essentially on that basic material.

Later twentieth-century literature on 1 Tim. 2.9-15 displays little evidence of hope that the text itself has anything new to offer. The morphology of some verbs has occasioned a few speculative observations and questionable arguments, but the general impression given is that it must be the historical background or the hermeneutic of the interpreter that unlocks the remaining enigmas. These assumptions invite re-examination.

---

23. See Köstenberger 1994: 263-67.

Concerned with the writing of women's history, Brooten says

> [The historian] cannot...use literature as a sort of attic archive, drawing out historical details and pasting together a collage which then passes as historical reality...[but] must respect the integrity of literature, recognizing that the very historicity of a literary document implies studying it for itself, in its present form, with its own contours. It would, therefore, be inappropriate to search the New Testament for snippets of information about women, cutting them out and placing them side by side with similar snippets about other first-century women painstakingly clipped from other literary and non-literary sources, glueing the whole thing together and passing it off as the reality of women's lives in the first century. (1985: 81)

The biblical exegete, too, must respect the integrity of the literature, seeking to understand a document 'for itself, in its present form, with its own contours'. But the historical 'collages' of which Brooten speaks frequently feature in a larger, circular exegetical process. Difficult New Testament passages about women are commonly interpreted against such collages, the resulting interpretations themselves pasted as focal points upon them, the whole then being employed as background for the interpretation of other difficult New Testament passages about women. It is of the utmost importance to note that historical reconstruction interacts with exegesis, and particularly when the meaning of the text is unclear. Lest such interaction distort rather than clarify, every linguistic, grammatical and contextual factor of that text must be scrutinized and reconsidered in the light of the latest scholarship before it can be made a convincing (let alone focal) feature of any historical reconstruction.

If ever the sources of antiquity were cut and pasted together to pass as historical reality which is then declared appropriate background for interpretation of a passage riddled with exegetical puzzles, they have been so cut and pasted for 1 Tim. 2.9-15.[24] Conversely, if ever a passage riddled with unresolved exegetical puzzles was pasted as a prominent feature on to historical 'collages', 1 Tim. 2.9-15 is that passage. This circular process is another reason for the diversity of its interpretation.

The need to consider more carefully the language of problem passages about women is now widely acknowledged. Kroeger, for example,

---

24. Kroeger (1987a: 25), e.g., reconstructs her background from 'many bits of evidence here and there that can be put together from many different sources'.

says that inadequate attention has been paid especially to their *hapax legomena*, and calls for careful scrutiny of context and contemporary attitudes and practice via the resources of those studying the classics, archaeology, epigraphy, papyrology, art history and numismatics (1987a: 38). As a classicist, however, her own contributions are reconstruction of a background and choices from linguistic options viewed as appropriate to that background. Both have been discredited.[25] M.Y. MacDonald agrees that 'the text itself must provide the primary starting point and focus for sociological investigations'. She objects, however, to Judge's argument that, until the work of mapping social identity and behaviour in primitive Christianty has been developed much further in juxtaposition with the conventions and practices of the society, the application of social models defined in terms of other cultures could prove a fundamental error. Historical 'field-work', claims MacDonald, is impossible without the use of models.[26] She apparently misses the point that much of the mapping of social identities and behaviours depends upon the adequacy of our appreciation of the language of the text. Only as that appreciation is sharpened by current and ongoing scholarship is there an appropriate control to ensure that texts are not misread or misunderstood historically when theoretical models are employed (Horsley 1992a: 164). If the content of the passage itself has been misunderstood, the conventions and behaviours investigated are accordingly skewed. So, too, are the 'collages' upon which they are 'pasted'.

5. *A Suggested Solution*

There is substantial reason to conclude that some components of 1 Tim. 2.9-15 have been universally misunderstood. All the general groups outlined above as 1–3 employ certain exegetical 'devices'. I use this term not to denote approaches, or methods, but tools to 'break open' the

---

25. For severely critical reviews of C. Kroeger and R. Kroeger (1992) see Yarbrough 1992: 25-30; Oster 1993: 225-27; Wolters 1993: 208-13; Baugh 1994: 153-71. See also Wilshire 1993: 53-54; Perriman 1993: 132-34; Köstenberger 1994: 271-72; Baugh 1995: 13-52; Schreiner 1995: 109-10, 119 n. 59; and at relevant points in the following study.

26. M.Y. MacDonald 1988: 24, 26-27, citing E.A. Judge, 'The Social Identify of the First Christians: A Question of Method in Religious History', *JRH* 11.2 (1980): 210-17.

meaning of the passage. First amongst these are decisions about authorship, and reconstructions of associated cultural–(general) historical background—all prominent and necessary aids for clearing away perceived obscurities. In addition to these, however, some combination from four other such devices is universally employed:

    I. **Immediate context**, with factors in 1 Tim. 1.18–3.15 seen as setting the concerns of 2.9-12 within the gathered assembly.

   II. **Broader context**, with 1 Tim. 1.3-4 and various passages from all three Pastorals about false teachers and women held to provide details of the specific situation occasioning the instruction at vv. 9-12.

  III. **Parallel teaching**, with 1 Cor. 14.34-35 viewed as a parallel for 1 Tim. 2.11-12 in the above congregational context (I) and specific situation (II).

  IV. **Theological foundation**, with 1 Tim. 2.13-14, via the conjunction γάρ, seen as presenting either reasons for, or illustration of the need for, the prohibitions of v. 12.

Three other passages or themes are similarly prominent in interpretations of 1 Tim. 2.9-15: at vv. 11-12 Gal. 3.28, and at vv. 13-14 both the Creation and Fall of Adam and Eve from Genesis 1–3, and 1 Cor. 11.3-16.

Gal. 3.28 becomes an exegetical device only to the extent that some who accept the Pauline authorship of the Pastorals argue that the Paul who wrote to the Galatians could not mean what 1 Tim. 2.11-12 appears to say, so must intend something much less restrictive or something required by particular circumstances. Here Gal. 3.28 becomes a catalyst for closer examination of 1 Timothy 2 itself rather than an interpretative device to unlock its meaning. Accordingly, Gal. 3.28 will not directly be addressed in this study.

Interpretation of Genesis 1–3 is certainly made a basis of some interpretations of 1 Tim. 2.11-15, but this is because 1 Tim. 2.9-15 itself partly comprises an interpretation of those chapters. Genesis is both the original source from which 1 Tim. 2.13-14/15 is constructed, and is made an exegetical device for it. Since the conjunction γάρ which introduces v. 13 is itself a major exegetical device (IV), I have chosen to consider the interpretation of Genesis 1–3 in vv. 13-14 under that heading. Relevant aspects of Genesis itself will be considered in an appendix to that discussion (Appendix 3).

Whatever view may be held about the authorship of 1 Timothy, 1 Cor. 11.3-16 is often said to reflect ideas about male–female pre-Fall relations parallel to those at 1 Tim. 2.13-14. It is therefore sometimes employed to delineate more clearly the Adam–Eve relationship envisaged, and thereby qualifies as an interpretative device. The passage was the subject of my unpublished MA Preliminary dissertation.[27] A re-working here would require an additional major section, the greater proportion of which would be irrelevant to the topic at hand. Pending an updating of that study for publication, therefore, I have here chosen to reduce the main factors to a further appendix to Parts II and IV (Appendix 2), therein keeping footnote examples to a minimum.

The devices designated **I–IV** above constitute a field of investigation relevant for all exegetical approaches. If those devices should be found false, or even in need of modification, it will mean that major factors in the text have been inadequately appreciated by all groups (1–3). The author's meaning will, to some extent, have been obscured no matter what decisions may be made about his identity or the cultural–historical background of the letter. The following study conducts such a re-examination. It is not a 'full', or commentary-type exegesis. It is not about the authorship debate. It reconstructs no cultural–historical (general) background. It does not enter the debate on women in ministry today. It does not apply the passage to any modern structures. My own views on those important subjects are unstated, although of course it would be remarkable if they did not emerge from time to time. My concern here is more basic, that is, *the identification of factors relevant to all exegetical groups* no matter what their views may be about authorship, background and women in ministry. Part I re-examines the immediate context and the effect it has on the passage (device **I**); Parts II and III re-examine materials commonly adduced in support of the usual interpretation of that context: that is, the broader context of the Pastoral Epistles (device **II**), and a perceived parallel (device **III**); and Part IV re-examines the relationship of vv. 13-15 to vv. 11-12 (device **IV**).

6. *Features of the Presentation*

1. Parts I and IV present the positive arguments. Parts II and III have been placed between them because the former further illuminates, and

---

27. 'Headship and Headcoverings in 1 Cor. 11.3-16', La Trobe University, 1988.

the latter partly depends upon, the conclusions of Part I, and because Parts I–III together clear the stage for the original approach found in Part IV.

2. Application of my conclusions will depend upon whatever decisions might be made about authorship and associated background. In all four parts, therefore, I consider alternative implications for those conclusions, proposing *both* 'if Paul wrote the Pastorals then…etc.' *and* 'if the Pastorals are pseudepigraphic then…etc.'

3. In view of the vast amount and diversity of the literature, I have chosen to survey it not as a whole but according to the themes of, and in the introductions to, the four Parts. In Part I, for example, the introductory chapter surveys and critiques interpretations of the immediate context. The devices to be re-examined have been employed either virtually universally or commonly, in at least some cases since very early in the Christian era. In the introductions to all four parts, therefore, *since the focus is upon those devices*, identification of trendsetters is generally inappropriate, and authors whose general approaches and conclusions are quite dissimilar or of widely varying force are grouped together. Originality, influence and derivation are, however, often noted in associated discussions about particular points relating to use of those devices.

4. Illustrations and examples are, where possible, drawn from across the exegetical spectrum. Two points should be noted in this regard:

(a) In some discussions examples are predominantly from one particular group because it is that group which uses, or most overtly or commonly uses, the particular device or argument in view. In Part I, Chapter 4 seeks to define key words in 1 Tim. 2.11-12. Group 2 in general terms simply accepts that, in accordance with contemporary thought, the passage in silencing women subordinates them to men. Groups 1 and 3, however, debate the implications, the former defending, and the latter explaining the prohibition. Arguments about the meanings of some words occur predominantly in the writings of those two groups, and this is reflected in my illustrations. In Part II group 3 is prominent, but since they advance ideas traceable in groups 1 and 2, those others are also cited. In Part III, Chapter 10, of the four basic ways 1 Cor. 14.34-35 is interpreted, generally speaking the second is employed by 'conservatives', and the third by 'liberals' but, although my discussions reflect those patterns, some exceptions and parallel references are noted.

(b) An attempt has been made to reflect in illustrations and examples something of the pattern of argument across *both the years and the exegetical groups*. This results in many footnotes listing representatives *chosen for those purposes*. Where appropriate, these are arranged chronologically. Inclusion or exclusion should be taken to indicate neither my support of, nor disgreement with, the general position taken by an author unless such judgments are expressly stated.

5. Recent work on Aspect in the Greek verb has been applied. The aspectual force of the non-indicative moods has long been recognized, but most definitions of the indicative are temporal or entail the idea that an objective kind-of-action ('Aktionsart') may be identified. No such definition is capable of universal application. The aorist, for example, is both 'timeless' and employed for past events in narrative. It is often defined as referring to 'completed' or 'punctiliar' action, but the 'gnomic' aorist does neither. The present may be 'historic' or even future in reference. The perfect, generally defined as showing present effect of aoristic action, sometimes occurs where an aorist or present might have been expected, and the effect may be perceived on either subject or object, or even as continuing in the Old Testament account.[28] These uneasy definitions have been reconsidered by K.L. McKay,[29] S.E. Porter,[30] and B.M. Fanning.[31] Debate between these three and about their research proceeds.[32] Silva advises that as little as possible be said about Aspect, arguing that he has not seen one example of good exegesis that '*depends* on the interpreter's ability to explain why one Aspect rather than another was used' (1993: 78, 81-82; emphasis his). The considerable disagreement between the writers in question makes such a warning understandable. Porter, who is primarily concerned to define essential rather than secondary semantic components, considers majority occurrences of aspectual choice in certain temporal contexts, but argues that verbs are essentially non-temporal, time being determined only by deictic markers (*deixis*), that is, persons, temporal terms

---

28. E.g. BDF, §§340, 342.

29. K.L. McKay has been working on this question for many years, e.g. 1965: 1-21; 1972: 39-57; 1974: 247-51; 1977: e.g. v-vi, 136-41; 1981: 289-329; 1985: 201-26; 1992: 209-28; 1994: 27-38.

30. Porter 1989a: *passim*; 1992: 26-28.

31. Fanning 1990: *passim*.

32. Carson and Porter 1993: 24-25, 34-43, 57-82; K.L. McKay 1994: §3.6.

or connectives.[33] McKay argues that, although time is not morphologically expressed, aspectual choice is part of the context and produces obvious temporal contributions.[34] Fanning says that aspect intersects with various lexical, contextual and discourse features, and finds temporality in the indicative almost always a major consideration, and in the non-indicative a secondary function.[35] I am not yet convinced that Porter is correct about the total absence of temporality in verbs. The temporal orientation of Dionysius Thrax (15.22-23) suggests that, even though his verbal categories are inadequate (as Porter argues: 1989a: 18-20), some people *may* have chosen a form for a perceived temporality. But if the debate on Aspect has a long way to go before definitions are widely accepted, it cannot simply be omitted from explication of Greek texts. McKay, Porter and Fanning are agreed about certain basic factors, and this agreement on matters long overlooked is of enormous importance (Carson and Porter 1993: 22). Two such factors present sufficient cause to consider whether aspectual choice sheds light on 1 Tim. 2.9-15:[36]

(a) Verbs in all moods primarily convey the writer/speaker's subjective view of action:[37] the aorist visualization of whole action,[38] the present of action in progress,[39] the future of expectation of action,[40] and the perfect in all cases of the state of the subject of the action.[41] Throughout this study I capitalize aspectual descriptions, that is Present,

---

33. Porter 1989a: e.g. 78-82, 98-107, 182, 252, 257; 1992: 25-26. Schmidt (1993: 70-71) argues that Porter has not proven absolute absence of the temporal dimension.

34. K.L. McKay e.g. 1992: 226.

35. Fanning 1990: 194-95, 323, 419. Cf. also Louw 1959: 47, 55, 57.

36. Some additional factors will be introduced in Part IV.

37. Cf. Silva (1993: 78), who doubts that the aspectual choices are conscious.

38. Porter 1989a: 91, 258; Fanning 1990: 97; K.L. McKay e.g. 1994: §3.3.

39. Porter 1989a: e.g. 91, 258; Fanning 1990: 103; K.L. McKay e.g. 1994: §3.2.

40. Porter 1989a: e.g. 414. K.L. McKay (e.g. 1992: 225; 1994: §3.5) says it expresses intention/expectation/volition. Fanning (1990: 120-24) doubts that the Future can properly be called an Aspect, saying it describes action subsequent to some reference point. He nevertheless agrees that it has something of the sense of intention about it.

41. K.L. McKay e.g. 1977: §23. 4.1; 1981: 310; 1994: §3.4; Porter 1989a: e.g. 91, 273-81; 1992: 40. Fanning (1990: 291-97) maintains that the result of the occurrence is present or simultaneous with the time of speaking, the state sometimes that of the object. His examples are not compelling in light of McKay and Porter.

or Aorist, the lower-case 'present', or 'future', being reserved for time.

(b) The morphological forms provide some indication of a structure in which the writer/speaker's emphases may be identified. McKay wisely urges that in all cases the context must be considered with the greatest care if the most accurate temporal and aspectual translation of that structure is to be achieved.[42] As does Porter, however, he provides some guidelines. The Present highlights transition to a new unit and factors therein (Porter 1989a: 196). In exposition, when the Perfect is employed with Aorist or other forms, its action is in some way focused.[43] For example, at Rom. 6.7-10 Aorists lay the fundamental events, Presents describe ongoing events, and Perfects emphatically introduce the section and highlight the state in which the Christian may live.[44] In narrative the Aorist is employed for background material, the Present/Imperfect for foreground, and the Perfect for an even more dramatic effect.[45] For example, at Acts 16.1-5 the Aorist establishes the framework of events, the Imperfect several significant (foreground) features, and Perfects draw to centre stage the common knowledge that Timothy's father was Greek (v. 3) and the determination by the Jerusalem leaders of the decisions which were being delivered (v. 4).[46] Porter calls the Perfect the 'frontground' aspect. I have chosen to describe this function as 'spotlighting'.

---

42. K.L. McKay e.g. 1992: 225.

43. K.L. McKay (1994: §4.5.2) cites Jn 3.32; 14.25. Porter (1989a: 251) lists possible exceptions, but at Lk. 9.45 and Jn 1.32 the Perfects are quite likely to present the foci, and 2 Cor. 3.12 seems to have been included in error. Only Jn 5.14 and Heb. 2.14 remain, and these are exposition rather than narrative, the characteristic emphasis muted. Fanning (1990: 193-94) tends to think that in conjunction with the Aorist the Perfect maintains its own characteristics.

44. Porter 1992: 22, also p. 303 for Rom. 5.1-5.

45. K.L. McKay e.g. 1981: 315-20; 1992: 226; 1994: §4.5.2; Porter 1989a: 92-93, 196-206, 247-51, 258-59. See also e.g. Mandilaras 1972: 16-17: 1973: §461. Fanning (1990) is confusing here. He says (p. 75) *perfective* verbs are used for foreground events, and (p. 191 with n. 119) 'the aorist can…narrate the… "foreground" events,…the [imperfective forms]…"background" '. He compares Turner, who says the Aorist advances the bare story, the Imperfect supplying details. However, Fanning also (pp. 230-31) writes that the Present often draws attention to crucial events or highlights new scenes or actors. Reed (1995: 84-85 n. 24) says Koine Greek is unique in that whilst the imperfective aspect is thematic, the role of the perfective is background. Cf. Silva 1995: 104-105.

46. Porter 1989a: 92-93. See also 1992: 302-303 for Mk 11.1-11.

To my knowledge, (a) and (b) have not previously been applied within a comprehensive reconsideration of 1 Tim. 2.9-15.[47]

6. Two common additional approaches to interpretation of this passage also invite attention. The first is methodological. The exegetical difficulties necessitate a 'construction' approach wherein each decision becomes the foundation for consideration of the next or some subsequent problem. The exegete becomes locked into progression from one 'solved' difficulty to the next. Options for difficulties other than the first-addressed depend upon which *is* first-addressed, and other possibilities are frequently not given due consideration. The second approach is more an associated problem of logic wherein a leap is made from '*x* may be the case' to '*x* being the case...etc.'.[48] With these two common approaches in mind, and given accumulating conclusions arising from re-examination of the four devices, the following study attempts to leave open as many doors as possible for evaluation according to decisions about authorship and dating.

7. Contextual exegetical problems lying outside the scope of the major concerns, whether in the passage itself,[49] the broader 1 Timothy,[50] or elsewhere in the New Testament, are considered only as they bear upon the task at hand.

8. It is assumed that all three Pastoral Epistles are the work of the same author or school of thought,[51] who/which, in the interests of

47. Porter (1993: 87-102) focuses on v. 15 only. See Part IV.

48. For a subtle example see Knight (1992: 141-42), who argues that since αὐθεντεῖν (v. 12) has no 'inherent' negative sense it refers 'then...to exercise of a leadership role or function'. No consideration is given to whether the context may supply the negative sense rejected, so the word 'inherent' masks what is essentially a leap from possibility to certainty. For a similar critique of Knight here see Köstenberger 1994: 264. Examples of others employing such logical leaps will be noted where appropriate.

49. As ἐν καταστολῇ κοσμίῳ μετὰ αἰδοῦς καὶ σωφροσύνης (v. 9), ὑποταγῇ (v. 11) and ἐν πίστει καὶ ἀγάπῃ καὶ ἁγιασμῷ μετὰ σωφροσύνης (v. 15).

50. As at 2.1-7 and 3.1b-16.

51. Cf. e.g. Murphy-O'Connor (1991: 403-18), who separates 2 Timothy. Some of the distinctions he notes are valid. See also, e.g., Bush (1990: 152-56), and my Part II. In my judgment, however, Murphy-O'Connor's argument falls short of proof, apparently predicated on the idea that an author will always employ the same terminology in the same way. Overall, statistical studies on the frequency of words used have not demonstrated different authorships: cf. e.g. Yule 1944: 281; Metzger 1958–59: 93-94; Michaelson and Morton 1971–72: 206-207; Kenny 1986: 95; Mealand 1988: 108; Prior 1989: 30.

simplicity, will henceforth be referred to as 'the Author' or 'he'.

9. When the people of a local Christian assembly are in view, since the word 'church' is today commonly associated with meeting-place or universally conceived entities, 'assembly' or *ekklesia* are employed.

Part I
1 TIMOTHY 2.9-12 IN ITS IMMEDIATE CONTEXT

Chapter 1

AN INTRODUCTORY LITERATURE SURVEY

There is today virtually universal acceptance that 1 Tim. 2.1-2, 8-12 deals with activities taking place in the congregation. This has not always been the case.

In the patristic era it is sometimes unclear whether 1 Timothy itself is in view. Material closely resembling portions of ch. 2 appears to draw upon shared tradition rather than directly to quote the Author. Clement of Rome writes προσέλθωμεν οὖν αὐτῷ ἐν ὁσιότητι ψυχῆς, ἁγνὰς καὶ ἀμιάντους χεῖρας αἴροντες πρὸς αὐτόν ('Let us then approach him in holiness of life, lifting up to him pure and undefiled hands', *1 Clem.* 29.1), for which cf. ἐπαίροντας ὁσίους χεῖρας (1 Tim. 2.8). Again he writes καὶ ἴδωμεν τί καλὸν καὶ τί τερπνὸν καὶ τί προσδεκτὸν ἐνώπιον τοῦ ποιήσαντος ἡμᾶς ('Let us attend to what is good and pleasing and acceptable in the sight of our Maker', *1 Clem.* 7.3), for which cf. τοῦτο καλὸν καὶ ἀπόδεκτον ἐνώπιον τοῦ σωτῆρος ἡμῶν θεοῦ (1 Tim. 2.3). It is widely accepted that such early Christian traditions lie behind (or behind some of) 1 Tim. 2.1-2, 5-6, 8 and 9-15.[1] Even in those patristic writings undoubtedly dependent upon 1 Timothy 2 the allusions and citations are often employed to support the writer's own instruction and do not constitute commentary. Perception of the setting in which it occurs is not always clear.

---

1. See e.g. Humphreys 1901: 96; Lock 1924: 28; Falconer 1937: 128; Easton 1948: 121-23; Leaney 1960: 50-51; Schmithals and Werbeck 1961: 146; Jeremias 1963: 16-17; Bartsch 1965: 13, 47; A.T. Hanson 1966: 31-34, 36; 1968: 56-64, 115; Brox 1969: 121-23, 128, 131; Dibelius and Conzelmann 1972: 41-42; Kelly 1972: 63-64; Houlden 1976: 67, 69; Knoch 1988: 25; Roloff 1988: 109-13, 120, 123, 126-31; Merkel 1991: 24-25. See further in Chapter 8, Section 5.2. Cf. Scott (1936: 21), who considers v. 5b more probably the writer's own comment on the familiar v. 5a but μεσίτης probably a term applied to Christ by the contemporary church, and Knight (1992: 123), who is unconvinced that vv. 5-6 are a citation.

There is certainly very early attestation to perception of a congregational context. In symbolizing prayer as incense which, together with 'loaves of faith', is placed before the Lord on the Sabbath day, Origen seems to have that setting in mind as he cites v. 8 in *Hom. in Lev.* XIII.5. He also cites v. 12 in *Frag. ex comm. in ep. ad 1 Cor.* 74.21 at 14.35 to support his claim that women should not speak ἐν ἐκκλησίᾳ. In allusions to v. 12 Tertullian writes *illa monstrosissima cui nec integre quidem docendi ius erat* ('that portent of a woman, who had no right to teach even correctly', *Bapt.* 1.3), and *[n]on permittitur mulieri in ecclesia...docere* ('it is not permitted to a woman in the church...to teach', *Virg.Vel.* 9.1). Nevertheless, the passage is also frequently applied to everyday life. In *Cels.* VIII.73.7-10 Origen cites vv. 1-2a, his context making restriction to the congregation unlikely. The pious life is highlighted as an effective help rendered to kings, and prayer as a service aligned with life in public affairs and the self-denial and meditation which teach Christians to despise and avoid pleasures. Some citations of or allusions to v. 8 cannot be restricted to the congregation. See for example Origen, *Hom. in Ex.* 3.3.23-24, *elevemus in oratione sanctas manus in omni loco sine ira et disceptatione* ('let us raise holy hands "in prayer in every place without anger and dispute" '), and in *Cels.* VII.44.38-39 'ἐν παντὶ' δὲ 'τόπῳ' εὐχόμενος ('and "in every place" praying') in a context speaking of a moderate and pure life in a world which is God's temple. At *Or.* 8.1 he writes οὐδὲ μετὰ ὀργῆς καὶ τεταραγμένων λογισμῶν ἐπὶ τὴν προσευχὴν ἐλθετέον ('or come to prayer in anger and distracting contentions') in a context speaking of those who give themselves continually to prayer (8.2). At *Or.* 31.4 (although making very clear that the congregation is especially conducive to prayer in 31.5) he writes

> καὶ περὶ τόπου δὲ ἰστέον ὅτι πᾶς τόπος ἐπιτήδειος εἰς τὸ εὔξασθαι ὑπὸ τοῦ καλῶς εὐχομένου γίνεται...λέγει κύριος...βούλομαι οὖν προσεύχεσθαι τοὺς ἄνδρας ἐν παντὶ τόπῳ. ἔχει δὲ καὶ τεταγμένον ὑπὲρ τοῦ ἐφ᾽ ἡσυχίας μὴ περισπώμενον τὰς εὐχὰς ἐπιτελεῖν ἕκαστον, ἐπιλεξάμενον τοῦ ἰδίου οἴκου, ἐὰν ἐγχωρῇ, τὸ σεμνότερον, ἵν᾽ οὕτως εἴπω, χωρίον, οὕτως εὔχεσθαι.

> On the question of place it is to be observed that every place is suitable for prayer for him who prays well: ...says the Lord...I will, therefore, that men pray in every place. It is enjoined that every man, in order to pray in peace and without disturbance, should choose a special place in his own house, if there is room for it—his sanctuary, so to speak, and there he should pray.

At 31.2 he speaks of prayer whilst ill or on a voyage, and at 32 again of prayer in one's own house. At *Or.* 24 Tertullian writes

> *Sed quomodo omni loco, cum prohibeamur in publico? Omni...loco, quem oportunitas aut etiam necessitas importarit. Neque enim contra praeceptum reputatur ab apostolis factum, qui in carcere audientibus custodiis orabant et canebant Deo, aut a Paulo, qui in naui coram omnibus eucharistiam fecit.*

> But what does it mean 'in every place' when we are forbidden to pray in public? 'In every place'...which appropriateness or even necessity enjoins. For neither is it considered done contrary to the precept by the apostles when they prayed in prison, in the hearing of their guards, and sang to God; nor was Paul contravening the precept when he offered up thanksgiving on shipboard, in the sight of all.

Eusebius in *Ps. Com.* 76 PG 23.889 adds to citation of v. 8 καὶ τοῦτ' ἔπραττον οὐ δι' ἡμέρας μόνον, ἀλλὰ καὶ διὰ νυκτός ('and this do not only by day, but also by night').[2] Bartsch makes clear that at v. 8 ἐν παντὶ τόπῳ marks use of a pre-existing rule[3] which in the patristic period was applied in both ecclesial and general instruction.[4] Clement of Alexandria cites v. 9 in general instruction at *Paed.* II.xii.127.2 (although as if from a letter of Peter), and at *Paed.* III.xi.64.3 where he combines at 4-5 reference to the generally referring 1 Pet. 3.1-4. Nor is a congregational context suggested for v. 9 in *Sent. Sextus* 235-36.[5] Cyprian *Hab. uirg.* and Tertullian *Cult. fem.* employ 1 Tim. 2 in argument about ordinary dress (Lock 1924: 31). There can be no doubt, therefore, that very early in the Christian era the context in which vv. 11-12 appears was not always viewed as congregational.

Subsequent interpreters show evidence of similar tendencies. In the thirteenth century, Aquinas at v. 8 stresses that man can pray in every

---

2.   Cf. the translation of *1 Clem.* 29.1 (see above) by Graham and Grant (1978: 34).

3.   Bartsch 1965: 47-59. See also e.g. Easton 1948: 123; Simpson 1954: 45; Jeremias 1963: 18; Kelly 1972: 65-66; P.H. Towner 1989: 206; Merkel 1991: 26. For Bartsch's conclusion that the rule is primarily cultic see below.

4.   Other references in *Bib. Pat.* are less clearly to 1 Timothy, and some appear in instruction about prayer without indicating the place of that prayer, e.g. Origen in *Hom. in Ex.* 11.4.28.

5.   Other patristic references to v. 9 cited in *Bib. Pat.* are less clearly to the passage. *Apoc. Pet. graeca* 475, e.g., simply speaks negatively of braided hair, although obviously not with only ecclesial behaviour in mind.

place, churches being built only to provide solitude and quiet. Verses 9-10 he takes to refer to women at prayer anywhere, and vv. 11-12 as referring generally (although citing 1 Cor. 14.34, 1862: 594-96). Luther finds v. 8 relevant for men's everyday lives, and believes women should normally wear modest clothing, but—although uncertain—favours the congregational context for vv. 9-12 (1527–28: XXVIII, 271-77). Calvin assumes that vv. 1-2, 8, 9-10 address prayers and demeanour anywhere, only v. 12 dealing with public ministry.[6] Fell writes even of v. 12:

> Here the apostle speaks particularly to a woman *in relation to her husband*, to be in subjection to *him* and not to teach nor usurp authority over *him* and therefore he mentions Adam and Eve. But let it be strained to the utmost, as the opposers of womens speaking would have it: that is that they should not preach nor speak in church, *of which there is nothing here...*[7]

By the nineteenth century unanimity is still not to be found.[8] Although voices dissenting from the congregational context are not often acknowledged in more recent literature, they had not altogether been stilled. Booth writes: 'we have never met with the slightest proof that this text has any reference to the public exercises of women...' (1859: 14-16). Booth cites Robinson, who claims that in connection with precepts about apparel and domestic position, especially in marital relations, the teaching in view is primarily that taking place at home (1859: 14-15). Another contemporary declares that the prohibition 'refers exclusively to the private life and domestic character of woman'.[9] Plummer and Bernard reject the non-congregational view without citing

6.   Calvin (1579: 11, 16-19) who, even though limiting the teaching etc. to a very few men called to an honourable—if burdensome—office, applies all this instruction to both all men's and women's everyday lives, only at v. 12 moving from that context.

7.   Fell (1666: 10). Fell's emphases, punctuation, and spelling are here reproduced. This part of her argument is either overlooked or disregarded by modern exegetes when citing her early rejection of the traditional interpretation. For additional fifteenth/sixteenth-century examples see Hugenberger (1992: 350 with n. 39).

8.   Those accepting the congregational context include Grimke 1838: 113-14; Weisinger 1866: 401; B. Weiss 1885: 107, 118; Plummer 1888: 82, 86, 94-103; Liddon 1897: 10, 15-16; Bernard 1899: 37, 43-44, 47.

9.   Booth 1859: 16 identifies this source only as 'a barrister'.

their sources.[10] Gordon does not state his own opinion, but cites with approval Garrat's non-congregational interpretation.[11]

A few twentieth-century scholars argue that, although vv. 1-8 deal with congregational concerns, vv. 9-15 or some parts thereof focus on marital relations.[12] Certainly ἀνδρός *could* convey 'husband', and the asyndeton between vv. 10-11 *could* indicate transition from one subject to another. Nevertheless, ἀνήρ (v. 8) clearly refers to all men, and γυνή (vv. 9-10) to all women. There is no sure foundation for a change of focus at vv. 11-12 from all women, not only to wives, but to wives in the domestic situation.[13] Powers takes a more radical approach, justifiably arguing that: whilst the prayers of vv. 1-8 include public worship, there is no justification for restricting application to that situation; at vv. 9-10 proper dress and adornment apply to the 'entire lifestyle and general demeanour'; and 'good deeds' presumably cannot be restricted to congregational activities.[14] Nevertheless, the conclusions he draws for vv. 11-15 are for the most part not compelling. The interpretation of vv. 13-15 which he follows will be addressed in Part IV, but he sees those verses as explaining what precedes: since Adam and Eve are husband and wife the primary reference of vv. 8-15 is marital (1975: 55-59). Details of his argument concerning vv. 11-12 are similar to those employed by others to be addressed in Chapter 4 below, but one difficulty is immediately apparent. The proper deportment and good deeds outlined in vv. 9-10 cannot be confined to the marital relationship any more than to the congregation.[15] Powers argues that at v. 8 men praying anywhere are in view. Since life in general and (presumably) women in general are in view in vv. 9-10, even though Adam and Eve feature prominently in vv. 13-15, his claim that the references and

10. See n. 10 above.

11. Gordon 1894: 916. Hugenberger (1992: 350-51 with n. 40) cites also Matthies.

12. E.g. Barrett 1963: 55; Hommes 1969: 7, 13; J.G. Baldwin 1973: 21-22; Ellis 1981: 217; Scanzoni and Hardesty 1982: 71; Fee 1984: 34; Nicole 1986: 47 n. 1 (a); Barnett 1989: 229. See also Gritz 1991: 131 and n. 78. For additional sources see Hugenberger (1992: 351).

13. Knight 1980: 30; Fung 1987: 200-01.

14. Winter (1988b: 93) argues that in inscriptions τὸ ἀγαθὸν ἔργον refers to public benefaction.

15. Hugenberger (1992: 351-52) points out that 1 Pet. 3.1-7 does limit command for prayer to husbands and requirement of modest adornment to wives. For critique see Schreiner (1995: 115-17).

allusions of vv. 8-15 are to the family sphere, and the primary reference to the marital situation,[16] is not forceful. In spite of these difficulties, however, Powers' observations about the context deserve more attention than they have received.[17]

The congregational context is often treated as more or less self-evident. Some are cautious about it, but stop short of considering the implications of the alternative. Moo decides that at vv. 1-2 the public setting is 'almost certain', noting '[s]o most commentators'. Whether ὡσαύτως (v. 9) indicates that women are to pray as are men, or simply links two separate regulations, he continues,

> *it is likely* that the context of public worship is retained...[I]nasmuch as vv11-15 *seem* to include a description of...[the required] 'good works,' and the learning and teaching activities described...are obviously communal, it is *almost certain* that...[the] instructions...must be taken as directed to...the congregational worship service.[18]

This makes a precarious foundation for subsequent exegesis. Others slide without explanation from a general to a formal setting of teaching and learning at v. 12.[19] The vast majority, however, register no sign of uncertainty, many (whether or not envisaging in some parts of the passage a wider reference) assuming or simply asserting that the background is the gathered assembly.[20] Some offer supporting argument, but

16. Powers 1975: 57-59. See also Banks 1976: 96.

17. Giles (1977: 64 and n. 7) rejects Powers on grounds of the allusion to Mal. 1.10-11 in v. 8, contemporary Jewish use of 'place' for 'place of prayer/meeting', the context, and Pauline usage (for all of which see points i-ix below). M.J. Evans (1983: 100) thinks Powers' argument possible, but judges a 'wider sphere' likely ('continued' prayer theme, ἐν παντὶ τόπῳ) with some ecclesiastical content. Liefeld (1986: 194-95 nn. 3, 5) briefly rejects Powers on linguistic and contextual grounds. Gritz (1991: 145 n. 11) reports Powers but, although allowing that the reference of vv. 1-8 could be wider than for public worship, ignores that possibility as she begins consideration of vv. 9-10. Hugenberger (1992: 352-54) utilizes Powers's argument; see n. 15 above.

18. Moo 1980: 62-63 (emphases mine). See also Kähler 1959: 11; Karris 1977: 206; Foh 1979: 125; Bruce 1982b: 10; Howard 1983: 40; Key 1984: 147; G. Davies 1986: 84-85; Nicole 1986: 47; Moo 1991: 182; Schreiner 1995: 113, 117 with n. 50.

19. E.g. Parry 1920: 11, 14-15; J.G. Baldwin 1973: 21-22; Williams 1977: 110-12; Osburn 1982: 10-11. Cf. Ridderbos (1977: 462 and n. 107), who argues that all women are in view because this is a 'liturgical' (not 'household') prescription.

20. E.g. Locke 1705-1707: 221; Grimke 1838: 112-14; Bernard 1899: 37-38, 43-47; White 1910: 83, 102; Bushnell 1919: §§42, 43 (followed by Penn-Lewis

few feel obliged to spend much time on the subject.[21] Such argument as has been offered features combinations of the following claims:

i.   public worship is in view throughout vv. 1-12;[22]

ii.   at 3.15 ἐν οἴκῳ θεοῦ... ἥτις ἐστὶν ἐκκλησία θεοῦ ζῶντος means the *gathered* assembly;[23]

iii. προσεύχεσθαι is not implied at v. 9, prayer being limited to the men and therefore public;[24]

iv. 'where Christians gather' (or similar) is implied after ἐν παντὶ τόπῳ;[25]

1919: 52); Meinertz 1931: 34; Scott 1936: 18, 24; Falconer 1937: 127-31; Leipoldt 1953: 124, 133; Hendriksen 1955: 91; Ryrie 1958: 71-72, 75-76; Barrett 1963: 49; Jeremias 1963: 16, 18; G.G. Blum 1965: 157-58; A.T. Hanson 1966: 31; Brox 1969: 122, 130-31; Kelly 1972: 59-60; Spencer 1974: 216; Barclay 1975: 58, 66-69; Houlden 1976: e.g. 63-65; Olthuis 1976: 142; Osborne 1977: 346; Hurley 1981: 197-98, 200-201; Payne 1981: 170, 187, 191; Stendahl 1982: 29; Scanzoni and Hardesty 1982: 70; Schüssler Fiorenza 1983: 290; Sigountos and Shank 1983: 283, 285; Howard 1983: 39; Woodhouse 1985b: 17; Scholer 1986: 201-202; Küchler 1986: 10; Fung 1987: 197; Witherington 1988: 118-19; Bilezikian 1989: 174, 179; Byrne 1988: 87; M.Y. MacDonald 1988: 179, 223-24; P.H. Towner 1989: 203, 205-16; Barnett 1989: 225; Harris 1990: 335-52; Guthrie 1990: 79; Gritz 1991: 125, 128; Oberlinner 1994: 82, 91-92; Jervis 1995: 54.

21. Exceptions include Holtz (1965: 52-73) and Roloff (1988: 107-38), who argue for a communion context throughout.

22. Weisinger (1866: 411-13), e.g., builds three steps on this foundation: i. βούλομαι οὖν (v. 8) refocuses on the concern of v. 1; ii. men and women are addressed separately; and iii. v. 9 begins with ὡσαύτως. Plummer (1888: 95) believes there is no reasonable doubt about this context, 'some of the directions' scarcely intelligible if private devotions or family prayer are in view. His reasoning is obscure because he offers no discussion about vv. 11-12. See also Holtz 1965: 52-73; Giles 1977: 73 n. 7 (for whom see also no. iv.); Roloff 1988: 107-42.

23. E.g. Foh 1979: 125; Roloff 1988: 107-108, 137; and Knight (1992: 128) whose modification will be noted below.

24. E.g. Prohl 1957: 34-35; Scott 1936: 24-26; N.R. Lightfoot 1976: 134 (for whom see also no. v.). See also Houlden 1976: 69-70.

25. E.g. Weisinger 1866: 412; Huther 1866: 126; B. Weiss 1885: 119; E.F. Brown 1917: 18; Marshall 1984: 191; Knoch 1988: 26. Lock (1924: 30) (for whom see also no. v.) in view of the orientation of vv. 4, 6 and 1 Cor. 1.2; 7.17; 14.33 also finds even more probable that this is a rule for all churches under the Author's influence. Cf. 'and wherever Timothy's supervision extends' (Parry 1920: 14), and 'every place where believers gather in and around Ephesus' (Fee 1984: 34). Claiming that 'place' in contemporary Jewish use means 'place of prayer/meeting place', and comparing 1 Cor. 1.2; 2 Cor. 2.14; 1 Thess. 1.8 are Scott 1936: 24; Barrett

v.   prayer, teaching, learning and authority are in view and proper clothing is required;[26]

vi. analogies occur at 1 Cor. 11.2-16 and 14.34-36;[27]

vii. credal or liturgical material is included;[28]

viii. later ecclesiastical orders were influenced by the passage;[29] and

ix. ecclesial problems caused by women led astray by false teachers are being addressed.[30]

With a congregational context thus supported or assumed, many argue that traditional household instructions are here adapted,[31] and often that

1963: 54; Kelly 1972: 65-66; Giles 1977: 73 (for the last of which see also no. i.). Hendriksen (1955: 91, 102, 105) believes v. 8 shows a close adherence to synagogue customs, elders 'naturally' leading the prayers (citing 5.17). Padgett (1987a: 22 and n. 14) establishes his claim by no. v., and Knight (1992: 128) combines the likelihood of his with nos. ii. and (partially) v.

26. Kelly (1972: 66) combines this claim with no. iv.; Padgett 1987a: 22 n. 14. See also Knight (1992: 130), but note his modifications below.

27. E.g. Houlden 1976: 71. 1 Cor. 11.3-16 will be considered briefy in Part IV App. 2, but it addresses both sexes, and v. 17 precludes restriction of reference in the foregoing section to the gathered assembly, so analogy is dubious. 1 Cor. 14.34-35 will be examined in Part III, but the many who see a parallel/relationship here include: Weisinger 1866: 415; Humphreys 1901: 97; Lock (1924: 30), for whom see also no. iv.; Dibelius and Conzelmann 1972: 47; Knight 1992: 140. N.R. Lightfoot (1976: 129, 134-35) thinks the parallel beyond question, the congregational context 'almost explicit', combining his claim with versions of nos. iii. and v., and reasoning that at v. 1 the plurality and multiformity of the prayer 'perhaps' suggests it is public.

28. Roloff 1988: e.g. 107, 110, 114, 120. Sometimes this reason is implied rather than stated: e.g. Knoch 1988: 25.

29. E.g. Bernard 1899: 37-38; Humphreys 1901: 92-93, 97-99; E.F. Brown 1917: 14. This reckons without the possibility of misinterpretation. See also Lock (1924: 29-32), who accepts that at times vv. 8-15 apply principles with wider application, and combines nos. i., ii. and iii. with vi. He also speculates, in the context of his consideration of ἐπαγγελλομέναις (professing)...κτλ., about an analogy to pagan priestesses, comparing ὁσίους χεῖρας (v. 8), ἱεροπρεπεῖς (Tit. 2.3) with an inscription 'describing the dress of ἱεραὶ γυναῖκες in the mysteries, μὴ ἐχέτω μηδεμία χρυσία...μηδὲ τὰς τρίχας ἀναπεπλεγμένας. Dittenberg[er], *Syll.* ii.[2] 653...; cf. Tert. [and] *de C.F.* ii.12, "*sacerdotes pudicitiae*".'

30. This claim will be examined in detail in Part II, but examples include Fee 1984: 34, 53; Padgett 1987a: 22-23.

31. E.g. Jeremias 1963: 15-16; Dibelius and Conzelmann 1972: 35, 39-41, 44-45, 47-49; Verner 1983: 91-92; Dautzenberg 1989: 196; Merkel 1991: 24, 26.

the Author to some extent still addresses aspects of non-congregational life.[32] Since nothing suggests that specifically marital/household relations are in view, the reference is therefore understood primarily to be to 'women in the congregation', but also partly to 'women generally'. General reference is identified especially at vv. 9-10, but also at v. 12b, aspects of v. 8, and even (rarely) at vv. 1-2. This dual reference has two difficulties:

    i.   there is little agreement about its precise mixture; and
    ii.   attempts to define it invariably betray an underlying tension.

Of authors drawn from across the exegetical spectrum surveyed for this study, every acknowledgment of dual (congregational–general) reference is marred by either inconsistency,[33] admission of opposing evidence,[34] assumption,[35] confusion,[36] indecision[37] or circular argument.[38]

32. See immediately below for examples.

33. Ellicott (1864: 32, 37) at v. 12 interprets αὐθεντεῖν *by* its context yet makes διδάσκειν the chief device *for establishing* the context of the preceding v. 8. Huther (1866: 132-33) acknowledges general reference at vv. 9-10, but is reluctant to permit it at αὐθεντεῖν. B. Weiss (1885: 121, 125) acknowledges some household reference at vv. 11-12, but denies general reference at vv. 9-10. Hurley (1981: 180, 198, 200-201) sees dual reference at vv. 8-10, but employs those verses with vv. 1-2 to render the prohibitions at vv. 11-12 ecclesial. G. Davies (1986: 85) acknowledges general reference at v. 8 but not vv. 9-10. Guthrie (1990: 84-87) is unwilling to restrict vv. 9-10 to public prayer, but tentatively so restricts vv. 11-12, his only textual support an unexplained choice of 'silence' for ἡσυχία (v. 12) cf. 'quiet' (v. 11).

34. Alford (1862: 318-19) cannot exclude congregational reference at a 'general' vv. 9-10 or the reverse at vv. 11-12. Meinertz (1931: 34, 37-38) must keep reminding the reader of a congregational context not obvious in the text. Knoch (1988: 24-27), accepting a congregational and even (hesitantly) eucharistic context, yet recognizes broader reference at vv. 1-4, 8-10.

35. Lock (1924: 31-32) believes ὑποταγῇ (v. 11) is directed to church officials and regulations, introducing ecclesiological terminology not found in the text. Dibelius and Conzelmann (1972: 5, 44-45, 47-48 with n. 20) acknowledge general reference at vv. 9-12, 15 (and 1 Pet. 3.3ff.), but with considerable diffidence claim that the context 'lets' v. 12 relate to the worship service (followed by e.g. Kähler 1960: 150).

36. Parry (1920: 11, 14-15) confuses ecclesial and non-ecclesial contexts. Easton (1948: 123-24, 126) acknowledges that vv. 1-2, 8 may not be limited to public worship, but claims they address only men. Yet, he claims, v. 8 dwells particularly on public worship, women at v. 9 pray in public, and at v. 12 he can only speculate.

Bartsch offers full discussion, arguing that in fact the Author does not here separate ecclesial and general activities. The primarily cultic reference, he says, is expressed by terms from popular philosophy and rabbinic Judaism concerning general behaviour, thus presenting a parallel to 1 Pet. 3.1ff. For him ἐν παντὶ τόπῳ has little contextual significance, being only a marker to a pre-existing rule associating eschatological, worldwide lordship and acknowledgment of God with rejection of the temple as the place of the cult.[39] He cites Mal. 1.11;[40] Ps. 102.22; *Jüd.*

37. White (1910: 106-109) employs v. 8 to confine διδάσκειν (v. 12) to public teaching, but suspects marital teaching may be in view. Scholer (1986: 201) cannot tell whether v. 9 instructs women at prayer or generally but, tending towards the latter, says 'the context is the church'.

38. Knight (1992: 115, 128-31, 138-49) recognizes broad perspectives at vv. 8-12, 15 and 3.15, but begins by assuming a congregatonal context at vv. 1, 8, for which he subsequently argues at v. 8 (citing vv. 11-12; 3.14-15, and likelihood of reference to places of meeting) and from there interprets vv. 11-12 as primarily congregational. For more detailed critiques of sources in my nn. 33-38 see my 1995: 26-34, for which see p. 9 above.

39. Bartsch 1965: 47-59. Dibelius and Conzelmann (see n. 35 above) agree that ἐν παντὶ τόπῳ has little contextual relevance, and declare ὁσίους χεῖρας to have been taken over from an earlier instruction. At vv. 9ff. they envisage regulations from a household rule 'somewhat artificially' applied at an earlier time to a church order about prayer (see also Brox 1969: 130-31, 134), the instruction 'doubtless intended for the worship service', and the combination of different rules explaining why (the implied) βούλομαι may be understood to refer either to (an implied) προσεύχεσθαι, or only to ἐν καταστολῇ κοσμίῳ...κοσμεῖν ἑαυτάς. The parallel at 1 Pet. 3.3ff., they emphatically note, is part of a household rule. Αὐθεντεῖν (interpreted as 'domineer over') is suspected of having a more general meaning originally (citing *BGU*, IV, 1208.37f. [...27–26 BC] 'self-assured, firm conduct'). Oberlinner (1994: 84-85, 90, 92, 97) similarly: 'die Situation der gottesdienstlichen Versammlung...ausgedehnt auf das ganze Leben' ('the situation of the religious meeting... extended to the whole life') until, citing Bartsch, 'mit V13 "der Zusammenhang gottesdienstlicher Regeln eindeutig verlassen" ist' ('with V13 is "the context of worship rules unequivocally departed from"').

40. See also Kelly (1972: 65-66), who calls 2.8 an 'almost technical' reflection of Mal. 1.11, and a lesser component. Lock (1924: 30) cites second century acceptance that Mal. 1.11 points to the universal offering of the Eucharist. The universality of Mal. 1.11, however, is that of worship unrestricted to a particular place, not of a Eucharist offered in many places. P.H. Towner (1989: 205-06) says ἐν παντὶ τόπῳ 'may' allude to a widely known rule about prayer sourced in Mal. 1.11, also suggesting the same connection by means of the same phrase with prayer at 1 Cor. 1.2 and mission at 2 Cor. 2.14; 1 Thess. 1.8. See also Easton 1948: 123; Simpson

Paläst. Corpus Inscr. ed. Sam. Klein. nos. 6, 8; Jn 4.22-24.[41] 1 Tim. 2.1, he says, requires that prayer be made for all people upon this basis (vv. 4-6; cf. also e.g. *Did.* 14.2). Whilst a decrease in eschatological expectation led to the waning of proclamation of God's omnipotence and omnipresence,[42] the Author understands the rule in light of an approaching *eschaton* (1965: 58-59 n. 10). In view of applications and developments of that underlying transformed rule in other early works, Bartsch is inclined to date the transformation earlier than the Pastorals. Claiming that βούλομαι οὖν προσεύχεσθαι (v. 8) dominates all that follows, he reasons that, although all the elements of vv. 9-10 appear in later sources in instructions for both congregational and general behaviour, the reference here is primarily cultic (1965: 60-69). The prohibitions of v. 12 for him therefore concern behaviour in the congregation, but he writes:

> Was für den Gottesdienst gilt, gilt für das ganze Leben… Dies ist jedoch nur von der ursprünglichen eschatologischen Erwartung der Gemeinde her zu verstehen. In dieser Erwartung verstand die Gemeinde jeden Augenblick als unmittelbar zu dem hereinbrechenden Ende… Von daher

(1954: 45) who also suggests allusion to Jn 4.21; Jeremias 1963: 18; Giles 1977: 73 n. 7; Merkel 1991: 26; Knight 1992: 128. Plummer (1888: 95), concerned to absolve the Author from Jewish–Christian antithesis (as are Alford 1862: 317 and Ellicott 1864: 33), similarly claims the emphasis is not on ἐν παντὶ τόπῳ but primarily on προσεύχεσθαι and secondarily on τοὺς ἄνδρας. Holtz (1965: 64) denies reference to Mal. 1.11.

41. Roloff (1988: 127, 131 and nn. 85, 104) declares Bartsch's thesis improbable, arguing that '[b]etont ist vielmehr die spiritualisierte Deutung des Opfers auf den christlichen Gottesdienst, und…das Verständnis der Reinheit des Herzens im Sinne kultischer Reinheit' ('rather, what is stressed is the spiritualized interpretation of the sacrifice in regard to the Christian worship service, and…the understanding of the purity of the heart in the sense of cultic purity'). Brox (1969: 131) questions whether v. 9 is meant that programmatically, claiming it concerns divine service.

42. Bartsch (1965: 51-54) writes that in *1 Clement* the Roman church intervenes in the Corinthian community to reverse a separation of the place of cult from that of the bishop, envisaging the bishop's function as that assigned to Old Testament priests. The Eucharist (meaning 'sacrifice') is to be offered οὐ πανταχοῦ, οὐκ ἐν παντὶ τόπῳ (citing 42.2 in the context of 40.5; 44.5). God is still viewed as Lord of the whole earth (54.3), but there is no longer a consciousness that service is not bound to the consecrated place. Some later ecclesiastical organization, he continues, reflects a wider development of the same reversal of the earlier rule, the 'church' described as the place where the Spirit thrives (e.g. *Const. Apost.* 62) and consecration of the bishop closely linked with that consecrated place.

musste das ganze Leben unter diesem Gericht und d.h. im Angesicht dieses kommenden Herrn verstanden werden... Darum gelten für den Gottesdienst die gleichen Regeln wie für das gesamte Leben... Wir haben damit zugleich eine Bestätigung unsrer Interpretation des Gebets für alle Menschen wie der Bedeutung des Gebets an allen Orten. Wie die Ausweitung der gottesdienstlichen Regeln auf das allgemeine Verhalten Ausdruck des Existenzverständnisses unter der Gegenwart Gottes ist, so hatten wir ja auch die Fürbitte für alle Menschen wie die Aufhebung der kultischen Gebundenheit des Gebets als Ausdruck für ein solches Existenzverständnis interpretiert, in gleicher Weise wurzelnd in der eschatologischen Erwartung der Gemeinde (1965: 70).

Whatever is valid for the worship service is valid for the whole life... However this can only be understood from the angle of the original eschatological expectation of the congregation. By virtue of that expectation the congregation understood every moment as immediately preceding the setting in of the end... On that basis the whole life had to be understood under the judgment and that is, in the face of this coming Lord... This is why the same rules apply for the worship service as do for the entire life... We thus have at the same time a confirmation of our interpretation of prayer for all people and of the meaning of prayer in all places. In the same way as the extension of the worship service rules to include general behaviour is an expression of the existential understanding under the presence of God, so we had also interpreted the intercession for all human beings and the abolition of the cultic constraint of the prayer as an expression of such existential understanding, rooted in the same fashion in the eschatological expectation of the congregation.

Although he persuasively demonstrates the pre-existence of an eschatologically based rejection of the temple as the place in which worship is to be carried out, and also the relevance of that pre-existing rejection to 1 Timothy 2, Bartsch overinterprets the dominance of προσεύχεσθαι. Even given the implication of that infinitive at v. 9 (and this, it will be argued in Chapter 2 below, is uncertain), he confuses 'the place of the cult' with 'the place in which prayer and worship may be offered': that the Author confines the latter to the former has not been demonstrated. Someone who (as Bartsch claims) consciously and literally accepts the pre-existing eschatological proposition seems likely to conceive of the prayer and worship potentially taking place literally ἐν παντὶ τόπῳ. The phrase may well be more than only a 'marker' to that proposition.[43] Its

43. Cf. Verner (1983: 167) who, presupposing that the Author is ordinarily purposeful, suggests that he here emphasizes that every locality is expected to conduct

use suggests a practical, universal outlook. In thinking of something which has hitherto happened in the temple, the Author may not now think in terms of some other religious and variously situated sphere (i.e. 'in church') but of something taking place in people's lives.[44] Since 1 Timothy may provide the earliest evidence of application of this underlying material to life in general, it is questionable whether those who had earlier accepted it made any narrower application. *Did.* 14.2, whenever dated,[45] confirms this. It is concerned that those gathering ἐν ἐκκλησίᾳ should have an appropriate attitude facilitated by an appropriate life; but it is unclear that the 'sacrifice'[46] in view is 'the eucharist' and not simply prayer. Since, as Bartsch demonstrates, subsequent references to these same views underlying both *Did.* 14.2 and 1 Tim. 2.1-4, 8 also address both ecclesial and general behaviour, it would be reasonable to assume that from its earliest appearance this eschatological recognition of God's omnipotence and omnipresence is viewed in terms of people's entire lives. Bartsch therefore unintentionally weakens the case for a (primarily) congregational context.

Some parts of 1 Timothy 2 obviously cannot be limited to congregational activities and, despite the unsuccessful nature of the above-noted attempts to acknowledge that fact, it should not be ignored or explained away. Why *does* its acknowledgment result in widespread disagreement about details and internal interpretative tensions? Because, I suggest, the congregational context itself is long overdue for thorough re-examination. Chapters 2–4 conduct such a re-examination.

its worship according to this universal rule. Alternatively he proposes that a number of different parts of a single assembly may be in view.

44. That prayer can be hindered by the inappropriate life is an idea Bartsch (1965: 55) traces in e.g. Mt. 5.23ff. Reicke (1957: 303-04) cites also 1 Cor. 11.20-29; 13.1; Jas 4.3; 1 Pet. 3.7.

45. For an early dating see J.A.T. Robinson (1976: 322-27). See also Niederwimmer (1989: 78-79) with n. 72.

46. See translation in e.g. Kraft (1978: 317).

Chapter 2

THE AUTHOR'S STATEMENTS OF PURPOSE,
STRUCTURE AND THEME

The Author's own statements of purpose at 1 Tim. 1.18-19a and 3.14-
15 sow the first seeds of doubt about a congregational context.[1] Although the rest of the letter cannot be divorced from these statements,
2.1–3.13 may usefully be considered as a unit.[2] The exegete may decide
the letter is an artificial construction[3] but, whatever the actual motivation for the whole, the controversial nature of 2.9-15 makes accurate
identification of the setting that the Author chose to delineate
imperative. He claims to write his instruction

(a) ἵνα στρατεύῃ...τὴν καλὴν στρατείαν ἔχων πίστιν καὶ ἀγαθὴν
συνείδησιν (1.18-19). Hymenaeus and Alexander (vv. 19-20) serve as
a measure of the depth of his concern that the reader understand the
importance of what is to follow.

(b) ἵνα εἰδῇς πῶς δεῖ ἐν οἴκῳ θεοῦ ἀναστρέφεσθαι (3.15).[4] Whether
'God's *oikos*' be understood as the local assembly, gathered or ungath-
ered, or something more universal,[5] and whoever may be the subject of

---

1.   In protest against claims that 3.14-15 furnishes *the* purpose of the letter, so
making it a 'suprasituational "church manual" ', Scholer (1986: 200) argues that
those verses are a 'summary statement' of directions for a particular local problem.
Both ideas will be examined in Part II. The question addressed here is simply
whether 3.14-15 is directed specifically to congregational behaviour.

2.   See, e.g., Jeremias 1963: 15; Holtz 1965: 53; Brox 1969: 121; Knight 1975:
84; Roloff 1988: 107; Bush 1990: 155.

3.   E.g. Dibelius and Conzelmann 1972: 5-6. Cf. Donelson (1986: 200), who
argues that the literary form of the Pastorals reveals an important historical moment
in the battle for orthodoxy.

4.   Some consider v. 16 the goal the Author has in mind and vv. 14-15 its introduction (Spicq 1947: 103; Jeremias 1963: 23); but see Verner (1983: 110-11).

5.   Full consideration of New Testament meanings for ἐκκλησία lies outside
the scope of this study.

εἰδῇς,[6] this verse displays the immediacy of the concern.

The instruction between these statements of purpose is thus marked as of the greatest importance. Verse 1.18 speaks quite generally of faith and good conscience. Verse 3.15 immediately follows the section dealing with the lives of local assembly officials, a context in which 'God's household' most naturally appears to be the lives of the people of the local assembly: at the least, it is uncertain that the gathered assembly or a universally conceived entity is in view.[7] Neither stated goal limits the context to worship or prayer meetings.

Between those goals chs. 2 and 3 are generally understood each to address one main topic. Chapter 3 certainly does so, presenting qualifications for ἐπίσκοποι, διάκονοι and certain women. The missing verbs at 3.8, 11 are supplied by δεῖ...εἶναι (v. 2), a construction requiring that three groups of officials be understood, not two with the wives of the second.[8] The topic underlying 3.1-13, therefore, is 'qualifications for assembly officials'. Any topic underlying ch. 2 is less easily identified.

The chapter division separates material about men and women from material about assembly officials. Even though there is considerable disagreement about the role of the women at 3.11, some versions choose headings suggesting that the chapters constitute two basic topics, for example:

	Chapter 2	*Chapter 3*
UBSGNT	Instructions concerning Prayer	Qualifications
NIV	Instructions on Worship	Overseers and Deacons
JB	Liturgical prayer	
	Women in the assembly	The elder in charge/deacons
TEV	Church worship	Leaders in the church

6.	Reed (1993: 108-17), contra the majority, and without implying anything about the identity of Timothy, argues that the latter is the primary subject.

7.	Houlden (1976: 62-63, 83) suspects that at 3.15, with the congregation immediately in view, 'the perspective naturally broadens to embrace the Church as a whole'. Verner (1983: 108-11, 128) notes that early Christian literature consistently employs ἀναστρέφεσθαι for the way individuals or groups habitually live, that throughout the Pastorals οἶκος refers to a social entity, and that the Author never separates household life from the life of the household of God.

8.	Hurley 1981: 229-31; Byrne 1988: 87. See also Stiefel (1995: 442-57), whose background reconstruction will be considered in Part II. Contra e.g. Verner (1983: 100, 132-33 and n. 17), who believes deacons' wives are in view, but does not explain why elders' wives are *not*.

Commentators sometimes take the same approach. Even though no claim may be explicitly made that the Author's thought progresses logically from πρῶτον (2.1) to δεύτερον (ch. 3), outlines imply that 2.1–3.13 comprises two major topics marked by the chapter division.[9] One factor reinforcing that impression is the parallel between the implied verbal constructions at 3.8, 11 and the need at 2.9 for βούλομαι, certainly,[10] and possibly also προσεύχεσθαι, to be understood from v. 8.[11] Such a construction does carry forward an underlying topic or theme. In ch. 2, however, vv. 10-15 (and, if προσεύχεσθαι is *not* implied, also v. 9), do not speak about prayer, so the carried-forward topic is generally identified as 'behaviour at public worship'. Beginning from 1.18 the section is interpreted along the lines of the following shortened paraphrase:

> I give you this instruction so that you may fight the good warfare.[12] *First of all*, I urge that prayers be made for everyone: i. men should pray thus; and ii. women should appear and act thus. (*Secondly*,) i. overseers must have certain qualities; ii. deacons must have certain qualities; and iii. certain women must have certain qualities. I am writing you these instructions so that you will know the conduct necessary in God's household.

But 2.15, however it may be interpreted,[13] is clearly concerned (as is 3.1-13) with character, not only with conduct in the assembly. The chapter division does not mark a simple change of context from behaviour at worship to qualifications for officials. The pattern of the Author's thought in ch. 2, therefore, is often conceived as shifting to some extent between ecclesial and non-ecclesial contexts. Some (as outlined in the previous chapter) claim to identify the first such shift at vv. 9-10, v. 8 or even vv. 1-2, but all agree it certainly occurs at least at v. 14b/15. To my knowledge it has never been argued convincingly that ch. 2 *as a whole* concerns the one topic 'behaviour in the gathered assembly'.

---

9.   E.g. Bernard 1899: 37, 51; Jeremias 1963: 15; Barrett 1963: 49-57; Knoch 1988: 23. See also some exegetes, e.g. T.D. Gordon 1995: 61. Cf. B. Weiss (1885: 107) who believes πρῶτον introduces the first of several matters.

10.   BAGD, s.v. ὡσαύτως.

11.   Cf. also 5.24 supplying εἰσιν for v. 25, and Tit. 2.2 supplying εἶναι for v. 3.

12.   Alford (1862: 311) points out that στρατεύεσθαι refers not merely to fighting but to the whole business of the employed soldier or the entire campaign.

13.   See Part IV for full discussion.

The obviously more general reference at v. 15, together with diversity of opinion about which portions of the rest of the chapter refer to congregational behaviour, furnish sufficient cause to reconsider two things:

(a) Do the two chapters present two basic ways to 'fight the good warfare' as the ensuring of:

    i.   appropriate behaviour at worship (ch. 2); and
    ii. appropriately qualified leaders (ch. 3)?

The continuous topic of 3.1-13 may only be identified as the Author's δεύτερον if he is found to be progressing logically from one major topic to another at that point. Yet, in spite of widespread assumption that one major topic *does* underlie the whole of ch. 2, no one has satisfactorily identified it. The chapter division does not complete a πρῶτον...δεύτερον structure. Of course, it is not essential that a δεύτερον argument occur at all, since the Author's thought may shift away from any structure he had in mind when he wrote his πρῶτον. I will return to this possibility later but, if it were so, chapter headings and outlines for ch. 2 in modern translations and commentaries should reflect the fact that at least at v. 15 the instruction is not about congregational behaviour.

(b) Is the topic carried forward by the implied verbal construction at v. 9 in fact 'congregational behaviour'? There is reason to conclude it is not. Within the framework bounded by 1.18 and 3.14-15 and divided at 2.15–3.1 by a shift of focus from men and women to assembly officials, 2.1-2 begins:

> Παρακαλῶ οὖν πρῶτον πάντων ποιεῖσθαι δεήσεις...ὑπὲρ πάντων ἀνθρώπων...

The Author is concerned that the prayers be made so that Christians may live peaceful, quiet lives in all εὐσεβείᾳ καὶ σεμνότητι. Οὖν indicates that the prayers are intended to contribute to the 'good warfare' (1.18-19). Precisely in accordance with the general address of that statement of purpose, no mention is here made of *where* they should occur. Nor is there any mention of activities one would normally expect at public worship such as communion and the exercise of spiritual gifts.[14]

---

14. Scott (1936: 19) suggests this may be because the Author is interested in practical life, here prayer on behalf of others. Prayer, however, surely cannot be

Τοῦτο καλόν (v. 3) is usually understood to refer to the prayer,[15] but the most obvious reference is that for which people are to pray.[16] The phrase serves as an introduction to a broadly focused, threefold exposition (vv. 3-7) on the importance of godliness and proper conduct, with πᾶς featuring prominently (vv. 1, 2 *bis*, 4, 6):

i. peaceful, godly lives are both good in themselves, and please God, who wants everyone to be saved and come into a knowledge of truth;
ii. God is one, and Christ, his only mediator, gave himself for everyone, being testified to at the proper time; and
iii. for this reason Paul had been appointed to teach the nations.

1 Tim. 2.4-7 is sometimes described as a 'digression' from the theme of prayer.[17] They are in fact part of a larger unit in which the focus shifts variously from the activity of praying to that which is to be prayed for (v. 2), to exposition upon that which is to be prayed for (vv. 3ff.), and within that exposition to God, Christ and Paul (vv. 4-7).[18]

At v. 8 the focus returns to prayer, οὖν this time linking not only with v. 7 but, via the topic, primarily with vv. 1-2:

Βούλομαι οὖν προσεύχεσθαι τοὺς ἄνδρας ἐν παντὶ τόπῳ ἐπαίροντας ὁσίους χεῖρας χωρὶς ὀργῆς καὶ διαλογισμοῦ.

envisaged as more 'practical' than communion (1 Cor. 11.17-34) or spiritual gifts (1 Cor. 12.1-31; 14.1-38). The omission of other elements of public worship stands unexplained.

15. E.g. Alford 1862: 314; Ellicott 1864: 28; Huther 1866: 119; Bernard 1899: 40; E.F. Brown 1917: 16; Meinertz 1931: 35; Scott 1936: 20; Jeremias 1963: 17; Kelly 1972: 62; Guthrie 1990: 81; Knight 1992: 119.

16. Murphy-O'Connor (1973: 1262) points out that this does not exclude the prayer, a necessary part of such a life. See also B. Weiss 1885: 111; Lock 1924: 27; Barrett 1963: 50; P.H. Towner 1989: 204. Cf. τοῦτο 'bezieht sich unmittelbar zurück auf die Weisung zum Gebet...(V1)... Das in V2b über die Lebensführung der Christen Gesagte wird jedoch mit aufgenommen' ('refers directly back to the instruction to pray... [VI] ...However that which is said in V2b abut the way of life of Christians is also taken up', Roloff 1988: 119).

17. E.g. Alford 1862: 312; Barrett 1963: 53; Byrne 1988: 87. See also for vv. 3-7 Huther (1866: 125) and Brox (1969: 122).

18. Correct are B. Weiss (1885: 118), who says there is no digression but that vv. 3-7 'die Begründung der ersten Ermahnung bildete' ('formed the reason for the first admonition'), and P.H. Towner (1989: 82), who calls vv. 1-7 'a coherent unit'.

In this study ἐπαίροντας ὁσίους χεῖρας will simply be understood as 'raising holy hands', and διαλογισμός as 'disputing'.[19] The Present aspectual force of βούλομαι and προσεύχεσθαι together convey:

I am in progress wanting/it is my custom to want

the men

to keep on/be in progress praying...etc.

Barrett argues that ἐν παντὶ τόπῳ is 'no mere literalism', in Jewish usage 'place' meaning 'meeting-place/place of prayer'. The same sense, he claims, is conveyed at 1 Cor. 1.2; 1 Thess. 1.8 (1963: 54). In fact it is not. Neither LSJ nor BAGD (which lists both of the texts Barrett cites under 'inhabited place, of a city, village, etc.') includes 'prayer-place' as a meaning. The phrase most naturally means either 'every location' (1 Cor. 1.2; *1 Clem.* 41.2) or 'every situation/occasion' (Heb. 12.17; Acts 25.16; Josephus, *Ant.* 16.258; *1 Clem.* 7.5 quoting Wis. 12.10).[20] In the context of the broad concerns of vv. 3-7, climaxing with mention of Paul's mission to 'the nations' (ἐθνῶν), the balance of probability already tips towards a geographical rather than a situational τόπος, but Bartsch's argument (see Chapter 1 above) confirms the paraphrase:

I want men in every location to be pray-ers, lifting up holy hands uncharacterized by anger or dispute.[21]

The Author is obviously not intending his adressee to infer that Christian men are at liberty to be angry and disputatious anywhere apart from meetings. Nothing suggests the reference is limited to 'every place

19. For the latter see Alford 1862: 317; Huther 1866: 127; B. Weiss 1885: 120; Parry 1920: 14; Lock 1924: 30-31; Scott 1936: 25; Bartsch 1965: 47; A.T. Hanson 1966: 35; Dibelius and Conzelmann 1972: 45; Guthrie 1990: 84; Knight 1992: 130. Cf. 'doubting', as Ellicott 1864: 33; White 1910: 107; E.F. Brown 1917: 18-19; Barclay 1975: 65-66; Hendriksen 1955: 105; Oberlinner 1994: 86-87. The context most naturally suggests 'debate' and, as Plummer (1888: 99) notes, the Pastorals frequently warn against quarrelsome conduct (e.g. v. 2b, and see Chapter 6, below).

20. BAGD, s.v. τόπος lists neither 1 Tim. 2.8 nor the meaning 'gathered assembly'. '[*I*]*n every region*, i.e. where the gospel is known' (Bernard 1899: 43) (italics his).

21. Bernard (1899: 44) notes that it is the irreproachable life which makes the hands of these men holy. Scholer (1986: 200-201) believes the instruction is about the posture and attitude proper for prayer. The holiness and harmony of those praying is more central.

where Christians gather'.[22] Anger at or disputes with family members, masters, slaves, friends, associates and the public at large is surely inappropriate for the maintenance of male holiness. The concern is for the character of men who pray.

Two things should therefore be noted:

i. Such concern must include marital, family, household, and social relationships with women, not only those with other men.

ii. Prayer may not be the sole focus of the verse. Certainly the primary position of προσεύχεσθαι makes clear that it is initially the main thought, but does it remain so?

Whilst the holy hands and cordiality may be understood as those of men while they are praying,[23] the primary position of προσεύχεσθαι together with the three following clauses suggests another option. The Author's focus may again shift as at vv. 2ff. from the activity of prayer. The options are set out below with main clauses in bold print and modifying material aligned with possible referents:

So I want

[option 1]   **the men to pray**
                        in every place
                        lifting up hands
                                    which are holy
                        without anger or debate

[option 2]   **the men**
                        in every place
                        lifting up hands
                                    which are holy
                        without anger or debate   **to pray**[24]

---

22. Powers (1975: 56-57) says that reading is completely gratuitous. Barton (1986: 230) notes the generality of the Greek phrase, drawing as it does 'no explicit dichotomy between οἶκος and ἐκκλησία'.

23. As e.g. Houlden (1976: 69-70), who says the Author considers the manner rather than content of prayer and favours the synagogue custom of vocal prayer being 'men's business'.

24. Alford (1862: 317) may suggest a third alternative. He argues that the primary position of προσεύχεσθαι requires close connection with ἐν παντὶ τόπῳ, τοὺς ἄνδρας being 'taken for granted'. It is unclear whether he includes ἐπαίροντας...

The Greek word order makes option 2 likely, a slight, but perceptible, shift of focus from the prayer to the men who pray emerging.[25]

Whether or not a refocus occurs within v. 8, does the theme of prayer underlie v. 9? The question of whether προσεύχεσθαι (v. 8) is implied in v. 9 along with βούλομαι arises at this point.[26] It should be noted, however, that there are those who believe that βούλομαι alone is implied but that the theme of prayer continues, and those who believe that προσεύχεσθαι is also implied but that women are not envisaged as praying audibly in the assembly. The debated implication of προσεύχεσθαι is obviously not the only factor taken into consideration when the theme of prayer is reckoned to continue into v. 9.

Of the various explorations into the question of an implied προσεύχεσθαι, conclusive argument has not been forthcoming. Those most closely considering the problem are the older commentaries, and on this point some are not easily followed, but two problems weaken every argument:

    i.   each assumes that v. 8 deals with prayer in the gathered assembly and is accordingly unpersuasive in carrying it into v. 9; and

    ii.   neither the claim that κοσμεῖν is the appropriate infinitive for an implied βούλομαι, nor the claim that προσεύχεσθαι is also

---

διαλογισμοῦ in this reference, but if so he takes option 1. If not, and since he takes prayer (not men) as the chief focus of the sentence, he seems to intend something like 'So I want the men, lifting up holy hands without anger and debate, to pray in every place'. But if (as he believes) the order of words is important, his separation of the three clauses is somewhat arbitrary. The relevant question appears to be whether they together qualify the subject or the praying done by that subject.

25. Parry (1920: 14) claims the stress is on the participial clause, i.e. that men should bring a holy character to their prayer. See also Huther 1866: 126; Kelly 1972: 65; Witherington 1988: 119; Moo 1991: 182. Cf. S.B. Clark (1980: 191-92, 196), who declares vv. 8-10 primarily an introduction to the main point, vv. 11-12, which features the subordination of women. However, since prayer clearly is identified as the first point, again emerges at v. 8, and may be implied at v. 9, it has more persuasively been viewed as the underlying theme, although see below.

26. Undecided are e.g. Lock 1924: 31; Dibelius and Conzelmann 1972: 45. Gritz (1991: 126) declares the question 'moot' because women did pray in public (citing 1 Cor. 11.5) and the principle established here has to do with the manner in which that prayer should be carried out.

implied, is sufficiently forceful to eliminate the possibility of the other.[27]

Implication of προσεύχεσθαι at v. 9 is uncertain, and must remain an open question. This should be borne in mind as interpretation of the whole proceeds. A decision based upon inconclusive evidence cannot clarify an already difficult context,[28] and the ambiguity may itself be significant.

Two other factors are of equal importance for the question of whether the theme of prayer continues into v. 9.

i.   Even if προσεύχεσθαι were implied, it would not require a congregational context.

ii. Options must be considered for v. 9 just as for v. 8. In this case there are three:

(and)
in the same way (I want)

[option 1]   **women**   **(to pray)**
                                   in modest demeanour
                 (and)   **to adorn themselves**
                                   with discretion
                                       and good sense
                                   not in…etc.

27. Those excluding implication of προσεύχεσθαι include Alford 1862: 317-18; Ellicott 1864: 34; Bernard 1899: 44. Those accepting it include Weisinger 1866: 409-14; B. Weiss 1885: 120-21; Giles 1977: 64. For summaries of all these, and also Knight (1992: 132), see my 1995: 42-44, for which see my preface. For others arguing similarly to Alford, Ellicott and Bernard see e.g. Grimke 1838: 112-13; Parry 1920: 14; Barrett 1963: 55; Holtz 1965: 65; Kelly 1972: 66; M.J. Evans 1983: 101; Witherington 1988: 119; Byrne 1988: 87; Oberlinner 1994: 89. For others arguing similarly to Weisinger, Weiss and Giles see e.g. Huther 1866: 128; White 1910: 106-107; Falconer 1937: 130. Brox (1969: 132) says v. 9 has no direct connection with v. 8.

28. Cf. e.g. Spencer (1985: 73) who, with Pauline authorship and comparison with 1 Cor. 11.5 in mind, observes that προσεύχεσθαι *may* be implied and leaps to the conclusion that it is.

[option 2]   **women**
                        in modest demeanour
                                to adorn themselves
                                        with discretion
                                                and good sense
                                        not in…etc.

                                                        (to pray)

[option 3]   **women to adorn themselves**
                                in modest demeanour
                                        with discretion
                                                and good sense
                                        not in…etc.

The clumsiness in option 1 due not only to the missing verb but the missing καί suggests that the Author's meaning has itself been missed. It cannot be denied that 2 is also clumsy, if less so, but the structure formed by vv. 1, 8 makes it a possibility. Both the more likely options (2 and 3) are concerned chiefly with character.

This strengthens the previous tentative conclusion that at v. 8, too, the first option (see p. 55 above) should be rejected.[29] The character with which both passages are concerned obviously has its outworking in lives, not simply ecclesial behaviour. Although at v. 8 the Author has just returned to the prayer of vv. 1-2, I therefore suggest that he is in fact already refocusing—this time upon the character of the men praying.[30] At the very least, it is unclear that the activity of prayer (not the

29. The recognition of P.H. Towner (1989) that mission is the main theme throughout ch. 2 makes him aware that v. 8 to some extent concerns general life. He says (pp. 206-207) that wrong relationships affect the acceptability of prayer, an idea that he, like Bartsch, traces from earliest Christian tradition. His description of the concern as a 'natural development' from vv. 1-2 suggests that he may also perceive a shift in focus from prayer to pray-er.

30. To obscure that shift one would have to disregard as incidental not only ἐν παντὶ τόπῳ (as Bartsch; see pp. 45-48 above) and ὁσίους χεῖρας (as Dibelius and Conzelmann: see p. 45 n. 39 above) but also ἐπαίροντας…χωρὶς…κτλ. Since the letter contains a number of other comfortably integrated traditions (see esp. Ellis 1987: 237-48), the shift of focus more convincingly explains the possibly implied double imperatival reference of βούλομαι than does the idea that two sources have clumsily been combined.

character of the men who pray) remains the central focus throughout v. 8. The alternative is a viable option.

When this factor at v. 8 is added to the uncertainty over whether προσεύχεσθαι is implied at v. 9, it may not be taken for granted that vv. 9-12 is to be interpreted in a context whose one underlying theme is prayer or behaviour in the gathered assembly. If as soon as the Author returns to his theme of prayer at v. 8 he refocuses on the character of those praying, his underlying topic carried forward with ὡσαύτως would be neither prayer nor behaviour at prayer but *the character of those who pray*. Within the terms of the stated goals, 2.8-3.13 would then address various groups who are required to pray for, and to live, peaceful, godly lives as members of God's household: all men and women, and officials of three kinds. This would explain why:

i.   Only three of the eight verses in ch. 2 that instruct in practical ways certainly speak of prayer (vv. 1-2, 8); five address other matters (vv. 9-12, 15).

ii. Allusions to 'behaviour in the gathered assembly' are absent from 1.18; 2.1-2, 8, 9-10, 15 and, of course, from the expositional vv. 3-7 and 13-14.

iii. At 2.9 προσεύχεσθαι need not be implied to maintain the topic and yet may be understood. This accords with the ambiguity noted above. Prayer remains the underlying topic only in the sense that certain things are required of both the men and the women practising it (vv. 1-2), but it is now obscured by a refocus upon their character.

Neither the statements of purpose, the structure nor the themes of 1 Timothy 2 require a congregational context. With this in mind, the next two chapters analyse vv. 9-10 and 11-12.

Chapter 3

1 TIMOTHY 2.9-10

ὡσαύτως [καὶ] γυναῖκας ἐν καταστολῇ κοσμίῳ μετὰ αἰδοῦς καὶ σωφροσύνης κοσμεῖν ἑαυτάς, μὴ ἐν πλέγμασιν καὶ χρυσίῳ ἢ μαργαρίταις ἢ ἱματισμῷ πολυτελεῖ, ἀλλ᾽ ὅ πρέπει γυναιξὶν ἐπαγγελλομέναις θεοσέβειαν, δι᾽ ἔργων ἀγαθῶν.

I also want women to dress modestly, with decency and propriety, not with braided hair or gold or pearls or expensive clothes, but with good deeds, appropriate for women who profess to worship God (NIV).

These two verses form the immediate prior context of the controversial vv. 11-12, so they here warrant careful consideration.

Restriction of their reference to the congregational context is never persuasive. Even Roloff, who believes the Author clearly addresses throughout the conduct of men and women in the worship service, is aware that vv. 9-10 sounds 'sehr allgemein und...Bezug auf den Gottesdienst allein durch den Kontext gesichert wird' ('general and...reference to the worship service is safeguarded through the context only', 1988: 126). Byrne justifies their restriction to the congregation at prayer by declaring them metaphorical (1988: 87-88). Others argue that modesty and appropriate appearance are particularly necessary at public worship.[1] None of these resolves the difficulty that the standard of appearance here required would almost certainly be thought by the Author (cf. contemporaries below) equally necessary in the community at large and even in extended household life.[2]

There is a good deal of speculation about the identity of the women in view. One influential discussion is that of Padgett, who argues that the selection of 'what not to wear' indicates that the women are

---

1. E.g. Plummer 1888: 100, 102; Hendriksen 1955: 105, 108.
2. Cf. Giles (1977: 64), who takes the emphasis on male behaviour and female dress as an indication that public gatherings must be in view.

wealthy.[3] These, he reasons, were 'probably' followers of the false teachers, 'likely' to have churches meeting in their homes and, 'naturally aspiring' to leadership, hiring false teachers as their tutors (here he cites 2 Tim. 4.3). Since a woman is to learn (μανθανέτω), they must be recent converts excluded from learning in the synagogues, whether as Jews or God-fearers. Padgett fails to account for the many female pagan converts who—like their male counterparts—must have been even more 'untaught' than those from the synagogues. More importantly for the present study, in focusing on what women are *not* to wear, he ignores the fact that vv. 9-10 are primarily positive and therefore cannot be directed only to the wealthy. The Author begins by stating that women *are to adorn themselves*—with respectability, discretion and prudence.[4] Although some exegetes focus for σωφροσύνη on the nuance 'chaste',[5] the word properly entails a sense of dynamic moderation. North defines it as 'the harmonious product of intense passion under control' (1966: x). It is a balance opposed equally to over-indulgence and to asceticism, or pride in pretended modesty.[6] Immodesty, indiscretion and lack of good sense have never been monopolized by the wealthy. Having begun so positively and all-inclusively, the instruction makes equally clear that such adornment as women *are* exhorted to employ includes or results from 'good works', as is fitting for women professing/proclaiming godliness. Again, it cannot be argued that only the wealthy are exhorted to do good works or expected to profess/ proclaim godliness. In other words, the instruction ends on the same positive and universally orientated note with which it begins.[7]

3.   Padgett 1987a: 23. See also Kelly 1972: 66-67; Countryman 1980: 153; Verner 1983: 180; Kidd 1990: 102-103. Barnett (1989: 226, 228) thinks there is no doubt about this, and (although he does not assume the instruction is limited to them) also takes for granted that they are educated. See Harris (1990: 336-39) for an able critique of this additional point.

4.   Hendriksen (1955: 106) persuasively argues that women are instructed to 'adorn themselves in *adorning*—that is, *becoming*—*attire*' with modesty etc. (emphases his).

5.   E.g. Dibelius and Conzelmann 1972: 46 and n. 14; Knight 1992: 134. Houlden (1976: 70) sees chastity as the main object of v. 9.

6.   Ellicott 1864: 35; Bernard 1899: 45; Hendriksen 1955: 106. See also Donelson 1986: 173 n. 153, 196 n. 242. Alford (1862: 318) says 'self-restraint' is too indicative of struggle, the true meaning involving establishment of the better nature. Lock (1924: 31) speaks favourably of 'self-government'.

7.   Cf. B. Weiss (1885: 122-23) who, by treating κοσμεῖν as epexegetic, argues

The negative component between the positive vv. 9a and 10 requires care. This adornment which women are to employ is not to comprise

πλέγμασιν καὶ χρυσίῳ ἢ μαργαρίταις ἢ ἱματισμῷ πολυτελεῖ.

The context suggests that πλέγμασιν refers to something more than ordinary plaiting. Whatever it is, however, Padgett's vague 'fancy hair-styles'[8] evokes confusion between 'elaborate' or 'extravagant', 'bizarre', and 'highly fashionable'.[9] There are at least three possible reasons why πλέγμα should not be interpreted as belonging exclusively to the domain of the rich:

(a) The connecting καί (cf. ἤ *bis*) may indicate a particular type of braiding incorporating the gold and pearls which was frequently affected not by the wealthy but by the courtesan.[10] This idea does have

that proper adornment is established at first negatively and then positively.

8. E.g. Padgett 1987a: 23.

9. Even when more precision is employed, as 'an elaborate type of coiffure' (S.B. Clark 1980: 194), the type and extent of the style remains uncertain. Meinertz (1931: 38) suggests 'artificial, showy', and Easton (1948: 127) 'extremely elaborate and artificial', but neither explains whether he means the braids themselves or their decoration (which 1 Timothy 2 does not mention). Others speculate. B. Weiss (1885: 122) believes a woman's hair is an adornment of Nature only artificially increased, and says that 'gemeint ist der künstliche Haarputz...also Haarflechten' ('meant is the artificial hair adornment...that is, plaits'). Apparently thinking of 1 Cor. 11.14-15, he seems to envisage that at public prayer the hair should be long and free but covered. It is unclear how the braiding of covered hair could constitute even a visible, let alone inappropriate, adornment. A further difficulty is that the Corinthian passage says 'long' hair is itself a form of mantle. If, however, he does not think the hair should be covered, it should be apparent that long, uncontrolled hair, generally impractical for everyday life, would have to be so for meetings, surely a problem for synagogue converts (Num. 5.18). Guthrie (1990: 85) says that, although Jewish women customarily wore plaits, elaborate types were fastened with ribbons and bows: apparently he equates ribbons with 'ostentation'. Two examples of elaborate arrangements are reproduced in *IBD* (II, 602-603), one significantly consisting of a coiled plait so long that artificial hair must be used. See others (although almost entirely of goddess images and imperial ladies) in Seyffert (1957: 266-68), who speaks of regular trade in German hair, nets (often gold), fastening needles (often ivory, gold etc.), and imported bleach. Cf. Tertullian, *Cult. fem.* 6 and 7. See also Balsdon 1962: 255-60.

10. Alford 1862: 319; Hurley 1981: 199 (followed by Witherington 1988: 119; Schreiner 1995: 119); Scanzoni and Hardesty 1982: 70; Fee 1984: 39; Oden 1989: 94-95; Knight 1992: 135. Philo, *Sacr.* 21 speaks of Pleasure in the guise of a harlot/courtesan περιέργῳ ποικιλίᾳ τὰς τῆς κεθαλῆς τρίχας ἀναπεπλεγμένη ('who has

immediate contextual support. The first term used for the required adornment is καταστολή, which refers to both clothing and lifestyle[11] and suggests rejection of a particular lifestyle or the appearance thereof. The Author may therefore reject as unsuitable for Christian women a hairstyle associated with the courtesan.[12] This, however, puts considerable weight on καί.

(b) Display of wealth may not be in view at all. The fact that not all commanded the services of an *ornatrix* (Carcopino 1956: 170-72) would never prevent women from experimenting with their hair. Unless it be argued that gold and pearls are incorporated (and I have suggested above that this is uncertain), or that styling considered inappropriate for any but the upper classes is entailed (a view I have found nowhere), it should not be assumed that only wealthy women are likely to be so adorned.[13] Since the term is at best vague it may not arbitrarily be so restricted.

(c) In view of this vagueness of terminology it should be considered whether the Author may have ordinary braiding in mind. The context

the hair on her head braided with elaborate artfulness', Clem. Alex., *Paed.* III.xi.62.3 αἱ περιπλοκαὶ τῶν τριχῶν αἱ ἑταιρικαί ('the meretricious intricacies of their hair'). Cf. Huther (1866: 130), who says no heniadys is indicated. Hendriksen (1955: 107) offers another alternative, claiming braids were sometimes fastened by jewelled tortoiseshell combs or pins of ivory or silver, bronze with jewelled heads often consisting of images of animals, idols etc., and represented great expense. Baugh (1995: 47-48) traces new Roman trends connoting imperial luxury and licentiousness copied throughout the Empire by the well-to-do.

11. As Padgett (1987a: 22) notes. See also e.g. Ellicott 1864: 34; Humphreys 1901: 98; White 1910: 108; Scott 1936: 25; Simpson 1954: 46; Dibelius and Conzelmann 1972: 45-46; Guthrie 1990: 84; Knight 1992: 133. Cf. however Bernard (1899: 45), who says that in contrast to καταστήμα (demeanour/ deportment) (Tit. 2.3), καταστολῆ means 'dress'. See also Huther 1866: 129.

12. Cf. *Apoc. Pet. graeca* 475 'Das sind die, welche sich Haarflechten gemacht haben nicht zur Schaffung des Schönen, sondern um sich zur Hurerei zu wenden, damit sie fingen Männerseelen zum Verderben' ('It is those who made plaits for themselves not for creating something beautiful but to turn to whoring in order to trap the souls of men for their destruction').

13. Barrett (1963: 54) reproduces a plate showing four maids 'at work on a lady's toilet', implying that the hairstyle is to be elaborate. Only one maid clearly works on the undressed hair, the others holding mirror and jars, and the style intended may be quite ordinary. The positions of the maids' own coiled braids show some individuality. Hesychius (IV, 2002) appears to equate πεπλεγμένοι with self-indulgence.

does seem to rule this out, but the idea will be reconsidered below.

Nor may χρυσίῳ and μαργαρίταις be limited only to wealthy women. Gold chains were worn by Roman barmaids, and some poor women in antiquity wore large pearl earrings.[14] The Author does not seem to have in view the specified substances so much as something else. Gold and pearls were not the only materials, or even the only expensive materials, used for jewellery, and so could here represent the costly variety (Friedländer n.d.: 180-81). Rejection of conspicuous wealth corresponds to rejection of the associated 'expensive clothing',[15] which could reasonably be expected to be made from imported luxuries such as cotton, muslin, or silk (perhaps worked with gold or woven with linen or cotton), or to be embroidered with gold, or dyed with valuable scarlet and the various purples.[16] Embroidery and other dyes do not belong in this category (Friedländer n.d.: 178-79). As some have noted, the negative component at 1 Tim. 2.9 is restrained in comparison with other contemporary views of what women should not wear.[17] The correspondence between the expensive clothing and jewellery suggests that adornments involving the less expensive metals and stones, beading, tooling etc. are not here rejected.[18] After all, a woman's *stola* was often fastened at the shoulders by brooches (Balsdon 1962: 253), and such are certainly adornments. One gains the impression that the Author is not declaring inappropriate all artificial adornment, and the 'balance' implied in his use of σωφροσύνη confirms that impression.[19] His prohibitions regarding jewellery and clothing appear to be about conspicuous wealth. On the other hand, his associated concern for modesty and good sense surely indicate that he would similarly be unimpressed with a surfeit of even inexpensive jewellery and decorative clothing. In the end, his generally positive focus suggests he is not too concerned with precise descriptions of women's adornment. What he

14. Friedländer n.d.: 182-83; Balsdon 1962: 264.

15. MM, s.v. ἱματισμός cite Tob. 10^{10} *aleph*, in *P Eleph* 1^4 (311–10 BCE) (= *Selections*, p. 2) used of a bride's trousseau/dowry. Accordingly, at 1 Tim. 2.10 Humphreys (1901: 98) suggests 'wardrobe', and Simpson (1954: 46) thinks of a complete outfit. See also Knight 1992: 135.

16. Friedländer n.d.: 173, 175-76; Balsdon 1962: 253-54. Cf. Rev. 18.12.

17. E.g. Knight 1992: 136. See also below.

18. Pliny, *Hist. nat.* 37.75-76 describes the lucrative manufacture of imitation jewels and the corresponding science of testing for genuineness.

19. See above. Contra e.g. Calvin 1579: Sermon 17 e.g. 199.

wants to say is that outer appearance should reflect an inner θεοσ-έβεια.[20] It may be that he simply wants women (no matter what hairstyles, clothing and jewellery they may wear) to be 'truly' adorned,[21] that is (and I paraphrase):

> I want women to adorn themselves with a modesty associated with discretion, good sense, and the good works befitting a woman professing/proclaiming piety. Braiding, gold, pearls and expensive clothing can never so adorn them.[22]

If this is the case it seems possible that πλέγμασιν may here refer to ordinary braids. It is more probable, however, that he considers expensive and elaborate self-adornment inappropriate, that is (and I again paraphrase):

> I want women to adorn themselves with modesty and not elaborate outer decoration, that is, I want them to show discretion, well-balanced sense and (as befits a woman professing/proclaiming piety) good works. I do not want them to be adorned with elaborate hairstyles and gold or pearls, or expensive clothing.

In either case, since the surrounding positive instruction of vv. 9-10 is clearly relevant for all women, and neither 'braiding', gold nor pearls can altogether be restricted to the wealthy, the instruction as a whole seems directed at all women.

Restriction of the reference to a congregational context has facilitated the common assumption that the Author is concerned about either:

    i.   women dressed both immodestly and ostentatiously; or
    ii.   some women dressed immodestly and others ostentatiously.

From very early in the Christian era instruction about women's appearance includes the view that a significant factor in their adornment is the intention to attract men. Tertullian writes

> *Quid enim est in capite feminae corona quam formae lena, quam summae lasciuiae nota, extrema negatio uerecundiae, conflatio inlecebrae?* (Cor. XIV.2)

> For what else is a chaplet on the head of a woman but a whoremistress of beauty, but a sign of the utmost wantonness, the utter denial of modesty, the excitement of seductiveness?

---

20. E.g. Scott 1936: 25; Dibelius and Conzelmann 1972: 46; Byrne 1988: 88.
21. See also 1 Pet. 3.1-6.
22. For similar interpretation see Foh (1979: 124).

Similarly, Augustine:

> *aurique circumpositio, et intortio crinium, et caetera hujusmodi quae vel*
> *ad inanem pompam vel ad illecebram formae adhiberi solent.* (Ep. 262)

> Wearing of gold and the plaiting of hair and other things of this kind are
> usually either for idle display or to add allurement to beauty.

The same idea appears in more recent times.[23] B. Weiss, for example,
says that the prohibited hairstyle 'in provocirender Weise die Blicke der
Umgebung auf die Trägerin lenkt' ('turns in a provocative manner the
gaze of those around towards the bearer', 1885: 122), and Witherington
speaks of ostentatious or suggestive apparel or hairstyles 'that could
attract the wrong sort of attention and compromise the moral witness'.[24]

Some find the key to the passage in contemporary literature. Knight
notes that Pliny, *Hist. nat.* 9.33.12; Juvenal, *Sat.* 6.502-3; Ovid, *Ars am.*
3.136ff.; Josephus, *Ant.* 8.185; Rev. 17.4; 18.12, 16 and Philo, *Sacr.* 21
connect such adornment not only with ostentation but with the
appearance of courtesans and harlots. He claims therefore that, with the
possible exception of the expensive clothing, the prohibitions at 1 Tim.
2.9 have a hyperbolic cast directed against excess and sensuality and

---

23. See also Mills (1984: 255-56), who says that the most widely accepted view
on the function of clothing is that it is primarily a means of enhancing the individual by asserting superiority. Historically, he continues, on a personal level ambivalence created by simultaneous hiding of shame and display of superiority results in
the promulgation of condemnation for asserting oneself too much: economic for
men, whose clothes were seen to enhance their social status; moral for women,
whose clothes made them more sexually attractive. Mills nevertheless points out
that the language of clothing can be quite complex, also expressing occasional (e.g.
wedding/funeral) mood, making statements of belief, symbolizing power or religious affiliation, social role/worth, facilitating social rituals. Cf. Culham (1986:
243) who argues that Roman and Greek clothing restrictions were intended 'to suppress competition for status and reinforce inward experience of *communitas* by
creating visible, outward *communitas*'.

24. Witherington 1988: 120. See also 'provocative and showy dress' (Brox
1969: 132); 'no (sexually) seductive adornment' (Küchler 1986: 51); 'denn mit
alledem würden sie sich in ein schiefes Licht setzen und Zweifel an ihrer Tugend-
haftigkeit und Keuschheit wecken...[und] die Aufmerksamkeit der Männer un-
keusch auf sich ziehen' ('for with all this they would show themselves in an
unfavourable light and awaken doubts about their virtue and chastity...[and] draw
the attention of men unchastely to themselves', Roloff 1988: 132-33); 'enticing,
seductive' (Schreiner 1995: 118-20).

towards good works.[25] Contemporary material does have its parallels with vv. 9-10, but there are also differences: this instruction is more restrained.

The Andanian mysteries forbid make-up, and specify particular head-coverings, the upper limit of expense for clothing for various groups, fabric from which shoes and garments are to be made, and the width of stripes on clothing (*LSCG*, 65, cited by Mills 1984: 259). An inscription at the Asklepieion at Pergamon requires those incubating to wear white and not to braid the hair, wear a ring, belt, gold or shoes.[26] The cult of Demeter near Patras forbade women to wear more than one obol of gold, brightly coloured or purple clothing, or cosmetics (*LSCGS*, 33, cited by Mills 1984: 258). The same cult at Lycosura stipulated that those entering the temple wear no gold, purple, brightly coloured or black clothing, shoes or rings, and women must have their hair loosened.[27] Other clothing regulations restrict garments included in the dowry, the number of items to be worn in public, and warn that offending articles will be confiscated (Mills 1984: 264). In contrast to those who draw attention to the loosened hair required at some mystery celebrations, Balch says that the way 1 Pet. 3.3-4 specifies how women should dress 'would be a great contrast with the practices in the cult of Artemis of Ephesus or with the cult of Isis'.[28] The close parallel between 1 Pet. 3.3-4 and 1 Tim. 2.9-10 suggests a shared tradition. Care should be taken before too hasty identification is made of parallels between that tradition and other contemporary regulations.

Others go even further than drawing such parallels, claiming that the Author's concern is that praying men not be distracted by improperly dressed women. Brown argues that the women of early Christian assemblies were accustomed to pagan worship involving the 'wildest

25. Knight 1992: 135-36, 138. See also Scholer (1980: 3-6), although it should be noted that he confuses vv. 9-10 with vv. 11-12 by interpreting the latter by contemporary instruction having its closest parallells with the former.

26. *LSAM*, 14, cited by Mills 1984: 258. Substantial restoration of this inscription should be noted.

27. *LSCG*, 68, cited by Mills 1984: 258-59. See also Culham 1986: 236; Horsley 1982–89: IV, 108-109.

28. Balch 1981: 101-102. He cites Xenophon of Ephesus, *Anthia and Habrocomas* I.11.2-6, where the hair is braided and so 'attractive', and Apuleius, *The Golden Ass* II.8.9, although in the latter the 'curiously set forth' and therefore 'fair' hair is that of the goddess.

orgies, and sometimes with the utter abandonment of shame'.[29] Kelly interprets αἰδώς as 'feminine reserve in matters of sex' and σωφροσύνη as having a 'definitely sexual nuance' (see also Verner 1983: 135 including n. 26), speculating that the Author is probably thinking of the

> impropriety of women exploiting their physical charms on such occasions, and…the emotional disturbance they are liable to cause their male fellow-worshippers.[30]

Whatever the degree of immodesty imagined, all the above interpretations evoke a picture of early Christian assemblies where some women wear provocative clothing—presumably the toga, which from the time of the early empire was not worn by respectable women (Balsdon 1962: 252), the diaphonous garments banned from certain mystery celebrations,[31] or at least the glittering hairstyle characteristic of the prostitute.[32] But is this idea present in the text? The Author speaks of 'expensive' clothing, jewellery and hairstyles, of modesty, discretion and good sense so that women might fittingly profess/proclaim godliness. Whatever πλέγμα may be taken to mean, it should not simply be assumed that κόσμιος, αἰδώς or σωφροσύνη convey 'decency'[33] rather than 'freedom from vanity' or 'simplicity' (*Macquarie Dictionary*, s.v. modesty).

The idea that v. 9 regulates women's appearance for the sake of the equilibrium of praying Christian men assumes a peculiarly male orientation for instruction in which men are not mentioned and for which there is no corresponding exhortation to self-control in v. 8. The assumption that 'indecency' is in view furthermore introduces the idea that woman is inherently dangerous and should be covered not only

29. E.F. Brown 1917: 19-20. See also Jeremias 1963: 18.

30. Kelly 1972: 66, followed by e.g. Gritz 1991: 126. See also Osborne 1977: 346; Marshall 1984: 192; Oden 1989: 94. P.H. Towner (1989: 208-209) is unable to decide whether this is the concern or whether, since the items prohibited are those found in contemporary society's caricature of wealthy women, it is to restore social (rather than male) balance. The goal would then be to prevent assembly women being 'typed' as the pagan caricature of ostentatiously dressed women 'perhaps' so as to persuade outsiders that the new life had tangible and desirable results.

31. For these see e.g. Mills 1984: 259; Culham 1986: 236.

32. C. Kroeger and R. Kroeger (1992: 74) without textual warrant suggest that some women may disrobe.

33. Contra e.g. Payne (1981: 191), who says that at least some were dressing indecently, and sees gold, pearls and expensive clothing as 'suggestive'.

decently but entirely lest some part of her should tempt a man. In the accepted context of the gathered assembly this imbalance invites construction of parallels with poor interpretations of the problematic 1 Cor. 11.3-16 featuring the 'veiling' of women 'in church'.[34] It also fails to recognize that early Christianity considered lust (and not only its incitement) a sin bearing personal responsibility (Mt. 5.28). Neither does it reflect the reality that male physical appearance may arouse temptation in women. But even if this were not the case, the context suggests that the Author is not thinking of sexual allurement. The contrast set up between the required καταστολῇ κοσμίῳ and μὴ ἐν πλέγμασιν...κτλ. suggests that at least the chief issue is ostentation or conspicuous wealth.[35] The context confirms this. The close connection previously noted between vv. 8 and 1-4 implies that the Author wants men to refrain from anger and debate so that they may demonstrate a quiet life attracting outsiders to salvation and a knowledge of the truth.[36] In a context consistently concerned for the salvation of outsiders (cf. also esp. 1.16; 3.2, 7, 16), the relevant vulnerability at vv. 9-10 would be that of those outsiders. In other words, whilst both Christian men and women would obviously be expected to wear decently covering clothing, just as men are exhorted to be holy, not angry and disputatious, women are exhorted to appear in a manner befitting their proclamation/profession of godliness, adorning themselves with good works and modest (i.e. simple, not expensive, sensible) hairstyles, jewellery and clothing. The vagaries of πλέγμασιν should not be over-interpreted in this context. Even if the hairstyle characteristic of the courtesan is in view (and this is unclear) the emphasis would appear to be more on its expense and ostentation than its sensuality.

But if speculation abounds about v. 9, v. 10 certainly presents three exegetical problems:

34. See e.g. Easton 1948: 124.

35. Osburn (1982: 11) correctly notes that the problem is 'over-' rather than 'under-dressing'. See also Keener 1992: 103-107.

36. Lock (1924: 30) suggests that although the reference is to v. 1 there may still be a slight connection with both God's universal salvation (citing vv. 4, 15) and the ideal of the true Christian life (citing vv. 2, 9-11). Murphy-O'Connor (1973: 1264-66) highlights the emphasis placed throughout 2.1-3.13 upon the 'kerygmatic value of the Christian life'.

(a) The relative clause ὃ πρέπει γυναιξίν has occasioned some
debate, some arguing that δι' ἔργων ἀγαθῶν should be understood in
connection with ἐπαγγελλομέναις θεοσέβειαν, the relative pronoun ὃ
indicating something like καθ' ὃ, or ἐν τούτῳ ὃ, for example:

> And, in the same way, [I want] women to adorn themselves in modest
> dress with discretion and prudence…which befits women professing
> godliness by means of good works.[37]

Alford says that this is 'on all grounds objectionable', whilst B. Weiss
finds it quite arbitrary, and White 'an awkward periphrasis for and
repetition of' ἐν καταστολῇ, κτλ.[38] In this study the antecedent will be
understood as the idea of adorning oneself (v. 9), with δι' ἔργων
directly connected, the relative clause being parenthetical.

(b) Θεοσέβειαν closely parallels εὐσέβειαν, which has evoked considerable discussion to be considered in Chapter 7, Section 1. Here the
meaning 'godliness' will be assumed.

(c) Although the overwhelming majority render ἐπαγγελλομέναις
'profess/claim to'[39] (as e.g. Philo, *Virt.* 54; Ignatius, *Eph.* 14.2), it may,
depending upon its context, also mean either 'announce/proclaim'
(1 Macc. 4.27) or 'promise[40]/offer' (Rom. 4.21; Jas 1.12; 2.5; 1 Jn 2.25;
Tit. 1.2; Acts 7.5; 2 *Clem.* 11.6).[41] In fact, at Heb. 6.13; 10.23; 11.11;

---

37. E.g. Huther 1866: 131. See also Scott (1936: 25), who notes that the
difficulty that charitable living cannot be inferred from devoutness in church could
be avoided in this way, but concludes that the meaning is that a life of known
uprightness and kindness is sufficient adornment.

38. Alford 1862: 319; B. Weiss 1885: 122 (although on p. 123 his careful
recognition that ἔργων ἀγαθῶν are not to be confused with ἐπαγγελλομέναις
θεοσέβειαν leads him to conclude that the former are appropriate appearances, not
charitable works; White 1910: 108. See also Ellicott 1864: 35; Humphreys 1901:
98; Parry 1920: 14-15; Kelly 1972: 67.

39. E.g. AV, RSV, NEB, TEV, JB, NIV, NASB, Phillips. See also Alford 1862: 319;
Ellicott 1864: 35-36; Plummer 1888: 102; Bernard 1899: 47; Humphreys 1901: 98-
99; White 1910: 108; Parry 1920: 14; Falconer 1937: 131; 'make pretension to'
(Simpson 1954: 46); Barrett 1963: 55; A.T. Hanson 1966: 36; Dibelius and Conzel-
mann (1972: 46) who suggest also 'confess'; Hendriksen 1955: 106-08; P.H.
Towner 1989: 208; Guthrie 1990: 85; Gritz 1991: 128; Knight 1992: 137.

40. Cf. ἐπαγγελίαν 'promise' in 1 Tim. 4.8.

41. E.g. 'preaching…enjoining…conducting public worship' (Grimke 1838:
113); 'preaching' (Mott 1849: 490). B. Weiss (1885: 123) rejects 'promise' for
'proof', citing Xenoph., *Mem.* I.2.7. For 'promise/proclaim' see (Bushnell 1919:
§§332-33, followed by Penn-Lewis 1919: 52-53).

12.26 it is difficult to separate ideas of 'promising' from 'proclaiming'. The word was used in the first century CE of candidates in Greek cities publicly announcing their plans for the public good if they gain popular support (MM, s.v). It was also a 'technical word for teaching any form of wisdom for pay'.[42] In 1 Tim. 6.20-21 it is used of those who set themselves up as teachers, so may be understood

> ...avoiding...what is falsely called 'knowledge', which some have *proclaimed* and lost their way concerning the faith.[43]

It is unclear at 6.20-21 whether, in fact, the Author has proclamation or profession in mind, or whether (cf. the author of Hebrews) the two ideas may merge, that is, anyone professing to have this 'knowledge' would be certain to proclaim it. BAGD includes 1 Tim. 2.10 with those passages to be translated 'profess, lay claim to, give oneself out as an expert in something' (BAGD, s.v., 2). MM contrast it (together with Philo, *Human.* I, ἐπαγγέλλεται θεοῦ θεραπείαν ['he commands service paid to God']) with the technical use in third-century BCE inscriptions announcing public sacrifices (MM, s.v). In view of general agreement that the context of 1 Timothy 2 is the gathered assembly, there has been a ready acceptance that, since the Author forbids women to teach or have authority over men, and requires them to be silent or at least quiet (ἡσυχία v. 12), these women 'profess' rather than 'proclaim'.

Ἐπαγγελλομέναις, however, tells nothing about the context: it must itself by defined by it. Only vv. 11-12 suggests 'profession' must be in view: women forbidden to teach or have authority over a man are unlikely to be envisaged 'proclaiming' or 'announcing' anything. A final decision for ἐπαγγελλομέναις must therefore be deferred until vv. 11-12 is considered, but three points are here to be noted:

- i. Verse 10 itself carries no necessary denotation of profession rather than proclamation.
- ii. Judging by 6.20-21 the Author may not clearly differentiate between the two.
- iii. Whether profession or proclamation is in view, nothing in vv. 9-10 requires attention to be restricted to women's behaviour ἐν ἐκκλησίᾳ.[44] Moreover, the implied βούλομαι and use

---

42. Colson and Whitaker (eds.) in Philo, *Poster. C.* 501 n. 139.
43. Contra e.g. White 1910: 108; Hendriksen 1955: 108.
44. P.H. Towner (1989: 207-208) is careful to note that: i. the underlying mission theme indicates that more is at stake in vv. 9-10 than tranquility within the

of the Present κοσμεῖν require recognition of full aspectual force, which may be paraphrased:

> …it is my custom to want women habitually to dress and adorn themselves in ways appropriate to their profession/proclamation of godliness.

Exegesis of the controversial vv. 11-12 must begin from this context.

church and its relationship with the world; and ii. such instruction is largely traditional (citing 1 Pet. 3.3-5).

Chapter 4

1 TIMOTHY 2.11-12

Since neither the statements of purpose at 1.18-19 and 3.14-15 nor the surrounding 2.1-2, 8-10, 15 confine the setting to the congregation, if an ecclesial setting is to be identified anywhere at all in this chapter, it must be in vv. 11-12:

γυνὴ ἐν ἡσυχίᾳ μανθανέτω ἐν πάσῃ ὑποταγῇ. διδάσκειν δὲ γυναικὶ οὐκ ἐπιτρέπω οὐδὲ αὐθεντεῖν ἀνδρός, ἀλλ᾽ εἶναι ἐν ἡσυχίᾳ.

A woman should learn in quietness and full submission. I do not permit a woman to teach or to have authority over a man; she must be silent (NIV).

It is universally accepted that obscure or controversial passages should be interpreted by their contexts or by clearer relevant material.[1] In this particular case, however, the question arises: which is the more obscure, vv. 11-12, or its context? As previously illustrated, some declare the context (at least primarily) congregational because they find vv. 11-12 the best indicator, but others declare vv. 11-12 (and often vv. 9-10) congregational because of vv. 1-2, 8. The conclusions reached in the previous three chapters make the latter approach questionable: vv. 1-2, 8, 9-10 nowhere restricts reference to the congregation. The former approach is equally debatable because the setting of vv. 1-2, 8, 9-10 and 15 is not, in fact, obscure: with the possible exception of ἐπαγγελλομέναις (to be reconsidered below) it is general, not congregational.

But does vv. 11-12 provide its own congregational reference? Laying to one side at this point the obvious difficulty that learning and teaching, at least, certainly appear most naturally to be things done in the gathered assembly, if there were no congregational reference, v. 12

1.   E.g. Ramm 1970: 104-106; Bromiley 1979: 71. For 1 Cor. 14.34-35, frequently declared relevant for 1 Timothy 2, see Part III.

(διδάσκειν δὲ γυναικὶ οὐκ ἐπιτρέπω οὐδὲ αὐθεντεῖν ἀνδρός) seems to prohibit women teaching or having authority over men in any situation at all.[2] Such broad prohibitions would clearly represent modifications to at least some earlier biblical practices. In the Old Testament some women have certain authority over some men (Gen. 21.11-12; Judg. 4.4-10). In the New Testament era, at least one Jewish woman is depicted as speaking to men in the temple in such a way as to suggest that she informs them about theological matters (Lk. 2.37).[3] Whatever 1 Cor. 14.34-35 may be understood to mean, the all-inclusive language of passages such as Phil. 4.3b and Col. 3.16 (whenever the latter is dated, and whatever is made of v. 18) not only accepts that women at least in some ways minister vocally, but encourages them to do so without restriction on the gender of those they address. 1 Corinthians 11.5 and chs. 12-14 in general (esp. 14.26, 39) suggest similar views. Paul clearly teaches that wives have certain marital authority paralleling that of their husbands (1 Corinthians 7, esp. v. 4), and his co-worker Priscilla teaches Apollos (Acts 18.24-26).[4] Many who restrict 1 Tim. 2.11-12 to the gathered assembly therefore conclude that it represents a departure from earlier Pauline teaching and practice. Any such departure might appear extreme if its prohibitions were to be interpreted in the context of the life rather than only in the congregation.

Despite all this, however, the interpreter should neither

    i.   conclude prematurely that the Author intends severely to restrict women's whole lives; nor

    ii.   in order to weaken the force of the prohibitions reject the natural context in favour of one traditionally accepted.

It will be argued below that the morphological choices at vv. 11-12 indicate an intention to present prohibitions that are neither broad nor harshly restrictive. At this point, however, *it should be noted very clearly that these two verses are to be interpreted in a congregational*

---

2.   As Knox 1558: 15, 22, 39-41; Alford 1862: 319.

3.   Grimke 1838: 104; Booth 1859: 20.

4.   Paul's association with and warm appreciation of a woman apostle, Junia (Rom. 16.7), cannot be excluded. See e.g. P. Lampe 1985: 132-33; Judge 1985: 14; Dunn 1988: 894-95. Contra e.g. Moo (1981: 207-208) and Fung (1987: 181-82) who caution that ἀπόστολος here 'probably' does not have the technical sense as Rom. 1.1. Whilst it is apparent that all apostles did not have the same function, even 'lesser' such officials may not simply be declared 'non-apostles'.

context only if they themselves require it. The general reference of 1.18; 3.14-15; 2.1-2, 8-10 neither creates it, nor should it be distorted by it.

A decision about whether vv. 11-12 provides its own congregational reference depends on how seven words are defined: γυνή, ὑποταγή, ἡσυχία, μανθάνω, ἐπιτρέπω, διδάσκω and αὐθεντέω. It should again be noted that debates about some of these words occur predominantly amongst those accepting Pauline authorship.

1. *γυνή (Verses 11, 12)*

As already argued, it is not possible in this context convincingly to restrict this to 'wife', so in this study it will henceforth be treated as the more general 'woman'.

2. *ὑποταγή (Verse 11)*

All agree that this should be translated 'obedience/submission',[5] but there is considerable debate about the object of that obedience,[6] the reference variously said to be men,[7] officials,[8] the teaching,[9] the social order in general (Dautzenberg 1989: 194), or some combination of

---

5. Barrett (1963: 55), however, renders 'maintain her due place'.

6. By contrast Ellicott (1864: 36) is concerned to point out that ἐν πάσῃ ὑποταγῇ is extensive, i.e. 'in all cases', not intensive, i.e. 'fuller'. Cf. Πάσῃ 'hat elativische Bedeutung: "völliges Schweigen" ' ('has elative meaning: "total silence" ', Roloff 1988: 135 n. 125) and 'voller Unterordnung' ('full subordination', p. 138 n. 144) .

7. E.g. Donelson 1986: 179; Dewey 1992: 355. See also Harris (1990: 340), who modifies by reference to the mutual submission of Eph. 5.

8. E.g. Stendahl 1982: 29; 'teachers' (Padgett 1987a: 24); 'Amtsträger' ('office bearers', Roloff 1988: 137-38); 'men in authority functions within the church' (Knight 1992: 139). See also Schreiner 1995: 124. For Barnett (1989: 230-33) the ἐπίσκοπος is equivalent to the διδακτικός (citing 2 Tim. 2.24), who would be hindered in household management if his own or anyone else's wife exercised authority (citing 3.1-7). In response to Barnett, Harris (1990: 341) points out the logical invalidity of the claim that, since women are prohibited from teaching, and the ἐπίσκοπος-πρεσβύτερος was a teacher, then women are here prohibited from serving in the office of the ἐπίσκοπος-πρεσβύτερος. Not all πρεσβύτεροι, he correctly notes, were teachers (1 Tim. 5.17).

9. E.g. 'Predigt und Schriftlesung' ('sermon and scriptural reading', Meinertz 1931: 38); 'manner of learning' (Blomberg 1988: 411); 'what is taught' (Gritz 1991: 130).

these.[10] The sentence, however, is not linguistically incomplete, so ellipsis may not be proposed (Llewelyn 1992: 132.). The obedience is to be directed to what is learned.

3. ἡσυχία *(Verses 11, 12)*

At v. 12b, the clause ἀλλ᾽ εἶναι ἐν ἡσυχίᾳ *is* (unlike v. 11) grammatically incomplete, but the ellipsis is here supplied by the immediately preceding subject γυνή and main verb ἐπιτρέπω (v. 12a). Because this would result in 'but [I do permit her] to be quiet/silent', the implied subject and object are generally understood as 'but I instruct her to be ἐν ἡσυχίᾳ' or 'but she must be ἐν ἡσυχίᾳ'.[11]

The importance of the word here is clear. Its dual use creates a contrast between the quietness and obedience with teaching and authority[12] and at the same time indicates that it is itself the primary emphasis of this instruction.[13] But does the Author intend 'silence' or 'quietness'?[14]

---

10. '[O]fficials and regulations' (Lock 1924: 32); both 'sound teaching' and 'men', the latter identified in wide terms as 'perhaps' including both husbands and church officials (Moo 1980: 64; see also 1991: 83); 'the teacher and his [sound] instruction' not excluding the subsidiary thought of submission to men (Fung 1987: 198); 'teaching and, by transference…the one giving the faithful teaching' (Witherington 1988: 120 and n. 208).

11. Ellicott (1864: 37) reports that such shortened forms occur most commonly in the case of antitheses introduced by adversative conjunctions.

12. Ellicott (1864: 37) notes the marked antithesis between each member of this verse and v. 11. Cf. B. Weiss (1885: 125), who claims that if the second ἡσυχία refers only to the first a 'conspicuous tautology' results, and argues that it refers to the ruling over the man, and renders 'silence' (v. 11) and 'stillness' (v. 12).

13. Bernard (1899: 48) notes its emphatic position in v. 12. Moo (1980: 64) places ἐν πάσῃ ὑποταγῇ at the heart of an ABCBA chiasm, with reference to both learning and men. See however Schreiner (1995: 124-25 with n. 88), who questions the presence of a chiasm, finding instead an inclusio. Fung (1987: 336 n. 186) discerns an ABBA pattern with two positive statements flanking two negatives, his accompanying argument about αὐθεντεῖν (see Section 7 below) making his the more persuasive case. For an ABCBA chiasm even less convincing than Moo's see Perriman (1993: 131), who argues that v. 12 is parenthetical, replacing ἐν ἡσυχίᾳ with a woman learning at A and the woman deceived at A', with vv. 13-14a at B, C and B', and v. 15 added to 'compensate' for the negative A'. See nn. 23, 49. Hurley (1981: 201) says the construction makes clear that the same situation prevails in both verses, the quiet and submissive learning inversely paralleled by the '(verbal) teaching' and exercising of authority. Others noting the word's importance include

The fact that he obviously intends the latter at v. 2 is not particularly helpful:[15] he is not restricted to one meaning. Spencer has demonstrated that, when employed by the rabbis and in the patristic period, ἡσυχία in conjunction with learning carried the positive nuance of a respectful, acquiescent manner.[16] There is reason to conclude that this is the meaning at both vv. 11 and 12: in v. 11 the ordinary relationship of learning to teaching suggests at least some verbal interaction, even if only affirmation. Nothing suggests that the same word should be translated as 'silence' in the verse immediately following,[17] since it does not automatically follow (in any context) that someone forbidden to teach or have authority must be silent. I conclude, therefore, that the idea conveyed is that of tranquility.

Fee 1984: 35-36; Liefeld 1986: 222; Barnett 1989: 229.

14. BAGD, s.v., 1 (e.g. Sir. 28.16; 2 Thess. 3.12; Josephus, *Ant.* 18.245). Contra Payne (1981: 169) and Gritz (1991: 129), Moo (1981: 198-99) points out that the first listed meaning in BAGD should not be confused with the 'primary' meaning. Preferring 'silence' or similar are e.g. Alford 1862: 319; Ellicott 1864: 36-37; Leipoldt 1953: 124; Dautzenberg 1975: 258; Swidler 1979: 336; Moo 1980: 64; 1981: 198-99; 1991: 183; Fung 1987: 198; Byrne 1988: 88 and n. 21; P.H. Towner 1989: 212-13; Dewey 1992: 355; Knight 1992: 138-39, 142; Schreiner 1995: 123. Preferring 'quietness' or similar are e.g. Powers 1975: 59; Payne pp. 169-70: 1986: 99-100; Scanzoni and Hardesty 1982: 70; Howard 1983: 39-40; Schüssler Fiorenza 1983: 290 and n. 19; Spencer 1985: 72-81; Padgett 1987a: 23-24; Blomberg 1988: 411; Roloff 1988: 138; Barnett 1989: 229; Gritz p. 129. Some are ambivalent. Humphreys (1901: 99) and Scott (1936: 25-26) employ both expressions, although the former renders 'quiet' in bold print and the latter appears to think of quietness as silence. Hendriksen (1955: 109) acknowledges as possible 'remain calm' but assumes 'silence'. Barrett (1963: 55-56) clearly prefers 'silence' but speaks of it as 'quietness'. '[N]ot necessarily *in silence*' (Fee 1984: 35: emphasis his).

15. Contra e.g. Giles (1977: 68), who imports the idea of 'all things being done decently and in order' from 1 Corinthians 14 and leaps from acknowledgment of the meaning at v. 2 and elsewhere to 'tranquil/peaceful' here (see also 1985: 60); Witherington 1988: 120 and n. 206; Wiebe 1994: 58.

16. Spencer 1985: 74-81, followed by Payne 1986: 97; Padgett 1987a: 24; Blomberg 1988: 411; C. Kroeger and R. Kroeger 1992: 75-76 and n. 25. Cf. S.B. Clark (1980: 195), who argues that ἡσυχία is here a disposition toward learning, a receptivity to direction probably corresponding to genuine submissiveness and requiring abstention not from speech but from direction/teaching.

17. Contra e.g. NIV; Guthrie 1990: 85-87. The claim of B. Weiss (1885: 125) (ref. my n. 12 above) dissolves when the two verses are seen as a chiasm.

4. μανθάνω *(Verse 11)*

All agree that this means 'learn'. Some argue that it has overtones of regulated instruction (cf. Jn 7.15).[18] Elsewhere in the New Testament, however, it can refer to learning by experience (e.g. Phil. 4.11; 1 Tim. 5.4, 13; Tit. 3.14; Heb. 5.8) or from someone who may not be an official teacher (1 Cor. 14.35; Acts 23.27).[19] Where the word occurs elsewhere in the Pastorals the distinction between types of learning is conveyed by reference either to an instructor (2 Tim. 3.7, 14) or an object (1 Tim. 5.4, 13; 2 Tim. 3.7; Tit. 3.14). Verse 2.11 refers to neither, so the definition must be arrived at in some other way. In the context outlined previously, only the closely associated διδάσκειν (v. 12) could suggest that 'schooling' is in view. In other words, that nuance would have to be projected back from the following verse. I will return to this below.

Debate occurs about whether the imperative constitutes a command or permission. Feeling secure in the belief that the Author at v. 12 believes women unsuited to teaching and having authority over men, most understand it as a command conveying something like the paraphrase:

Women should learn what they are taught in the congregation.[20]

Such a view also appears to suggest that the Author implies a female resistance to what is taught. Rarely is it noted that if he does believe women prone to certain things he must also believe men prone to argument and debate.[21] There is, however, a close parallel between tranquility in which learning should occur (v. 11) and holiness excluding argument and debate (v. 8).[22] The object of both is that people act peaceably.

---

18. E.g. Spencer 1985: 74; Padgett 1987a: 24.

19. Rengstorf (1967: 405) says Josephus often conveys 'to experience'. See also BAGD, s.v., 4; Vine 1975: 324.

20. E.g. 'learn, i.e. at the public ministrations; in antithesis to διδάσκ. ver. 12' (Ellicott 1864: 36).

21. Cf. however Roloff (1988: 132) 'Der Grund...dürfte schwerlich gewesen sein, dass ihm Zorn und streitsüchtige Gedanken als ein ausschliesslich männliches Laster galten...' ('this imperative is addressed to the congregational leaders'). See also Kähler 1960: 149; Keener 1992: 102.

22. Alford (1862: 317) writes of v. 8 that men are to pray 'in tranquillity and mutual peace'.

Others argue that the imperative represents permission (cf. Mt. 8.32; 10.13; 26.45), that is 'Allow a woman to learn...etc.'[23] This, then, is presented as the Author's chief concern and in direct opposition to some contemporary views. The argument generally features the contrast with rabbinic ideas about women learning *torah*, ideas themselves contrasting with Deut. 31.12; Josh. 8.35.[24] The key role played by ἡσυχία makes this view untenable even in the context of the gathered assembly. The Author does not begin a new topic at v. 11. He approaches one begun at v. 9 from a different perspective. Just as he wants men who pray to be holy etc., he wants women to be characterized by (amongst other things) tranquility, a state in which learning of some sort should occur, and in which instruction and authority-taking of some sort should not. As demonstrated above, the primary role of ἡσυχία makes clear that at v. 11 his main focus is upon the tranquility in which the learning is to be done. The 'learning' itself is a secondary concern, at least to the extent that μανθανέτω may not legitimately be highlighted as his chief point.[25] He is not saying 'allow a woman to learn and she must do so peacefully and obediently', but rather (literally) 'a woman in tranquility should learn in all obedience'. If the final phrase had been omitted perhaps 'permission' might have been understood, but the imperative is modified by ἐν πάσῃ ὑποταγῇ. The Author wants women to learn not only peacefully but obediently. *That* they learn is taken for granted. The permissive 'Let a woman learn...etc.' derives from English translation. The Greek itself is strongly directional (Porter 1992: 55).

But if this is a command, the context so far has not suggested that the learning must be that which takes place in the congregation. The ques-

23. E.g. M.J. Evans 1983: 101. For the legitimacy of imperatival permission see e.g. Robertson 1923: 948. Perriman (1993: 129-31) (see n. 13 above), by declaring v. 12 parenthetical, arrives at a similar conclusion.

24. E.g. G. Davies 1986: 86; Barnett 1989: 229; Gritz 1991: 128; C. Kroeger and R. Kroeger 1992: 75.

25. Contra e.g. Stouffer 1981: 258; Fung 1987: 197; Wiebe 1994: 59. For this reason also the claim of Spencer (1985: 74) is to be rejected, i.e. that this command to learn is 'the third (cf. prayer, consistent lifestyle) way to help people reach a knowledge of the truth'. See similarly Kroeger 1986: 237. Contra also Payne 1986: 96. Witherington (1988: 120) claims that the imperative indicates that the Author sees women's learning as important, but points out (n. 207) that the manner of learning rather than the learning itself is in focus. See also Moo 1991: 183; Schreiner 1995: 122.

tion is, then: should that context be projected back from v. 12, the learning defined as regulated instruction of some sort? The answer will depend upon conclusions about v. 12 reached in sections 5–7 below, so I will return to μανθάνω.

5. ἐπιτρέπω *(Verse 12)*

In recent times this word has attracted considerable attention, notably in the Moo–Payne debate. This exchange is now a standard reference amongst those accepting Pauline authorship for the Pastorals, so is here outlined briefly. In response to those claiming that no more than a personal preference or particular circumstance is conveyed by the present tense,[26] Moo argues that

> the first person singular…renders the present tense necessary and can have almost a gnomic timeless force (cf. also 2:1 and 2:8). This, of course, does not prove that it *does* here, but any limitation will have to be inferred from the context and not on the basis of tense alone (1980: 65; emphasis his).

Payne responds that other constructions would more appropriately suggest a continuing prohibition, claiming that

> ἐπιτρέπω, particularly in the first person singular present active indicative usually does not refer to a continuing state and can only be determined to have continuing effect where there are clear indicators to that effect in the context (1981: 170).

Paul, he continues, typically employs the word to express his own personal position, the New Testament only rarely employs it in reference to a continuing state and nowhere in the first person, and 1 Tim. 2.12 does not claim to be either 'from the Lord' or for all the churches:

> when [Paul] occasionally…did express a continuing state using the first person he typically included some universalizing qualifier (1981: 171-72).

The usual English translation 'I do not permit', he claims,

> is misleading since [it]…implies a continuing state where *the Greek does not*. [Preferable]…is 'I am not permitting' since it preserves the nuance of the Greek, favoring the normal present reference without excluding the possibility of a continuing state (1981: 172-73; emphasis his).

---

26. As e.g. Kaiser 1976: 11; Williams 1977: 112; Osborne 1977: 347. See also e.g. Wiebe 1994: 59; Jervis 1995: 59.

He concludes that the instruction is restricted to particular circum-stances,[27] continuing effect only determinable by the context (1981: 172). Moo's rejoinder argues that the tense is chosen for its note of per-sonal appeal, and maintains that 'the sense of temporal limitation does not adhere to the word as such'.[28] Payne's surrejoinder maintains that there is substantial evidence of use of ἐπιτρέπω predominantly for par-ticular, not universal permissions (1986: 96-97, 100-101).

Two observations about this debate should be made at the outset. First, Moo is correct when he notes that the real point at issue is 'what the construction *allows*' (1981: 199; emphasis his). The reader, how-ever, wants to know *what the Author himself intended*. Both men acknowledge that Moo's position does not rest entirely upon grammati-cal factors,[29] but Payne insists that temporal limitation may be identi-fied on the grounds of Paul's consistent usage. His claim will fail to persuade not only those unconvinced about Pauline authorship, but also those who recognize the possibility that Paul *could* here depart from his usual practice. Secondly, it is extremely difficult to see how the English 'I am not permitting' could, as Payne claims, more appropriately con-vey a less continuous meaning than 'I do not permit': both depend upon their contexts for identification of the extent of application. As Moo argues, ἐπιτρέπω is similar.

Moreover, Payne and Moo both neglect the aspectual nature of the Greek verb.[30] Their debate occurred prior to publication of much of the work on that subject cited in my Introduction, so both are to some extent confused by now-outdated conceptions—Payne particularly so. Moo is correct insofar as he recognizes that temporal limitation does not adhere to ἐπιτρέπω, but he does not capture its visualization of continuity.[31] If the recent studies on aspect cited in my Introduction are

27. He is followed by e.g. Padgett (1987a: 25), Liefeld (1987: 50 n. 2, 52), and Witherington (1988: 120), although the latter notes the important role played by the context. Taking a similar position are Stouffer 1981: 14; Roberts 1983: 20, 22; Fee 1984: 39; Harris 1987: 32; Perriman 1993: 130. See also the Phillips translation.

28. Moo 1981: 199-200. See also 1991: 185.

29. Moo 1981: 199; Payne 1986: 100.

30. As does Knight (1992: 140), who argues on the basis of Paul's use of other 1st person singular Present indicatives (e.g. Rom. 12.1; 1 Tim. 2.8) that universal and authoritative instruction is in view. See also Scholer (1986: 203 n. 28), who rejects Moo's conclusion that the instruction is normative, but on the basis of Pauline usage sides with him against Payne about ἐπιτρέπω.

31. Cf. however Blomberg 1988: 411. Cf. also Spencer (1985: 84-86), who says

correct, Payne, those following him, and those arguing similarly, are wrong: the Greek here (despite Payne's italicized claim) *does* convey the Author's visualization of an ongoing command.

Of course this does not mean that the context cannot set limitations to that continuity. If sufficient reason should be found to conclude that the instruction is directed at particular circumstances, the Author may visualize prohibitions whose relevance is continuous only so long as those circumstances prevail. This question will be addressed below and in Part II.

6. διδάσκω *(Verse 12)*

It is almost universally[32] agreed that this must refer to some kind of teaching, but the nature of that teaching remains a point of widespread contention, as does the question of whether it is intended to be normative.[33] Acts 18.24-26 is frequently adduced to demonstrate that Paul permits women to exercise a teaching ministry over men at least in private.[34]

the Present 'principally denotes continuous present action' (i.e. 'I am not presently allowing…etc'.), but overshadows that continuity by a temporal emphasis which she then employs rather as background for the imperative, itself featured as the main point of v. 11 (see my Section 4 above) and the chief interpretative device for v. 12.

32. Some rare exceptions will be noted below.

33. Liefeld (1987: 51), e.g., calls for definition taking into account that women were not included in the unique and highly visible teaching functions of Judaism and the Graeco-Roman world, concluding that the prohibition is not permanent. See at n. 47 below for αὐθεντεῖν.

34. E.g. G. Davies 1986: 87; Knight 1992: 140. E.F. Brown (1917: 20) also cites Tit. 2.3 and refers to 2 Tim. 1.5 as evidence that teaching other than that in the congregation is not prohibited. Payne (1986: 102-104) also argues on the grounds of Pauline authorship that only a particular type of teaching is prohibited, citing Tit. 2.3; 2 Tim. 2.2 with 1.5 and 3.14-15; 1 Cor. 14.26 and Col. 3.16. With the same authorship in mind, Liefeld (1987: 53) is unclear, apparently because of a typographical error. He suggests that Aquila's presence may have been what made Priscilla's teaching acceptable, but questions why in 1 Tim. 2.12 Paul does not specify that women are forbidden to teach only if their husbands were ['not'?] present. In interesting (if dubious) contrast, Moo (1981: 201) reduces Priscilla's presence to its barest possible minimum significance, claiming that it remains unproven that she 'taught' Apollos at all. Cf. Saucy (1994: 80) 'Priscilla…instructing Apollos in what must have been considerably advanced theology'.

Many shades of meaning are suggested and debated, including the teaching of the woman's own husband,[35] or also her family (Windisch 1930: 421-22), or the heretical nature of the message.[36] It is commonly said to refer to teaching which is public[37] or official, especially as an elder.[38] Howe and Knight, arguing from very different positions, both more convincingly claim that a function rather than an office is in view.[39] That the function was public nevertheless proves difficult to demonstrate. Hommes says that teaching in early Christian congregations was inter-communal and always implied some proof on the basis of scripture (citing Col. 1.28; 3.16; Eph. 5.19; Rom. 15.14; 1 Cor. 14; Acts 20.7-12), so was incompatible with the subjection required from married women (1969: 7-8, 13-14). Yet restriction here of address to married women is arbitrary, and congregational discussion remains unproven in early congregations: see Part III for 1 Corinthians 14. Of other texts cited, the first four are unrestricted to the congregation, and the last suggests an address rather than a discussion—Paul may well be the only speaker until the Eutychus incident.[40] At v. 11 the singular

35. Powers 1975: 59. See also 'teaching that would constitute a failure of the requisite wifely "submission" ' (Hugenberger 1992: 358) .

36. Kroeger 1986: 225; C. Kroeger and R. Kroeger 1992: 81. See also e.g. Harris 1987: 32, and further in Part II below. Liefeld (1986: 245) justifiably argues that Kroeger goes beyond the text.

37. E.g. Ellicott 1864: 36-37; Scott 1936: 26.

38. E.g. Meinertz 1931: 39; Simpson 1954: 46-47; G.G. Blum 1965: 157; S.B. Clark 1980: 195-97; Moo 1980: 65-66; 1981: 200; 1991: 185; Tucker and Liefeld 1987: 460; P.H. Towner 1989: 215; Schreiner 1995: 127. G. Davies (1986: 86-89), e.g., envisages a formally structured hierarchy unsubstantiated in the early period in which he believes the letter is written, confuses the teacher with the elder (cf. 5.17), and to support the 'great honour' involved cites 1 Pet. 4.11, which concerns not teaching but speaking which is unrestricted to assembly meetings; Jas 3.1; Heb. 13.17; and 1 Thess. 5.12, only the last of which speaks of esteem whilst all feature responsibility and hard work. Authority in all the cited letters has its basis not in bestowal of office, but in recognition of gifted ministry, which is itself service, and is limited to the particular ministry, the place in which it is exercised irrelevant. Harris 1987: 21-27. See also e.g. Woodhouse 1985b: 16-17; Fee 1985: 149-50; Liefeld 1987: 53-60. Saucy (1994: 79-97) considers different kinds of teaching in New Testament assembly life, concluding (p. 93) that only authoritative teaching over men is prohibited, but see re οὐδέ at pp. 87-89 below.

39. Howe 1979: 271-72; Knight 1992: 141. See also Harris 1990: 341.

40. i. The singular παρέτεινεν (v. 7); ii. Paul's imminent departure suggests his desire to impart and the congregation's desire to receive instruction; and iii. Euty-

Aorists suggest that an ordinary meal-break is taken, not another
'communion' (v. 7). At that hour, especially following such a dramatic
demonstration of the effects of prolonged teaching, and in view of
Paul's planned departure, extended informal discussion rather than
formal address could in all probability be assumed. Moreover, would
sons, daughters, female household dependants, and slaves of both
sexes, not be equally as prone to unsubmissive behaviour in inter-communal discussion as wives? Finally, as will be demonstrated below,
διδάσκειν not only did not always involve scriptural proof, but was not
always official, formal, public or even an address.

Amongst those few who acknowledge that in the hellenistic era
διδάσκειν is employed for activities other than 'teaching' directed at
'pupils', Hugenberger, who claims that in this 'marital' context it
acquires a strident or perjorative connotation, alone (to my knowledge)
says it approximates 'tell/order/boss' (1992: 358 n. 72). His 'marital'
context has, however, above been rejected. Grimke declares it here 'to
dictate'—tenuous indeed in the ecclesial context she envisages.[41]
Others assume the same context and conclude it must mean 'to teach'.
Nevertheless, Payne says that the word itself is a general term
applicable to all sorts and levels of teaching which cannot be limited to
public assemblies.[42] Knight notes that it is used quite generally at Col.
3.16; 1 Cor. 11.14; and Rom. 2.21 (1992: 141) Witherington finds the
only indication of the type of instruction in the 'worship' context.[43]
Since vv. 1-2, 8-10 cannot persuasively be restricted to the congregation, and the learning of v. 11 by itself conveys no necessary reference

chus is more likely to fall asleep with one ongoing voice than several variously situated and pitched. See BAGD, s.v., 2; MM, s.v.

41. Grimke 1838: 114. See further in Parts II and III.

42. Payne 1981: 174. See also Liefeld 1987: 51.

43. Witherington 1988: 121. Harris (1990: 342-43 and n. 27) is careful not to
introduce assembly structures unidentifiable in the letter, and strongly argues that
the word may not convincingly be restricted to official roles. He, too, notes its
ambiguity, but means that the Author—in current circumstances—may prohibit
women even from teaching women or children. See further in Part II. Saucy (1994:
90) rejects Witherington's claim that διδάσκω itself has a general meaning on the
grounds that in the Pastorals teaching 'clearly suggests...authority', but see below
for Tit. 2.3-5 and his supporting argument (following Payne 1986) that διδάσκω
and αὐθεντέω convey a single idea.

to that kind of context, possible broader meanings for διδάσκειν should be noted.

In Mt. 28.15 it conveys the idea of ordering someone (Rengstorf 1964: 138). In 1 Cor. 11.14 nature 'teaches' simply by its existence. The LXX translators of Job chose διδάσκω four times for similarly non-formal concepts: *ḥāvāh* 'make known/tell' at 36.2 (NIV 'show'), and *yadha'* 'make known/declare' at 37.19 (NIV 'tell') and 42.4 (NIV 'answer'), and at 10.2, although apparently misunderstanding the Hebrew, in the sense of 'charge'. MM translate P. Oxy 1.40.8 (second/third-century CE) '*tell* me what is…?' (MM, s.v.). At P. Oxy 22.2342.25 (102 CE), where a woman lying to the *strategos* is under pressure by her sons to conceal a ledger, Horsley and Lee translate 'coach'.[44] In the patristic period it could mean 'give directions/orders' (Thdt., *Ps.* 118.100 [1.1463]) (*LPGL*, s.v., 3). Clearly it does not always involve an address by a teacher.

The Author elsewhere shows one indication that the word for him could mean something rather broader than 'teach'. At Tit. 2.3-5 he wants older women to be qualified in various ways ἵνα σωφρονίζωσιν τὰς νέας certain things required for daily marital and household life. Σωφρονίζω here is variously interpreted as 'encourage', 'advise', 'urge' or 'train'.[45] One of the qualifications required by such older women is that they be καλοδιδασκάλοι. They are therefore envisaged carrying out a type of teaching function as they advise the younger women, even though what they are here instructed to impart may be partly by example and is practical rather than doctrinal or theological. It seems that for the Author the major component of this qualification did not necessarily involve anything more formal than direction, encouragement or advice.

Since the context in which 1 Tim. 2.12 appears is more appropriately interpreted as addressing women's lives than a formal setting in which 'teach' would be the obvious choice, these alternative options must be given due consideration. See further below.

---

44. Horsley and Lee 1997: 71. See also for e.g. διδάσκαλος at FD 3.2.48.18 (97 BCE) '*trainer* of the great choir', and P. Oxy 41.2971.15 (66 CE) 'maintained and clothed by the *master-craftsman* Seuthes'.

45. BAGD, MM, and LSJ, s.v. English translations render variously 'train' (NIV, TEV, RSV), 'show' (JB), 'school' (NEB), 'teach' (AV).

7. αὐθεντέω *(Verse 12)*

The literature on this word is deeply divided. The reference is variously said to be to authority in a general sense,[46] or to usurped[47] or domineering[48] authority. After extended debate,[49] the most thorough lexical study

---

46. E.g. NIV. See also Parry 1920: 15; S.B. Clark 1980: 198; Moo 1981: 202; Knight 1984: 154-55; G. Davies 1986: 86; Fung 1987: 198 and n. 190; Blomberg 1988: 412. Similarly, Hurley (1981: 202 n. 4), whose previous acknowledgment that the context (rather than the word) makes clear that the authority in question is 'not proper' suggests the more logical conclusion that some form of 'improper' authority is focused.

47. E.g. AV. See also G.G. Blum 1965: 157; Foh 1979: 126-27; P.H. Towner 1989: 216. Liefeld (1987: 52) tentatively suggests 'self-arrogated authority' in the context of a claim that διδάσκειν conveys a temporary prohibition. Does this not imply only temporary prohibition of self-arrogated authority?

48. E.g. NEB. See also Alford 1862: 319; Humphreys 1901: 99; Scott 1936: 26; Falconer 1937: 131; 1941: 375; Simpson 1954: 47; Barrett 1963: 55; Hommes 1969: 16-19; Powers 1975: 59; Williams 1977: 112; Scanzoni and Hardesty 1982: 71; Osburn 1982: 12; M.J. Evans 1983: 103; Spencer 1985: 86-87.

49. Knight (1984: 154-55) finds no overtone of improper authority. See also Moo 1981: 202; G. Davies 1986: 86. Scholer (1975: 7-8; 1983: 13; 1986: 202-208) says the word's rarity indicates a different nuance from the ἐξουσιάζω group. Payne (1986: 108-10) denies that in the relevant period it ever clearly meant 'to have authority over'. Others criticizing Knight include Giles 1985: 60-61 n. 28; Tucker and Liefeld 1987: 460. Knight (1992: 141-42) maintains 'the word shows no *inherent* negative sense' (italics mine). Wilshire (1988: 120-34) demonstrates from the TLG program that it often means 'exercise authority', and by late fourth century CE could be defined by ἐξουσιάζειν, although he notes that everywhere else in the New Testament where teaching and authority are coupled ἐξουσία is employed. Witherington (1988: 121) shows that the letter from Tryphon which Knight cites does imply questionable use of authority, and when Chrysostom advises the husband μὴ...ἐπειδὴ ὑποτέτακται ἡ γυνὴ αὐθεντεῖ it is rightly translated 'do not play...the despot/act arbitrarily'. Kroeger (1979: 12-15) interprets 'to engage in fertility practices', but see Panning 1981: 185-91; Osburn 1982: 4-8. Payne (p. 110), who sees 'extensive hints of sensual activity throughout 1 Timothy' e.g. 2.9 (for which see Chapter 3) and 15 (see Part IV), and frequent focus on illicit sex in αὐθέντης, nevertheless also is unconvinced that here this is so. '[R]epresent herself as the originator/source (of man)' (Kroeger 1986: 229-32, 235). See similarly 'to exert evil influence over' (Stouffer 1981: 258). Kroeger uses older dictionaries, projects backwards from developed Gnosticism, and neglects the broader context. See further at n. 56 below, and in Part II. Identifying a negative notion are Harris 1990: 342-43; Gritz 1991: 135; Wiebe 1994: 59. G. Davies (p. 87)

is undoubtedly that of H. Scott Baldwin, who conclusively demonstrates that various shades of meaning are possible, and that only the context can determine which is intended.[50] I will return to this below·

When the above conclusions about these seven words are considered, in spite of the several remaining obscurities one overall conclusion does emerge: no word or combination of words in vv. 11-12 demands a congregational context. In fact, ἐπαγγελλομέναις, μανθανέτω, διδάσκειν and αὐθεντεῖν all require interpretation within the general reference of vv. 1-2, 8-10, 15. It should also again be noted that ἐπαγγελλομέναις and μανθανέτω depend for their meanings largely upon whatever is decided about διδάσκειν and αὐθεντεῖν.

8. *How Many Prohibitions?*

Within the context of general reference there is also the question of whether v. 12 prohibits one thing or two.[51] It has often been suggested that it is the teaching of a man by a woman which here constitutes the taking of authority over him, that is, that the prohibition is essentially against only one action—some type of authoritative or domineering teaching. The claim frequently amounts to little more than assertion,[52] and confusion is evident about the relationship of each factor to the other.[53] A few of those accepting Pauline authorship do address the

---

says that in that case, since vv. 13-14 indicate that the actions are permissable for men, Mt. 20.25-28 (cf. 1 Pet. 5.3) would be contravened. See further in my Conclusion to Part I n. 3. Wilshire (1993: 43-55) 'instigate violence' fails to consider the role of ἀνδρός and speculates about the situation addressed (see Part II below). Perriman (1993: 136-42) undermines 'act authoritatively' by making v. 12 a parenthesis, which he says is prompted and to some extent shaped by his (unconvincing) 'chiasm'. See nn. 13, 23 and further below.

50. H. Scott Baldwin 1995: 65-80 with App. 2, pp. 269-305.

51. Payne (1986: 104) sees this as the 'single most crucial question for a proper interpretation of 1 Tim. 2:12'.

52. See e.g. Leipoldt 1953: 124-25; Osborne 1977: 346; Giles 1977: 67; Marshall 1984: 192.

53. Panning (1981: 191) and P.H. Towner (1989: 216) see διδάσκειν as a specific instance of αὐθεντεῖν. See also Köstenberger (1995: 165 n. 16). Cf. the reverse in Parry (1920: 15) 'a general rule supported by the particular case, the assumption of authority to teach'. Barnett (1989: 232) notes that οὐδέ *need* not introduce a completely new thought, and immediately leaps to '[t]his means that "to

matter in detail, but in the end unconvincingly.

Payne, for example, compares each occurrence of οὐδέ in Paul's letters, observing that, of those occasions when related items are so joined, in most cases the elements help make specific a single idea, and elsewhere they are closely interrelated, much more even than at 1 Tim. 2.12. There is, he argues, no Pauline parallel for separating two prohibitions by this conjunction, so it would be appropriate to translate with a single idea in view (1986: 104-108). Even granted Pauline authorship and not only the close relationships in each pair in his study but also at 1 Tim. 2.12, Payne here fails to convince. Not only are some of his lexical examples tenuous,[54] but Köstenberger now demonstrates from a wider database that οὐδέ does not subordinate one action to another.[55] Payne does correctly note that claims that two prohibitions of action directed at men are in view must deal with the fact that 'man' occurs in the sentence at some distance from 'to teach', and that this is hardly conducive to limiting the restriction to teaching directed at men. The reason for the assumption that such a transference is necessary, he properly suggests, is the practical modern need to restrict the first prohibition reasonably to allow women to do any teaching at all (1986:

teach"...signifies "to exercise authority over"...' See other inadequate arguments in Booth 1859: 14-15; B. Weiss 1885: 125. Hendriksen (1955: 109) equates αὐθεντεῖν with official preaching. Hurley (1981: 201) (followed by G. Davies 1986: 87-88) concludes that women are not to be authoritative teachers. Bilezikian (1989: 296 n. 43) sensibly questions the value of *un*authoritative teaching.

54. At 1 Cor. 11.16 two distinct parties are discernible. At Gal. 1.16-17 Payne argues that Paul does not deny he talked about the faith with 'Ananias and the other disciples in Damascus' right after his conversion (citing Acts 26.12-20, although presumably with 9.19 in mind), but by using οὐδὲ specifies the particular consulting he had in mind, i.e. σαρκὶ καὶ αἵματι, the apostles. There is, in fact, no evidence in Acts 9.19 that Paul *did* '*consult* about the faith' in the sense that doctrines were accepted/rejected: the text allows for agreement with Gal. 1.17, suggesting that two separate parties are in view. Following Payne are Hugenberger (1992: 344 with n. 9, 357-58 with n. 71), who says 'even if some of the examples cited...admit an alternative explanation' (p. 358), and Saucy (1994: 90 with n. 50).

55. Köstenberger 1995: 156-79. See also Köstenberger, Schreiner and Baldwin 1995: 81-103. Cf. Fung (1987: 337 n. 197), citing Thayer (1961: 461*b*), and arguing that, whilst οὔτε combines mutually complementary clauses, οὐδέ has a looser connection. Köstenberger, however, demonstrates that actions coordinated by οὐδέ are always viewed as either both positive or both negative. Köstenberger concludes that 1 Tim. 2.12 must prohibit either teaching and having authority, or false teaching and domination, but there are other possibilities (see below).

107-108). But he assumes that there must be either two prohibitions of actions directed at men, or one overall prohibition, and he does not consider another alternative suggested below. He furthermore highlights the singular ἀνδρός in order to reject the argument that the prohibition permits one-to-one instruction (1986: 104, 108), but again fails to consider a factor discussed below.[56]

The Greek word order suggests that the Author begins with one prohibition in mind but adds another, literally:

> But to instruct I do not permit a woman—neither to exercise authority over a man.[57]

---

56. Blomberg (1988: 412-13) is even less convincing, his language betraying his own lingering doubts. At least some of his 'double' references are potentially misleading: in v. 4 salvation is not necessarily the same thing as coming to a knowledge of the truth; in v. 7a 'herald' and 'apostle' may not be identical (Murphy-O'Connor [1973: 1266] points out that the first has a purely verbal function but the second not exclusively so), and in v. 8 anger is distinguishable from dispute. In the immediately preceding v. 11 quietness and full submission are also distinguishable. C. Kroeger and R. Kroeger (1992: 80-84, 102-103, 230 n. 29; see also Kroeger 1986: 225-44) build on Payne's argument here. Having argued that elsewhere in the letter διδάσκω is always qualified by other verbs, and in the Pastorals generally appears in contexts which express/imply its content, they suggest that αὐθεντεῖν here takes that function, meaning 'to represent oneself as the author, originator, or source of something', a value they claim disappears from classical dictionaries when 1 Tim. 2.12 was challenged by nineteenth-century feminists. They translate ἀλλ᾽ εἶναι ἐν ἡσυχίᾳ 'but she is to be in conformity [with the Scripture]'. New Testament lexicographers are in fact not inclined to so react: Lee (1997: 174-76) writes that their characteristic tendencies include uncritical derivation from predecessors' material, and demonstrates how even a 'strong build-up of contrary evidence can escape notice entirely'. On the basis of outdated lexicography, uncited and no longer extant classical texts, a discredited background (see my Introduction n. 25), and the introduction of an ellipsis into a clause which is itself complete, the Kroegers rewrite v. 12. A less likely option, they suggest (1992: 37, 190-92), is that οὐδέ *may* simply intensify one prohibition only, and that αὐθεντεῖν *may* be an infinitive of indirect discourse, so they render 'I categorically forbid a woman to teach [anyone] to maintain that she is responsible for the origin of man'. This is grossly speculative.

57. As e.g. Moo 1980: 68; 1981: 202. See also Gritz (1991: 131), who nevertheless sees a relationship between the two, the teaching giving the impression of 'lording it over'.

It is true that the first prohibition appears on the surface to be definable partly as limited to the teaching of men, a component which (as Payne notes) is actually stated only in the second. This, however, is not necessarily because ἀνδρός is projected back from that second prohibition with the object (like the parallels Payne cites) taking the case required by the second verb.[58] It is because Tit. 2.3-4 makes clear that elsewhere the Author *does* want women to instruct other women and children. It seems quite reasonable, therefore, to limit that first prohibition to some action directed towards men only. On the other hand, with general life rather than the congregation in view, Timothy himself (as Payne also notes) is depicted as having been taught by women with no indication of an age at which such teaching should cease (2 Tim. 1.5; 3.15). Could it be that the 'instructing' prohibited at 1 Tim. 2.12a, in contrast to αὐθεντεῖν, may not be directed at men alone, but be of a more general nature?[59] Whether or not this is the case, however, it is reasonable to conclude that, whilst (as Payne argues) ἀνδρός should not be transferred conceptually to the first clause, two distinct prohibitions are (contra Payne) nevertheless discernible.

9. *The Author's Morphological Choices*

Before it may be decided that, since the context is general rather than simply congregational, women are here broadly and harshly prohibited from anywhere 'instructing' (in some way), or 'taking authority over' men, another factor must be evaluated. The Author himself provides a clear guideline to the definition of both διδάσκειν and αὐθεντεῖν by choosing, or maintaining from an earlier source, the imperfective aspect. This factor is generally ignored[60] or noted only in passing.[61] Those few who do acknowledge the continuous action indicated by this

58. E.g. Smyth 1963: 364-65. Robertson (1923: 510) says verbs of ruling take the genitive. Cf. Spencer (1985: 87) who says that, since διδάσκειν takes the accusative, 'man' is 'most likely' the object only of αὐθεντεῖν. From this possibility, together with the rarity of the second infinitive, she leaps to the conclusion that it '[t]hus...signifies "to domineer" etc.'

59. Fung (1987: 198-99 and n. 193) points out that if ἀνδρος were intended to refer to both verbs, more probable would be either διδάσκειν ἄνδρα...οὐκ ἐπιτρέπω οὐδὲ αὐθεντεῖν ἀνδρός or διδάσκειν ἄνδρα...οὐκ ἐπιτρέπω οὐδὲ αὐθεντεῖν [sc. ἀνδρός].

60. E.g. Bernard 1899: 48; Barrett 1963: 55-56.

61. E.g. Dibelius and Conzelmann 1972: 47; Fee 1984: 35-36, 39.

choice interpret the passage in a congregational context and conclude that the prohibition is against women being recognized and ongoing teachers. Foh and Hurley accordingly argue that the ban is not upon all authoritative, ecclesial roles or all teaching roles in the congregation, and speculate about what that might mean in practice.[62]

Aspectual choice for infinitives has long been acknowledged as significant. The Present is generally said to describe action which may involve notions of attempting or continuing or beginning to do something, or to represent a series of repetitions of the action as parts of a whole.[63] It is also recognized that (as with imperatives) Present infinitives are normally chosen when attention is being drawn to one of these kinds of notions.[64] Two decades ago McKay wrote:

> Sometimes the distinction between, say, process and whole action, was of little concern to the writer or speaker in the context before him, and so the choice he made would be based on a purely personal (or even capricious) appreciation of its fitness; but often the choice of aspects was fully significant, showing how he wanted the event to appear to his hearers or readers (1977: §23.1.4).

Yet few ask whether the aspectual force of the Present infinitives at 1 Tim. 2.12 clarifies the passage, presumably because, with an ecclesial context in mind, the well-known fact that they convey the idea of action in process is taken here to express ongoing prohibition. This idea of continuity, however, derives from ἐπιτρέπω, which together with these infinitives conveys visualization of continuous prohibition of ongoing actions.

Some make lexical distinctions between verbs which describe actions (run, say etc.) and those which describe states of being (have, remain etc.). If the distinction is valid,[65] it is not always clear which is intended. As McKay says,

> Language is never so simple that it can be treated like simple arithmetic, with the expectation that a little mechanical calculation will produce clear results... The test of any hypothesis...is not that it resolves all doubts but that it offers the most consistent explanation, leaving few anomalies (1977: §214 n. 2).

---

62. Foh 1979: 126; Hurley 1981: 242-52. See also Key 1984: 14.
63. E.g. Goodwin 1879: §§1253, 1255; 1889: §25; K.L. McKay 1977: §23.2.
64. E.g. Thorley 1988: 199.
65. Porter (1989a: 49) believes it is not.

Διδάσκω and αὐθεντέω are both active rather than stative, although the latter would probably qualify for either. But someone able to teach will tend (or be expected) to do so when necessary, and someone equipped to take authority will tend (or be expected) to take it when required. A state-like condition, therefore, may apply for both. However, even if allowed a degree of stative meaning, activities of teaching or having authority over someone expressed with imperfective aspect (according to the lexical view accepted for the sake of this argument) may be conceived variously as single actions in process at the time of reference, or as actions attempted, continued or begun. Choices would be complicated further by the need to decide whether διδάσκω here means something less formal than 'teach'.

Since, however, there is nothing in either vv. 11-12 or their context requiring restriction to the gathered assembly, these Present infinitives suggest that a preliminary attempt to amplify v. 12 should include the following paraphrased options:

I customarily permit a woman

        neither continuously to instruct
                /tell

        nor continuously to dominate[66]
                /usurp authority over
                /exercise authority over   a man.

The Author does not say 'I customarily never permit a woman to instruct/tell or to dominate/have authority over men.' He says that he customarily prohibits women from some form of instruction, and some form of authority-taking over a man, both of which he envisages as *continuous*.

Should it be maintained that, regardless of its general reference, v. 12 must have some outworking in the congregation, the significance of these aspectual choices may not be ignored. The prohibition would then not be upon women *ever* teaching or exercising authority over a man, but upon some ongoing form of those actions. The Author shows no sign of wanting to prevent them from taking *any* teaching or authoritative roles in meetings or administration. If any boundaries to those

---

66. H. Scott Baldwin (1995: 73 n. 19) helpfully distinguishes this from the intransitive and necessarily negative 'domineer'.

activities *are* implied (and I doubt this: see below), in the structures discernible in New Testament assemblies[67] the teaching prohibition would simply be against too-frequent instruction of the same man. In other words, if a woman teaches a man for a certain period, or occasionally, she cannot be described as *continuously* instructing him. Similarly in regard to αὐθεντεῖν. Prohibition of continual domination, or continual ursurpation of authority, is unlikely to be in view because domination and usurpation would surely be inappropriate even if they were only occasional. The authority prohibited must be envisaged as continual, not occasional or temporary. A woman commissioned for particular tasks who performs them in humility and in combination with other ministries would not be in contravention of such a prohibition as this. Her authority would be specific and occasional, not general and continuous.

However, the ecclesial and administrative contexts assumed for the sake of argument in the previous paragraph have no real basis in the text. Certainly it is valid to consider the implications of general counsel for congregational behaviour and structures. But, if the continuous actions prohibited are not congregational teaching and administrative authority, the interpreter is well-advised to tread carefully. The Author himself makes no transition from everyday to congregational contexts. He is concerned with peaceful, holy ways of life which will please God. Christian men should not be angry and disputatious, and Christian women should appear and act in accordance with their proclamation and/or profession of godliness. In everyday life (which obviously includes the congregational context) that peace and holiness should be in evidence. No matter what conclusions are reached about the authorship and dating of the letter, or about the cultural–historical circumstances in which it is written, it is in this everyday context that these prohibitions should be interpreted. Three options are:

(a) The Author does not explicitly state that some women at the place of address are attempting or continuing in some way which he finds unacceptable to instruct or take authority over men. Nevertheless, if the letter should show evidence that he addresses specific circumstances (see full discussion in Part II), it would be reasonable to conclude that the continuous force of ἐπιτρέπω is limited to the duration of that

---

67. See warnings about interpreting the prohibitions in the context of structures unsupported by the New Testament text in e.g. Foh 1979: 249; Harris 1987: esp. 23-28; 1990: 342; Liefeld 1987: esp. 53-60.

situation. Should this be the case, however, although it would also be reasonable to conclude that some women have been acting inappropriately somewhere, there is no reason to conclude that they necessarily do so in the gathered assembly.

(b) If the Author is judged to be outlining rules he believes relevant for any Christian community, he intends to forbid women generally to take part in these actions. In this case ἐπιτρέπω indicates that it is his customary practice so to prohibit Christian women. In a general context, and in terms of the hitherto limited appreciation of the Greek verb, this sounds not only harsh but also unrealistic. Appreciation of his aspectual choice changes all that. The Author has chosen to prohibit the *continual* practice of those actions, not the actions themselves.

(c) If the Author is found to be compiling material from earlier sources into a letter or the form of a letter, and v. 12 is judged part of that source material, the choice of aspect may be that of some other author perhaps in some other period. It should be noted, however, that the compiler either chooses or retains from his source these Present infinitives. If he chooses them he intends to convey either meaning i. or ii. If he retains them from his source then that source intends that same meaning and he, with his own sensitivity to aspectual distinctions (cf. e.g. 1.3), chooses to leave it in place.

Attention to the aspectual forms of these infinitives contributes significantly to the way the passage is to be understood, and is ignored at the cost of appreciation of the Author's own intention. Even without clearer definition the distinction is helpful. The prohibitions may be against attitudes or practices he visualizes as taking more than one form (cf. 2.8; 3.2-3 etc.). However, since they concern constant or repeated actions in a woman's everyday life, I suggest that in fact his meaning is reasonably clear. First, he prohibits 'continual instruction', and in everyday life this can surely be little else than 'going on and on', or 'nagging'. There is (as previously argued) at least a possibility that this is seen as directed not only at men.[68] In a context concerned with character, a woman's constant berating of female relatives, slaves etc. would surely be viewed as being as inappropriate as that directed at males. Secondly, he prohibits the continual exercise of some form of authority over a man. As noted above, it seems unlikely that he wants

---

68. Note again that the rejected anger and disputation of the men themselves is unlikely only to refer to that directed at each other.

only to prohibit *continual* domination or the *continual* usurpation of authority. The alternative

> ...nor (continually) to exercise authority over a man

is also inappropriate because many women in antiquity exercised varying degrees of legitimate household or economic authority over some men on a continual basis.[69] On the other hand, the only way most women could continually 'exercise authority' over men would be by 'acting authoritatively', that is, by being self-assertive or 'bossy'.[70] The Author assumes his prohibitions relevant for all, so translations must be found that capture both continuous and negative aspects of these actions without implying that their occasional (or even unusual) exercise may be appropriate. In line with Köstenberger's findings on οὐδέ, the two actions prohibited are negative.

In this context there is no reason to restrict ἐπαγγελλομέναις (v. 10) to 'professing' rather than 'proclaiming', although (cf. 6.21) the idea of an associated 'profession' should not altogether be abandoned.

Also in this context, and in a trio of letters where the learning inherent in μανθάνω is more often that gained by experience than 'schooling', the verb obviously cannot be confined to formal tuition.

I suggest that vv. 11-12, along with the remainder of the chapter, is concerned with women's whole lives, not limited to their behaviour only in the congregation. Any attempt to define what this might imply for their behaviour in an ecclesial setting must reckon with the fact that congregational teaching and adminstrative authority-taking are not the topics in view.

---

69. Dixon 1988: e.g. 174-79, 188; 1992: 151.
70. See above Perriman at n. 49, and Hugenberger on p. 84.

CONCLUSION TO PART I

At 1 Tim. 2.11-12 the Author does not intend to prohibit women from teaching or taking authority over men anywhere. His goal is much milder than this: the sensible regulation of everyday behaviour.

Whilst no δεύτερον need follow his πρῶτον (2.1), one theme does underlie the whole of 2.1–3.14: peaceful, quiet lives lived in godliness and holiness. Within that overall theme a natural δεύτερον is, after all, discernible as in the following shortened paraphrase:

> I give you this instruction so that you may fight the good fight. **First of all**, I urge that prayers be made for everyone that we may live a peaceful and quiet life in all godliness and holiness. (**Secondly**,)[1] men praying should be holy and peaceful, women similarly should be godly and peaceful, and *episkopoi* and *diakonoi* should run their households well and, along with [certain] women, must be godly. I am writing you these instructions so that you will know how it is necessary to behave in God's household.

The thought from 2.8–3.13 progresses through groups required to live peaceful, quiet lives in godliness and holiness. The shift of topic does not occur at the chapter division, but in the transitional v. 8[2] where two topics merge. Two ways to 'fight the good warfare' are the closely related 'pray for peaceful and holy lives' and 'live peaceful and holy lives'.

1.   Parry (1920: 11-14) appears to see this division, but obscures it by introducing the gathered assembly at vv. 8-12. See also n. 2. By contrast Spencer (1985: 72, 74) sees in ch. 2 three ways the quiet life may be gained: prayer, quiet lifestyle, and the pursuit of education, this last derived from v. 11 (for which see Chapter 4).

2.   Parry (1920: 13-15) divides vv. 1-7 from v. 8–3.1a, 1b-13, apparently including ch. 3 in the concern for the character of 'the several members'. Knight (1992: 130), in consideration of *UBSGNT* (1975), argues that v. 8 is best understood as transitional because of its close connections with both what precedes (picking up on and concluding vv. 1-7 with a practical perspective) and follows (supplying the main verb for vv. 9ff.).

The widely accepted congregational context of 1 Timothy 2 has no real foundation in the text. When it is made an interpretative device for vv. 11-12 it does not clarify the language. It distorts it. 1 Timothy 2.9-12 addresses actions occurring in various situations. In a context in which men are expected to make sure that the hands they raise anywhere in prayer are holy, not those of angry disputants, vv. 9-12 is best translated:

> And in the same way I want women to adorn themselves in unaffected dress with simplicity and good sense, not in braids and gold or pearls or expensive clothing, but by means of good works, which is fitting for women proclaiming godliness. A woman should learn quietly in all obedience. I also permit a woman neither constantly to direct, nor to dominate[3] a man. She should be tranquil.

---

3. Contra G. Davies (see n. 49 above), men have no permission so to act. For Davies' reasoning about vv. 13-14 see Part IV.

Part II
1 TIMOTHY 2.9-12 IN ITS BROADER CONTEXT

Chapter 5

AN INTRODUCTORY LITERATURE SURVEY

Quite apart from the question of the authorship and dating of the letter, reconstruction of the broader context in which 1 Timothy must be interpreted requires the identification of evidence for the circumstances to which it is addressed. Accordingly, this brief chapter has two purposes:

    i.   to outline factors commonly employed in reconstructions of those circumstances, and which some have made a major exegetical device for 2.11-12; and

    ii.   to introduce three chapters in which views underlying those reconstructions will be re-examined.

The letter is commonly viewed as a church order designed to combat false teaching.[1] It has been pointed out that in fact it gives no clear definitions of offices and functions, the focus being upon behaviour.[2] Although it sets out qualifications for those in official roles (3.1-13), and requires that they be disciplined (5.19-20), the roles themselves are nowhere described. Some argue that the Author more directly responds to the dangers of heresy at the place/s of address.[3] It is generally agreed, however, that false teachers are the most influential background factor in the three Pastoral Epistles. In spite of wide acknowledgment that descriptions are vague, many envisage a more or less unified type of

    1.   E.g. A.T. Hanson 1966: 47; 1982: 23-24, 42; Dibelius and Conzelmann 1972: 5; S.B. Clark 1980: 192; Byrne 1988: 86; Beker 1991: 45. See also Guthrie 1990: 39, 62; Knight 1992: 10.

    2.   E.g. Schüssler Fiorenza 1983: 288. Holtz (1965: 53) claims the accent is on the liturgical–sacramental, not ecclesiastical–legal order.

    3.   E.g. Fee 1984: xx-xxi (incl. n. 16), xxxii, 25-26; 1985: 141-46; Scholer 1986: 199, 201; Liefeld 1986: 220; Kroeger 1986: 226; C. Kroeger and R. Kroeger 1992: 42-43; Payne 1986: 97, 99, 109; Padgett 1987a: 20; M.Y. MacDonald 1988: e.g. 173, 226; P.H. Towner 1989: 21-45, 248; Wiebe 1994: 55; Schreiner 1995: 108, 112.

false teaching which, although no longer precisely identifiable, has its source and/or operates within the assemblies addressed.

It is also widely held that the Author of the Pastorals confronts actual problems at the places of address of the three letters. In 1 Timothy it is claimed or suggested, for example, that 2.1-2 indicates that an exclusivism has developed, or that prayer is being neglected,[4] 2.7 that Pauline authority is being denied,[5] 2.8 that men are angry and disputatious[6] or fail to provide spiritual leadership,[7] 2.9-10 that women are dressing inappropriately,[8] 5.3-16 that some families are neglecting their widows,[9] and overall that the rules are dictated chiefly by pressures from pagan accusations of anti-social behaviour (A.T. Hanson 1966: 31). Most importantly for the present study, it is claimed variously from combinations of 2.11-12; 4.3; 5.3-16; 2 Tim. 3.6-7; Tit. 1.11; 2.3-4 that heretical depreciation of marriage at the places of address has resulted in troublesome behaviour including confusion of male–female roles,[10] that some women are acting presumptuously, are causing or perceived as causing trouble,[11] are immoral, weak in faith and sinful,[12] and some

---

4.   E.g. Plummer 1888: 82-85; Lock 1924: 24; Simpson 1954: 39; A.T. Hanson 1966: 31; Kelly 1972: 60; Murphy-O'Connor 1973: 1261. See also Easton 1948: 125. Cf. Houlden (1976: 63) who is unsure that prayer is neglected, and Merkel (1991: 24-25) who believes that gnostic claims and 2 Tim. 3.11ff. are significant here.

5.   E.g. Meinerz 1931: 37; Kelly 1972: 65; Guthrie 1990: 83.

6.   E.g. Weisinger 1866: 412; M.J. Evans 1983: 101; Spencer 1985: 83; Witherington 1988: 118.

7.   E.g. S.B. Clark 1980: 194.

8.   E.g. Calvin 1579: 209-10; Weisinger 1866: 415; Simpson 1954: 45; Osborne 1977: 347; Payne 1981: 182, 185, 187, 191; Moo 1981: 218; Osburn 1982: 11; Spencer 1985: 83; Roloff 1988: 134. Cf. Harris (1990: 339 and n. 15), who denies that this is necessarily the case.

9.   E.g. Kelly 1972: 115; Verner 1983: 137; M.Y. MacDonald 1988: 184.

10.   E.g. Jeremias 1963: 18-19; Hommes 1969: 17; Brox 1969: 133; Kelly 1972: 65, 68, 70; Williams 1977: 109-10; Johnston 1978: 252; Moo 1981: 217-18; 1991: 181; Verner 1983: 178; Perkins 1987: 20-21; M.Y. MacDonald 1988: 176; Bilezikian 1989: 180-82, 299 n. 46; Merkel 1991: 27; Beker 1991: 84-85.

11.   E.g. Calvin 1579: 209-10; Grimke 1838: 113-14; Weisinger 1866: 414; Simpson 1954: 45-46; A.T. Hanson 1966: 31; Olthuis 1976: 142; Giles 1977: 67-68; 1983: 58; 1985: 42, 60; Payne 1981: 183, 185, 187, 191; Osburn 1982: 11; Scanzoni and Hardesty 1982: 71; Howard 1983: 40-41; Verner 1983: 137, 178; Padgett 1987a: 23, 25, 27, 30; Witherington 1988: 126; Bilezikian 1989: 180-81,

widows are licentious, idle and gossips.[13] Some believe 1 Tim. 2.9-15 has both traditional and *ad hoc* components.[14] Even in this case, however, those explaining the prohibitions at vv. 11-12 by local or regional behaviour treat all passages in the three letters touching upon false teaching and women as important potential sources for the isolation of those circumstances.[15] In the absence of express statements about particular conditions some are cautious,[16] but a growing number (amongst which those designated in my Introduction as group 3 are prominent) claim that the Author responds to the activities of women influenced by false teachers to translate their liberty in Christ into freedom from contemporary social structures and who are attempting to teach and take authority over men. Such a response, they argue, is non-normative. The following re-examination is occasioned by the widespread and increasing support for this view.

Against versions of such reconstructed background, implications of the statements of purpose at 1.18-19a and 3.14-15 are (where addressed) variously explained. Some believe that the Author responds to a particular situation, but that at 3.14-15 he assumes general relevance.[17] It has been argued that at 1.18 παρατίθεμαι indicates the transmission of traditions (Ellis 1987: 245 and n. 51), again suggesting universal applicability. Others, however, trace close connections back from οὖν (2.1) to 1.18 and then to 1.3-7, arguing that ch. 2 responds to

299 and n. 46; Gritz 1991: 133. Cf. Houlden (1976: 63) who is unsure. Despite my n. 8 above, Harris (1987: 32-33) is convinced that the concern is for a specific situation.

12. E.g. Witherington 1988: 118.

13. E.g. Jeremias 1963: 18-19; Payne 1981: 185, 187, 190; Spencer 1985: 83. Cf. the more cautious Houlden (1976: 63), and Alford (1862: 351) who argues that the widows at 1 Tim. 5.15 are those Paul has encountered during his ministry in general.

14. E.g. S.B. Clark 1980: 193-94, 199-200 and n. 10; Oden 1989: 93; Knight 1992: 115-16.

15. Harris (1987: 32), e.g., claims that exegetical questions about 1 Tim. 2.11-15 depend on prior investigation into the background scenario and that the more pressing problems at the place of address require 'virtually no speculation'.

16. E.g. Hendriksen 1955: 103; Dibelius and Conzelmann 1972: 64.

17. E.g. Moo (1980: 82; 1981: 218-21) argues that, although its 'occasion' is the local false teaching, the 'situation' is unambiguously universally applicable. See also S.B. Clark 1980: e.g. 199-200. Others see here universally applicable prohibitions effective only while a woman is untrained: e.g. Bilezikian 1989: 180-81 with n. 45. See also Stouffer 1981: 15; Spencer 1985: 86.

circumstances arising from the activities of particular false teachers.[18]

A number of such arguments will be discussed in the following chapters, but three recent examples demonstrate initially that those circumstances are in no case convincingly isolated.

P.H. Towner exercises caution. Well before beginning his detailed exegesis of 2.9-15, however, he has concluded that the assembly at the place of address is troubled by an over-realized eschatology, and that misunderstanding of the Pauline equality tradition has resulted in emancipatory excesses (1989: 33-45). At 2.9-15 itself he correctly notes that the main motive is mission, the behaviour prohibited being parallel to that associated with false teachers, and the standards required being largely traditional (1989: 201-22). However, in ch. 2 he can ascertain with certainty no fact about the situation at the place of address, claiming probability only for indifference to prayer and disturbance between socio-economic groups, and possibility only for the idea that αὐθεντεῖν signifies an unusual situation of women taking upon themselves the teaching role.

Oden is bolder, clearly articulating views which others introduce simply by reference to the same texts. There is 'solid internal evidence *in the letter itself*' (emphasis mine), he claims, that false teachers are affecting a few vulnerable Ephesian women (2 Tim. 3.6-7) insufficiently committed to sexual chastity (1 Tim. 5.6, 13), who may also constitute a serious problem of ostentation and lack of commitment to the poor. 1 Timothy 2.12 primarily concerns a local problem, perhaps 'some sort of boisterous public display or unconventional touting of heresies' (1989: 93, 97-98). Yet it is misleading to represent 2 Tim. 3.6-7 as 'solid evidence' for 1 Timothy 'itself', and it will be demonstrated in Chapter 7, Section 1 that its illuminatory value is dubious indeed. Furthermore, since at 1 Tim. 2.9 it is unclear that chastity is in focus (see Chapter 3, pp. 65-69), it should not simply be assumed that the notoriously problematic 5.3-16 (for which see Chapter 8, Section 5) makes a more acceptable source for such illumination. These widows, who are clearly amongst the poor about whom Oden believes the Author is concerned, surely cannot be the most significant factor in a problem of ostentation. Finally, Oden simply speculates about 2.12.[19]

---

18. E.g. Fee 1984: 21-23, 25-26, 36; Harris 1990: 339-40.

19. At vv. 8-9 Oden (1989: 97) even more dubiously claims that the Author challenges resistance to and protest about the limitations of male/female sexuality.

Padgett's speculation is extreme. The male anger and argument about which the Author is concerned, he suggests, is most likely caused by false teachers and their women converts. The latter must not tell old wives' tales (4.7) causing that anger and disputation, but must be modest and sensible in speech and dress.[20] At 4.7, however, nothing suggests either that 'old wives' tales are being told in the congregation or that the anger and debate at 2.8 result from the telling of those tales anywhere. The catalyst for any anger and debate liable to impair male holiness is nowhere identified as reaction to either false teachers or women.[21]

Each attempt at such 'explanatory' reconstruction faces problems similar to those above. This is because all are based upon some combination of six erroneous views about 1 Timothy and the other Pastoral Epistles which will be examined in the next three chapters. Many from my groups 1 and 2 (who do not attempt so to explain 1 Tim. 2.11-12) hold the same six views. Those who accept Pauline authorship distort the language of the texts they employ, and those who reject Pauline authorship minimize in the same texts factors which together cast considerable doubt on the projected background. Four of these errors will be considered in Chapter 6, the fifth in Chapter 7, and the sixth in Chapter 8.

---

20. Padgett (1987a: 20-22), cautiously and only partly followed by Schreiner (1995: 112-13).

21. Padgett's subsequent speculation about vv. 11-12 is not strengthened by his acceptance of Payne's claims about ἐπιτρέπω (see Chapter 4, Section 5).

Chapter 6

1 TIMOTHY AS A LETTER:
FOUR COMMON MISCONCEPTIONS

1. *Genus*

No matter how useful the Pastoral Epistles may have proven to those
other than the originally intended recipients, they do not present themselves as 'church manuals'.[1] Congregational behaviour is nowhere
addressed (for 1 Timothy see Part I above), and functions (distinct from
the required behaviour) of officials other than the delegates addressed
are not described. 2 Timothy is generally viewed as a (literary) 'testament' written (as though) just prior to Paul's death.[2] Whatever the identity of the Author, however, all three Epistles have been written in the
form of personal letters.[3]

The personal approach is particularly clear in 2 Timothy if Pauline
authorship is accepted. With the exceptions of the concern that others

1.   Fiore (1986: 1-9) ably outlines the problems of viewing them as such.
2.   E.g. Ellicott 1864: 107-108; Parry 1920: 66; Lock 1924: xix, xxv; Kümmel
1965: 271; A.T. Hanson 1966: 47; 1982: 30, 47, 153; Käsemann 1968: 87; Brox
1969: 263; Dibelius and Conzelmann 1972: 40, 71, 115, 121; Fee 1984: xxv-xxvi;
Meade 1987: 135, 137-38; Wolter 1988: 222-24; Quinn 1990: 9, 15; Beker 1991:
47. Cf. Prior (1989: 92-112), who argues that 4.6-8 has in view Paul's release from
prison.
3.   Fiore (1986: 191-232) demonstrates their place in a long tradition of
Graeco-Roman epistolary exhortation literature. Donelson (1988: 108-12) identifies
coherence, consistency and presupposition of logic shared with a specific readership. Reed (1992: 140-46) traces interacting and unifying themes. Contra 'a miscel-
laneous collection...[with] no unifying theme...[or] development of thought' (Hanson 1982: 42). Burridge (1992: 255) says genre is 'a major literary convention,
forming a "contract" between author and reader...[, its] appreciation...crucial as a
major "filter" through which the author "encoded" his message, and through which
we may "decode" the same'.

be trained to teach (2.2),[4] and the plural greeting (4.22), the exclusive concern is Timothy.[5] Verse 2.14 is generally understood to be indirectly aimed at Timothy's congregation but, since there is no accusative of person (cf. Tit. 3.1), it is Timothy himself who is addressed.[6] The aspectual choices convey

> *Keep on calling* these things to mind, *being continually warned* before God not to word-fight...

1 Timothy and Titus certainly focus more upon both the people to whom the addressees are to minister and the false teaching endangering those people (1 Tim. 1.3-7; chs. 2–3; 4.6, 11, 16b; 5.4, 7, 14, 16, 20; 6.1-2, 17-19; Tit. 1.5, 10-14; 3.1). Nevertheless, address remains consistently personal (1 Tim. 1.2-3, 18-19; 3.14-15; 4.6-16; 5.21-23; 6.11-14, 20; Tit. 1.4-5; 2.1, 7, 15; 3.8), and imperatives are uniformly second person singular (1 Tim. 5.1-20; 6.17, 20; Tit. 2.1, 6, 15; 3.9-13). At no point apart from final greetings (1 Tim. 6.21b; Tit. 3.15) are assembly members addressed. Even in those final greetings, as at 2 Tim. 4.22, the plurals may indicate:

  i.   scribal interference—in light of Pauline practice, or of acceptance of the letters as canonical (note the textual variants registered in *UBSGNT*);
 ii.   semantic insignificance; or
iii.   ancillary address (Reed 1993: 97-101).

All three letters are personal, the primary concern being that the addressees understand how their own commissions are to be carried out.[7] Nowhere is sight of those addressees lost,[8] so even if the letters

---

4.   Payne (1986: 103) correctly notes that these faithful people are not necessarily only male, comparing 1.5; 3.14-15. Contra Donelson 1986: 169.

5.   Prior 1989: 63. Falconer (1937: 19) correctly says the purpose of the letter is to appeal to the addressee to rekindle his divine gift and to fulfil his ministry.

6.   So Prior 1989: 63, 159. Contra e.g. Alford 1862: 383; Bernard 1899: 122; Fee 1984: 204.

7.   Contra e.g. Fee (1985: 145), who claims that 1 Timothy 'betrays evidences everywhere that it was intended for the church', personal words 'totally subservient' to the task of restoring its order. For less extreme but similar argument see Knight 1992: 193. See also White 1910: 102; Williams 1977: 109-10; Payne 1981: 183, 185-90.

8.   Furnish 1968: 93 n. 47. Cf. Barrett (1963: 48) who, although noting the continuing personal tone, says 1 Tim. 3.2-6.21 has a more than personal reference.

were read to their congregations it is at least unclear that this was their primary purpose.[9]

If Pauline authorship is denied the personal address is viewed as a literary device. Nevertheless, 2 Timothy remains directed to those represented by the addressee, the Author's chief concern being to warn them not to engage in controversy with false teachers etc. (see above regarding the object of 2.14).[10] In 1 Timothy and Titus the same personal address (see above regarding the plural greetings) again indicates that the primary concern is for those represented by the addressees, and that it is not at all clear that these two letters are intended to address (or be read to) their congregations.[11]

This personal address should not be obscured by the 'church order' concept which facilitates the artificial introduction of both a congregational setting for 1 Timothy 2 and a Christian community setting for passages to be discussed below in Chapters 7 and 8.

2. *Primary Background Factor*

It is questionable that the most influential background factor of the Pastorals is false teaching. Certainly it features in comparative terms more clearly than do official roles, but both are reflected in the focus upon other matters. At 1 Tim. 1.3-4, for example, false teaching is

9.   Contra e.g. Kelly 1972: 42-43, 235; Banker 1987: 5. See also Guthrie (1990: 83, 200) who nevertheless points out that Tit. 1.12 renders a semi-official purpose unlikely.

10.   See also Brox (1969: 246, 250) who says 'Dieser Imperativ geht an die Adresse der Gemeindeleiter…(2.2)' ('This imperative is addressed to the congregational leaders [2.2]'), but at vv. 20-21 sees individual paraenesis contrasting return to leaders in v. 22. Stenger (1974: 264 n. 79) concludes (on other grounds) that 2 Timothy is addressed to 'weniger die nachapostolische Kirche allgemein… als eine bestimmte Gruppe innerhalb dieser Kirche: die der Amtsträger' ('not so much the post-apostolic church in general…but a certain group within that church: that of the office-bearers'). Contra e.g. Scott 1936: 107; Dibelius and Conzelmann 1972: 110; Houlden 1976: 120.

11.   Contra e.g. Schmithals and Werbeck 1961: 146; Dibelius and Conzelmann 1972: 35; Stenger 1974: 263 with n. 74; Murphy-O'Connor 1991: 405. It could be taken as a confirmation of the above argument that Skeat (1979: 173-77) with some force suggests that μάλιστα (Tit. 1.10-11) should be rendered 'in other words', a phrase characteristic of direct speech or dictated letters. Such a phrase seems unlikely in pseudepigraphic address to (post-Pauline) assemblies but less so to their leaders.

clearly stated as the reason for the addressee's commission. Overall, however, the focus consistently returns to the causal role of foolish talk, controversy etc., the addressees directed in the context of cause and not only effect (1 Tim. 1.4, 7; 6.4, 20; 2 Tim. 2.16, 23; 3.7; Tit. 1.10-11; 3.9). A more basic background factor than the false teaching, therefore, is *the foolish and godless chatter and controversy* from which heresy emerges.[12] The undoubted presence and effects of false teachers at the assemblies to which the letters are addressed should not obscure this.

3. *Distinctive Characteristics*

The Pastoral Epistles are often treated as though they were one letter or unit of instruction[13] addressing one group of assemblies.[14] But, no matter how similar they may be in date, style and subject matter, they do not purport to address one uniform situation (Prior 1989: 61-67). The differences involve more than Paul's imprisonment and the commonly noted more personal address in 2 Timothy.[15]

When Pauline authorship is accepted, although Hymenaeus[16] appears

12. Whilst not identifying chatter and controversy as the primary focus, some do note their importance: e.g. Easton 1948: 55; Barrett 1963: 105; Fee 1984: 204; Harris 1987: 32; Oden 1989: 73; Guthrie 1990: 42. Kelly (1972: 12) says much of the polemic is directed against the general contentiousness false teaching encouraged. It will be argued in Chapter 7, however, that at least at 2 Tim. 2.14-26 the false teaching developed from the contention (cf. 1 Tim. 1.19).

13. Lock (1924: xiii) finds this legitimate. Dibelius and Conzelmann (1972: 8, 71) identify 'three expressions of one and the same concept', 'imply[ing] a unified, consistent conception', 2 Timothy providing personal, historical background and representing Paul's ecclesiastical and ethical authority. Padgett (1987a: 20) calls 1 and 2 Timothy 'an *ad hoc* response'. Even when differences are noted some fall into this trap: e.g Harris (1990: 349) and further examples below.

14. E.g. 'the church of the Pastorals' (Verner 1983: 127, 137, 139, 165, 179-80). See also Jeremias 1963: 18-19; G.G. Blum 1965: 159; Scholer 1975: 8; 1986: 197-99, 203-204; Bassler 1984: 31; Payne 1986: 97-99; M.Y. MacDonald 1988: 23, 165-66, 168, 175; Kidd 1990: 190-91; Oberlinner 1994: 94.

15. As e.g. Kümmel 1965: 271. Those noting additional differences include Kelly 1972: 10, 233-35; Fee 1984: xxv-xxvi. Bush (1990: 152) speaks of 'the artistry of the individual letters'. Collins (1988: 260) writes 'Each of the pseudepigrapha represents a unique actualization of the apostolic tradition...[A]lthough there is a...commonality among the pastoral epistles, the real differences...must not be overlooked.'

16. The uncommon name presumably (although not necessarily) designates the

at 1 Tim. 1.20 with Alexander and at 2 Tim. 2.17-18 with Philetus, it is uncertain whether either Hymenaeus or Philetus were ever at Ephesus, and the Alexander of 1.20 may be neither the metalworker of 2 Tim. 4.14 nor the spokesman of Acts 19.33.[17] Timothy's location at the time 2 Timothy is written may not simply be assumed to be Ephesus.[18] At the time Titus's letter is written he is stationed on Crete, where there are various assemblies (1.5). Errors involving myths (Tit. 1.14; cf. 1 Tim. 1.4), greed (Tit. 1.11; cf. 1 Tim. 6.5) and Jewish influence (Tit. 1.14; cf. 1 Tim. 1.8-11) are apparent both in the Ephesian (1 Timothy) and Cretan assemblies, so false teaching may be identical. Nevertheless, there are significant differences in:

i. the commissions of the addressees (Timothy to reform, Titus to appoint);
ii. the ages and number of assemblies (that at Ephesus established, those on Crete new);
iii. the degree of urgency (e.g. Titus is not repeatedly urged to 'fight the good warfare', 'guard the deposit' or pay attention to his ministry);
iv. the focus (for Titus less upon false teachers and more upon God's people in the world) (Fee 1984: xxiii-xxvi).

same person, as e.g. Alford 1862: 312; Ellicott 1864: 133; Liddon 1897: 9; Scott 1936: 110; Barrett 1963: 106; Dibelius and Conzelmann 1972: 111; Kelly 1972: 184; Fee 1984: 206; Harris 1990: 349 n. 40; Guthrie 1990: 40; Knight 1992: 413.

17. Guthrie 1990: 78. Liddon (1897: 9) believes ὁ χαλκεύς (2 Tim. 4.14) probably distinguishes Alexander from Hymenaeus's associate (see also B/A⁶, s.v., 4), but Parry (1920: 11) thinks that although these may be the same person he may not be the Alexander of Acts 19.33.

18. Contra e.g. Hendriksen 1955: 264; Spencer 1974: 216; P.H. Towner 1989: e.g. 29-32; Guthrie 1990: 160; Gritz 1991: e.g. 111, 115; C. Kroeger and R. Kroeger 1992: 42. Fee (1984: 245) admits to speculation in identifying Alexander, but speaks (pp. xxv, 203-204) as if the second letter is certainly directed to Ephesus, and believes 3.6-7 fills in 'all kinds of blanks in 1 Timothy about the false teachers and their relationship to the women in the church' (p. 221). Knight (1992: 10) argues for an Ephesian destination not only because of Hymenaeus and Alexander but because Tychicus is sent there to replace Timothy (4.12), and Onesiphorus, Prisca and Aquila, all of whom are at the place of address (4.19), have rendered service (1.18) or lived there (Acts 18.19). It is unclear, however, that Tychicus is Timothy's replacement, that Onesiphorus renders help in the city in which his household is situated, or that the widely travelled Prisca and Aquila are still at Ephesus.

These are three individual letters to two different addressees, at two or three different places at only one of which is there evidence of various assemblies. Definitions of purpose must allow for such differences.

When Pauline authorship is denied the fictitious nature of the situation envisaged cannot justify blurring the above differences. Whilst similarities are clear, the Author does depict three distinguishable sets of circumstances. Definitions of his purpose should reflect this.

As pointed out in my general Introduction, the three letters are most naturally to be seen as written by the same Author/s. They may, therefore, shed light upon each other, but it can be misleading to speak of 'the' church of the Pastorals as though this were a single entity. It is certainly misleading to treat the three letters as if, or almost as if, they were one. This is an important factor for interpretation of passages to be discussed in Chapters 7 and 8 below, and so for reconstruction of background for 1 Tim. 2.9-12.

4. *Purpose*

Any claim to identify a purpose other than those stated in the letter must be treated cautiously. Amongst those proposed have been:

 i.   concern about wealthy assembly members;[19]
 ii. concern for obedience to those in authority;[20]
 iii. minimization of the impact of false teaching on marital relations by the transfer from domestic to ecclesiastical life of principles for the government of women (Verner 1983: 90-91, 107, 175-80, 182-83).

However, challenge to the rich is obviously only part of a broader concern for the behaviour of all members of God's household. In Part I it was argued that 1 Timothy 2–3 is concerned that the lives of all members be godly, and that at 2.11 the submission enjoined is directed to what a woman learns, not to her husband or teachers. Other passages cited in support of ii. and iii. will be addressed in Chapters 7 and 8, but one motif in the Pastorals that receives more attention than either patri-

19. Kidd (1990: 92-93, 155-57, 180), who nevertheless declines to claim a decisive role for the penultimate position of 6.1-2.

20. Schüssler Fiorenza 1983: 289. See also Byrne 1988: 86; M.Y. MacDonald 1988: 220.

archal order or marital relations is the life and doctrine of the addressees and other officials. The prominent feature is their required godliness, not the principles by which they are to govern. Although 'household' behaviour is central to the focus of 1 Timothy, and leaders are certainly in evidence, neither hierarchical nor patriarchal order are the primary focuses. See further in Chapter 8.

Whatever the Author's actual motivation for writing, he states three concerns, the second and third of which overlap in joint reference to 2.1–3.13. Altogether the addressee is

   i.   to deal with certain people who are teaching different doctrine etc. (1.3-7); and

   ii.   now to receive instruction both

       a)   relevant for 'good warfare' (1.18-19a); and

       b)   indicating conduct necessary in God's household (3.14-15).

But is the 'good warfare' the local/regional battle against those promoting heresy (1.3-7); and consequently is 1.8-17 a digression from that primary concern? Or is the 'good warfare' a way of life paralleling Paul's own display of Christ's patience as a pattern to those who would believe (1.16)? The answer depends upon establishment of the relationship between i. and ii.

It is generally held that 1.3 is a statement of purpose about the writing of the letter.[21] The sentence is unfinished, the καθώς clause having no apodosis, so the consensus is that the Author omits something like οὕτω καὶ νῦν παρακαλῶ or οὕτω ποίει,[22] or that προσμεῖναι has imperatival force.[23] NIV, for example, translates

---

21. E.g. Ellicott 1864: xx; Hendriksen 1955: 56; Spencer 1974: 216; 1985: 88; S.B. Clark 1980: 192; Fee 1984: 4; Donelson 1986: 116; Payne 1986: 97, 99; Padgett 1987a: 21; Wiebe 1994: 56. For further examples see below.

22. Bernard 1899: 22. See also Ellicott 1864: 3; B. Weiss 1885: 75; Humphreys 1901: 82-83; Falconer 1937: 120; Easton 1948: 108-109; Holtz 1965: 33-34; Knight 1992: 71; Oberlinner 1994: 9 n. 2, 11 with n. 5. Lock (1924: 7) suggests that ἵνα παραγγείλῃς is elliptical. Scott (1936: 7) says the sentence is 'plainly meant to lead up to some new admonition', the writer losing himself in fresh ideas, only taking up the thread again at 2.1. See also Kelly 1972: 43; Dibelius and Conzelmann 1972: 15 n. 1; Oden 1989: 55. Cf. Falconer (1937: 26-27), who says the treatment of false doctrine is secondary.

23. Lock (1924: 7 [followed by Easton 1948: 109]) and Hendriksen (1955: 56-57 n. 25) also suggest that the act of writing may substitute for the omitted words.

> As I urged you when I went into Macedonia, stay there in Ephesus so
> that you may command certain men not to teach false doctrines...etc.[24]

Here 1.3-4 confirms or reissues the previous order. NEB, however,
allows the infinitive its natural force but lays to one side comparison in
the unfinished καθώς introduction:

> When I was starting for Macedonia, I urged you to stay on at Ephesus.
> You were to command certain persons to give up teaching erroneous
> doctrines...etc.[25]

Here the Author *recounts* the previous order. The context suggests that
this more accurately captures his intention. His morphological choices
together with time *deixis* (πορευόμενος εἰς Μακεδονίαν) indicate that
he visualizes himself as/depicts the writer as visualizing himself having
already in a whole action (παρεκάλεσα) urged the addressee to remain
(προσμεῖναι, whole action) for the purpose of commanding (παραγγείλῃς, whole action) certain things. He now launches into an exposition on the goal of that task, that is that the troublemakers the
addressee had been urged to command might experience or display love
from a pure heart, etc. (v. 5). Nothing requires that either appointment
or task are being 'confirmed'. The purpose appears to be to make clear
the goal of a *previously* given commission. Verse 3, I suggest, although

---

24. See also AV, TEV, JB, RSV, NASB, *Inter-Linear Greek–English NT* 1975
(London: Bagster), and (to a lesser degree) Phillips; Jeremias 1963: 11; Kümmel
1965: 259; Roloff 1988: 62-63; Guthrie 1990: 39-40.

25. A.T. Hanson (1966: 22) uses NEB but writes 'At once the author launches
into his main theme, a warning against the false teaching'. Barrett (1963: 39) also
uses NEB, but it is unclear if the command is seen as reissued. Dibelius and Conzelmann (1972: 15) translate similarly to NEB but in both suggested translations
envisage the order reissued. Knoch (1988: 19) 'Bei meiner Abreise nach Maze-
donien habe ich dich gebeten, in Ephesus zu bleiben...' ('On my departure for
Macedonia I asked you to remain in Ephesus...'), seeing καθώς as an 'Erinnerung
an den Auftrag' (a 'reminder of the order'). Meinertz (1931: 26) '(Denke doch
daran), wie ich dich aufgefordert habe' ('[Remember, please] how I asked you'),
sees it as 'eine Ermunterung' ('an encouragement'), but also writes 'so errinnert er
ihn' ('thus he reminds him'). Similarly Merkel (1991: 18) 'Wie ich dich ange-
wiesen habe, in Ephesus zu bleiben...' ('As I instructed you to remain in Ephesus...') describes this as an 'Erinnerung an eine früher gegebene Anweisung' (a
'reminder of an instruction given earlier'), but adds 'um deren bleibende Gültigkeit
einzuschärfen' ('in order to emphasize its enduring validity').

revealing the task set, is not a statement of purpose for the writing of the letter. It simply introduces its first concern.[26]

The relationship between the false teaching at 1.3-4 and that at v. 19, moreover, is indirect. There are two 'commands' in the unfinished vv. 3-4: the παράκλησις to the addressee, and the παραγγελία he is to administer. In the new sentence at v. 5 the latter is still in view (παραγγελίας together with vv. 6-7). Neither the παραγγελία (vv. 3, 5) nor the παράκλησις (v. 3) is to be identified with ταύτην τὴν παραγγελίαν at v. 18. Instead, v. 18 refers forward to the instruction following 2.1,[27] which is here passed on (παρατίθεμαι) to the addressee in accordance with the waging of the 'good warfare'. In fact, παρατίθεμαι suggests that what is passed on is traditional instruction, and similarly at 6.20 τὴν παραθήκην φύλαξον (cf. also 2 Tim. 2.2 ταῦτα παράθου).[28] Some argue that the expression evokes a sense of the addressee's responsibility for the authenticity and intactness of the material so entrusted.[29] The instruction which constitutes the παραγγελία at 1.18 is distinguishable from the commission of the addressee. Certainly the good warfare, closely connected as it is with the faith and good conscience which some have pushed aside, is thereby also closely connected with the false teaching and the command to be administered in 1.3-7:

πίστιν καὶ ἀγαθὴν συνείδησιν, ἥν τινες ἀπωσάμενοι περὶ τὴν πίστιν
ἐναυάγησαν, ὧν ἐστιν Ὑμέναιος καὶ Ἀλέξανδρος...κτλ. (1.19-20)

26. Note again Scott at n. 22 above. Note also that this 'introduction' weakens the idea that this is a semi-official letter buttressing the addressee's authority as claimed by e.g. Kelly 1963: 43; Guthrie 1990: 83, 99. Gritz (1991: 107 and n. 17), who also treats Tit. 1.5, 10-16 as an 'authorization', fails to note that there again the addressee is reminded of an earlier commission and its goal.

27. E.g. Alford 1862: 311; Weisinger 1866: 402; 'basically means the whole letter' (Ellis 1987: 245). Contra e.g. Holtz 1965: 50. See also Knight (1992: 107) who, although noting that at v. 5 παραγγελίας has a wider, more positive perspective than only correction of false teachers, argues that ταύτην τὴν παραγγελίαν naturally refers back to vv. 3-5 rather than forward to the ἵνα clause which introduces the purpose of the charge, not its content.

28. Ellis 1987: 245 and n. 51. Cf. Horsley (1982–89: II, 85), who says that at 6.20 παραθήκη is used figuratively although the writer clearly draws on literal usage found e.g. in P. Mich. 671.5.

29. Maurer 1972: 164; 'I commit (as a deposit, to be faithfully guarded and kept...)' (Alford 1862: 311). Bush (1990: 154) says that 1.12-20 and 6.11-16, 20-21 constitute an inclusio, a function of which is progression from the former (which passes on the message) to the latter (which emphasizes the source of the authority).

...συνειδήσεως ἀγαθῆς καὶ πίστεως ἀνυποκρίτου, ὧν τινες ἀστοχήσαντες ἐξετράπησαν...κτλ. (1.5-6)

This connection, however, is not with the original commission but with the exposition beginning at v. 5, that is, within the present communication, not between the letter and the original commission. It is a contrast—between the faith and conscience which the addressee must exercise in his warfare, and the faulty faith and conscience of those who have pushed such things aside (v. 19) or have 'missed the mark' (v. 6). The link between vv. 19 and 5 falls short of identifying the good warfare with the original commission. Furthermore, although 2.1ff. constitutes τὴν παραγγελίαν of 1.18, and is obviously intended to enable the waging of the good warfare, that warfare initially is said to be fought κατὰ τὰς προαγούσας ἐπὶ σὲ προφητείας,[30] not by that παραγγελίαν. Those prophecies may very well concern the addressee's general calling rather than a particular part of it (cf. 4.14; 2 Tim. 1.6).[31] But whether or not this is the case, 3.14-15 confirms that 1.18-19a = 2.1ff. functions quite distinctly from 1.3 as a statement of purpose for the letter.

Fee's attention to 3.14-15 as it refers to chs. 2–3 unintentionally illustrates this separate function. Consistently interpreting the false teachers as Ephesian elders,[32] he claims that both chapters respond to local circumstances. Although declaring disorders reflected in ch. 2 to have surfaced in worship gatherings, he recognizes that ch. 3 has everyday life in view. Noting that the Author claims (v. 14) to write chs. 1–3 in case he is delayed, the real urgencies, says Fee, are focused at 3.15. The

30. Alford (1862: 311) says 'as clad in them, as if they were his defence and confirmation'.

31. A.T. Hanson 1982: 64-65; Knight 1992: 107-109.

32. Fee 1984: 21-22. Fee (1985: 142-44) argues that the key to the purpose lies in 1.3; 3.15; and a now-fulfilled Acts 20.30. Granted Pauline authorship, and in appreciation that the latter verse either suggests knowledge after the fact or a true prediction (143 n. 7), the defection of elders 'in the 60s' is scarcely (as claimed) 'a piece of solid historical datum'. Acts 20.29-30 distinguishes between those who will 'come in among' the Ephesians, and elders who can be expected to 'arise', so Timothy (1.3) may be left there before the latter begins to occur. Neither is it clear that such false teachers are either 'insiders' or now elders. If elders have by now defected, presumably 'wolves' have also 'come in' but, even if now 'insiders', these are not necessarily elders. Whilst elders certainly teach it is not necessarily the case (as Fee implies) that teachers are elders. Fee has here simply omitted 1.18-19b from data to be taken 'with full seriousness'.

church is at stake, and people entrusted with the truth must know how to behave, so false teachers must be stopped and the people put back in touch with that truth. To emphasize this point, he says, metaphors are mixed and '*conduct...in God's household...is* not...[behaviour] "in church" '.[33] But if (as Fee argues) the Author includes ch. 2 in such required conduct, surely all people entrusted with the truth ought to behave accordingly.[34]

Scholer argues that 3.14-15 is not a statement of purpose but a 'summary statement' of directions for the particular problem faced (1986: 199-200). That 'summary', however, states that what has just been written sets out appropriate behaviour for Christians (2.1) who are subsequently particularized as men (2.8), women (2.9-15), ἐπίσκοποι (3.1b-7), διάκονοι (3.8-10, 12-13) and certain women (3.11). No regional situation is mentioned in either ch. 2 or ch. 3. In ch. 3 the parallels between vv. 1-13 and Tit. 1.6-9 could indicate requirements of the same author or school of thought at about the same time, but each is independent of its context,[35] and their parallels with Household Codes make it improbable that either is designed only for a present situation. At 3.1a πιστὸς ὁ λόγος indicates that there, too, an idea with wide currency is employed. Note again that it is widely agreed that ch. 2 uses traditional material: in vv. 1-7 with their intrinsically universal concerns;[36] and in v. 8 with its concern for activities taking place ἐν παντὶ

33. Fee 1984: 53-54 (italics his). See also 1985: 143. Fee's bold introductory claim (1984: xx) that sense is made of every detail in the letter by the assumption that everything has to do with 1.3 throws into contrast his argument at 2.12, which inclines towards the speculative.

34. Roloff (1988: 107) calls 2.1–3.16 'einen in sich geschlossen Teil...die... Weisungen als grundsätzlich an die ganze Kirche gerichtet gelten sollen. Und in der Tat handelt es sich hier um allgemein das Gemeindeleben betreffende Anordnungen' ('a self-contained section...the...instructions are meant to be understood as being directed as a general principle to the whole church. And indeed here are orders which concern generally the congregational life').

35. Ellis 1987: 244. Verner (1983: 104-107), also noting close parallels with Tit. 1.6-8, concludes that the Author makes his own emphasis by combining traditional and non-traditional material.

36. Many reject the claim (made by F.C. Baur) that the plural βασιλέων (v. 2) indicates a time after 137 CE, holding the reference to be general: e.g. Ellicott 1864: 26; B. Weiss 1885: 109; Easton 1948: 121; Jeremias 1963: 16; Dibelius and Conzelmann 1972: 36-38; Guthrie 1990: 80. Cf. Lock (1924: 25), who suspects here response from Paul the Roman citizen to a danger that Christians may follow Jewish tendencies to rise against the Empire.

τόπῳ. In accordance with the most recent work on Aspect, note again at vv. 8 (and therefore 9) and 12 the visualization of (to some extent) ongoing intention (βούλομαι) and ongoing command (ἐπιτρέπω). Even laying to one side at this point the difficult vv. 13-15, where it is also widely agreed that traditional thought is apparent, 3.15 certainly appears to summarize something which the Author envisages as more universally relevant than instruction for a particular situation.[37]

At 1.3 neither the order to the addressee nor the command to the troublemakers is identifiable with the instruction of 1.18 = 2.1ff., and if 3.14-15 refers to both chs. 2 and 3, 1.18 = 2.1ff. surely cannot refer only to a particular regional 'warfare'. Permitted their own reference, 1.18-19a and 3.14-15 together indicate that the 'good warfare' is a way of life which the Author believes is universally relevant.[38] At v. 18 στρατεύῃ conveys

> I am setting this instruction before you...in order that you might go on fighting...the good warfare...etc.

The goals of this letter are distinguishable from the goal of the addressee's commission, and 2.9ff. should be interpreted accordingly.

When 1 Timothy is taken seriously as a letter, whether understood as directed to Timothy himself or to later leaders, its personal address, its primary background factor, its differences from the other Pastorals, and its statements of purpose are all important for reconstruction of its occasion. All, as demonstrated above, are commonly misunderstood. Together with misconceptions to be outlined in Chapters 7 and 8 below, this has contributed significantly to distortion of the background against which 2.11-12 is so often interpreted.

---

37. Scholer (1986: 201) himself seems to recognize this for 2.9-10.

38. Parry (1920: 10) writes 'not merely the strife with the ἑτεροδιδασκα-λοῦντες but the whole work...'

Chapter 7

REFLECTIONS OF HERESY:
A FIFTH COMMON MISCONCEPTION

The heresy in the Pastoral Epistles is generally treated as a more or less loosely unified body of thought which, although no longer precisely identifiable, has its source and/or operates within the Christian assemblies at the places of address at the time of writing.[1] It is widely held to include prohibition of marriage (1 Tim. 4.3 cf. 2.15; 5.14; Tit. 2.4) and teaching specifically directed at and acted upon by women (2 Tim. 3.6-7; 1 Tim. 2.9-15; 5.13; Tit. 2.3-5), abstinence from foods (1 Tim. 4.3 cf. 5.23), spiritualization of the resurrection (2 Tim. 2.18), and various gnosticizing and/or Judaizing (2 Tim. 3.13; 4.4; 1 Tim. 1.4; 4.7; 6.4, 20) and emancipatory (1 Tim. 2.11-12) tendencies.[2] Re-examination of the evidence adduced reveals a more diverse picture.[3]

1. E.g. Bernard 1899: xlv-lv; Humphreys 1901: 45-53; Easton 1948: 3; Brox 1969: 33, 38, 41; Yamauchi 1973: 50; Donelson 1986: 118-22; Kroeger 1986: 226, 236; M.Y. MacDonald 1988: 173; Wiebe 1994: 55; Oberlinner 1994: e.g. 174, 180, 232-33. Some, noting local Cretan features, nevertheless discern parallels throughout: e.g. Holtz 1965: 22-23; Dibelius and Conzelmann 1972: 135; Kelly 1972: 10-12, 95, 184, 233-35; Guthrie 1990: 42-43. Verner (1983: 176-77) (followed by M.Y. MacDonald 1988: 178) recognizes tensions in descriptions of the heresy, and is cautious about its Christian origin. However, although noting that 1 Tim. 4.1ff.; 2 Tim. 3.1ff. are associated with the future, he employs both to reconstruct the situation contemporary with the letter. In considering 2 Tim. 3.6-7, he claims prohibition of marriage is a prominent feature of the false teaching, and he finds a similar situation probable in Tit. 1.11 (his n. 175).

2. E.g. Dibelius and Conzelmann 1972: 65-66; Kelly 1972: 11; Yamauchi 1973: 49-50; Payne 1986: 98-99; Harris 1987: 32-33; 1990: 349; Padgett 1987a: 20-21; M.Y. MacDonald 1988: 179; P.H. Towner 1989: 24-28; Moo 1991: 180-82, 189. See similarly those noting differences between the letters, e.g. Fee 1985: 142-43; Knight 1992: 296 cf. 11-12, 295-98, 301-303, 412, 414.

3. See e.g. 'a many headed heresy' (Bauer 1972: 90). Brox (1969: 38) says the heresy 'hat nicht den Charakter einer Zusammenfassung, so dass hier schon eine

If the Author is Paul, his language describes various false teachings.[4]
1 Timothy 4.1-3a, 2 Tim. 3.1-9, 4.3-4 and Tit. 1.15-16 include some
false teachers who originate and/or operate outside the assemblies, and
some not yet in evidence at the time of writing.[5] If Pauline authorship is
rejected, the language remains significant. Although the pseudepigra-

Art Widerlegung aller denkbaren Häresien…vorläge' ('is not in the nature of a
summary so that there would already be a kind of refutation of all conceivable
heresies…here'). See also Koester 1982: 302-303. Gunther (1973: 4-5) demonstrates the vagueness of description by identifying 19 different diagnoses of the
false teaching; Barrett (1974: 240-41) sees various trends 'lumped together'; De
Boer (1980: 371 n. 47) finds evaluation difficult; Kidd (1990: 97-98) can identify
scant evidence of a coherent theological system.

4.   Amongst those acknowledging some diversity Hatch (1898: 351) cites without details Reuss, Credner, Thiersch and Hilgenfeld. See also Colson 1917–18: 271;
Parry 1920: lxxxi-lxxxix; Lock 1924: xvii (who is unsure about authorship);
Michaelis 1930: 102-28. Guthrie (1990: 41-42, 103, 168-70) believes 2 Tim. 3.5;
4.3 are 'pre-visions' and 1 Tim. 4.1-5 foretells tendencies outside the community,
food laws having already emerged at Colossae (Col. 2.16, 20-22), but employs
1 Tim. 4.1-4 with 5.22 to describe 'a general contemporary tendency', and at 2 Tim.
3.5 suspects καί may refer to the people in 2.23 who clearly emerge from the
church membership. See also Fee (1984: xxi-ii) who (cf. at my n. 2 above), in
describing the elements of the teaching at Ephesus, cross-references from 2 Tim.
2.18 and, although noting the speculative nature of the reconstruction (pp. 223-24),
is attracted to the idea of emancipation tendencies amongst the women of 2 Tim.
3.6-7. He claims (p. xxxix n. 17) that it is generally assumed that opponents are
outsiders, but I find no evidence of such a general assumption.

5.   Parry (1920: lxxxi-lxxxvii) has little doubt that that which *is* internal and
current is of one kind. He also demonstrates, however, that it is described with reference to method and moral defect, its doctrinal content (with the exception of
2 Tim. 2.18, which refers certainly only to two people) always being vague (see
also Guthrie 1990: 42). Such method, argues Parry, should be envisaged against a
contemporary shared Graeco-Judaic background of self-appointed teachers, μῦθοι
(speculative narratives) and γενεαλογίαι (legends about heroes etc.) which he
concludes are predominantly of Jewish origin. See also 'a pseudo-hellenic Judaism'
(Colson 1917–18: 269), and Guthrie (p. 40), who sees more evidence for the
influence of Jewish legend than Greek speculation. At 1 Tim. 1.7-8 the words νομο-
διδάσκαλοι and καλὸς ὁ νόμος…κτλ. suggest Parry may be correct with respect to
the place to which 1 Timothy is addressed, but it does not necessarily follow that
shared Jewish method or even specific speculations and legends result in identical
teachings. Since 'myths' and 'genealogies' were broadly accepted terms for a type
of approach despised by others as frivolous and useless (Colson p. 266), the Author
may envisage widely varying teachings.

pher may contrive to give the impression he writes in an earlier period,[6] this should not simply be assumed. Of particular importance for the present study are 2 Tim. 3.1-9 and 1 Tim. 4.1-3, both frequently asserted to provide details explaining the need for the instruction at 1 Tim. 2.9-15.[7]

1. *2 Timothy 3.1-9*

Regardless of authorship, nothing requires this group of false teachers to be Christian, either currently, or in the past.[8]

This opposition differs from that of 2.14-26 in two ways:

i. their descriptions; and
ii. the ways the addressee is instructed to deal with them.

1.1. *Descriptions*

The opposition at 2.14-26. These are godless babblers, indulging in foolish, quarrel-producing arguments, who can be expected to grow more and more ungodly (ἐπὶ πλεῖον γὰρ προκόψουσιν ἀσεβείας),[9] their teaching spreading like gangrene. They appear to be diverse.

At v. 14, having restated the gospel, featured the importance of endurance for the sake of the elect, and emphasized all of this by a faithful saying (vv. 11-13), the Author directs the addressee to continue to call these things to mind and reminds of an ongoing solemn charge before God not to fight with/about words (v. 14: see Chapter 6, Section 1). Hymenaeus and Philetus (vv. 17-18) illustrate the dangers inherent in such talk (v. 16), their heresy being proof that godless chatter spreads.

---

6. As e.g. Brox 1969: 41, 253, 256; Karris 1973: 562-63. See also Dibelius and Conzelmann (1972: 65-66), who believe that the view that the letter is genuine presupposes definite allusions and factors comprehensible only to the addressees (cf. the argument below), and Scott (1936: e.g. xxix, 47, 110), who nevertheless notes differences between Titus and the other letters (p. 157), and the existence of various forms of Christian gnosticism (p. 158). Houlden (1976: 43) says the letters are directed against all kinds of deviationists, so implying deviation from Christianity.

7. For Tit. 1.14-16 and 2 Tim. 4.3-4 see Appendix I.

8. Contra e.g. Easton 1948: 63; Barrett 1963: 110-11; Brox 1969: 253-54; Verner 1983: 176-78; Fee 1984: xxi; Scholer 1986: 204, 218-19; Kroeger 1986: 237; Harris 1987: 32-33; 1990: 349; M.Y. MacDonald 1988: 165; Oden 1989: 78.

9. Humphreys (1901: 184) notes the same words as at 3.9, claiming that there an advance beyond what appears in 2.16 is in view. At 2.16, however, προ-κόψουσιν is modified by ἀσεβείας; at 3.9 the meaning is simply 'advance/get far'.

At 2.16 περιΐστασο indicates first that the addressee is *consistently* to avoid this godless babbling,[10] and secondly that the elliptical future tense (ἐπὶ πλεῖον…προκόψουσιν ἀσεβείας καὶ ὁ λόγος αὐτῶν ὡς γάγγραινα νομὴν ἕξει) is to be understood as timeless: anyone indulging in godless talk can be expected to grow more and more godless, etc.[11] Whilst those who claim that Hymenaeus's and Philetus's heresy develops from an eschatological misunderstanding of Pauline teaching may be correct,[12] and the error may now be widespread (vv. 17, 18c), τινων (v. 18c) gives no idea of the numbers so subverted.[13] The development and spread is one action occurring before the backdrop of godless talk and contention. There are other such actions.

First of all, at centre stage the addressee appears to be in some difficulty. He is encouraged (1.6-8, 13-14; 2.1-3, 8-13). He is also not only reminded of his responsibility, but instructed (vv. 16, 23-25), and (noting the strongly marked τοῦτο δὲ γίνωσκε, ὅτι…3.1) the same theme is returned to at 3.10–4.5. Patterning himself upon Paul, he is to base his teaching on the scriptures so that he may be thoroughly equipped, to preach and be ready in and out of season, to refute, etc., because the time will come when Christians will not want sound teaching. All of

---

10. Ellicott (1864: 133) claims that the false teachers (not the babblers) will grow worse and worse. The Author, however, focuses on the fact that word-fighting and godless chatter lead to false doctrine, and is concerned that his addressee avoid those errors.

11. Cf. future reference at 4.3-4 in Appendix 1. Cf. also Ellicott (1864: 133) who interprets the tense as time-specific and claims that the Future indicates the error is not yet in its most developed state.

12. E.g. Barrett 1963: 106; Fee 1984: 206-207; P.H. Towner 1989: 36-38. Ellicott (1864: 134) suggests that (in his opinion general) asceticism very probably led on to contempt for the body and false views about death and thence the resurrection.

13. Ellicott 1864: 134. Bernard (1899: 123-24), although warning against confusion with later gnostic teaching, notes the existence of similar error at Polycarp, *Phil.* 7, ὃς…λέγει μήτε ἀνάστασιν μήτε κρίσιν ('whoever…says [there is] neither resurrection nor judgment…'), and 2 *Clem.* 9, μὴ λεγέτω τις ὑμῶν ὅτι αὕτη ἡ σὰρξ οὐ κρίνεται οὐδὲ ἀνίσταται ('let none of you say that this flesh is not subject to judgment or that it does not rise again'), but argues that, in the *Acts of Paul and Thecla* 14, the probably direct reference to 2 Tim. 2.18, ἡμεῖς σε διδάξομεν, ἣν λέγει οὗτος ἀνάστασιν γενέσθαι, ὅτι ἤδη γέγονεν ἐφ' οἷς ἔχομεν τέκνοις ('we will teach you about that resurrection which he asserts has already occurred in the children which we have'), furnishes no additional evidence for prevalence.

this builds to the climax of 4.6-8, which sets before him Paul's own example. The Author seems to believe his delegate (or those he represents) is involved in 'word-fighting'.[14]

Secondly, doctrines taught by false teachers other than Hymenaeus and Philetus (ὧν) are unspecified.[15] Various types of heresy may have emerged, linked only by their shared indulgence in godless chatter and their infectious nature.

The words ὁ...στερεὸς θεμέλιος τοῦ θεοῦ (v. 19) and μεγάλη... οἰκίᾳ (v. 20) are often interpreted as referring to the visible church[16] in which false teachers continue as members. It has also been suggested that the building may represent the assembly at Ephesus.[17] Quite apart from the fact that location is unspecified in this letter, either reference would be curious in view of the fact that utensils used for unclean purposes are already useful.[18] This does not necessarily mean that the

14. This is true whatever meaning is preferred for λογομαχέω, e.g. Scott 1936: 107-108. Contra e.g. Meade (1987: 127-28), who sees the addressee focused as Paul's authoritative interpreter. Simpson (1954: 141) argues that 2.22-23 are 'wholesome cautions, not veiled censures'. With v. 14 directed to the addressee, however, at least vv. 23-25 seems to respond to actual tendencies.

15. Contra e.g. Barrett 1963: 106; P.H. Towner 1989: e.g. 31, 38. Humphreys (1901: 174-75, 213) claims οἵτινες indicates the class to which Hymenaeus and Philetus belong (see also Ellicott 1864: 133), which could imply that those of vv. 16-17a teach the same doctrine. This is untrue in the *koine*. BAGD, s.v. ὅστις 3, lists this instance as simply taking the place of ὅς and the antecedent appears to be the two named and not the 'they' implied in προκόψουσιν. Bernard (1899: liv) approves Weiss's warning that perversions of individuals constitute no direct evidence for the general character of erroneous teachings, but nevertheless claims that Hymenaeus's and Philetus's error was a natural accompaniment to the heresy Timothy had to oppose.

16. E.g. Alford 1862: 385-86; Ellicott 1864: 135-36; Bernard 1899: 124; Lock 1924: 101; Scott 1936: 112-14; Easton 1948: 54-61; Hendriksen 1955: 266-67, 270; A.T. Hanson 1968: 31-32; Brox 1969: 249; Dibelius and Conzelmann 1972: 133; Roloff 1988: 215; Oden 1989: 71-72; P.H. Towner 1989: 129-36; Beker 1991: 85. See also Simpson 1954: 138-40; Knight 1992: 417; Guthrie 1990: 163-64. Humphreys (1901: 175-76) argues that the thought is the difference between true and false teachers, not the whole church.

17. E.g. Kelly 1972: 186-87; Fee 1984: 207. For various less widely accepted interpretations see e.g. Alford 1862: 385; Lock 1924: 100; Scott 1936: 112; Hendriksen 1955: 266-67; A.T. Hanson 1966: 19; 1968: 34; Houlden 1976: 122; Fee 1984: 207; Guthrie 1990: 162.

18. Easton 1948: 57; Barrett 1963: 107; Guthrie 1990: 164.

Author has chosen his metaphor unwisely.[19] The different settings at
1 Cor. 3.12 and Rom. 9.21 warn that care is required. Uncertainty about
the antecedent of τούτων adds to the difficulty of the passage.[20] The
contrast at v. 20 (ἃ μὲν...ἃ δὲ) suggests that the uses to which the utensils are put are due to their nature, that is, they are honourable because
they are gold or silver, or dishonourable because they are wooden or
clay.[21] The latter kinds cannot be transformed by cleansing, so in the
closely associated v. 21 (οὖν, τούτων) the analogy should not be pressed:[22] a person may be so cleansed. This could certainly be taken to
mean that formerly dishonourable members may be made useful, but in
fact nothing demands that interpretation.

Sometimes adduced to evoke forbearance towards internal church
error here are the parables of the Tares and the Dragnet (Mt. 13.24-30,
36-43, 47-50).[23] In the former, however, the 'field' is 'the world'
(v. 38). In the latter, since the image of the kingdom of heaven is used
variously throughout the series of parables,[24] and represents 'the
church' in no other, it should not be assumed that the Dragnet is the

19. Contra e.g. Scott 1936: 113-14; Easton 1948: 57; Kelly 1972: 187. See also
Fee (1984: 211) but note p. 212.

20. Amongst those claiming it refers to the false teachings/teachers are
A.T. Hanson 1966: 89; Fee 1984: 211-12. Lock (1924: 101) believes this is the
primary reference. Barrett (1963: 108) is attracted to the same conclusion. Arguing
that the antecedent is ἃ δὲ εἰς ἀτιμίαν are Alford 1862: 387; Ellicott 1864: 137
(who nevertheless interprets these as the ψευδοδιδάσκαλοι); Scott 1936: 114;
Kelly 1972: 188. Dibelius and Conzelmann (1972: 113) are uncertain.

21. Contra e.g. Knight (1992: 418), who says they are regarded as dishonourable because of the uses to which they are put.

22. '[T]he reality rises above the figure' (Hendriksen 1955: 271). Simpson
(1954: 140) seems to believe that the less valuable wares, if cleansed, are acceptable in the household. Although v. 20 certainly pictures both kinds as useful, it does
not speak of cleansing: instead it seems to be the nature of some utensils to be noble
and others ignoble. It is only in v. 21, where people are in view, that cleansing is
introduced.

23. E.g. Bernard 1899: 124; Easton 1948: 60-61. Referring only to the former
parable are Alford (1862: 386), Simpson (1936: 140) who also introduces the
Gibeonites in the congregation of Israel, and Hendriksen (1955: 270). Humphreys
(1901: 176) refers to the latter parable.

24. France (1984: 38) writes 'Jesus uses "the kingdom of God" in such a variety
of linguistic connections and in relation to such varied subject-areas that it is impossible to identify any specific situation, event or "thing" which *is* the Kingdom of
God.'

exception. The gospel message is the more likely subject. Also adduced here to evoke internal error is 1 Tim. 3.15, where the assembly is described as στῦλος καὶ ἑδραίωμα τῆς ἀληθείας.[25] Even if this is the assembly and not a reference to the following sentence,[26] and even if the building component is a 'foundation',[27] and neither is certain, the absence of the article could indicate that the assembly is viewed as 'a' foundation. At 2 Tim. 2.19, therefore, ὁ...στερεὸς θεμέλιος τοῦ θεοῦ does not necessarily refer to that assembly at 1 Tim. 3.15.[28] The claim that the 'great house' is the assembly rather than the world has no real basis.[29]

The point of vv. 19-21 is that in spite of false teaching God's strong foundation continues to stand. The most obvious contrast and therefore 'foundation' would be *sound* teaching (so clearly featured throughout the Pastorals).[30] There are sayings (v. 19) 'inscribed' on this stone, with vv. 20-21 immediately preceding a return to the dangers of foolish arguments etc. marked again by second-person imperatives. The first inscription quotes Num. 16.5, and the second alludes possibly to v. 26 of that same chapter or to Isa. 52.11 or 26.13.[31] Interestingly, 2 Tim.

25. E.g. Humphreys 1901: 175; Scott 1936: 113; Brox 1969: 249-50; Kelly 1972: 187; Knight 1992: 415, 417.

26. E.g. Simpson 1954: 19. Guthrie (1990: 100) rules this out because of the awkwardness of the Greek and the anti-climax of thought. Cf. Reed (1993: 114 n. 1), who suggests that Timothy may be the subject.

27. A.T. Hanson 1968: 5-20. See also AV, TEV, NIV, Phillips, JB, RSV and NEB. Guthrie (1990: 100) prefers 'bulwark'; NASB 'support'. BAGD, s.v. ἑδραίωμα *'foundation*, perh. *mainstay'*. MM, s.v. report that Hort strongly advises 'bulwark'.

28. Hendriksen (1955: 266 n. 142) is confused when he sees contradiction in rejection of the church as the foundation at 2 Tim. 2.19 but acceptance at 1 Tim. 3.15.

29. Lock (1924: 101) says many patristic commentators interpreted it as the world.

30. Lock (1924: 100) cites Hillard: 'the truth/deposit'. See also A.T. Hanson 1966: 19. Scott (1936: 112) rejects this interpretation. Others come close to it: Humphreys (1901: 175) (ref. n. 25) defines the foundation as 'the Church built on apostolic doctrine', citing Mt. 16.18. Oden (1989: 70), who fails to note that only the foundation is mentioned in v. 19, and like Humphreys believes that vv. 20-21 refer to the church, writes of v. 19: 'the church is compared to a building...whose foundation is...built on the word of truth...the foundation is essentially the...purpose of God'.

31. See e.g. Houlden 1976: 122; Guthrie 1990: 162-63. Barrett (1963: 106) says Numbers 16 is probably in mind throughout. See also Alford 1862: 386. Knight

2.20-21 speaks of σκεύη χρυσᾶ καὶ ἀργυρᾶ, with which cf. τὰ σκεύη κυρίου LXX Isa. 52.11, so there may be a close relationship between the second quotation and the following analogy. Kelly argues that τούτων can refer only to 'these latter utensils', v. 16 being too remote an antecedent (1972: 188). The two are not necessarily altogether distinct (Ellicott 1864: 137). The 'godless babbling' at v. 16 is contrasted (μέντοι) with the firm foundation stone of God. The analogy of the great house may be a third saying and thus a further 'inscription', and be complete in v. 20. Verse 21 would then be the Author's development from it, probably with some reference to the addressee,[32] and mark a return to the main topic. In this case τούτων would refer both to the immediately preceding ἅ...εἰς ἀτιμίαν and to v. 16. The imperfection of the analogy would then be apparent only, v. 20 saying nothing about cleansing and, with the personal direction at v. 14 in mind, the meaning of vv. 19-21 would be as in the following expanded translation:

> Nevertheless, the firm foundation of God stands, having this seal:
> The Lord knows who are his,

and

> Let all those naming the name of the Lord desert unrighteousness.

And[33]

> In a great house there are not only gold and silver utensils but also wooden and clay, and some are for honourable but some for dishonour-

(1992: 415-16) suggests the second involves a modification of a phrase from Joel 3.5. Lock (1924: 100) believes each is modified by sayings of Jesus (Mt. 7.23/Lk. 13.27). Bernard (1899: 124) adds Jn 10.14, 27, for which see also Ellicott 1864: 135. For the second passage Humphreys (1901: 176) too sees a parallel in Lk. 13.27, Kelly (1972: 186) adds Lev. 24.16; Josh. 23.7; Ps. 6.8, and Fee (1984: 208) Ps. 34.14 and Prov. 3.7. Cf. those arguing that rather than the LXX the Author quotes: early Christian poetry (Dibelius and Conzelmann 1972: 112); a proverbial saying (Kelly 1972: 186); an early Christian hymn (A.T. Hanson 1966: 88); an early gospel or collection of sayings (Lock 1924: 101).

32. Ellicott 1864: 136; Fee 1984: 211. See also Dibelius and Conzelmann 1972: 113. Lock (1924: 101), however, believes τις refers especially to anyone wanting to be a teacher. Contra A.T. Hanson (1968: 30-35), who argues that vv. 20-21 are the Author's own adaptation of Rom. 9.14-33.

33. Ellicott (1864: 136) sees antithetical force here but (as will be argued in Part IV, Chapter 12) a citation may include a conjunction whose original force has no real bearing upon present context.

able use; so if someone [such as you, Timothy] purges himself from [the tendencies of] these [sorts of people] he will be an honourable utensil, useful to the master, having been prepared for every good work.

In any case, in v. 21 the metaphor shifts to a direct statement of truth,[34] and the three passages following the reference to the foundation and preceding the return to the main topic make a single point: in contrast to others, God's people turn away from wickedness. The intention may not be to contrast differences between assembly members but between people in general. At least, it is unclear that apostates are tolerated as members and, if not, they would no longer be liable to correction and would hardly accept instruction.

There are, therefore, two related types of opposition even in 2.14-26. First there are those assembly members engaging in ignorant, godless and quarrel-producing controversy, with whom the addressee is to deal in humility (v. 25). Secondly, there are those from amongst that first group who have grown more and more godless to the extent that their heretical teachings (of whatever type) destroy the faith of others, and who seem already to be outside the fellowship. There may be considerable diversity of teaching amongst these related groups.

The opposition at 3.1-5. These are described in much more general terms.[35] This is because τοῦτο δὲ γίνωσκε introduces citation of an apostolic prophecy as a traditional saying (cf. Jude 18; 2 Pet. 3.3) elaborated here to incorporate a somewhat chiastic vice-list.[36] The original prophecy appears to have foretold the sinful nature of people (not nec-

---

34. Barrett 1963: 108. Dibelius and Conzelmann (1972: 113) note the shift in 'an unmistakably paraenetic direction'.

35. Scott (1936: 118) says the heresy of the previous section is regarded as the outcome of a general corruption in society. Houlden (1976: 124), although identifying the two groups as one, notes that 3.2-5 embraces the wider social scene. Knight (1992: 428-29) heads 3.1-9 'the character of mankind in the last days' and sees vv. 2-4 as reflecting 'the evils of a pagan society' and 6-9 as applying those characteristics to particular false teachers. See also Fee 1984: 218.

36. Ellis 1987: 243; Knight 1992: 429-32. Cf. Holtz (1965: 179-80), who suggests a hellenistic origin passing into Jewish tradition; Kelly (1972: 193-95) a Jewish tradition shared with Philo; Guthrie 1990: 168. McEleney (1974: 211-17) concludes that a theme rather than a particular list is drawn upon. See also Lock 1924: 105; Easton 1932: 5, 7-8; Scott 1936: 119; A.T. Hanson 1966: 92; Houlden 1976: 125; Verner 1983: 176; Fee 1984: 218-19.

essarily Christians) of the future.[37] It is adapted elsewhere, in 2 Peter to speak of those who can be expected to scoff at the *parousia*, and in Jude of people who slip in amongst Christians and divide them. Although the citation expresses expectation (ἐνστήσονται), ἐσχάταις ἡμέραις are clearly seen as having begun (vv. 5b, 6a, 8): see also Jude 4, 12, 19-20; 2 Pet. 3.8.[38]

Whilst the opposition in 2.14-26 arises from amongst the assembly membership, the same is not necessarily true of the people of 3.1-5.[39] Certainly (v. 8) they resist the truth (as τοὺς ἀντιδιατιθεμένους 2.25), have minds in a depraved state (κατεφθαρμένοι τὸν νοῦν, cf. 2.16, 25-26), and are ἀδόκιμοι (cf. 2.25-26), that is, people 'failing to meet the test', but the adaptation of traditional material warns that this is not simply a description of those with whom the addressee has to do. In fact, those in 2.14-26 appear to fulfil in particular what had some time earlier been prophesied in general terms (Kelly 1972: 193).

At 3.5, in ἔχοντες μόρφωσιν εὐσεβείας τὴν δὲ δύναμιν αὐτῆς ἠρνημένοι the Perfect marks a stative condition of denial of power (Humphreys 1901: 183). There is no indication that the people making that denial necessarily claim to be or are Christians.[40] It will be argued below that v. 5 continues what is widely agreed to be an ordinary vice-list in vv. 2-4,[41] and that there is no reason in this context to assume that

37. '[T]he majority' (Ellicott 1864: 142); 'members of the human race' (Hendriksen 1955: 283). Kelly (1972: 193) speaks of a general situation, Barclay (1975: 184) 'a godless world', and Guthrie (1990: 168, 170) a time when society would be corrupt, moral decadents attempting to join the church. Knight (1992: 429) claims the Future here expresses certainty. In a prophecy, however, it most naturally expresses expectation.

38. E.g. Ellicott 1864: 141-42; Humphreys 1901: 180; Easton 1948: 63-64; Kelly 1972: 193; Fee 1984: 219; P.H. Towner 1989: 65; Guthrie 1990: 168; Knight 1992: 428. Knight (p. 433) claims εἰσιν and ἐνδύνοντες (v. 6) are temporal but, whilst this is now questionable (ref. my Introduction pp. 30-33), present person *deixis* occurs at v. 5b. Contra e.g. Bernard (1899: 129), who believes only the germ of the evil is present; Simpson 1954: 143, 145-46; and those interpreting as in the time of a post-Pauline Author: e.g. Scott 1936: 116; Barrett 1963: 110; Houlden 1976: 124-25. See also Lock 1924: 104.

39. Contra e.g. Humphreys 1901: 182; Kidd 1990: 191.

40. Contra e.g. Parry 1920: 62; Barrett 1963: 111; Holtz 1965: 180; Brox 1969: 254; Kelly 1972: 195; Knight 1992: 432.

41. Contra those denying the continuation, e.g. A.T. Hanson 1966: 92; Brox 1969: 254; Kelly 1972: 195; Dibelius and Conzelmann 1972: 116; Houlden 1976: 125; Fee 1984: 220.

εὐσέβεια has a Christian connotation.[42]

Various definitions have been offered for εὐσέβεια.[43] Von Lips envisages a relation to God in which knowledge of him as creator and of his creation outworks in the life as 'Respektierung der natürlichen und geschichtlichen Ordnungen... Die einzelnen Textstellen zeigen, dass beim Gebrauch von εὐσέβεια mal der eine, mal der andere Aspekt mehr betont wird' ('respect for the natural and historic structures... The separate text passages show that in the use of εὐσέβεια sometimes one aspect and at other times another is more emphasized', 1979: 83-84). Following von Lips, Towner believes that at 2 Tim. 3.5 the Author speaks of people who have a genuine knowledge of Christ but whose conduct is inappropriate to that knowledge.[44] Even though he notes differences between the heresies of Ephesus and Crete, Towner here treats the three Pastorals as a unit, and herein lie the weak links in his argument. Long before addressing the meaning of εὐσέβεια he has linked 1 Tim. 6.20 to the resurrection heresy of 2 Tim. 2.18. False teachers at Ephesus, he reasons, 'almost certainly' employ the term γνῶσις and believe salvation to be fully attainable at the present time, their asceticism (1 Tim. 4.3) linked with that over-realized eschatology. He concludes that they claim to possess special knowledge about resurrection heresy.[45] Upon this basis he interprets εὐσέβεια thus:

42. For εὐσέβεια generally see e.g. Horsley (1982–89: II, 55-56) citing *SEG* 24 (1969) 1081; (IV, 35-36) citing *IG*, XIV (Berlin, 1890) 1976, and (IV, 74-82) citing *IBM*, III.2 (Oxford, 1890) 482 (+ addendum on p. 294); and see also (I, 78-79) citing a deed of surety published by J.R. Rea, *CPR*, V, 2.17, 40-43 (pl. 16). See also Dibelius and Conzelmann 1972: 39. Fee (1984: 27) and P.H. Towner (1989: 167) suggest the word is picked up from the opposition.

43. White (1910: 103) says it is 'almost a technical term for *the Christian religion as expressed in daily life*...more general[ly]...*religious conduct* in 1 Tim. vi.11 and in 2 Peter' (italics his). For Lock (1924: 26) it connotes 'the true reverence towards God which comes from knowledge', perhaps including 'true respect and reverence for human superiors'. Foerster (1959: 217) concludes that in the Pastorals it is employed as 'einer ehrenden Anerkennung der Ordnungen, als...einer Ehrfurcht, die in der Ehrfurcht vor Gott ihre Wurzel hat' ('a respectful recognition of the structures as...a respect which is rooted in the reverence for God').

44. P.H. Towner 1989: 148-49. See also Knight 1992: 432.

45. P.H. Towner 1989: 29-31. Cf. e.g. Lock (1924: xvii), who suggests '[r]abbinical pride in knowledge of the law'. Colson (1917/18: 270) concludes that ἀντιθέσεις refers primarily to the legal and dialectical side of the γνῶσις. See also Guthrie 1990: 42. Reicke (1957: 300) points out that at 1 Pet. 3.7 γνῶσις is recogni-

    i.   At 6.5 the false teachers suppose gain is εὐσέβεια,[46] so their teaching is motivated by desire for financial gain,[47] and they 'apparently' conceive of godliness primarily as knowledge of the divine.

    ii.   2 Tim. 3.5, 'almost certainly' envisaging some positive attribute other than outward behaviour, confirms i.

    iii.   Tit. 1.16 implies that 2 Tim. 3.5 conveys the idea that these people regard their knowledge of God as their εὐσέβεια.

    iv.   In its various appearances in the Pastorals εὐσέβεια supports the above (1989: 148-50).

Certainly εὐσέβεια in the Pastorals generally conveys the idea of conduct issuing from a proper relationship with God based upon sound teaching, and many of Towner's supporting texts cited in what I have here called iv. are best understood in this light.[48] However, it is not at all certain that the false teachers of 6.20 employ the term γνῶσις. Even should it be granted both that they do and that 2 Timothy is addressed to Ephesus, 1 Tim. 6.5 and 20 do not establish that they conceive of εὐσέβεια as the possession of knowledge of the divine. The idea is read into the text on the assumption that the false teaching in both letters is one general group. At ii. Towner neither explores the relationship with the vice-list preceding 2 Tim. 3.5 nor demonstrates that these false teachers necessarily make the same claims as those in 1 Tim. 6.6. The unspecified 'form'[49] of godliness may not consist of a claim involving γνῶσις (see below). At iii. those featured in Tit. 1.16 should not be assumed to be Christians (see Appendix 1). In summary, Towner does not establish that at 2 Tim. 3.5 εὐσέβεια has Christian overtones.

tion/attention/consideration, citing also Mt. 17.12; 1 Cor. 8.3; 13.12; 2 Cor. 6.9; Gal. 4.9; 1 Jn 3.1.

    46.   The text, having the article with εὐσέβειαν, says the reverse, i.e. 'supposing godliness to be gain', but the meaning is obviously intended to be negative.

    47.   At this point, having excercised caution about the idea that at Tit. 1.16 the profession to know God, associated with denial of that knowledge by inappropriate deeds, indicates a claim to possess special knowledge (p. 31), Towner unnecessarily introduces Tit. 1.11 to suggest the possibility of amplifying πορισμόν. The context itself suggests the gain is financial.

    48.   See an exception below: 1 Tim. 4.8.

    49.   LSJ, s.v. μόρφωσις cites both Rom. 2.20 and 2 Tim. 3.5; BAGD, s.v. separates them, the former under 'embodiment'.

As von Lips points out, the facet of εὐσέβεια stressed must be gleaned from the particular reference. At 1 Tim. 3.16, in the context of 2.1–3.15, the concern is with the everyday lives of the people of God's household (see Part I), which is a pillar and foundation of the truth. Both respect for appropriate regulations and knowledge of the truth are in view, and εὐσέβεια is a 'great mystery'. When the three Pastorals are treated more or less as a unit and false teachers envisaged as of one general type, 2 Tim. 3.5 easily takes on the same dual viewpoint, but in its own context that duality is not at all clear. Γνῶσις is not mentioned. What precedes is a vice-list amplifying a well-known apostolic prophecy. What follows is a command that envisages the people answering to the foregoing description as contemporary. If v. 5 said 'have nothing to do with those who have a form of godliness but deny its power', it would be plain that the Author takes up where a familiar vice-list leaves off.[50] Instead μόρφωσιν εὐσεβείας…κτλ. is closely connected with vv. 1-4 by ἔχοντες. Moreover, since there is no previous command to avoid the people described in vv. 1-4, καί seems to convey simply 'and' rather than 'also', creating something of a hiatus between the description and the command, almost as 'so'.[51] *UBSGNT* divides it from the description with a colon. If μόρφωσιν εὐσεβείας…κτλ. is not part of the original vice-list, it nevertheless appears intended to amplify the prophecy together with that list. As demonstrated above, the prophecy speaks of 'people' to be avoided, not specifically of Christians.

BAGD renders μόρφωσις 'outward form, appearance'.[52] In the New Testament the word occurs elsewhere only at Rom. 2.20, where it is commonly interpreted positively, for example:

because you have in the law the *embodiment* of knowledge and truth…[53]

---

50. Dibelius and Conzelmann (1972: 115-16) in fact understand him to do so.

51. Guthrie (1990: 170) says that if καί is equivalent to 'also' it could refer to those of 2.23. That verse, however, says that controversies (not the opposition) are to be avoided.

52. BAGD, s.v., 2. See also μορφή, citing Mk 16.12, where the form is clearly outward. Cf. Bernard (1899: 131), who says μόρφωσις (distinct from σχῆμα, the outward fashion/bearing) is an affectation of the μορφή of godliness, the μορφή itself a manifestation of the inward nature of godliness.

53. As e.g. L. Morris 1988: 134. See also NIV, RSV, 'full content' (TEV), 'the very shape' (NEB).

But since ἐν sometimes conveys 'a cause/reason',[54] it is appropriate to render

> having the *outward appearance* of knowledge and the truth because of the law.[55]

In any case, the people of 2 Tim. 3.5 have a 'form' of εὐσέβεια. It seems likely that they in fact appear pious, but although they may then live in accordance with knowledge of received regulations,[56] they 'are in a state of having denied' (ἠρνημένοι) the power of that piety. They do not deny the εὐσέβεια itself. Perhaps for the Author they deny what empowers such knowledge, that is, Christian truth. Even if this is not the case and the denial is to be understood as a state of failure to live a life appropriate to received regulations (cf. Tit. 1.16),[57] the context suggests that those regulations are not specifically Christian. The only reason to assume that εὐσέβεια in this context has Christian content is the prior assumption that the people of vv. 1-5 are defecting assembly members.[58]

1.2. Instructions
The opposition at 2.14-26. Two interwoven problems occur here. First, who are τοὺς ἀντιδιατιθεμένους (v. 25)? If the participle is a passive form the addressee is required to deal with those disaffected by the opposition,[59] but if it is a middle form he is to deal with the opposition itself[60]—a diverse group. Secondly, what is he expected to do?[61] Does

54. BAGD, s.v., III.3a cites e.g. Mt. 6.7 ('because of'); Heb. 10.10 ('by'), and Rom. 1.24 and Heb. 11.18 (both quoting Gen. 21.12, 'through').

55. E.g. AV, JB, and 'a certain grasp on the basis of' (Phillips).

56. Contra von Lips 1979: 83.

57. Alford (1862: 391), e.g., believes they have repudiated the 'living and renewing influence (of εὐσέβεια) over the heart and life'.

58. Contra e.g. Ellicott 1864: 144; Simpson 1954: 144-45; Barrett 1963: 111; A.T. Hanson 1966: 92; Fee 1984: 220-21. Dibelius and Conzelmann (1972: 115) regard the passage as a variant of the theme of 1 Tim. 4.1ff.; but see below for differences.

59. Bernard 1899: 126-27, followed by Fee 1984: 216-17.

60. E.g. Alford 1862: 388; Kelly 1972: 190. Fee (1984: 215) with some indecision thinks the false teachers may be included here with those they have influenced.

61. For the debate about whether αὐτοῦ and ἐκείνου (v. 26) refer to the same subject/s and its/their identity see e.g. Alford 1862: 389-90; Ellicott 1864: 140-41; Humphreys 1901: 179; Lock 1924: 103; Hendriksen 1955: 276; A.T. Hanson 1966: 90; Kelly 1972: 191; Dibelius and Conzelmann 1972: 114; Knight 1992: 426-27.

ἐν πραΰτητι παιδεύοντα indicate humbly administered instruction, training or discipline? The sense conveyed by παιδεύω at 1 Tim. 1.20 and Tit. 2.12 is 'discipline' as elsewhere in the New Testament, except for Acts 7.22; 22.3, where it is 'train', but even there in the context of formal schooling (Humphreys 1901: 178-79). It does seem likely that the Author is thinking of something stronger than 'instruction' at 2 Tim. 2.25. At Tit. 3.10 he wants the unrepentantly divisive excluded (cf. 2 Jn 10).[62] In 1 Tim. 1.20 Hymenaeus has already been 'handed over to Satan', so it would be reasonable to conclude that at 2 Tim. 2.17-18 he and Philetus are no longer members.[63] Although in this case it would be inappropriate to direct the addressee to train or discipline them and those like them, he could be expected to take any opportunity humbly to *instruct* them in the hope that they too would regain their senses (v. 26).[64] Nevertheless, the parallel between the purpose clauses ἵνα παιδευθῶσιν μὴ βλασφημεῖν (1 Tim. 1.20) and μήποτε δώη αὐτοῖς ὁ θεὸς μετάνοιαν εἰς ἐπίγνωσιν ἀληθείας...κτλ. (2 Tim. 2.25-26) suggests that, in the latter, correction or discipline rather than simple instruction is in view.[65] Those who are no longer assembly members would obviously now be beyond the sphere of correction.

62. Oden (1989: 62-63) concerning Tit. 1.10 (cf. 3.10) says 'silencing' is bridling by proper argument and rechannelling energies, and Scott (1936: 160) that Titus is to play the part of stern physician rather than judge to make them sound in the faith. Both miss the fact that those to be sharply rebuked (v. 13) are not the teachers but the households they have ruined. See Appendix 1.

63. As e.g. Parry 1920: 11; Barrett 1963: 107. Contra e.g. Scott (1936: 110), who thinks the results of Hymenaeus's teaching (if not the man himself) may still be active; Easton 1948: 18; Dibelius and Conzelmann (1972: 111-12) who nevertheless find the sharp criticism supposes loss of legitimate authority; Kelly (1972: 184) who thinks the ban (1 Tim. 1.20) may not have been immediately effective. Alford (1862: 312) finds no necessary assertion of excommunication at 1 Tim. 1.20 (even cf. 1 Cor. 5.5). But, even if at 2 Tim. 2.17-18 Hymenaeus is seen as having been an Ephesian assembly member, nothing suggests he and Philetus have not been 'handed over' well beforehand. See e.g. Guthrie 1990: 41, 161.

64. Parry (1920: 11) says that at 1 Tim. 1.20 παιδευθῶσιν in reference to Hymenaeus (and Alexander) implies punishment with reformation in view.

65. E.g. Alford 1862: 388. See also NEB, and 'correct' in RSV, JB, Phillips, TEV. Perhaps adding to the impression of discipline is the contrast with ἀπαιδεύτους (v. 23), which Fee (1984: 214) e.g. translates 'uninstructed/ill-informed', and Guthrie (1990: 166) 'ill-educated', but which could equally be understood as 'undisciplined'.

The opposition at 3.1-5. These, by contrast, are to be shunned (ἀποτ-ρέπου), suggesting that they are (at least now) outsiders.

The differences between the instructions at 1.2.1 and 1.2.2 could of course mean that there has been an ongoing defection continuing outside as a heretical faction, but it at least warns that false teachers are not simply one group. The addressee is dealing with different kinds of people.[66] This is particularly obvious if 2.25 speaks of 'instruction', but even if (as seems most likely) 'discipline' is in view, and even if that involves expulsion, differences remain. Some opposition in ch. 2 may presently be within the assembly, but that at 3.1-5 is not.

Even though, therefore, the opposition of 2.14-26 represents in particular forms those foretold in the prophecy adapted in 3.1-5, and even though present time *deixis* (vv. 5b, 8) occurs in relation to the second group, the two passages are not simply complementary descriptions of the same people. The opponents in 2.14-16 are erring Christians, a number of whom seem to have already been expelled, but those in 3.1-5, 8-9 have not necessarily ever been Christians. Their state (κατεφθαρ-μένοι v. 8) and the direction to have nothing to do with them (v. 5b) indicates that the Author does not count them as such (Humphreys 1901: 174, 184). They are not presently operating within Christian assemblies. In view of the traditional nature of their description, they are a type which may be found anywhere, not a particular regional phenomenon.

It is clear, however, from the present time *deixis* together with ἐνδύνοντες and αἰχμαλωτίζοντες (v. 6), that some of this second type (not necessarily only male[67]) currently prey upon women who are loaded down with sins and swayed by all kinds of desires, women who are always learning but never able to come to a knowledge of the truth (3.6b-7). The identity of these women will more appropriately be considered in Chapter 8; but it is unclear that their 'capture' is either the

---

66. Ellicott (1864: 139, 144-45) explains the difference by a future time reference, but believes the heretical seeds are already present. Scott (1936: 115-16), supporting the translation 'educating with gentleness' (2.25), is struck by the lenience, arguing that the adversaries there include those within and without, but (with Kelly 1972: 195) claims this has in view Timothy's personal relations cf. 3.5b his official relations. Murphy-O'Connor (1991: 410) uses 2.26 as evidence that the author is not the same as for the other Pastorals, without comparing 3.5b.

67. Contra e.g. NIV, and Knight (1992: 434-45) who claims ἄνθρωποι is used in 'its more restricted masculine sense'.

primary goal or the chief result of the false teaching.[68] The series of pronouns (vv. 5b, 6, 8) suggests that the teachers are variously occupied. The antecedent of οὗτοι (v. 8) is τούτων (v. 6), which refers to τούτους (v. 5b). The referent of the latter is not simply those with a form of godliness who deny its power but, because of the close connection created by ἔχοντες and the hiatus at the imperative at v. 5b (see above), the whole group described in vv. 2-4. These people seem chiefly to be resisters of the truth who, in their infiltration of households, do entrap certain women. They are people who appear godly but are in fact depraved, and they may be encountered anywhere at any time in the 'last days'.

I conclude that 2 Tim. 3.1-9 is an inappropriate source for the identification of false teachers who, operating within Christian assemblies, lead astray significant numbers of female members.

2. *1 Timothy 4.1-3*

Many find here a key to the interpretation of 1 Tim. 2.9-15.[69]

The formula τὸ...πνεῦμα...λέγει may introduce citation from the Old Testament (e.g. Heb. 3.7-11; cf. 1 Tim. 5.18), or current prophetic announcement (Acts 21.11). Most agree, however, that in this case a prophecy originally spoken in the past is in view (cf. Acts 28.25). It is also widely agreed that those who can be expected to abandon the faith are nevertheless the Author's contemporaries, ὑστέροις καιροῖς (v. 1)

---

68. P.H. Towner 1989: 26-27, 39; Schreiner 1995: 112. Contra Dibelius and Conzelmann (1972: 116 and n. 10), who confuse these teachers with the Gnostic Marcus: μάλιστα γὰρ περὶ γυναῖκας ἀσχολεῖται καὶ τούτων τὰς εὐπαρύφους καὶ περιπορφύρους καὶ πλουσιωτάτας ('for particularly he is busy with women, and of these, ones who wear fine clothes edged with purple and extremely opulent'). See also Alford 1862: 392; Scott 1936: 121; Barclay 1975: 192; Gritz 1991: 111-12 n. 51. Contra also Bernard 1899: 131; Brox 1969: 255; Schüssler Fiorenza 1983: 312; Talbert 1984: 106-107; Payne 1986: 97-98; Byrne 1988: 90; Roloff 1988: 147; Bilezikian 1989: 299 n. 46. Verner (1983: 176-77) is inclined to believe that the Author regards women as less capable than men of knowledge of the truth. Hendriksen (1955: 286) by contrast finds only '*fickle*' women at risk (italics his).

69. E.g. Barrett 1963: 55-56; Ford 1971: 340; Payne 1981: 185, 190-91; Moo 1981: 218; Verner 1983: 177-80; Fee 1984: 61; Scholer 1986: 202; Kroeger 1986: 237, 243; M.Y. MacDonald 1988: 179-80; Oden 1989: 58; Bilezikian 1989: 299 n. 6.

being the equivalent of ἐσχάταις ἡμέραις in 2 Tim. 3.1.[70] Others believe the reference is to times future to the speaker,[71] and some take a middle path, envisaging a time when error already present would be developed more fully.[72]

Those accepting or allowing for Pauline authorship[73] who claim that these 'later days' are 'present days' overrule their Author's morphological choices. Since λέγει (visualizing continuous action) reports speech constructed around ἀποστήσονται (expressing expectation) and a comparative adjective, the reference is most naturally to the future.

Parry declares contemporary prophecy uncertain, but assumes that τὸ...πνεῦμα ῥητῶς λέγει is part of the report, not the Author's own introduction (1920: lxxxvii, 24). Lane and many others interpret the asceticism largely by 2 Tim. 2.18,[74] assuming the two letters address one general situation and that Hymenaeus's and Alexander's heresy is widespread. Knight (citing 2 Tim. 3.1ff. [discussed above]; 4.3-4 [see Appendix 1]; Acts 20.28-31) confuses Aspect with temporality, claiming that λέγει expresses the present reality of the communication.[75] Towner says the present tense ὑποτιθέμενος (v. 6) and interest

70. E.g. Easton 1948: 139, 141; Lane 1964–65: 164 n. 1; Brox 1969: 166-67; Dibelius and Conzelmann 1972: 64; P.H. Towner 1986: 428, 431-33, 441; 1989: 65; Oberlinner 1994: 174. See also Lock 1924: 47; Scott 1936: xxix, 44; Barrett 1963: 67; A.T. Hanson 1966: 48; Kelly 1972: 93-94; Oden 1989: 57-58; Kidd 1990: 190; Knight 1992: 188-89. See also Fee (1984: 60-61, 63) who is nevertheless not easily able to see how the asceticism relates to 1.4, and Houlden (1976: 87) who notes that ἔσχατος is the more common term.

71. Bernard (1899: 65) says ὑστέροις is in opposition to προτέροις (cf. LXX 1 Chron. 29.29), not a synonym for ἐσχάτοις. Alford (1862: 335-37) renders 'after times', finding 'later' too closely connected with 'the last times' even though the seed was probably being sown at the time of the writing of the letter. See also Liddon 1897: 39; Humphreys 1901: 113; Parry 1920: lxxxvii, 24. Some see future action imminent, e.g. Simpson 1954: 64; Guthrie 1990: 41, 103.

72. Ellicott 1864: 54; Hendriksen 1955: 145-47.

73. To avoid repetition, where relevant others will also be included in the following notes, with discussion on their viewpoint at the end of the present section.

74. Lane 1964–65: 165-66. Lane also identifies 4.8b as of paramount importance because of πιστὸς ὁ λόγος (v. 9), but that is more a marker of tradition than of structural emphasis, and refers to the whole of v. 8. The Author is primarily concerned with his addressee (vv. 6-7), so v. 8b is not (as Lane claims) 'the key to the entire passage'.

75. Knight (1992: 188) cites 1 Tim. 5.18 as a similar communication where (as he notes) the ongoing nature of the scriptural reference is clear. There are, however,

in the present (vv. 6-8) is virtually inseparable from vv. 1-5, to which ταῦτα (v. 6) obviously refers. Present danger, he reasons, is implied at v. 3.[76] Dividing vv. 6b-8b into positive (vv. 6b, 7b, 8b) and negative (vv. 7a, 8a) elements, Towner traces contrasts throughout and connections with vv. 1-3, concluding that the myths of v. 7a 'almost certainly' refer to the doctrines of vv. 1-3 and so, too, does σωματικὴ γυμνασία (v. 8a) (1986: 433). He is here chiefly concerned (and justifiably so) to demonstrate that in the Pastorals the present age is also 'the last days'; but the interactions between vv. 6-8 and 1-3 are neither as close as he suggests nor do they negate the future orientation of the earlier section. Again, some links in his argument are tenuous. At v. 6 present time is introduced by person *deixis*, not by ὑποτιθέμενος. The danger implied at v. 3 is not necessarily a present reality, and Towner's 'almost certainty' betrays lingering doubt. Verse 8 is a 'faithful saying' with γάρ added to link it to the context, with πρὸς ὀλίγον envisaging exercise as of some (if little) use.[77] Whilst there is a contrast between v. 8a and b, the former may therefore illustrate rather than contrast with v. 7b, being a more positive than negative structural component. Furthermore, ἡ σωματικὴ γυμνασία is not easily identifiable with the

differences in both the subjects and the ways they communicate, the one itself the written word and the other by spoken word. At 5.18 the Author envisages the scriptures in ongoing action. At 1 Tim. 4.1 the given subject is τὸ πνεῦμα, not (as Knight implies) the Spirit's speech. Although such ongoing action *could* be shown by its context to have begun at some past time (cf. as Knight, Acts 20.28-31), the formula does not appear at 2 Tim. 3.1-9, and it will be argued below that at 1 Timothy 4 a current 'speaking' is in view.

76. P.H. Towner 1986: 431-33. See also e.g. Knight (1992: 189) who nevertheless (pp. 192-93) argues that vv. 1-7 are a compact unit; Haykin 1985: 295. Concerned to identify whether the prophecy was made in the past or at the time of writing, Haykin, with a view to re-examining theology and practice in relation to the Holy Spirit in the Pastorals, supports the past reference, fulfilment of the prophecy being at the time of writing.

77. '[E]ither for a little while, or for a limited range, as affecting only the body' (Parry 1920: 26). Knight (1992: 196, 198-99) says either 'for a little' meaning 'is of some value', or 'for little' meaning 'is of no value', are possible, the focus upon the ὀλίγον/πάντα + ζωή contrast, not precise identification of ὀλίγον. The consensus, as he notes, is 'for a little'. Yet 'little value' is not necessarily 'no value'. '[A] small department of a man's being' (Alford 1862: 339); 'extent rather than duration' (Ellicott 1864: 60). See also Humphreys 1901: 118; Scott 1936: 47; Simpson 1954: 68.

asceticism of v. 3.[78] Others claim ordinary bodily exercise is in view.[79] Ellicott argues that a spiritual bodily exercise or self-discipline seems indicated because:

i.   γύμναζε (v. 7) is spiritual rather than physical;
ii. the context contrasts external/internal observances; and
iii. asceticism is well-attested in the first century.

Such activity, he suggests, may be defined in very general terms as distinguishable from the specific and extreme actions of v. 3.[80] However, although the disciplining of oneself unto godliness (v. 7b) would certainly be spiritual, σωματικὴ γυμνασία at v. 8a is itself contrasted with (δέ) εὐσέβεια (v. 8b) (Knight 1992: 196-97, 199). It is not immediately clear that a distinction is made between a (spiritual) form of discipline which leads to godliness (v. 7b) and a physical form of discipline which is of some use (v. 8a). As a 'faithful saying' (v. 9),[81] however, v. 8 is a unit in its own right, and in that unit σωματικὴ γυμνασία most naturally appears to be ordinary physical exercise.[82] In its present context, therefore, that exercise is distinguishable both from the asceticism of v. 3 and from the kind of exercise which leads to godliness (v. 7b). Towner's argument in support of the 'later days' as identical with the 'last days = present days' therefore has a number of problems.

The reference is more naturally to a current prophecy,[83] the whole to be expanded literally:

78. Contra also e.g. Houlden 1976: 88. See also e.g. Easton 1948: 145.

79. E.g. Alford 1862: 339; Liddon 1897: 43-44; Swete 1917: 3; Parry 1920: 26; Scott 1936: 49; Falconer 1937: 142-43; Simpson 1954: 68; Kelly 1972: 99-100; Fee 1984: 66, 71; Guthrie 1990: 107. Lock (1924: 51) finds this probable. Cf. 'training in the palaestra' giving the rhetorical student grace of movement (Colson 1917–18: 270-71). Dibelius and Conzelmann (1972: 68) say it was doubtless originally physical but possibly here directed to asceticism.

80. Ellicott 1864: 60. See also Bernard 1899: 69; Humphreys (1901: 117) who prefers the metaphorical meaning evident in 2 Pet. 2.14; Heb. 5.14; 12.11; and Jeremias 1963: 27.

81. See the persuasive argument in Knight (1968: 62-79). See also Kelly 1972: 101.

82. See e.g. Kelly 1972: 100.

83. Bernard 1899: 65-66. Humphreys (1901: 113) makes this point but believes the distinction should not be pressed too far because John calls his period (which Humphreys dates 25 years later than 1 Timothy) the 'last hour' (1 Jn 2.18). See also Fee (1984: 60) who, although noting the prophetic form, relates it to the present.

> The Spirit in an on-going fashion is clearly saying that in later-than-now
> times some can be expected to depart from the faith...etc.

In other words, the present day = last days will later on see Christians apostasize because of demonic teachings with familiar non-Christian ascetic features (cf. Col. 2.16, 20-22; Pliny, *Hist. nat.* 5.15).[84] As Ellicott persuasively argues, in 4.2

> ἐν [is]...instrumental,...[and κωλυόντων γαμεῖν κτλ. v. 3a] seems far
> too direct an act of the false teachers suitably to find a place in...an indi-
> rect definition of the falsely taught (1864: 55).

Those depicted in v. 1 as departing from the faith having given themselves to beguiling spirits and teachings of demons are Christians of the future (no matter how close that future may be). They are distinguishable from those who will teach them, the latter being hypocritical liars in a state of having seared (κεκαυστηριασμένων) their own consciences, who forbid people to marry and teach abstinence from certain foods.[85] Nothing suggests that these liars are present or former assembly members.

1 Timothy 4.1-3 (unlike 2 Tim. 3.1-9) does speak of Christians defecting under the influence of outsiders, but that defection is expected to occur in the future. The Author wants to make clear the importance of 'holding on to faith' (1.19) and the results of 'abandoning' it (4.1),

---

John, however, makes his time-setting clear; context clarifies the present time of 2 Tim. 3.1; and although 1 Tim. 4.1 in its own context shows by aspectual choice as well as time *deixis* that the Author has future events in mind, this may very well indicate something much less than 25 years. Dibelius and Conzelmann (1972: 64) note that ῥητῶς is found in prophecies. Lock (1924: 47) says it implies quotation of someone else's prophecy. Kelly (1972: 93-94) notes that the belief that false teaching and apostasy would occur before the *parousia* was deeply embedded in primitive Christianity (citing Mk 13.22; 2 Thess. 2.3, 11f.).

84. Lane (1964–65: 165 n. 1) says forms of these proscriptions appear in pagan philosophies and cults, citing e.g. Josephus, *War* 2.8.2; Philo, *Vit. Cont.* 4. See also Ellicott 1864: 60; Parry 1920: lxxxviii-lxxxix.

85. Parry (1920: lxxxvii-lxxxviii) correctly argues that to mix this external false teaching, whose subject matter is so described and denounced, with the vaguely described and internally conceived false teaching of other passages is 'perverse and confusing'. Against this introductory background, however, he is himself (pp. 23-25, 77) again confusing (cf. Chapter 1 n. 36), believing these external false teachers claim to be Christian, although are not, and cause the apostasy (which nevertheless 'originates' within the church; cf. pp. lxxxvii, 24). Liddon (1897: 40) suggests the ascetic doctrines specified may represent a larger body of error.

and directs the addressee to tell the people that future apostate Christians will adopt these doctrines taught by outsiders.[86] He makes morphological distinctions between that future asceticism and the current godless myths, old wives' tales and genealogies of 1.3b-4, and returns at 4.7 to those present errors (τοὺς...βεβήλους καὶ γραώδεις μύθους).[87]

The above discussion on 1 Tim. 4.1-3 assumes acceptance of Pauline authorship. When that authorship is rejected the future orientation is seen as a literary device accusing this opposition of teaching asceticism[88] or describing what is in fact a late first/early second-century phenomenon.[89] As demonstrated, however, the Author chooses to distinguish between apostate Christians (v. 1a) and those liars influencing them (vv. 1b-3a). Nothing in the text suggests that the liars are or have been Christians, and the focus is more upon the demonic, beguiling nature of their teachings than their asceticism. On the other hand, since asceticism is well documented early in the first century, and the particular ascetics focused here in 1 Timothy 4 are not Christians but outsiders, their teaching of it tells nothing about the date of the letter. The Author shows every indication of intending to warn that hypocritical, lying outsiders teaching demonic and ascetic doctrines can in the future be expected to beguile away from the faith some Christians.

I conclude that the teachers of 1 Tim. 4.1b-3 make unconvincing players in reconstructions of a specific regional assembly background.

The idea that the false teachers of the Pastoral Epistles constitute a more or less loosely unified group which emerged and continues to function within the assemblies at the places of address at the time of writing is a misconception. They are of various kinds. Passages dealing

---

86. Ellicott (1864: 58) believes ταῦτα most naturally refers to vv. 4-5 and the principles and dissuasive arguments involved, but the argument of Ellis (1987: 243-46) on the formulaic ταῦτα suggests this is somewhat forced. Parry (1920: 26) and Fee (1984: 70) believe the reference is to 2.1–4.5.

87. Parry 1920: 26; Hendriksen 1955: 152. Contra Lock 1924: 47. Ellicott (1864: 59) says the article may indicate well-known character.

88. Dibelius and Conzelmann (1972: 67) say the ethical reproach belongs to the style of polemic.

89. As e.g. Scott 1936: 44, 48; Verner 1983: 176 n. 169. Dibelius and Conzelmann (1972: 64) argue that vv. 3c-5 betrays awareness of present danger, but this is doubtful since the first heresy is either (as they also argue) not refuted at all, or (as suggested by Lock 1924: 48; Knight 1992: 190; and allowed for by Liddon 1897: 41) if ἅ includes marriage, only in the most general way.

with them which are commonly employed to argue that female assembly members are vocal adherents of their teaching describe neither specifically current nor internal teachings.

Chapter 8

PARAENESIS ON WOMEN:
A SIXTH COMMON MISCONCEPTION

Passages about women from all three Pastorals feature in many reconstructions of background for 1 Timothy. Payne, for example, writes

> Paul repeatedly identifies women as especially influenced by the false
> teaching in the Ephesian church. 2 Tim. 3:6 refers to silly women,
> 'always learning but never able to acknowledge the truth'… Women and
> especially widows are the particular group most significantly influ-
> enced… No other book of the New Testament devotes such a high pro-
> portion of its content to problems specifically related to women as does
> 1 Timothy (note especially 2:9-15; 4:7; 5:2-7, 9-16). The continuity of
> the problem as specifically tied to the false teachers is evident from
> 2 Tim. 2.16-17… [I]t is this peculiar appeal to women…that explains
> why Paul specifically says he does not want *women* to teach.[1]

Such reconstructions reckon without the fact that paraenesis does not
specifically address problems at the place of address unless there is
contextual evidence to that effect.[2]

---

1. Payne 1986: 97-99 (emphasis his). See also e.g. Dibelius and Conzelmann
1972: 48; Kelly 1972: 115; Houlden 1976: 125; Scholer 1975: 8; 1986: 197-99,
203, 205, 211, 213, 218; Karris 1977: 206-208; Verner 1983: 137, 178, 180; M.Y.
MacDonald 1988: 176; Moo 1991: 181; Porter 1993: 101-102; Wiebe 1994: 55-56;
Oberlinner 1994: 93-94, 103; Schreiner 1995: 109. Some inconsistency is apparent.
Plummer (1888: 82-83, 99) says the letters (incl. 1 Timothy 2) deal with conditions
at the place of address but that there is no need to assume at vv. 8-12 'any special
need of warning'. Harris (1987: 32-33) believes false teachers successfully concen-
trate on women but (1990: 339) notes that vv. 9-10 do not require that Christians
are dressing in the way rejected. P.H. Towner (1989: 38) finds no evidence that
false teachers make special efforts to win women who then proceed to teach false
doctrines etc., but reasons that vv. 9-12 show some commotion amongst women.
2. See e.g. discussions in Bradley 1953: 238-46; Crouch 1972: 121, 151;
Schrage 1974: 3-5; Verner 1983: e.g. 2, 79. Moo (1981: 219) notes in Galatians the

One cautious example is Karris, who accepts that such instruction responds to the situation of the early church in general, and demonstrates the methodological soundness of evaluating the polemic of the Pastorals as traditional.[3] From 1 Tim. 1.9-10;[4] 6.3-5, 20-21 he concludes that nothing at all may be deduced about local conditions, from 4.1-7 only that opponents forbid marriage and prescribe abstinence from certain foods, and from Tit. 1.10-16; 3.8-9 only that the teaching of the opponents is Jewish. Noting the currency of the reference at 2 Tim. 2.16-17, he nevertheless says that 3.1-9, 13 tell very little about present opponents. Yet, he believes, the use of such material reveals the Author's purpose. Although arguing, therefore, that 2 Tim. 3.6-7 is a redaction of a traditional polemical charge, like many others he believes that 1 Tim. 2.11-15; 5.13 and Tit. 2.5 'emphasize' the 'proper role of women', and he suggests that the opponents of 2 Tim. 3.2-9 may have had 'significant success among the womanfolk' (Karris 1973: 560, 563). Elsewhere he *does* include 1 Tim. 4.3 as evidence of women creating problems (1977: 206). Moreover, since he assumes that the three letters constitute a single literary unit describing a general situation, his conclusion is accordingly flawed. Even though the Author treats women differently to men and employs different amounts of space in addressing various groups, none of the passages cited 'emphasizes the proper role of women' in the sense that the 'proper roles' of others are *not* emphasized. In no case, moreover, is the instruction directed to a specific situation. It will be argued below that any such 'collage' of selections from 1 Tim. 2.11-15; 4.3; 5.3-16; 2 Tim. 3.2-9, 13; Tit. 2.5 is similarly flawed. The controversial 1 Tim. 5.3-16 will be considered last.

1. *1 Timothy 2.11-15*

As the primary text of the present study, brief remarks only are in order here. The modern predisposition to allot equal time for contrasting

close connection between teaching and situation yet undoubted universal applicability. See also 1991: 189.

3. Karris 1973: 563 n. 58. Cf. Donelson (1986: e.g. 5, 164, 200), who sees the pseudepigrapher's descriptions as fiction and the deposit he 'hands on' as his own creation.

4. Verner (1983: 179), in responding to Karris, argues that in fact ἀνυποτάκτοις (v. 9) does not belong to traditional polemic, and concludes that a challenge is being mounted from a subordinate position. There is, however, no reason to suppose that these people are assembly members.

views should not obscure the fact that although vv. 9-12 is considerably longer than v. 8, it does roughly correspond to it, and appear second in order. In Part IV linguistic, grammatical, and contextual markers in vv. 13-15 will be discussed with a view to demonstrating the Author's deliberate refocus there upon behaviour required of both sexes. The 'emphasis' on the roles of women at v. 12 is more apparent than real. Nowhere does the context indicate that a specific regional situation is addressed. Not only does this passage look very much like traditional teaching, but its controversial parts make it a questionable exegetical device for the elucidation of any other, including 2 Tim. 3.2-7.

2. *1 Timothy 4.3*

This passage has already been addressed in Chapter 7, but further brief remarks are pertinent here. It has been argued that times later than Paul's are in view. If his authorship is accepted nothing suggests that asceticism, and particularly female asceticism, is a current problem in the Ephesian assembly.[5] If Pauline authorship is rejected this passage should be employed with caution in reconstructing regional conditions. The asceticism in view is not only that of women.

3. *2 Timothy 3.6-7*

Further to the discussion in Chapter 7 on the immediate context of these verses, whether Pauline authorship is denied or accepted, and whatever appeal asceticism had for second-century Christian women,[6] nothing suggests that these women are or have been Christians, let alone at the place of address.[7] They are women[8] in a state of having been weighed down (σεσωρευμένα) with sins,[9] the subsequent present participles

5. Contra e.g. Payne at n. 1 above.
6. As e.g. D.R. MacDonald 1979: 169-84; 1983: 39-40; Bassler 1984: 23-41; Thurston 1989: 38.
7. Contra again Payne at n. 1 above, and e.g. Brox 1969: 132; Barclay 1975: 192-93; Fee 1984: 221; Perkins 1987: 20-21; Knoch 1988: 26; M.Y. MacDonald 1988: 179; Gritz 1991: 111-13. Bassler (1984: 31 n. 33) admits this possibility.
8. Lee (1993: 2) points out that γυναικάριον has a derogatory connotation only because of its context.
9. Some see their burden as a guilty conscience (e.g. Bernard 1899: 131; Humphreys 1901: 183; Hendriksen 1955: 286-87; Barrett 1963: 111; Oden 1989: 78; Guthrie 1990: 170; Gritz 1991: 112), but this reads more than is warranted into

describing how they act in that state. The Author's choice of the Perfect indicates his intention to portray them as already incapable of acknowledging the truth before the type of person described in vv. 1-5 ever worms his or her[10] way into their houses, that is as deeply sinful women predisposed to error.[11] Like those apparently godly but in fact depraved people who prey upon them, they may be anywhere at any time in 'the last days'. Those people with whom they are associated are paralleled with Jannes and Jambres (v. 8), figures from Jewish oral and pagan traditions,[12] suggesting that already-existing material has been adapted throughout. Whatever conquests false teachers may have made amongst the women of antiquity, it is impossible to tell from this passage if they enjoy a similar success specifically amongst Christian women at the place/s to which 2 Timothy is addressed.

4. *Titus 2.3-5*

The concern here is no more with the proper roles of women (vv. 3-5) than the proper roles of men (vv. 2, 6-8) or slaves of either sex (vv. 9-10). Nor is there evidence that it reflects women taught by false teachers that they should no longer be restricted to motherhood and subordination.

The instruction is again directed to the addressee, who is to teach sound doctrine, and to teach older men, older women (who will then train younger women), younger men and slaves to live appropriate lives. He is contrasted (δέ 2.1) with the rebellious people, mere talkers, etc. who are disturbing households. Certainly the groups to be taught, including those at 3.1-2, will include members of these households, but these are in secondary focus (cf. 2.1, 7-8, 15; 3.1, 8b, 9-10). Again traditional material is freely adapted, the concern in this case being not with the relations of the addressee with each group but with what he should teach them. It reflects, rather than reproduces, the concerns of

---

σεσωρευμένα. It is also unacceptable to represent them as more sinned against than sinning in their vulnerability due to sin-burdened consciences and desire-controlled lives, contra e.g. Hitchcock 1927–28: 351; Spencer 1985: 84; Knight 1992: 434.

10. That some may be female was suggested in Chapter 7.

11. The target is a particular type. Contra e.g. Verner 1983: 177; M.Y. MacDonald 1988: 179-80.

12. See e.g. Alford 1862: 393; Parry 1920: 63; Dibelius and Conzelmann 1972: 116-17; Odeberg 1977: 192-93; Guthrie 1990: 171; BAGD, s.v. Ἰάννης.

the Household Codes.[13] Since 2.1 sets the principle that what follows is in accordance with sound teaching (Knight 1992: 317), and λάλει indicates that the addressee is continuously to speak, etc. (Banker 1987: 73), it is difficult to avoid the conclusion that the Author himself views his instruction as permanently valid. There is no indication that he is concerned specifically with conditions at the assemblies at which the addressee is presently ministering.[14]

Women are not here restricted to particular roles. The instruction they are to give is the kind which would take place in everyday situations.[15] There is, however, no indication that older women are restricted to teaching young women;[16] that they may teach them only in domestic privacy;[17] or that the things they are to teach them are the only things women are permitted to do.[18] Although the teaching of young women is clearly in view, the major focus here is the idea that they should be

---

13. So Dibelius and Conzelmann 1972: 139.

14. Contra e.g. Ellicott (1864: 194-95), who argues that Cretan women are particularly liable to unfaithfulness (see pp. 67-68 above for argument that σωφρονίζωσιν has no necessary reference to chastity), and Guthrie (1990: 205), who wonders if the exhortation to train young women to love their children pinpoints some special Cretan weakness.

15. See Chapter 4, Section 6 re διδάσκω, and e.g. Fee 1984: 141, 145.

16. Scanzoni and Hardesty 1982: 63; Payne 1986: 103; C. Kroeger and R. Kroeger 1992: 81. Contra e.g. Houlden 1976: 148; Moo 1980: 74; 1981: 201; 1991: 186 with n. 17; Schüssler Fiorenza 1983: 290; Donelson 1986: 178. Bilezikian (1989: 176-77) also makes this point but sees these older women as formally appointed specialist teachers.

17. Contra Ellicott 1864: 193; Bernard 1899: 166; Scott 1936: 164; A.T. Hanson 1966: 180; Kelly 1972: 240; Payne 1986: 103; Guthrie 1990: 205, and also Hendriksen 1955: 364; Fee 1984: 141, 145. Contra also Banker (1987: 77-78) who, although relating ἵνα most directly to καλοδιδασκάλους rather than to v. 3 generally, and so highlighting the exhortative and not just exemplary nature of the training, nevertheless declares it informal.

18. Contra e.g. Hendriksen 1955: 365; Verner 1983: 135; Donelson 1986: 178; Byrne 1988: 89; M.Y. MacDonald 1988: 187. Neither is there sufficient evidence to support the idea that older women here constitute a kind of priesthood (contra A.T. Hanson 1966: 113 ἱεροπρεπεῖς), or (as Lock 1924: 139-40 notes) an official position. Banker (1987: 76) tends to exclude the 'priestly' inference in favour of holiness of character. Easton (1948: 91) assumes older women are to 'supervise' younger women, while Titus may supervise the older women themselves, and (citing 1 Tim. 5.2) handle 'particularly difficult cases' amongst younger women—an unsupported and unnecessarily hierarchical view.

counselled about their marital, parental and household duties only by qualified teachers. In contrast to vv. 2, 3, 6, 9, the addressee is not depicted in that role.

These women must be viewed in accordance with both historical and literary contexts. First, the old/young division should be interpreted with some fluidity, 'young' in antiquity sometimes meaning well beyond 30,[19] but 'old' requiring assessment with the shorter life expectancy of the period in mind, perhaps by our standards 'mature' or 'middle-aged'.[20] Some relativity and therefore some overlapping cannot be excluded. Secondly, no one would seriously suggest that slaves, all of whom are included in the instructions to men and women (Banker 1987: 85), are restricted here to the activities mentioned in vv. 9-10;[21] and although the relationship between men and their children is unmentioned, men are obviously not restricted from loving those children. Instructions to women must be interpreted in the same common-sense way.

This passage has its parallels with 1 Tim. 2.9-15, and to that extent serves as a sounding-board for conclusions about its more controversial fellow, but it does not suggest that the Author restricts women to household-related duties and subordination. Nor does it imply that he combats false teaching that women are suited to teach in the assembly.

5. *1 Timothy 5.11-15*

The exegetical difficulties of this passage call for much lengthier consideration than those above. Its primary focus is upon an administrative modification of earlier practice. In that context, v. 13 does not (contra e.g. Karris: see p. 141 above) 'emphasize a proper role'—it *reflects* roles which are assumed. Such a reflection requires the interpreter to proceed with caution.

The widows in this passage are generally viewed as:

19. LSJ, s.v. νέος, 1; Irenaeus, *Adv. Haer.* 2.22.5.

20. Oden 1989: 115. Banker (1987: 73) says the dichotomous age differentiation makes 'older' rather than 'elderly' appropriate. Cf. Fee (1984: 140), who cites Philo, *Spec. Leg.* 2.33 where the word refers to women over sixty.

21. For the wide variety of conditions under which urban slaves lived see e.g. Bartchy (1973: 42-43 incl. n. 108).

    i.   including some who have rejected remarriage and traditionally-accepted female roles;[22] and

    ii.   being members of the assembly/ies to which the letter is directed.[23]

These ideas facilitate interpretation by contemporary parallels,[24] and furnish convenient detail for reconstruction of historical background against which 1 Tim. 2.9-15 may be interpreted. Yet both are problematic. The first is extrapolated from a deeply controversial context. The second assumes that the paraenesis is directed at a situation at the place/s of address. The remainder of this chapter deals with these matters.

5.1. *Rejection of Marriage*

No study known to me demonstrates that some of these widows reject remarriage.

    It is commonly claimed that the Author here speaks of an order or group of widows with official duties.[25] Four points taken together suggest otherwise:[26]

22. As e.g. Müller-Bardorff 1958: 127 with n. 41, 131-32; Moo 1981: 218; Fee 1984: 61, 75; Bassler 1984: 31-33; Scholer 1986: e.g. 218-19; Knoch 1988: 26.

23. M.Y. MacDonald (1988: 21) designates the passage a direct disclosure of the *Sitz im Leben*, presupposing a community problem. See also e.g. Payne 1981: 183, 185, 190-91; Fee 1985: 144; Padgett 1987a: 20-21, 24. D.R. MacDonald (1979: 178) adds the families of vv. 4, 8. Schüssler Fiorenza (1983: 289-90) unconvincingly asserts that at vv. 1-2 the older men and women are elders and the younger deacons. See also Bailey (n.d.: 8-11), who assumes that 4.6–5.22 throughout discusses 'ministry' positions.

24. See e.g. Bartsch 1965: 112-43, esp. 117.

25. Those visualizing an 'order' include Bernard 1899: 81, 83-84; Lock 1924: xx-xxi; Scott 1936: 57; Easton 1948: 153; Müller-Bardorff 1958: 113-33; Schmithals and Werbeck 1961: 145; A.T. Hanson 1966: 57-59; 1982: 37, 96-100; Käsemann 1968: 88; Brox 1969: 186; Kelly 1972: 115; Dibelius and Conzelmann 1972: 74-75; Stählin 1974: 453, 455 n. 44; Houlden 1976: 92-93; Verner 1983: 165; Byrne 1988: 89; Thurston 1989: 41, 44-55; C. Kroeger and R. Kroeger 1992: 91. Finding insufficient evidence for an order but identifying a group with special duties are Simpson 1954: 74-75; Oden 1989: 153, 156; Guthrie 1990: 114. Oberlinner (1994: 221, 227, 234, 247) calls them e.g. 'unofficial', 'semi-official'.

26. Barrett 1963: 73, 75; Bassler 1984: 40 n. 60. See also Fee 1984: 80, 85. Hatch (1898: 349) notes that later sharp distinctions between offices, officers and others are not yet developed. Brox (1969: 194-95) frankly writes of the widows in the Syriac *Didascalia* (third-century CE), commonly employed to illuminate 1 Tim.

(a) Throughout the Pastoral Epistles the τιμή/τιμάω word-group conveys the idea of respect (1.17; 6.1-2, 16; 2 Tim. 2.21) rather than payment. 1 Timothy 5.17 is the only clear exception, as indicated by the supporting Deut. 25.4 (cf. also 1 Cor. 9.9) and a saying of Jesus (Lk. 10.7; Mt. 10.1). Although the honour to be paid widows involves financial support (vv. 4, 8, 16), there is no good reason to conclude that it is intended as payment for services rendered.[27] It appears primarily to be the return of honour and heightened status customarily bestowed upon a benefactor by those to whom a service had been rendered.[28]

(b) Official duties are nowhere mentioned, and should not be confused with qualifications.[29]

(c) Καταλεγέσθω (v. 9) refers to classification within a sphere, not membership of an official order.[30]

5.11-12, 'Manches, das man in 1 Tim 5 zwischen den Zeilen lesen muss, ist hier ergänzt und verdeutlicht' ('Much of what one has to read in 1 Tim. 5 between the lines, is here added and explained').

27. Verner 1983: 162-63. See also Brox 1969: 187. Those seeing in this context both respect and its material proof include Ellicott 1864: 68; Liddon 1897: 51; Bernard 1899: 78; Barrett 1963: 74. Stählin (1974; 455-56) highlights the importance of 'active care'. Envisaging a wage are e.g. A.T. Hanson 1966: 57; Thurston 1989: 45. See also Easton 1948: 152; Müller-Bardorff 1958: 114-15, 121; Bartsch 1965: 112. Dibelius and Conzelmann (1972: 73) unconvincingly claim there is probably no monetary connotation here.

28. Kidd 1990: 55. See also Winter 1988b: 90-91.

29. Verner 1983: 164-65; Fee 1984: 80, 85. Contra e.g. Ellicott 1864: 72-73; Scott 1936: 60-61; A.T. Hanson 1966: 57; Kelly 1972: 115-17; Dibelius and Conzelmann 1972: 74-75; D.R. MacDonald 1979: 177; S.L. Davies 1980: 70-73; Guthrie 1990: 114-15. Thurston (1989: 50-53) claims duties are implied. See also Stählin 1974: 457; Knight 1992: 222. Easton (1948: 153-54) thinks the duties correspond largely to those of deacons, but Plummer (1888: 155-68) denies this. Ryrie (1958: 83-84) believes only the ministry of prayer is clearly indicated. See also Müller-Bardorff 1958: 122-25; Brox 1969: 189; and Bartsch (1965: 117) who (p. 134) says 'Unsere Regel sucht...eine Beschränkung der Tätigkeit der Witwen auf den Dienst des Gebets...jede andere Tätigkeit als mit diesem...unvereinbar zu verhindern' ('Our rule seeks...a limitation of the activity of the widows to the service of prayer...to prevent any other activity as...incompatible with it'). Liddon (1897: 56) argues that the advanced age of 60 implies contemplative–devotional rather than practical–philanthropic duties. Ref. also Winter (1988b: 93) in my Chapter 1 n. 14 above.

30. Simpson 1954: 74; Müller-Bardorff 1958: 118-19 and n. 11; Barrett 1963: 73; Verner 1983: 163; M.Y. MacDonald 1988: 185; P.H. Towner 1989: 183. Contra Liddon 1897: 55; Brox 1969: 190; Kelly 1972: 115; Stählin 1974: 456; Houlden

(d) Similarities between qualifications for officials and widows reflect standards required of all believers, not parallel groups.[31]

A group with official duties is therefore unlikely. Two factors nevertheless render the identity of the widows problematic:

(a) Does ἑνὸς ἀνδρὸς γυνή (v. 9) require the enrolled widow to have been only once-married,[32] or to have been faithful to her husband during his life-time?[33] It is unclear that the late second-century concept of monogamous widowhood being spiritually superior to remarriage is

1976: 93; S.L. Davies 1980: 71; Thurston 1989: 45, 49; Kidd 1990: 104. Scott (1936: 59-60) speaks of 'technical' terms but does not identify them. Dibelius and Conzelmann (1972: 75) highlight the technical character without conclusion. Although supporting the existence of an order, Ellicott (1864: 72) and Parry (1920: 31) note that the nature of the list may be deduced only by its context.

31. P.H. Towner 1989: 183-84. Contra Hendriksen 1955: 173-76; Bartsch 1965: 130; Brox 1969: 190; Verner 1983: 163-64; M.Y. MacDonald 1988: 185-86; Thurston 1989: 44; Kidd 1990: 105. See also Müller-Bardorff (1958: 118, 121-22), who admits the weakness of the claim that χήρα (vv. 9a, 11a) is better understood as complement than subject. Knight (1992: 30) notes that qualifications required in ch. 3 only enlarge and specify those already required in Acts 6.3, suggesting a continuing tradition.

32. As e.g. Alford 1862: 346-47; Plummer 1888: 122-25; Bernard 1899: 81; Easton 1948: 212-15; Kelly 1972: 75, 115-16; D.R. MacDonald 1979: 177-78; Verner 1983: 130-31; M.Y. MacDonald 1988: 211; Guthrie 1990: 114; Dewey 1992: 357.

33. As e.g. Humphreys 1901: 127; Hendriksen 1955: 174; Barrett 1963: 58-59; Dibelius and Conzelmann 1972: 75; Houlden 1976: 93; Knight 1984: 223; Winter 1988a: 95 and n. 64. Barrett (pp. 58-59, 75) suggests that at 3.2 μιᾶς γυναικός ἄνδρα may quote a qualification for public office, interpreting 'faithful to his one wife', with the corresponding 'faithful in marriage to one man' at 5.9. Fee (1985: 148 n. 21, 150) tends to find marital fidelity probable, and see also 1984: 80. Lock (1924: 60) is undecided. Easton (1948: 214) and A.T. Hanson (1966: 59) support 'undivorced'. Oberlinner (1994: 232) suspects this idea may be present. Müller-Bardorff (1958: 121 n. 17) finds more likely a ban on sexual offence, possibly including polygamy. For various views see Saucy 1974: 229-40. It has also been suggested that μιᾶς γυναικὸς ἄνδρα prohibits polygamy, or requires marriage (Ford 1971: 345 n. 2; BDF, §247 [2]). The latter idea seems too strong. Verner (1983: 129) notes that the former is improbable because of Graeco-Roman monogamy (to which Jews conformed), but even if this were not the case 5.9 would require a non-corresponding interpretation to 3.2: women never took more than one husband. Brox (1969: 191) suggests that a subtle form of polyandry may be in view in which 'eine Scheidung aus nichtigen Gründen rechtmässig sein konnte' ('a divorce for trivial reasons could be lawful').

involved (cf. also 3.2b and Tit. 1.6b).[34] Opposition to asceticism at 4.3-5 and the instruction at 5.14 suggest that marital faithfulness is the more likely meaning, but the expression itself is ambiguous.[35]

(b) 1 Timothy 5.11-12 appears to assume a group of widows pledged to life-time celibacy.[36] P.H. Towner points out that ἀθετέω may simply convey the idea of rejection rather than nullification of a public agreement (Lk. 7.30; 10.16 *quarter*; Jn 12.28; 1 Cor. 1.19; Gal. 2.21; 1 Thess. 4.8 *bis*; Jude 8), and that the important role of πίστις in the Pastorals makes improbable the static idea of an 'oath'.[37] Nevertheless, the setting aside of this former πίστις involves not only wantonness which alienates these widows from Christ (v. 11b) but also an associated desire to marry (v. 11c). It is not even the act of marriage but simply the *desire* to marry together with their wantonness which brings these widows under judgment (v. 12).[38] The normalcy associated with remarriage at v. 14 makes it difficult to understand how such a desire could be seen as a setting aside of former πίστις unless there had been some kind of officially recognized pledge to remain single.[39] It has been

---

34. Contra Lightman and Zeisel (1977: 26-27), who quote the certainly late imperial epitaph (publ. E. Diehl, *ILCV* [Berlin, 1923-27] no. 1581 = A. Ferrua-D. Mazzoleni, *ICUR*, IX [Rome, 1985] no. 24120) 'Rigine...que se|dit uidua annos LX et eclesa | numqua grauauit unibyra que | uixit annos LXXX...' ('Regina...who lived as a widow for 60 years and never burdened the church, who had one husband alone, and lived 80 years...') to demonstrate the emergence of continent widowhood as an honoured status; but Regina appears to have been honoured more for never having burdened the church than for remaining a widow.

35. Verner (1983: 129-31) points out that since the phrase occurs without explanation or defence the addressee is probably expected to both know and agree with it.

36. E.g. Alford 1862: 347, 349; Easton 1948: 154; Bartsch 1965: 133; Kelly 1972: 117; D.R. MacDonald 1979: 177-78; Schüssler Fiorenza 1983: 312; Bassler 1984: 40; M.Y. MacDonald 1988: 186.

37. P.H. Towner 1989: 184. See also Humphreys 1901: 129. Contra Lock 1924: 60; Dibelius and Conzelmann 1972: 75; Knight 1992: 226, and cf. the more cautious Simpson 1954: 75; Müller-Bardorff 1958: 120 and n. 14; Stählin 1974: 454 with n. 136.

38. Liddon 1897: 58, 60; Bernard 1899: 83. See also Easton 1948: 154; Müller-Bardorff 1958: 119.

39. As e.g. Ellicott 1864: 75; Parry 1920: 32; Lock 1924: 60; Scott 1936: 61; Easton 1948: 154; Barrett 1963: 76; A.T. Hanson 1966: 57, 59-60; Brox 1969: 194; Dibelius and Conzelmann 1972: 75; Kelly 1972: 117; Trummer 1978: 219; Bassler

argued that the condemnation is upon the breaking of the pledge, not the desire for marriage.[40] It has also been argued that the intention is to mark the ethical connection between the two, weariness of Christ's yoke involving a further, more decided lapse (Ellicott 1864: 75). Since ἔχουσαι κρίμα, κτλ. is more clearly in apposition to γαμεῖν θέλουσιν than to καταστρηνιάσωσιν τοῦ Χριστοῦ, the latter argument is more convincing. Two things at least equally alienate these widows: their wantonness and their desire to marry. The pledge of celibacy has seemed the only adequate way to explain that further alienation. It is, however, nowhere directly indicated.

The two factors, (a) and (b), raise further difficulties. If the widows of vv. 11-15 *are* pledged to life-time celibacy, what of those in vv. 3-10, 16? Is such a pledge a prerequisite for enrolment on the list when the age of 60 is reached? Might ἑνὸς ἀνδρὸς γυνή in fact require a 'true' widow to have been married once only? Or are the widows of vv. 3-10, 16 a different group to those in vv. 11-15?

The entire section (vv. 3-16) does appear intended to address one major topic.[41] Widows remain the subject throughout, and v. 16 reverses the order of ideas introduced in vv. 3-4.[42] Bassler says that the internal logic conflicts with that impression of unity: if enrolment on the list (v. 9) is viewed as a precondition for financial support and is governed by the criteria of vv. 9-10, poor widows under 60 would be disqualified.[43] If ἑνὸς ἀνδρός does mean 'once-married', widows obeying v. 14 only to be widowed again would also be disqualified. Speculation abounds here. Some claim or assume that widows apparently affected would no doubt in any case be assisted financially, but they offer no decisive argument.[44] Many conclude that two sorts of widows are in

1984: 40; Byrne 1988: 90; Knight 1992: 222, 226; Oberlinner 1994: 237. See also Müller-Bardorff 1958: 120.

40. Hendriksen 1955: 175; Barrett 1963: 76; Barclay 1975: 114; D.R. MacDonald 1979: 178; Fee 1984: 81-82.

41. Dibelius and Conzelmann 1972: 73-74; P.H. Towner 1989: 181-82; Oberlinner 1994: 221.

42. Bassler 1984: 33; Müller-Bardorff 1958: 113-16.

43. Bassler 1984: 34. Cf. Müller-Bardorff 1958: 116-17.

44. See e.g. Bernard 1899: 81-82; Scott 1936: 60; Ryrie 1958: 83; A.T. Hanson 1966: 57-58; 1982: 37, 96; Oden 1989: 153; Thurston 1989: 54; Guthrie 1990: 115. Knight (1992: 222-25) argues that with qualified widows no longer able to care for themselves the church enters a permanent agreement for 'mutually accepted commitments and possible responsibilities', it being wrong to conclude that no others

view, the destitute (vv. 3-8, 16) and a particular group (vv. 9-15).[45] Bassler justifiably argues that such explanations are more concerned with the preservation of early Christian honour than the unity of the passage, but her own solution is speculative. The Author, she says, is concerned to deny the freedom and equality preached by Paul (Gal. 3.28) but which had resulted in negative reaction in the surrounding culture. By now, she argues, the widows' circle probably includes large numbers of married, divorced and single women choosing the esteem, remuneration and freedom from patriarchal family structures and responsibilities, that are associated with membership.[46] This would open the door to heretics also advocating celibacy.[47] The Author, she claims, does not intend simply to locate and honour the true widow but, by controlling the number to be supported, also to reduce the offence they cause. He therefore develops criteria both affirming contemporary social norms and rendering women immune to the heresy.[48] Maintaining the unity of the passage, Bassler concludes that the second-century

are helped. Quite apart from the fact that the women he describes could hardly carry out the duties he outlines, in effect Knight argues that the qualified are where possible to earn their keep but the unqualified would receive it freely (if only occasionally or temporarily). Müller-Bardorff (1958: 117) says 'Dennoch geht es...um die Einprägung sozialer Unterhaltspflicht der Gemeinde Hilfsbedürftigen gegenüber nicht an sich....[s]ofern nur feststeht, dass sie nicht als Witwe in einem besonderen Sinn Anspruch auf diese Unterstützung hat als einen ihr gebührenden "Sold" ' ('Nevertheless it is not a matter...of inculcating a social maintenance duty on the part of the congregation relative to those in need of help *per se*...provided only that it has been established that as a widow she does not have in any particular sense a claim for this support as a "pay" which is due to her') but (p. 121, although rejecting καταλεγέσθω as supporting proof) believes 'diese Witwen...sind...als Trägerinnen eines besonderen kirchlichen Amtes angesehen' ('these widows...are...regarded as bearers of a particular ecclesiastical office').

45. Alford 1862: 346-47, 350; Ellicott 1864: 73; Plummer 1888: 153-54; Liddon 1897: 51, 55-61; Bernard 1899: 80; Humphreys 1901: 124; Parry 1920: 29; Scott 1936: 57, 59; Leipoldt 1953: 136; A.T. Hanson 1966: 57-58; Verner 1983: 95, 165; Fung 1987: 181-82; M.Y. MacDonald 1988: 186. Lock (1924: 56) is unsure.

46. Bassler 1984: 34. See also S.L. Davies 1980: 72-73; Schüssler Fiorenza 1983: 312; Thurston 1989: 39-40.

47. Bassler 1984: 35-37. See also Müller-Bardorff 1958: 131-32; Byrne 1988: 90.

48. Bassler 1984: 32. See also Dewey 1992: 357.

defection of widows to ascetic heresies resulted from their exclusion at 1 Tim. 5.3-16 (1984: 34, 39).

Before turning to reasons why Bassler is unpersuasive, one factor she does not deny should be kept in mind. The initial contrast in the passage is between the widow left alone and ἡ σπαταλῶσα (vv. 5-6). Σπαταλάω often appears with τρυφάω, 'lead a life of luxury or self-indulgence, to carouse', but has somewhat worse associations (cf. Jas 5.5 'self-indulgence' NIV, 'wantonness' AV) (MM, s.v. σπαταλάω). Ellicott claims that although the two are sometimes almost synonymous σπαταλάω highlights prodigality and wastefulness more than the luxury and effeminacy of τρυφάω;[49] but others do not make this distinction. The LXX translators employed σπαταλάω at Ezek. 16.49 for an idle and luxurious life contrasting with care of the poor and needy, and the compound κατασπαταλάω at Prov. 29.21 for 'pamper' and at Amos 6.4 for 'stretch languidly and effusely'.[50] At Sir. 21.15 σπαταλάω denotes abandonment to pleasure and comfort (Kelly 1972: 114). Hort concludes that generally the leading idea is probably luxurious feeding.[51] At 1 Tim. 5.6, therefore, it is appropriate to view the self-indulgence as luxurious rather than licentious.[52] The widow left alone is at least initially not contrasted with women choosing to be celibate, or even women abandoning celibacy, but with sumptuously self-indulgent

49. Ellicott 1864: 70. Liddon (1897: 53) accepts synonymity at Jas 5.5, rendering at 1 Timothy 5 'dissipated'. Humphreys (1901: 126) also stresses prodigality. Alford (1862: 345) cites Wetstein σπαταλᾷ, λίαν τρυφᾷ, ἀσώτως ζῇ.

50. *TWOT*, II, 728. See e.g. NIV. Hort (1909: 107-109) demonstrates that Symmachus used forms of σπάταλος at Deut. 28.54 for 'tender and delicate' and at Eccl. 2.8 and Song 7.7(6) for 'delights', for all of which the LXX uses forms related to τρυφάω.

51. Hort 1909: 109. Ps. Chrysostom, *de poen.* ix.777 E calls the rich man of Lk. 16.19 (there described as εὐφραινόμενος καθ᾽ ἡμέραν λαμπρῶς) ὁ σπαταλιστὴς ἐκεῖνος ('that self-indulgent man'). See also ὡς οὖν καιρὸν ἔχεις, λοῦσαι, μύρισαι, σπατάλησον | καὶ χάρισαι, δαπάνησον, ἅπερ δύνασαι ('so as you have opportunity, bathe, perfume yourself, live in comfort and indulge yourself, spend what you can', Kaibel 1965: no. 646a 5-6).

52. Barrett 1963: 74. See also Parry 1920: 30; Simpson 1954: 73; Kelly 1972: 114. Contra e.g. Plummer 1888: 154; Hendriksen 1955: 170; and esp.: 'plunge into dissipation', 'loose-living' (Scott 1936: 59); 'prostitution' (Easton 1948: 152; followed by Bartsch 1965: 128 n. 22); 'one whose sexual behaviour is unsatisfactory' (A.T. Hanson 1966: 58; see also 1982: 97); 'licentiousness' (Gritz 1991: 111). See also Barclay 1975: 105; Guthrie 1990: 113; Knight 1992: 219.

widows.[53] This self-indulgence, moreover, involves a kind of death (ζῶσα τέθνηκεν).[54]

Against this background Bassler fails to convince for two reasons. First, she produces from the text no evidence that deserting wives, divorcees or single women *have* swollen the widows' numbers, so her subsequent argument has no foundation.[55] Secondly, she too easily accepts that there is a conflict between the structure and content of the passage. Like many others she begins from the assumption of two premises:

i.   that the τιμή due to 'true' widows continues the pattern of Acts 6.1, itself patterned upon earlier Jewish practice;[56] and
ii. that the wantonness of the widows in vv. 11-12 is sexual.

The 'logical conflict' which Bassler perceives derives from these common premises, both of which require detailed consideration.

The nature of τιμή. If the τιμή due to 'true' widows *does* continue the pattern of Acts 6.1 and Jewish practice, widows ineligible for the list are not excluded from financial assistance.

As noted above, τιμή in the Pastorals characteristically means 'honour'. The goal at Acts 6.1 clearly includes an honouring recognition of widows. 1 Timothy 5.3-16 certainly continues this same pattern. I suggest, however, that in contrast to Acts 6.1 the focus here is upon honour

53. Lock 1924: 58; Simpson 1954: 73-74; Hendriksen 1955: 170; Kelly 1972: 114.

54. Alford 1862: 345; Hendriksen 1955: 170; Stählin 1974: 454; Knight 1992: 219.

55. Cf. the similarly unsubstantiated D.R. MacDonald (1979: 177-79), who assumes not only a widow's order, and (v. 16) women receiving financial assistance from the church to keep them, but young virgins enrolled in the order (vv. 3, 16). For additional refutation of MacDonald see below.

56. Fee (1984: 76) traces from the Old Testament e.g. Exod. 22.22; Deut. 24.17 to Acts, incl. 9.36, 39, 41; Jas 1.27. See also e.g. Hendriksen 1955: 167-68; Barrett 1963: 74; Brox 1969: 185; Oden 1989: 154; Knight 1992: 216. Schüssler Fiorenza (1983: 165-66) argues that, since the widows in Acts 6 are not said to be poor, and διακονεῖν τραπέζαις (v. 2) refers to table service, they may be neglected in assignment for service at or in participation in the eucharist. This seems unlikely: the care of poor widows had been customary amongst Jews, and the apostles believe the serving in question interferes with their ministry of the word but Jesus himself had broken and served bread to them.

rather than the assistance, and it is that honour which is being restricted.[57]

In Graeco-Roman society a wife's dowry was intended for her maintenance, and widows not in control of their own finances were supposed to be maintained by those inheriting its management.[58] Although upper-class widows were expected to remarry they did not always do so,[59] and all classes honoured the widow *univira*.[60] There is plenty of evidence of concern that aged parents be honoured. Children were widely regarded as owing them an obligation of thanksgiving.[61] At Athens their care was legally enforced, and men aspiring to public office were questioned accordingly.[62] At Rome mothers (including the widowed, divorced or remarried) were considered entitled to regular visits not only from daughters but also from adult sons who were otherwise liable to public censure (Dixon 1988: 169-70, 192-93, 218, 221-22). Philo criticized men who neglected their parents (*Dec.* 115-20). Parents expressed the hope that they would be supported and comforted by adult children in return for parental effort and anxiety (Dixon 1988: 191-92; 1992: 133, 138, 157). On the other hand, there is no evidence of any private or public support of the elderly except by children for their own parents.[63] Despite legal provisions some κύριοι found ways to exploit the system

57. Alford (1862: 344) asks if only honour is in view why the destitute should be held in more honour than those with families. But whether practised by assembly or family the honour would be of the same kind.

58. Winter 1988a: 83-84. Cf. Plummer (1888: 159-60) who argues that provision for the widow (as distinct from children) is attibutable to Christianity. Dixon (1988: 47-51) discusses widows inheriting life interests in at least a large part of their husband's estates and therefore controlling/sharing administration of that wealth unless they remarry. Cf. Plutarch, *Praec. coniug.* 36, which observes that mothers favour sons because they will give them aid.

59. Winter 1988a: 85. Rawson (ed.) (1986: 31-32) notes upper-class non-enforcement of Augustus's re-marriage legislation, believing enforcement amongst lower classes improbable since their birth-rate is not the target, and suggests *univirae* may gain praise because traditional attitudes survived unpopular legislation, or as a form of congratulation that a marriage survived.

60. Lightman and Zeisel 1977: 19-32. See also van der Horst 1991: 103.

61. Kidd (1990: 54-55, 138) cites Dio Chrysostom, *Orat.* 75.7-8.

62. Simpson (1954: 73) cites Aristotle, *Nic. Eth.* ix.2; cf. Euripides, *IA* 1230, Plato, *Laws* 717. Barclay (1975: 106-08) cites also Aeschines (who quotes Solon) and Demosthenes. Finley 1981: 167; Henderson 1987: 111; Winter 1988a: 85; Dixon 1992: 153.

63. Finley 1981: 167-68. See also Henderson 1987: 111.

(Winter 1988a: 87-88), and many widows without dowries (Dixon 1992: 150-57) were dependant on food distributions.[64] The synagogues distributed weekly to travellers and the resident poor (Winter 1988a: 88-89). Acts 6.1-7 reports an early Christian attempt to get the balance of a similar distribution right on a daily basis. Although attention there is upon neglected widows, 2.5 and 4.34-35 suggest that the distribution itself, like that made by the Jews, is not only to widows but to all the poor.

1 Timothy 5.3-16 modifies similar procedures apparently involving no means test and concerning widows only.[65] Christian κύριοι are to practice εὐσέβεια first in their own households (vv. 4, 8) (Winter 1988a: 90). In v. 16 believing women,[66] who are not legal managers of dowries, are in addition to κύριοι called upon, whatever their marital status, to care for widows.[67] In contrast to κύριοι (v. 8) these are not

---

64. Garnsey (1988: e.g. 275-76) writes that outside Rome euergetism, not government, was the source of such distribution.

65. I take the subjects of both μανθανέτωσαν (v. 4) and ὦσιν (v. 7 and therefore v. 8) here to be the children and grandchildren, as e.g. Liddon 1897: 52; Verner 1983: 137 n. 36; Fee 1984: 77-79. Contra e.g. Bartsch (1965: 127) who says v. 8 'ist eine an die Witwe gerichtete Forderung...so dass von daher für das Verständnis von...[v4] als Weisung an die Witwen sich eine grössere Wahrscheinlichkeit ergibt' ('is a demand directed to the widow...so that the result is thus a stronger probability for the interpretation of... [v. 4] to be an instruction for the widows'). Cf. Holtz (1965: 117), who says v. 8 is directed to widows *and* children. Oberlinner (1994: 229-30) says at v. 7 '...hat...diese Mahnung an die Witwe beispielhafte Bedeutung: sie gilt für alle in der Gemeinde' ('...is...this exhortation directed to the widow of exemplary importance: it goes for everybody in the congregation'), and at v. 8 'die Witwe selbst...als Adressatin anzusehen ist' ('the widow herself...has to be regarded as the addressee').

66. Liddon (1897: 61) and Easton (1948: 154-55, 157-58) believe, and Stählin (1974: 458 n. 166) and Guthrie (1990: 116-17) appear to suspect, that πιστός ἤ πιστή is correct here. See also Alford 1862: 351. Supporting πιστή only are Ellicott 1864: 78; Humphreys 1901: 131; Parry 1920: 33; Hendriksen 1955: 178; Barrett 1963: 77; A.T. Hanson 1966: 60; Kelly 1972: 120-21; Metzger 1975: 642; Verner 1983: 139 incl. n. 40; Knight 1992: 229. Less sure are Scott 1936: 63; Müller-Bardorff 1958: 115 n. 9; Dibelius and Conzelmann 1972: 76. Bartsch (1965: 137) and Dewey (1992: 357) suggest communities of widows here, but the text provides no evidence for this. Cf. Oberlinner 1994: 243 with n. 67.

67. Winter 1988a: 93-94. Knight (1992: 229) speculates that this is to enable husbands and households 'to do what God calls them to do' (see also Kelly 1972: 121, and cf. Holtz 1965: 122). Verses 4-5, 7-8, however, indicate that κύριοι are not to shirk such ongoing care to which *all* are 'called by God'. Padgett (1987a: 21)

censured, v. 16 apparently introducing something new. Although nowhere in 1 Timothy is support for the poor apart from widows mentioned, 6.6-10, 17-19 make it difficult to imagine that they are of no
concern. Perhaps the Author envisages them being assisted by individual patronage (cf. Acts 9.36, 39) or by assembly arrangements unfocused in the letter. What he *is* concerned about here is that a particular
sector of those poor be properly honoured. Children and grandchildren
should learn first of all to serve their own family and return payment to
their forebears (v. 4).[68] Since parents expend much more than money on
children this is unlikely to be intended to be solely financial (Oden
1989: 154). The widows of vv. 3, 10, 16 therefore appear to be a particular group amongst the poor considered worthy of honour including
(but not consisting only of) an official assembly allowance[69] distinguishable from help for the poor in general.

The ἰδίων/οἰκείων distinction (v. 8)[70] may support this view. If ἴδιοι
include slaves, freedman etc., οἰκεῖοι would be family living at home,
including widows.[71] But if ἴδιοι are widows, οἰκεῖοι are widows living
at home distinct from those residing elsewhere whose dowries would be
managed by someone else.[72] Since widows are the subject throughout

implies that some young widows have abandoned elderly relatives, and places the
major emphasis on v. 16, the Author specifically urging women. The chief focus,
however, is upon household heads, v. 16 appreciating that in some cases the responsibility would fall to women.

68. Knight (1992: 218) notes the Present infinitives here. The Author envisages
ongoing actions.

69. Oden (1989: 143) says genuine regard, sympathy and recognition of service
and personal dignity are implied. See also n. 27 above. Lock (1924: 57) suggests
special seating in meetings and rank in ecclesiastical hierarchy may be included, but
his evidence is late.

70. See e.g. Hendriksen 1955: 171; Verner 1983: 138. See also Stählin (1974:
453) who outlines various views on μανθανέτωσαν, stating (n. 123) that ἰδίων
makes more sense in relation to widows serving in their own homes. Here μάλιστα
with καί clearly means 'especially' (cf. Skeat 1979: 173-77).

71. Winter 1988a: 91-92. Simpson (1954: 73) takes this view.

72. Winter 1988a: 91-92. Ellicott (1864: 71) notes that the omission of the second article tends to bind the two into one class, but concludes that the former are
relations but the latter family. See also Alford 1862: 346. Humphreys (1901: 126)
makes a similar observation, but concludes that this means relatives and dependents
living in the same house. See also Knight 1992: 221. Lock (1924: 59) suggests the
two may refer to the same persons. Καὶ μάλιστα makes this improbable. Verner
(1983: 138) objects to division of widows into those living with/apart from rela-

vv. 3-16 the latter seems most likely, in which case κύριοι are expected to care not only for those whose dowries they manage but also in whatever ways are appropriate for family widows whose dowries are managed by others. This reflects the same broad concern for parents and grandparents seen above in both the thought of the day and the idea that τιμάω consists of more than monetary support. In accordance with vv. 7-8, avoidance of such responsibility would deny the faith, offend against both the fifth commandment and the expectations of contemporary society, and be worthy of the condemnation of outsiders (Winter 1988a: 93).

It emerges, then, that the widow over 60 years of age without a dowry (and therefore lacking a responsible κύριος), who puts her hope in God, spends her time in prayer, has lived a reputable life, and has no other patronage, is to be honoured by grateful care which would normally be given by her family (cf. vv. 1-2). Other poor Christians including widows failing to meet these requirements do not qualify for this honour. However, if care for the poor followed by the earliest Christians is patterned after the Jewish model, these others (although to some extent responsible for their own welfare) would presumably be financially assisted at the discretion of individuals or the local assembly in accordance with available resources. Enrolment on the list does not appear to be the precondition for financial assistance but for honour transcending such assistance.

But if the section deals with the one subject of honour due to certain widows, are those widowed more than once disqualified? It will be argued below that they are not. Before that, however, the second premise adopted by Bassler and most others requires attention.

The nature of καταστρηνιάω. A compound of στρηνιάω 'run riot, wax wanton' (LSJ, s.v.), καταστρηνιάω (v. 11) appears nowhere else in the New Testament, the LXX, the apocrypha, or any Greek writer prior to the Christian era (MGM, s.v.). In this context of 'desire to marry' most interpret it as the exercise of at least sensual desire,[73] and sometimes of

---

tives, arguing that the latter would be in greatest danger of neglect, but Winter (p. 91 n. 47) points out that the widow living elsewhere should be in the care of whoever manages her dowry.

73. E.g. NIV, TEV, Phillips, JB, NEB. BAGD, s.v. cites Ps. Ignatius, *Ad Antioch* 11: 'to feel sensuous impulses'. See also Hendriksen 1955: 176; Müller-Bardorff 1958: 119; Barrett 1963: 76; Kelly 1972: 117, 121; Hurley 1981: 136; Fee 1984:

sexual wantonness.[74] Wantonness, however, may be self-indulgent.[75] The simplex verb is certainly not limited to the sexual variety. Hesychius (IV, 2002), equates it with πεπλεγμένοι. δηλοῖ δὲ καὶ τὸ διὰ πλοῦτον ὑβρίζειν, καὶ βαρέως φέρειν ('[it shows] arrogance because of wealth, and being hard to bear'). Revelation 18.7, 9 conveys the idea 'to wax wanton through wealth' (cf. στρῆνος v. 3 'luxury'). The LXX translators employed it at 2 Kgs 19.28 for *sha'ᵃnān* 'arrogance'.[76] In the first half of the third century CE, *P. Meyer* 20. 29 records μὴ στρηνιάτω Λουκιᾶς, ἀλλά ἐργαζέσθω ('let Loukias not act wantonly, but let him work'), so unless we are to envisage more or less full-time sexual occupation, this again suggests 'self-indulgence'. Ellicott says the word implies 'restiveness', thence 'fulness of bread or wanton luxury' (1864: 75). Compounds, moreover, do not always alter or even intensify verbal meaning. The κατα- prefix may simply indicate the direction of an action (against a genitive object), as at Mt. 9.24; Mk 14.60; Jas 2.13.[77] Souter translates 'exercise...vigour against',[78] Lock 'to grow restive against the limitations of Christian widowhood',[79] and Scott speaks of impatience with staid routine (1936: 61). Ellicott notes the possibility of the simple rather than sexual meaning.[80] In support of the sexual nuance here is the fact that in modern Greek dialects

81; Guthrie 1990: 115. Knight (1992: 225-26) also interprets vv. 14b, 15 as possibly indicating 'a fall into sexual temptation'.

74. Humphreys 1901: 129. Simpson (1954: 75) says the simplex (e.g. Rev. 18.7, 9) speaks of perversity bred of lustihood. Ellicott (1864: 75, 78) claims the sexual reference cannot be excluded because of γαμεῖν θέλουσιν, subsequently referring to the action as sensual/swerving from the path of purity and chastity. AV, RSV 'wanton' is liable to be understood as sexual. Alford (1862: 349) approves Jerome, *ep.* 23 [11] ad Ageruchiam [Gerontiam] 'quae fornicatae sunt [-cantur ?] in injuriam viri sui Christi' ('who are fornicators of Christ, by virtue of the injury each has committed against her own husband').

75. For the English distinction see e.g. *Concise Oxford Dictionary* 1959: s.v. 1; *Macquarie Dictionary* 1985: s.v. 4, 5.

76. *TWOT*, II, 894. See e.g. NIV.

77. Winter (1988a: 97 n. 68) writes that κατα- simply enforces the meaning 'to run riot/become wanton'. See also Ellicott 1864: 75; Humphreys 1901: 129. Müller-Bardorff (1958: 119) points out that κρίμα (v. 12) has the content of κατάκριμα.

78. Souter 1960: 129. See also Bernard 1899: 82.

79. Lock 1924: 60. Liddon (1897: 58-59) says the phrase is the equivalent of στρηνιᾶν κατὰ τοῦ Χριστοῦ ('behave unseemingly against Christ'). See also Oden 1989: 157.

80. Ellicott 1864: 75. Cf. at n. 74.

στρηνιᾶν means 'to be in heat'; it is so used of men and women in modern Cypriot (Shipp 1979: s.v.). Certainly, at Rev. 18.7, 9 there is a close connection between self-indulgent and sexual wantonness, but even there the ideas are distinguishable.

There is good cause to conclude that at 1 Tim. 5.11 self-indulgence is the sense in view.[81] When sexual wantonness is inferred these widows are a most curious group for three reasons:

(a) Their wantonness is not only directed against Christ rather than *towards* some object, but a desire for marriage constituting an additional alienation from Christ then develops. The order of the action does not suggest that, having supposed their sexuality controllable, they now experience such an unexpectedly strong resurgence that marriage seems the only option. The text does *not* say 'whenever they want to marry they act wantonly against Christ', which might suggest (even though no object is specified) that a particular man aroused that desire.[82] Instead it says 'whenever they act wantonly against Christ they want to marry', suggesting that the first alienation is a general wantonness. It is odd that this should be thought to lead to desire to marry rather than to promiscuity. But if we accept for the moment the unlikely proposition that the widows hope to channel their lust within the bounds of matrimony, further problems emerge.

(b) 1 Timothy 5.11-12 remains problematic whether or not a pledge of celibacy is envisaged. When it is denied there appears to be no way to define the nature of the further alienation. The suggestion that the desire is to marry an unbeliever is speculative:[83] it is their wantonness and desire to remarry—not their wantonness and choice of marriage partner—which alienate them (Knight 1992: 226). But if the pledge *is* assumed, although the alienation then appears to be caused by breaking

81. As e.g. 'to wax wanton with wealth, success, prosperity, shutting out the thought of humility and service' (Parry 1920: 32).

82. Contra e.g. D.R. MacDonald (1979: 178) who says 'Apparently some younger "widows" who had made a pledge of chastity to Christ had later desired to marry, and therefore, in the author's opinion, had incurred judgment'; and Guthrie (1990: 115), who says 'younger women would not wish to be tied to church duties if further opportunities came for marriage'.

83. Contra Humphreys 1901: 129-30; Fee 1984: 81; Oden 1989: 157-58; P.H. Towner 1989: 184. See also Winter 1988a: 97. Barrett (1963: 76) finds πίστις meaning 'original profession of faith' possible, but doubts this could be broken by a desire for marriage.

it, more is explained away than resolved. It again seems peculiar that (in numbers sufficient to warrant a general rule) formerly married women, presumably with some degree of sexual self-knowledge, having found it appropriate to make a pledge of life-time celibacy, should then develop not only a compulsive desire but one apparently aimed more against Christ than towards a particular man. Moreover, in spite of this latest development (and its curious accompanying urge to marry), much of their waking time is spent in ways oddly out of character for such a compulsion. They flit from house to house talking foolishness[84] and being busybodies, and they are lazy. None of this may require restriction to female quarters, but it would most naturally suggest at least a good deal of time spent with other women present. Their sexual obsession seems remarkably restrained for at least much of each day. It is not obvious in what way such transparent idleness and gossip, both of which must inevitably discourage eligible men, would serve their apparently overwhelming physical need. Widows intent upon locating a respectable marital cover for their newly awakened desire would more productively be engaged in either assuming the appearance of matronly respectability, or frequenting places where men are more likely to be found.

---

84. Fee 1984: 83; 1985: 144 n. 9. Some suggest the 'gadding about' is related to pastoral-type visitation (e.g. Ellicott 1864: 76; Barrett 1963: 76; Dibelius and Conzelmann 1972: 75; Kelly 1972: 118; Stählin 1974: 455; D.R. MacDonald 1979: 177, 179), but, as argued above, no official order is identifiable. See also e.g. Müller-Bardorff 1958: 123; Brox 1969: 195. Oberlinner (1994: 239-40, 245-46) claims that λαλέω in the widest possible sense involves proclamation and pastoral care, but draws upon Tit. 1.11 ἃ μὴ δεῖ for interpretation via false teachers of τὰ μὴ δέοντα and speculates 'wobei *möglicherweise* ein Teil dieser Frauen gnostisch beeinflusst war' ('whereby *possibly* some of these women were...gnostically... influenced', emphasis mine), admitting '[e]s fehlt allerdings ein ausdrücklicher Hinweis darauf, dass der Verfasser die Witwen tatsächlich in die Nähe der von ihm so massiv bekämpften gnostischen Irrleher rücken wollte' ('What is missing though, is an explicit reference to the author actually intending to position the widows in the vicinity of the gnostic heresies which he was so strongly fighting against'). Ellicott observes that the idle habits are acquired through the running from house to house rather than the more likely reverse, but whilst his translation 'they learn to be idle, going about...etc.' is persuasive (see also Dibelius and Conzelmann 1972: 75; Alford 1862: 349; but cf. the less persuasive Humphreys 1901: 129), the participle together with ἅμα indicates coincidental action. Holtz (1965: 120) and A.T. Hanson (1966: 60) suggest, and Müller-Bardorff (1958: 123) rejects, the idea that περίεργοι, λαλοῦσαι τὰ μὴ δέοντα hints at magical spells.

(c) The age of some of these widows is remarkably advanced.[85] Some interpret the Author as simply believing that passion or lust is more common amongst younger than older widows,[86] but those excluded from the list on the grounds that they are likely to become lustful are younger than 60. They are not necessarily 'young'.[87] It has been argued that νεωτέρας here refers to the younger of the excluded widows.[88] This fails, however, to take into account not only that those no longer young but not yet 60 would then be unmentioned, but that v. 11a reverses the instruction at v. 9 to enrol only those not less than 60. It seems that widows right up to 59 years of age are to be excluded on the ground of their liability to wantonness. The indefinite clause and its projected result associated with participial and ὅτι clauses (v. 11b, c,

85. Knight (1992: 222) notes the significance of the age criterion in first place in the list of qualifications (vv. 9-10), emphasized form (μὴ ἔλαττον), and reiteration (v. 11). Porter (1989a: 249) interprets the Perfect as marking the primary requirement. Kajanto (1968: 16-17) points out that in antiquity precise age may not always be known.

86. Plummer 1888: 160; Dibelius and Conzelmann 1972: 40; Hurley 1981: 136; Verner 1983: 165-66; P.H. Towner 1989: 185. Kelly (1972: 116-18) speaks here of women still 'in the prime of life', 'at a…susceptible age', 'still active and full of energy', and 'young enough to be in the social swim', Stählin (1974: 454) of 'women who still have much of life before them', and Müller-Bardorff (1958: 119) says 'das sexuelle Brennen jener Frauen in der Vollkraft ihres Leibes zum Ausdruck bringt' ('gives expression to the sexual arousal of those women in the full bloom of their body').

87. Scott 1936: 61. Contra e.g. 'in the natural exuberance of physical life' (Parry 1920: 32); Hendriksen 1955: 176; Fee 1985: 146; M.Y. MacDonald 1988: 167-68, 180, 186-89; 'incontinent' (Guthrie 1990: 116). Knight (1992: 225) indicates that, although νεωτέρας implies those up to 60, the primary focus is in v. 14 (remarriage and child-bearing). He nowhere addresses those well under 60 but past the activities so focused. Nor does Scholer (1986: 197). D.R. MacDonald (1979: 178-79) concludes that at v. 14 marriage (not re-marriage) is urged upon only these 'young' members of the widow's order which itself furnishes the tellers of oral traditions the Author is attempting to silence. Building upon his historical foundation already based on sources other than this text (cf. n. 55), MacDonald further distorts the letter by: i. this separation of widows; ii. suggestions that Ephesian bearers of myths and genealogies (1.3-4, 6-7) are older widows; iii. his inference from 4.7 that only women tell such stories (although even the addressee is warned against them), which he links with asceticism not even clearly yet taught; and iv. support of the whole by selection from Titus 2 of vv. 3-5 but not 2, 6-7a.

88. E.g. Ellicott 1864: 74, 77; Liddon 1897: 58; Bernard 1899: 82; Humphreys 1901: 129; Parry 1920: 32.

12) clearly do not argue that *all* under 60, when honoured by enrolment on the list, behave wantonly towards Christ and so want to marry. Nevertheless, v. 11a does not deny enrolment only to the sexually wanton, but to all under 60. This implies that, when widows up to 59 have been enrolled, sexual wantonness accompanied by the urge to remarry has been such a common development that it has been found necessary to restrict the list to those 60 and over. The bizarre nature of what is involved here must be squarely faced.

Such explanations as are offered as to why 60 should be the minimum are speculative. Some simply state or assume that 60 was considered the beginning of old age.[89] Some note that 60 was the age set for priests and priestesses in Plato's ideal state,[90] and that orientals thought it the appropriate age for contemplative retirement.[91] Others cannot help sensibly observing that people over 60 are not less inclined to gossip and be idle.[92] It has been suggested that women were considered capable of working until the age of 60 (Winter 1988a: 95 n. 63). It is true that many aged women were midwives, nurses, doorkeepers, saleswomen etc.,[93] so it is not difficult to see why 60 might be seen as a suitable age for retirement. Nevertheless, since death and incapacity were for the lower classes the only perceived dividing-lines between work and retirement (Finley 1981: 160, 168), such an arrangement would be, to say the least, innovative. The problem is: *why should the age of 60 be thought to mark (even approximately) a transition from a condition in which honour bestowed by the assembly would so frequently result in physical desire compelling marriage that it is deemed advisable to exclude all widows under that age?* It has been suggested that at 60 a woman's sexual passions might be thought less dangerous,[94] that she

89. E.g. Parry 1920: 31; Brox 1969: 190; Fee 1984: 80; Oberlinner (1994: 231) citing Str–B, III, 653.

90. Lock (1924: 59) citing *Laws* 759 D; Barclay 1975: 109.

91. Lock (1924: 59) cites Ramsay, *Expositor* 1910: 439. Oden 1989: 156. See also Kelly 1972: 115; Barclay 1975: 109. Knight (1992: 222-23) cites both arguments and Str–B, III, 653, but the role he has in mind is clearly not contemplative.

92. Scott 1936: 62; Kelly 1972: 118; Guthrie 1990: 116.

93. Henderson 1987: 121-25; Bremmer 1987: 197, 200. Contra those arguing it was 'next to impossible' for widows or single women to earn their living except by prostitution, e.g. Bartsch 1965: 128; Barclay 1975: 114, 250; Guthrie 1990: 111, 113.

94. Kelly 1972: 115. See also Bartsch 1965: 129; Thurston 1989: 47.

would have abandoned the idea of remarriage,[95] or that 'worldly pleasures' and interests would cease to beckon (Scott 1936: 60). The literature of antiquity plainly describes some aged women living self-indulgently.[96] Why should we believe that the Author imagines that at (at least approximately) the age of 60 (not 50, or 40, or 70) widows would no longer be attracted by frivolous activities, or that their sexuality has lately waned?

Just as old men in antiquity were sometimes ridiculed and treated with contempt,[97] old women were sometimes mocked and portrayed as lustful and/or drunken,[98] but they were more often represented sympathetically (Henderson 1987: *passim*). Not everyone imagined them to be lustful, and *univirae*, although highly regarded, were not unusual.[99] The Author wants older women treated as mothers (1 Tim. 5.2), and believes them capable of all kinds of good deeds (5.10) and constant prayer (5.5). Elsewhere he considers them appropriate teachers for younger women (Tit. 2.3). Overall he deals with them as rational people, like older men and young men and women (1 Tim. 5.1-2; Tit. 2.2-10) capable of responding to moral teaching. He does not seem to have a low opinion of them. Moreover, the normal female ageing process suggests that it is not only improbable but impossible that he believes them to be so commonly sexually wanton as is implied by the traditional interpretation of 1 Tim. 5.11.

Few of either sex lived until 60 in antiquity,[100] but in relation to this passage a consideration of the physical condition of those women who did is long overdue. The literature ignores the subject, and some facts appear to need plain statement. In developed societies during the last century the median age of menopause has been—with considerable variation—around 50. In Third World societies, probably because of

95. Lock 1924: 59; Easton 1948: 153; Fee 1984: 80; Oden 1989: 156; Knight 1992: 223.

96. Bremmer 1987: 201-202, 204-205; Henderson 1987: 118-20; Dixon 1992: 156, 238 nn. 121, 122.

97. Henderson 1987: 110; Dixon 1992: 152.

98. Finley 1981: 164-65; Griffin 1985: 21-22; Henderson 1987: 110, 117-20; Esler 1989: 172-82; Dixon 1992: 152; Brecht n.d.: 64-65.

99. Lightman and Zeisel 1977: 19-32; Dixon 1992: 152. Note e.g. Lk. 2.36-38.

100. Barrett 1963: 75. Dixon (1992: 145-46, 149-50, 235 nn. 82, 85) writes that few lived to see their grandchildren, the median life expectancy being around 37 for men and 27 for women. See also Finley 1981: 156-71. Cf. Dean-Jones (1994: 106) who sets the average female lifespan at 36–37.

differing health and nutrition, and again with considerable variation, it may be several years earlier.[101] Ancient evidence conforms with these patterns. Amundsen and Diers cite six sources, claiming that the later three present the best evidence. Oribasius[102] (fourth-century CE) sets it around the fiftieth year, with very few as late as 60, but the obese from about 35; Aetius[103] (sixth-century CE) at 35–50 with few at 60; Paulus Aegineta[104] (seventh-century CE) either quoting Oribasius or a common source. The other three sources are, however, instructive. Aristotle[105] (fourth-century BCE) sets it at around 40, Pliny the Elder[106] (first-century CE) the majority at 40, and Soranus[107] (first- to second-century CE) the majority between 40 and 50. In the classical period a woman was considered old when she stopped bearing children and was no longer a source of anxiety for the men of her household. At 40 women were credited with reliability, gaining them a degree of autonomy (Henderson 1987: 108). This implies that, in the classical period, at 40 most women had stopped bearing children.

At a conservative estimate more than half the women living to 60 in the first to second century CE would have been post-menopausal for ten to twenty years, some for longer, and most of the remainder for 5–9 years. Even a high proportion of those rare late 50 year olds still peri-menopausal would be feeling the usual results of decreased oestrogen.[108] Ancient medical records say little about the subject. Dean-Jones, who groups together all conditions associated with menopause, argues that since it signalled reassimilation to the more tractable male

---

101. E.g. WHO 1981: 17-20; van Keep 1983: 11; Greene 1984: 3; Goodman 1990: 137-38; Kono *et al.* 1990: 43-49; Sukwatana *et al.* 1991: 217-28; Moore and Kombe 1991: 229-34. Some claim increased numbers of pregnancies or extraordinary environmental conditions may extend the median age for a year or two, but this remains unproven.

102. Amundsen and Diers (1970: 82) citing *Eclogae medicamentorum* 142.

103. Amundsen and Diers (1970: 82) citing *Tetrabiblos* XVI.4.

104. Amundsen and Diers (1970: 83) citing *Epitome* III.60.

105. Amundsen and Diers (1970: 80) citing *Historia animalium* VII.5.585a, and note the possibility of third-century BCE pseudepigraphic authorship. Cf. Dean-Jones (1994: 106), who cites *HA* 545b.26-31 as putting the age at 45-50.

106. Amundsen and Diers (1970: 81) citing *Hist. nat.* VII.14.61.

107. Amundsen and Diers (1970: 82) citing *Gynaeciorum* I.4.20.

108. Mackay *et al.* (1983: 85) report that today at least 75–85% experience significant symptoms.

body no medical explanation was required, and women saw compensations in their changing status and therefore suffered few difficulties (1994: 106-108). Post-menopausal problems, however, fall into two categories: those caused by oestrogen depletion, and those which may be caused by coincidental life changes or cultural expectations.[109] The silence in ancient medical writings could suggest that women accepted conditions related to the former as signs of a new liberty from childbearing, or that they consulted each other.[110] It could also mean that male doctors were concerned with women only as they affected the lives of men,[111] and many post-menopausal women would already be widowed. Whatever their cultural expectations, long before the age of 60 many would experience symptoms almost certainly common to all races, cultures and classes.[112] They would be unable to conceive the

109. Danforth *et al.*, 1977: 183; Steiner 1983: 152. See also Cooper 1976: 34; WHO 1981: 23-35; Greene 1984: 5; Whitbourne 1985: 109-11.

110. See e.g. Rousselle 1988: 24-25.

111. Rousselle (1988: 25-27) claims that doctors had little knowledge of female reproductive organs, there being only two cases of vaginal examination in the Hippocratic Collection. Soranus says he writes essentially for the midwives, who were the ones with access to female patients. Rousselle (p. 40) calls his gynaecological writings and those of Rufus of Ephesus 'manuals on fertilization written for husbands'.

112. Recent studies show that a phytoestrogen-rich diet (e.g. soy, linseed and to a lesser extent rye) may prevent such symptoms. See Murkies *et al.* 1995: 189-95; Pansini *et al.* 1996: P312; Dalais *et al.* 1996: P315; Murkies *et al.* 1998: 297-303. In antiquity such a diet would not have been common: Fussell 1965: 20-21; Cowell 1972: 77; Heiser 1981: 73; Rawson 1986b: 426; Sauer 1994: 70-71, 222-23. Palaeopathological studies so far yield little relevant information for antiquity (e.g. Bisel 1980: 41-43, 48-59; 1984: 598-606; 1986: 11-23; 1987: 123-29; M. Grant 1990: 121-24), but slight to moderate arthritis was fairly common (Bisel 1986: 15; 1987: 125). Mackay *et al.* (1983: 88-89) report that today, by the age of 60, 25% of women suffer compression fractures of the vertebrae. For the (today) relatively common vaginitis (Mackay *et al.* p. 87) in antiquity see e.g. Bremmer 1987: 203; Esler 1989: 172-73. For other likely difficulties see Novak *et al.* 1972: 629, 631; Danforth *et al.* 1977: 179. Dean-Jones (1994: 108) refers to some cultures in which women view menopause positively and report few symptoms, but her source (Flint 1982) does not discuss vaginitis, dyspareunia etc. Flint (pp. 364-70) says that although the First International Congress on Menopause (1976) identified universal symptoms, her own study of 483 women of the Rajput caste (1975) found few, so she concludes that culture defines what symptoms will be exhibited. Whilst this is undoubtedly to some extent true, some Rajput women did report some symptoms. Even if they had not there is a considerable leap from the failure of one group to

children Augustus's remarriage laws were designed to produce. Some would almost certainly choose to avoid remarriage. Post-menopausal widows manifesting a compulsive sexual wantonness could scarcely be the norm. Modern surveys find degrees of lessening sexual interest in both men and women from about the age of 50,[113] and there is no reason to think that this did not occur in antiquity.

It therefore seems impossible that such a proportion of widows up to the age of 60 should be thought to have proven sexually wanton as is implied in the usual reading of 1 Timothy 5. In fact, it seems very likely that *univirae* would include not only those choosing to remain faithful to deceased husbands but a significant number already post-menopausal and therefore either unsuitable as prospective child-bearers or simply preferring to remain single.[114] Should the Author be ignorant of any of this, it nevertheless seems incredible that someone who elsewhere treats ageing women as normal human beings should think widows of any age—let alone the middle to (in that era) advanced aged—so commonly prone to compulsive lust as to prompt an across-the-board exclusion from any kind of list. Nor does it seem credible that anyone at all should choose the advanced age of 60 as the approximate point at which the widow's sexual fire finally burns itself out.

If, however, the wantonness is self-indulgent, each of the above three problems dissolves: self-indulgence would obviously be directed against Christ but towards no third party; no pledge of celibacy is required to make sense of the passage;[115] and the advanced age of some excluded widows causes no difficulty. Whilst it is unlikely that honour and

report any to the conclusion that all such symptoms are due to cultural values and attitudes. Suggestions made above about ancient medical records could be relevant for unreported symptoms in some twentieth-century cultures. Datan *et al.* (1981: 149) report that 47% Arab and 43% North African respondents thought the worst thing about menopause was its effects on physical health (pp. 103, 85), and that 49% Arab and 41% North African respondents found less pleasure in sexual relations after menopause (p. 177).

113. Mackay *et al.* 1983: 88; Steiner 1983: 156; Semmens 1983: 173-80; Bachmann and Leiblum 1991: 47; Sukwatana *et al.* 1991: 225.

114. Lightman and Zeisal (1977: 31) note that claims to faithfulness may mask preference for singleness.

115. The idea that a pledge is made to Christ as bridegroom is therefore superfluous, contra e.g. Leipoldt 1953: 136; Holtz 1965: 119; Kelly 1972: 117; Stählin 1974: 454; Houlden 1976: 94; Oden 1989: 158.

support by the assembly of many widows up to the age of 60 could be thought so frequently to lead to their becoming sexual wantons, it is easy to see that it could be thought that, without families to care for them (and for whom to care), many so honoured would be likely to become self-indulgent. Self-indulgence is the natural environment for idleness and foolish talk, and is here envisaged as developing an ongoing (θέλουσιν) desire for marriage. The benefits of that state may be perceived variously as social, household, economic or sexual, but the key factor here is that the desire springs from self-indulgence. This obviously could be thought to constitute an additional alienation from Christ. There may be no realistic hope of achieving the goal. Always supposing that suitable husbands are readily available, and this seems unlikely (Rawson [ed.] 1986: 53 n. 94), those of any age without dowries[116] and those post-menopausal even at 35–45 must have difficulty finding them.[117] However, the dream or plan to marry results from an alienation from Christ encouraged by idleness and foolish talk, and may well disregard reality. The primary offence is that featured in v. 6[118] where a 'living death' parallels the alienation and judgment of v. 13. The contrast is consistently between widows worthy of honour and self-indulgent widows.

Since v. 14 urges remarriage and 4.2-5 opposes asceticism, as noted above ἑνὸς ἀνδρὸς γυνή (v. 9) already seems likely to mean 'a woman faithful to her husband during his lifetime'. This probability is confirmed by the fact that when the 'wantonness' is envisaged as self-indulgent the much-touted 'vow of celibacy' has no foundation. There is no reason to suppose that those widowed more than once are disqualified from the list.

As signalled by its unified structure, then, 1 Tim. 5.3-16 deals with one major topic: widows to be honoured as aged parents—those eligible to be honoured by the assembly, those who should be honoured by

116. Winter (1988a: 97) points out that the direction to remarry (v. 14) presupposes its existence. Rawson (ed.) (1986: 53 n. 94) says that insufficient is known about mortality rates for certainty about the remarriage market.

117. At v. 14a the Author may counsel those widows *who can* to remarry and bear children.

118. Humphreys (1901: 126, 129) makes this connection, but links the idea of lust. Fee (1984: 79) says vv. 11-13 expose in detail the self-indulgence at v. 6. Stählin (1974: 454) cites Ps. Ign. *Ad Antiochenses* 11.1: αἱ χῆραι μὴ σπαταλάτωσαν, ἵνα μὴ καταστρηνιάσωσι τοῦ λόγου.

responsible κύριοι or πισταί, and those ineligible for the honour.
Rejection of marriage is not an issue.

5.2. *Location of the Widows*

I now turn to the second difficulty commonly underlying exegesis of
1 Tim. 5.11-15: the questionable nature of the assumption that a regional problem is addressed.

The Author, although obviously concerned about conditions at the
place of address, makes extensive use of traditional material.[119] It is
widely agreed that he adapts the Christian Household Code—not only
at 2.9-12; 3.1-13, 15 and 6.1-2 but also at 5.1-20 (notably vv. 1-3)—to
the point where it is difficult to identify just where that code starts and
finishes.[120] It is also widely agreed that this extensive adaptation leaves
clear traces of the characteristic concern of that code that wives, slaves
and children should submit to the hierarchical structures of contemporary society (cf. Eph. 5.21–6.9; Col. 3.18–4.1 and 1 Pet. 2.13–3.7).[121]
One such reflection is commonly identified at 1 Tim. 5.14.[122] But is an
existing code used in 5.1-16 with a local situation in mind? Even
though teaching about widows is unknown in non-Christian duty-lists
(Dibelius and Conzelmann 1972: 73), and appears nowhere else in the
New Testament,[123] it will be argued below that the Author freely adapts

119. E.g. Ellis 1987: *passim*. In the Pastoral Epistles generally Dibelius and
Conzelmann (1972: 6) cite e.g. 2.8; 5.1-2, 5f.; 6.1ff.; Tit. 2.1-6, 7f., 9f. P.H. Towner
(1989: 29) notes the sometimes modified traditional formulations scattered throughout the letters. Easton (1948: 15-16) lists citations from Old Testament, New Testament, hymns, liturgy, doxologies, hellenistic sources, popular sayings and ethical
lists. A.T. Hanson (1966: 15-16) believes the theological language quotes hymns,
creeds, liturgy, and much of the moral-teaching contemporary pagan ethics. See
also 1982: 42-45.

120. For the Pastorals see e.g. Donelson 1986: 176-77 with n. 162. For
1 Timothy generally see Crouch 1972: 12; P.H. Towner 1989: 170-71. See also
Fung (1987: 338 n. 200), who says 2.8-12 is '*Haustafel*-like'. For the widows see
Müller-Bardorff (1958: 113 and n. 5, 121 n. 18), who suggests that traditions lie
behind v. 8 and (less confidently) v. 10b; Bartsch (1965: 13, 128), who identifies
evidence of tradition in vv. 4, 7, 15, 16; Stählin (1974: 455), who suggests that v. 3
may be a traditional rule; and Verner 1983: 23, 95, 99, 101, 106.

121. E.g. Kamlah 1970: 241 n. 14; Crouch 1972: 12, 29. See also Lock 1924: xv-
xvi.

122. E.g. Byrne 1988: 90.

123. Acts 6.1-7 reports on organization for their care.

known Christian views about conditions anticipated at any location. He may very well be aware that some at the place/s of address are in need of such instruction, but nothing suggests this is the chief reason he writes this section. On the contrary, he is concerned to pass on widely accepted principles for commonly encountered problems.

But what *are* the principles he passes on? Various attempts have been made to define the nature and primary concern of this type of instruction.[124] Although the conflicting theses[125] do not establish the process by which the New Testament codes developed (Verner 1983: 22), it is generally agreed that 1 Tim. 5.1-3 adapts such a code in the context of the life of the *ekklesia*, and that v. 14 reflects ideas widely accepted as characteristic of it, that is, that women are expected to be domestic and subordinate. The primary concern of the Christian Household Code, however, is more profound than the subordination of wives, slaves and children. Crouch and Balch, both of whom have made a significant con-

---

124. For a full discussion see Crouch (1972: 9-21). See also Verner (1983: 16-25).

125. Dibelius and Greeven (1976: xi-xii) say paraenesis is traditional: e.g. in James local conditions are undetectable; and Dibelius (1964: 239) says that in Paul's letters 'Vor allem fehlt ihnen eine unmittelbare Beziehung auf die Briefsituation. Die Regeln und Weisungen sind nicht für bestimmte Gemeinden und konkrete Fälle formuliert, sondern für die allgemeinen Bedürfnisse der ältesten Christenheit. Sie haben nicht aktuelle, sondern usuelle Bedeutung' ('Above all they lack any immediate relation to the situation of the letter. The rules and instructions are not formulated for particular congregations and actual cases in point but for the general needs of oldest Christendom. Their importance is not actual but usual') (see also the more cautious Schrage 1974: 3); (1975: 149) in the Pastorals' instruction (incl. for widows) is 'nicht für den Moment, sondern für...die Dauer des Gemeindelebens' ('not for the moment, but for...the duration of congregational life'). Weidinger (1928: 12-13, 18-19, 48-50) and Dibelius (1953: 49) claim codes were developed from Stoic duty lists in the interests of conformity because of the delayed *parousia*. For those concurring see Crouch (1972: 21 n. 42). Rengstorf (1953: 136-37) says codes concern the οἶκος and emphasize household heads. See further re n. 128. Schroeder (1959: 88-89) finds subordinates and their protection foremost. Crouch (1972: e.g. 144, 149) sees emphasis on subordinates, and identifies Jewish and Stoic ethics and distinctively Christian reciprocity, claiming the codes counter excesses by women and slaves resulting from Gal. 3.28. Balch (1981: 81-116) sources codes in the ancient topos on household management already influential among Jews and, via 1 Pet. 2.13-17, identifies a focus on that part of the Graeco-Roman ethic which Christians were accused of violating and governors were concerned to preserve.

tribution to the question in the last generation, consider the characteristics of those codes in reference to their development.

Crouch convincingly demonstrates their hellenistic Jewish heritage and (like Dibelius and Weidinger) believes they do not necessarily reveal conditions at the place addressed. Their relatively late appearance and the non-existence of others with precisely the same concerns leads him to assume a general situation in the hellenistic assemblies giving rise to the Christian form, it being legitimate to speak of an 'occasion' for which existing ethical material was adapted (Crouch 1972: 120-21): that is, excessive enthusiasm by women and slaves. Of course, if Ephesians and Colossians are judged to be genuinely Pauline, and 1 Peter genuinely Petrine, the origin of these codes must lie in early Judaic Christianity, not in the general situation of later assemblies. If Ephesians and Colossians are viewed as deutero-Pauline the ideas may yet be Paul's own and therefore an early development.[126] 1 Peter is commonly said to draw heavily upon Paul.[127] But if the codes *are* judged a later development, not only has Crouch downplayed the important role of the household (Kidd 1990: 79) but, based upon passages from 1 Corinthians and the Pastorals, his claim that the motivating cause is excessive enthusiasm by women and slaves is unconvincing.

His foundation is twofold:

(a) the major emphasis of the New Testament codes is upon subordinate parties; and

(b) the demands of the codes are similar to 1 Cor. 7.20—ἕκαστος ἐν τῇ κλήσει ᾗ ἐκλήθη, ἐν ταύτῃ μενέτω being the principle Paul applies whenever the social order is threatened by outbursts of religious enthusiasm (1972: 121-23).

Crouch's (a) is simplistic and, although (b) is accurate, it leads him to unconvincing conclusions. Since both (a) and (b) touch upon concepts which appear again and again in interpretations of New Testament passages on women, detailed demonstration of my claims is called for here. Crouch provides the departure point to which I return several

---

126. M.Y. MacDonald (1988: 102-105, 117-18) argues that the codes do not stand out sharply as non-Pauline.

127. E.g. Hort 1898: 4-5; Selwyn 1946: 21; Beare 1958: 25; Marshall 1991: 20; Goppelt 1993: 30.

times for discussion on (a), and remains more steadily the focus of attention for (b).

(a) A number of scholars argue that the true focus of the New Testament code is fundamentally different from pre-Christian parallels.[128] Some go so far as to claim that the subordination required is of a different kind.[129] Crouch declares that attempts to bestow upon ὑποτάσ- σεσθαι a specifically Christian flavour are only an appeasement of modern sensitivities. For him, the essence of what the New Testament demands of wives is the same view displayed by Josephus (*Apion*

---

128. E.g. Rengstorf 1953: 132; 1954: 31-32.

129. Kähler (1959: 7, 10; 1960: 82, 156) via 1 Cor. 15.23-28 rejects the degrada- tion of ὑποτάσσεσθαι 'zu einem Befehls- und Gehorsamswort' ('to an imperative and obedience term', 1959: 10-12) 'Der Mann wird in seinem Sollen fast über- fordert: wie könnte er seine Frau *so* lieben, wie Christus seine Gemeinde geliebt hat!...Die Frau ist nicht dem Manne "ausgeliefert", sondern Christus, wie auch der Mann in seiner Liebe nicht der Frau "ausgeliefert" ist, sondern Christus' ('The man is nearly overtaxed in what he is supposed to do; how could he love his wife *in the way* that Christ loved his congregation! ...The wife is not "at the mercy" of the husband but of Christ, just as the husband, too, in his love is not "at the mercy" of the wife but of Christ') (emphasis hers), but does not find this kind of relationship in the Pastorals, believing the balance of 1 Corinthians 7 and Eph. 5.21 is there disturbed, ὑποτάσσεσθαι now 'eine starr festgelegte, die Frau degradierende "Seinsordnung"' ('a rigidly fixed "order of being" which degrades the wife'). See also Wendland 1970: 97; Schrage 1974: 12 n. 1. See however Kähler 1960: 156, 170. Müller (1989: 295) points out, however, that it is precisely at 1 Cor. 15.27 that ὑποτάσσεσθαι 'hat...den unbestreitbar aggressiven Sinn gewaltsamer und sieg- reicher Unterwerfung' ('has...the indisputably aggressive sense of forcible and victorious subjugation'). Goppelt (1972: 289-93 with n. 7; 1982: 168-71) and Yoder (1982: 174-75) argue that the codes accept contemporary social orders, and focus more on the root of ὑποτάσσεσθαι than the prefix. Goppelt highlights the flexibility of such a principle and its fostering of responsible, critical conduct, and Yoder the new and meaningful motivation, the revolutionary implications of recognition of subordinates as moral agents, and their first placement. See also Balch 1981: 90. Müller (p. 297), however, demonstrates that in pre-Christian antiquity ὑποτάσ- σεσθαι should not be accused of being 'en bloc eine autoritäre und ungemilderte Sozialethik' ('en bloc an authoritarian and unmitigated social ethics'). See further below. Kroeger (1987b: 280-82) draws attention to difficulties faced by the first- century Christian whose marriage was *sine manu* and the wife's father a pagan, suggesting that the codes urge such a wife to membership of her husband's house- hold, 'identifying with' him, or 'coming under his influence' (citing Rom. 8.20; Lk. 2.41-51). Despite shedding light on such marriages, Kroeger here goes well beyond the text of the Household Codes.

2.201): woman is in all things inferior to man and must obediently be directed by his God-given authority (1972: 10, 29, 31, 109-11 incl. n. 61, 121-22, 149). But whilst ὑποτάσσεσθαι and ἀγάπη themselves are not specifically Christian, their contexts here make them so. Schrage correctly says that the focus of the New Testament code is upon the humility required by both members, Christ

> die entscheidende Instanz und eigentliche Bezugsgrösse der Haustafel-mahnungen. Er ist nicht nur das Motiv, sondern auch das Urbild, das dem Verhalten in den Strukturen der Welt Richtung und Orientierung gibt...[S]pielt...die Christus- Konformität eine nicht unerhebliche Rolle...κατὰ Χριστόν mit κατὰ ἀγάπην wechseln kann... Einmal soll der Gehorsam gegenüber den übergeordneten Instanzen...begründet werden,...Zum anderen aber sollen die Träger familiärer oder staatlicher Autorität daran errinnert werden, Gott nachzuahmen.[130]

> the decisive authority and real reference force of the Household Table exhortations. He is not only the motif but also the archetype which gives direction and orientation for behaviour in the structures of the world. Thereby lies within the Household Table probably a truly two-fold connection. On the one hand there is already in Paul the Christ con-formity playing a not unimportant role... κατὰ Χριστόν with κατὰ ἀγάπην can alternate... On the one hand obedience to the higher author-ities...is to be justified...on the other hand, however, the bearers of family or state authority are to be reminded to imitate God.

Presumably referring partly to codes or passages reflecting codes, Judge writes that Paul's generalizations about government, slavery or mar-riage always have Christ as their starting-point and behaviour as their end, and all proposed social relations derive from the mystery of sacri-fice and service. None matters in the Kingdom, but none need be destroyed at all costs, all providing occasion to surrender one's own interest for the sake of others (1974: 193, 203).

Crouch ignores clear implications of submission as it appears in the New Testament. At Eph. 5.21–6.9, although outworking variously and realistically, and falling short of suggesting equality, it is intended to be mutual.[131] 1 Peter 2.13a, best translated 'submit yourselves to every

---

130. Schrage 1974: 15-16. See also Schroeder 1959: 122-31; Kamlah 1970: 237-43; Wendland 1970: 93, 103; Yoder 1982: 180-82; Goppelt 1973: 105.

131. E.g. Kähler 1959: 7; Schrage 1974: 12. Contra e.g. Stouffer (1981: 13) who, although seeing the emphasis on 'in the Lord', claims care is taken 'not to upset the delicate cultural fabric' of the day; and M.Y. MacDonald (1988: 105, 118), who

human creature...'[132] (not '...to every authority instituted among men...'),[133] presents the first of a series of examples for vv. 11-12,[134] with submission an expression of the humility expected of all for others.[135] Teaching about self-submission is characteristic of Christianity throughout the New Testament (e.g. Mt. 5.38-41; 20.25-27; Jn 13.1, 12-15; Rom. 13.1-5; 1 Cor. 6.7-8; Phil. 2.3-8; Tit. 3.1-2). Comparison of 1 Tim. 6.1 (cf. 1 Pet. 2.18) with Rom. 12.10 (cf. 1 Pet. 3.8) and 1 Pet. 3.7 reveals that the honour the slave should show the master, and the husband his wife, is that which all should show others.[136]

Such mutual submission obviously is not meant to be mindless (Mk 12.17; Acts 4.19; 5.29; 16.36-37; 1 Pet. 2.20b-25; cf. e.g. 1 Sam. 25.14-42, and see also Col. 3.22; Eph. 6.5-6).[137] Schrage identifies in the New Testament House Codes 'eine wesentlich kritischere Weltsicht' ('a substantially more critical world view') free of 'kriecherischer Servilität und unkritischem Untertanengeist' ('grovelling servility and uncritical subservient spirit'). Christians are not to be ἀνθρωπάρεσκοι to their earthly lords, 'die denn auch durch den Zusatz κατὰ σάρκα...eine deutliche Abwertung erfahren' ('who then also through the addition of κατὰ σάρκα...experience a marked devaluation'). Moreover, 'die Annahme

claims the divinely ordained subjection of wife to husband is stressed, the 'clearly stated aim' a justification and clarification of v. 22.

132. Bartsch 1965: 175 and n. 22; Kamlah 1970: 237; Kelly 1972: 130; Foerster 1977: 1034-35; E.A. Blum 1981: 233; Porter 1990b: 121.

133. As e.g. Balch 1981: 96; M.Y. MacDonald 1988: 107. See also 'every ordinance of man' (AV); 'every human authority' (TEV); 'every man-made authority' (Phillips); 'the authority of every social institution' (JB); 'every human institution' or similar (RSV, NEB, NASB).

134. See also Schrage 1974: 12; Balch 1981: 98.

135. Kamlah (1970: 242-43) notes that James at 4.6 cites Prov. 3.34 Ὁ θεὸς ὑπερηφάνοις ἀντιτάσσεται, ταπεινοῖς δὲ δίδωσιν χάριν, the immediately following οὖν indicating that submission to God is an expression of that humility. At 1 Pet. 5.5c (towards the close of this long section exhorting to self-submission; see esp. v. 5a linked by ὁμοίως to the service of the overseer for his flock vv. 1-4) he notes that the same Proverb is cited, the subject at vv. 5b and 6a again humility.

136. Kamlah 1970: 243. Recognition that in the New Testament the instruction to submit oneself means to honour/show humility does not, as Crouch (1972: 31) implies, necessarily involve the ameliorating concept that the submission is contingent upon the love/care received, nor the love/care upon the submission. The instruction to each, although to be interpreted in light of that to the other, is an appropriate, personal, independent responsibility.

137. For Rom. 13.1-5 see Porter 1990b: 115-39.

einer völligen Kongruenz von urchristlicher und antiker Ethik verbietet'
('the acceptance of a total agreement of early Christian and classical
ethics is forbidden'): Plutarch takes subordination so far as to forbid a
wife to have gods other than those of her husband (*Praec. coniug.* 19),
but 1 Pet. 3.1 encourages submissive wives to win their husbands to the
faith (Schrage 1974: 10-12).

Even the submission of contemporary social structures was not as
rigid as it is commonly represented, being considered possible even in
the act of disobeying bad parental advice.[138] Plutarch's oft-quoted *Mor.*
142.33 is instructive:

> τοῦτο συμβαίνει καὶ περὶ τὰς γυναῖκας. ὑποτάττουσαι μὲν γὰρ
> ἑαυτὰς τοῖς ἀνδράσιν ἐπαινοῦνται, κρατεῖν δὲ βουλόμεναι μᾶλλον
> τῶν κρατουμένων ἀσχημονοῦσι. κρατεῖν δὲ δεῖ τὸν ἄνδρα τῆς γυναι-
> κὸς οὐχ ὡς δεσπότην κτήματος ἀλλ᾽ ὡς ψυχὴν σώματος, συμπαθοῦντα
> καὶ συμπεφυκότα τῇ εὐνοίᾳ. ὥσπερ οὖν σώματος ἔστι κήδεσθαι μὴ
> δουλεύοντα ταῖς ἡδοναῖς αὐτοῦ καὶ ταῖς ἐπιθυμίαις, οὕτω γυναικὸς
> ἄρχειν εὐφραίνοντα καὶ χαριζόμενον.

> So it is with women also; if they subordinate themselves to their hus-
> bands, they are commended, but if they want to have control, they cut a
> sorrier figure than the subjects of their control. And control ought to be
> exercised by the man over the woman, not as the owner has control of a
> piece of property, but, as the soul controls the body, by entering into her
> feelings and being knit to her through goodwill. As, therefore, it is pos-
> sible to exercise care over the body without being a slave to its pleasures
> and desires, so it is possible to govern a wife, and at the same time to
> delight and gratify her.

Balch properly argues that Plutarch here adheres to subordination even
though elsewhere he argues for some equality (1981: 141-47). Nevertheless, βουλόμεναι indicates that Plutarch's objection is to a *continuously* controlling woman, and he is careful to define with some
delicacy the control he believes the husband should exercise. His primary concern is not to uphold the right of the husband to that control,
but to moderate an assumed control in such a way that it would be neither domineering nor even necessarily one way.[139] In accordance with

---

138. Balch (1981: 99-100) cites Musonius, *Must One Obey one's Parents under
All Circumstances?* (*Or.* XVI 85, 15-86, 8 Hense; 104, 9-21 Lutz; 86, 19 and 87, 8-
10 Hense; 104, 30 and 104, 37-106, 1 Lutz).

139. Hillard (1989: 165-82) argues that women whose actions could be interpreted as consistently domineering were a political liability to their menfolk.

my observation here, Müller identifies other contemporary examples of 'einen pragmatischen Mittelweg...eine verantwortungsvoll ausbalancierte Stellungnahme für ein gemässigt fortschrittliches und milde humanisiertes sozialethisches Verhaltensmuster' ('a pragmatic middle course...a responsibly balanced statement for a moderately progressive and mildly humanized social ethical behaviour pattern', 1989: 288-89). There was, he argues, no such thing as 'eine einverständliche "Ethik der hellenistischen Popularphilosophie", aus welcher das Christentum (und zuvor das Judentum) nur hätte zu "entnehmen" brauchen' ('a mutually agreed "ethics of Hellenistic popular philosophy" from which Christianity [and Judaism prior to that] would have only had to "draw"', 1989: 308). The Christian code adapts one particular contemporary model which promotes ethical responsibility, appealing to partnership and reciprocity in the conventional structures of ancient households (1989: 310, 314).

Crouch's first claim is therefore simplistic. New Testament House Codes have a dual emphasis: on the one hand on the active self-submission of those whose roles are universally accepted as rightfully submitted and to some extent legally enforced; on the other hand on the humility and imitation of Christ's self-sacrificing love required by those universally recognized to hold positions of authority in existing, but not necessarily sanctioned, social structures (Schrage 1974: 12, 22).

(b) Crouch's second foundation argument involves the idea that the social order at Corinth is threatened by a type of situation necessitating an emphasis on the first-mentioned parties of each pair in the Codes. Women, he says, have been indulging in cult-like pneumatic enthusiasm, and slaves expecting manumission. Since children could not be incited to social revolution by anything in Pauline freedom-teaching, the code must later have been expanded to include them along with husbands, fathers and masters.[140]

The context of ch. 7, he argues, suggests that the problematic v. 21 discourages slaves from seeking emancipation (1972: 124-25, 150). He fails, however, to demonstrate either that slavery is an issue at Corinth, or that Christian slaves anywhere are expecting manumission. Manumission does not appear to have been an issue in the first century CE.[141]

---

140. Crouch 1972: 104, 123, 144-45, 149. For critiques of Crouch's argument see Schrage 1974: 1-22, esp. 4-5; Müller 1989: e.g. 282-84.

141. Bartchy 1973: e.g. 19, 64-67, 85-87, 116-19, 129-31 and n. 468, 162-63.

1 Corinthians 7 is introduced by περὶ δὲ ὧν ἐγράψατε...κτλ., widely understood to begin a series of replies to the Corinthians each beginning with περὶ δέ.[142] Verse 25 also begins with that formula, which might suggest that a completely new matter is taken up if it were not that almost the entire chapter deals with marriage. Verse 17 states Paul's general rule. As Crouch acknowledges, vv. 18-23 may simply illustrate that rule, again stated in v. 24. 1 Corinthians 7.2-17 deals with the married in relation to the citation, and vv. 25-40 consider whether the unmarried should remain so. These apparently constitute one general (or two or more related) responses to Corinthian over-interpretation of Paul's own earlier teaching which they have quoted to him, that is 'it is good for a man not to touch a woman'. Paul now carefully modifies (without denying) that citation.[143] Verses 18-23 appear to be no more than additional illustrations of the rule applied. Crouch believes that the problem of divorce is at least a live possibility at Corinth (vv. 10-16), prior address indicating its 'more acute' occurrence amongst women.[144] According to this reasoning, vv. 12, 15b would suggest that it is predominantly male Corinthians who desert unbelieving partners, but

Following Bartchy are M.Y. MacDonald 1988: 111-13; Kidd 1990: 162. See also Balch 1981: 106. Cf. also *1 Clem.* 55.2.

142. See further in Chapter 9.

143. Crouch (1972: 130) acknowledges this. See here Baasland (1988: 78-79).

144. Crouch 1972: 130-31. Bartchy (1973: 128-30), having demonstrated that slavery was not an issue, nevertheless believes that 'the bold activity of the women and the curious sexual practices in the congregation' were, citing 5.1-2; 6.15-16; 7.1-5, 36-38; 11.5-16; 14.34-35. For the last-cited see full discussion in Part III. In every other case men are either the offenders or at least equally as guilty as women. Bartchy seeks to buttress his argument about slavery by following Stendahl in arguing that at Gal. 3.28, where no 'women problem' is apparent, Paul could use the pairs 'Jew–Greek, slave–free, male–female', but in 1 Cor. 12.15 he omits the last pair because he has just finished addressing a problem caused by women. He would not, Bartchy claims, use the 'slave–free' pair if slaves create the problems. He is followed here by e.g. Balch (1981: 107) who nevertheless notes the absence of evidence in 1 Peter that wives are attempting to gain equality. 1 Cor. 11.3-16, however, speaks of practices involving both sexes, and about men first. Witherington (1981: 598-602) persuasively argues that at Gal. 3.28 the third pair is included precisely because trends in those assemblies create difficulties for women. It is questionable that it is omitted at 1 Cor. 12.15 for any significant reason, or that the inclusion of the slave–free pair at 1 Corinthians 7 supports Bartchy's (already persuasive) argument.

Crouch does not confront this difficulty.[145] Even more significantly, the form of the citation indicates that male asceticism plays a (dominant?) role in the Corinthian position. On the other hand, however, Paul's calm, reasoned approach throughout the chapter suggests that few of either sex have actually deserted their spouses or inappropriately handled the marriage of virgins. It has been argued persuasively that περὶ δέ passages further previous oral teaching and do not concern threats to community solidarity (Baasland 1988: 82-83). It seems likely, then, that ideas based on a misunderstanding are being debated before much action has been taken. Even if vv. 18-23 do introduce additional subjects, the calm approach still suggests the problems are perceived as rectifiable. However, the first and at least primary concern is for individual sexuality and marital responsibility. Paul certainly captures here a very early moment in emerging Christian asceticism and reveals the rule by which he handles misdirected zeal. Nevertheless, Crouch demonstrates from ch. 7 neither that Corinthian women are any more attracted to asceticism than men, nor that Corinthian slaves or women are creating acute problems.

At 1 Cor. 11.3-16, Crouch claims, the ultimate concern is the subordinate position of woman to her husband (1972: 131 incl. n. 52). Yet subordination is nowhere mentioned in that passage. In a context concerned with the honour of both members of each of three pairs (v. 3), and in which the behaviour of men is the first addressed, 'headship' (a term evoking different things to different people: Harris 1990: 343 n. 27) may not simply be assumed to envision general hierarchical rule (see Appendix 2). Crouch's handling of 14.34-35 will more appropriately be addressed in Part III, but his belief that Paul here expressly forbids women to speak in the gathered congregation (1972: 137-39) is notoriously problematic. In addition to this, vv. 23, 27-28, 31-32 make clear that Corinthians of both sexes may be guilty of 'pneumatic enthusiasm'. Neither 11.3-16 nor 14.33b-36 adequately support the claim that it is the behaviour of women that calls forth the development of a code emphasizing their subordination.[146]

---

145. Wire (1990: 83-87) presents a more sophisticated support of address to a predominantly female problem, but is still not compelling.

146. Crouch (1972: 141-44) claims that the form of the code also originates in tension between Hellenistic religiosity and Jewish morality, but for my response to his descriptions of 'ecstatic utterances...under the influence of the deity' see Chapter 10, pp. 204-206.

Crouch's identification of similar tendencies in the Pastorals is just as unconvincing (1972: 139). 1 Timothy 6.1-2 may suggest that some Christian slaves are attempting to capitalize on new relationships with Christian masters, or even pressing their new awareness of personal worth as far as possible with non-Christian masters, but it may simply anticipate those actions in accordance with patterns elsewhere. In any case, it does not suggest that slaves are agitating for manumission. Crouch's consideration of passages about women reckons without factors addressed already in the present study. It is at least doubtful that the women of 2 Tim. 3.6 are or have been Christians. Nothing except the assumption that the three Pastorals may legitimately be treated as one work would suggest (as Crouch implies) that 1 Tim. 4.4 limits ascetic tendencies to women. The concern in 1 Timothy 2 is for every-day living, not for congregational behaviour. None of those passages provides a sure foundation for the idea that 'excesses related to an enthusiastic–pneumatic movement' are in view. Against this back-ground there is at least some doubt that 5.15, as Crouch claims, is to be explained as concerning women led astray by false teachers and indulg-ing in excess.

Crouch has neither appreciated that the primary goal of the New Tes-tament Codes is the different kinds of mutual submission of various parties, nor proved that women and slaves provide the catalyst for their development.

Balch's argument that the code in 1 Peter responds directly to socio-political tension with the general community is attractive, but the same explanation is less satisfying for the other codes. In some contrast to 1 Peter, Col. 3.18-4.1 and Eph. 5.21-6.9 presuppose Christian house-holds[147] and, although the context of each does show some concern for the opinion of outsiders (Col. 4.5-6 and to a lesser extent Eph. 5.15), the focus is more didactic than apologetic. The Pastorals do have clearer parallels with 1 Peter (e.g. 1 Tim. 2.2-3; 3.7; 4.16; 2 Tim. 2.10). At Tit. 2.3-10[148] (in passages to a greater or lesser degree reflecting Household Codes) certain behaviour is required so that:

---

147. Goppelt 1972: 293; M.Y. MacDonald 1988: 109. Balch (1981: 96) does point out that in 1 Peter the primary concern is for the slaves and wives of non-Christians.

148. Barrett 1963: 133, although cf. 'the similarities are merely surface at best' (Fee 1984: 138-39).

i.   the word of God may not be maligned (v. 5 cf. Rom. 2.24 quoting Isa. 52.5; Ezek. 36.22);

ii.   those opposing may be ashamed and have nothing bad to say (v. 8); and

iii. the teaching about God may be attractive (v. 10).[149]

The object of 1 Tim. 5.14 is that the enemy have no occasion for slander,[150] and vv. 24-25 suggest the same concern with outside impressions.[151] This makes plausible the idea that the underlying code may, as Balch argues, originally have been intended to demonstrate to outsiders that Christianity in fact taught the respectful self-submission it was accused of destroying. The focus is upon the members upon whom so much depends in witness before others and for whom nonconformity to accepted household customs means significant danger.[152] Even in 1 Peter, however, the concern is not only apologetic but also missionary[153] and (like the codes of Colossians and Ephesians) didactic. But in

149. Barrett (1963: 134) notes parallels in Tit. 2.14; 3.2.

150. All the foregoing texts from the Pastorals are noted in Balch 1981: 92. Fee (1984: 86) argues that the enemy here is Satan (cf. his pp. 143, 145 re Tit. 2.8) because outside opposition at Ephesus is suggested nowhere in 1 and 2 Timothy. Even though it is unclear that Timothy is at Ephesus when he receives the second letter, so that the outside opposition of 3.1-9 may be irrelevant for 1 Timothy, that opposition is viewed as occurring everywhere. In 1 Timothy Hymenaeus and Alexander have already been excluded (1.20). 5.24-25 together with parallel concern with outside impressions in Titus suggests that outside opposition is at least partly in view in 5.15.

151. Müller-Bardorff (1958: 121 n. 19) claims '3,7 denkt dabei vorzüglich an den Ruf, den die Betreffenden auch bei den Aussenstehenden haben. Dagegen scheint 5,10,...zunächst und vor allem an den Ruf zu denken, den die Witwen in der Gemeinde geniessen' ('here 3,7 prefers to think of the reputation which the persons concerned also have with outsiders. By contrast, 5,10...appears to think first and above all of the reputation which the widows enjoy in the congregation'), but with the possible exception of εἰ ἁγίων πόδας ἔνιψεν each qualification would surely be apparent to outsiders.

152. Balch 1981: 94. Kidd (1990: 139) also notes the apologetic motif. Cf. Crouch (1972: 149 n. 18), who argues that omission of masters, children and fathers in 1 Peter confirms the optional nature of those sections.

153. Balch (1981: 87) denies that ἐν ἡμέρᾳ ἐπισκοπῆς (2.12) refers to a day of conversion, and argues persuasively that the day of judgment is in view, and (pp. 105, 109) recognizes that the goal of 3.1 is both apologetic and missionary. However, with some force he argues (p. 108) that at 1 Pet. 2.18-24 slaves do not seem expected to convert their masters.

the Pastorals the relevant passages are not codes as such: they adapt and reflect such material. Certainly some closely resemble codes: 1 Tim. 2.9 (cf. 1 Pet. 3.3-5) and 6.1-2; Tit. 2.9-10 (cf. Eph. 6.5-8; Col. 3.22-25; 1 Pet. 2.18-21). The previously noted evidence for the Author's use of traditional material strongly suggests that existing codes have been applied to various relationships within the community. Other passages are more accurately described as 'code-like': 1 Tim. 2.11-12, 15; 3.2-12; 5.1-2, 14; Tit. 1.6-8; 2.2-8. Nevertheless, in the same context of those evidences of use of tradition, independent development is un-likely in view of:

  i. close connections between 1 Tim. 2.11-12, 15 and Tit. 2.3-4; 1 Tim. 3.2-12; Tit. 1.6-8;
  ii. the traditional concern for the individual's relations with vari-ous types of others at 1 Tim. 5.1-2; and
  iii. the simple assumption of traditional women's roles at 1 Tim. 5.14 and Tit. 2.4-5.

The Author *is* concerned with the perceptions of outsiders (1 Tim. 2.4; 3.7; 5.7-8; Tit. 3.1-2), but his *primary* concern is for relations between the addressees and members, and between those members. It seems unlikely that he independently develops responses to conditions at the place of address directly based upon an ancient rather than an already-developed Christian *topos*. At p. 184 below, and in Part IV, evidence will be presented that the same kind of differing but mutual submissions underlying the more formal New Testament codes is reflected in the Pastorals, and this makes it even more unlikely that he responds independently from that now-traditional code.

Whilst both Crouch and Balch shed some light on aspects of developing New Testament Household Codes, neither adequately explains that development. The differences and perceived strengths in their theses nevertheless influence their successors in the quest for the motivating cause of the distinctive Christian Household Codes.

Although Verner believes that Balch weakens Crouch's argument that the code is a peculiarly Christian development reflecting conditions in the church, he agrees with Crouch that internal conflicts are their motivating cause, the relationships being those of superior–inferior (1983: 21-22, and e.g. 91). The distinctive role of the Pastorals in that development, he claims, is the extension of governing principles beyond the family unit (1983: 107). He seeks to discover whether social structures and relations in household and church reflect a focus on issues faced by the Author's church, or traditions which may not be particularly current. He then considers the Household Code as early Christian paraenesis, including an excursus on paraenetic discourse which demonstrates the not always immediately obvious internal and contextual coherence of that type of instruction. Issues of coherence and generality, he concludes, should be kept distinct (1983: 79-125). His following chapter, based upon those findings, nevertheless presumes that the Author 'writes purposefully and coherently in addressing *the general situation of the church of the Pastorals*' (italics mine). The Author's own ideas and actual conditions at 'the church' are distinguishable,[154] Dibelius's dictum (that paraenesis responds to a *general* situation) leading to undue restriction to generalities (Verner 1983: 16). This attempt to combine aspects of two conflicting and largely unsatisfying theses in new argument is itself unsatisfying. Verner's claim that Balch weakens Crouch's argument is valid if pre-Christian ideas and an apologetic function are the *only* characteristics of New Testament codes. They are, however, recognizably Christian, and didactic. Verner fails to consider whether material about social structures and relations deriving from traditions may be employed in focus on issues which, although currently live in Christian assemblies in general, do not necessarily, or particularly, occur at the place of address. As previously argued, the Author only secondarily addresses the *ekklesia* at the place of address whilst detailing how 'the good warfare' may be fought, giving every indication of envisaging it as a way of life. Verner leaps, in effect, from his able demonstration that paraenesis is frequently purposeful and coherent to the conclusion that 1 Tim. 5.8, 11ff. suggests problems in 'the church of the Pastorals'.[155] He also says, however, that the configuration of household and church as the unified sphere of the Christian community in the Pastorals corresponds to that in Polycarp, *Phil.* and Ignatius, *Pol.*, and may well reflect conditions 'general in the church...during a limited period and perhaps...area'

---

154. Verner 1983: 127-28. It is not always clear whether Verner refers to the Christendom of the day or the Christians at the place of address, but when in doubt I am guided by his introduction: 'the Pastorals...contain information about the social strata...structure and...tensions of the church to which they are addressed' (p. 1).

155. Verner 1983: 137. See also M.Y. MacDonald 1988: 184.

(1983: 23-24). To this extent he acknowledges the generality of the issues addressed. The role he defines for the Pastorals in the history of the development of the codes is also problematic. Whilst the concern in the Pastorals certainly extends beyond the family unit characterizing the codes themselves, the overarching concern of those codes (unlike the traditional household *topos*) is not rulership[156] but differing kinds of self-submission. 1 Timothy 5.1-3[157] precisely reflects that concern. The Author reworks by-now conventional Christian behaviour codes in a broad community context in accordance with conventional Christian thought.

P.H. Towner, although agreeing with Balch that the Christian code had an apologetic function, basically supports Crouch, arguing that the aim is to encourage or restore assemblies disturbed by emancipatory tendencies. He admits, nevertheless, that internal disorder is unprovable, and argues that the required order is not simply for the benefit of pagan onlookers and concerned with disruption to social structures. It also seeks to ensure the survival of the church and the mission (1989: 172, 175, 180, 187-90, 195-99). Towner apprehends something of the depth of the New Testament Household Codes, but his acceptance that the excessive behaviour of slaves and women is the motivating factor in their development prevents him following it to its logical end.

To state the obvious, such characteristically Christian codes emerged in particular conditions. Although arriving at different conclusions about the nature of the subordination required, Yoder and Crouch agree that a major factor was the earlier affirmation of the dignity of the subordinate parties.[158] But if the dual focus of those codes is permitted its logical force, just as in non-Christian circles relations between wives and husbands, children and fathers, slaves and masters called forth instruction to those ranks, so too amongst Christians. They were, after all, the

---

156. Contra also Kidd (1990: 102), who here follows Verner although believing that the claim that gender stratification is *the* issue is an overstatement. For Kidd money is always a factor, but he accepts that gender stratification is pivotal to an understanding of the Pastorals, 1 Tim. 2.11-15 seeing women teaching in the assembly as a threat to a primordial and fundamental order, and 'rulership' the overarching rubric of the houshold topos employed.

157. See Section 4 above for discussion on Tit. 2.3-5, and Part IV for 1 Tim. 2.13-15.

158. Yoder 1982: 175-79. For Crouch see above.

given social realities. But whatever may have been the motivation behind the Christianization of such traditions, it does not necessarily follow that repetition or adaptation of those concerns constitutes evidence of contrary conditions at the place of address. The point of the foregoing discussion has not been simply to argue that men, fathers and masters are as much in focus in the codes and their adaptations as are women, children and slaves, and are therefore viewed as equally in need of instruction. The aim has been to demonstrate that the traditional (albeit now distinctively Christian) nature of the instruction must be recognized as such. The fact that the roots of those New Testament codes lie in non-Christian thought, their similarities and differences, and their own characteristic Christian emphases, together suggest that each employs already-conventional Christian teaching.[159]

Failure to appreciate the duality and depth of the reference in New Testament Household Codes has played its part in setting the background against which 1 Tim. 5.3-16 is interpreted. With its minimal reflection of those codes (vv. 3, 13-14), the passage has been seen by those with whom my Part II is concerned primarily as a reflection of local or post-Pauline assembly conditions incorporated into an adaptation of a behaviour-code about relations with older and younger men and women, and πρεσβύτεροι.[160] In other words, although viewed as part of the adaptation rather than as part of the tradition itself, it is also viewed as reflecting the traditional concern about the 'proper roles of women'. However, since the concern of the Christian Household Code is for different kinds of submission of each to the other, unless this context shows contrary evidence that same underlying concern must be assumed. The primary focus is upon widows, but any 'proper roles for women' that *are* reflected should be envisaged as ideally functioning in association with household heads who are correspondingly (appropriately) self-submitted. That such ideal conditions would not always exist (1 Pet. 2.18-25; 3.1, 6b) is as self-evident at 1 Timothy 5 as it is at Eph. 5.25-33 and Col. 3.19.

159. Even in Col. 3.18-4.1 the considerably longer instruction to slaves, placed as it is in the fifth of six positions, suggests some adaptation of a shorter version. Contra Crouch 1972: 150. M.Y. MacDonald (1988: 114-15) also argues contra Crouch here.

160. As e.g. Dibelius and Conzelmann 1972: 73; Kelly 1972: 115. See also Easton 1948: 91-92.

Whatever the motivation for the development of Christian Household Codes, they certainly teach that parties traditionally viewed as rightfully submissive are expected to continue to be so, and that parties understood to be in authority should be so in humility. Such is clearly the nature of the code adapted and reflected in 1 Timothy 5. The addressee is to treat older and younger men and women with respect (vv. 1-2) and to see that widows are properly cared for (vv. 3-16). Witness to outsiders is of obvious concern (v. 14,[161] cf. vv. 7-8), and the focus is upon parties both responsible (the addressee: imperatives at vv. 3, 7, 9, 11; κύριοι: vv. 4, 7-8; certain women: v. 16) and dependent (widows). It should also be noted that, as elswhere in the Pastorals, at v. 7 ταῦτα may be formulaic, referring to preformed material.[162] On the whole it seems likely that underlying 1 Tim. 5.3-16 is a customary concern about widows and their care. There is a close relationship between vv. 1-2 and 3-5, and both the structure and argument of vv. 3-16 point to the unity of the passage as a whole. Even though there is clearly some concern in 1 Timothy for the situation at the place of address, even though widows would presumably constitute part of the membership, and even though real events have contributed to the perceived need for this particular instruction (v. 15), there is no mention of a particular situation here. The underlying traditional concerns suggest that this passage does not specifically describe widows at that place but widows in general.

At v. 14, moreover, the Author selects βούλομαι, conveying visualization of continuous action:

> So I (customarily) want younger widows to marry…etc.

In this context this cannot be confined to a particular situation. The aim throughout is behaviour giving no opportunity to the outsider to speak evil of Christians (v. 14).[163] When Pauline authorship is rejected this

161. I here take ἀντικειμένῳ as 'enemy' as e.g. Alford 1862: 350; Liddon 1897: 60; Parry 1920: 32; Hendriksen 1955: 178.

162. Ellis 1987: 243-44 and nn. 40, 41. At 1 Tim. 4.6 ταῦτα refers to vv. 1-5, also introduced by τὸ…πνεῦμα…λέγει; at 4.11 it apparently refers to v. 8, v. 10 being parenthetical (see Chapter 12 n. 19 for support of Knight against Ellis, who believes the reference is to v. 10); at 6.2b it refers either to vv. 1-2 (cf. Eph. 5.21–6.9; Col. 3.18-4.1), to ch. 5, or even to all the instructions of the letter; at 3.14 it refers to 2.1f., 8-15, and to 3.1b-13 which is independent of its context and has close affinities with Tit. 1.6-9; see also 5.21 and 6.11.

163. P.H. Towner 1989: 175-99. See also M.Y. MacDonald 1988: 167-70.

general orientation should be recognized. When Pauline authorship is accepted Paul's normal viewpoint prevails.[164] As 1 Corinthians 7 makes clear, although celibacy is his ideal he realistically encourages marriage where preferred, and his choice of Aorists in vv. 8, 40 (cf. vv. 11, 19, 24) confirm what the context (v. 26) strongly suggests: the Corinthian situation requires special advice.[165] Writing here to Timothy, however, he gives no indication of the locality of these self-indulgent widows, and places no emphasis on them, mentioning them just before returning to his main point from vv. 9-10 in v. 16. The widows of v. 15 may have strayed, but not necessarily—and certainly not specifically—at Ephesus.[166]

Whether Pauline authorship is accepted or rejected, 1 Tim. 5.11-15, although drawing upon real events in unspecified contemporary assemblies,[167] like the rest of the chapter presents general teaching considered by the Author relevant anywhere. It is an inappropriate source for the identification of female asceticism and rejection of traditional roles so frequently included in reconstructions of background for the Pastorals.

164. Contra some denying Pauline authorship, e.g. Scott 1936: 62; Dibelius and Conzelmann 1972: 75-76; Schüssler Fiorenza 1983: 312; M.Y. MacDonald 1988: 118. Contra also Wendland (1970: 98), who draws substantial conclusions from the difference between 1 Corinthians 7 and 1 Timothy 5; Kelly (1972: 119), who claims 1 Cor. 7.25ff. is a general ruling and 1 Timothy 5 a special case; and Fee (1984: 83), who explains the differences by the Ephesian situation.

165. Simpson 1954: 76; Oden 1989: 59. Contra Barrett (1963: 67), who argues that 1 Corinthians 7 scarcely shows a positive attitude to marriage. See also Weidinger 1928: 10.

166. Bernard 1899: 84. It is not altogether clear at v. 15 that it is in fact widows who have strayed after Satan: τινες could be masculine or gender-inclusive, the antecedent being τῷ ἀντικειμένῳ, and the turning away by those who have slandered widows for inappropriate behaviour outlined in vv. 11b-13 and implied in v. 14. This would depend upon the number change being due to τῷ ἀντικειμένῳ describing a class.

167. Fee 1984: 79; P.H. Towner 1989: 188.

Conclusion to Part II

The background for explanation of 1 Tim. 2.9-15 commonly reconstructed from various passages about false teachers and women in the three Pastoral Epistles is fallacious. False teaching at the place of address is clearly a major concern, but there is no convincing evidence in those passages that the Author believes that significant numbers of Christian women specifically at that place are rejecting traditional female roles. Nor is there in those passages any evidence that he believes women are in general unsuited to teaching or characteristically prone to deception by false teachers. The first of the three options for 1 Tim. 2.12 presented in Part I (pp. 93-94) is therefore to be rejected and ἐπιτρέπω to be understood to convey unlimited continuous force. The third option there presented must then preserve the intention of the second. No matter who wrote it, and whatever the details of its meaning, 1 Tim. 2.9-12 presents instruction that the Author himself believes is universally relevant.

Part III
1 CORINTHIANS 14.34-35: A PARALLEL?

Chapter 9

AN INTRODUCTORY LITERATURE SURVEY AND OUTLINE
OF THE CORINTHIAN BACKGROUND

The third exegetical device here to be re-examined is the parallel with
1 Tim. 2.11-12 commonly perceived at 1 Cor. 14.34-35.

αἱ γυναῖκες ἐν ταῖς ἐκκλησίαις σιγάτωσαν: οὐ γὰρ ἐπιτρέπεται
αὐταῖς λαλεῖν, ἀλλὰ ὑποτασσέσθωσαν, καθὼς καὶ ὁ νόμος λέγει. εἰ
δέ τι μαθεῖν θέλουσιν, ἐν οἴκῳ τοὺς ἰδίους ἄνδρας ἐπερωτάτωσαν:
αἰσχρὸν γάρ ἐστιν γυναικὶ λαλεῖν ἐν ἐκκλησίᾳ.

Women should remain silent in the churches. They are not allowed to
speak, but must be in submission, as the Law says. If they want to
enquire about something, they should ask their own husbands at home;
for it is disgraceful for a woman to speak in the church (NIV).

Certain similarities are undeniable. In both passages women are forbidden some sort of speech, are urged to submission and either quietness
or silence, and appeal is made to an authority—in one to the Adam–Eve
narratives, in the other to the 'law'. There are also significant, although
inexact, linguistic parallels:[1]

1 Timothy 2.12	*1 Corinthians 14.34-35*
ἐπιτρέπω	ἐπιτρέπεται
ἡσυχία	σιγάτωσαν
διδάσκειν	λαλεῖν
ὑποταγῇ	ὑποτασσέσθωσαν
μανθανέτω	μαθεῖν

1.   E.g. B. Weiss 1885: 124-25; Ellis 1981: 214; P.H. Towner 1989: 40 n. 100.
Witherington (1988: 117) adds ἐν παντὶ τόπῳ/ἐν πάσαις ταῖς ἐκκλησίαις (1 Cor.
14.33b), but see Part I and Chapter 10 below.

1. *An Introductory Survey of the Literature*

Although a few exegetes minimize the parallels outlined above,[2] since each passage is in its own way problematic, the one is frequently referred to,[3] aligned with,[4] or directly employed in interpretation of the other, sometimes taking a circular approach.[5] For this study the chief focus must be on those interpreting 1 Tim. 2.11-15 by 1 Cor. 14.34-35. Since, however, some people believe the former intensifies the instruction of the latter,[6] others that it modifies it,[7] and many that it clarifies it,[8]

2. For Kähler (1959) see n. 17 below. Karris (1977: 206-207) cites the διδάσκειν–λαλεῖν distinction and says the situations seem quite different, but his interpretation of λαλέω will be rejected in Chapter 10 below as was some of his background for 1 Timothy in Part II. Dautzenberg (1975: 260) nevertheless concludes 'Es handelt sich an beiden Stellen um Abhängigkeit von der gleichen Regeltradition' ('Both passages concern the dependence on the same rule tradition'). Roloff (1988: 128-30) nevertheless sees 1 Tim. 2.11-15 as 'eine überarbeitete, präzisierte und situativ zugespitzte Neufassung von 1 Kor 14, 33b-36' ('a revised, more precisely stated and pointedly sharpened new version of 1 Cor. 14.33b-36'). See also Windisch 1930: 420-21.

3. E.g. Liddon 1897: 18; Humphreys 1901: 99; E.F. Brown 1917: 19; Parry 1920: 15; Barrett 1963: 55.

4. E.g. Ellicott 1864: 36; Huther 1866: 131-33; Robertson and Plummer 1911: 325; Allworthy 1917: 97-98; Moffatt 1941: 232; Spicq 1947: 70; Easton 1948: 127; Brox 1969: 133-34; Trummer 1978: 144-49; Moo 1980: 64; 1981: 221; Grudem 1982: 255; Dewey 1992: 355; Baugh 1994: 156 n. 13.

5. Locke (1705–1707: 221) introduces 'in the churches' to 1 Tim. 2.12, and employs διδάσκω to interpret λαλέω at 1 Cor. 14.34-35. Knight (1980: 37) also introduces 'in the church' to 1 Tim. 2.12, and employs its Genesis reference to interpret 'law' at 1 Cor. 14.34. Prohl (1957: 31) interprets the passages together.

6. E.g. G.G. Blum 1965: 157. See also above at n. 1 Weiss, and at n. 2 Roloff and Windisch.

7. E.g. Witherington 1988: 117-18.

8. Hendriksen (1955: 109) interprets ἐπιτρέπω by ὁ νόμος; Moo (1980: 67-68) defines and Scott (1936: 26) restricts διδάσκω; Gritz (1991: 130) limits γυνή to wives; Guthrie (1990: 85) is inclined, and Lock (1924: 29) more confident, to restrict the context to public worship, but Weisinger (1866: 415-16) and Leaney (1960: 53) simply 'proof-text' it. Weisinger (p. 415) similarly 'proof-texts' the 'usurped' authority and the required 'silence'. P.H. Towner (1989: 40-41) employs linguistic similarities together with links with the Household Code to reconstruct similar backgrounds featuring problematic women. For similar approaches see also e.g. Knox 1558: 15; Alford 1862: 319; Meinertz 1931: 38; Falconer 1937: 131; Jeremias 1963: 19; Weeks 1972: 23; Ridderbos 1977: 462.

interpretations of 1 Cor. 14.34-35 itself must be considered here.

There is a wide range of views about the nature of the perceived parallel between the two passages.

Of those rejecting Pauline authorship for the Pastorals: a high percentage believe 1 Cor. 14.34-35 itself to be an interpolation, and most conclude that in both passages the required submission, silence/ quietness, and appeals to law/scripture, constitute a post-Pauline school of thought;[9] but those who hold the Corinthian passage to be authentically Pauline consider its thought either a conservative development,[10] another perspective (Houlden 1976: 64, 71), or a misunderstood aspect,[11] which is taken up in 1 Timothy 2 by the pseudepigrapher.

Of those accepting that the Author of the Pastorals is Paul, it is generally assumed that the two passages must be in accord,[12] but some either limit the application of 1 Cor. 14.34-35,[13] or declare it an interpolation.[14] In both these latter approaches, in accordance with what is then believed to be Paul's generally liberal approach to women, local reasons are sought for maintaining that 1 Tim. 2.12 is not intended to be normative.[15]

All these views are to some extent problematic for two reasons:

(a) The conclusions already reached in Part I are relevant, namely that, although 1 Cor. 14.34-35 is set in a congregational context, 1 Tim. 2.9-12 is not. The similarities must therefore be evaluated together with certain differences. In 1 Cor. 14.34-35 women ἐν ἐκκλησίᾳ are (at least in some way) not to speak, are to be submissive, and should ask questions of their husbands at home. Anything else is considered disgraceful. In 1 Tim. 2.11-12 women are to live their lives learning quietly and submissively, and are neither continually to instruct, nor to

9.   E.g. Fitzer 1963: 37-39 with n. 103; Scroggs 1972: 284; Conzelmann 1975: 246; Swidler 1979: 325; Knoch 1988: 26. See also Allworthy 1917: 98; A.T. Hanson 1966: 37.

10.   Schüssler Fiorenza 1983: 232-33. Meeks (1973: 204) suggests this as an option.

11.   Kähler (1959: 4), for whom see Chapter 10 n. 67 below.

12.   In addition to those to be discussed in Chapter 10 see e.g. Weisinger 1866: 415-16; White 1910: 108; Simpson 1954: 46-47.

13.   Some early examples are E. Wilson 1849: 155; W.K. Brown 1887: 105-108. See further in Chapter 10, Sections 1 and 2.

14.   E.g. Fee (1988: 699-708), for whom see Chapter 10, Section 3.

15.   See Part II. Cf. Holtz (1965: 68-69, 72-73), who argues that both passages are interpolated.

play the dictator over a man. The one passage draws strict rules for congregational behaviour, the other provides broad guidelines for the life.[16] The Corinthian passage appeals to the 'law' in support of ecclesial behaviour closely associated with, and apparently based on, a hierarchical marital relationship.[17] 1 Timothy comments in a broad context which (as has been argued in Part II) occasionally reflects the reciprocity of a *distinctive* Household Code tradition, and the submission it enjoins is to be directed to what is learned. Curiously, after forbidding *continual* instruction, and *continual* authority-taking over a man, it makes selective reference to clearly identifiable scripture which paradoxically features a *single* action, that is, to Adam and Eve in Genesis 3. In whatever way that paradox is resolved, in whatever way 1 Cor. 14.34-35 is interpreted, and in spite of the above-mentioned parallels it should be assumed neither that the two passages present identical views nor that the one may simply be employed to interpret the difficulties of the other. This is not to claim that they have nothing to say about each other: see my General Conclusion. The claim here is simply that greater caution is called for than is usually in evidence.

16. Barton (1986: 230) notes that, unlike 1 Cor. 14.34-35, 1 Tim. 2.11-12 makes no locative distinction between οἶκος and ἐκκλησία.

17. Some see a close connection between 1 Cor. 14.34-35 and the Christian Household Code (e.g. Delling 1931: 124; Crouch 1972: 111; Küchler 1986: 57; P.H. Towner 1989: 40-41), but see Chapter 8, Section 5.2. Kähler (1959: 4) argues 'Ein *Lehr*verbot..., wie in 1 Tim. 2,12, ist hier nicht zu finden; denn von einem *Lehren*wollen der Frau ist hier nicht die Rede. Hingegen ist sie voller *Lernbegier*... So gilt...ὑποτασσέσθωσαν noch für die Gemeindeversammlung, in der der Frau soeben das "Reden" verboten wurde. In diesem Zusammenhang ist durch nichts angedeutet, dass sich ὑποτάσσεσθαι auf den οἶκος...bezieht. Vielmehr erscheint hier ὑποτάσσεσθαι als "Ordnungsbegriff" in bezug auf den Gottesdienst. Dadurch, dass die Frauen das ungeordnete Dazwischenreden unterlassen...' ('A *teaching* prohibition as in 1 Tim. 2.12 cannot be found here; after all, nothing is being said here about a *teaching* desire on the part of the woman. However, she is still full of *eagerness to learn*... Thus ὑποτασσέσθωσαν still applies to the congregational assembly where the woman has just been forbidden "to talk". In this context there is no hint that ὑποτάσσεσθαι is in relation...to the οἶκος. Rather, ὑποτάσσεσθαι appears here as a "notion of order" in relation to the worship service. By virtue of the fact that the women refrain from any disorderly interjecting...'). Kähler fails to demonstrate, however, what 'law' silences women for interjection, leaving the likelihood that the submission required is the marital variety transferred to the assembly and applicable to all women. Contra also Stouffer 1981: 258.

(b) Interpretation of 1 Cor. 14.34-35 requires:

i. reconciliation with 11.5, which appears to assume that women pray and prophesy with men;
ii. definition of 'the law' in the context of Pauline thought;
iii. explanation for placement after v. 40 in the pre-Vulgate Western text;[18]
iv. a decision whether v. 33b belongs in sense with v. 33a or v. 34;[19] and
v. explanation for the masculine pronoun at v. 36.

Again, there is considerable scope for diversity. The literature reveals four general approaches to i., with the problems of ii.–v. resolved accordingly:

1. Interpretation of 11.5 by 14.34-35, Paul being seen as consistently envisaging women silent ἐν ἐκκλησίᾳ.
2. Interpretation of 14.34-35 by 11.5 and the general context, Paul being seen as forbidding women only some speech ἐν ἐκκλησίᾳ.
3. 14.34-35 declared to be a later interpolation.
4. 14.34-35 declared to be a citation by Paul of a Corinthian slogan which he rejects at v. 36.

---

18. *UBSGNT*; N/A[27]; Metzger 1975: 565; Fee 1988: 699; Payne 1995: 240-41. Fee (1994: 274-75) demonstrates the equal value of these Western texts to the Greek text. Wire (1990: 149-51) argues that all these MSS placements originate from a single displacement.

19. *UBSGNT*, although reporting the contrary at TR and WH, choose to place the full stop after v. 33a, as e.g. NIV, TEV, RSV, JB, NEB; L. Morris 1971: 200-201; Grudem 1982: 13; Orr and Walther 1982: 311-12; Bruce 1983: 135; Fee 1988: 697-98 (although cf. 1994: 279 where he assumes that v. 34b is part of the original text but says 'in the churches' [v. 34] appears nowhere else in Paul [but cf. v. 33b]); Carson 1988: 122. Some explain the resulting repetition of ἐν ταῖς ἐκκλησίαις in vv. 33b-34 by referring the first to other assemblies and the second to those of the Corinthians: e.g. N.R. Lightfoot 1976: 133; R.P. Martin 1984: 75, 83-84; Fung 1987: 333 n. 149; Witherington 1988: 96. Cf. J. Weiss (1910: 342), who at v. 34 suggests 'der Schreiber...ganz allgemein von sämtlichen Versammlungen sämtlicher Gemeinden verstanden hätte' ('the writer...had understood quite generally of all assemblies of all congregations'). Placing the full stop at the end of the verse are e.g. AV; Phillips; RV; NASB; Robertson and Plummer 1911: 324; Barrett 1971: 330; Murphy-O'Connor 1986: 90.

This diversity (to be illustrated in Chapter 10 by examples of each) warns that care should be exercised before even referring 1 Cor. 14.34-35 to 1 Tim. 2.11-12, and even more when using it as an interpretative device. It is not simply the 'clearer' passage by which one which is 'more obscure' may be interpreted. It is itself problematic. The opposite approach (that is, interpreting 1 Cor. 14.34-35 by 1 Tim. 2.11-12), with the greater number of controversial components involved, obviously demands an even greater caution. But having recognized this, the similarities remain and the exegete must attempt to explain them. For this study this first requires evaluation of 1–4 above. Each has its problems, but the pertinent questions here are: which may safely be rejected? and how do those remaining affect the passage as a comparison or interpretative device for 1 Tim. 2.9-15?

Before turning to those questions, however, some preliminary guidelines may be found in the background at Corinth.

2. *An Introductory Outline of the Corinthian Background*

It has been argued that the difficulties that Paul addresses in 1 Corinthians are caused by Gnostics[20] or Judaizers.[21] Despite mention of dissensions (1.12) and address to many errors, however, no particular 'opposition' is identifiable (Grudem 1982: 55). Since Paul uses his gospel as the basis for his argument (15.1-3) the Corinthians appear to continue to share it, but their tendency towards spiritualization of the self is indicative of an early form of developing second-century Gnosticism.[22] This shift together with their enthusiasm adequately explains the development of ideas amongst them which some exegetes have related to Gnosticism.[23] Nor do Judaizers seem to be the problem. Certainly Acts 18.12-13 suggests that a substantial number of their foundation converts were Jewish. Crispus (whose household presumably included other Jews) has considerable status (Acts 18.8). 1 Corinthians 1.14 and Rom. 16.23 suggest that Gaius and Titius Justus (Acts 18.7)

20. E.g. G.G. Blum 1965: 153-54; Parvey 1974: 124-25; Barton 1986: 236, 242.
21. E.g. Bushnell 1919: §214.
22. Ellis (1975: 288) points out that even in 2 Corinthians there is still no trace of the mythological speculation of second-century Gnosticism. See also Conzelmann 1975: 14-15; Fee 1988: 8, 11, 14.
23. This point is made by Conzelmann (1975: 15-16) and Fee (1988: 14).

may be one and the same and, if so, the assembly continues to meet in the home of this former proselyte to Judaism. The Petrine party (1.12) may be predominantly Jewish but, even if it is not, the unexplained technical terms τὸ ποτήριον τῆς εὐλογίας and τὸν ἄρτον ὃν κλῶμεν (10.16), and reference to the Passover (5.8), suggest the Corinthians are acquainted with Passover language (Winter 1978: 78). Yet there is little trace of response to Judaizing tendencies. The outsiders of 2 Corinthians 10–13 do not yet appear to have invaded the assembly.[24]

Fee argues that 'although there are certainly divisions within the community itself (probably along sociological lines)', the most serious division is between the Corinthian majority and Paul—his authority being the key issue. Also important, says Fee, is their modification of the gospel, and (probably closely related to that) they are likely to have an 'overrealized' eschatological view of their present existence, understood in strictly spiritual terms and following directly from a perception that they are people of the Spirit. Part of the problem in chs. 7 and 11, he believes, is with some 'eschatological women' already living as if totally in the new age (1988: 6, 12, 269-70, 497). There are three difficulties in Fee's argument. First, neither 1 Corinthians 7 nor 11 suggest there is a problem specifically with female 'people of the Spirit'. Each is concerned with both sexes (for 1 Corinthians 11 see Appendix 2). Secondly, it is unclear that Paul's major concern is the division between himself and the Corinthians.[25] A comparison lies at hand in the letter to the Galatians, which is occasioned by modification of Paul's gospel (1.6-9; 3.1–5.12) and accusations against him by those making those modifications (1.10–2.21). Paul spends about four-fifths of that letter confronting the modification and the division from him, and returns to those subjects in 6.12-17. In 1 Corinthians the division from him becomes evident only in the portion (less than one quarter) of the letter addressing the nature of true spiritual wisdom and the quarrelling parties. He then moves on to various matters, returning to their division from him in ch. 9. He is substantially concerned about the Corinthians themselves. He undoubtedly is still considered a key authority at Corinth: there is a Pauline party (1.12); members have written to him; and Chloe's people have reported to him (cf. Gal. 1.6). Thirdly, although acknowledging significant divisions, Fee here blurs them

24. See e.g. Fee 1988: 8.
25. Carson (1988: 18-19) also makes this observation.

when he suggests they have sociological causes.[26] Some may well do so. There are, however, not only contentions on the one hand about leadership parties (1.10-12) and the nature of true spirituality (12.1-16), but also on the other hand about male–female appearance (11.16), the resurrection of the dead (15.12), apparently about the use of spiritual gifts (12.14-31; 14.39b),[27] and certainly some involving lawsuits (6.1-9). Whilst some of the latter group may contribute to the former pair, the divisions amongst the Corinthians are complex.[28]

Fee reconstructs the Corinthian situation largely upon a threefold foundation:

(a) archaeological evidence that the homes of the rich could accommodate only about 9–11 people reclining in the *triclinium*, while the *atrium* on average seated about 30–50;[29]

(b) ἕκαστος γὰρ τὸ ἴδιον δεῖπνον προλαμβάνει ἐν τῷ φαγεῖν (11.21) interpreted as referring to the wealthy eating 'private meals', either their own or privileged portions or taken before the common meal;[30] and

26. Cf. e.g. Barton (1986: 237-39), who argues that divisions are between households or groups of households.

27. Contra Fee (1994: 147 n. 222, 150 with n. 232), and cf. him envisaging (pp. 259-60) re 14.37 address predominantly to leaders.

28. Murphy-O'Connor (1983: 158) acknowledges more diverse divisions, suggesting that, since assemblies such as that meeting in the Ephesian home of Prisca and Aquila were sub-groups of larger communities, the Corinthians probably made the same arrangements, a meeting of the 'whole' assembly exceptional (Rom. 16.23; 1 Cor. 14.23). See also Banks 1981: 46. However, Romans is addressed πᾶσιν τοῖς οὖσιν ἐν Ῥώμῃ...κλητοῖς ἁγίοις (1.7), ch. 16 speaking of various house assemblies and nothing suggesting that all regularly meet together, and Galatians ταῖς ἐκκλησίαις τῆς Γαλατίας (1.2), directed to a province rather than a city. 1 Corinthians is directed τῇ ἐκκλησίᾳ τοῦ θεοῦ τῇ οὔσῃ ἐν Κορίνθῳ (1.2). This assembly may still gather in the home of Titius Justus (Acts 18.7) but, even if not, 11.17–14.40 speaks of the whole (11.18; 14.23), suggesting it meets together at least regularly enough to develop a reputation for disorder. There is no mention in the letter of smaller house-assemblies so, whatever other meetings the Corinthians conduct, they are the assembly at Corinth because they meet together on some regular basis.

29. Fee 1988: 533-34 with n. 11. See also Murphy-O'Connor (1983: 156), who uses the dimensions of four first- to fourth-century CE houses. Cf., however, 'We simply do not know' (Fee 1994: 242).

30. Fee 1988: 534. Theissen (1982: 151-53 n. 14) cites a plate illustrating such a division, but admits it is not even certainly of that supper (p. 171). Barton 1986: 237.

   (c)   observation of human nature.[31]

Such combinations have suggested to Fee and others that the Corinthian host invites his own class to eat in the dining room, the remainder eating in the *atrium*,[32] and that the supper is 'in danger of becoming the occasion for demonstrating social differences' (Theissen 1982: 60). That danger is real in 11.17-34, but not one of the three factors forming the foundation for this version of those divisions is conclusive, and their combination, whilst giving the impression of strength, is merely speculative:

   (a) From the second century BCE the Roman *domus* was frequently enlarged by the hellenistic peristyle garden or courtyard,[33] opening towards which was frequently the elaborately decorated *oecus*, often used as a dining room.[34] At Pompeii the house of the Vetii had an *atrium* of 42 m^2, a *triclinium* of 25.2 m^2, a peristyle courtyard approx. 500 m^2, and an *oecus* almost as large as the *atrium* but (without the *impluvium*) more spacious. *Triclinium, oecus* and *atrium* all opened broadly to the peristyle.[35] Also at Pompeii, at the House of the Silver Wedding, the broadly opening *oecus* and summer dining-room faced each other across one end of the peristyle, at the other end of which was a further dining room with close proximity to an open air *triclinium* (A.G. McKay 1975: 34-35). At Ptolemais (Cyrenaica) one house had two adjoining *oeci*, one approximately 96 m^2 with two doors to the

   31. Fee 1988: 534; Theissen 1982: 153 and n. 20; Murphy-O'Connor 1983: 159.
   32. Theissen 1982: 147-74; Fee 1988: 15, 534. Cf. also Barton 1986: 237-39. Criticizing Theissen's argument (and reported by Fee n. 13) are Winter 1978: 76; Malherbe 1983: 84. Fee (pp. 537-38) accordingly finds v. 19 puzzling, reasoning that it most likely anticipates vv. 28-32 in referring to divisions that would separate true from false believers, but is something of an aside. But if vv. 17-34 simply have to do with sociological differences, v. 19 appears to say that God's approval rests on certain social groups—obviously not Paul's intention.
   33. Wycherley 1970: 531-32; Carrington 1970: 532. The peristyle is absent from two of the four plans Murphy-O'Connor consults (first- and fourth-century CE; see my n. 29 above), and unmentioned for the only house for which he provides no plan (second-century CE). The fourth is the house of the Vetii: see below. Wallace-Hadrill (1991: 212) reports that, of houses sampled at Pompeii–Herculaneum, 36 (64%) had both *atrium* and peristyle, the very largest houses with two of each.
   34. Ward-Perkins and Claridge 1980: 41. Wallace-Hadrill (1991: 202) warns of uncertainty about the use of rooms.
   35. Murphy-O'Connor (1983: 157) reproduces the plan but mentions neither extra dining space nor 'open' plan.

peristyle, and the other approximately 59.5 m² opening right across the peristyle end (A.G. McKay 1975: 226-27). Similar houses had such generously proportioned rooms that four sets of dining couches could easily be accommodated with plenty of room for serving and entertainment. Folding doors, and windows opening as folding doors, ensured not only garden views from the couches (A.G. McKay 1975: 41, 50) but access to and from the peristyle. Now, it cannot be demonstrated that the Corinthian host owned such a house, but neither can it be assumed that he could accommodate only 9–11 people reclining. It may well be that he not only had considerably more space than Fee and others permit, but that there was little division in physical terms between those reclining—perhaps in two or more adjoining or accessible rooms—and any who may spread out into the courtyard.

(b) It has not been demonstrated adequately that at 11.21 the wealthy eat in a separate location or prior to others. One alternative is at least equally possible. Winter argues that nowhere else in the New Testament does προλαμβάνω (11.21) mean 'take before' (cf. Mk 14.8; Gal. 6.1), and that in a second-century CE inscription, in the context of taking food, it cannot be so understood.[36] Paul, he suggests, here intends to convey 'to devour', ἐν τῷ φαγεῖν best understood 'during the meal'.[37] Although ἐκδέχομαι (v. 33) elsewhere in the New Testament is understood as 'wait for', the LXX and papyri provide a basis for the meaning 'to receive one another' in the sense of sharing.[38] Some Corinthians may be eating their own food in the presence of those who have brought none and who are left only with bread and wine.

(c) The human nature observed may be irrelevant to the text at hand. 5.8 and 10.16 (as already noted) suggest that Corinthians are well acquainted with Passover language and, because Crispus is amongst them, Winter concludes that the supper is patterned in some way on the Passover meal. If Gaius is Titius Justus, he himself is a Jewish proselyte. Winter justifiably finds it inconceivable that any Jewish Christian would exclude anyone actually sitting at the table from full participation in such a meal (1978: 80). It is similarly inconceivable that such a host would divide guests into two distinct social parties meeting in separate areas. This is not to claim that all are in one room; only that

36. Winter (1978: 73-82) citing *SIG*³, 1170.7, 9, 16. By the first century CE, he suggests, προ- had lost its temporal force. See also MM, s.v.; BAGD, s.v., 2 with a.

37. Winter 1978: 74-78; BAGD, s.v. ἐν II, 1, a.

38. Winter (1978: 79) cites *P. Tebt.* 33 1.7.

whatever structural divisions there are—and they may well be minimal—the gathering is conducted as one. Paul intends at vv. 23-24 not
simply to remind the Corinthians of Jesus' death but to bring out its
significance and their obligation to pattern their actions upon it (cf.
12.25). Verse 11.29 reflects their failure to do so at the supper.[39] Such a
reconstruction satisfyingly reflects and further illuminates something
which surfaces throughout the letter: the failure of the Corinthians to
understand how they should relate to one another (1.11; 3.3; 6.1; 8.9-
13; 10.23-11.1; 12.4-31; ch. 13; 14.12).

These Corinthians are not simply different social groups further
divided into leadership factions. They are a collection of people who
have not yet learned they are one body. Paul does not immediately confront them with the division from himself as he does the Galatians, so
their letter does not appear directly to set even the majority against him.
It seems rather to have made clear to some extent that adaptations of
hellenistic thought are modifying the gospel he had taught, a situation
further illuminated by Chloe's people. One major outworking of their
failure to grasp the concept of their unity is in damage to inter-personal
relations. Although Paul is combative in most sections of the letter (Fee
1988: 9-10), he is chiefly so with failure to recognize their relationship
with one another. Whilst the split from him is significant, these multiple
internal divisions with their primary effect of failing relationships must
take their place as another significant factor in the background against
which 14.34-35 is to be interpreted.

A second factor follows from the last: that not every subject
addressed is the result of either Corinthian spiritualization of the self or
enthusiasm. Disorder at the meal, for example, stems from a combination of ignorance, contemporary social practice, and thought-
lessness.

Additional background factors are provided by details of the structure
of the letter. Hurd claims to identify those parts answering questions
from the Corinthians' own letter and others responding to things Paul
has heard by word of mouth. He argues that the introductory formula
περὶ δέ at 7.1, 25; 8.1; 12.1; 16.1, 12 marks an abrupt shift from each
preceding section and commences a calm and systematic response
characterized by concern only with the future; establishment of as
strong an authority as possible; frequent slogans quoted from the

---

39. Winter 1978: 79-80. Fee (1988: 533) notes that abuse of the 'body' is abuse
of Christ himself.

Corinthian letter (although cf. 6.12-18); and promotion of awareness of the need for loving concern for weaker members. These passages, Hurd argues, respond to the Corinthian letter. By contrast, in those sections identifiable as responses to information 'heard' about the Corinthians (1.11; 5.1; 11.17) the tone is aroused; the treatment is direct and one-sided; past behaviour is condemned; generally no appeal is made to supporting authorites; and the approach is unsympathetic, censorious and authoritative (Hurd 1965: 65-82).

It is now clear from literary and epistolary sources that, despite Hurd's claims, περὶ δέ may introduce topics broached orally, in writing, or combining both, and that, not only does the phrase indicate that each is readily known to the Corinthians from some experience shared with Paul, but also that some debate has occured with him.[40] Nevertheless, Hurd's observations about the different approaches remain pertinent. Paul's approach to topics that the Corinthians have debated with him is distinguishable from that to matters about which he has heard. Hurd also argues that one broad topic lies behind chs. 12–14: the relative value of speaking in tongues and prophesying. The length, complexity and singleness of purpose of the whole (in accordance with the more recent findings on περὶ δέ above) suggest persuasion of those holding a contrary view rather than an answer to a request for information. The Corinthians, Hurd concludes, present a defence of their own position, using Paul himself as a justification, that is 'you yourself, Paul, speak in tongues' (14.18).[41] Wire points out that the argument may have concerned spiritual 'people' (cf. 12.1, 14.37 with 14.1).[42] Paul *could* be introducing a topic of his own choice (Mitchell 1989: 247-50), but it is more likely that he is concerned about Corinthian

---

40. Baasland 1988: 76; Mitchell 1989: 231-56.

41. Hurd 1965: 193-95. Forbes (1995: 261-64) argues that vv. 29-32 address the domination of ministry by official prophets who deny others the right of evaluation, and who leave no opportunity for a simple gift of prophecy. Cf. Fee 1988: 694-95.

42. Wire (1990: 135-36), who also points out that, since other responses to the Corinthian letter open with slogans which Paul immediately qualifies, not only after 12.1 does he question answers rather than answer questions, his careful rhetoric in fact being wariness (p. 80). Hart (1975: 181) argues that chs. 12–14 are Paul's 'corrective and instruction for' some who claim to be πνευματικοί. Paul seems, however, more concerned to teach the whole assembly about such claims, πνευμα-τικοί in secondary focus at 14.37. Hart herself (pp. 325-26) appears inconsistent in her claim that the concern at 14.34-35 is 'the women', who have a 'natural liking... for talk and discussion' and 'some' who view themselves as emancipated.

ignorance which they will recognize from some previous exchange (12.1, 31b; 14.20, 36-38, 40).

Each of the four approaches to interpretation of 1 Cor. 14.34-35 outlined on p. 192 above as 1–4 must therefore be evaluated bearing in mind a background of various kinds of divisions which are not necessarily due either to spiritualization of the self or enthusiasm, and in a context responding to argument rather than questions. The following chapter makes such an evaluation and considers the different effects of each approach when the passage is treated as an exegetical device for 1 Tim. 2.11-12.

Chapter 10

INTERPRETATIONS OF 1 CORINTHIANS 14.34-35

Approaches 1 and 2 seek to reconcile 1 Cor. 14.34-35 with 11.5. Approaches 3 and 4 find such reconciliation impossible. It should again be noted that my discussions below reflect the fact that, although there are exceptions (some of which will be noted), 2 is generally employed by 'conservatives', and 3 by 'liberals'.

1. *14.34-35 as an Interpretative Device*
for its Context (11.5; chs. 12, 14)

This approach is deeply flawed. Some claims made in its defence have no justification, e.g. that in contrast to 14.34-35, 11.5 refers to actions

   i.   taking place somewhere other than the gathered assembly,[1] or
  ii. in a private part of the meeting with only Christians present.[2]

Certainly the absence of any reference to the *ekklesia* before 11.17-18 indicates that limitation to that context should not be assumed at 11.3-16.[3] Nevertheless, the *ekklesia* is obviously one place where its instruction is relevant, since prayer and prophecy would certainly occur. But

---

1.   E.g. Hodge 1857: 304-305; Ridderbos 1977: 461-62; Mare 1981: 277.
2.   E.g. Prohl 1957: 31-34; Scanzoni and Hardesty 1982: 68; Almlie 1982: 41-55.
3.   Cf. Almlie (1982: 41-55), who argues that v. 17 is transitional, τοῦτο referring to vv. 3-16 as another aspect of the Lord's supper meeting, and περὶ δέ at 12.1 marking a shift to the teaching meeting at the same location but with rearranged seating and different focus. To make the 'Supper' meeting 'priestly' Almlie downplays the place of prophecy ('God's speaking to man') and its teaching component (see below), and for the 'teaching' meeting he ignores hymns (14.26), assumes prophecy and tongues–interpretations are necessarily instructional (cf. v. 13-17; Acts 2.11b), and downplays the place any prayer may have had. For the meeting division he employs (pp. 50-51) a dubious interpretation of Acts 20.6-12 for which see Chapter 4, Section 6 above. See pp. 208-209 for discussion on seating practices.

Paul nowhere else advises differing behaviours in private and public[4] or modified group behaviour when outsiders are present. Moreover, he clearly intends prophecy to be both for the common good (12.7)[5] and partially an evangelistic tool $(14.24\text{-}25)$.[6] Also unjustified is the claim that 11.5 speaks of uncontrollable inspiration but 14.34-35 of regular practice (Falconer 1937: 131). In ch. 14 Paul plainly views all vocal contribution as controllable.

Other suggestions are also unpersuasive. It has been claimed that the purpose of the covering in ch. 11 should not be assumed to be to enable women to participate audibly (W.J. Martin 1970: 240). It has also been argued that v. 5 only grudgingly permits women to participate[7] or does not condone such action, only illustrating the issue of the 'coverings' before forbidding it in ch. 14.[8] Support has been sought in the claim that vv. 26, 39-40 address only males.[9] It has been suggested that a

4.   Dautzenberg (1975: 267) says the categories are those of a later time.

5.   Robeck (1975b: 43-44, 53) points out that it normally takes place when believers gather. See also Forbes (1995: 200) 'public', although (p. 288) '[normally] to the church, not to the world'.

6.   Longenecker (1986: 77) says there is no evidence that first-century services were split. See also Crouch 1972: 133; Osborne 1977: 344; Foh 1979: 119; Hurley 1981: 187; Sigountos and Shank 1983: 284; Forbes 1995: 270.

7.   E.g. Kelly 1972: 68.

8.   Knox 1558: 16; Ryrie 1958: 76-77; G.G. Blum 1965: 149, 150-51; Crouch 1972: 133-36 incl. n. 61. See also Robertson and Plummer 1911: 325. Weeks (1972: 21-27) argues that ch. 11 teaches that women should not pray or prophesy in the assembly, but is unconvincing partly because he assumes those activities necessarily involve the exercise of rule. For additional critique of Weeks see Carson (1988: 122 n. 31), and below. Wire (1990: 231, 155) argues that 11.3-16 begins restriction furthered at 14.34-35. This is predicated upon a hierarchical view of 11.3-16 in which women should be veiled to shield male glory, and verges on the speculative, and the idea that the material following ch. 5 deals largely with male sexual sin and female rejection of marriage. Verses 6.1-11, however, (esp. vv. 10-11) suggest a wider than only sexual concern, 7.1 with vv. 2-9 significant if not predominantly male asceticism, and chs. 8–10 that topics addressed are not necessarily directly connected. 1 Corinthians 11.3–16 addresses the need for men and women to appear as such, each honouring their respective heads and the woman both having a glory of her own and straightforwardly assumed at least to pray and prophesy publicly. Cf. Liddon (1897: 18), who believes 14.34-35 overturns a former liberality (11.5; 14.26) in deference to 'the law'.

9.   E.g. Knox 1558: 16; Barnes 1975: 782.

parallel occurs as Paul deals with eating meat in an idol's temple, mentioning it with what appears to be approval in 8.10 but condemning it at 10.20-22 (Hodge 1857: 148). The 'parallel' is tenuous. At 8.9 Paul warns that such eating may become a stumbling block to others so, when at 10.20-22 he claims it amounts to participating in sacrifice to demons, his thought, although certainly more extreme, is not entirely unconnected. Verse 11.5, however, occurs immediately following the commendation of v. 3. Two factors in any case render unpersuasive claims that 11.5 does not envisage women audibly praying and prophesying in mixed company. First, the whole point of 11.3-16 is to outline requirements for communal prayer and prophecy.[10] Secondly, something more substantial than assertion is required to establish 14.34-35 as the 'clearer' passage by which the 'more obscure' 11.5 should be interpreted. The fact is that 11.5 has much more in common with its general context than does 14.34-35, and for that reason this particular aspect of the otherwise troublesome 11.3-16 is quite clear. The letter is addressed to the assembly, obviously including both sexes (1.2) with ἀδελφοί consistently having a generic sense (1.10-11, 26; 2.1; 3.1; 4.6 etc.).[11] In 10.14 Paul similarly addresses ἀγαπητοί μου. Although ἀνδρίζεσθε (16.13) might suggest masculinity,[12] the LXX translators used it at Deut. 31.6, 7 in a call for courage to all Israel and, at Prov. 31.10, ἀνδρείαν for the 'noble woman'.[13] In this general context of address to all members of the assembly, 1 Corinthians 7 and 11.3-16 detail matters concerning both sexes, as more generally do 11.17-35, chs. 12, 13 and 14.1-25. Nothing signals a change in this regard at 14.26-40. Chapter 12 gives no indication that spiritual gifts are restricted to men, and there would be little point in women receiving them 'for the common good' (v. 7) only to be forbidden contribution in open fellowship.[14] Verse

---

10. Foh 1979: 100, 118. Barrett (1971: 331) correctly writes 'Only special pleading...can deny that chapter xi concedes the right of women...to pray and prophesy in...church'. See also e.g. Booth 1859: 5; Allworthy 1917: 92; Windisch 1930: 414-17; Grudem 1982: 72; R.P. Martin 1984: 83; Carson 1988: 122-24.

11. Fee (1988: 52 n. 22) notes the same generic use in Phil. 4.1, immediately followed by pleas that Euodia and Syntyche agree.

12. E.g. '[B]e men of courage' (NIV).

13. Bushnell 1919: §§627-33; BAGD, s.v. ἀνδρεῖος; Fee 1988: 828 n. 13.

14. Witherington 1988: 96. See also e.g. Allworthy 1917: 94; Windisch 1930: 415-16; Grudem 1982: 247.

14.26 appears to assume that women contribute such gifts when 'all come together'.[15]

But if the context consistently gives the impression that women take varied vocal part ἐν ἐκκλησίᾳ, 14.34-35 requires that at least in some way they remain silent. This awkwardness is compounded by the enigmatic reference to 'law', doubt about whether the ruling includes v. 33b, and the masculine pronoun at v. 36. These difficulties make it inadmissible to declare this passage a suitable exegetical device for its otherwise consistent context including 11.5. 14.34-35 must itself be interpreted within that context.

2. The Context as an Interpretative Device for 14.34-35

This approach has three basic forms. The first two have nothing to recommend them.

(a) Assertions or suggestions that the passage allows for exceptional cases[16] or seeks only to order without prejudice to the Spirit's freedom[17] are desperate attempts to weaken what at v. 34 certainly looks like a double and absolute command buttressed by an appeal to law and further reinforced in v. 35.[18]

(b) Although it is, in principle, valid to interpret by Corinthian circumstances, such appeals here prove futile,[19] each reckoning without the universal relevance assumed in the context (vv. 26, 37, and 33b whether belonging to v. 33a or v. 34).[20]

---

15. The value of argument from silence is admittedly dubious, but at Acts 2.5-13 no Jew present is reported as singling women out as particularly 'disgraceful', and nothing suggests that women are silent in the prayer meetings of Acts 4.23-31; 12.12-17; 16.13.

16. E.g. Robertson and Plummer 1911: 324-25; Ryrie 1958: 76-78.

17. E.g. Locke 1705–1707: 222, 245, 442, 453.

18. Conzelmann 1975: 246 n. 58; N.R. Lightfoot 1976: 134; F. Stagg and E. Stagg 1978: 177-78; Sigountos and Shank 1983: 287; Fee 1988: 706; Bilezikian 1989: 145.

19. L. Morris (1971: 201) suggests that Paul is concerned to avoid the 'faintest suspicion of immodesty' in 'morally-lax' Corinth. The writer of Rom. 12.2 and, in 1 Corinthians itself, 2.5a, 13-16, however, is likely to view the opinion of the 'morally lax' with considerable caution.

20. As is noted by Conzelmann 1975: 246 n. 58; Knight 1980: 38. This criticism applies to e.g. Mott 1849: 491; 1872: 552; W.K. Brown 1887: 106, 110; Parvey 1974: 123-25, 128-32; Hart 1975: 327; Howard 1983: 38-39; Forbes 1995: 274-77.

Sometimes adduced are women's local religious practices. Here the 'ecstatic' vocal contributions of chs. 12 and 14 are highlighted, beginning from 12.2-3, which is said to allude to the frenzied ecstasy of some contemporary cults.[21] Forbes has recently demonstrated the unlikelihood of this idea in view of the fact that perceptions of the existence of that contemporary frenzied ecstasy itself have depended upon both generalization across the centuries and blurred distinctions between cults.[22] Moreover, 12.2-3 emphasizes former Corinthian practices without specifying behaviour. Paul recognizes that inspired utterance is not unknown to these former pagans, and is concerned to establish as a foundation for his three subsequent chapters that it is the content of speech, rather than its inspiration, which produces appropriate evidence of the Spirit of God.[23] In spite of the many faults of the Corinthian Christians, the letter provides no real evidence of any of them (male or female) indulging in frenzied cultic practices. They may be unruly ἐν ἐκκλησίᾳ,[24] quite apart from their excesses at the supper, but even this is questionable since 14.23-25 does not necessarily address a situation in which 'everyone' *does* speak in tongues at once, often without interpretation, and in which prophets *do* speak 'over one another'. It seems more likely that Paul projects a situation which *will result if* certain gifts are not manifested in a disciplined manner. At 11.3-16, the 'coverings' (however interpreted) are the subjects, not some accompanying behaviour, and both sexes are addressed. 'Frenzy' is nowhere indicated.

Others argue that it is lack of education which makes these women

Barrett (1971: 332-33) considers that Paul in the interest of peace and order could command women to be silent just as he could silence unedifying male prophets, but is uncertain exactly what speech is forbidden and, in the end, reluctant to localize relevance.

21. E.g. W.C. Klein 1962: 7; C. Kroeger and R. Kroeger 1978a: 331-38; 1978b: 6-7, 9-11; C. Kroeger 1987a: 34. Criswell (1976: 213-14) unconvincingly claims that tongues-speaking is forbidden here, linking it with the ecstatic frenzy of the cult of Aphrodite.

22. Forbes 1995: e.g. 169-70, 180 with n. 68, 211, 280-89.

23. Fee 1988: 577-78 with n. 41. For alternative interpretations rejecting 'ecstatic frenzy' here see Grudem 1982: 163-65; Carson 1988: 24-31. Keener (1992: 78) writes: 'Typical ancient views on womens' frenzy do not tell us how women acted and texts on how women acted suggest that too many men acted in similar ways for us to apply this background only to female[s]...'

24. See e.g. *MAMA* 10 (1993: no. 330) for the gross behaviour and excessive noise of congregations of a later period, including chattering women.

unsuited to theological discussion or contribution.[25] Yet, if this were the problem, why would all women apparently be included in the prohibition when some in antiquity were, in fact, educated,[26] and why would the many uneducated men not similarly be silenced? More importantly, standards of education are beside the point in a letter consistently assuming everyone at Corinth capable of understanding and being faithful to Paul's teaching (1.18–3.23).

Paul is also said here to apply 9.19-23 in a milieu caught between progressive ideas about women and valued traditional practices.[27] The absolute 14.34-35 in no way resembles that 'principle of accommodation' (cf. e.g. 8.9-13). See again also Paul's views at Rom. 12.2 and 1 Cor. 2.5a, 13-16.[28] The context suggests that any attempt to soften the impact of 14.34-35 by limiting it to a Corinthian situation is bound to fail.

(c) A more promising form of this approach might appear to be the limitation of the prohibition at 14.34-35 to some sort of 'out-of-order' speech (sometimes said to be that of particular women), often envisaged as resulting from eschatological trends. An immediate contextual basis for this is found in the three-stage sequence in ch. 14: Paul regulates speaking in tongues (to prevent all so speaking at once, vv. 23-28), prophecy (to prevent incorrect use, vv. 29-33) and women's speech (vv. 34-35). Women, it is reasoned, must have been speaking in some unacceptable way.[29] There are three difficulties here.

25. E.g. Olthuis 1976: 136, 140-41; Keener 1992: 83-84; Forbes 1995: 277 n. 57. See also W.K. Brown 1887: 105-106, 109; Scholer 1983: 13.

26. E.g. Friedländer 1965: 230-31; Sigountos and Shank 1983: 286-87; Verner 1983: 81; Horsley 1982–89: V, 12-14, 45, 48, 111. Forbes (1995: 277 n. 57) objects that educated exceptions were few. It nevertheless remains difficult to see why those few should be silenced.

27. Sigountos and Shank 1983: 293-95.

28. Whether or not Col. 2.8 and Eph. 4.17-18 are believed written by Paul, each is relevant. See Chapter 8, Section 5.2 for discussion on Christian Household Codes.

29. E.g. Grimke 1838: 110-11; G.G. Blum 1965: 150, 153; Hart 1975: 326; Knight 1975: 87-88; 1980: 36; Giles 1977: 61; Osborne 1977: 345; Hurley 1981: 188-90; Key 1984: 146; Witherington 1988: 96, 103; Gritz 1991: 89; Keener 1992: 72. See also Jervis 1995: 65, 71. Also noting contextual linguistic connections is Bartsch 1965: 69. See also Ellis 1978: 27 n. 25; 1981: 218. Grudem (1982: 242-44) also says that σιγάω never implies total silence, the context always specifying the kind intended, and such is sometimes the case for λαλέω. See n. 30 below.

i.   Each topic Paul addresses is not necessarily caused by either enthusiasm or eschatological trends: see the Corinthian background outlined in Chapter 9.

ii. Even though behaviour ἐν ἐκκλησίᾳ remains in view, the ideas and rhetorical patterns in vv. 34-35 differ significantly from those preceding. Verses 34-35 subordinate rather than order people, reverse the main verbs (silence, speaking), and occur after vv. 32, 33 (the former in principle including tongues-speaking, and the latter a rhetorical climax). Verse 34 appears to forbid all, not specific, speech, and is triply reinforced—by an appeal to law and, in v. 35, an addendum on question-asking and a repetition of the original command, this time warning of disgrace. Contextual similarities are therefore superficial.[30]

iii. Definition of the forbidden speech proves elusive. The following demonstration divides such definitions into five sub-categories.

1. *Disorderly Speech*

This is variously envisaged as chatter or gossip, disruption by asking questions or calling them out to husbands from a gallery or across an

---

30. Allison 1988: 30, 37-39. Windisch (1930: 418) notes that, although key-words closely tie the passage and context, there is no apparent connection to spiritual gifts. See also Leipoldt 1953: 125-26; Dautzenberg 1975: 264-65; Barton 1986: 230; Wire 1990: 153; Fee 1994: 280. The observations of Grudem (1982: 242) (see n. 29) should therefore be treated cautiously. So should Allison's additional observation that disallowing some to contribute conflicts with the contextual principle (v. 27). Tongues-speaking even with interpretation is limited, so πάντα πρὸς οἰκοδομὴν γινέσθω is concerned not so much that all should be absolutely free to speak but that, when so many do, it should be with a view to strengthening the ἐκκλησία. On the other hand, since gifts are intended for the common good (12.7), it is difficult to see how the ἐκκλησία could be strengthened by excluding so many. See also Meeks 1973: 203-204. Witherington (1988: 91) cites Robinson, who argues that Paul here follows a pattern of exhortation (cf. Col. 3.18ff.; Eph. 5.19ff.) about inspired speech followed by commands to women, connected by ὑποτάσσεσθαι. The passages cited, however, both have a broader focus. The spiritual songs etc. preceding Col. 3.18 are sung etc. as the word of God is allowed to dwell richly within, v. 17 setting vv. 18–4.1 (incl. husband, children etc.) in the context of 'whatever you do'. Eph. 5.19-20 in the context of 5.17–6.18 is one aspect of understanding the will of the Lord, one other being mutual if differing submissions (v. 21), again also by husbands, fathers etc.

aisle or other barrier.[31] Both historical and textual contexts present challenges here.

The assemblies of which the New Testament speaks meet in the homes of wealthy Christians (Acts 18.7; Phlm. 2) where furniture is sparse by modern standards.[32] Eutychus, for one, sits with some informality on a window sill (Acts 20.7-12). Certainly Jesus and Paul address synagogues in accordance with normal practice (Lk. 4.16-21; Acts 13.14-45), and Paul teaches by discussion at the lecture hall of Tyrannus (Acts 19.9-10). Nonetheless, in 1 Cor. 11.17ff. Christians gather for a communal meal and to contribute their various gifts of the Spirit. Nothing suggests that women are divided from men. Such evidence as there is external to 1 Corinthians provides no indication of such a division. There is no archaeological evidence in the first century CE for women's galleries even in synagogues,[33] and pre-70 CE synagogues in fact generally met in houses or multi-purpose meeting places.[34] The women may have sat in those gatherings at the back or to one side, but there is no evidence of this.[35] Although they were not permitted into all parts of the temple, Anna certainly appears to have been free to prophesy and address men in its precincts.[36] In New Testament synagogues women appear able to hear without difficulty (Acts 17.1-4; 18.26), and at least one is visible to and able to approach the speaker

31. E.g. Gordon 1894: 914-15; Robertson and Plummer 1911: 324-26; Allworthy 1917: 95; Moffatt 1941: 232-35; Kähler 1960: 76-78; Parvey 1974: 128; Scanzoni and Hardesty 1982: 68-69; Howard 1983: 38; Jervis 1995: 60-61. Some who believe the prohibition absolute nevertheless envisage a physical division (e.g. Leipoldt 1953: 125-27; N.R. Lightfoot 1976: 133), and others no physical division but chatter/questions (e.g. Stouffer 1981: 258; Orr and Walther 1982: 313; Witherington 1988: 103). For contemporary literature in which women questioning men in public is considered inappropriate see Forbes (1995: 274-75 incl. n. 52).

32. Ward-Perkins and Claridge 1980: 40. Cf. Vitruvius, VI.5.2, where reference is made to space for audiences in rhetoricians' homes.

33. Brooten 1982: 137-38. Contra e.g. Fitzer (1963: 19 with n. 36), with which cf. Brooten pp. 123-24.

34. Kee 1995: 481-500, although cf. Lk. 7.5. Kee (p. 491) somewhat speculatively argues that Acts 18.7 probably means that the Corinthian Jewish meetings were in a house, and more persuasively (p. 496) that excavation at Dura Europos shows that synagogue, church and Mithraeum all evolved from houses.

35. Safrai 1976: 939; Wilcox 1991: 10. Contra e.g. Jeremias (1969: 374) who speaks of a lattice barrier; Spencer 1974: 217; Dautzenberg 1989: 188.

36. If Jewish women are free so to act at least in some public places this may explain n. 15 above re Acts 2.5-13.

(Lk. 13.10-13). The claim that New Testament Christian *ekklesia* divide the sexes is without relevant contemporary foundation.[37] Neither should it be assumed that some significant part of the female component of the Corinthian assembly chatter, gossip or ask questions while their menfolk stalwartly carry on the meetings.[38] These gatherings occur in a culture much less regulated by time than our own[39] and, whilst it should not be supposed that all contribute vocally, all *may* do so.[40] Murphy-O'Connor calculates that there must be at least 50 people present (1983: 156-58), but proportions of some homes noted in Chapter 9 above suggest that there may be substantially more. Unless the home in which they gather has an auditorium,[41] such a crowd may at least in part be seated around the *impluvium* between columns and statues, or in a courtyard, near a fountain or pool, again amongst columns, statuary, garden beds, trellised vines or even very large trees.[42] The Corinthian assembly includes many immature individualists who are free to speak but fail to grasp that the purpose of their gathering is mutual edification (12.7; 14.12, 26). Assuming that the vocal disorder so often envisaged is present (although see above), they seem to be concentrating on their own personal experience (R.P. Martin 1984: 78).

Against that background the speculation that women 'chatter and gossip' fails on two counts. First, although λαλέω (v. 34) *could* mean 'chatter',[43] that nuance is absent everywhere else in the New Testament. Throughout this chapter the word means 'speak' (cf. vv. 27-29), so

---

37. Philo (*Vit. Cont.* 9.32, 68, 80, 83-88) describes Therapeutae dividing the sexes, but appears to consider this unusual, called for by the celibacy practised, and in no way excluding the women from participation. Lane Fox (1986: 559 and n. 25) describes the segregation of a later period in *Didascalia Apostolorum* and John Chrysostom. See also Grisbrooke 1990: 13-14.

38. S.B. Clark (1980: 185) correctly points out that the instruction is issued not because women are disorderly but because they are women.

39. Carcopino 1956: 147, 151-52, 154; Banks 1985a: 7; 1985b: 100-101.

40. Forbes (1995: 276) claims that limitation of time is Paul's motive for restricting tongues and prophecy, and that questions by women might extend discussion. The stated motivation, however, is desire to correct disorder. R.P. Martin 1984: 79.

41. See n. 32 above.

42. A.G. McKay 1975: 41; Ward-Perkins and Claridge 1980: 41-44.

43. BAGD, s.v. Horsley (1982–89: I, 28) cites *Sammelbuch griechischer Urkunden aus Aegypten*, V.2 (1938) 7835, for translation of which see Nock 1972: 415. See also Horsley pp. 68-69.

there is inadequate cause to conclude that it does not do so here.[44] Secondly, it is presumptuous to exclude women from the general commotion and depict them in quite different ignorant behaviours unstated in the text. In fact, women chattering would hardly be noticable in what would be no more nor less than an undisciplined babble of male and female voices.[45] The text offers no support for claims that women are chattering amongst themselves or calling out to their more dignified husbands.

Others limit the forbidden speech:

> only to wives;
> to teaching;
> to asking questions in dialogue instruction; or
> to public evaluation of what the prophets say.

Before proceeding to each of these individually, a general critique of three common factors will avoid repetition.

First, there is insufficient evidence to conclude that question-asking is part of the format of Corinthian meetings.[46] It is at least doubtful that

44. Bushnell 1919: §197 (3); Barrett 1971: 332; Grudem 1987: 20 n. 13. Allison (1988: 36) notes that, since public speech was a male occupation considered shameful for women, there is no reason to assume that only the latter would chatter disruptively. See also Forbes 1995: 271. Contra E. Wilson 1849: 151; Booth 1859: 8-10; Scanzoni and Hardesty 1982: 69. R.P. Martin (1984: 85-87) claims that in this context λαλεῖν is glossalalic. At vv. 27-30 (cf. here), however, it is modified to convey that meaning. C. Kroeger and R. Kroeger (1978a: 335; 1978b: 10) argue that it here denotes meaningless utterance. Cf. however v. 29.

45. Fee 1988: 703. Wire (1990: 140-47) writes: 'the Corinthians' priority is speaking in the Spirit, and it thrives on the expression and interaction of many voices'. It is questionable, however, that significant 'interaction' is taking place. Jervis (1995: 60-65 and n. 39) envisages unspiritual and uninspired speech about prophecy. Beginning from a possibility (which p. 62 appears to shift to assumption) that Corinthian spirituality resembles Philo's, she concludes that Paul wants to disabuse the women/assembly of the perception that the women's contribution is 'spiritual'. Her argument is more speculative than forceful.

46. Neither does it follow that, if women *do* ask questions, they are impertinent, presumptuous, ignorant or foolish. The questions mentioned are non-specific, and the context provides no additional information. S.B. Clark 1980: 185. Contra e.g. Witherington 1988: 103; Keener 1992: 81-82, 88. Nor is there sufficient reason to suppose that some such questions would not be directed to other women. Leipoldt 1953: 125; Barton 1986: 231.

there was some kind of discussion or public evaluation.[47] It is not at all clear at v. 29 that the prophets' messages are publicly discussed: διακ-ρίνω may mean 'weigh carefully', not 'arbitrate' in the sense of a public hearing[48] or discussion (cf. 11.29, 31). The only other suggestion anywhere in the letter of extended interaction (formal or informal) is v. 35, but it is difficult to see upon what basis the already double prohibition in v. 34, repeated in a stronger form at v. 35b, may validly be defined as the asking of questions by its more particular reinforcement in v. 35a.[49] The prohibition here seems to be upon speech, even the asking of questions with a view to learning.

Secondly, identification of 'the law' is always a problem. When Paul elsewhere appeals to Old Testament law he cites the relevant passage.[50] That he does not do so here is not surprising: the Old Testament neither forbids women any sort of public speech nor says they must be subordinate in such a way as to provide sufficient foundation upon which they might be so silenced.[51] Apart from Gen. 3.16, marital headship in

47. Bushnell 1919: §197 (4). Contra e.g. B. Weiss 1885: 124; Windisch 1930: 419; Kähler 1959: 4; Héring 1962: 154-55; Hommes 1969: 7; Hart 1975: 325; N.R. Lightfoot 1976: 134; Osborne 1977: 344-45; Karris 1977: 206; Trummer 1978: 146; S.B. Clark 1980: 186-87; Ellis 1981: 218; Hurley 1981: 190; Grudem 1982: (cautiously) 61, 65-66 n. 126; Sigountos and Shank 1983: 284-85; Schüssler Fiorenza 1983: 232; R.P. Martin 1984: 80; Wire 1990: 148-49.

48. BAGD, s.v. Dunn (1983: 82, 89) moderately interprets but subsequently assumes public discussion. For discussion on the identity of those who are so to discern see e.g. Robeck 1975b: 45-47; Grudem 1982: 58-62; Carson 1988: 120. See also Dunn (1983: 82, 88-96), R.P. Martin (1984: 80-82, 86), Wire (1990: 148), and Forbes (1995: 265-69 incl. nn. 27-33), none of whom prove their claim that this discernment is the spiritual gift διακρίσεις πνευμάτων (12.10). Cf. the more cautious Robeck who, although (e.g. n. 56) speaking of the 'gift of discernment' (without modification) in relation to prophecy, says 'discerning of spirits...may at times be properly used to test a prophet' (p. 53).

49. See also Crouch 1972: 134-35 n. 61. Contra e.g. Fung 1987: 194-97.

50. Murphy-O'Connor 1986: 91; Fee 1988: 707; 1994: 279.

51. Fee 1988: 707; Bilezikian 1989: 149. For an earlier similar observation see E. Wilson 1849: 153. Cf. Prohl (1957: 45-47), who unconvincingly argues that Exod. 20.14; Est. 1.20 capture the law in question; i.e. male marital headship; and Jervis (1995: 56-58, 66-67, 71-72 with nn. 21, 62, 63, 78), who suspects that the law concerns control of inappropriate speech (e.g. Deut. 27.9; Exod. 4.12), women 'possibly' more prone than men to be disruptive ἐν ἐκκλησία. Exod. 4.12, however, is directed to Moses, and whilst Deut. 27.9 addresses all Israel, since evidence is lacking elsewhere in 1 Corinthians that women, specifically, are disruptive,

the Old Testament is specified only at Numbers 5 and 30, and there defined: wives must be sexually faithful, and family heads are responsible (under specific circumstances) to veto a woman's vows (Bushnell 1919: §§173-80). Numbers 5.9-20 is not necessarily an expression of general subjugation, the context suggesting 'under your husband's authority (to expect sexual faithfulness)'.[52] Whatever practices evolved by the hellenistic era, and whatever dating is preferred for Numbers, chs. 5 and 30 do not themselves imply the total subjection of women, particularly in any way relevant to silencing them in Christian *ekklesia*. Genesis 3.16 itself[53] will be examined in Part IV, Appendix 3, but two things should here be noted: it foretells, commanding neither woman nor man; and in Greek versions such as would be read at Corinth,[54] in the context of ἀποστροφή (Hebrew *t°shûqāh*), κυριεύσει (Hebrew *māšal*) may convey something very different from 'rule over' meaning 'subjugate'. Whether Gen. 3.16 foretells, introduces, or maintains some form of marital hierarchy (and Appendix 3 will argue that each is problematic), there is a considerable leap from it to the ecclesial silence required at 1 Cor. 14.34-35. It has been reasoned that, since Paul bases 11.3-16 on the creation narrative of Genesis 2, in ch. 14 he means 'because God made man first, and woman to be his helper, she must be obedient'.[55] Eve's leading of Adam (Gen. 3.17) is sometimes seen as

speech prohibited at 14.34-35 is not convincingly so defined.

52. Cf. also Ezek. 23.5 (where AV, NIV translate 'mine' when God is the husband), AV and NIV for Num. 5.19-20 picturing simply a married woman (but NEB 'owing obedience'; Sturdy 1976: 44, and RSV 'under your husband's authority', Noth 1968: 48), Deut. 22.22 *ba'al*, translated by AV 'a woman married to an husband', and NIV 'another man's wife', and Rom. 7.2 ὕπανδρος for which AV, TEV, NIV, Phillips, JB, RSV, NEB all translate 'a married woman'. Each passage deals with real/analogous sexual faithfulness, not total subjugation. Cf. the fuller *kāna'* Judg. 3.30; Gray 1976: 54. Cf. Binns 1927: 33.

53. Suggesting this as the law in view are e.g. Str–B: III, 468, but see at my n. 61 below; Bachmann 1936: 425; Leipoldt 1953: 125; Ryrie 1958: 79 with n. 34; L.Morris 1971: 201; Barrett 1971: 330; Stendahl 1982: 29-30; Orr and Walther 1982: 312. Mare (1981: 276) suggests also 1 Cor. 11.3; Eph. 5.22; 1 Tim. 2.12; Tit. 2.5, all of which are either from the same letter or not yet written and cannot be viewed already as 'law'. Osborne (1977: 344-45, 347) aligns Gen. 3.16 with 1 Cor. 11.8-9 but subsequently introduces 'the fall'. 'Gen. 3' (Dautzenberg 1975: 261).

54. Bushnell (1919: §198) notes that Paul almost exclusively employs the LXX in this letter.

55. E.g. Ryrie 1958: 79; Ridderbos 1977: 462; Knight 1980: 37-38; Moo 1980: 74; Grudem 1987: 22; Fung 1987: 192-93; Carson 1988: 129. Olthuis (1976: 135

the connection, that is 'God made the woman helper, so (because when she stepped out of that submissive role she led the man astray) women must not vocally minister to men'.[56] Others combine Genesis 2 and 3.16.[57] However such interpretations of Genesis are viewed, the consistent impression elsewhere in 1 Corinthians that Paul *does* accept that women may contribute vocally ἐν ἐκκλησίᾳ creates difficulties for this 'law' even when the speech prohibited is declared limited. It has been suggested that, since Old Testament law permits women to prophesy, Paul here wants them to submit only as that law says (Foh 1979: 120-21). This is more ingenious than forceful, accounting neither for the apparently absolute nature of the command nor the absence of Old Testament definition of the extent of submission required. Laws beyond the Old Testament are therefore suggested, each of them similarly problematic. Some argue that in accordance with Rom. 3.27 a principle of Paul's own is in view,[58] picked up again in v. 37 as 'what I write to you is from the Lord'. This presupposes a previous ruling for which there is no evidence, and dilutes the immediacy of v. 37.[59] Those who claim that the appeal is to Jewish oral law cite the associated use of the rab-

---

with n. 2, 140) argues that this leads to confusion, but envisages the co-partnership of the creation story without explaining what obedience is there directed. He also sees the submission directed to God rather than men. Although, however, v. 35 does not specify that the 'law' in view is marital, its restriction of ministry to men implies an even more general subordination. Carson (1991: 148-49, 152) claims that the 'law' is identifiable as 'scripture' from 11.8-9 and 1 Tim. 2.13, i.e. Gen. 2.20b-24. Unless we assume that Paul had personally assured the Corinthians that his instruction about women's roles is always based on that passage, however, it is unlikely that as the letter is read they would reach the same conclusion: 11.8-9 has been left well behind; 14.34 is more specific than Gen. 2.20b-24, and by contrast to it (see Appendix 3) is clearly hierarchical; and 1 Tim. 2.13 has not yet been written.

56. E.g. Meinertz 1931: 39. See also my Part IV and Appendix 3 for full discussion.

57. E.g. G.G. Blum 1965: 152-53; N.R. Lightfoot 1976: 133; Grudem 1982: 253-54. Some are vaguer: e.g. 'Torah, i.e. the first section of Hebrew scriptures' (Woodhouse 1985b: 17). See also Windisch 1930: 417; Jeremias 1963: 19; Foh 1979: 118.

58. R.P. Martin 1984: 76, 87. Martin also cites Gal. 6.2, but this refers to the 'law' of Christ.

59. Unconvincing too are e.g.: E. Wilson (1849: 151), who speaks of Corinthian church law barring unqualified interruption by both males and females (see also J.G. Baldwin 1984: 154); and 'custom or pattern of behaviour of women in all the churches... (33b)' (Hart 1975: 326).

binic formula ἐπιτρέπεται[60] and such passages as *Gen. R.* 18.1; *Yoma* 43b; *Meg.* 23a.[61] Not only must these account for Paul's otherwise generally liberal attitude to women, but they must also explain why, although critical of Peter's observance of Jewish custom amongst Gentiles (Gal. 2.14), he himself now appeals to such laws. Some claim the appeal is to conventional values.[62] Conventions, however, vary, and even later rabbinic practice (not necessarily reflecting first century CE)

---

60. Aalen (1964: 513-25) demonstrates the Jewishness of ἐπιτρέπεται, but not that Paul equates the law with the ἐντολή (v. 37). In the New Testament the latter is not, as Aalen argues for Judaism, reserved for prescriptions from the 'written torah' (cf. e.g. Jn 15.10a; Acts 17.15), and ἃ γράφω ὑμῖν refers to the whole foregoing instruction, not just that to women. Allison (1988: 43), citing J.Weiss, also notes that ἐπιτρέπεται is a common rabbinic formula relating the Torah to contemporary situations, occurring in the epistles only elsewhere at 1 Tim. 2.12. It should be noted, however, that in the latter the verb is in the active voice.

61. E.g. Fung 1987: 192. See also Str–B (III, 468), who warn that words from tradition are words of Torah. Cohen (1949: 161) demonstrates that restrictive rabbinic views about women's intellectual capacity are not unanimous. Crouch (1972: 110-11, 138-39) believes hellenistic law to be in view. Olthuis (1976: 148 n. 7) suggests Jewish law about prayer as an alternative (cf. n. 61 above). Prohl (1957: 33, 35) confuses rabbinic law, Greek custom, and the Old Testament. Parvey (1974: 128-32) anachronistically declares a parallel with the Talmud (codified 600 CE) and claims that Paul has no command from the Lord (cf. however v. 37). The old law invalid, some women celibate, and some apparently violating established boundaries, he wants neither to suppress genuine gifts nor have women address the congregation, so he gives practical advice about ecstatics, calls the prophets to account, challenges the genuineness of their gifts (v. 36), and puts his own authority to the test (vv. 37-38). But if Corinthian women pray and prophecy and Paul is reluctant to limit genuine gifts, he is indecisive and confused, clutching his personal authority, lashing out at (of all places) v. 36 for no apparent reason at prophets but not tongues-speakers, reluctantly allowing women to be grateful for the small liberties of prayer, or prophecy (which gift 12.29 indicates all did not have). Such 'advice' is more obscure than 'practical'.

62. E.g. 'custom' (Scanzoni and Hardesty 1982: 69; see also Falconer 1937: 131; Parvey 1974: 129), a meaning found nowhere in the New Testament (Gutbrod 1967: 1059-83). Scanzoni and Hardesty do not even claim to establish adequately that the passage only requires orderly meetings, not that women may not minister, speculating that: i. meetings may be held in synagogues/orthodox homes; and ii. highborn women may be offended by outspoken lower-class women. See, however, Acts 18.7; 1 Cor. 11.22. Contra also Schüssler Fiorenza (1983: 231-32), discussed below.

is diverse.[63] Moreover, for Galatian women Paul resists reversion to restrictive customary practices (Witherington 1981: 593-604) (see also 1 Cor. 7.4, 34). Rom. 16.1-7, 12-13, 15; Phil. 4.2-3; Acts 16.13-15 all picture women in Pauline circles associating with men other than their husbands or sons. This is clearly not unique in the period, but it does contrast with 1 Cor. 14.34-35. It has also been suggested that the law is general—either Jewish, Gentile, or both.[64] The New Testament nowhere else makes such general legal reference (A.F. Johnson 1986: 159), and contextual appeals to both universal Christian practice (vv. 34b, 36) and the 'word of the Lord' (v. 38) make it unlikely here. Finally, in the immediate context of a strong claim to divine authority (v. 37), appeal to law of any sort appears rhetorically superfluous (Allison 1988: 43). In short, this reference is both unlike Paul and obscure.[65]

The third factor to be noted in a preliminary general critique of the sub-categories on p. 210 above is the dubious nature of conclusions which result from interpreting this difficult passage by others which are themselves problematic.

With these points in mind, I now turn to the remaining sub-categories.

2. Wives Only

When the prohibition is limited to wives[66] there does, on the surface, appear to be a foundation for credibility: women are to 'ask their own husbands at home', and the resulting restricted prohibition would be familiar. Philo, although believing women generally unsuited to public life and discussion, approves of female Therapeutae participating, their celibacy enabling them to abandon the irrational, passive, matter-bound

---

63. See e.g. Jeremias 1969: 359-76; Jacobs 1971: 625-27; Meeks 1973: 174-79; Brooten 1985: 65-91. Pryor (1993: 5) notes there is no record of the Jews criticizing Jesus in this regard. See also Wilcox 1991: 9-10. Cf. Forbes 1993: 14. For restrictive views see e.g. Philo, *Spec. Leg.* 3.169; Plutarch, *Praec. coniug.* 31-32, *Mor.* 138a-146a, esp. 18; Livy 34.2.9. See also Bushnell 1919: §202. Cf. however Brooten (1982: *passim*), and Verner (1983: 55-56) citing Xenophon Eph. *Eph.*

64. E.g. Liefeld 1986: 149; Kroeger 1987a: 30.

65. Allworthy 1917: 97; S.B. Clark 1980: 187-88; Murphy-O'Connor 1986: 91; Fee 1988: 707.

66. In addition to those discussed below see e.g. E. Wilson 1849: 154; W.K. Brown 1887: 107; Robertson and Plummer 1911: 325; Moffatt 1941: 232-34; Prohl 1957: 32-34; Kähler 1960: 74; Barrett 1971: 331; Orr and Walther 1982: 312-13; Giles 1985: 56; Gritz 1991: 89-90.

female nature for the rational, active, spiritual male role.[67] Schüssler
Fiorenza accordingly reasons that in 1 Corinthians 7

> The single-minded dedication of the unmarried woman and virgin, but
> not the unmarried man...is qualified...(7:34). Paul here ascribes a spe-
> cial holiness...We therefore can surmise that Paul is able to accept
> the[ir] pneumatic participation...in the worship service..., but argues in
> 14:34f. against...active participation [by]...wives.

1 Corinthians 14.34-35, she claims, orders glossalalists, prophets and
wives, but its strictness in comparison with Paul's attitudes to women
elsewhere surprises her. Here, she argues, he takes over bourgeois
moral concepts denoting conventional rather than absolute values, presupposing that 'wives had dared to question other women's husbands or
point out some mistakes of their own during the congregational interpreting of the Scriptures and prophecy'.[68] There are several problems
here. First, Paul's male–female distinctions at 7.32-34 describe the
same dedication and holiness, which for him involves both body and
spirit for both sexes (1 Thess. 4.4), and is unaffected by marital status
(1 Cor. 7.7). He says the unmarried are free (7.32-34), not that they are
specially holy.[69] In Graeco-Roman first century CE, where daughters are
not accorded freedoms denied their mothers,[70] it seems unlikely that he
would deny to the married the ministry he allows the (sometimes
immature) single person. The apparently absolute nature of the prohibition with its appeal to 'the law' suggests that all women are in view,
and that they are expected privately to question whatever menfolk they
may have.[71] Secondly, if a wife's public judgment of the ministry of her
κύριος is considered disgraceful, what of other conventionally subordinate household members: female dependants of any age including wid-

67. Cf. Philo, *Spec. Leg.* 111, 169, 171; *Vit. Cont.* 32, 68, 80, 83-88. See also
Mortley 1981: 14-15.

68. Schüssler Fiorenza (1983: 230-32), the inset quotation from p. 231. See also
Hayter 1987: 130-31.

69. Bartchy 1973: 144; Bloesch 1982: 33; Allison 1988: 40.

70. Murphy-O'Connor (1986: 91), who concludes that Schüssler Fiorenza's
harmonization of 14.34-35 with 11.5 is meaningless. See also Grudem 1982: 247-
48 n. 24; Forbes 1995: 271 with n. 43. Cf. Prohl (1957: 33) claiming that Paul
responds to an actual situation where only married women are speaking, 'maiden
ladies' of the day not daring publicly to address a male speaker. This ignores
widows and divorcees.

71. See also Jervis 1995: 51 n. 3.

ows, sons, grandchildren, freedmen/women, and slaves and clients of either sex?[72] Not only does Paul not forbid these any sort of speech, but he wants (a non-specific) 'each' to contribute for the upbuilding of all. Thirdly, (as argued above) conventional wisdom was not unified, and Paul shows plenty of evidence elsewhere of non-restrictive practice. Fourthly, Paul elsewhere claims to have opposed Peter to his face for choosing to please Judaizers (Gal. 2.11-14).[73] If in 1 Corinthians 14 he reverts to convention in conflict with his own teaching and practice elsewhere, he stands accused by his own words of hypocrisy (Gal. 2.13). One difficulty here is that the prohibition itself, together with appeals to the 'law', and to πάσαις ταῖς ἐκκλησίαις (v. 33b, whatever its reference), suggests an intention to deliver something more absolute than Schüssler Fiorenza acknowledges. Finally, as argued above, there is no convincing evidence of public congregational evaluation at these Corinthian meetings. The difficulties of 1 Cor. 14.34-35 cannot adequately be explained by declaring it a requirement that wives keep quiet and not question husbands, whether their own or someone else's.

Ellis argues that the passage shares with 1 Tim. 2.12 an underlying Christian exposition of Genesis 1–3.[74] Gen. 3.16, he says, stipulates a wife's subordination to her husband, and 1 Cor. 11.3, 9 teaches subordination, so marriage is part of the rationale Paul uses to regulate women's ministry. 1 Corinthians 14.34-35 is therefore Pauline, prohibiting a woman's co-participation in prophetic ministry with her husband present since testing his message would be disgraceful. Such a ruling, Ellis claims, is essentially no different to vv. 26-33 and 11.2-16. Codex Fuldensis (sixth-century CE), he says, places the passage after v. 40 but includes a marginal reading after v. 33,[75] the scribe having access to two readings. Because it is unclear whether v. 33b belongs with v. 34 or v. 33, and the subject matter continues more smoothly

72. See also Wire 1990: 229.

73. If Pauline authorship is accepted for Colossians, 2.8 is noteworthy; if that authorship is rejected, the continuing differentiation between 'human tradition and the principles of this world' and life in Christ is still noteworthy. See Chapter 8, Section 5.2 for discussion on Household Codes such as 3.18–4.1.

74. Ellis 1981: 213-20, followed by Barton 1986: esp. 229. Also appealing to common tradition are Bartsch 1965: 69; Sigountos and Shank 1983: 287.

75. Ellis (1981: 213 n. 1) cites Metzger's 1971 edn of 1975: 565. Payne (1995: 241-42, 45), however, demonstrates that Metzger, not having actually viewed the MS, was mistaken. See further p. 227 below.

without vv. 34-35, he reasons that they are a marginal note written
either by Paul or at his instruction.[76] Again there are several problems.
Ellis too easily accepts that public discussion-type testing of prophecy
even occurred, and boldly interprets one difficult passage by others just
as problematic. Even granted that Gen. 3.16 'stipulates' marital hierarchy (although see above and Appendix 3) and constitutes the relevant
'law', and so forms a basis upon which silence may be commanded, a
logical leap of some magnitude is still required. 1 Corinthians 14.34-35
itself apparently intends to silence women in public meetings, and this
exceeds the extent of marital submission demonstrated elsewhere in
either Testament. Whatever 1 Cor. 11.3-16 teaches, it is at least argu-
ably not 'subordination' (see Appendix 3). Whilst Ellis is very likely
correct in seeing a single Christian tradition behind 1 Cor. 14.34-35 and
1 Tim. 2.12, the inexactness of the linguistic parallels (which he himself
notes) together with the differing contexts, warns against too-hasty
identification of shared details of that tradition. This is especially so if
(as he suspects) 1 Timothy 3.1a is backward-referring (see Part IV). In
addition to this problem of cross-interpretation of various difficult passages, 1 Cor. 14.34-35 *does*, in fact, 'essentially' differ from vv. 26-33
and 11.2-16, prohibiting (absolutely) 'speech', including even the asking of questions, and regulating only the activities of women. Finally,
why would Paul write 11.5, ch. 13, and 14.1-26 and what follows, apparently with all women in view, only to insert into that otherwise
smoothly flowing extended section two later sentences which drasti-
cally alter the application of much of it by forbidding a large proportion
of women vocal participation? If he had intended all along that women
be excluded, he could hardly have omitted that detail as he originally
wrote. Ellis proves neither that only wives are in view nor that only certain speech is prohibited.

3. Teaching

Amongst those presenting this interpretation Knight is prominent.[77]
Although sensibly interpreting λαλέω in light of the context and previ-

---

76. See also Moffatt 1941: 233. Ross (1992: 156) finds the resulting connection
between v. 33b and v. 36 unlikely. He speculates that an early copyist omitted
vv. 34-35 because of apparent inconsistency with 11.5, perhaps preserving them in
the margin from where they were later restored, but again Payne is instructive: see
n. 75 above.

77. See also e.g. Meinertz 1931: 38. R.P. Martin (1984: 87-88), who interprets

ous use as public communication, he is generally unconvincing. First, he finds it 'most appropriate' to draw a parallel with the correlation of speaking and silence at (a Pauline) 1 Tim. 2.11-14, where the teaching of men violates the divinely established role relationship (1975: 87-88; 1980: 30, 36-37). Even granted Pauline authorship for the Pastorals, his interpretation of one difficult passage by another[78] assumes familiarity with the subject matter of 1 Timothy, if not the letter itself, when the Corinthians obviously were expected to construct definitions from the context and practices Paul had taught amongst them. Secondly, although teaching is one of several activities featured at v. 26, the primary subjects throughout the section are prophecy and speaking in tongues, summarized in v. 39, so it seems unlikely that they would conclude at vv. 34-35 that the subject is teaching. Thirdly, by limiting 1 Tim. 2.11-12 to public assemblies Knight negates conflict with Acts 18.26; but 1 Cor. 14.26 suggests that Paul does accept women bringing instruction even in public mixed company. Fourthly, the continual instruction forbidden at 1 Tim. 2.12 is not the speech ἐν ἐκκλησίᾳ at 1 Cor. 14.34-35, where the context suggests, not only (as Knight correctly argues) an absolute application, but an absolute prohibition against speech. Fifthly, Knight recognizes that 11.5 allows women prayer and prophecy, claiming that these entail no authority over others, but also that the latter involves an essentially passive instrumentality.[79] He himself argues that prophecy is the result of God's Spirit acting in

---

substantially by 1 Tim. 2.8-15, envisages women wrongfully aspiring to be charismatic teachers of revelations at odds with apostolic proclamation. For refutation see Carson (1988: 126-27). Less sure about teaching being the subject are e.g. 'preach or at any rate ask questions' (Robertson and Plummer 1911: 324); 'primär das lehrende Sprechen' ('primarily the teaching speech', Dautzenberg 1975: 258); and 'teach, preach or ask questions' (N.R. Lightfoot 1976: 133).

78. Knight (1975: 89-90) claims that 1 Corinthians 14 and 1 Timothy 2 are the relevant didactic passages by which 1 Cor. 11 must be interpreted; but the latter surely cannot be viewed as non-didactic.

79. Knight 1980: 46. Hopeful he will not be considered offensive, he compares Balaam's ass (Num. 22.22ff.), but she did not prophesy: she spoke (v. 28). Also distinguishing between the authority involved in prophecy and teaching are G. Davies 1986: 89; Fung 1987: 208-209. Grudem (1982: 66-73, 254; 1987: 11-15) reduces New Testament prophecy to 'merely human words' contrasting the Old Testament variety, 'the very word of God'. He is followed by Harris (1987: 24), but see n. 82 below.

and through a person to produce a revelation.[80] In fact, the styles and personalities of Old Testament prophets are discernible precisely because prophecy involves *active* instrumentality.[81] The distinction between teaching and prophecy, moreover, is not that between the engaged and disengaged or passive mind, any more than prayer is the activity of a passive mind. Paul assumes prophecy is part of the teaching process (14.4-5).[82] Teaching itself does not necessarily entail headship (cf. Priscilla and Apollos). Nor does prophecy. Verse 14.26 similarly implies no necessary headship or authority for whoever may minister. Finally, Knight assumes that Eve was created subject to Adam, claiming that Paul develops this argument and its implications in 1 Corinthians 11, and that 14.34-35 cites that foundational incident to show that the reversal of established order 'manifestly had a disastrous effect' (1980: 31). For the role relationship of the creation records see Part IV, Appendix 3, but note here that Knight's key words 'authority', 'dominion' and 'subjection', do not occur in Genesis 1–2 for male–female relations. For 1 Cor. 11.3-16 see Appendix 2, but note here that Paul focuses on the differentiated honour of each member of the second pair from v. 3. The creation order (however interpreted) falls short of an adequate basis for banning women from public teaching. The speech prohibited cannot convincingly be so defined.

4. *Asking Questions during Public Dialogue Instruction*

Foh reasons that, when the passage is placed after v. 40 as in the Western tradition, it becomes a new section in the category of things to be done decently and in order. The speech is then definable as the asking

---

80. Knight 1975: 90 n. 35; 1980: 46 n. 27. See also Witherington 1988: 94-95.

81. Mt. 17.5 and Jn 12.28 show God communicating without the medium of a human voice, so when he uses one various factors may be at work.

82. Wiles 1974: e.g. 9, 59, 69, 86-90, 172-73, 182-83, 213-14, 225, 247-48; Osborne 1977: 343-44; R.P. Martin 1984: 80. See also W.C. Klein 1962: 14-15; Robeck 1975b: 47, 51; Witherington 1988: 95. Filson (1941: 332) argues that every leader in the primitive church is to some extent a teacher. Giles (1989: 146) says clear distinction between New Testament prophet and teacher is not always evident. Harris (1987: 24-25; 1990: 344) says the authority of both derives from God: for prophets coterminous with inspiration, for teachers with received tradition, and neither more authoritative than the other. Payne (1986: 102) says the teacher's authority, founded upon the tradition, is more derived than that of the directly inspired prophet. See also Banks 1976: 92-93. For recent discussion on distinctions between the two functions see Forbes 1995: 225-29.

of questions in dialogue instruction and, in line with 1 Tim. 2.12, for a woman to participate would be tantamount to teaching (1979: 120-21 with n. 71). Such transposition may simplify the troublesome 'flow' and make the masculine pronoun at v. 36 more readily understandable, but even placed after v. 40 the prohibition remains absolute and maintains linguistic connection with its context, requires explanation why the majority of MSS place it in the more difficult traditional position, and cannot establish that dialogue instruction took place. Secondly, as argued in Part I, 1 Tim. 2.12 says nothing about teaching ἐν ἐκκλησίᾳ. Finally, if (as 1 Cor. 11.5; 14.26 imply) women could prophesy and bring instruction, why should asking questions be considered either teaching or disgraceful? If women had been *answering*, the proposition may gain a measure of credibility, but this is nowhere suggested. Even under Old Testament law some women prophesy and address men, and at 1 Thess. 5.21 Paul assumes all capable of 'testing everything'. His reason for wanting to forbid women a place in discussion remains obscure.

5. *Public Evaluation of the Prophets' Speech*

This may now be the most popular view amongst those believing Paul responsible for 1 Cor. 14.34-35.[83] Hurley has been influential here, although he admits that the focus on the prophets themselves and the unrestricted σιγάτωσαν (v. 34) at first obscures this meaning. He argues, however, that Paul uses σιγάω at vv. 28, 30 without general restriction on vocal contribution, the context, rather than the words used, limiting the application. If vv. 33b-35 are about judging the prophets, he reasons, their context would naturally restrict the application.

> The speaking...constituted...exercise of authority...inconsistent with the subordinate...role...Paul believed women should play in the assembled church... [T]he participation of women in...judgment of male and female prophets within the context of the church is certainly an exercise of authority.

83. E.g. W.C. Klein 1962: 8; Thrall 1965: 102; Giles 1977: 62-63; Dumbrell 1977: 20; Moo 1980: 74; Grudem 1982: 250-55; 1987: 21-23; Bruce 1982b: 10; Key 1984: 146; Carson 1986: 40; 1988: 129-30; 1991: 151-53; Liefeld 1986: 150; Fung 1987: 194-95; Witherington 1988: 101-102; Kidd 1990: 165; Gritz 1991: 89. Attracted but doubtful is N.R. Lightfoot (1976: 133-34).

Hurley believes that the Old Testament supports such silencing, its whole structure teaching male headship at home and worship. Paul, he says, most likely here, as elsewhere, appeals to the relationship of Adam and Eve before the fall, but may be reminding the Corinthians that men are called to exercise authority and render judgment at home and in the religious life of Israel.[84] Numerous factors undermine Hurley's view. Some of these have been addressed above: he begs the question by supposing that public judgment of prophets is in view and proceeding on that basis; the differences between vv. 34-35 and 23-33 are greater than he recognizes; and an appeal to the relationship of Adam and Eve here would make a questionable basis upon which to authorize the silencing of women. Moreover, the distinction between authority to prophesy and to evaluate prophecy is arbitrary,[85] and the implication that any man has the authority publicly to criticize the prophets evokes scenes of chaos precisely such as Paul is trying to avoid. Furthermore, male headship in the Old Testament has no apparent connection with the silencing of women. Deuteronomy 13 provides instruction for dealing with false prophets, addressing three types of offenders.[86] Execution is the penalty for each. In the first the method is unstated, but 17.2-7 indicates that anyone worshipping other gods is to be stoned, provided there is more than one witness. As at 13.9 the first stone is to be cast by the witness for the prosecution. It seems quite clear that false prophets are to be stoned by 'all the people' (17.7). Although by the New Testament era Jewish women generally are

84. Hurley 1981: 189-92, the direct quotation from p. 191. See also Liefeld (1986: 149-50), who cites Deut. 18.15; Num. 12.1-15, and further at n. 91 below.

85. So Sigountos and Shank 1983: 285; R.P. Martin 1984: 86; Bilezikian 1989: 283; Forbes 1995: 273 with n. 48. Carson (1988: 130; 1991: 153) argues that the distinction involves no inconsistency because Paul grants lesser status to New Testament prophecy than to that of Old Testament prophets, elevating teaching above it (see also Grudem 1982: 66-73), but see nn. 82 above and 86 below. Robeck (1975a: 36-37) concludes that Luke sees an intrinsic relation between Old Testament prophecy and that in Acts and, although (1975b: 39, 52) distinguishing between New Testament varieties, advises caution in view of apparent fluidity.

86. Craigie 1976: 222-26. Dunn (1983: 80-87) demonstrates the consistent pattern of universal responsibility for evaluation of prophecy in both Testaments. See also Binns 1927: 105; *TWOT*, II, 832. Distinctions between Old and New Testament prophets (see my n. 85) therefore require circumspection, the authority of all depending upon the purity of the message without necessarily involving authoritative position or function. Cf. e.g. 1 Kgs 13.18.

excluded as witnesses,[87] there are exceptions[88] and they had not always been excluded from reading the Torah.[89] The mother of a persistently rebellious son is certainly required under Old Testament law with her husband to take hold of that son, bring him to the elders, denounce him, and hand him over for stoning (Deut. 21.18-21). There is no indication in Deuteronomy that women are excluded from either making the necessary judgments about prophets or casting the first stone when appropriate. Deuteronomy 18.20-22 itself tells how to identify a false prophet, again nothing suggesting that women do not need to know (5.1). The fact that they are not specifically mentioned should not be over-interpreted:[90] they are not to be afraid of such prophets (v. 22).[91] Elders and judges (including Deborah) are ultimately responsible for judgments, but the law administered by those leaders as represented in Deuteronomy implies that individual Israelites are responsible to judge the words of the prophets with whom they have contact. Women therefore appear as witnesses and executioners (*TWOT*, II, 832) of false prophets under Old Testament law. Headship does not confer exclusive right to judge error. Finally, the religious life of Old Testament Israel may not be simplistically divided. Certain women do exercise public religious leadership, authority and judgment (Exod. 15.20-21 cf. Num. 12.1-2; 2 Chron. 34.22-28; Judg. 4.4–5.31 cf. 1 Sam. 3.20; 7.15). The 'law' at 1 Cor. 14.34 therefore remains problematic, and the speech forbidden cannot convincingly be defined as the public judgment of prophecy.[92]

87.   Josephus, *Ant.* 4.219; Jeremias (1969: 374) cites (the later) *M. Shevu.* iv.1; *Sifre Deut.* 19.17, 190; *b. B.K.* 88a.

88.   Baumgarten (1957: 267 with n. 3) cites *m. Soṭ.* 6.2.

89.   Jeremias (1969: 374) cites *b. Hag.* 3a *Bar.*, and *par.*; *y. Hag.* i.I, 74d.35, and notes that at Sardis Jews 'met in their local shrine "with wife and children"', *Ant.* 14.260'.

90.   See also the tenth commandment, where it is no more likely that women would not understand that they must not covet a neighbour's house, land, servants, stock or anything else including husband than it is that men would not realize they are not to covet their female neighbours' servants or possessions.

91.   Liefeld (1986: 149-50) (ref. n. 84 above) does not allow for the fact that (whilst she is certainly singled out for punishment) Miriam disobeys a command about a particular prophet. Men prophesying in New Testament *ekklesia* are not Moses. Bilezikian (1989: 284) notes that Miriam does not evaluate prophecy: she undermines legitimate leadership with a view to usurpation.

92.   Witherington (1988: 102-103), who follows Hurley, reduces the judgment

Until such time as a more convincing limited definition of the speech prohibited than those discussed above should be presented, 1 Cor. 14.34-35 stands as a self-reinforcing and isolated prohibition against women uttering any speech at all ἐν ἐκκλησίᾳ, and does so in a context that not only envisages universal application but conflicts with that prohibition. This internal tension makes it reasonable to question whether Paul is its source. If he is, its doubtful meaning and its differences from 1 Tim. 2.11-15 render it a dubious exegetical device for its even more problematic fellow (whether or not the latter is viewed as Pauline). If Paul is not the author of 1 Cor. 14.34-35, the merits of the two remaining ways it has been interpreted must be weighed.

3. *The Interpolation Argument*

The conflict with 11.5 and the general context, the problematic 'law', and the 'rough seams' of 14.34-35 (i.e. doubtful reference at v. 33b; masculine pronoun at v. 36) lead many to conclude that the passage is an early scribal gloss reflecting the same thought as 1 Tim. 2.12, itself frequently envisaged as pseudepigraphic. Its excision, it is suggested, leaves a smoother-flowing text.[93] The most obvious difficulty here has always been that 1 Cor. 14.34-35 was thought always to appear somewhere in the MSS, either in the traditional position or at the end of the

---

of prophets to the asking of questions. He believes 'the law' associated with an objectless ὑποτασσέσθαι is not marital, but the Old Testament principle of silence and respect to be shown when another speaks, citing esp. Job 29.21. His argument, however, is predicated on the idea that vv. 34-35 in context address a disorder. See however pp. 206-207.

93.   E.g. Fitzer 1963: 9-10; Scroggs 1972: 284; 1974: 533; Conzelmann 1975: 246 and n. 53; D.R. MacDonald 1980: 266-67; Murphy-O'Connor 1986: 92; Payne 1986: 100; 1996: 248, 260; Byrne 1988: 63-65 n. 6; Fee 1988: 705; Munro 1988: 28-29; Oberlinner 1994: 93-94. Meeks (1973: 203-04, 206) is less sure. See also Leipoldt 1953: 126; A.T. Hanson 1966: 37; F. Stagg and E. Stagg 1978: 178-79; Swidler 1979: 324-25, 337; Jewett 1979: 55; Walker 1983: 108, 110; Knoch 1988: 26; Merkel 1991: 27. The solution sometimes attracts even when it does not convince and MSS evidence is judged uncompelling. See e.g. Allworthy 1917: 95-97; Barrett 1971: 332-33; Giles 1977: 59-60; Howard 1983: 37-39. Cf. Jervis (1995: 54-55), who doubts that someone whose environment had been influenced by the Pastorals would make such an interpolation. She assumes, however, both that Paul forbids unspiritual speech concerning prophecy (her pp. 60-61), and that the Pastorals address assemblies (see my Chapter 6, Section 1).

chapter (see further below). Furthermore, the extent of the interpolation is debated.

(a) It is generally limited to vv. 34-35. Fee, for example, argues that v. 33b parallels other conclusions (4.17; 11.16 etc.), and v. 36 makes better sense when referred directly to it. The Western tradition, he points out, indicates an early understanding to that effect[94] and, when included in the interpolation, v. 33b produces the awkward repetition of ἐν ταῖς ἐκκλησίαις .[95]

(b) Some do include v. 33b.[96] It has been strongly argued that v. 33a is rendered awkwardly anticlimactic by the addition of v. 33b, which cannot introduce v. 36.[97]

(c) Conzelmann also includes v. 36, finding the transposition of vv. 34-35 only to after v. 40 a secondary simplification.[98]

(d) Dautzenberg further includes vv. 37-38, arguing that although it 'textkritisch nicht nachweisbar sein kann...[, u]nter redaktionellen und gattungsmässigen Gesichtspunkten ist der Platz dafür geschickt gewählt' ('text critically cannot be provable...[, u]nder editorial and genre-specific points of view its position is very suitably chosen').[99]

Wire suggests that this ever-widening scope indicates that vv. 34-35 do, after all, have a close relationship with their immediate context (1990: 231).

Many adopting the interpolation solution largely interpret by 1 Tim. 2.11-15,[100] presupposing that it and the Christian Household Code are

---

94.   Fee 1988: 697. See at Chapter 9 n. 18. See also Metzger 1975: 565. Fee (n. 49), citing Chrysostom, *Hom.* 36, 37 in 1 Cor., writes that conjunction with v. 34 seems to be a modern phenomenon. Robertson and Plummer (1911: 324) report more desperate options: vv. 32-/33 are parenthetical, or ὡς ἐν πάσαις ταῖς ἐκκλησίαις goes with what preceeds but τῶν ἁγίων with αἱ γυναῖκες κτλ. Fung (1987: 333) cites one translation of the latter: 'the wives of the saints'.

95.   Fee 1988: 698. See also Barrett 1971: 330; Murphy-O'Connor 1986: 90.

96.   E.g. Robertson and Plummer 1911: 324; Conzelmann 1975: 246; Wolter 1988: 44 n. 74.

97.   Allison (1988: 30), who sees the passage as a redaction, not an interpolation. His explanations for the unchanged position of v. 33b in the Western MSS and the repetition of ἐν ταῖς ἐκκλησίαις (vv. 33b-34) will be considered below.

98.   Conzelmann 1975: 246 and n. 54. Murphy-O'Connor (1986: 90) points out that the masculine pronoun makes this improbable.

99.   Dautzenberg 1975: 262, 270-73, 291-98; 1989: 193.

100.   E.g. Barrett 1971: 332; Scroggs 1972: 284; Conzelmann 1975: 246; D.R.

not only non- but post-Pauline. In Part I it was argued that (whatever may be made of vv. 13-15) 1 Tim. 2.9-12 (although addressing a wider context) is no more restrictive than are 1 Cor. 14.28, 30: the passage simply requires behaviour to be reasonable. As outlined in Chapter 9 above, 1 Cor. 14.34-35 differs significantly from 1 Tim. 2.9-15. Since MSS evidence for interpolation of 1 Cor. 14.34-35 has been said to be non-existent (although see below), conjectural emendation has had to rely solely upon its content, and the latter does have parallels in Paul's own day.[101] Any case for interpolation resting on the arguments proposed above has therefore been uncompelling. Two additional arguments are, however, more forceful.

Fee observes that interpolation best explains variants. If the autograph included vv. 34-35 between vv. 33 and 36, it is generally suggested that scribes moved the passage to improve the flow from v. 33 to v. 36, but there are no other such displacements in the epistles, and no adequate reason has been produced for it. If the displacement did occur, the responsible party failed to resolve the problems of the enigmatic reference to 'law' and the absolute prohibition in conflict with 11.5. Furthermore, a close relationship has been maintained with the context by common address to speaking and silence, and a long didactic discourse (12.1–14.33b) is left introduced by περὶ δέ but suddenly interrupted by vv. 36-38. If the autograph included vv. 34-35 after v. 40, it seems doubtful that any scribe would shift them to the traditional position in view of the masculine pronoun at v. 36, the awkward repetition in vv. 33-34, and the interruption of the subject matter of tongues and prophecy. But if vv. 34-35 were originally a scribal marginal gloss,[102] they could have been inserted in two different positions at a date early enough to preclude MSS evidence.[103] In this case, Paul at vv. 36-37 challenges the Corinthians to note that other assemblies reflect the char-

MacDonald 1980: 266; Murphy-O'Connor 1986: 92; Byrne 1988: 63; Munro 1988: 28.

101. E.g. Plutarch, *Praec. coniug.* 31-32. See also Aune 1987: 72, 98; Forbes 1995: 274-75 with nn. 52-53. Metzger (1981: 183-85) warns against premature conjectural emendation since relatively abundant evidence for the New Testament text reduces its necessity to the smallest dimensions.

102. Conzelmann (1975: 246) suggests the gloss is a comment on σιγάω with 1 Tim. 2.11 in mind.

103. Fee 1988: 699-700; 1994: 272-81. See also F. Stagg and E. Stagg 1978: 178-79; Allison 1988: 54 n. 6.

acter of God in their order, and that those believing themselves πνευμα-τικοί who fail to acknowledge that what he now writes is from God should themselves be ignored.

By itself, Fee's valid argument still confronts difficulties. Even if the passage is judged to be non-Pauline, it is not necessarily post-Pauline.[104] Furthermore, since other marginal glosses in the New Testament (e.g. Jn 5.3b-4; 1 Jn 5.7) are omitted in some MSS, but 1 Cor. 14.34-35 has been understood always to be included somewhere, interpolation would (as Fee acknowledges) require a very early date, even before the turn of the first century.[105] Yet, Paul's geographically wide influence, as well as that of his close associates, including a number of women, makes it improbable that only the interpolated version would be reflected in extant MSS.[106]

Recently, however, Payne has drawn attention to marginal text-critical sigla in Codex Fuldensis (sixth-century CE) which indicate that its editor had MS evidence leading him to believe that vv. 34-35 were interpolated. Payne demonstrates that vv. 34-35 do not, as Metzger (followed by Ellis and others) had claimed, appear in Fuldensis both after v. 40 and in the margin after v. 33. *In the main text they follow v. 33*, and in the same hand *in the lower margin*, in what Payne convincingly argues is replacement text for the whole of vv. 34-40, *they are omitted*.[107] Furthermore, he demonstrates, marginal sigla at the same verses in B (second-century CE) indicate very early acknowledgment of a textual variant (1995: 250-62). This important contribution for the first time identifies a credible textual foundation for the interpolation argument.

Two problems nevertheless linger. First, the reader would ordinarily expect a gloss to reflect the thought of the context, but here, despite the above-noted contextual linguistic links, the ideas differ (see p. 207).[108] Secondly, exclusion of vv. 34-35 appears to leave an even 'rougher

---

104. Fee (1988) does not claim it is. Ellis (1981: 215) persuasively questions the validity of automatically interpreting theological differences in terms of chronological distance, finding the assumption that Christian thought moved forward as a block an undemonstrated oversimplification, and envisaging various developments over different time spans.

105. Fee 1988: 705; 1994: 281. See also e.g. Ross 1992: 155.

106. See also Wire 1990: 230; Carson 1991: 142.

107. Payne 1995: 240-50. Metzger concurs in Payne's n. 18.

108. See also Carson 1991: 142.

seam' than those presented by inclusion of those verses (see the beginning of this section). This remains true whether or not v. 33b is viewed as part of the original text. According to the pattern which Hurd identified (see pp. 198-99 above), one would expect throughout this three-chapter-long περὶ δέ passage a calmly systematic response and the establishment of strong authority. Instead, not only does Paul appear annoyed at v. 36, but vv. 37-38 also have more in common with non-περὶ δέ passages. Paul's tone is angry, he speaks authoritatively, is unsympathetic and censorious, and he makes a particularly strong appeal to authority, claiming that what he writes is the Lord's command. He neither deals with the future nor condemns past behaviour. The section fits neither of Hurd's categories. Something different is happening here.

The implications of this break in an otherwise consistent pattern appear not to have been appreciated fully to date,[109] even though it occurs not only when the passage is omitted, but also when it is placed either in the traditional position or after v. 40. Paul is, of course, perfectly free to respond calmly and systematically to a Corinthian communication in 11.1–14.33/35 but, remembering what he also knows about their disorder (11.17-18), rebuke them at vv. 36-38.[110] Such would certainly be understandable if chs. 12–13 do respond to a stated but (to him) unacceptable position on οἱ πνευματικόι rather than to a question. He does, however, mildly teach his way almost to the end of the three chapters, and his sudden annoyance is noteworthy (cf. 5.2; 11.17).

Despite all previous claims that 1 Cor. 14.34-35 always appears in the text somewhere, Payne demonstrates that at least one very early MS version excluded it. For him, an 'already strong case for interpolation' is now even stronger[111] but, as striking as his evidence is, it falls short of being compelling:

    i.   an adequate explanation for the eclipse of the 'uninterpolated' text at such a necessarily early date has not been forthcoming;

---

109. See, however, Dautzenberg (1975: 291-92), who notes the change of atmosphere from the 'threatening' vv. 37-38 to the 'conciliatory' vv. 26-33a, 39. My own observation here includes those considered at 4 below.

110. As e.g. Witherington 1988: 98-99.

111. Payne 1995: 240. Payne's argument (pp. 247-48) from the silence of many early Christian writers re vv. 34-35 is, in the end, speculative.

ii.   inclusion of vv. 34-35 presents the more difficult, and there-
      fore the more preferable, reading (Carson 1991: 143);

iii. the thought expressed has ample contemporary parallels;

iv.   the 'flow' from v. 33a/b directly to v. 36 remains problematic;
      and

v.   whether vv. 34-35 are included or not, vv. 36-38 alter a con-
      sistent pattern in an otherwise calmly didactic περὶ δέ section.

One further option should therefore be evaluated.

4. *The Quotation Argument*

The claim that Paul quotes 1 Cor. 14.34-35 from the Corinthian letter
only to reject its argument at v. 36[112] has not met with extensive
approval. It *is* widely accepted that there are a number of quotations in
1 Corinthians.[113] NIV, for example, sets in inverted commas 6.12 *bis*;
6.13; 8.1 note 'a'; 8.5; 8.6; and 10.23. Others are at 7.1; 8.4b (RSV,
NEB) and 8.8. 11.2 has been considered a quotation with the pronouns
reversed: 'We remember...etc.'[114] Some argue at 6.13 that ὁ δὲ θεὸς
καὶ ταύτην καὶ ταῦτα καταργήσει is part of the quotation at v. 12, and
at 6.18b πᾶν ἁμάρτημα ὃ ἐὰν ποιήσῃ ἄνθρωπος ἐκτὸς τοῦ σώματός
ἐστιν is another.[115] There is considerable force to the idea that each of
these is something Paul has said which the Corinthians misunderstood

---

112. E.g. Bushnell 1919: §§201-206, 215; Montgomery 1924: 465; Sidlow Baxter 1973: VI, 115; Kaiser 1976: 10-11; Flanagan and Snyder 1981: 10-12; M.J.
Evans 1983: 99-100; Odell-Scott 1983: 90; 1986: 100-103; Talbert 1984: 105-106;
Bilezikian 1989: 146-53, 284-88. Allison (1988: 43-52) argues similarly, but claims
that vv. 34-36 are a deutero-Pauline redaction from an earlier Pauline letter inserted
because of linguistic parallels, v. 33b added to smooth the transition.

113. Hurd 1965: 67-68, Table 5. See also e.g. Bushnell 1919: §205; Hurley
1973a: 113; Bartchy 1973: 143 n. 499; Murphy-O'Connor 1978: 394; Bilezikian
1989: 286.

114. E.g. Barrett 1971: 247.

115. Hurley 1973a: 92; Murphy-O'Connor 1978: 394. Hurley (p. 114) argues
that v. 18c should be included, but Murphy-O'Connor (p. 395) is more convincing.
Some argue that 14.22 is constructed from a citation: e.g. Sweet 1966-67: 241-44.
See also Talbert (1984: 102), who says vv. 21-22 cite Corinthian quotation of Isa.
28.11-12 with a two-stage interpretation (v. 22a, b) to which Paul responds in
vv. 23-25. It should be noted, however, that Paul does not immediately reject what
precedes v. 23 and in no way reinterprets the Old Testament passage. See further at
n. 137.

and used to support their own position.[116] This would certainly explain the reasonable way in which Paul corrects them, even though in ch. 6 he addresses a matter about which he has heard, not one which the Corinthians debate with him. 1 Corinthians 14.36ff., however, presents no such reasonable correction.[117] Demonstration of citation and rejection in this case rests upon the content of vv. 34-35 and the language of v. 36.

To date, attempts at such demonstration have generally not been judged compelling.[118] Underlying each is the foundation claim that ἤ commonly establishes a disjunctive or comparitive conjunction between ideas, and more sharply so in questions.[119] Two additional arguments have been constructed upon that foundation:

  i.   Paul's ἤ *requires* an antithesis, sharply rejecting the viewpoint of vv. 34-35;[120] and

  ii. the masculine pronoun illuminates the ἤ constructon, that is '...or are you (men) the only ones it has reached?'[121]

116. Hurd 1965: 278. See also the Corinthian background in Chapter 9 above. In regard to 7.1 see also Bartchy 1973: 143 n. 499.

117. Carson 1986: 38; Witherington 1988: 99; Keener 1992: 76.

118. See e.g. critiques in Carson (1986: 38-39; 1991: 149-50). Carson himself accepts that 'the law' refers to Gen. 2.20b-24, and that the prohibition concerns judgment of prophecy (for both of which see above). He also shifts (1986: 39-40) from demonstration that Kaiser's (1976: 10-11) argument is weak to assumptions, first that v. 36 'cannot' refer to rabbinic tradition, and secondly that νόμος must be employed according to Paul's pattern. See also 1988: 127-28.

119. Grammarians cited are BDF: §§446, 440; Smyth 1963: §2861; Thayer e.g. 1961: 276. See e.g. Odell-Scott 1983: 90. Allison (1988: 46) similarly argues that it introduces a rebuttal of something implicit in the immediately preceding clause, something presumably not perceived by its proponents. Carson (1988: 128) acknowledges the disjunction but refers it to an attitude of independance from other churches (vv. 33b-34). Fee (1994: 258-61, 279) declares vv. 36-38 'something of an aside', rejecting the AV, RSV translations, but sees the rhetoric as confrontational, sarcastic, biting.

120. Allison e.g. 1988: 47. See also the implication of Odell-Scott (1983: 90).

121. E.g. Odell-Scott 1983: 91-92. See also AV; RSV; Kaiser 1976: 11; Talbert 1984: 105-106; Allison 1988: 51; Bilezikian 1989: 151-52, 286-88. Barton (1986: 232) translates similarly, but assumes that μόνους addresses either the women or the whole assembly. Assuming women are addressed are e.g. G.G. Blum 1965: 151; Key 1984: 145. Others argue that the whole assembly is in view: e.g. Grudem 1982: 70-71 and n. 132; Orr and Walther 1982: 313; R.P. Martin 1984: 87; Carson 1988: 128-29 and n. 56; Witherington 1988: 98. Cf. Wire (1990: 154) who refers v. 36a to

Both these additional arguments are ill-founded: ἤ frequently *reinforces* a previous statement (Carson 1991: 151); and Corinthian women may not simply be excluded from this rebuke whose pronoun may very well include them. Nor may it be assumed that they, in contrast to the men, would either uniformly want to minister ἐν ἐκκλησίᾳ or wish to break with former tradition.[122]

The foundation argument itself has come under heavy and generally effective fire. Carson demonstrates how two of its proponents (Kaiser and Bilezikian) fail to appreciate the sense of the examples they quote from grammars as parallels (1991: 149-51). Although such incorrect evaluation of cited examples is regrettable, it is noteworthy that it was the grammarians' language which set the stage upon which the failure occurred. Thayer indicates that ἤ may introduce something 'contrary' to what precedes, that is 'if one be denied or refuted the other must stand' (1961: 275 [1c]). This has apparently led some to the idea that something preceding ἤ has been opposed, but, as Carson argues, none of Thayer's examples (e.g. Mt. 20.15; Rom. 3.29; 1 Cor. 9.6; 10.22) are contrary in that sense; they simply offer different perspectives. Again, Smyth writes that ἤ 'often introduces an argument *ex contrario*' (1963: §2861), but his sole example (Demosthenes 31.14) does not negate; it takes another point of view.

On the other hand, Carson appears to go too far when he declares it

the women but v. 36b more generally. In reply to Odell-Scott, Murphy-O'Connor (1986: 92) claims that v. 36 condemns the situation in vv. 26-33. Odell-Scott (1986: 102) responds, considering and rejecting the possibility that the original unaccented H was intended as the adverb 'truly'. Munro (1988: 28) argues that since at 6.1-2; 11.20-22 ἤ disjoins undesirable states of affairs from the writer's view, here it could disjoin the practice of women speaking. This would be reasonable if vv. 34-35 were Pauline, but Munro herself believes them interpolated, in which case the disjunction would incongruously be with v. 33.

122. Some of Odell-Scott's additional arguments (1983: 91-92) are similarly unpersuasive. 1 Cor. 11.20-21, he notes, is structurally identical and it would be absurd to argue that v. 22 summarizes that passage. The parallel is questionable: μὴ γὰρ οἰκίας οὐκ ἔχετε εἰς τὸ ἐσθίειν καὶ πίνειν a question, vv. 20-21 indicating that Paul is not teaching but criticizing, and the disjunction in ἤ clear. Verses 14.34-35, however, can be read as though Paul continues to teach, the disjunction at v. 36 not so clear. Odell-Scott also explains the 'law' in terms of a debate on the status of Jewish law when there is no evidence of any such debate at Corinth at that time. Also unpersuasively, Bilezikian (1989: 146-47) argues that arrogant members are 'competing for conspicuous ministries'. Cf. however v. 23.

'brute fact' that '*in every instance in the New Testament*' where ἤ is used in a construction analogous to 1 Cor. 14.36, '*it reinforce*[s what]... *precedes*' (1991: 151; italics his). At 1 Cor. 6.1 Τολμᾷ τις ὑμῶν πρᾶγμα ἔχων πρὸς τὸν ἕτερον κρίνεσθαι ἐπὶ τῶν ἀδίκων καὶ οὐχὶ ἐπὶ τῶν ἁγίων Carson claims that τολμάω 'proves beyond contradiction' that Paul assumes the answer 'No!', that is '*the question itself...* forbid[s]...litigation' (1991: 150; italics his). Yet some *had* dared to take disputes before the ungodly, and may well respond (whether or not shamefacedly) 'Actually, we did!'[123] In this case ἤ (v. 2) would not reinforce, but sharply disjoin. Again at v. 8 Paul's ὑμεῖς ἀδικεῖτε καὶ ἀποστερεῖτε, καὶ τοῦτο ἀδελφούς Carson reads as concern that they should not do these things, with v. 9 an emphatic reinforcement (1991: 150). Paul may, however, expect an admission, that is 'well, yes, we have done these things', and sharply disjoin his reminder that the wicked will not inherit the kingdom of God.[124]

At 14.36, then, the grammatical basis upon which the citation-rejection solution is constructed, although considerably reduced from the claim that ἤ 'commonly' negates what precedes to the lesser proposition that it *may* so negate, has to date not effectively been altogether discredited. Until it has, it should be asked 'does sharp, contrary disjunction occur here?' Only the context can settle that question.

Like Carson, Murphy-O'Connor finds citation less probable than interpolation. This is partly because:

i. the responsible scribe probably failed to recognize the negating effect of v. 36, and interpreted v. 33 as a good introduction to a community rule about women; and

ii. Paul dismisses Corinthian slogans only when confronted with a situation about which he has heard and apparently about which the Corinthians are quite comfortable. He never elsewhere dismisses them with the 'brutal passion' of v. 36.[125]

---

123. Also requiring a negative answer is 1 Cor. 9.6.

124. If, as Hurley claims, 6.18c should be included with b as part of a citation (although see n. 115 above) then ἤ (v. 19) would also sharply negate.

125. Murphy-O'Connor 1986: 91-92. Several others similarly reject the quotation solution. For Munro (1988) see n. 121. Witherington (1988: 99) claims the negation anticipates response to the foregoing teaching, but his unconvincing alternative (see nn. 83, 92) renders that speculative. Liefeld (1986: 149 and n. 40) claims the negation is of assumed disobedience of vv. 34-35 as at 'the structurally similar' 6.18-19. See also A.F. Johnson 1986: 159. As noted above, however, 6.18-19 itself looks

Odell-Scott is justifiably dubious about the scribal ineptitude Murphy-O'Connor implies, and baffled that Paul is denied passion except when addressing situations about which the Corinthians are unconcerned (1986: 101-102). Nevertheless, Murphy-O'Connor's ii. should be taken to its logical conclusion: in no other περὶ δέ passage in the letter does Paul so heatedly rebuke his readers. As argued above, the combative vv. 36-38 break an otherwise consistent pattern. Chapters 12–14 may (as Hurd argues) respond to a different kind of Corinthian approach than other περὶ δέ passages, although (as suggested above) other sections may also respond to stated positions. But if 'slogans' are Paul's own teachings, vv. 34-35 may be a different kind of quotation: a factional view (cf. 4.[14/]18-20) incidentally and *negatively* reported to Paul within a sustained argument which defends preference for speaking in tongues over prophecy. In other words, the Corinthians may have written in effect, 'So you see, Paul, (because of the aforementioned spiritual approach) our general practice is to aim at speaking in tongues, although some amongst us do incongruously argue "the women should remain silent ἐν ἐκκλησίᾳ…κτλ."!'

Allison argues that v. 33b is an editorial addition designed to smooth the introduction of vv. 34-36 from an earlier letter, the redactor having assumed that the decree is Paul's own.[126] It is difficult to reconcile the implied necessity that this redaction take place early enough to preclude survival of unaltered letters, yet late enough to make reasonable such interpretation of Paul's thought and practice. Allison's argument here is partly based upon observations that:

very like a citation-rejection. Liefeld (p. 151) also notes that v. 39, in summarizing the chapter, mentions only prophesying and tongues, and infers that vv. 34-35 are not part of Paul's major thought. Citation-rejection would also explain this omission. Schüssler Fiorenza (1987: 403 n. 52) finds the prohibition consistent with a 'patriarchal' 11.3f., for which see above. Wire (1990: 229-30) argues that the silencing occurs in a sequence of three, and that Paul elsewhere attributes refuted argument to others (1.12; 15.12; cf. 6.12, 13; 7.1; 8.1-7; 10.23), but see above for the 'sequence', and the attribution of citations compared (cf. 1.12; 15.12) is so obscure that until recently they were not recognized as such. Gritz (1991: 88) claims that the argument deals inadequately with the text and context, but she shows no evidence of having seriously considered it, nor does she prove her conclusion that evaluation of prophets is in view.

126. Allison 1988: 53. Cf. Windisch (1930: 417, 420) who suggests that chs. 12–14 are a later letter or that a dictation pause occurs after ch. 11.

   i.   v. 33b is only structurally parallel with the εἰ δέ clause intro-
        ducing the second part of the passage; and
  ii.   Paul's rebuttal in no way acknowledges or responds to it.

But neither does Paul respond to vv. 34-35. The interpolation solution
would hardly have gained its current popularity if he did. His rhetoric
(as Allison argues) certainly presumes his readers must admit that no
one has an exclusive claim to speech, and is directed at those pro-
pounding the view, but he chooses not to dignify them with argument.
Allison also claims that, in the letter into which vv. 34-36 is inserted,
Paul reflects the Corinthian response to the passage in its original context (e.g. ch. 13 counters resentment by the men he had opposed) (1988:
52). However, the long and unified argument of chs. 12-13 lays the
foundation for the outline of mutual, *ekklesia*-strengthening, orderly
ministry which at 14.1 Paul identifies with the 'way of love', a way
from which the Corinthians have strayed in their approach to spiritual
matters. Verses 14.34-35 departs from that way, being divisive,
assembly-subverting, and legalistic. Citing that view at the close of this
long section, Paul believes it calls only for contempt.[127] Furthermore,
that v. 36 should together with vv. 34-35 be regarded as part of a redaction is unsatisfying in view of its continuity with vv. 37-38. The MSS
are divided about whether v. 38b should read ἀγνοεῖται, ἀγνοεῖτε, or
ἀγνοείτω. Whatever the original (but particularly with the passive preferred by *UBSGNT*), in confrontation absent elsewhere in 12.1–14.33,
vv. 37-38 place the Corinthian community under God's command,
making them responsible before him. Verse 36, read as contemptuous
of a minority attempt to silence women, leads naturally into this pre-
conclusion confrontation with those who might reject the 'command of
the Lord' so carefully begun at 12.1 and specified at 14.1.[128] Verses 34-

---

127. Carson (1988: 130) highlights the unity of the section, noting at 12.3; 14.37
dual references to the lordship of Jesus and tests for spirituality. See also the outline
of Grudem 1982: 57 incl. n. 114; Wire 1990: 135. Baasland (1988: 76-81) demonstrates that Paul in 1 Corinthians employs the περὶ δέ formula primarily for debate
on topics which for him 'put brotherly love into concrete terms'.

128. Carson (1988: 131-32) nevertheless correctly points out that Paul is unlikely
to have intended chs. 1–11 to be less authoritative. Bartsch (1965: 69-70) claims
that v. 37 refers back only to v. 26. R.P. Martin (1984: 83) is undecided whether the
reference is to the proper spirit of worship or to v. 26 itself. Dautzenberg (1975:
293, 296-98) argues that to give such a wide, undefined meaning is rare and not
easily comprehensible, but he considers ch. 14 *either* a unity *or* to include an

36 are, I submit, an essential part of the original text. Neither is there any MSS evidence that v. 33b is an editorial addition. Allison's argument that it is awkwardly anticlimatic following v. 33a is persuasive, as is his implication (1988: 48) that Paul could scarcely fail to object to an appeal to universal Christian practice he knows is untrue. But if it was, after all, part of the autograph, how is the repetition of ἐν ταῖς ἐκκλησίαις to be explained?[129] In fact the repetition may be more apparent than real. The prohibition of v. 34, justified as it is by an appeal to law,[130] and associated with the impersonal and rabbinic-sounding ἐπιτρέπεται,[131] resembles known Jewish oral law[132] and emanates from an assembly with some Jewish membership. As part of a citation from an unknown original context, and in language used by Paul nowhere else (πάσαις ταῖς ἐκκλησίαις τῶν ἁγίων),[133] v. 33b may refer to the synagogue, but v. 34 to Christian meetings: that is 'but some are actually arguing "as in all the gatherings of those set apart for God[134] the women

interpolated vv. 33b-37f. If, however, vv. 34-35 are a citation readily recognizable to the Corinthians, κυρίου ἐστὶν ἐντολή is neither (as he claims) 'in excess' nor contradicts the relation of apostle and community in general.

129. Witherington (1988: 98) believes v. 33b goes with v. 34, but says that even if it does not v. 34 itself speaks of 'all the churches'. But vv. 34-35 without 33b make no universal or even widespread claim apart from problematic appeals to law and custom.

130. Conzelmann (1975: 246) cites Val. Max. *Fact. et dict. mem.* 3.8.6 'What have women to do with a public assembly? If old-established custom is preserved, nothing'. One might suspect that the law of the ἐκκλησίαι of the Greek *demos* is employed at 1 Cor. 14.34 were it not that the appeal to πάσαις ταῖς ἐκκλησίαις τῶν ἁγίων (v. 33b) together with v. 34a seems to require throughout a religious rather than secular basis.

131. Ref. Aalen at n. 60 above.

132. Dautzenberg (1975: 257) writes 'Der Gebrauch der dritten Person bei den Imperativen: *sigatosan, ypotassesthosan, eperotatosan* ist Gesetzesstil und entspricht dem Regelcharakter' ('The use of the third person with the imperatives: ...is legal style and corresponds to the character of the rule'). Bilezikian (1989: 148) notes the appeal to general practice, not authority, at 7.17; 16.1; and the combination at 11.16.

133. E.g. Ellis 1981: 213-14.

134. Cf. some at Chapter 9 n. 19 who interpret v. 33b as referring to other Christian assemblies. Bilezikian (1989: 147-48) unconvincingly argues that 'saints' originally designated the Jewish Christians of Jerusalem and Palestine and was only later extended to others.

should remain silent in the (/our) assemblies…etc."!'[135]

Fee validly argues that there is no precedent either for the length or argumentativeness (γάρ *bis*) of such a quotation.[136] Nevertheless, 6.12-13a, 18b offer a comparison. Here we find πάντα μοι ἔξεστιν (*bis*) with retorts, v. 13a most likely including ὁ δὲ θεὸς καὶ ταύτην καὶ ταῦτα καταργήσει with a balanced parallel response at vv. 13b-14 (Murphy-O'Connor 1978: 395), followed by the related v. 18a, the slogan (v. 18b) and the retort of vv. 18c-20. These four quotations together approximate to the length of 14.33b-35, with ὁ δὲ θεὸς καὶ ταύτην καὶ ταῦτα καταργήσει a supporting argument resembling the repeated explanatory γάρ. It may also be that, in an exchange with Corinth requiring a three-chapter reply, their report on a minority claim, although incidental, may yet be substantial. In this case Paul's version may be more a summary (Allison 1988: 48) than a direct quotation, differing yet again from slogans.[137]

135. Allison (1988: 49) believes the goal is the synagogue model where women could not speak, teach, conduct prayer, prophesy, or sit with men, the 'law' based on Genesis 2 and 3.16. That model, however, is more extreme than contemporary evidence allows (see pp. 208-209, 211-15 above) and, if the Genesis accounts *are* so employed, the exegesis is questionable. See Part IV, Appendix 3. Osborne (1977: 345) argues that the reference is unlikely to be Jewish because the New Testament nowhere distinguishes oral from written law. In Part IV evidence will be presented for just such a distinction, but there is no reason to expect that a citation must conform to other New Testament practice.

136. Fee 1988: 705. See also Fung 1987: 334-35 n. 171; Jervis 1995: 59 n. 31. Fee also argues that v. 34 gives no hint of quotation to follow (see also Munro 1988: 28), and that the otherwise quite pro-women Corinthians are unlikely to forbid women to speak (see also Jervis). But cf. 6.18, where Fee (p. 262 n. 60) reasons that the Corinthians would recognize their own slogan, and 7.1; 11.3-16, where trends towards sexual abstinence and rejection of characteristic gender-related attire do not necessarily embrace sexual equality: 7.1, e.g., implies defilement of men by women, not the reverse (cf. Lev. 15.18). Greek misogony seems to have (re-) emerged amongst Corinthian πνευματικοί. Phipps 1982: 125-31. Jervis also objects that Paul's other slogan-retorts concern contextual issues, but assumes that here that must be 'gender-specific actions in worship', when the more general issue 'behaviour ἐν ἐκκλησία' clearly continues. See further below.

137. If vv. 21-22 are another citation (see n. 115), the absence of rejection and reinterpretation could be due (as with slogans elsewhere) to the fact that Paul responds to misinterpretation of his own teaching, the length of vv. 34b-36 comparable. There are, however, other persuasive explanations for apparent conflict

When vv. 33b-35 are read as a rejected citation, πάντα (v. 40) is definable by the subject underlying the entire section: spiritual gifts in general and speaking in tongues and prophecy in particular. Verse 39 confirms this. Λαλεῖν should be defined by this same underlying subject. There is no trace elsewhere in this letter of anyone being forbidden to speak in tongues (v. 39): rather the reverse (v. 23).[138] I suggest that although the Corinthians generally see the personally edifying tongues-speaking as the sign of the πνευματικός, and seek it more than prophecy and with little concern for interpretation, some remember how women are required to behave in other circles. Retaining or adopting common contemporary ideas about women, and possibly about wives in particular,[139] they seek to establish a kind of order of their own (Allison 1988: 50) by attempting to forbid them any vocal contribution ἐν ἐκκλησίᾳ. In view of Paul's own teaching and their own enthusiasm for vocal gifts, Corinthian Christians generally could be expected to reject such a proposition. If, however, they negatively reported it as a minor aside in their argument that it is preferable for spiritual people to speak in tongues than to prophesy, Paul's reply may well display the linguistic continuity but conceptual *dis*continuity outlined above. His primary concern is to rectify an imbalance in the goals of Corinthians of both sexes, so at the very end of that extended address[140] he quotes the factional view (which he knows is not generally held), angrily rebukes its proponents, states his own authority, exhorts everyone to be eager to prophesy, and commands that no one forbid anyone to speak in tongues.

Whilst the length of the citation puts certainty beyond grasp, the citation solution at 1 Cor. 14.33b-35 alone to date satisfactorily explains the combination of: conflict with 11.5 and the general context; the enigma of 'the law'; the otherwise puzzling outburst and choice of gender at

between vv. 22 and 25. See e.g. Fee 1988: 676-88; 1994: 240-42; Forbes 1995: 97-99, 175-81.

138. Carson (1988: 18) with some force argues that a faction does prefer no one at all to speak in tongues (see also Orr and Walther 1982: 314). It is, however, not only unclear that chs. 12–14 are (as Carson claims) a 'yes-but' argument, but citation-rejection at vv. 33b-36 suggests a more restricted factional exclusion in the immediate context.

139. When the passage is viewed as a citation precise reference is obscure.

140. Grudem (1982: 247) calls vv. 34-35 a minor note preceding Paul's conclusion. Cf. Wire (1990: 155), who believes v. 37 shows that vv. 34-35 are not parenthetical but the turning point in Paul's argument about the spiritual.

v. 36; and the continued confrontation at vv. 37-38. It may also suggest how vv. 34-35 found their way to the end of the chapter in some MSS. The Western tradition's placement of those verses after v. 40, together with the textual variant/s implied in Codex Fuldensis and B, suggest that an early scribe, confronted only with MSS including these problematic verses, and holding similar views to the rejected Corinthian faction, attempted to reconcile ideas believed to be Paul's own with the difficulties of the repeated ἐν ταῖς ἐκκλησίαις and the masculine pronoun and negation at v. 36. That no other New Testament passage has been so shifted is not really surprising.[141] There is no other quite like 1 Cor. 14.34-35ff.[142]

---

141. Contra Fee 1994: 272-79.
142. For alternative explanations of displacement see Wire 1990: 151-52.

Conclusion to Part III

Explanations for such similarities as do exist between 1 Cor. 14.34-35 and 1 Tim. 2.11-15 must still be found: see my General Conclusion. For the present, however, two things are noteworthy:

(a) The passages differ significantly. 1 Cor. 14.34-35

    i.   presents rules for the gathered assembly;

    ii.   presupposes unmodified marital hierarchy; and

    iii. appeals to unspecified law which cannot comfortably be identified with anything in the Old Testament but parallels known contemporary thought.

1 Timothy 2.9-15, in a general context which occasionally reflects the Christian Household Code and its implied balance,

    i.   presents guidelines for a woman's life;

    ii.   enjoins obedience to what is learned and abstinence from continually dictatorial behaviours; and

    iii. appeals to identifiable Old Testament scripture, but selectively and in such a way as to require careful evaluation (see Part IV).

(b) To date, in its own context 1 Cor. 14.34-35 has not been reconciled persuasively with 11.5 and associated passages, so it conflicts with Paul's own views and practices. It appears to be either an interpolation or a citation from the Corinthian letter which is rejected at v. 36. It has been argued that thus far the latter remains the more satisfying solution.

If Paul is held to be the source of both 1 Cor. 14.34-35 and 1 Tim. 2.9-15, in spite of their similarities the tenuous nature of all interpretations of 1 Cor. 14.34-35 renders it an inappropriate interpretative device for the even more problematic 1 Tim. 2.9-12, and potentially misleading even as a comparison. If Pauline authorship is accepted for 1 Timothy but rejected for 1 Cor. 14.34-35, again despite their similarities the differences and non-Pauline character of the Corinthian passage (particularly when viewed as a rejected citation) alone present good cause to reconsider the traditional interpretation of 1 Tim. 2.9-12. If Pauline authorship is rejected for 1 Timothy, the differing context and (to some extent) content of 1 Cor. 14.34-35 warn that the same school of thought is not necessarily in view. When the latter is viewed as an interpolation the Pauline approach to women remains unmodified. When viewed as a rejected citation 1 Cor. 14.34-35 forcefully contradicts the traditional interpretation of 1 Tim. 2.9-15 and cannot be viewed as emanating from the same school of thought. In all cases, unless its differences are recognized, 1 Cor. 14.34-35 will inevitably obscure rather than validly illuminate the even more problematic 1 Tim. 2.9-12.

Part IV
THE ROLE OF γάρ AT 1 TIMOTHY 2.13-15

Chapter 11

An Introductory Literature Survey

Ἀδὰμ γὰρ πρῶτος ἐπλάσθη, εἶτα Εὔα. καὶ Ἀδὰμ οὐκ ἠπατήθη, ἡ δὲ γυνὴ ἐξαπατηθεῖσα ἐν παραβάσει γέγονεν. σωθήσεται δὲ διὰ τῆς τεκνογονίας, ἐὰν μείνωσιν ἐν πίστει καὶ ἀγάπῃ καὶ ἁγιασμῷ μετὰ σωφροσύνης.

For Adam was formed first, then Eve. And Adam was not the one deceived; it was the woman who was deceived and became sinner. But women will be saved through childbearing—if they continue in faith, love and holiness with propriety (NIV).

With rare exceptions 1 Tim. 2.13-15 is interpreted within a combination of three fixed parameters:

   i.   v. 12 concerns congregational behaviour and is to some extent restrictive: see, however, Part I.

   ii.   At v. 13 γάρ introduces either reasons for,[1] or illustration of the need for,[2] those ecclesial restrictions, or both.[3]

1. I.e. it is illative. Most take this view, e.g. Calvin repr. 1983: 212; Ellicott 1864: 37; Huther 1866: 133; Meinertz 1931: 39; Scott 1936: 26; Hendriksen 1955: 109; Kähler 1959: 11; Barrett 1963: 56; G.G. Blum 1965: 157-58; A.T. Hanson 1966: 37; Brox 1969: 133-34; Kelly 1972: 68; Dibelius and Conzelmann 1972: 47; Powers 1975: 57; Giles 1977: 68-69; 1985: 40, 57; Foh 1979: 127; Knight 1980: 29, 31-32; S.B. Clark 1980: 195, 198-99, 201-203; Moo 1980: 68-70; 1981: 202-203; 1991: 190; Hurley 1981: 202; Stendahl 1982: 29; Schüssler Fiorenza 1983: 289, 336 n. 24; Fee 1984: 36-37; Küchler 1986: 12; Byrne 1988: 88; Roloff 1988: 147; Guthrie 1990: 87-88; Dewey 1992: 356; Hugenberger 1992: 345, 358 n. 72; Waltke 1992: 22, 26; T.D. Gordon 1995: 61-63 with n. 15; Schreiner 1995: 134-35. Cf. Oberlinner (1994), who, although seeing a reason based on creation theology here (pp. 95, 97), says (p. 98) that the creation account 'hat...allerdings nicht die Funktion, die vom Verfasser vorgelegte Anweisung zu *begründen*...die Begründung ist vielmehr ausschlaggebend die Autorität des "Paulus"...' ('does not have... however the function of *giving a reason* for the instruction put forward by the author...rather, the reason is decisively the authority of "Paul"...'; italics his).

iii.　At 3.1a πιστὸς ὁ λόγος refers to what follows.[4]

Treated in this way as a major exegetical device, γάρ renders vv. 13-14 a foundation–introduction to v. 15, where the kind of life that the Author believes is appropriate for women contrasts the activities rejected at v. 12. Despite this broad agreement about the context and general nature of vv. 13-15, meaning proves disconcertingly elusive. At vv. 13-14 the implications of the Author's selections from the Genesis record are widely debated. Some claim or imply that he reflects contemporary Jewish ideas that the woman was physically seduced by the serpent (ἐξαπατάω) or was responsible for the introduction of sin and/ or death (citing e.g. Sir. 24.25 and *Apoc. Mos.*).[5] Others see a focus on, or implication of, woman's inferiority,[6] gullibility or vulnerability;[7]

2.　I.e. it is explanatory/analogous. E.g. Stouffer 1981: 15; Payne 1981: 175-77 (but see n. 3 below); Spencer 1985: 89-91; Scholer 1986: 208, 211; Bilezikian 1989: 179 and n. 44; Keener 1992: 115-17.

3.　Gritz 1991: 136. See also Harris 1990: 349-50 with n. 42; Knight 1992: 131, 142, 144. Payne (1986: 110-13) argues that the two often overlap. Undecided about the function of γάρ here are Williams 1977: 112-13; Walker 1983: 107. Exceptions to nn. 1-2 above and here are e.g. B. Weiss (1885: 125) who says the reference is also to v. 11 (see also Perriman 1993: 130); Blomberg (1988: 414) who claims v. 13 presents a reason but v. 14 reflects the following thought. C. Kroeger and R. Kroeger (1992: 117-25) argue that vv. 13-14 refute a heresy, but see Chapter 13 n. 18 below.

4.　For the few exceptions see Chapter 12.

5.　E.g. Thackeray 1900: 55-57; Lock 1924: 32; A.T. Hanson 1968: 76-77; 1982: 73; Brox 1969: 135; Malina 1969: 24; Dibelius and Conzelmann 1972: 47-48 with n. 23; Hayter 1987: 132; Byrne 1988: 88 with n. 24; Roloff 1988: 139; Merkel 1991: 27; Oberlinner 1994: 99. See also Kähler 1959: (apparently) 10-11; Knoch 1988: 27; Dautzenberg 1989: 200 n. 44; Dewey 1992: 356. Swidler (1976: 47-48) traces the ideas in first-century CE Judaism. See also Urbach 1975: I, 421.

6.　E.g. Luther 1527–28: 278; Liddon 1897: 19; Bernard 1899: 48; White 1910: 109; Windisch 1930: 421-22; Falconer 1941: 375; Spicq 1947: 70; Ryrie 1958: 79; Leaney 1960: 54; Jeremias 1963: 19; Holtz 1965: 70; Meeks 1973: 206; A.T. Hanson 1982: 73; Wolter 1988: 44 with n. 74; Merkel 1991: 27.

7.　E.g. B. Weiss 1885: 126-27; Meinertz 1931: 39; Scott 1936: 27; G.G. Blum 1965: 158; A.T. Hanson 1966: 37; 1968: e.g. 76; 1982: 73; Houlden 1976: 71; Trummer 1978: 149; Hurley 1981: 216; Key 1984: 147-48; Hayter 1987: 133; Roloff 1988: 137, 140; Byrne 1988: 88; Merkel 1991: 27; Keener 1992: 116. S.B. Clark (1980: 203-207) suggests that she is more susceptible to spiritual influences and so less capable of leading. From Rom. 5.19, however, he also declares the man vulnerable to disobedience—a dubious leadership qualification. In the end Clark is appeal to the consequences of reversed created roles;[8] or reference to the principle of primogeniture.[9] It has been suggested that he links the lack of education for women contemporary to himself with Eve's second-hand acquaintance with God's prohibition and so to the inadvisability of women being teachers.[10] Others oppose items from the foregoing.[11] At v. 15 some argue that woman is confined to domesticity.[12] Others are sure she is not.[13] Some believe v. 15 to be a corrective to vv. 13-14.[14] Many grapple with the unexpected number change between σωθήσεται and μείνωσιν,[15] the rare and in this context problematic

---

inclined to see the deception more as typological than as empirical generalization, but notes that the two are not mutually exclusive. In similar train of thought Schreiner (1995: 145-46) claims that women (who generally speaking are 'more relational and nurturing', 'kinder and gentler') are 'less likely to draw a line on doctrinal non-negotiables', so that false teaching would enter the church. Church history is in fact littered with records of male disagreement about placement of those lines.

8. E.g. Knight 1980: 31; 1992: 143; Hurley 1981: 216; Woodhouse 1985b: 17. See also Moo 1980: 70; 1991: 190; Oden 1989: 100; Schreiner 1995: 145.

9. E.g. G. Davies 1986: 90; Fung 1987: 201.

10. E.g. Guthrie (1990: 88), who admits this is 'somewhat forced'. See also Bushnell 1919: §§342, 338.

11. E.g. Bruce 1982b: 11; Harris 1990: 347; Gritz 1991: 138; Hugenberger 1992: 346.

12. E.g. Swidler 1979: 337; M.Y. MacDonald 1988: 223. Meeks (1973: 206) says the sole proper function is procreation. See also Windisch 1930: 421.

13. E.g. Foh 1979: 128.

14. E.g. Kelly 1972: 68-69; Giles 1977: 70; Küchler 1986: 51; Oberlinner 1994: 100-101.

15. W.K. Brown (1887: 108) sees here irregularity typical of emendation. Moo (1980: 72 and n. 70) calls the shift 'natural'. Küchler (1986: 12) calls it unconscious, deriving from a change from 'Praxis zur Theorie, von der Beobachtung zur Regel' ('practice to theory, from the observation to the rule'). C. Kroeger and R. Kroeger (1992: 172) see stress on the paraenetic quality of the condition. See also Hendriksen 1955: 112; Roloff 1988: 142 n. 170. Some suggest a movement to 'man and woman/husband and wife': e.g. White 1910: 110; Prohl 1957: 40; Barrett 1963: 56; Brox 1969: 137; Powers 1975: 58; Giles 1977: 70-71; R.P. Martin 1984: 76. Seeing this as a possibility are Parry 1920: 15; Lock 1924: 33; Barrett p. 56, but Huther (1866: 137) calls it quite arbitrary; B. Weiss (1885: 129) denies it; Witherington (1988: 124) finds it least likely; and Guthrie (1990: 90) says the Author is not dealing with husbands. See also Porter (1993: 98). Some suggest the plural refers to or includes children: e.g. Meinertz 1931: 40; Leaney 1960: 54; Barrett p. 56; Houlden 1976: 72; Procksch 1977: 113; Witherington pp. 123-24. See also

τεκνογονίας with the article,[16] a non-specific σωτηρία,[17] and a wonderfully malleable διά.[18] AV translates literally 'she...they...'; but NIV and Phillips 'woman...she...'; TEV, RSV and JB 'women...they...'; and NEB 'she...women...' (although footnoting: '...if only husband and wife continue'). The chief characteristic of interpretations surveyed for the present study is their diversity. Allowing for variations, the Author is said to envisage here women who (contingent upon certain behaviours) are:

   i.   saved by bearing children;[19]
   ii.   saved through the midst of the pain now suffered in childbearing (Alford 1862: 320);

Luther (1527–28: 279), for whom the salvation does not seem to rely upon the children, and who attempts to aim some of his interpretation at men. Denying reference to children are: e.g. Ellicott 1864: 39; Huther p. 137; Weisinger 1866: 419; B. Weiss 1885: 129; Liddon 1897: 20; Lock 1924: 33; Brox p. 137; Porter 1993: 99. Spencer (1985: 93) claims the reference is to male instructors and female students.

16. Understanding 'child-bearing' are e.g. Alford 1862: 320; Barclay 1975: 68-69; Byrne 1988: 88-89. For child-bearing as typical of women's activities: e.g. Moo 1980: 71 with n. 69 (although noting dissension in MM). Moo's (1981: 205) response to Payne's criticism is difficult to reconcile with this, apparently because of a misprint. Also unable to exclude child-rearing are e.g. Meinertz 1931: 40; Falconer 1941: 377; Brox 1969: 136; Dibelius and Conzelmann 1972: 48. See also Olthuis 1976: 143; Hurley 1981: 223. Payne (1981: 178, 181; see also 1986: 113) claims that a generic meaning would be unusual and require defence.

17. Instances in MGM ΣΩΖΩ demonstrate a range of meanings. Powers (1975: 57-58) sees here 'physical deliverance', Byrne (1988: 88-89) 'salvation', Alford (1862: 320) both the foregoing, and E.F. Brown (1917: 22) 'preserved from sin'. Interpreting primarily in accordance with acceptance of Paul as the Author and his otherwise consistent meaning of 'spiritual salvation' is e.g. Payne (1981: 178). Roberts (1983: 20) leaps from the possibility of reference to an earthly, non-eternal salvation to 'saved into ecclesiastical wholeness'.

18. E.g. 'Means/agency' (Knight 1992: 147); 'during' (Powers 1975: 58); 'attendant circumstances' (Weisinger 1866: 418-19; B. Weiss 1885: 128; White 1910: 110); 'a condition' (Scott 1936: 28); 'efficient cause' (Moo 1980: 72 with n. 67). Payne (1981: 180-81) says agency is the expected meaning with the genitive, questioning whether 'efficient cause' is even grammatically possible, and pointing out that 'attendant circumstances' would more naturally be included with v. 15b rather than alone directly stated. Porter (1993: 97) notes that the most convincing temporal examples have accompanying temporal words, absent here.

19. E.g. A.T. Hanson 1968: 72, 76 (but cf. with n. 20 at iv. below); Parvey

iii.   saved even though they must bear children (Scott 1936: 28);

iv.   working out their salvation in their roles as mothers;[20]

v.   kept safe during childbearing;[21]

vi.   saved by The Childbearing (i.e. the birth of Christ);[22]

vii.   saved from deception by their role of motherhood;[23]

1974: 136; D.R. MacDonald 1979: 177; Swidler 1979: 337; Küchler 1986: 51; Perkins 1987: 21; M.Y. MacDonald 1988: 223; Wolter 1988: 44 n. 74; Dewey 1992: 356. Scanzoni and Hardesty (1982: 133) are undecided between this and vi. It is unclear whether Dibelius and Conzelmann (1972: 48) take this or view iv.

20.   E.g. Weisinger 1866: 418-19; B. Weiss 1885: 127; Humphreys 1901: 100; White 1910: 110; E.F. Brown 1917: 21; Parry 1920: 15 (apparently); Meinertz 1931: 40; Falconer 1937: 131; 1941: 376-77; Easton 1948: 125, 129; Hendriksen 1955: 111; Barclay 1975: 68-69; Osborne 1977: 347; Foh 1979: 128; Moo 1980: 71; 1981: 205; 1991: 192; Stendahl 1982: 29 (apparently); A.T. Hanson 1982: 73-74 (apparently); Roloff 1988: 141-42; Witherington 1988: 124; P.H. Towner 1989: 221; Harris 1990: 350 n. 43. Bernard (1899: 49 n. 1) combines v. Seeing iv. as possible are e.g. Lock 1924: 32-33; Nicole 1986: 48 n. 1 (cf. vi.). Luther (1527–28: 279) appears to support it by confusing the agency and goal of the salvation. Fee (1984: 38) seems to see childbearing as typical of the good works required of godly women. See also Jeremias (1963: 19). Kelly (1972: 69-70) claims the key is the prediction of motherhood as woman's appointed role at Gen. 3.16. See also Oberlinner 1994: 101. It would be more accurate to say that the predicted role is *painful* childbirth, woman clearly having been intended to bear children from the beginning.

21.   Simpson 1954: 48; Powers 1975: 58; Keener 1992: 118-19 with n. 137. See also NEB note [q] b. A.T. Hanson (1966: 38) is tempted here even though doubtful it can be extracted from the Greek. P.H. Towner (1989: 221) suggests it may be included (cf. iv.). Bernard (1899: 49) combines it with iv. Arguing against it on the grounds that it is untrue to reality are e.g. Bushnell 1919: §343; Scanzoni and Hardesty 1982: 134; Foh 1979: 128; Fee 1984: 37; Nicole 1986: 48 n. 1; C. Kroeger and R. Kroeger 1992: 171. Keener points out, however, that not all sick are healed despite Jas 5.14.

22.   E.g. Ellicott 1864: 38-39; Liddon 1897: 20; Bushnell 1919: §§327, 343; Spencer 1974: 220; 1985: 92-94; Williams 1977: 113; Nicole 1986: 48 n. 1 (cf. iv.); Oden 1989: 100-101; Knight 1992: 146-47. See also NEB note [q] a. Payne (1981: 177-81, 188) traces the link between Mary's child-bearing and salvation through the patristic period. Some see vi. as possible: Falconer (1937: 132); but (1941: 76, where he reports that Latin commentators interpreted thus but Greeks in general gave it no place) says it destroys the point of v. 12 and does not harmonize with v. 15b; Barclay (1975: 68) prefers iv; Hurley 1981: 222. Guthrie (1990: 89-90) suggests it has the least difficulties.

23.   G. Davies (1986: 94-95) argues that the deception is the desire to lord it over husbands. Cf. 'saved...from being branded a false teacher' (R.P. Martin 1984: 76).

viii.   preserved from seizing authoritative roles by marital life;[24]
ix.   saved in the eschatological sense by accepting the role of motherhood;[25]
x.   saved even though they give birth (and, by implication, are sexually active).[26]

Every one of these ten interpretations has its difficulties, and these are compounded when combined. At i. the conditional clause requires some mental gymnastics (Hendriksen 1955: 111 n. 57), and the interpretation implies ignorance of Paul's doctrine of salvation by grace through faith. Such a claim is unacceptable for those believing Paul to be the Author and, for those who do not, the pseudepigrapher's use of his name appears self-defeating. View ii. places some strain on διά, may suggest that childbirth could be viewed as a hindrance to salvation (Knight 1992: 145), and emphasizes the suffering rather than (as the text) the childbearing itself (Dibelius and Conzelmann 1972: 48). View iii. again takes a less than obvious meaning for διά[27] and suggests that child-bearing could be thought to endanger salvation. View iv. is popular, but makes a great deal out of both σῴζω,[28] which the Author elsewhere employs for spiritual salvation (1.15; 4.16), and τεκνογονία, which at 5.14 is differentiated from marriage and household management and contrasts with τεκνοτροφέω for childrearing (Porter 1993: 96). Again common, v. has even greater difficulties: the Author elsewhere employs ῥύομαι for 'keep safe' (Fee 1984: 37); nothing in the context addresses danger in childbirth (Knight 1992: 145); and an explanation is required for the conditional clause (Moo 1980: 71). The obscurity of the much-

---

24. Hurley 1981: 222-23. See also Blomberg 1988: 414-15 (apparently). Jebb (1970: 221) combines vii-viii.

25. E.g. Houlden 1976: 72; Fung 1987: 203-204.

26. Gritz 1991: 143-44; C. Kroeger and R. Kroeger 1992: 172-77. See also Marshall 1984: 192; Merkel 1991: 28. Blomberg (1988: 416) combines it with iv. Kelly (1972: 70) (cf. iv.) suspects it is a subsidiary goal. See also Lock 1924: 33 (cf. vi., iv.); Falconer 1941: 377 (cf. iv.); Brox 1969: 136; Olthuis 1976: 143 (primary interpretation unclear); Moo 1980: 72 (cf. iv.); Roloff 1988: 142, 147 (cf. iv.); Guthrie 1990: 88-89 (cf. vi.).

27. Meinertz 1931: 39-40; Guthrie 1990: 89; Porter 1993: 96-97.

28. Knight 1992: 145-46. Cf., however, Schreiner (1995: 152-53), who claims that the Author responds to the false teachers, comparing 4.11-16 'you will save both yourself and your hearers' which probably included criticism of bearing children. This is speculative.

supported vi. is often noted,[29] and particularity can be established only by context, not by the presence of the article (Porter 1992: 104-105). View vii. is highly unlikely without some qualifier.[30] View viii. has the dual problem that v. 12 is a considerable distance from v. 15, and σῴζω in the New Testament (including the Pastorals) so frequently refers to spiritual salvation.[31] View ix. introduces thought not clearly present. View x. again stretches the meaning of διά and introduces thought not immediately suggested.

This confusion exemplifies and crowns that broader variety commonly encountered in interpretations of New Testament passages about women. Answers depend upon starting points, which in this case are generally, via the influential γάρ, a congregationally viewed vv. 9-12/11-12, increasingly supported by invalid historical reconstruction of that setting derived from passages about false teachers and women (see Chapters 7 and 8 above), and frequently with reference to the potentially misleading 1 Cor. 14.34-35 (see Part III). Most refer to Genesis 1–3, sometimes with a view to setting hermeneutical guidelines for vv. 13-14 and so 15. Of these, however, Genesis 1–3 (or the particular interpretation of it in 1 Timothy 2) is often viewed through the lens of dubious interpretations of New Testament passages, chiefly 1 Cor. 11.8-9[32] (for which see Appendix 2). It is here, on the threshhold of vv. 13-15, that diverse exegetical 'winds' converge to reap their 'whirlwind'.

1 Timothy 2.13-15 itself provides some long-neglected indications that the Author intended something different from any of the above interpretations. It has been argued in Part I that the first of the fixed parameters in which it is viewed is inappropriate. Since vv. 9-12

---

29. E.g. Parry 1920: 15; Simpson 1954: 48; Leaney 1960: 54; Foh 1979: 128; Fee 1984: 38; Blomberg 1988: 414; Guthrie 1990: 89 (despite his comment at n. 22 above). Hurley (1981: 222) believes it also an interruption. '[A] pious and ingenious flight...of fancy' (Bernard 1899: 49); 'foreign to the...context' (Hendriksen 1955: 111 n. 57); 'improbable' (Houlden 1976: 72); 'not the most natural explanation', noting 5.14 (Moo 1980: 71). Roberts (1983: 19) questions 'incarnational soteriology'. Roloff (1988: 140) denies Gen. 3.16 was understood as the Protevangelium prior to the second century CE, but see my Appendix 3.

30. Fee (1984: 38) calls it 'nearly inconceivable'.

31. Roloff 1988: 141; Porter 1993: 93-94.

32. E.g. Knox 1558: 13; Calvin 1579: 212; Alford 1862: 320; Williams 1977: 113; Moo 1980: 68; 1981: 204; Knight 1980: 31-34, 43; 1992: 143; Payne 1986: 111-12; Scholer 1986: 209; Fung 1987: 202; Barnett 1989: 234.

address women's lives in general, vv. 13-15 must be reappraised, and the conjunction γάρ subjected to close scrutiny.

Three factors should be taken into consideration:

i. Πιστὸς ὁ λόγος (3.1a) may be backward-referring.
ii. Temporal rather than aspectual translations of verbs can distort the action visualized by the Author.
iii. During the hellenistic era interpretations of the Genesis Creation–Fall were diverse, and each must be assessed according to its own content and context (Levison 1988: 160-61). See Appendix 3 for relevant aspects of the Genesis record itself.

With the above three factors in mind, Chapters 12–14 below will each consider one of three markers in the text of vv. 13-15 to the Author's meaning (context; aspectual choices; Jewish character) which together suggest that γάρ here introduces neither reasons for, nor illustration of the need for, v. 12.

Chapter 12

THE FIRST MARKER: CONTEXT

Details of the Genesis record employed at 1 Tim. 2.13-14 are few: Adam was created first and was undeceived, but the later-formed and subsequently deceived Eve became a transgressor. The interpretations outlined in Chapter 11 derive from perceived implications arising not only from what *is* selected from Genesis but from what is *not*. Identification of the Author's particular emphasis plays a prominent role. It has been pointed out that the contextual needs determine that selection and emphasis (Scholer 1986: 211). The difficulty here is that if the context is misunderstood so too will be that selection and emphasis. The ecclesial context in which the passage has long been viewed is unconvincing; so, too, are common background reconstructions supporting that context. The exegetical domination of these devices must be halted and the language of the passage re-examined with a view to allowing any genuine emphases to emerge naturally.

The first-occurring apparent marker to the Author's meaning is γάρ. It has been noted that this conjunction is sometimes simply a connective requiring no translation.[1] In this context, however, it invariably creates the expectation that 'womanhood' is the issue somewhere in vv. 13-15. The exegetical diversity resulting from that expectation nevertheless warns that nothing should be taken for granted. The function of γάρ should be interpreted by the context, not the reverse.[2]

If γάρ is causal, the link in the Author's mind between a *non*-congregational v. 12 and vv. 13-14 is obscure. Why should it be thought necessary to support prohibitions for women roughly paralleling instructions for men with such a deeply theological basis when the immediately preceding instructions to those men have no such support?

---

1. Witherington 1988: 122; K.L. McKay 1994: §15.3.
2. Padgett 1987a: 25; Harris 1990: 350 n. 42. See also Robertson 1923: 1191; Payne 1981: 176.

It is similarly unconvincing solely on the basis of background recon-struction to assert that γάρ here 'can' (or 'does') illustrate what happens when a woman falsely teaches a man: see Part II, and Chapter 11 n. 2. How, then, is a legitimate decision made about its function?[3]

The matter for which a reason or illustration introduced by γάρ is given is not necessarily identifiable in what precedes. At 2 Tim. 2.11a, for example, although γάρ would normally be understood to link directly with πιστὸς ὁ λόγος, it is generally accepted by English trans-lations that the formula is forward-referring.[4] In this case γάρ connects with the original context, the recurring συν- prefix suggesting some ref-erence to Christ.[5] At 2 Tim. 2.11, then, γάρ is redundant.[6] Such unal-tered citation is not unusual.[7] Fanning suggests that in various New Testament letters catechetical material and LXX quotations duplicate Aorists where Present imperatives, conveying the idea of continued action, would normally be expected (1990: 377-79). K.L. McKay says that at 2 Tim. 2.19 ἔγνω differs from the usual gnomic use and suggests that Num. 16.5 may be unadapted to the expected Perfect.[8] At 2 Tim. 2.11 Knight argues that although some claim that the immediate context stresses martyrdom and that 2.11b-13 is included because v. 11 con-cerns dying with Christ,

---

3.   Pierce (1987: 3-10) properly challenges the conjunction's exegetical control, but argues from a perceived Old Testament analogy that at 1 Tim. 2.11-15 bound-aries for leadership are set arbitrarily and should be understood 'typologically', there being no logical link between the restriction and the ancient event. See also Wiebe 1994: 60. Pierce's recognition of the poverty of any attempt convincingly to identify causal or explanatory functions in γάρ at 1 Tim. 2.13 appears to be unique, but he leaps from recognition that *the conjunction* does not serve as a link between vv. 12 and 13-15 to an assumption that no link exists, and since 'religious leader-ship' is not addressed in ch. 2 his analogy is inherently inappropriate.

4.   E.g. NIV, TEV, Phillips, JB, RSV, NEB.

5.   Swete 1916: 1-2; Knight 1968: 113.

6.   See also at 1 Tim. 3.16 Ὅς, its antecedent clearly excluded from the quota-tion. Bernard 1899: 62. See also Origen, *Frag. ex comm. in ep. ad 1 Cor.* 74.21, who supports 1 Cor. 14.34-35 by 1 Tim. 2.12 καὶ διδάσκειν δὲ γυναικὶ οὐκ ἐπιτρέπω...κτλ., with δέ obviously redundant.

7.   On the other hand, for modified quotations see e.g. Ellis 1978: 147-48, 152, 174-81; Stanley 1990: esp. 75-76. See also New Testament citations diverging from LXX to serve the purpose of the writer: e.g. Rom. 10.11 adding πᾶς; Gal. 4.30 sub-stituting 'son of the free woman' for 'my son Isaac'.

8.   K.L. McKay 1981: 308-309. As an alternative, he suggests a semitic perfec-tive may have been translated clumsily.

> ...the preceding context does not speak of a martyr's death...[but] of
> suffering...and...enduring...[I]t is [the]...stress on 'enduring' that
> forms...the...bridge to the saying...[The Author]...quotes the saying at
> the natural transition point...in its original setting. In so doing he in-
> cludes...its unity...[O]ther lines must not be artificially interpreted just
> to fit into this context but must be viewed in their normal interrelation-
> ships to one another. The saying is quoted because it commends endur-
> ing and warns against its negative opposite, denial (1968: 116).

Porter argues that the negative opposite is by far the most potentially
devastating clause, the Future creating an expectation that, if denial
occurred, exclusion from God's kingdom would result.[9] The saying
does significantly conclude ἀρνήσασθαι γὰρ ἑαυτὸν οὐ δύναται, but
the arguments of Knight and Porter here are not mutually exclusive.
Although denial is the chief focus of the original, in the mind of the
Author the connection between what he has just written and the citation
is not only that denial, but also endurance. He is confident, however,
that his addressee will both recognize the saying and the emphasis in
the original context *and* appreciate the significance of the quoted portion in the new context. He therefore maintains from the original each
verbal form together with the now-redundant γάρ.

If πιστὸς ὁ λόγος at 1 Tim. 3.1a were backward-referring, γάρ at
v. 13 may again be redundant. In this case the formula would be a more
significant marker to the Author's meaning than the conjunction. I have
nowhere found this possibility considered, and now proceed to explore
it.

Certainly those concerned with vv. 13-15 who claim that 3.1 is backward-referring are few and unpersuasive. Some make no attempt to
explore implications.[10] Lock pays somewhat closer attention, arguing
that v. 15 is the saying, included with a view to moderating the implications of vv. 13-14, which he believes are quoted from 'some Jewish
apocrypha' to provide reasons for v. 12.[11] However, he neither makes

---

9. Porter 1989a: 313. See also Knight 1968: 136.

10. E.g. von Soden 1893: 232; White 1910: 110; Parry 1920: 15; J.G. Duncan
1923: 141; Holtz 1965: 72; Brox 1969: 112, 141.

11. Lock 1924: 29, 32-33. E.F. Brown (1917: 22) somewhat confusedly both
claims that v. 15 quotes 'some current Jewish or Christian writing' and suggests
that the Author himself is probably thinking of how Eve was deceived before she
had children. See also Falconer (1937: 132; 1941: 377-78), who suggests a Jewish
v. 15a with the conditional clause a Christian addition. Cf. Barrett (1963: 57), who
finds backward reference more likely than forward reference, but, having indicated

believable the Author's appeal to a Jewish source which must immediately be modified by a further saying, nor considers the possibility that γάρ is redundant.[12] Ellis, although unsure about the reference of the formula, argues that 1 Cor. 14.34-35 and 1 Tim. 2.11-15 derive from an exposition on Genesis 1–3 which circulated amongst Pauline churches.[13] This requires considerable caution in view of the differences between 1 Cor. 14.34-35 and 1 Tim. 2.11-15 (see Part III) on the one hand, and Ellis's apparent assumption on the other that the Genesis record subordinates woman to man at creation (see my Appendix 3). His further apparent assumption that γάρ makes vv. 11-12 part of the citation is also questionable in view of their close connection with vv. 9-10 and, via the even more closely connected v. 8, the chapter as a whole. He does not consider the possible implications here of the redundant γάρ at 2 Tim. 2.11.

In spite of the unconvincing nature of previous attempts to explain some part of 2.13-15 as the faithful saying of 3.1a, *UBSGNT*, Westcott and Hort (1882: 132), and Metzger (1975: 640) are amongst those preferring the backward reference.[14] The substitution of ἀνθρώπινος for πιστός in some MSS, and in one case even omission of the formula,[15] points to scribal and patristic discomfort about the relationship of the phrase to 3.1b. Scholars throughout the Christian era have been divided about the reference.[16] The sayings at 1 Tim. 1.15 and 2 Tim. 2.11-13

that the latter does not require a Christian origin, proceeds as though that *is* the correct reference.

12. See also Giles (1977: 69-72; 1985: 42-43, 57) who, without reference to the formula, argues that vv. 13-14 (and their 'corrective' at v. 15) are drawn from rabbinic interpretation with the readership in mind. Giles's acceptance of Pauline authorship (which implies that Timothy is the primary reader) already renders this improbable. It remains unclear, furthermore, why anyone intending to support prohibitions here would appeal to prejudices based upon what Giles declares are 'not very strong' arguments only immediately to 'correct' that appeal. Giles identifies a parallel at 1 Corinthians 11, where vv. 11-12 ensure that improper deductions are not made from vv. 3-4. There is a considerable difference, however, between that modification of a theological foundation, and correction of dubious rabbinic argument 'justifying' earlier prohibitions.

13. Ellis (1987: 239 with n. 16, 241-42 and n. 26; 1981: 213-16) followed by e.g. Gritz 1991: 145-46 n. 15.

14. For discussion on the need to make contextual judgments about the presence of citations see K.L. McKay (1994: §12.1).

15. See App. crit. in *UBSGNT*.

16. Knight (1968: 52-53) summarizes the division. A.T. Hanson (1982: 64, 75,

Text in a Whirlwind

follow πιστὸς ὁ λόγος-type introductions, but Metzger says that Tit. 3.8 must relate to what precedes.[17] Knight persuasively argues that 1 Tim. 4.9 is also backward-referring,[18] but his conclusion that 1 Tim. 3.1a is not is less convincing. The question, he correctly notes, is not which reference fits some scheme for 'faithful sayings'[19] or is regarded as the better statement,[20] but which is in fact the saying: immediate context is the primary indicator. Verse 3.1b, he notes, is an important statement upon which is placed great emphasis (cf. development from vv. 2ff., οὖν in v. 2), and without πιστὸς ὁ λόγος it appears abruptly. There is also considerable interest in church order in 1 Timothy 3, 5.17ff.; Tit. 1.5ff., many passages in Acts, Paul's letters, and other New Testament letters. He therefore cites Kelly:

> neither ii.15 nor any of the verses immediately preceding strikes one as a maxim which might have been current in the apostolic Church, whereas iii.1b has all the style and ring of a proverbial saying...[21]

The traditional nature of the material following 3.1b is not in question here: it is concluded by and forms the immediate referent of the ταῦτα formula (v. 14), is independent of its context, and its close affinity with Tit. 1.6-9 suggests a common origin (Ellis 1987: 244). Nor is it questioned that 'church order' (i.e. the lives of the people of the *ekklesia*) is important in the Pastorals. But in the context of a general concern to 'live holy lives', 3.1b is hardly 'abrupt': the focus on holy living continues in reference to other groups. Knight's failure to see anything in vv. 13-15 resembling a 'faithful saying' is not compelling. In effect,

91) claims the reference need not be either forward or backward, but is intended to add solemnity to an otherwise pedestrian text.

17. Metzger 1975: 640. See also Swete 1916: 2.

18. Knight 1968: 62-65. See also Swete 1916: 2; Fee 1984: 66-67. Cf. Ellis (1987: 239 n. 15), who tends to conclude otherwise. Lock (1924: xxxi-ii), citing Turner, suggests the formula may in each case be editorially introduced, but Ellis's demonstration of the use of traditional material renders this unacceptably speculative.

19. As e.g. Parry and von Soden at n. 10 above.

20. As e.g. Scott (1936: 29), who rejects the 'pedantic allegory' about Eve. See also Weisinger 1866: 423.

21. Knight 1968: 53-54. See also 1992: 152-53. Swete (1916: 2) arrives at much the same conclusions. See also B. Weiss (1885: 129-30) who argues that 2.15 is not the saying because it is 'so eng verwachsene, also von dem Briefschreiber selbst herrührende Aussage' ('such a closely related, that is a statement originating from the writer of the letter himself'). See also Oberlinner 1994: 112 with nn. 6, 7.

then, on the basis only of agreement with Kelly, Knight has declared 3.1b the 'better statement', a procedure he himself rejects. An adequate assessment of 1 Tim. 2.15 depends upon conclusions reached about its relation to 3.1a, and that deserves closer attention than Knight and the overwhelming majority give.

Although relatively frequent in the Pastorals (1 Tim. 1.15; 3.1; 4.9; 2 Tim. 2.11; Tit. 3.8), the πιστὸς ὁ λόγος formula is not a common one. Close parallels have been identified, but nowhere else is the meaning 'the saying is faithful'. The sense 'the report is credible' occurs in Josephus, *Ant.* 16.100; 19.132 and Dio Chrysostom, *Disc.* 45.3. The Hebrew *nkwn dbr* of 1Q27.1.8 is similar, that is 'certain is the word (to come to pass)'. Cf. in Revelation οὗτοι οἱ λόγοι πιστοὶ καὶ ἀληθινοί εἰσιν (21.5) and οὗτοι οἱ λόγοι πιστοὶ καὶ ἀληθινοί (22.6).[22] Even though 1 Tim. 1.15 and 2 Tim. 2.11-13 are obviously well-known sayings circulating amongst Christians, other 'faithful sayings' *could* simply draw attention to the truth of something said by the Author himself.[23] There are, however, other indications that traditional material is being extensively used in the letters (Ellis 1987: 237-48). One thing is undeniable: without the 'introductory' formula, 3.1b makes perfectly good sense and loses none of its impact. When the formula is taken as forward-referring, however, 2.13-15 is notoriously difficult. One is surely forced to consider whether the formula might hold a key to its meaning.

Since, however, the previously outlined interpretations accepting that the formula is backward-referring are unsatisfying, γάρ may not simply be declared redundant on the grounds of an assertion to that effect. Something more substantial is required. It will be necessary, therefore, as part of an evaluation of the role of γάρ at vv. 13-15 to ask whether those verses give any indication that they, or some part of them, may be a 'saying'. Before that, however, a second marker requires attention.

---

22. Ellis 1987: 239-40 nn. 18-19. See also Swete 1917: 1; BAGD, s.v. πιστός, 1b.

23. As e.g. J.G. Duncan 1923: 141; Fee 1984: 42, 159.

Chapter 13

THE SECOND MARKER: ASPECTUAL CHOICES

The recent work on Aspect cited in my Introduction sheds some light on portions of the debate about 1 Tim. 2.13-15.

It is sometimes claimed that, although Eve remains the subject throughout v. 14, γυνή and/or the Perfect γέγονεν, with its implication of ongoing effect, indicate that she is to be understood as the representative of her gender:

> ...but the woman, having been led astray, has fallen into sin (and remains there).[1]

All believe that at least by v. 15 attention has shifted to 'Woman'. In a difficult passage at the end of a controversial context, the number change between σωθήσεται and μείνωσιν deserves close attention. Such explanations as have been given for that change lack force.[2] All are based on interpretations of vv. 11-12 in a congregational context, and at v. 13 are influenced by a conjunction which (as demonstrated in Chapter 12) is of doubtful application, so the number change warns that the Author's meaning may have been missed.

---

1. E.g. Bernard 1899: 49; Humphreys 1901: 99; Lock 1924: 32-33; Falconer 1937: 131; 1941: 376; Wolter 1988: 44 n. 74; Gritz 1991: 141. See also Scott 1936: 27. Cf. those seeing here only Eve's abiding state: e.g. Ellicott 1864: 38; von Soden 1893: 232; Spencer 1985: 89; Guthrie 1990: 88. Fung (1987: 339 n. 209) suggests 'this is a Perfect of Allegory...a standing warning against being deceived by the devil'. Arguing without recourse to the Perfect that γυνή means 'Woman' are e.g. Alford 1862: 320; Liddon 1897: 20; White 1910: 109; Parry 1920: 15; G. Davies 1986: 93, 95.

2. Easton (1948: 125) says the awkwardness is slight, Barrett (1963: 57) that the lapse is easily committed in writing, Holtz (1965: 72) that it is not conspicuous, Brox (1969: 137) that it 'keine unerträgliche Härte darstellt' ('does not constitute an intolerable hardship'), and Gritz (1991: 145 and n. 203) that it is not unusual when the singular is generic.

The LXX translators introduce the name 'Eve' only after the judgment at Genesis 3, prior to that using ἡ γυνή. It is not clear, therefore, that at 1 Tim. 2.14 the Author has anyone other than the first woman in mind. The traditionally understood 'ongoing effect' of the Perfect often cannot be identified. Some Perfects are widely accepted as aoristic, although there is little agreement about where this actually occurs.[3] Moulton doubts that γέγονα in every case conveys the Perfect sense.[4] Zerwick writes

> It is to be noted that the choice between aorist and perfect is…determined by…the writer's wish to connote the special nuance of the perfect; if this be not required, the aorist will be used. The use of the perfect in the New Testament thus shows that the author has in mind the notion of a state of affairs resultant upon the action (1987: §288).

Zerwick almost always finds explanations for apparent New Testament aoristic Perfects, but notes his own doubts that γέγονα always has either the full sense of the Perfect or is the evolved 'I am' (e.g. Mt. 25.6; 1 Cor. 13.11) (1987: §289 and nn. 10-11). Although most New Testament occurrences of Perfect forms of this verb *may* be understood to convey present effect of past action (MGM, s.v.), they have, then, sometimes been identified as aoristic even by those supporting that traditional general definition. Some Perfects, moreover, have been understood from the classical period onwards to take on present meaning, for example οἶδα.[5] Others are perceived occasionally to do so.[6] Attractive arguments have been presented claiming that some are used in the same way as the vivid 'historic present'. Moulton claims

---

3.   Cf. e.g. Burton (1898: 39, 42-44), who says those at e.g. Lk. 9.36; 2 Cor. 12.17; Heb. 7.13; Rev. 3.3 may convey existing result, but claims that Matthew, and possibly Mark, regularly uses an aoristic γέγονα. See also BDF: §343. Jannaris (1968: §§1872, 1875) notes a steady spread of the use in the *koine* (see also Schwyzer 1988: 287), including the New Testament; but Fanning (1990: 303) says they are 'rather rare in the New Testament'.

4.   Moulton (1908: I, 145-46), citing Josephus, *Apion* 4.21; *P. Oxy* 478; *BGU* 136. Moulton says ἔσχηκα (2 Cor. e.g. 2.13; Jn 4.18; Mk 12.23) means 'possessed', maintaining true Perfect meaning, that some Perfects 'belong to the formula which tells us that the abiding significance…lies in its having been anticipated in prophecy', but that the author of Revelation may see εἴληφεν and εἴρηκα as actual aorists.

5.   BDF, §341; Mandilaras 1973: §462; Fanning 1990: 299.

6.   Jannaris (1968: §1866) cites Jn 20.29; 1 Tim. 6.17; 2 Cor. 1.10; Jude 6, but the traditionally understood Perfect nuance may be understood in each.

that in the great majority of New Testament cases γέγονα 'has obviously present time' (1906: 146). Robertson, reluctant to accept that New Testament writers used aoristic Perfects, nonetheless identifies 'dramatic historical present perfects' (Jn 1.32, 41; 5.33; Acts 7.35; 21.28; 2 Cor. 1.9; 11.25; Jas 1.24) (1923: 896-903). Other examples occur in Mt. 13.46 ἀπελθὼν πέπρακεν πάντα ὅσα εἶχεν; Mt. 25.6 μέσης δὲ νυκτὸς κραυγὴ γέγονεν; and Lk. 10.36 τίς τούτων τῶν τριῶν πλησίον δοκεῖ σοι γεγονέναι. Some which *could* be understood as 'aoristic' *may* also be understood as 'historic presents', for example Jn 12.29-30, where the voice from heaven appears no longer to be speaking, yet γεγονέναι, λελάληκεν and γέγονεν appear; Heb. 12.3 ἀναλογίσασθε γὰρ τὸν [Christ] τοιαύτην ὑπομεμενηκότα; 1 Jn 4.14 ὁ πατὴρ ἀπέσταλκεν τὸν υἱόν. More than a century ago Weymouth noted:

> ...there are [New Testament] passages where it is not easy to see any permanent result as having followed the action, there being some Old Testament narrative either quoted or alluded to, and the Perfect being so used as to bear a certain resemblance to the Historical Present (1890: 25-26).

Examples he adduces are at Acts 7.35; Heb. 7.6 *bis*; 8.5; 11.17. BDF §342 supplies Gal. 3.18; 4.23. These will all be discussed below, but note here that in none of them is the claim convincing that present effect of aoristic action is expressed. Since 1 Cor. 11.8 and Rom. 5.14 both employ the 'historic Present' in reference to the creation story, it seems—on the face of it—that these Perfects are indeed used in the same way. The use is not confined to the New Testament. In the LXX there seems little point in assuming present effect in, for example, either Josh. 1.3 εἴρηκα (cf. the consistent Aorist use for Moses throughout) or 2 Macc. 2.11 βεβρῶσθαι. Either could be understood as equivalents of the 'historic present'. Again, Philo writes Μελχισεδὲκ βασιλέα τε τῆς εἰρήνης—Σαλὴμ τοῦτο γὰρ ἑρμηνεύεται—(καὶ) ἱερέα ἑαυτοῦ πεποίηκεν ὁ θεός ('Melchisedek King of Peace—for this translates as Salem—[and] God made him his priest', *Leg. All.* 3.25). Clement of Alexandria writes Ἀδὰμ τέλειον μὲν ὡς πρὸς τὴν πλάσιν γεγονέναι φαμέν ('we say that Adam was born perfect with respect to the way he was formed', *Str.* 4.23). Athanasius similarly writes Ἀδὰμ μόνος ὑπὸ μόνου τοῦ θεοῦ διὰ τοῦ λόγου γέγονεν...εἰ μόνος μὲν αὐτὸς ὑπὸ μόνου τοῦ θεοῦ πεποίηται καὶ πέπλασται... ('Adam was the only one who was brought to birth by God alone through the agency of the word...since he alone has been made and moulded by God alone...', *Decr.* 8). Weymouth argues that New Testament Perfects of this type are best translated as 'historic presents', that is, in past tense (1890: 26). BDF claim that they retain present effect, but reason that Gal. 3.18 indicates that believers still possess the promise given to Abraham, and Heb. 11.17 that Abraham offered Isaac as an abiding example (§342). Both these explanations are interpretative, not based on grammatical principles.[7] The argument that these Perfects function in the same fashion as 'historic presents' is more satisfying than that they represent abiding examples. None of them, including those not in the context of Old Testament narrative but apparently or possibly used as 'historic presents', conveys any sense of present effect of past action.

At 1 Tim. 2.14 γέγονεν parallels those Perfects occurring in the context of seminal Old Testament events. Even if, therefore, the Perfect is generally defined as showing present effect of past action, this parallel with other New Testament and wider contemporary use suggests that it should be understood here as one of those exceptions to be translated by past-tense reference to Eve. It has always been misleading simply to assert that this γέγονεν conveys present effect of past action.

The work on Aspect cited in my Introduction, however, now makes clear that temporal definitions are inadequate for Greek verbs and fail to account for many 'exceptions'. The Perfect is not used 'in place' of either Aorist *or* Present: it consistently conveys its own characteristic stative aspect. No matter how many New Testament parallels may be marshalled to demonstrate that it may be used precisely as the 'historic present', the pattern is illusory. The 'historic present' conveys visualization of action in progress and, when occurring in narrative, indicates intention to mark significant or foreground action. Not only does the Perfect in every case grammaticalize the state of the subject of its clause as visualized but, in narrative, its heavy marking spotlights the action of that subject.[8] This explains the recurring pattern of New Testament Perfects used for some events taken from Old Testament narrative, and their identification as 'equivalents of historic presents'. They

7.   Cf. Dods (1910: 358), who rejects Blass's argument in favour of an aoristic meaning at Heb. 11.17, and Rendall (1910: 181) who claims that the Perfect at Gal. 4.23 presents a scripture record now in existence, comparing Heb. 11.17, 28.

8.   Porter 1989a: 251, 258-59. See also K.L. McKay 1992: 226; 1994: 4.5.2. For Fanning see my Introduction n. 45.

are indeed vivid, just as action visualized in progress is vivid in comparison with that visualized as whole. The Present and Perfect both feature actions against broader narrative backgrounds but, although both appear in settings deictically marked as either past or present, and although both render action vivid, the similarities must not be permitted to blur essential differences. The characteristic force of each must be recognized. The Perfect conveys visualization of the state of the subject of the action, not of progression of the action, and by its heavier markedness spotlights that action more dramatically than do the imperfective forms. In the following discussions these differences will be marked where appropriate by bold print for the Perfect (and its subject), and by italics for imperfective forms. It should be noted that the Perfects cited above from the LXX, Philo, Clement and Athanasius are not equivalents of the 'historic present', but fully significant 'spotlighting' Perfects.

It is widely accepted that in the brief narrative at 1 Tim. 2.13-14 the emphasis is upon the man's primary creation or non-deception,[9] or the woman's (and sometimes therefore women's) deception.[10] A temporal element in v. 13 cannot be denied: Adam is first-created. Nevertheless, γέγονεν not only visualizes Eve's state but, against a background of Aorist forms, directs the spotlight:

> For Adam was formed first, then Eve. And Adam was not deceived; but **the woman**—who had been led astray—**came into a state of being** in transgression.[11]

As a preliminary step in considering the implications of these aspectual choices, it should be noted that γίνομαι could convey literally '*in/into*

---

9. Believing priority is stressed are e.g. Weisinger 1866: 416; Houlden 1976: 72; S.B. Clark 1980: 201. Schüssler Fiorenza (1983: 235) and Hayter (1987: 133) say fidelity is also stressed. Barnett (1989: 234) says the material about Eve is 'gratuitous and parenthetical'. See also Fung 1987: 202.

10. E.g. Ellicott 1864: 38; Huther 1866: 134-35; Liddon 1897: 19; A.T. Hanson 1968: 72; Malina 1969: 24; Olthuis 1976: 143; Williams 1977: 113; Moo 1980: 69-70; modified 1981: 204; but see also 1991: 189; Fee 1984: 37, 40; Harris 1987: 33; 1990: 345-50; Witherington 1988: 123; Gritz 1991: 138; Keener 1992: 115; Perriman 1993: 130; Schreiner 1995: 141. Payne (1986: 112) sees the greatest stress marked by repeated use of 'deceived' and its heightened form regarding Eve.

11. Spencer (1974: 218) misses the mark with '[v.]14 emphasiz[es]...that the woman..."became" a transgressor...' by adding '...because of her deception'. The reason is not emphasized.

transgression was in a state of *being/(be)coming'*. The reference is almost universally understood to be to the woman's progression from innocence through deception and disobedience to the Fall: that is 'the woman...fell into a sinful state'.[12] In the language of v. 14, however, the 'spotlight' falls more directly upon a state described by γέγονεν than ἐν παραβάσει. Regardless of whether the verb is rendered '(be)coming' or 'being', the focus could be upon a perceived transitional state of transgression between deception and Fall: many do so interpret the woman's condition prior to the actual taking and eating of the forbidden fruit (see Appendix 3, Section 2). The fact that Adam's subsequent sin, which is identical to the subsequent sin of the woman, receives no attention could reinforce this idea. The actual Fall, that is, the taking and eating of the forbidden fruit, may not directly be in view at all. In this case the passage would convey:

> but **the woman,** having been led astray, **was in a condition tending** towards transgression.

I will return to this possibility below.

The Perfect marking conveys a tone of extreme gravity,[13] further emphasized by the end position in the clause (K.L. McKay 1972: 52). Moreover, the Perfect sometimes expresses responsibility for action.[14] McKay writes that this occurs sometimes in action verbs (1965: 17; 1977: §23.4.2; 1994: §3.4.5).[15] Γίνομαι certainly refers to Eve, whether or not the focus begins to shift to Woman, and Eve moved from one state to another—obviously an action. Responsibility therefore may well be expressed. If Woman is focused, a state must be implied, and it is difficult to see how the one verb could at once be both active and stative. Porter suggests that in fact such lexical division is invalid.[16] In summary, the aspectual choices in v. 14 require the reader seriously to

---

12. For A.T. Hanson (1968) on παράβασις see my Appendix 3 n. 54.

13. Gildersleeve (1908: 396) says the Perfect belongs to drama, oratory and dialogue, in history appearing only in speeches or reflective passages where the author has his say. Fanning (1990: 297) says 'perfect indicatives are more characteristic of a reflective and discursive style in which the significance of events is dwelt upon, and they occur less in straightforward narrative'. See also BDF, §340; K.L. McKay 1965: 17; Mandilaras 1973: §§461, 470-71, 473.

14. Porter 1989a: 279; Fanning 1990: 148.

15. K.L. McKay 1965: 17; 1977: §23.4.2; 1994: §3.4.5.

16. Porter 1989a: 87, 259. K.L. McKay (1981: 297 n. 18; 1994: §3.1.4) is himself careful about the distinction. See also Fanning 1990: 129-40 with n. 4.

consider the condition which the woman was responsible for entering. This woman is Eve. Whether or not the context indicates that the Author intends to extrapolate something about women in general, 1 Tim. 2.14 itself is concerned with the state of the first woman against a background of basic differences between her and Adam. In short, there is no necessary shift of focus from Eve to Woman in v. 14 .[17] Γάρ may or may not be redundant, and πιστὸς ὁ λόγος may or may not be backward-referring but, according to the research on Aspect cited in my Introduction, the goal of vv. 13-14 is not to highlight the primacy or non-deception of Adam or the subsequent creation or deception of Eve. Those details are secondary to the focus on Eve's condition,[18] and interpretations based upon their primary emphasis are misdirected. Any instinct to minimize or maximize the implications of this emphasis as either Pauline or non-Pauline should be resisted until other markers are in place; but the aspectual choices must be permitted their natural force.

Does the language of v. 15 suggest that attention, here, at any rate, does shift from Eve to women in general? Standard definitions of conditional clauses with ἐάν, Aorist subjunctive protases, and Future indicative apodoses, state that whilst reference is normally specific and future it is also commonly general with no particular future application.[19] Decisions about specificity or generality must be made from the context, since there is no linguistic or grammatical distinction between the two (Zerwick 1987: §327). If Eve were the subject of σωθήσεται it would not immediately be clear upon whom her σωτηρία depends. It is therefore universally concluded that this is a general statement about Woman with no particular future application, the focus having returned from the digression to Adam and Eve. In the context of vv. 9-12, even though γέγονεν does not express present effect, its marking of Eve's

17. Keener (1992: 115 with n. 113), although noting rabbinic links between Eve and all women, also makes this observation. See also e.g. Weisinger 1866: 418, and at n. 1 above Ellicott, von Soden, Spencer and Guthrie.

18. This concentration by itself renders dubious the argument of C. Kroeger and R. Kroeger (1992: 122-25) that the Author is refuting heresy about Eve's primal creation and/or Adam's deception and/or Eve's non-deception and superior knowledge. However, see also my Introduction n. 25.

19. Zerwick 1987: §322, and see other references below. See also e.g. BAGD, s.v. δέ 1e; BDF, §373 (3). Cf. Burton (1898: §250), who argues that such conditional clauses referring to future time suggest some probability of fulfilment of the condition, and Jannaris (1968: §1970), who says the supposition is emphasized.

sinful state against a background of her differences from Adam could nevertheless suggest her representation of all women. The possibility noted above that the concern is about her transitional pre-Fall state may reinforce this, that is, she may represent deceived Woman's perceived tendency towards transgression. In any case, when the conditional clause is viewed as having general application, γάρ certainly appears intended to connect vv. 13-14 directly with the prohibitions of v. 12.

One alternative to the general-statement interpretation is suggested by the claim that protases combining ἐάν with the Aorist subjunctive occasionally refer to something impending in past time, as at Acts 9.2 (BDF, §373 [3]). At 1 Tim. 2.15 this could indicate 'but Eve would be saved...if they [Adam and Eve] would continue in faith...etc.' However, at Acts 9.2 it is the context which makes clear that the Future condition is to be set in the past. At 1 Tim. 2.15 the context itself creates the difficulty. Any claim of past time-setting simply on the basis of this alternative could have little force because of:

i.   temporal definitions of this type of condition;
ii.   the paucity of parallels set in the past;
iii. the influential γάρ; and
iv.   the fact that it is not obvious why the Author would include such a discourse immediately following instructions about women roughly paralleling those previously given about men.

Even though it has been argued in Part I that the congregational restrictions traditionally envisaged in v. 12 are not in view, at v. 13 women have nevertheless just been forbidden to direct (constantly) and to have authority over a man (constantly). Against a background of differences between herself and Adam, the first woman is vividly featured as responsible either for entering a state tending towards, or falling into a state of, transgression. A singular subject is to be saved by continuing (in company with some other person/s) in faith, etc. Not surprisingly, the unidentified subject of σωθήσεται is concluded to be Woman. Only the number change in μείνωσιν suggests there may be something wrong with this reasoning, but that alone requires exploration of the possibility that Eve herself may be the subject of σωθήσεται.

The type of conditional clause employed conveys limited information. Turner states that protases with ἐάν and the Aorist subjunctive involve 'a definite event occurring only once in the future, conceived as taking place before the time of the action of the main verb' (1963: 114-

15). Thorley, however, defines this kind of protasis simply as indicating that the action of the verb is regarded as completed at the time of the main clause. He can find no aspectual reasons for the Aorists at Mt. 5.20, 46; Jn 8.51, 52, and notes that the Vulgate in most instances translates with a Future Perfect, and rarely with a simple Future.[20] It has now been demonstrated, however, that the Aorist conveys visualization of 'whole' rather than 'completed' action. Of the five New Testament conditional clauses in Turner's list of such protases featuring μένω, four (Acts 27.31; 1 Cor. 7.8 and 40 cf. v. 26; 1 Jn 2.24[21] cf. v. 26) refer to whole actions. 1 Timothy 2.15 is the fifth. In fact, of the 118 times μένω occurs in the New Testament (together with 24 occurrences of ἐπιμένω, παραμένω and καταμένω; MGM, s.vv.), whenever the Aorist is used contextual evidence indicates perception of whole action. Every New Testament protasis with ἐάν with the Aorist subjunctive of μένω (MGM, s.vv.) may be understood as a whole rather than a definite event. Of the aspectual 'exceptions' which Thorley notes, Mt. 5.46 is the first of two such conditional constructions, and since that at v. 47 is apparently understood as one greeting, ἀγαπήσητε is likely similarly to envisage a whole act of love (cf. Lk. 7.47 in context). Mt. 5.20 and Jn 8.51, 52 both appear in the context of God's future judgment. Each could, in point of fact, be understood in terms of the Latin Future Perfect to which Thorley parallels these constructions, that is, as whole actions. At Mt. 5.20, for example, we could read: 'unless your righteousness *will have exceeded* that of the scribes and pharisees, you will certainly not enter into the kingdom of heaven'. In this case the righteousness in view would be that evident at the judgment. Rom. 10.9, closely resembling the language and construction of 1 Tim. 2.15, may be understood to refer to the particular acts of 'confession' and 'believing' which bring the subject into a state of salvation.[22]

However, Greek must be interpreted according to its own (not Latin) grammar. K.L. McKay classifies this type of clause as an open condition in which the protasis may be particular or general, and notes that

20. Thorley 1988: 201-202. In correspondence with me (5.7.90) Dr. Thorley pointed out that the two examples from John were accidentally omitted from his article. Turner (1963: 114) also says the Aorist subjunctive is like the Latin Future Perfect in relation to the main clause.

21. The shifting 'tenses' here parallel 2 Tim. 2.5 and Rev. 3.2-3.

22. E.g. L. Morris 1988: 384-86. At 1 Tim. 2.15 Alford (1862: 321) similarly renders 'if they...shall be found in that day to have remained'.

the possibility of fulfilment depends upon the context, although protases with ἐάν + subjunctive *normally* occur in general conditions.[23]
Porter argues that protases ought to be divided into two aspectual
classes. 1 Timothy 2.15b represents his class 2a: those making projec-
tions with no statement of probability.[24] Normal aspectual force is
maintained, so the Aorist subjunctive conveys visualization of whole
action, projecting a condition without indicating whether or not it ever
came or will come to pass. This is unaffected by the presence of ἐάν (εἰ
+ ἄν) (1989a: 307). According to Porter, verbs in apodoses function as
they do in other contexts (1989a: 166, 316), so the Future indicative at
1 Tim. 2.15a states what could be expected if the condition were to be
met. Since the Future appears in past and present as well as future time
contexts, only *deixis* indicates the time setting (1989a: 416, 421).
Although McKay rejects Porter's approach for conditions (1992: 18
n. 45), they are in general agreement that only the context can clarify
whether the reference is general or specific. Porter, however, draws
attention to the fact that in the third person the translator must consider
the visualization of the writer/speaker (1989a: 415): for example in Mt.
7.6 pigs 'can be expected' to trample; in Jn 10.28 no one 'can expect'
to seize. Whether Eve or Woman be taken as the subject of the apodosis
at 1 Tim. 2.15, therefore, the interpreter is confronted with choices:

> But she   could expect/could be expected   to be saved…
> …if they   continue/continued…etc.[25]

Deixis is the only guide to the original thought, but this is precisely
where the problems of this passage lie.

Although the aspectual choices in vv. 13-14 provide important evidence for the proper emphasis, v. 15 therefore proves more intractable.
If the Author had provided only the two markers to his meaning considered in the previous and present chapters (the possibility only that
γάρ may be redundant, and aspectual choices at vv. 13-14), several
problems would remain. Does his focus shift back to 'Woman' at v. 15?
Could the expectation be that of Eve or of someone else? If women
were *not* the subjects of μείνωσιν, who could be, and what then could

---

23. K.L. McKay 1994: §§19.1; 21.1.3 (emphasis mine).

24. Porter (1989a: 307-11; 1993: 100), cf. (1992: 262) 'class 3', projection for
hypothetical consideration. See also Carson 1986: 81.

25. Porter (1993: 100-101) does not confront these choices because he dismisses Eve as an unlikely subject. See further in Chapter 14 n. 93.

be the purpose of vv. 13-15? What significance is to be found in the background details of vv. 13-14 expressed in Aorist forms? Finally, as has frequently been noted, although vv. 13-14 select from rather than quote Gen. 2–3.13, Adam *is* created first there, and Eve *does* say she was deceived (3.13b). Differences between 1 Tim. 2.13-14 on the one hand and, on the other, Rom. 5.12-21; 1 Cor. 15.22; 2 Cor. 11.3 do not amount to actual disharmony, so there is no compelling reason to conclude that the Author does not share Paul's view of Adam's responsibility for the introduction of sin.[26] Nevertheless, when v. 15 is understood to address women generally, and when it is reasoned that γάρ directly links what follows with the prohibitions of v. 12, the approach differs from 2 Cor. 11.3 in that Eve seems to serve as support for prohibitions for women only.[27] But, if (as argued in Part I) the prohibitions of v. 12 are neither harsh nor broadly restrictive in comparison with the instructions given to men, what is the connection in the Author's mind between those prohibitions and the Creation–Fall? If (as I have argued) the instruction to women *does* amount to no more than a more diverse counterpart to instruction to men, why should it inspire selections which both stress some parts of the Genesis story whilst ignoring others, and serve as a background for a colourful highlighting of Eve's personal responsibility for a grievous entry into a state of transgression? The third marker to the Author's meaning holds a key to all these problems.

I therefore take up again the questions of whether vv. 13-15 may be, or contain, the 'saying' referred to at 3.1a, and so whether γάρ may be redundant.

---

26. Weisinger 1866: 417; B. Weiss 1885: 126; Liddon 1897: 19; Meinertz 1931: 39; Scott 1936: 27; Osborne 1977: 347; S.B. Clark 1980: 202; Moo 1980: 70; Guthrie 1990: 88; Knight 1992: 143-44. Contra e.g. Kähler 1959: 12; Roloff 1988: 140.

27. E.g. Byrne 1988: 88.

Chapter 14

THE THIRD MARKER: JEWISH CHARACTER

The characteristically Jewish nature of 2.13-14 or 13-15 is often noted.[1] Some argue that the Author uses Jewish material,[2] but the possibility that he incorporates *unmodified* some such material has received little, and inadequate, attention.

Such incorporation is not without precedent. Of sayings in the Pastorals marked by the πιστὸς ὁ λόγος formula, 1 Tim. 4.8-9 has no necessarily Christian character[3] and may have been current amongst, or inherited or adapted from, another community.[4] With a view to the identification of any substantial evidence in 2.13-15 that 3.1a may be backward-referring, the idea that a saying concerning Adam and Eve may originally have been Jewish is worthy of exploration.

1.　See e.g. Windisch 1930: 421-22; Scott 1936: 27; Müller-Bardorff 1958: 127 n. 41; Jeremias 1963: 19; Bartsch 1965: 165; Brox 1969: 134; Dibelius and Conzelmann 1972: 47-48; Houlden 1976: 71; Swidler 1979: 337; Scholer 1983: 13; 1986: 210; Hayter 1987: 132-33; Witherington 1988: 123; Roloff 1988: 138-39, 147; Oden 1989: 99-100; Merkel 1991: 23-28; Dewey 1992: 356; Oberlinner 1994: 95. Cf. Ellicott (1864: 37) who denies Jewish character, A.T. Hanson (1968: 112) who sees here additions to a Pauline midrash, and Payne (1981: 188-89) who argues that vv. 13-14a are sayings of Ephesian Judaizers. See also Küchler (1986: 27, 30).

2.　E.g. Dibelius and Conzelmann 1972: 48.

3.　I accept backward reference for this formula. See Knight 1968: 77-79 (although see pp. 127-30 above for the meaning of εὐσέβεια). Cf. Ellis (1987: 239 n. 15) who is undecided about the reference here.

4.　Knight (1968: 59, 77-78), who argues that the formula is used for special Christian sayings, admits that here it may refer to a proverb of either Jewish or Gentile origin. Bloch (1990: 25) demonstrates the continuance of the view, quoting Maimonides: 'A person must distance himself from those things which weaken the body, but rather must become accustomed to (pursuing) things which make the body healthy', and '...to have a healthy...body is the way of Hashem (God)'. Cf. Easton (1948: 130), who, although guessing that 3.1a is forward-referring, says 3.1b 'could easily' be current in civic circles. See also at Chapter 12 n. 11, Barrett.

With such an origin in mind perhaps it may seem more appropriate that παράδοσις (commonly used for the oral handing on of traditions)[5] be used than λόγος (cf. Mt. 15.2; Mk 7.5), particularly since the former was similarly used of Christian traditions (1 Cor. 11.2) and teachings (2 Thess. 3.6; *1 Clem.* 7.2).[6] However, in 2 Thess. 2.15 παράδοσις is conveyed by λόγος or letter, and in 1 Thess. 2.13 ἀκοή is also to be understood as 'tradition'(Schippers 1966: 224-30). Most importantly, λόγος is part of a formula used throughout the Pastorals for sayings which had achieved general status.[7] Why should a saying originating in Judaism and carried over to Christianity not be described by the same word?

Before one reasonably could posit a Jewish origin for 1 Tim. 2.13ff., it would be necessary

1. to trace parallels with known Jewish or Jewish Christian thought;
2. to find the saying intelligible as a unit or part of a unit distinct from its present context; and
3. to identify the relevance in the present context.

This chapter explores each of these.

1. *Jewish Parallels*

During the hellenistic era Jewish views about Adam and Eve were diverse. Levison argues that this diversity has been ignored because the focus has been on uncovering the background for Paul's views, a focus which unjustifiably assumes both a restricted Adam cycle and a single Semitic Vorlage (1988: 14-31). In fact,

> ...each [early Jewish] author employs and adapts Adam according to his *Tendenz*. The result...is...portraits of Adam which express the viewpoints of individual authors and not an Adam myth or a unified corpus of Adam speculation.[8]

---

5. See the inscription published by Horsley (1992b: 121) and associated discussion (p. 145).

6. I am indebted to D. Sim for this observation.

7. Λόγος may also mean 'teaching' or 'message' (Lk. 4.32; 10.39; Acts 4.4; 10.44) or 'statement' (e.g. Mt. 15.12; Acts 6.5; Josephus, *Ant.* 15.81; BAGD, s.v., 1β, γ).

8. Levison 1988: 14. Stone (1992: 64) nevertheless finds a Semitic Vorlage possible. Goulder (1992: 226-29) traces some common threads in first-century CE Jewish and Christian interpretations.

New Testament interpretations of Adam and Eve should therefore be assessed as contributions to a diverse body of thought in which parallels may occur when similar perspectives control those interpretations (Levison 1988: 159, 161).

The non-conflicting differences between the interpretations at 1 Tim. 2.13-14 on the one hand, and Rom. 5.12-21 and 2 Cor. 11.3 on the other, require neither that the particular perspective of the former passage is different from nor identical with the latter two. When Paul is accepted as the author of all three, although his perspective of the Genesis record could reasonably be expected to remain constant, his focus for differing contexts may not. Whoever wrote 1 Timothy, the object here is to explore whether 2.13-15 or some part thereof may be a 'faithful saying' *not original to the Author*. It is therefore inappropriate to presuppose its meaning.

It is commonly claimed that the Author shares perspectives which control known Jewish interpretations of the Genesis record, and from this a Christian school of thought reflecting Jewish views has been postulated.[9] However, whilst there is evidence that some Jews in the hellenistic period believed women to be inferior to men,[10] evidence also exists that others may not have held that view. Some certainly did not believe Eve to be the cause of sin and death: see Appendix 3.

Sirach, so often employed in demonstration of Jewish belief that woman was that cause, may have been misunderstood. Comparing the woes caused by an evil wife with the joys of a good one, he writes

ἀπὸ γυναικὸς ἀρχὴ ἁμαρτίας, καὶ δι' αὐτὴν ἀποθνήσκομεν πάντες. μὴ δῶς...γυναικὶ πονηρᾷ παρρησίαν· εἰ μὴ πορεύεται κατὰ χεῖράς σου, ἀπὸ τῶν σαρκῶν σου ἀπότεμε αὐτήν (LXX Sir. 25.24-26, S and A).[11]

From a woman was the beginning of sin;
And because of her we all die.
Give not...to a wicked woman freedom of speech.
If she go not as thou wouldest have her,
Cut her off from thy flesh (RV).

9. E.g. Malina 1969: 24, 33. See also my Appendix 3.
10. Keener (1992: 114-15) traces these views through to later rabbinic times, but notes that some saw Eve deceived partly because Adam had misrepresented the command to her.
11. I am indebted to A.E. Gardner for drawing my attention to the context of Sir. 25.24 in this form. For παρρησία cf. Acts 2.29; Phlm. 8. BAGD, s.v.

B, however, reads

μὴ δῷς...γυναικὶ πονηρᾷ ἐξουσίαν.

Lampe lists παρρησία as an example and synonym of ἐξουσία in the patristic period. In the same context Sirach writes

ἀνάβασις ἀμμώδης ἐν ποσὶν πρεσβυτέρου, οὕτως γυνὴ γλωσσώδης ἀνδρὶ ἡσύχῳ...ὀργὴ καὶ ἀναίδεια καὶ αἰσχύνη μεγάλη γυνὴ ἐὰν ἐπιχορηγῇ τῷ ἀνδρὶ αὐτῆς (25.20,22).

As the going up a sandy way is to the feet of the aged,
So is a wife full of words to a quiet man...
There is anger, and impudence, and great reproach,
If a woman maintain her husband. (RV)

Verse 20 parallels LXX Prov. 21.19

κρεῖσσον οἰκεῖν ἐν γῇ ἐρήμῳ ἢ μετὰ γυναικὸς μαχίμου καὶ γλωσσώδους καὶ ὀργίλου,

It is better to live in a desert than with a woman who is quarrelsome, a chatterbox, and irascible,

and Prov. 27.15

σταγόνες ἐκβάλλουσιν ἄνθρωπον ἐν ἡμέρᾳ χειμερινῇ ἐκ τοῦ οἴκου αὐτοῦ, ὡσαύτως καὶ γυνὴ λοίδορος ἐκ τοῦ ἰδίου οἴκου.[12]

Constant dripping casts a man out of his home on a stormy day, as likewise an abusive wife (casts him) from his own home.

Noting that interpretation of Sir. 25.24 as referring to Eve conflicts with Sirach's view of the origin of death (41.3b, 4a; cf. 40.11; 17.1-2a), Levison concludes that the 'evil wife' remains the subject throughout 25.24-26. Ἀποθνήσκομεν, he argues, is hyperbolic, the subject limited to Sirach and his audience (25.16; 24.23 cf. 44.1; 48.11), and he renders

From the [evil] wife is the beginning of sin, and because of her we [husbands] all die.[13]

---

12. Both Sirach and Proverbs should be understood in the literary–historical context of Sir. 8.3; 9.18; 25.20 and LXX Ps. 140.11, all dealing with incessantly talking men (cf. 1 Tim. 2.8).

13. Levison 1985: 617-23. Contra e.g. Vermes 1992: 223. Cf. also the less convincing von Rad (1972b: 262) who, although believing Eve to be in view, says sin and mortality are touched on only in passing, not intended as subjects for instruction, and S.B. Clark (1980: 694 n. 11) who says the passage is a humorous lament, not a theological statement.

An allusion to Eve having introduced sin and death, he claims, would interrupt the context, concerned as it is with the effects of the evil wife upon her husband (1985: 618). The interruption is questionable, the allusion illustrating that woman has ever been a source of trouble to man. Nevertheless, a parallel to Levison's translation does exist in a fragment from a poem at Qumran which, making no allusion to Eve, describes the effects of an evil woman upon men:

> *why 'h r'šyḥ kwl drky 'wl*
> she is the beginning/foremost of all the ways of perversity. (4Q184.8)

Sirach's allusion *may* be to Eve, but this should not simply be taken for granted (Porter 1990a: 17). If the allusion is present, the claim ignores Adam's role and what God is recorded as having said in Gen. 3.17-19. Parts of the Genesis story would have been selected as a basis for restriction upon, or divorce of, a sinful wife. Since Sirach emphasizes elsewhere that mankind was created mortal, he would also partly be inconsistent. 1 Timothy 2.13-14 similarly selects only parts of the Genesis story. Since both appear to see links between a man's peace and quiet, the question of woman's freedom of speech and/or authority, and the Genesis story, it could be said that 1 Tim. 2.13-14 is not unlike some Jewish thought already in evidence in pre-Christian times. That is, discussion about the need for women to be quiet and submissive in their relationships with men triggers in the Author's mind the subject of Eve. Nevertheless, although Sirach's connection between what he saw as Eve's role and the 'evil wife' of his day would then seem clear (viz woman had, from the start, been a source of grief for man), a similar clarity is not evident in 1 Timothy. The Author's reference to the Genesis record is certainly selective but, since his prohibitions for women parallel exhortations about men, the reason why he would turn for support to these particular selections for the women's prohibitions only is difficult to isolate. Does he, as some believe, show evidence of a Sirach-like belief in the basic inferiority and sinfulness of women? His focus *is* upon the deceived/fallen state of the woman. But it is unclear that Sirach *does* allude to Eve in 25.24-26. The argument that 1 Tim. 2.13-14 resembles roughly contemporary Jewish thought needs to be based upon something more than solely Sir. 24.25.

The *Apocalypse of Moses* is also commonly invoked as reflecting the Jewish view that Eve was responsible for the introduction of sin. It certainly does so at 9.1-2; 10.2; 11.1-3; 14.2; 32.2, but it also contains what was originally a separate account (15-30). Although the differences in this section are ignored by those seeking negative views of women, here deception is portrayed as beginning in Adam's portion of Paradise (15.2-3), and Adam claims sole blame for sin (27.2).[14]

Other Jewish sources also feature Adam as the one who introduced sin (*4 Ezra* 7.118; *2 Bar.* 48.42), or regard death as decreed by God from the beginning (Wis. 15.7-13; Sir. 17.1-2a; 41.3-4): see Appendix 3.

At 1 Tim. 2.13-14, therefore, it is dangerous to declare that the few and enigmatic selections from Genesis are parallel to particular Jewish views when those views presented are themselves either doubtful or do not represent all perspectives. If the passage is in fact Jewish in character, that relation must be traced somewhere other than Sir. 25.24 and the *Apocalypse of Moses*.

2. Intelligibility as a Unit

Since the chief characteristic of thought about Adam in antiquity is selection according to individual *Tendenz*, this particular *Tendenz* must be identified before attempting to interpret that selection. As argued above, however, when the passage is understood as the Author's own words, that identification is difficult indeed. An adequate explanation for his connection between vv. 12 and 13-14 is not immediately clear. But if vv. 13-14 were a quotation, the point in its original context may differ from that in which it now appears. Plutarch, for example, in applying Homer sometimes preserves only the loosest connection with the original narrative contexts (Stanley 1990: 71). In accordance with contemporary practice and, indeed, his own at 2 Tim. 2.11-13 (see Chapter 12, pp. 251-52)), the Author may choose a quotation not because of the particular emphasis in the original context but because the portion in some way illustrates the point of his own discourse. Neverthless, it would be futile to hazard identification of such a point unless it can be demonstrated that vv. 13-14/13-15 are in fact a 'saying'.

New Testament quotations from the Old Testament are introduced by ἐρρέθη (e.g. Rom. 9.12), εἴρηκεν (e.g. Heb. 4.3), ῥηθέν (e.g. Mt. 1.22), εἰρημένον (e.g. Lk. 2.24), and γέγραπται (e.g. 1 Pet. 1.16).[15]

---

14. Levison 1989: 150 with nn. 13-14. See also Wells 1979: 123; M.D. Johnson 1985: 249, 251 and n. 14. Stone (1992: 14, 23, 64) critiques Levison (1988) but without challenge to this part of his argument.

15. Daube 1949: 260 with n. 77. For the exception at Gal. 4.22 see below.

Oral traditions are identified by other markers, some of which occur in the Pastorals, the πιστὸς ὁ λόγος formula being prominent among them (Ellis 1987: *passim*). The case for a backward reference at 3.1a would be greatly strengthened if some other linguistic marker of tradition could be identified in what precedes. Such a marker, I submit, does exist.

As at 1 Tim. 2.13-14, and as noted in Chapter 13, three New Testament authors narrating (rather than quoting or expounding upon) Old Testament stories use Perfect forms which spotlight the state of certain subjects. The full list comprises: Acts 7.35, 44; Gal. 3.18; 4.23; Heb. 7.3, 6 *bis*, 9; 8.5; 11.12, 17, 28.[16] Two things should be noted about these passages:

(a) Early Christian preachers and teachers are represented in Acts as restricting references to the Old Testament almost exclusively to audiences familar with those scriptures. All the passages in the above list address, or are reported as addressing, Jews, Jewish Christians or Christians under the influence of Judaizing teaching.

(b) Each passage is set in a context suggesting that Jewish thought has to some extent been adapted. The following necessarily lengthy illustration of this claim in passages outside the Pastoral Epistles

   i.   does not attempt exhaustive interpretation, but draws attention only to points relevant for the present purpose;

  ii.   does not attempt precise identification of the source of the thought, being content to demonstrate its Jewishness; and

---

16. According to the material cited in my Introduction, in each case the spotlight falls on the subject, and not (as frequently claimed) upon an earlier record. Attridge (1989: 196 n. 128, 334 n. 9) calls those in Hebrews 'exegetical', but includes 8.13 (which is theological discourse rather than narrative) and 10.9 (where εἴρηκεν introduces partial quotation from LXX Ps. 39.8). J.B. Lightfoot (1905: 180) writes of Gal. 4.23 ' "is born, as we read": comp. 1 Tim. 2:14'. K.L. McKay (1981: 318) includes Heb. 11.17, 28 amongst those speaking of something 'significantly on record', and stresses the characteristic significance of the use in its context. Moule (1986: 14-15), followed by Fanning (1990: 305), lists all as 'Perfects of Allegory', claiming this is a logical extension of the Perfect for a past but still relevant event. Porter (1989a: 255, 264-65), however, uses those from Hebrews to demonstrate stative aspect rather than present result of past action and to establish further the essentially non-temporal nature of the Perfect. He includes μετέθηκεν (11.5), which features God as the one taking Enoch away. This, however, is a direct quotation from LXX Gen. 5.24 A. Cf. again (see Chapter 13, p. 258) also LXX Josh. 1.3 and 2 Macc. 2.11.

    iii.   does not suggest that semitisms are employed, appreciating that spotlighting in narrative is normal Greek aspectual practice.

The New Testament evidence suggests that writers and speakers addressing Jewish Christians and Christians under the influence of Jewish teaching sometimes use material from Jewish oral tradition which, by use of the Perfect, spotlights focal points of Old Testament narrative. It is probable that Greek-speaking Jews before them made those aspectual choices.

Acts

Many conclude that Acts 7 contains semitic elements.[17] Stephen's theme of God's patience with a disobedient and stubborn people, their admonition by prophets, and their judgment, was certainly familiar to the Jews (e.g. Joshua 24; Neh. 9.30; Ezekiel 20; Zech. 7.11-12; Josephus, *Ant.* 9.265-66) (Conzelmann 1987: 57). At v. 35, where ἀπέσταλκεν occurs, the simple narrative style changes to a passionate indictment of contemporary Jewry[18] featuring a series of demonstratives (τοῦτον v. 35 *bis*, οὗτος vv. 36, 37, 38) and stylized expressions (the Perfect, the semitic σὺν χειρὶ ἀγγέλου) introducing a Moses typology (ruler v. 35, deliverer or wonder-worker v. 36, mediator v. 38; cf. for example Philo, *Vit. Mos.* 2.166).[19] Some of this material about Moses not found in the Old Testament does appear in contemporary Jewish writers. At v. 22, for καὶ ἐπαιδεύθη Μωϋσῆς [ἐν] πάσῃ σοφίᾳ Αἰγυπτίων cf. Philo, *Vit. Mos.* 1.5, and more extreme claims in Jewish legends.[20] At v. 23, for τεσσερακονταετὴς χρόνος cf. the evidence in

17. For a summary see Hemer 1989: 420-23. Haenchen (1971: 287) claims that Stephen's speech is based on a synagogue-type history-sermon. Hill (1992: 100) argues that it copies no known history. Wilcox (1965: e.g. 159-61, 181) concludes that the author draws, at least for Old Testament quotations and allusions, upon a source reflecting a semitic tradition having parallels in the *Targumim* and other traditions but written in Greek, and whose deviations from the LXX he chose not to alter. For a critique of source theories for Acts 7 see Hill (pp. 50-101), who (e.g. p. 94) nevertheless accepts that certain points originate in tradition.

18. Foakes Jackson and Lake (eds.) 1922–42: V, 69, 77; Haenchen 1971: 288-89.

19. Foakes Jackson and Lake (eds.) 1922–42: V, 77; Bruce 1982a: 178; Conzelmann 1987: 54. Cf. also Stephen's closing words (v. 53), and Heb. 2.2. See below for Gal. 3.19-20 where ἐν χειρὶ μεσίτου appears.

20. Jeremias 1977: 850; Schürer 1979: 350.

Strack–Billerbeck, II, 679-80. At v. 38, for τοῦ ἀγγέλου τοῦ λαλοῦντος αὐτῷ (cf. Gal. 3.19 and Heb. 2.2) cf. Philo, *Somn.* 1.22; *Test. XII Patr. T. Dan* 6.2; Jub. 1.29; Josephus, *Ant.* 15.136 (where, however, the editor suggests ἄγγελοι may be men); and rabbinic sources.[21] At v. 35, then, the Perfect occurs at a pivotal point in the record of a speech directed against Jews, reported (if not spoken) in Greek and including ideas not found in the Old Testament record but familiar to contemporary Jewry. In an allusion to the Old Testament, it spotlights in the narrative God himself as the one who sent the Moses whom the Jews had rejected. The aspectual choice may be that of the author or his source, but in this context it seems likely that the emphasis is taken directly from tradition familiar both to Jews and to any oral or written source the author may have employed.

At v. 44, ἑωράκει occurs in an allusion to Exod. 25.40. A quotation from the same passage in Heb. 8.5 (which uses a Perfect for another word in narrative about Moses: see below) has the Aorist δειχθέντα, simply stating that Moses had been shown the pattern. However, LXX Exod. 25.40 spotlights that action with δεδειγμένον. Acts 7.44, therefore, appears very like an expositional form of the LXX version. Since there seems to be no reason to choose to spotlight this particular action in this context, quotation from familiar tradition appears likely.

Galatians

The Jewish character of the rabbinic-sounding exegesis on the word σπέρμα in Gal. 3.16, 19 and the inversion of the Hagar–Sarah allegory[22] in 4.21-31 have long been noted.[23] Barrett argues that in these

---

21. Str–B, III, 556. Thackeray (1900: 204) says the speech embellishes the narrative by legendary accretions as Haggadah. Longenecker (1981: 340) says it contains conflations and inexactitudes of popular Judaism using commonly understood language. Craigie (1976: 393) suggests that Deut. 33.2 lies behind the New Testament view that the law was mediated through angels in Acts 7.53; Gal. 3.19; Heb. 2.2. Foakes Jackson and Lake (eds.) (1922–42: V, 78) say Jewish tradition introduced an angel as mediator. Vermes (1975: 177) argues that Stephen speaks as a leader of the Hellenists and expresses differently the claim of the Minim that the *torah* was delivered by angels rather than God. Writing of Gal. 3.19 (see re n. 32 below) Bruce (1982a: 176-78) claims that at Acts 7.38, 53 Stephen (as Paul) refers to it as well known. Foakes Jackson and Lake (p. 75) say that ἀστεῖος (v. 20) does not reflect the Old Testament record, citing instead Philo, *Vit. Mos.* 1.9 and Josephus, *Ant.* 2.9.6-7. Cf. however LXX Exod. 2.2.

22. For the question of whether this should be called 'typology' see e.g. A.T.

two chapters Paul quotes substantially the words of the Galatian Judaizers so as to refute their view

> that the Abrahamic covenant had been redefined by the Sinaitic. The
> promise was made to Abraham and his seed; and the obligations of the
> seed were revealed in the law, fulfilment of which was made the neces-
> sary condition for receipt of the promised blessing…Only the Sarah-
> Isaac line could count as seed; this was the line that included Moses and
> therefore the law, and it had its seat in Jerusalem…[24]

In support of Jewish argument, in Galatians 3 Barrett notes for example
καθώς (v. 6), which he takes to mean 'in accordance with', and which
takes up the passage the opponents quote; the quotation from Deut.
27.26 (v. 10); the allusions to Genesis (v. 16); and mention of the law
having been delivered by angels (v. 19c; see Acts above); and in ch. 4
γέγραπται (v. 22) introducing a summary of Old Testament material
from several chapters of Genesis instead of the quotation one might
expect (cf. Paul in Romans; 1 and 2 Corinthians; Galatians). Barrett
concludes that from 3.16b (excluding v. 19c) and 4.24 Paul makes his
own responses.[25] It could be added that Judaizing Christians may have
seen themselves as a spiritual Jerusalem over against traditional Jewry.
I suggest, however, that not only are quotations at both Gal. 3.15-20
and 4.21-31 more extensive than Barrett argues, but that Paul makes his
own use of oral tradition.

At Gal. 3.15 κατὰ ἄνθρωπον λέγω is essentially Jewish, and Paul
always uses the construction to apologize for otherwise too-bold statements and in defence against strict Jewish attitudes (cf. Rom. 3.5; 6.19;
1 Cor. 9.8).[26] One would therefore expect it to introduce an assertion
that he feels requires some modification, that is 'I speak according to

---

Hanson 1974: 94-95; Longenecker 1975b: 126-29; Kepple 1976–77: 239-49. See
also Ellis 1957: 53; Dodd 1965: 6; Bruce 1982a: 217; Koch 1986: 216-20.

23. E.g. J.B. Lightfoot 1905: 181; Burton 1920: 504; Reid 1964: 79; R.P.C.
Hanson 1970: 412; A.T. Hanson 1974: 102; Longenecker 1975b: 127-29.

24. Barrett 1976: 15. Koch (1986: 204 n. 12, 209-11 nn. 35, 45, 224 with n. 20,
230-31), who believes the allegory is Paul's own, nevertheless writes e.g. 'hier
überschneiden sich zeitgenössisch-jüdische und vorpaulinisch-frühchristliche
Schriftinterpretation' ('contemporary Jewish and pre-Pauline early Christian interpretation of Scripture intersect here').

25. Barrett 1976: 6-12. Thackeray (1900: 161-63) also traces Jewish thought at
3.19.

26. Daube 1956: 394-400. Contra Burton 1920: 37-38, 178.

men:...' The assertion that follows, however, is primarily concerned with the permanence of covenants in general and that to Abraham's posterity in particular (vv. 15b-16a).[27] It requires no apology or defence. On the other hand, the rabbinic method of v. 16b is unlike Paul, but his κατὰ ἄνθρωπον λέγω suggests that vv. 15b-16b are one piece, a quotation from Jewish tradition[28] for the consideration of the Galatian Judaizers.

The Jews did sometimes interpret 'seed' (v. 16b) in the singular (*Jub.* 16.17).[29] Jer. 33.21-22 and the Targum to Ps. 89.4 identify the 'seed of Abraham' with the 'seed of David' and so the Messiah (cf. Lk. 1.68-69; Acts 3.25). 4QFlor 1.10-13 interprets 2 Sam. 7.12-16 messianically. 2 Samuel 7.12 and Psalm 89 may underlie, for example, Acts 2.30-31 and 13.22a (cf. 13.33 ἀναστήσας and LXX 2 Sam. 7.12; cf. also Gal. 4.6b and Ps. 89.27). Gen. 3.15, according to *Targ. Neof.* and *Targ. Ps.-J.* is to take place 'in the Day of King Messiah', and although *Targ. Onq.* reads 'seed' there as 'sons', it interprets 'he will remember what you did to him from the beginning, and you will be watching him at the end'. *Jub.* 4.7 'on the earth' hints at the same messianic interpretation of Gen. 4.25 found in *Gen. Rabbah* and various *midrashim*.[30] Philo, *Quaest. in Gen.* 3.60 and *Gen. R.* 53.12 link Isaac with the future world. In Galatians 3 Paul, who in v. 17 follows rabbinic calculations concerning the Deuteronomic prediction, appears influenced throughout this section by Jewish identification of Isaac as the 'seed' in Gen. 15.13.[31]

But Jewish thought is not abandoned at v. 16b. The adversative τοῦτο δὲ λέγω (v. 17) introduces the modification signalled in v. 15a. The two Perfects of theological discourse in Paul's contrast between v. 17a and

27. But cf. Daube 1956: 395.

28. Bammel (1959–60: 313-19) says the legal approach is the Jewish Mattanah.

29. Cf. parallels in the Jubilees passage with what appears to have been the Galatian Judaizers' argument above.

30. For all these examples see Wilcox 1979: 2-20.

31. Daube (1956: 438-41) confidently assumes that Paul employs a rabbinic Midrash quite possibly known to his readers. For Jewish calculation of 430 years see also Thackeray (1900: 58-75, 79). Ellis (1978: 193, 216) suggests that method reflecting a type of first-century CE Jewish exegesis is influential from v. 6 (which cites a midrash on Gen. 15.6) to v. 29. Dahl (1969: 23-24) sees vv. 13-14 as a fragment of Jewish-Christian origin derived from a midrash on Genesis 22. Swetnam (1981: 93-118) finds dependence on haggadic tradition probable, identification of σπέρμα with Christ being otherwise arbitrary.

b appear to be his own, highlighting the previous ratification of the first covenant and the temporal lateness of the law. He proceeds, however, by way of Jewish numerical calculation, apparently stationing himself within the thought world of those with whom he argues in order to persuade them from their own material. Some Jews believed that the Torah would be changed/modified (invalidated?) in the days of Messiah (v. 19b) (W.D. Davies 1989: 84-93). Moses was commonly called 'mediator' (v. 19c; e.g. Philo, *Vit. Mos.* 2.166) (J.B. Lightfoot 1905: 146). Although references to the angelic administration of the law are difficult to isolate prior to the writing of Galatians, Paul treats it as something well known.[32] See also below for the allusion in the context of Heb. 8.5 (cf. 2.2). The phrase ἐν χειρὶ μεσίτου is a semitism[33] also reminiscent of Acts 7.35, 38, and again see the context of Heb. 8.5 below. The assistance of angels in the giving of the law holds an important place in later rabbinic speculations.[34]

With all of this Jewish background in mind, the heavily marked narrative κεχάρισται at Gal. 3.18b looks very much like a reference to the tradition quoted in v. 16a:

> But I say this: the law, which appeared 430 years later, does not annul a covenant which had been previously established by God, so as to render the promise ineffective. For if the inheritance is by law, it is no longer by promise. But '**God graciously gave** to Abraham by means of promise'. So, what is the law? It was added because of the transgressions, until the seed to whom it has been promised might come, having been commanded through angels by a mediator. But a mediator is not of one, but God is one.

The aspectual choice of the narrative Perfect could be Paul's own, but there is a close relationship with v. 16a, and evidence that at vv. 17-20 he is to some extent still using Jewish tradition. It cannot be excluded that at vv. 15b-16a he is quoting Jewish material.

At 4.21 Paul may refer to the *torah* as a whole rather than to written law. The evidence again suggests that not only is quotation more extensive than Barrett claims but that Paul himself makes use of Jewish oral tradition. For Paul, normally γέγραπται γὰρ would introduce quotation

---

32. Bruce 1982a: 176-77. See also at n. 21 above.

33. J.B. Lightfoot 1905: 145. See also Bruce 1982a: 178-79.

34. J.B. Lightfoot 1905: 145. Segal (1977: 211) says that against such speculation the rabbis, in defence of monotheism, argued that God himself gave the law, but Paul, opposing the same polemic, said the law is inferior.

from the Old Testament in accordance with rabbinic practice, but at v. 22 material from several chapters in Genesis is summarized (Barrett 1976: 9 with n. 18). The context suggests that a Jewish source is responsible for this exception. The pattern throughout 4.21–5.1 suggests that the whole is drawn from a Genesis midrash similar to *Jubilees* or the Qumran Genesis Apocryphon.[35] Barrett's claim that vv. 22-23 quote the Galatian Judaizers is persuasive, but Paul calls what he writes 'law'. The Judaizers themselves appear to have quoted from their oral law about Abraham, a quotation which Paul has reproduced. Γεγέννηται (v. 23) should be interpreted in this context.

As he proceeds into v. 24 Paul does not appear to have ceased quoting. Barrett, although arguing that Paul now responds, nevertheless draws attention to the allegorical interpretation (v. 24) and Jewish exegesis involved in both the reinterpretation of the name Hagar (v. 25) and the explanatory text (v. 27).[36] It is generally agreed that, since ἅτινά ἐστιν ἀλληγορούμενα (v. 24) refers to statements taken substantially from scripture, it means 'which things are allegorical utterances'.[37] There is, however, no other New Testament example of a Present participle used as a noun with reference to scripture (Burton 1920: 256). The phrase would most naturally be translated 'which things are being allegorized/are being given a deeper meaning'.[38] Barrett, who pictures Paul here interpreting the Old Testament, says that in effect there is little difference between 'are written in allegorical form' and 'are (here and now) being allegorically interpreted' (1976: 11). The imperfective aspect, however, visualizes the continuance of the action, and the passive voice is employed. The action may not be Paul's own. Philo's use of the same points in his allegory from Sarah and Hagar

35. Ellis (1978: 156), who notes the introduction and initial text at vv. 21f., exposition with additional citation linked to initial and final texts by ἐλευθέρα (vv. 22, 23, 26, 30), παιδίσκη (vv. 22, 23, 30, 31) and υἱός = τέκνον (vv. 22, 25, 27, 28, 30, 31) at vv. 23-29, and final text and application referring to the initial text in vv. 30ff. Cf. Koch (1986: 227 n. 12), who denies the pattern here.

36. Barrett 1976: 10-12. Ellis (1978: 160-61) includes v. 24 with vv. 22-23 amongst passages containing the equivalent *pesher* formula 'this is' with an eschatological perspective.

37. J.B. Lightfoot 1905: 180; Burton 1920: 253-57; A.T. Hanson 1974: 91-94; Bruce 1982a: 217. See also Barrett 1976: 11.

38. E.g. 'capable of (and...actually receive)...allegorical interpretation' (Thackeray 1900: 196).

suggests a common educational background.[39] It is unclear, therefore, whether the Judaizers state that it is their practice to read a deeper meaning into what has just been said, or whether Paul himself notes current allegorization (v. 24a). In either case vv. 24b-26 is that allegory, and one which Paul finds an excellent springboard for his own argument at v. 28. At v. 26 ἡ...ἄνω Ἰερουσαλήμ takes the Hebrew spelling (cf. 1.17-18; 2.1 and Paul's other epistles) (J.B. Lightfoot 1905: 181-82). Wis. 9.8; 2 Bar. 4.2-7 reflect this idea.[40] For a restored Jerusalem see Ezekiel 40ff.; Zechariah 2; Hag. 2.6-9, Sir. 36.13ff.; Tob. 13.9-18; 14.5; *Pss. Sol.* 17.33; *1 En.* 90.28-29; and see also *4 Ezra* 7.26; 13.36; *2 Bar.* 32.2 (Burton 1920: 263). Interpretation of Isaiah 54 as referring to the restored Israel of a new age is found in 4QpIsa^d. Jewish writers connected Isa. 51.2 (1-8) with 54.1,[41] so Abraham and Sarah may well be in view at Gal. 4.27 (Burton 1920: 264). I suggest that, with the possible exception of v. 24a, 4.24-27 is the Galatian Judaizers' own exposition of their tradition quoted in vv. 22-23.[42] Taking up the inverted allegory, Paul responds from the framework of that Jewish thought. This is evident in his use of ἐδίωκεν (v. 29), which considerably expands the Hebrew *m^{e}ṣaḥēq* in Gen. 21.9 (LXX παίζοντα) in the same way that later rabbinic traditions imply that violent or sinful action occurred (e.g. *Gen. R.* 53.11).[43] In Gal. 4.22-27, therefore, Paul re-

39. J.B. Lightfoot 1905: 198-200. Citing e.g. Philo, *Vit. Cont.* 28 (pp. 180-81, 198), Lightfoot speculates that ἀλληγορέω may refer to recognized modes of interpretation.

40. By means of an alternative vocalization at Ps. 122.3 'Jerusalem, built like the city which is its fellow', Bruce (1982a: 221-22) compares *Targ.* and *Midr. Tehillim*, and *b. Hag.* 12b. See also Thackeray 1900: 199-200. Bruce also notes that ἥτις ἐστὶν μήτηρ ἡμῶν has its parallels in LXX Ps. 87.5 μήτηρ Σιων, ἐρεῖ τις and 2 Esd. 10.7, both, however, speaking of the earthly Jerusalem.

41. Thackeray 1900: 200; J.B. Lightfoot 1905: 182.

42. For textual variations in v. 25a see e.g. J.B. Lightfoot 1905: 192; Kepple 1976–77: 248-49. Lightfoot (p. 181) suggests that at v. 25 συστοιχέω in the rabbinic schools may have referred to a recognized method of interpretation. Thackeray (1900: 197) finds insufficient evidence for this. Cf. Koch (1986: 205 n. 14) who notes that the word 'ist als term. tech. bei Aristoteles belegt' ('has been proven to be a *terminus technicus* appearing in Aristotle') and is employed by Paul 'offenbar als Fachausdruck' ('obviously as a technical term').

43. Thackeray 1900: 212-14; A.T. Hanson 1974: 98-99; Bruce 1982a: 223-24. Cf. Rendall (1910: 182-83) who unconvincingly argues that, although Paul adopts the traditional Jewish view of ἐδίωκεν, he speaks of a disposition rather than actual persecution.

presents the Judaizing argument based on oral tradition, but uses it to demonstrate that those who would inherit the promise would be children of the free woman. In ch. 5 he proceeds to contrast that freedom with the keeping of the law. Γεγέννηται appears to be part of the Jewish tradition upon which the Galatian Judaizers constructed their argument.

> ...**the (son) of the slave woman was born** by earthly descent, but **the (son) of the free woman (was born)** as the result of promise.

Hebrews
Four of the eight Perfects in narration about Old Testament events occurring in the letter to the Hebrews are in ch. 7[44] in the context of the interpretation of Gen. 14.8-20 by Ps. 110.4. Whatever the precise identity of the recipients[45] (who may be otherwise untraceable), ch. 7 reflects oral tradition. Verse 1 uses standard Jewish interpretation for the name Melchizedek (cf. Philo, *Leg. All.* 3.79; Josephus, *War* 6.438), and v. 3 makes scriptural silence an interpretative device as do Philo and the rabbis.[46]

---

44. Attridge (1989: 186) says εὐλόγηκεν is stylistically preferable to εὐλόγησεν in v. 6.

45. Yadin (1958: 44) says they are Christians converted from the community at Qumran, and notes the Jewish approach of the Melchizedek material. Bruce (1968–69: 263) says the letter itself does not suggest that the recipients thought Melchizedek anything other than a very great human being, and was written to Jewish Christians from nonconformist Judaism of which the Qumran tradition is one representative. Longenecker (1978: 172 and n. 39) finds the Qumran hypothesis probable. J.W. Thompson (1979: 222-23) concludes that this Melchizedek is closer to Philo than Qumran. Lindars (1991: 4-15) assumes that paraenesis in ch. 13 addresses a particular situation, and his reconstruction (involving a dissident group of converted Jews returning to synagogue meetings for reassurance of forgiveness for ongoing sin) is accordingly unpersuasive. For the question of whether the letter displays Alexandrian philosophy see e.g. Barrett 1956: 363-93; Caird 1959: 44-45.

46. Reid 1964: 94-96; Longenecker 1978: 176 and n. 50; Attridge 1989: 189-90. Attridge (pp. 186-87, 189-90) furthermore finds at v. 3 contemporary speculation, and at v. 1 introduction of interpretative techniques differing from earlier chapters. See also the more speculative Longenecker (p. 177), who suggests that v. 3 may be poetry from a hymnodic or catechetical midrash of Gen. 14.18-20; Schröger (1968: 258), who says various rabbinic rules of interpretation are employed and calls the method 'Midrasch-Pescher'; and Reid (pp. 80-93) who suggests that the *gezerah shawah* may be employed at 5.5f., probably because the author expects the recipients to be convinced by that rabbinic device, and to provide a foundation for the

Early rabbinic Judaism is strangely silent about Melchizedek. A lacuna appearing at *Jub.* 13.25 where his meeting with Abraham should occur, together with later negative rabbinic attitudes, suggests reaction against unaccepted exegesis.[47] Early Jewish views about Melchizedek do, however, survive in 11QMelch ii.6, 8, 13[48] and *2 Enoch* 71–72,[49] where he appears as an eternal or heavenly figure. The fragmentary Nag Hammadi tractate *Melchizedek* (NHC 9.1), which underwent Christian revision, although dated second to fourth century CE is earlier in origin and has similarities to *2 Enoch* (Attridge 1989: 193-94). Philo is typically allegorical at *Leg. All.* 3.25-26 (see Chapter 13, p. 258 above), and does not show Melchizedek as a heavenly figure, but may offer support for the idea that other early references were deleted. Although his Perfect does not envisage Melchizedek still functioning as king and priest, something caused Philo to spotlight the fact that it was God who made Melchizedek both king of peace and his own priest. Citation from tradition is not unlikely. Early Christian and Gnostic speculation reflect the above Jewish views.[50]

Since Melchizedek seems to have been the subject of some contemporary Jewish debate, and exposition of Psalm 110 forms a major part of the structure of the letter,[51] the antecedent of the neuter relative pronoun at 5.11 is probably the immediately preceding 'Melchizedek' rather than 'Christ as typified by him' (Longenecker 1978: 174). In this

---

argument at ch. 7. He also notes the use of *a fortiori* argument (7.16), commonly employed by the rabbis, as also Philo and Paul.

47. Suggesting this was Christian are Charles 1902: 100-101; Moffatt 1979: 91. Alternatively, Longenecker (1978: 162-63) suggests Hasmonean employment of the title of Melchizedek, identification of the dynasty with the Messianic age, and probable use of Psalm 110 to defend priestly/royal claims, and suggests that the reaction resulting in the lacuna and later rabbinic polemic was against Hasmonean–Sadducean speculation. For a parallel rabbinic reaction see Vermes (1975: 174, 177), who also compares Heb. 2.1-2 with argument in that parallel. See also at n. 21 above.

48. Attridge 1989: 192-93. Longenecker (1978: 167-69) discusses whether 11QMelch is correctly interpreted here.

49. Attridge (1989: 193) argues that this composition is probably first-century CE and, although some doubt exists about whether the Melchizedek material is authentic, it is certainly not a Christian interpolation and is probably original to the work. See also Andersen 1985: 95-97.

50. Westcott 1892: 201-203; Attridge 1989: 194-95.

51. Longenecker 1978: 175. See also Caird 1959: 47-51.

case, the author is concerned from that point to explain matters concerning the order of Melchizedek. The community at Qumran saw Melchizedek as an angelic warrior–redeemer figure. In Hebrews he is only the precedent and prototype for a greater high priesthood.[52] Although it is unclear that the author is committed to the entire argument of 7.3,[53] like Paul in Galatians, and the Stephen of Acts, he seems to employ contemporary speculation, speaking from the thought world of his addressees (Longenecker 1978: 178). It has been argued that Melchizedek is not represented in Hebrews 7 as a historical figure, the participles ἀφωμοιωμένος (v. 3) and μαρτυρούμενος (v. 8) being literary allusions.[54] These aspectual choices in this context, however, suggest that he is to be understood (v. 3) as (in a state of) **being likened to** the Son of God, and (v. 8) (currently) *being attested* as living. Each could, of course, be translated in past time according to person *deixis*, but in the former the Perfect seems to require a present tense since it is followed by μένει ἱερεὺς εἰς τὸ διηνεκές and in the context of Jesus' eternal highpriesthood (6.20; 7.20, 28 cf. Ps. 110.4).[55] The Present participle (v. 8), together with the gnomic-sounding v. 7,[56] may naturally take the same tense.[57] In v. 6, where person *deixis* requires translation into past tense, Melchizedek is described as (in states of) **having exacted a tithe** from Abraham, and **having blessed** the one having the promise. In v. 9 δεδεκάτωται spotlights the remarkable fact that by means of Abraham even **Levi paid [him] tithes**, a view of heredity evident amongst the Jews.[58] The recipients of the letter to the Hebrews may well have an exalted view of Melchizedek.[59] Each of these

---

52. Cf. A.T. Hanson (1988: 296-97), who believes that in Hebrews Melchizedek is seen as an appearance of the pre-existent Son.

53. Contra Longenecker (1978: 177, 182) who, although (p. 185 n. 51) noting argument to the contrary, believes Melchizedek is considered a divine/heavenly figure.

54. E.g. Westcott 1892: 173, 199-200. See also Dods 1910: 308.

55. Dods (1910: 306, 308) says the chief reason for introducing Melchizedek is to emphasize the 'for-everness' of Christ's high priesthood.

56. Attridge (1989: 196 n. 134) notes that this verse reflects inaccurately e.g. Job. 31.20; 2 Sam. 14.22; 1 Kgs 1.47.

57. Dods (1910: 310) assumes a present-tense translation, claiming the writer here gives scriptural silence the force of assertion: 'of whom it is witnessed'.

58. Dods (1910: 310) citing e.g. Ramban on Gen. 5.2.

59. Contra Bruce in n.45 above.

Text in a Whirlwind

Perfects may be quoted from oral tradition still influential amongst them.[60]

One narrative Perfect occurs at 8.5. Verse 1 refers to the ancient Hebrew notion of the heavenly throne (Pss.11.5; 47.8; Isa. 6.1; 66.1; Jer. 17.12; Ezek. 1.26), and μεγαλωσύνη is a common rabbinic name for God, 'the power' (Westcott 1892: 213). The distinction in v. 3 between sanctuary and tabernacle is Jewish (*1 En.* 14.10-20), as is the notion of a heavenly pattern for the tabernacle (Exod. 25.40; 1 Chron. 28.19) appearing in literature from the Persian, Hellenistic, and Roman periods (*1 En.* 14.10-20; *T. Levi* 3.2-4; 4QShirShabb and in rabbinic writings (*b. Hag 12b; Gen. R. 55.7; m. Cant* 4.4) (Attridge 1989: 222). The relationship of earthly and heavenly sanctuaries in Hebrews is simpler than Philo's elaborate temple symbolism, but the parallels point to a common Jewish background here transformed in a Christian context (Attridge 1989: 223). Note also the 'mediator' comparison in v. 6 and cf. Acts 7.38 (p. 274); Gal. 3.19c (p. 278). The quotation from Exod. 25.40 in v. 5 is not exactly that of the LXX, which is generally held to be the version used by the author of Hebrews.[61] He may have used a variant text, πάντα being an addition,[62] and δεδειγμένον replaced by δειχθέντα. Cf. also 8.8-12 with 10.16-17 and LXX Jer. 38(31).31-34. Westcott suggests that 10.16 is quoted from memory (1892: 240-41). If, however, these passages were taken from oral traditions, variants could be expected. The Present construction μέλλων ἐπιτελεῖν (v. 5) introduces the narrative style, strengthening the impression that the writer has some traditional wording in mind: 'just as **Moses was warned** (by God) when he was about to build the tabernacle...' Note again Acts 7.44 (p. 275). Following the Old Testament quotation, Heb. 8.6 (marked by the emphatic νυν[ὶ]) takes up the main point from vv. 1-2 with two Perfects of discourse: '[Christ]...received a superior service', and 'a covenant...which is founded on better

60. Note, on the other hand, Perfects of theological discourse at 7.11, 13, 14, 16, 20, 22, 23, 26 and 28, all featuring the state of their subjects. Note also what Dods (1910: 311) calls the 'peculiar' passive at 7.11, in this context possibly a traditional expression.

61. E.g. Moody Smith 1972: 59. 'Hebr. ist nicht nur von LXX abhängig, sondern kennt offenbar auch andere Übersetzungen' ('Hebr. does not depend only on LXX but obviously also knows other translations', Michel 1966: 401-402 n. 3).

62. Attridge (1989: 220) cites Philo, *Leg. All.* 3.102 and several passages from Irenaeus, *Adv. haer.*

promises'.[63] Verse 5 is an illustration (καθώς) of an illustration (priestly service) of the main point of the passage (Christ is servant of the true tabernacle). The narrative κεχρημάτισται hardly constitutes a spotlighted action in this context. In view of contextual parallels with Jewish thought it seems to have been directly quoted from oral tradition.

Three further examples appear in Hebrews 11 in a list treated in the manner of Jewish apocalyptic, which itself has antecedents in extended treatments of heroes of the past (Sirach 44–50; Wis. 10.1; 1 Macc. 2.51-60; *4 Maccabees*; Acts 7; Jas 5.10-11) (Swetnam 1981: 87). The first is in v. 12, in a context consistently focusing on the faith of various people, but here returning to Abraham in ἀφ' ἑνὸς ἐγεννήθησαν. However, at v. 11, reflecting the contemporary idea of female seminal emission, the σπέρμα is Sarah's own (Van der Horst 1990: 287-302). Sarah's own faith is the subject here. Nevertheless, at v. 12 νενεκρωμένου highlights her husband's state of impotence. The Author has not spotlighted Abraham in vv. 9-10, speaks of Sarah in v. 11, and in v. 12 the subsequent birth of her husband's innumerable offspring is closely related to (διό) her faith. He does not seem to want to spotlight Abraham at this point, so the Perfect may be retained from some other context.

The second example is at v. 17. It concerns the Aqedah, which takes an important place in pre-Christian Jewish tradition (e.g. Sir. 44.20; Jdt. 8.25-27; *Jub.* 17.15–18.19; *1 Macc.* 2.52; *4 Macc.* 16.18-20; Wis. 10.5; Josephus, *Ant.* 1.222-36; Philo, *Abr.* 167-207; *Sacr.* 110; Ps.-Philo, *Liber Antiquitatum Biblicarum* 32.1-4).[64] It was used especially to encourage Jews in times of persecution (cf. Heb. 12.1-12), and it featured Abraham's faith (Swetnam 1981: 81). By the first century CE there did already exist a Jewish tradition that the principal merit of the Aqedah was Isaac's self-sacrifice. It was seen as a true sacrifice and Israel's chief title to redemption, others being intended to remind God of it, and was associated with the Passover and eschatological salva-

---

63. Schröger (1968: 258) says that, employing the conclusion *a minori ad maius*, the argument is rabbinic. That form of argument, however, is not necessarily Jewish.

64. E.g. Thackeray 1900: 214-15; Michel 1966: 401; Daly 1977: 55-59; Swetnam 1981: 23-80; Vermes 1983: 193, 197-204; Segal 1984: 169-84; Attridge 1989: 333 with n. 4.

tion.[65] A later Jewish tradition shows Isaac as actually having died and
been raised.[66] Although the Aqedah was nowhere a prototype of messianic suffering,[67] to the extent that Paul, in his letters, worked with
inherited materials in developing his interpretation of the death of
Christ (Vermes 1983: 220-21), he did so according to the oldest pre-
Marcan stratum of Christianity (Acts 3.25-26; Mk 1.11; Mt. 2.17 and
Lk. 3.22; Mt. 12.18 cf. Isa. 42.1).[68] Paul's messianic interpretation contrasts the Jewish tradition (Segal 1984: 178). Heb. 11.17, however, uses
the narrative just as did the earlier Jewish tradition,[69] the fate of each
hero related in some way to death, with Abraham, not Isaac, in focus.[70]
Genesis 22 does not say that Abraham believed God would raise Isaac
from the dead (Heb. 11.19), although it may hint at it in 'we' (Gen.
22.5), but raising from the dead does feature in *Gen. R.* 56.2 and the
second of the *Shemoneh Esreh*.[71] 2 Corinthians 1.9, Jn 5.21 and (especially) Acts 26.8 suggest that Christians adapted a Jewish formula
describing God as the one who raised the dead.[72]

Swetnam believes that for the author of Hebrews 11 the promise to
Abraham involves a unity of spiritual descendants 'in Isaac': the sharing in Abraham's faith in the face of death is 'spiritual', so the 'seed' is
singular. To the possible objection that the position of vv. 17-19 is not
commensurate with the importance of such a profound meaning, he
replies that, although the genre requires chronological listing, v. 39
implies that Abraham is in some sense central because those living
prior to him had not received 'the promise'.[73] To a second possible

---

65. Vermes 1983: 204-11, 215-18. See also Dahl 1969: 20-22; Daly 1977: 46,
50, 53-55, 63-65; Segal 1984: 173-74. Cf. Swetnam 1981: 79-80.

66. Str–B, III, 746; Vermes 1983: 205-206.

67. Dahl 1969: 20; Daly 1977: 74-75; Segal 1984: 77.

68. Dahl 1969: 17, 26-28; Vermes 1983: 223; Segal 1984: 178.

69. Drury (1973: 377) calls v. 19 a midrash, but Longenecker (1975b: 185)
claims that, although common midrashic techniques are used, the author apparently
bases himself upon Christian exegetical tradition.

70. Michel 1966: 401; Swetnam 1981: 89.

71. See also Str–B, III, 212. For dating of *Shemoneh Esreh* see Heinemann
(1971: 839-40).

72. Attridge 1989: 335 and n. 25. 'Wahrscheinlich ist der Inhalt des Schlusses
aus einem feststehenden Bekenntnis geschöpft (Rom. 4.17)' ('It is likely that the
content of the conclusion has been drawn from an established creed [Rom. 4.17]',
Michel 1966: 402).

73. Swetnam 1981: 95-97. Michel (1966: 401) also finds vv. 17-19 particularly

objection that something requiring such elaborate and indirect argument for its establishment cannot be depended upon to convey the author's meaning, he responds by examining the use of 'seed' elsewhere. At Heb. 11.11, he argues, since εἰς καταβολὴν σπέρματος is a standard expression for the male, Sarah 'assumes the function of the male with regard to Abraham's spiritual offspring', and he traces evidence of a pre-Christian tradition that Abraham's seed was spiritual at Rom. 9.7, 10-13; 4.12-13, 17, 19-21 (the last two verses said to be either from the same tradition as Heb. 11.11-12 or to have some interaction with it); Galatians 3-4; Jn 8.31-59; *2 Bar.* 57.1-2; and *4 Maccabees* (Swetnam 1981: 97-118). Noting the careful language of Hebrews, he suggests that προσενήνοχεν (in contrast to the 'conative' προσέφερεν) conveys the idea that the action, so far as Abraham was concerned, was complete.[74] For this study the following three points should be noted about Swetnam's two responses to possible objections.

(a) The Perfect at v. 17 could be perceived as spotlighting Abraham in a way commensurate with the importance of vv. 17-19 at what Swetnam believes is the heart of the chapter—if it were not for the two other narrative Perfects in the context: at v. 12 (as previously noted) the spotlighting appears *in spite of*, not *because of*, the primary focus; and at v. 28 Moses is similarly spotlighted (see below).

(b) Swetnam's argument that there was an early (even pre-) Christian interpretation of σπέρμα as spiritual is generally sound.[75] However, Heb. 11.11 does not support that spiritual reference: the notion of female seminal emission is well-attested (Van der Horst 1990: 287-302). At v. 12 physical 'seed' is at least partially in view. Furthermore, Sarah, whose faith was exercised *after* the giving of the promise, appears in the list *before* vv. 17-19. Abraham's centrality is again questionable.

---

important. Dods (1910: 358) suggests that the article accompanying Isaac's name in Heb. 11.17 calls attention to his importance. The article is, however, commonly used with names.

74. Swetnam 1981: 122, 128. See also e.g. Dods 1910: 358; Daly 1977: 67; Moffatt 1979: 176. Cf. 'Das Perfekt hat "vorbildliche" Bedeutung... Dies Imperfekt sieht die Absicht Abrahams als vollzogene Handlung an' ('The Perfect has "exemplary" significance... This Imperfect regards the intention of Abraham as a carried-out action', Michel 1966: 401-402).

75. Ellis (1978: 155) in fact traces midrashic method in Rom. 9.6-29. See above re Galatians 4.

(c) Although capturing the imperfective aspect of προσέφερεν, Swetnam misses not only the stative aspect of the Perfect but the differing emphases in the narrative style. The Perfect highlights Abraham's state as he acted, and the Imperfect (which Swetnam calls 'conative') fixes attention (if somewhat less than the Perfect) on the *extended* nature of that action:

> By faith, (when) being tested, **Abraham sacrificed** Isaac. The one who received the promises, to whom it was said 'In Isaac shall your seed be called', *was sacrificing* his beloved son, having reckoned that God was even able to raise from the dead, for which reason he received him, also in a foreshadowing.

Together with evidence of widespread Jewish use of the Aqedah and belief that Abraham believed God would raise Isaac from the dead, the fact that the writer to the Hebrews wrote in accordance with an early reinterpretation of Abraham's seed suggests that 11.17-19 and its context is significantly composed of what had been Jewish oral tradition. The Perfect may well be quoted from that tradition.[76]

The final such narrative Perfect appears in v. 28—πεποίηκεν: by faith **[Moses] established** the Passover... Again it is unclear why, in a context consistently featuring faith, this verb should be highlighted. On the other hand it is easy to see why it should be made a central focus in a Jewish context. I suggest that this, too, is a quotation from familiar tradition.

The spotlighting Perfect is not at all *de rigeur* in New Testament references to Old Testament people such as Adam, Abraham and Moses:[77] witness Mt. 1.2 (genealogy); Mk 7.10 (introduction to Old Testament quotation); Mk 10.3 (conversation); and 1 Cor. 15.22 (theological discourse).[78] Neither are Perfects used in some narrative passages about Old Testament events (e.g. Lk. 20.37; Jn 3.14; 2 Cor. 3.13, 15; 2 Tim.

---

76. Note that in v. 18 the quotation from Gen. 21.12 is introduced by πρὸς ὃν ἐλαλήθη ὅτι, in contrast to the allusion to the same promise in Gal. 3.16 above.

77. Cf. MGM, s.vv. It could not be expected in accounts of the Transfiguration (Mt. 17.3-4; Mk 9.4-5; Lk. 9.30-33) and the rich man and Lazarus (Lk. 16.22-30), which are not Old Testament narrative.

78. See also 1 Cor. 10.1-11, where the narrative tends to become theological discourse, and where at v. 4b a reflection of Jewish legend is discernible (Thackeray 1900: 205-12). Note also that in Jn 6.32; 7.19, 22 and Rom. 4.1, all of which are more discourse than narrative, the Perfects suggest use of oral tradition.

3.8;[79] 1 Pet. 3.6). On the other hand they *are* sometimes used to spotlight contemporary identities against background featuring Old Testament characters. Examples occur at: Jn 9.29 (οἴδαμεν [*bis*] and λελάληκεν for the Pharisees' certainty that it was God himself who spoke to Moses in contrast to their state of suspicion as to Jesus' identity);[80] Heb. 3.3 (ἠξίωται for Jesus' worthiness of greater honour than Moses); Acts 6.11 (ἀκηκόαμεν for the perceived weight of the evidence of the false witnesses against Stephen speaking about Moses and God). Nevertheless, there is sufficient evidence to conclude that Christians not uncommonly marked facets of seminal Old Testament narrative by the spotlighting Perfect. In every case above where they do there is cause to conclude that the narrative is quoted, or to some extent adapted, from Jewish oral tradition. It seems likely, therefore, that, although the grammatical form and its function were normal in Greek, the narrative emphasis so marked was taken over from Greek-speaking Jews. The fact that this particular kind of emphasis is employed only when addressing or reported as addressing Jews, or Christians substantially under the influence of Judaizers, also suggests an expectation of recognition of the source and an appreciation that the original emphasis may not be significant in the present context.

The Author of 1 Timothy, I suggest, expects his reader to recognize the Jewish origin of 2.13-14.[81] His retention of the Perfect also anticipates recognition that, as part of a saying perceived as an apt conclusion to what precedes (3.1a), γάρ refers back to something in its original context.[82]

---

79. In this verse Jewish legend is certainly used.

80. Cf. e.g. Zerwick (1987: §286) who says that the highlight is upon Moses' resultant dignity and the immutability of what God said.

81. Cf. also later Christian apologists employing classical texts in argument with non-Christians. Leadbetter 1992: 10.

82. A search in *The Complete Concordance to Flavius Josephus* under Adam, Moses etc. leads me to conclude that Josephus (who writes for Gentiles) does not use the Perfect in this way. The non-existence of a concordance to Philo hinders a similar search but, although he uses oral traditions (Wolfson 1962: I, 189-94), he seems rarely to employ the Perfect in this manner. His *Quaest. in Gen.* was written for Jews, but more than 90% of it has survived only in Armenian (R. Marcus, Suppl. I, *vii*). In *Spec. Leg.* he uses Palestinian sources found in Tannaitic literature, but writes primarily for Gentiles (Belkin 1940: 27, 29-30). A search in the works of Justin with a view to comparing his aspectual practice when addressing the Jewish Trypho has not uncovered any relevant parallel.

A New Testament Parallel?

The so-called imperatival participle (e.g. Rom. 12.9-21) may offer a partial parallel to the above conclusion. The ongoing debate on this New Testament use revolves around whether the form results from employment of Jewish moral codes involving laws distinguished from Old Testament instruction,[83] or were a genuine development in the *koine*.[84] Porter argues that they were never more or less than participles and simply extend capabilities implicit in Greek from earliest times.[85] Fanning, however, argues that early Mishnaic codes may have smoothed the way for rare Greek use by Christians (1990: 386-88). Such rarely used Greek imperatival participles were certainly found useful by both pre-Christian Jews and Christians to reduce the force in directives they wished to distinguish from Old Testament commands or teachings of Jesus. Porter correctly argues that the evidence disallows conclusive identification of Christian use of Jewish moral codes. Nevertheless, it remains plausible at least that Christians continued the Jewish use of a rare but genuine Greek form to distinguish types of instruction. In accordance with this, Kanjuparambil finds the ideas of Rom. 12.9-21 expressed in 1 Thess. 5.13b-22 and 1 Pet. 3.8-9; 4.7-13, but notes that neither employs the reduced imperatival force of the infinitives at Rom. 12.15 and 1QS which could derive from either Greek or Hebrew, and 1 Peter only employs imperatival participles (3.9; 4.8, 10). Paul, he concludes, does not use the 'Jewish' imperatival participle for the predominantly Gentile Thessalonians (cf. Rome), and Peter was known as 'the apostle to the Jews' (Gal. 2.8) (1983: 287-88). Whilst there was no 'Jewish Greek', such choice of occasional terminology known to be meaningful to a specific readership does not appear unlikely.

In light of the above, the background nature of the reference to the woman's deception at 1 Timothy 2 renders unconvincing several claims outlined in Chapter 11. The Jewishness of the passage *does not require* the presence of ideas that Eve was physically seduced by the serpent,[86]

83. E.g. Daube 1946: 467-88; W.D. Davies 1965: 130-33; Moule 1968: 179-80; Kanjuparambil 1983: 285-88.

84. E.g. Moulton 1906: I, 180-83; Salom 1963: 41-49. See also Meecham 1946–47: 208; Furnish 1968: 39-41.

85. Porter 1989a: 370-77; 1989b: 591-92.

86. A.T. Hanson (1968: 72-73) demonstrates that ἐξαπατάω *can* denote seduction, but neither that it does here nor that ἐν παραβάσει γέγονεν therefore means

responsible for the introduction of sin, or judged for her independant action. These ideas neither appear in Genesis 3 itself (see Appendix 3), nor were universally held by hellenistic interpreters of that material. They may not simply be assumed here.[87] 1 Timothy 2.13-14 are primarily concerned with Eve's entry into a state of (tending towards?) transgression. The undoubtedly selective nature of the background material against which that primary concern is featured should not be overinterpreted. Nonetheless, it is instructive. In contrast to the 'inspirational' approach at Qumran and Alexandria, pre-70 CE 'scribal' exegesis (including that of the Pharisees and Sadducees) was characterized by concern for context (as at 1 Tim. 2.13-14), and by the virtual absence and deliberate rejection of ultra-literal or 'hidden meaning' modes of interpretation.[88] Traditions evident in later writings incorporating other exegetical techniques seem very likely to have been rejected by the party responsible for this interpretation at 1 Tim. 2.13-14.

If, then, vv. 13-14 show evidence of citation from another source, is v. 15 part of that same citation? The widespread debate about the significance of the number change between σωθήσεται and μείνωσιν and the meanings of σῴζω, διά and τὴ τεκνογονία has resulted in various

'fell into a condition of ('living in') sin'. See Appendix 3 n. 54. Küchler (1986: 35-39) argues that by the hellenistic period ἀπάτη was synonymous with e.g. ἡδονή, but reasons that, since v. 14 leaves out of account rather than features the Gen. 3.17 speech of Eve to Adam, it cannot intend to ground v. 12 but rather v. 11. He furthermore notes that although some hellenistic sources clearly feature the sexual nuance, in LXX, Josephus and the New Testament itself 'die klassische Bedeutung vorherrscht' ('the classical meaning predominates'). He claims (pp. 41-42) that at 2 Cor. 11.2f. Paul introduces a sexual action between the serpent and Eve, supporting this largely (pp. 42-50) by 4 Macc. 18.7-9a (which, although like 2 Cor. 11.2b-3 makes use of the Genesis account, with assistance from Deut. 22.25 shows a much clearer concern with marital fidelity); Sir. 25.23 (for which see Section 1); and Philo, *Op. Mund.* (for which, although he notes that Philo's allegories 'sind zwar eine Welt für sich innerhalb des Judentums der Antike und müssen in ihren Eigenheiten respektiert werden' ['admittedly are a separate world within the Judaism of classical antiquity and need to be respected in their peculiarities'], he relies heavily on Sirach). Eve is nowhere at 2 Cor. 11.2-3 said to be 'seduced' from her relationship with Adam: it is her mind (cf. τὰ νοήματα ὑμῶν) which is the serpent's goal. It seems clear that the sexual nuance cannot be assumed in hellenistic interpretations of Genesis 3. See further in n. 101 below.

87. On the other hand, contra e.g. Oden (1989: 99), this is not a statement of Adam's limitation without Eve.

88. Brewer 1992: 2, 159, 208-209, 212-13, 218-19, 223.

unsatisfying interpretations.[89] There are two reasons for this: first, the
faulty character of the fixed parameters within which that debate occurs
(i.e. v. 12 in fact being unrestricted to the congregation, 2.13-14 being a
'saying' and so a likely referent for 3.1a, and γάρ in that case probably
redundant); and secondly, the ambivalence of the key words. Words
which *can* mean various things are too easily moulded to fit inappropriate contexts. Several factors must be taken into consideration:

   i.   The colon introduced editorially in *UBSGNT* after γέγονεν
       marks the end of one clause and the beginning of the next. It
       implies no change of subject.

   ii.   The virtues in the conditional clause are not specifically
       female.[90] This is true even of σωφροσύνη,[91] a quality often
       used to describe males[92] and which the Author enjoins upon
       men of every age (Tit. 2.2, 6) and specifies for the bishop (Tit.
       1.8; 1 Tim. 3.2) (North 1966: 317).

   iii. δέ links γέγονεν (v. 14) with σωθήσεται, and no subject other
       than Eve is introduced. Since she appears in vv. 1-14 in con-
       junction with Adam, they together would be the most obvious
       subjects of μείνωσιν.[93]

   iv.   Many early exegeses cannot be understood without reference
       to the context of the quoted text (Brewer 1992: 169). Whilst
       v. 15 is not a direct quotation, the text in view is obvious.
       Definition of σώζω must take into consideration that selection
       is made from Genesis 1–3, which culminates in the 'curse'.
       The Hebrew of Gen. 3.15 accommodates messianic interpreta-

---

89. See Chapter 11.

90. Spencer (1985: 94) notes this about the first three. Εάν 'nennt... Beding-
ungen, die ihrer Natur nach allen Christen gelten' ('names...conditions which by
their nature apply to all Christians', B. Weiss 1885: 128). Contra e.g. 'maternal
qualities' (C. Kroeger and R. Kroeger 1992: 171, 177).

91. Contra e.g. Huther 1866: 137; Bernard 1899: 50; Moo 1980: 73; MacMullen
1980: 216.

92. Robert 1965: 39; North (1966: 253) citing Kaibel no. 288a; Horsley (1982–
89: II, 53) citing Raffeiner no. 11 (= Peek, *GVI*, 1729; Kos, II/I), and especially (IV,
151) citing e.g. *I. Eph.* IV.1311 and V.1606.10; *IGB* 395; *IGM* 2.

93. As e.g. Giles 1977: 71. Contra A.T. Hanson 1982: 74. Cf. 'husband and
wife, picking up the idea of Adam and his wife' (Powers 1975: 58). Porter's dis-
missal of Eve as the subject (see Chapter 13 n. 25) does not allow for citation from
another source.

tion, and the LXX translators utilized that possibility: see Appendix 3.

v. Previous debates about the meaning of τεκνογονία with the definite article have failed to consider the possibility that what may be in view is the ongoing process of the bearing of children, that is, over generations.[94]

With the Jewish nature of the two preceding verses acknowledged, when viewed upon a basis of these additional observations (i–v), are the key words of v. 15 not virtually self-defined?

> …but she (Eve) could expect/could be expected to be saved by the (ongoing process of) childbearing if they (Adam and Eve) continued.

What we have here in 1 Tim. 2.13-15, I suggest, is a Jewish messianic interpretation of Gen. 3.15b-c, in accordance with the idea of retrospective salvation at Galatians 3 and Hebrews 11 (for both of which see above) offered in response to a question or argument implied by vv. 13-14.

This possibility would be strengthened if vv. 13-15 could be shown to conform to a known Jewish hermeneutical pattern. Although rules governing Jewish hermeneutics were formally drawn up during the first two centuries CE, the rabbis inherited a large body of oral law they believed came from Moses. In reality it is likely to have been either part of common law or projected from the written Torah (W.S. Towner 1982: 103-105). Patterns specified in later hermeneutical rules were

---

94. An exception is 'Das Kindergebären Eva's hat zur Geburt des σωτήρ geführt' ('the child-bearing of Eve led to the birth of the σωτήρ', von Soden 1893: 231). Others come close. Lock (1924: 33) notes that childbearing became the channel of salvation. Fee (1984: 38) points out that τεκνογονία has to do with the activity of 'bearing', not a single birth/child. See also Fung 1987: 203; Gritz 1991: 141; Wiebe 1994: 61. Oden (1989: 101), although envisaging 'the Childbearing', observes that salvation would 'in due time appear'. Guthrie (1990: 89) says the article could be generic rather than definitive (see also Moo 1980: 72), but relates this to childbirth in general, not the ongoing process. Knight (1992: 147) notes textual doubt that the article should be stressed but claims that even without it the noun 'could well stand for the birth of the promised seed'. See also Origen, *Ier. hom.* 4.5.17-19 καὶ ἀληθῶς ὁ δυνατὸς θεὸς ἤγειρε τέκνα τῷ ᾿Αβραὰμ ἀπὸ τῶν λίθων, ἐὰν 'μείνωμεν ἐν τῇ τεκνογονίᾳ' καὶ τηρήσωμεν 'τὸ πνεῦμα τῆς υἱοθεσίας' ('and truly the powerful God raised children to Abraham from the stones, if "we remain in the childbearing" and we observe "the spirit of adoption" ').

already in evidence. One such rule declares that two contradictory texts may be harmonized by a third. For example,

> R. Akiba says: 'One scriptural passage says: "And thou shalt sacrifice the passover-offering unto the Lord thy God, of the flock and of the herd" (Deut. 16:2), and another scriptural passage says: "from the sheep or from the goats shall ye[...] take it" (Exod. 12:5). How can both these verses be maintained? You must say: This is a rule about the interpretation of the Torah: Two passages opposing one another and conflicting with one another stand as they are, until a third passage comes and decides between them. Now, the passage: "Draw out and take you lambs according to your families, and kill the passover lamb" (Exod. 12:21) decides in this case, declaring that from the flock only and not from the herd may the passover sacrifice come.[']^{95}

Some hermeneutical practices are common to Old and New Testaments, but the consensus is that the formal rules developed by the rabbis do not occur in the New Testament (W.S. Towner 1982: 133-35 with nn. 65-66). 1 Timothy 2.13-15 does have some affinities with the above pattern:

i.   Two statements (v. 13, v. 14) with their source in Old Testament narrative are linked by καί;
ii. δέ (v. 15) may represent 'but there is a solution to this dilemma:...etc.';
iii. δέ also introduces an allusion to a third passage occurring in the Old Testament in close proximity to the source of the first two, that is 'she could expect/could be expected to be saved by the childbearing', cf. Gen. 3.15.

Yet, in spite of the above, 1 Tim. 2.13-15 does not exactly follow the Jewish pattern cited. There is no direct quotation from the Old Testament, and it is very difficult to see a real contrast or incongruity between vv. 13 and 14. Moreover, v. 15 not only makes an unconvincing resolution, but neither its conditional clause nor a reference to the woman's salvation is found in the Old Testament passage in question. Since, however, Jewish oral tradition was extremely varied, and the saying may have been an early example, it is appropriate to allow that some contrast may be present which, although not exactly following the fully developed hermeneutical rule, may nevertheless recognizably conform to the same general pattern and represent its developing outline.

---

95. W.S. Towner (1982: 126) citing *Mek. Pisha* 4.42-49 (I, 32).

Verse 13 does present one contrast between Adam and Eve, and v. 14 another, the emphasis upon the state into which the woman had fallen. Some Jews taught that woman, who could not be circumcised and was regularly ceremonially unclean, could assume a place in the covenant community only by connection to her husband or son (Witherington 1981: 595). Against a predominant background of contemporary belief in the inherent inferiority of woman,[96] and in light of obvious differences in the Genesis record between Adam and Eve's creation and fall, a concern amongst such Jews may have been: could Eve be saved? The question is not explicitly asked anywhere in vv. 13-14, but it is implied by the adversative δέ at v. 15.[97] If such a question had been asked, we might have expected such Jews to answer 'but she would be saved by means of childbearing (i.e. bearing Adam's children)'. Instead we find the definite article with τεκνογονία, and a fourfold condition having a plural subject. Although v. 15 does not explicitly say so, the implication is that Adam's own salvation depends on the same fourfold condition, a view quite likely amongst those interpreting Gen. 3.15b-c as messianic. What evidence there is suggests that Jews in the hellenistic era would conclude that Adam and Eve did remain faithful to one another (Gen. 4.1-2, 25). The godly/messianic line is consistently traced from them (Gen. 4.25; ch. 5; 10.1, 21-31; 11.10-32; 21.1-7; 25.19-26; 35.23-26; 46.8-27; Ruth 1.24; 1 Chron. 2.1-14; 3.1–4.21).

Parallels between the hermeneutical rule and 1 Tim. 2.13-15 are insufficient to establish that the passage is an early example of that form of argument. Yet the passage does reflect the principle underlying not only that rule but all early 'scribal' exegetical techniques: scripture is to be interpreted by scripture.[98] The question–answer format is found in the *yelammedenu rabbenu* ('let our master teach us') in later rabbinic writings dealing with textual problems, at Qumran occasionally proceeding from a current event, and, Ellis claims, also in the gospels, e.g. Lk. 10.25-37 (1978: 158-59, 218). With certain parallels to Galatians

---

96. Lloyd (1984: 2-9) traces the idea from the earliest Greek thought through to Plato and beyond.

97. Giblin (1971: 514-15) points out that a reported question may not be an adequate norm for grasping a given answer. Owen-Ball (1993: 13) demonstrates at Lk. 20.25 the transcending significance for the answer of the addition 'and to God…etc.'. It follows that an answer given may not provide definitive information about an uncited question.

98. W.S. Towner 1982: 124; Brewer 1992: e.g. 165, 167-69, 212, 216, 222-23.

3–4, 1 Tim. 2.13-15 may be a well-known Christian response (v. 15) to Jewish or Judaizing Christian argument (vv. 13-14), quoted as a whole saying. It is noteworthy, however, that v. 15 has no distinctively Christian character. Its ground for projecting Eve's salvation lies in the coming seed rather than in that seed as realized in Jesus, and the virtues required are not necessarily Christian.[99] It is a thoroughly Old Testament and Jewish argument built upon the idea that resolution of a question concerning Eve's salvation is to be found in the Genesis record.

Characteristic of Jewish hermeneutical method in the hellenistic period was a synthetic view of scripture manifesting in a 'telescoping' around certain events (Patte 1975: 67). The principle has been expressed: 'There is no before and after in Scripture'.[100] In the Targum on Isa. 42.12 this approach reduces history to a series of privileged events, the targumist referring exclusively either to the sacred history or the eschatological time, with no reference to present events (Patte 1975: 71-72). Employing the Perfect in the same manner as elsewhere in the New Testament, 1 Tim. 2.13-15 presents in the background a selection of differences between Adam and Eve reminiscent of (if not precisely identifiable with) known contemporary views about the nature of woman. If the concern is not simply about Eve, but about whether women generally would, in the end, be saved, Eve may (as suggested earlier) be employed as the representative of all women in reference to eschatological salvation, that is: 'Could women, whose prototype, in contrast to that of men, tended towards (or fell into a state of) transgression, ever be saved?' In this case the answer in v. 15 is not only affirmative but recalls the joint requirements for anyone at all to be saved. That is, the saying as a whole ignores the implication that woman is in a state other than is man, choosing to focus on the shared basis of their joint salvation.[101] If Adam and Eve themselves remain the subjects, the question implied still seems to be: 'Could such a woman be saved?' In view of the fact that the concern appears to be for the possibility of Eve's salvation, and not her own opinion about her salva-

99. Contra e.g. B. Weiss 1885: 129; E.F. Brown 1917: 21; Parry 1920: 15; Falconer 1941: 377; Barrett 1963: 57; Kelly 1972: 70; Roloff 1988: 142; Barnett 1989: 235; Guthrie 1990: 90; Gritz 1991: 144; Knight 1992: 144. Scott (1936: 28-29) says the last virtue is not specifically Christian.

100. Daube 1956: 410-12; Patte 1975: 68.

101. If the 'sexual nuance' were to be maintained at v. 14 (despite my n. 86 above), it too is ignored.

tion, the choice between 'she *could expect/could be expected* to be saved' is best resolved by the latter.

Whether this Eve is a prototype or simply herself, the Author's non-challenge to the low interpretation of woman suggested by the background material in vv. 13-14 parallels Paul's use of his opponents' allegorization of Hagar–Sarah, and the use by the writer to the Hebrews of his addressees' speculation about Melchizidek. As at Heb. 7.3, οὐκ ἠπατήθη is based on the silence of Scripture (Liddon 1897: 19). Note also at v. 5 the 'mediator' language found elsewhere only at Heb. 8.6 (for which see p. 284 above); 9.15; 12.24. I conclude that 1 Tim. 2.13-15 not only reflects Jewish concerns known to be extant in the early Christian era, but is intelligible as oral tradition from the early 'scribal' school of thought.

Oral tradition was designed precisely for development and adaptation to changing circumstances (Safrai 1987: 49, 51-52). If a tradition such as has been suggested above existed, it would obviously lend itself to development towards the idea that women generally could be members of the covenant people only by association. There is but a small step from the idea that the first woman would gain her salvation by means of the childbearing process set in train by her union with her husband to the idea that women generally would be saved by means of their union with their husbands and the bearing of children. Something very like 1 Tim. 2.13-15 may well lie behind the development of this idea.[102] It should be noted again, however, that no claim is there made that Adam could be saved by some other means than Eve. The question is implied against a background of differences between them. The answer nevertheless transcends that weighted background by highlighting the unique and important roles of both partners in the beginning of the childbearing process which would lead to the future αὐτός (LXX Gen. 3.15). The seed born to Eve would be generated by Adam, so together they must live in faithfulness, love and holiness with sound judgment.[103] Whatever differences there were in their creation and fall, they remain one flesh with one mandate, their salvation coming in exactly the same way from the same seed, whose generation depended on their union. The

102. See e.g. Witherington (1981: 595) for rabbinic Judaism. Kugel and Greer (1986: 101) argue that implications of early exegesis can often be grasped only by reference to later sources.

103. Lock (1924: 33) suggests the first and last qualities may be marital fidelity and right relations.

argument supporting the implied question is selective and suggests a low view of woman in her created state, and possibly after her deception, let alone her fall; but the response reflects a messianic interpretation of the Genesis record closely adhering to the LXX.

3. *Relevance in the Present Context*

Disciples of early Jewish masters learned their oral traditions by rote in phrasing designed for memorization.[104] Greek-speaking Jews would presumably repeat such traditions as had been translated into and developed in that language with the same precision. In quotations in the Mishna, connective particles and words understandable in some other context may be preserved (Safrai 1987: 77). If 1 Tim. 2.13-15 originally answered a question about Eve (influenced at its heart by a low view of women) by messianic interpretation of Gen. 3.15, γάρ at v. 13 emerges as part of that rote learning and redundant in its present context. The Author is concerned throughout ch. 2 that both men and women should present before the world lives which would attract others to Christ. It seems likely that he faithfully quotes the whole of the original saying for the sake of its final part, the heavily marked (Future indicative + Aorist subjunctive) argument that Adam and Eve had joint responsibility to live appropriately.[105] In other words, his exhortation to men and women to live godly lives triggers in his mind a conclusion from a Jewish tradition well-known amongst Christians, or possibly a well-known Christian reply to a Jewish argument. Both genders were, from the beginning, to be saved through the seed which would in due course result from the harmonious union of their first parents. Confident that the addressee will recognize it for what it is, he therefore quotes that tradition verbatim with the context which identifies its subjects, in the belief that, for Christians as for Jews, πιστὸς ὁ λόγος.

---

104. Patte 1975: 13; Safrai 1987: 76.
105. Scholer (1986: 196) sees v. 15 as the climax of the unit. Porter (1993: 93) suggests it is the concluding statement of vv. 8-15.

CONCLUSION TO PART IV

Interpreted as a well-known saying, 1 Tim. 2.13-15 reflects both known contemporary Jewish concerns about the nature of woman and the traditional Jewish concern of the early 'scribal school' of thought to interpret scripture by scripture. In common with contemporary Christian literature employing Jewish material, it spotlights by use of the Perfect a particular focus in narrative about Old Testament characters. As a whole it serves admirably as a conclusion to 2.1-12. In fact, it shows every indication of being the 'faithful saying' of 3.1a. In view of the exegetical confusion resulting from alternatives outlined in Chapter 11, I conclude that the 'saying' at 3.1a is 2.13-15, and that γάρ, which must be interpreted by its context, is best left untranslated.

In the context of non-congregational prohibitions at vv. 11-12, with its verbal forms treated aspectually rather than temporally, and understood as Jewish oral tradition presumed by the Author to be well-known to the addressee, 1 Tim. 2.13-15 takes on a simpler form. Regardless of the identity of the Author, it makes good sense as one quotation:

> Adam was formed first, then Eve. And Adam was not deceived, but the woman, having been led astray, entered a state of transgression. But she would be saved by means of the childbearing process if they (together) remained in faith and love and holiness with sound judgment.'

The saying is trustworthy.

GENERAL CONCLUSION

The foregoing study rejects the proposition that 1 Tim. 2.12 prohibits women in the gathered assembly from teaching (and having authority over) men. It has been argued that 1 Tim. 2.9-15 is composed of two parts: instruction about women (vv. 9-12), and a conclusion to vv. 8-12 as a whole (vv. 13-15). In the same way that, in their general lives, the Author wants men everywhere not to be angry or to dispute so that the hands they raise in prayer may be holy, he wants women who proclaim godliness to dress appropriately, learn obediently and tranquilly, and not constantly to go on and on (at anyone?) or to play the dictator over a man. Having drawn this parallel, he is reminded of a saying which captures such mutual male–female responsibility to live godly lives, a saying which recalls that both Adam and Eve must live in faith, love and holiness with good sense if the promise of Gen. 3.15 were ulti-mately to be fulfilled. Such mutual responsibility for godliness, he believes, remains relevant for Christian men and women if the true faith is to reach people everywhere (vv. 2b-4, and v. 8: οὖν, etc.). Assuming the familiarity of the reader with that saying and its Jewish background, he quotes it verbatim with its contextual identification of the subjects and its now-redundant γάρ and, in accordance with his practice else-where, seals his perception of its appropriateness with the πιστὸς ὁ λόγος formula.

Two questions call for brief consideration here, both entailing some degree of speculation.

(a) As signalled in the conclusion to Part III, an explanation must be sought for the partial parallels between vv. 11-12 and 1 Cor. 14.34-35 when the former is understood as above but the latter as a citation which Paul rejects.

The Corinthian background holds a key. At 1 Cor. 11.2 Paul says he has previously delivered to the Corinthians traditions amongst which there is reason to suppose were some concerning male–female relations and roles. They have certainly been taught sufficiently along those lines for some to quote as authoritative the slogan 'it is good for a man not to touch a woman' (7.1) and for Paul to modify it at considerable length. He also writes extensively at 11.3-16 about male–female behaviour in such a way as to suggest that Corinthians are in danger of jeopardizing the consistency of a Christian practice. Although this latter instruction is additional to the παράδοσις at v. 2, δέ (v. 3) suggests that something in that παράδοσις has been misunderstood. Some Corinthians, therefore, have improperly grasped widely accepted Christian teachings about male–female roles. In accordance with this, 14.34-35 suggests that some converted Jews or proselytes have concluded that women should be silent ἐν ἐκκλησίᾳ. Was this faction misinterpreting some aspect of Christian teaching about women by means of a more familiar tradition? Is there any evidence that the Corinthians had received such Christian teaching? The later 1 Tim. 2.11-12 suggests so. The section in which it occurs is heavily influenced by tradition. The Author introduces that section at 1.18a with its implication of παράδοσις, and concludes it at 3.14a with a ταῦτα reference followed by citation of a hymn (v. 16). He includes a 'faithful saying' which, I have argued in Part IV, is a Jewish oral tradition or at least a widely accepted Christian response to Jewish oral law. Verse 2.2a reflects ideas spelled out at Rom. 13.1-7; 1 Pet. 2.13-17; Tit. 3.1-2. Traditional material occurs at 2.5-6.[1] Verses 2.9-10 parallel 1 Pet. 3.1-6 and reflect ideas from contemporary thought. There are parallels between 3.2-7 and Tit. 1.6-9. Another underlying tradition at 2.8 is traceable from the pre-Christian era on to the *Didache* and patristic writings: the rejection of the temple as the place of prayer and worship, associated with proclamation of 'every place' as suitable for that purpose, and the need for people to live in full recognition of that everywhere-present God.[2] Such traditions seem likely to have been taught earlier at Corinth and, however they were applied to men, women may well have been counselled along lines of submission and abstention from playing the dictator. This would create a basis, however dubious, upon which a faction dedicated both to the law and contemporary views about the place of women might be encouraged to demand their silence in the congregation. The limited but undeniable similarities between 1 Cor. 14.34-35 and 1 Tim. 2.11-12 may be the result of a shared tradition having been applied in quite different ways: the one distorting it to suppress all speech ἐν

1. See p. 36 above.
2. See pp. 45-48 above.

ἐκκλησίᾳ, the other accurately reflecting it in moderation of behaviour in all spheres of life.

(b) How could the contextual, linguistic and grammatical markers to the meaning of 1 Tim. 2.11-15 outlined in Parts I and IV have become so quickly and totally obscured as is evident in the writings of subsequent Christianity? Since the aspectual force of the verb remained constant until long after the New Testament era,[3] how could Greek-speaking exegetes identify the continual instruction and authority-taking at v. 12 as congregational? By the first century CE the Latin verb had temporal rather than aspectual force, so it should not be expected that the implications of Greek morphology would always be appreciated. But what about those whose own writings in Greek suggest a continuing aspectual approach?

An answer is probably best found in a combination of factors. In this passage the full significance of the aspectual choices and the markers pointing to citation is apparent only if the context is seen to be the entire lives of the members of the *ekklesia*, and not limited only to their gathering together. Only then do the infinitives of v. 12 take on non-congregational implications. Only then do clear questions surface about the appropriateness of vv. 13-15 and its introductory conjunction. Although evidence has been presented in Part I that not all patristic exegetes interpreted the entire chapter as necessarily congregational, Origen's support of the restrictive and congregational 1 Cor. 14.34-35 by citation of 1 Tim. 2.12 (*Frag. ex comm. in ep. ad 1 Cor.* 74.21) exemplifies the diminishing appreciation of the consistency of that general-life context in the latter passage. The stage was set for further confusion by the assumption that it was Paul himself who silenced women at 1 Cor. 14.34-35. The continual instruction and authority-taking prohibited at 1 Tim. 2.12 may simply have been seen—as they are today—as occurring in the *ekklesia*. The spotlighting of Eve's entry into transgression has an undeniable background of negative contrasts between her and Adam which provided effective ammunition in cultures concerned with preserving gender-based hierarchy. In that context there was little likelihood that γάρ would continue to be seen as redundant. As private letters, or letters to individuals purporting to be private correspondence from Paul to earlier leaders, rather than as letters to congregations, the Pastoral Epistles may have been privately held, or at

---

3.   No significant change occurred in aspectual framework before at least the fourth to fifth centuries CE: K.L. McKay 1981: 289; Porter 1989a: 84 n. 7, 273.

least circulated only to a limited degree, for some time. The fact that they are not widely attested throughout the second century CE suggests that this might be the case.[4] Whenever they did begin to circulate, however, they were, like all other New Testament letters, appropriated by people other than those to whom they were directed. But in this case the original readership was very specific. The Author assumes that his reader will recognize the essentially Jewish vv. 13-15 and their original context, and so too the transcendence of v. 15 over the suspicion of women underlying vv. 13-14. Subsequent readers could not be expected to have been so discerning. They understandably saw vv. 13-15 as either a 'faithful saying' or Paul's own instruction, and in both cases as uniformly appropriate teaching for Christians. In cultures where women were customarily subordinate, the connection with vv. 11-12 (themselves interpreted in a congregational setting) was assured by the convenient γάρ. Verses 13-15 were thus transformed into a theological justification for a prohibition against women teaching and having authority over men in the *ekklesia*, and the significance of the number change in the two verbs in v. 15 was obscured. Largely on the basis of this combination of contextual confusion and uninformed appropriation, the ecclesial roles and relations of women and men were developed and justified for the better part of two millennia.

The authorship of the Pastoral Epistles and the reconstruction of a cultural–historical background appropriate to that authorship are obviously critical issues in any interpretation of 1 Tim. 2.9-15. This study has laid them aside only for the purpose of re-examining four exegetical devices which converge in a relentless exegetical whirlwind that confuses such interpretation. It has been argued that:

I. Although the idea that the immediate context of vv. 11-12 limits the prohibitions to the gathered assembly is virtually universal, the context in fact indicates rather that the prohibitions concern life in general. When, moreover, the Author's aspectual choices are taken into consideration, this general-life context suggests an interpretation which differs significantly from those previously offered.

4. For post-Pauline late first-century to very early second-century dating see e.g. Barrett 1974: 238; de Boer 1980: 360 n. 4; A.T. Hanson 1981: 403; Quinn 1981: 496; Beker 1991: 36.

II.   Despite the increasingly common claim that 1 Tim. 2.11-12 is localized to the place of address, the Author intended his instruction to be normative everywhere.

III.   Undoubted linguistic similarities between 1 Cor. 14.34-35 and 1 Tim. 2.11-12 do not, as is commonly claimed, constitute a relevant parallel, but instead mask what is in fact an opposing viewpoint.

IV.   1 Timothy 2.13-15, again despite virtually universal claims, provides neither foundation for, nor illustration of the need of, the preceding prohibition, but instead concludes the whole of ch. 2, and vv. 8-12 in particular, having its chief focus on both genders.

Some combination from the four exegetical devices re-examined has been employed in all interpretations of 1 Tim. 2.9-15 surveyed for this study. Whatever may have been decided about the authorship and the relevant cultural–historical background, therefore, I suggest that those interpretations are universally misdirected.

These findings have implications reaching far beyond the scope of the present study: that is, for analyses of assembly structures in the Pastorals and the roles of the men and women in them, of the daily lives of those people, and of subsequent practices aspiring to a basis in the New Testament record. A general comment must here suffice. The Author of 1 Timothy views the peaceful, godly life which he requires both men and women to live as mandatory, not only for the fighting of the 'good warfare' (1.18-19) and for general life in that pillar and foundation of the truth, 'God's household' (3.14-15), but also for proclamation of the 'true faith' (2.1-7). To the extent that his meaning at 2.8-15 has been lost, presumably he would view the warfare which has been fought as not good, the foundation and construction of the 'household' as inadequate, and the faith which has been proclaimed as untrue. Any structures and roles for men and women he has in mind seem likely to differ substantially from those which have characterized practices and analyses based upon misinterpretation of his instruction.

Appendix 1

FALSE TEACHING AT TITUS 1.14-16 AND 2 TIMOTHY 4.3-4
(see Chapter 7 n. 7)

Two passages not directly relevant for the present study nevertheless illustrate the diversity of the false teaching reflected in the Pastorals.

1. *Titus 1.14-16*

If Pauline authorship is accepted, the Cretan assemblies are in the early stages of organization. Titus must straighten out unfinished business (1.5), appointing elders according to standards employed elsewhere (cf. 1 Tim. 3.1-7), and teaching various groups appropriately (Tit. 2.1-3.8). He can expect difficulties (3.9), but the divisive are to be warned once or twice and then excluded (παραιτοῦ 3.10). This is an unqualified instruction (cf. 1 Tim. 5.9) suggesting expulsion, the reason given being that their persistence betrays their corrupt state (ἐξέστραπται) and self-condemnatory sin (v. 11). He is therefore to identify and exclude some people (cf. 1 Tim. 1.20). If Pauline authorship is rejected, those represented by Titus are expected to carry out those tasks. In neither case may it be assumed that false teachers are tolerated as ongoing assembly members.

Some of these false teachers may never have been members. Titus 1.10-16 speaks of many ἀνυπότακτοι, ματαιολόγοι and φρεναπάται, 'in other words'[1] (or 'especially') those of the circumcision, who are subverting (ἀνατρέπουσιν)[2] whole households for the sake of dishonest gain. The addressee is to refute (v. 9c)—indeed to silence (v. 11)[3]—these people. The purpose of the rigorous rebuke[4] at v. 13b is that 'they' be sound in the faith, but who are 'they'? Knight argues that,

---

1. Skeat 1979: 174. If this is correct, in contrast to that in the other Pastorals this opposition consists specifically of Jews. Banker (1987: 53) says that in all five New Testament occurrences of οἱ ἐκ περιτομῆς Jews who have believed in Christ are in view.

2. Banker 1987: 54. See also 'perverting' (Alford 1862: 412).

3. Banker (1987: 50) says οὓς δεῖ ἐπιστομίζειν is not the major focus of the addressee's task but appears in a focus on the opposition itself.

4. Banker (1987: 57-58) points out that 'rigorous' here means 'uncompromising'. Hendriksen (1955: 355) interprets 'decisively'. Dibelius and Conzelmann (1972: 71) use 'briefly', but also 'strictly' (p. 137). Parry (1920: 76) chooses 'without parley or qualification', believing 'sharply' hardly strong enough.

since 'they' are distinguishable from those turning away from the truth (v. 14), they are the Cretan believers. Here those 'turning away' are the opposition of vv. 9c-11, the Author at vv. 11-13 looking away to the households and at vv. 14-16 back to the false teachers.[5] Certainly the Jewish component at v. 14 (and v. 15?) (cf. v. 10b) could suggest this.[6] On the other hand, at v. 11, with the exception of the object in οἵτινες ὅλους οἴκους ἀνατρέπουσιν, the Author remains focused on the opposition (Banker 1987: 56). At vv. 12-13a, therefore, his citation and confirmation of the Cretan prophet may illustrate the character of those who are upsetting households etc.[7] In this case the refutation is to be administered to the opposition mentioned in vv. 9c-11,[8] who would then be distinguished from those turning away from the truth (v. 14) and described so harshly at vv. 15-16.[9] Knight himself notes that the critique and evaluation at vv. 15-16 is even more radical than at vv. 9c-11,[10] and acknowledges that many Jews lived on Crete.[11] Despite the Jewish component in each, then, vv. 9-11 and 14-15 may speak of different people.[12] If so, the Author appears hopeful that some of the first group (who are to be refuted ἵνα ὑγιαίνωσιν ἐν τῇ πίστει) might successfully be redirected. But, since in their overturning of households they are clearly divisive, 3.9-11 infers that some might require exclusion. The Author's morphological choices are instructive in regard to what would then be a second group of troublemakers who continually[13] turn away from (ἀποστρεφομένων) the truth, are in a state of defilement (μεμιαμμένοις) shared by their minds and consciences (v. 15), are ἄπιστοι, unbelievers,[14] or unfaithful people, claiming to know God but denying him by their actions, detestable, disobedient and disqualified for any good work (v. 16). Unlike those of vv. 9c-11, these apparently

---

5.   Knight 1992: 300-304. See also Alford 1862: 413. Banker (1987: 48-49, 57), who prefers this reading, suggests the Author may blur together deceivers and deceived. See also Fee 1984: 134. Brox (1969: 289) says the Author speaks now of the one, now the other.

6.   Kelly (1972: 237) argues that at v. 16 the claim to know God, whilst almost certainly alluding to esoteric knowledge, in no way contradicts a Jewish boast.

7.   Cf. Banker (1987: 49) who suggests that v. 12 describes both the opposers of sound doctrine and those deceived by them.

8.   E.g. Bernard 1899: 161; Hendriksen 1955: 355; Kelly 1972: 236; Guthrie 1990: 201.

9.   Contra e.g. Banker (1987: 57) who finds it highly probable that they are all one group, and Fee (1984: 134) who assumes they are.

10.   Knight 1992: 295. Alford (1862: 414) claims ὁμολογοῦσιν 'necessarily contains an implication of the subjective truth of the thing given out', i.e. their true knowledge of God is belied. Since, however, they are continually turning away from God etc., and especially since their minds are defiled, their ongoing denial suggests that here ὁμολογοῦσιν is only the claim of the troublemakers. See e.g. Hendriksen 1955: 357.

11.   Knight (1992: 297) citing Acts 2.11; 1 Macc. 15.23; Philo, *Leg. Gai.* 282.

12.   As Parry 1920: 75-78.

13.   Banker 1987: 59. See also Alford 1862: 414.

14.   E.g. Parry (1920: 77-78) who (comparing 5.8) concludes these are Jewish, anti-Christian controversialists; Banker 1987: 61-62; Knight 1992: 302.

lie beyond the addressee's responsibility. If, however, the refutation is to be administered to the Cretans, and the opposition at vv. 9c-11 identified with that at vv. 14-16, nothing suggests that opposition is necessarily expected to change. They may never have been assembly members, but only have maintained influence over some who are.[15] Whether or not they have been Christians, and whether or not they may yet relinquish their error, their description suggests they are at least now operating from outside the assemblies.

If the 'uncompromising refutation' is to be directed at the Cretans, we have here:

   i.   an opposition at least now outside the assemblies which must be refuted, indeed silenced (vv. 9c-11, 14-16); and
   ii.   assembly members affected by that opposition:
      a)   some who may respond to refutation (vv. 11b, 12-13); and
      b)   some who should be excluded (3.10-11).

Alternatively we have:

   i.   an internal opposition to be rigorously refuted (vv. 9c-11, 13b, c):
      a)   some of whom may respond and become sound in the faith (v. 13b, c); and
      b)   some who may continue to be divisive (v. 11) and should be excluded (3.10-11);
   ii.   Cretan households upset by that opposition (v. 11b); and
   iii.   people influencing the opposition from outside the assemblies (vv. 14-16).

In either case, the errors of the external group are described very generally. No matter how tempting it may be to see parallels with the false teachers of the other Pastorals, their doctrines are not necessarily universally in alignment either with each other or with those at other locations.

2. 2 Timothy 4.3-4

At v. 3 ἔσται indicates that the Author is to be visualized as expecting something in the future.[16] He speaks of a time when Christians will no longer want sound teaching but will turn away from it, accumulating for themselves those who will teach

---

15. Knight (1992: 304) persuasively argues against Hendriksen and Parry that those turning away from the truth are not Pharisaic Jews influencing Jewish Christians (v. 10), their error being too esoteric and ascetic, but he fails to demonstrate that they are not outsiders.

16. E.g. Bernard 1899: 141; Kelly 1972: 206-207; Guthrie 1990: 178-79; Murphy-O'Connnor 1991: 413. Parry (1920: 66) points out that no remoteness is implied, simply that the situation is sure to arise. Hendriksen (1955: 311-12) says there are always such teachers. Believing these teachers are presently operating are e.g. Dibelius and Conzelmann 1972: 120-21; Fee 1984: 234; M.Y. MacDonald 1988: 174; Bilezikian 1989: 299 n. 46. See also Scott 1936: 130; Barrett 1963: 116-17. Barclay (1975: 206-207) says the warning is for a coming day, but describes contemporary sophists.

them what they want to hear, and straying after myths. The content of the false teaching may not differ from that already present (μύθους v. 4) (Parry 1920: lxxxix, 66), but there are new elements: the *general* impatience *and* the accumulation of such teachers. The passage is closely linked by γάρ (v. 3) to the solemn charge (διαμαρτύρομαι) before God that in all patience and instruction the addressee preach the word, stand by at all times,[17] refute, rebuke and encourage. This is because at some time in the future it will no longer be possible to find many who will listen to sound teaching, and false teachers, already emerging, will abound. When Pauline authorship is rejected the pseudepigrapher might describe conditions prevailing in his own period. When Pauline authorship is accepted nothing suggests that this situation already prevails.

---

17. Malherbe 1984: 235, 242-43 (following e.g. Ellicott 1864: 158; Scott 1936: 129; Barrett 1963: 116; Kelly 1972: 205-206) claims ἐπίστηθι 'seems naturally to point to' κήρυξον, the addressee commanded 'to have "an attitude of prompt attention that may at any moment pass into action" ', and concludes that 'irrespective of the condition of the listeners' teaching is directed to those not expected to respond. M.Y. MacDonald (1988: 172, 174), however, points out that 2.24-26 indicates some possible response. It seems likely that ἐπίστηθι is a separate command, the addressee in contrast to the opposition (σù δέ v. 5) to 'stand by' (not to preach) εὐκαίρως ἀκαίρως, as e.g. 'not only in regard to preaching, but to all...duties' (Bernard 1899: 140).

Appendix 2

1 CORINTHIANS 11.3-16
(see pp. 27-28, 177, 248)

This controversial passage is generally understood to address something that Corinthian women were doing incorrectly ἐν ἐκκλησίᾳ. The ongoing debate focuses on whether:

    i.   γυνή means 'wife' or 'woman';
    ii.   the point at issue is cultural or normative;
    iii. v. 3 speaks of authority relations or origins; and
    iv. the 'coverings' are veils/mantles, or hairstyles.

Universally recognized causes of this confusion are questions about the references of κεφαλή (v. 3), κατὰ κεφαλῆς ἔχων (v. 4), κατακάλυπτος and its negative (vv. 5-7, 13), ἐξουσία and ἀγγέλος (v. 10), and ἀντί (v. 15). For exegesis of 1 Tim. 2.9-15, with the exception of 1 Cor. 11.3, 7b, c-9, this debate has only tangential relevance, but, in order to set a background against which to consider those relevant verses, major contextual problems must here be briefly addressed. As signalled in my Introduction, details and full critiques of the literature are left for a subsequent publication.

1. *Some Exegetical Presuppositions*

(a) It is questionable that the passage responds to behaviour actually occurring at Corinth.[1] Controversy about 'coverings' has probably occurred (v. 3 θέλω δὲ, v. 16 εἰ δέ τις δοκεῖ φιλόνεικος εἶναι), but only at v. 17 does Paul rebuke the Corinthians, and vv. 3-16 immediately follow his commendation (v. 2). His matter-of-fact style suggests clarification, not rebuke.

(b) That Paul responds to specifically female error is also questionable. Since he clearly addresses male behaviour here (vv. 4, 7, 14), women are unlikely to be his sole focus.[2]

1.   Contra e.g. Longenecker 1986: 72; Fee 1988: 491. See also (apparently) Conzelmann 1975: 191.
2.   Scroggs 1972: 302; Murphy-O'Connor 1988: 266; Oster 1988: 483. Contra e.g. Hurley 1973b: 201; 1981: 170; Conzelmann 1975: 184; Fee 1988: 491, 495, 505; 1994: 145; Schreiner 1991: 125, 137-38.

(c) The generally assumed ecclesial setting[3] cannot be excluded, but is actually mentioned only at v. 17. Prayer and prophecy (vv. 4-5) may occur elsewhere (cf. Acts 2.46b-47; 12.12; 16.25; 21.11), and the general context includes public feasts (ch. 10, Murphy O'Connor 1976: 616). The focus is on headship, which is not easily limited to the *ekklesia*. The settings may be various.

Paul, I suggest, clarifies both male and female practice, possibly in a setting wider than the *ekklesia* only.

2. *Debated Factors*

(a) The context indicates that γυνή–ἀνήρ are not wife–husband, but woman–man (vv. 4-5, 12, 14).[4]

(b) Paul's strong theological basis (v. 3) and argument from universal practice (v. 16) suggest that the point at issue is not simply cultural. Elsewhere συνήθεια (v. 16, cf. 1 Cor. 8.7; Jn 18.39) and φύσις (v. 14, cf. Rom. 1.26; 2.14) have other connotations.[5]

(c) Κεφαλή (vv. 3-5) here is variously said to be: authority;[6] pre-eminence/prominence;[7] or source.[8] The lexical improbability of the two latter options has now been convincingly demonstrated (Grudem 1991: 425-68, 534-41), but 'authority' is not easily applied consistently throughout.[9]

    i.   Since both genders are required to serve Christ, he is woman's authority also.

    ii.   The only way all (even Christian) men could have authority over all (even Christian) women would be in some honorary, not easily defined capacity.[10]

    iii.   Christ's submission was voluntary (cf. Lk. 22.42; Jn 5.19-30; Phil. 2.6-8; Heb. 9.7–Ps. 40.7-8). The Father's authority is clear, but the 'upward',

---

3.   E.g. Schreiner 1991: 131, 138. Fee (1994: 145 with n. 214) notes some exceptions.

4.   Conzelmann 1975: 184; Schreiner 1995: 116. Contra e.g. Fee 1994: 144 n. 211. Hurley (1973b: 190-220; 1981: 180), although acknowledging that it is difficult to restrict the passage to married persons, writes as though that restriction is valid.

5.   Contra e.g. Barrett 1971: 256-57; Fee 1988: 526-27.

6.   E.g. Hurley 1973b: 202-203; 1981: 164, 168; R. Jewett 1979: 67-68; Grudem 1985: 49-80; 1991: 425-68; Küchler 1986: 95.

7.   Cervin 1989: 112. See also Liefeld 1986: 139-40.

8.   E.g. Scroggs 1972: 298; 1974: 534; Murphy-O'Connor 1980: 492-93; Bruce 1983: 103; Fee 1988: 503; 1994: 145 n. 212. Cf. Schüssler Fiorenza (1983: 229), who sees hierarchy subtly introduced into 'source'. See also Barrett 1971: 248-49.

9.   1 Corinthians 11.3 is not a chain of command, not even in reverse. The more reasonable (if still problematic: see further below) view is that it features three separate authority relations, woman ontologically equal to man and directly responsible before God. Grudem 1991: 462.

10.   For implications for the view (rejected above) that husbands–wives only are addressed, see below for Eph. 5.22-23.

active flow of voluntary submission warns that when defining headship a focus upon *that authority alone* may miss the mark.[11]

It remains unclear why one nuance only should be chosen for this word which manifestly connotes several.[12] On most occasions it is used metaphorically in the New Testament it has multiple application: authority-unifier (Eph. 1.20-23; 5.22-23); origin-unifier (Col. 2.19; Eph. 4.15); origin-unifier-authority (Col. 1.15-20). Exceptions are 'authority' alone (Col. 2.10), and 'the sum of all things' (Eph. 1.10). The focus, however, is consistently upon an *honoured* (certainly authoritative) *position*. At Eph. 1.10 authority is apparent but position paramount; at vv. 20-23 authority is one outworking of majesty; at 4.15, in the context of the same exalted position, origin and union are in view, but position dominates. At Col. 1.15-20 Christ is God's image, certainly as origin, authority and unifier, but his pre-eminent position is again manifest; in ch. 2, vv. 10, 19 are in the direct context of v. 9, where all the fullness of the deity lives in Christ in bodily form.

The only other 'headship' passage (and the only other than 1 Cor. 11.3 addressing a man–woman/husband–wife relationship) is Eph. 5.22-23. The context considers submission in various relationships, but 4.17 precludes assumptions either that the status quo is to be maintained, or that ὑποτάσσω and κεφαλή conclusively determine one another's meanings.[13] Husbands, fathers and masters are certainly authority figures here, but a three-way balance must be maintained between: that underlying authority; the contextual object that the attitude of mind should be renewed; and v. 21.

At Eph. 5.23 κεφαλή is obviously 'head over', but total hierarchical rule is equally obviously not intended. Although masters, husbands and fathers (unlike slaves, wives and children) are not directly instructed to submit, not only is there a sense in which each serves those who are here so instructed, but v. 21 indicates that submission should be essentially mutual. Since wives are morally responsible adults with their own decision-making powers, and primarily answerable to God, their submission 'in everything' (v. 24) should not be taken more literally than the context requires.

Those attempting to define the marital authority underlying Eph. 5.22-23[14] face a

11. Letham (1990: 72-73), Piper and Grudem (1991: 68) and H. Brown (1995: 198) now challenge past distortions of male headship in which 'power over' has been the dominant nuance, but see below for even such 'modified' acceptance of the meaning 'authority'.

12. E.g. Grudem (1991: 435, 443, 447-48, 458, 465, 468) says that, although overtones of 'growth from' and 'pre-eminence' may occasionally be detected, 'authority/rule' is always present. Yet he slides to that (important) nuance as 'the' meaning. Schreiner (1991: 127 with n. 9) rejects the meaning 'honour', arguing that what is given to an authority should not be confused with the status of that authority. Yet he confuses authority with the status/headship which includes not only authority but responsibility and honour.

13. See also discussion on New Testament submission in Chapter 8, Section 5.2.

14. See e.g. Hurley (1981: 150-51) who, having cited Eph. 5.22-23 (p. 147), writes '[h]eadship...most often involve[s] initiative rather than command...[but there will be

critical problem: words associated with rule must be defined by their contexts.[15] In this case, however, *the context does not contain the word*: authority is only an unfocused implication. It is questionable that its definition is either practical or appropriate. The analogy with Christ and the assembly should not be pressed too far. There is no trace of the idea that marital submission is to be imposed from above.

At 1 Cor. 11.3-16 the focus throughout is on the δόξα (vv. 7 *bis*, 15) or its negatives (καταισχύνω vv. 4, 5, αἰσχρόν v. 6, ἀτιμία v. 14) of each of three heads and of the woman. As demonstrated above, all but one other New Testament headship focuses to some extent more widely than on authority alone upon the honoured position of the head. The exception (Eph. 5.23-33), in focusing on submission, profoundly modifies the authority of the head to loving, self-sacrificing responsibility. There can, therefore, be little doubt that at 1 Cor. 11.3 κεφαλή is something more nuanced than *simply* 'authority'. Following 10.31–11.1, where the glory of God is the goal of every action, it is non-coercive and deserving of voluntary honour.

(d) At 11.4, κατὰ κεφαλῆς ἔχων is generally translated literally 'having (something) *down from* (the) head', commonly understood as a mantle[16] or the Jewish practice of veiling.[17] Yet:[18]

   i.   the ex Pharisee Paul seems unlikely to declare headcoverings disgraceful for praying or prophesying men (Exod. 28.4, 37, 39-40; 39.28; Ezek. 44.18); and

   ii. if Paul (vv. 5-6) has been arguing that a woman without a covering may just as well be shaved, the normal substitutionary force of ἀντί (v. 15) produces the unlikely concluding argument that long hair itself replaces that covering.[19]

occasions when] the responsibility of the husband to lead and the wife to respect his intitiative requires her to yield to his decision'.

15. *TWOT*, I, 534. See my Appendix 3 n. 3.

16. E.g. Schreiner 1991: 126.

17. E.g. Ydit 1971: 6; Byrne 1988: 39-40.

18. It has been argued that evidence for veiling practices is too obscure to be sure either that oriental women were veiled in public or that Greeks were not (e.g. Hurley 1981: 267-78. See also Fee 1988: 507-508 with n. 64). Oster (1988: 489-505) demonstrates that in Roman Corinth male converts may well, as v. 4 suggests, have felt it appropriate to pray and prophesy *capite velato*, and furthermore argues that some non-Roman women may have been uncovered. However, although providing convincing historical background, he does not address the following questions (a) and (b).

19. BAGD, s.v., 1 substitution; 2 (citing 1 Cor. 11.5) equivalence. Some interpret such 'equivalence' as e.g. 'an analogical inference' (Bruce 1983: 108); 'Verse 15 *can be* explained in such a way that Paul is not rejecting his earlier call for a shawl', ἀντί *'probably'* indicating equivalence (Schreiner 1991: 126; emphases mine). BAGD, s.v., 2, however, subdivides *'for, as, in place of '*, and the examples suggest substitutions, e.g. Mt. 5.38; Rom. 12.17. See also Porter 1992: 145 with n. 3.

Alternative interpretations often compare LXX Num. 5.18, the strongest arguing that the uncovering is 'long, loosed hair'.[20] None is altogether satisfying:

i.   the woman in Numbers 5 is 'uncovered' only when her hair is loosened, but 1 Cor. 11.15 claims that long hair itself 'covers';

ii. despite v. 4, long hair for men had traditionally been neither dishonouring to God nor personally shameful (cf. Song 4.1 and esp. 5.11 and 6.5; 2 Sam. 14.25-26; Num. 6.5; Judg. 16.13),[21] and Paul himself appears to have made a Nazirite vow (Acts 18.18); and

iii. since some Jews wore long hair, and ancient Greeks were well known to have done likewise (e.g. Homer, *Iliad*: 4.268), no matter what the custom in Paul's Corinth it seems unlikely that he could usefully argue that 'nature' teaches that long hair is a disgrace to a man.

Exegetical attention has previously been fixed upon vv. 3-7, 14. At v. 15 κομάω is always translated 'grow the hair long', and κόμη 'long hair'. There is, however, ample evidence that the verb could mean 'plume oneself/give oneself airs'; it was used of horses and metaphorically for trees and plants. The noun could indicate simply the hair of the head, the gill of the cuttlefish, foliage or a comet's tail.[22]

In the eleven LXX occurrences of this word-group,[23] only at Num. 6.5 could it indicate length of hair. At Lev. 19.27; Job 1.20b; *3 Macc.* 1.18; 4.6; Jdt 13.7; Bel 36 G/TH, English versions translate simply 'hair'. Job 38.32b appears to have the comet's tail in mind,[24] and 16.12 the scruff of the neck.[25] At Ezek. 44.20[26] '[a.] they must not shave their heads or [b.] let their hair grow long, but [c.] they are to keep the hair of their heads trimmed' (NIV), LXX renders b. 'and they shall not bare their hair', and c. 'they shall certainly cover their heads'. In the context of priests entering the sanctuary, b. 'or put away their covering' is valid. At c. (the literal) 'clipping they shall clip their heads'[27] with alternative pointing is 'like a horse they shall clip their heads'.[28] At Ezek. 24.23 κόμη translates *pe'er*, which can be a head

20.   E.g. Hurley 1973b: 197-99, 201-203, 215; 1981: 254-71; Murphy-O'Connor 1980: 484-89; 1988: 267-68.

21.   Köhler 1953: 26-27; *IBD*, II, 600-601.

22.   LSJ, s.vv. κομάω, κόμη. The adjective κομήτης may similarly describe a feathered arrow, a grassy meadow or, with the article, a comet.

23.   Hatch and Redpath 1954: s.v. κόμη.

24.   *IBD*, III, 1485; *IDB*, I, 216.

25.   *TWOT*, II, 698: '*orep* has been linked with the manes of horses.

26.   Links with 1 Cor. 11.3-16 are notable: both feature κεφαλή, κόμη and χυρέω. Hurley 1973b: 197-98.

27.   a. precludes 'shearing' here.

28.   Since from ancient times manes were clipped and decorated with head-dresses (Baskett 1980: 22, 42-43, 47), perhaps the translator associated the head-dress with the shaping and decking.

dress/turban (v. 17), an adornment (Isa. 61.10), or a wreath/crown of beauty (Isa. 61.3).[29]

The wordgroup therefore not uncommonly connotes grooming or decoration. At 1 Cor. 11.4 Paul's use of κατά with the genitive suggests 'having [something] *against* the head',[30] and in the Graeco-Roman world that is a fair description of how women generally arranged their hair. Since φύσις teaches that κόμη is their glory/honour given instead of a mantle, and at Num. 5.18 the *un*-loosed hair is viewed as the covering, I suggest that at 1 Cor. 11.14-15 κόμη should be translated along the lines of 'ornamentally arranged' hair.[31] The difficulty in this context is to find an appropriate English noun and verb applicable, but not excessive, for both the negative-for-men and positive-for-women views expressed. Perhaps they are best distinguished: 'prettified hair' for men and 'dressed hair' for women.[32] Here we have definition for, rather than conflict with, vv. 4-7, 13.[33]

(e) For present purposes, the focus at vv. 7-12 must be limited to the two difficulties at v. 10, with a brief suggestion as to how that fits with vv. 7b, c-9.

i. the appeal to ἄγγελοι[34] has three possible biblical grounds. Angels will be judged by men and women (6.3); have a role in judging sexual purity (Gen. 18.20-22; 19.1-29); and in the Pauline tradition watch God's unfolding plan for the *ekklesia* (Eph. 3.10; 1 Tim. 5.21).

ii. In the New Testament, ἐξουσία consistently appears in the active voice indicating the authority of the subject, so here is the woman's own.[35]

---

29. *TWOT*, II, 713-14. If κόμη here refers to hair, LXX instructs 'keep your hair upon your heads...'. In the context of mourning this might indicate that they were not to shave it, if it were not for the obvious parallel with v. 17. The idea of 'hair' therefore seems improbable. Colson and Whitaker (III, 54) note that κομάω also means 'to be proud'. See also LSJ, s.vv. κομμόω, κομμωμα, ὁ κομμωτής, κομμώ, κομμῶ, κομίζω, cf. κομέω and κομιδή, cf. κομέω. *LPGL*, s.v. κομάω demonstrates in the patristic period 'flourish/abound in'.

30. Murphy-O'Connor 1980: 484. See also Oster (1988: 486) who argues that in contemporary Greek literature κατὰ κεφαλῆς ἔχων 'can refer to something resting on the head'. Porter (1992: 163) says that at Mt. 12.30 κατά indicates 'position away from'. Opposition is therefore apparent, an idea close to 'abutment'.

31. Vine (1975: 189), although denying this interpretaton, does acknowledge its validity elsewhere. Strong (n.d.: §2864) includes 'locks as ornamental'.

32. This could clearly allow for wide cultural variations, but implied is the idea of what would broadly be accepted as feminine-type decorative hairstyles of whatever length.

33. In some cultures male/female hairstyles are identical, but this is rare and often involves characteristic male/female head-dress. It seems to be a general truth that men and women naturally wear their hair differently.

34. Gen. 6.1-4 makes at best a tenuous tool (see the cautious approach of Küchler 1986: 107-14), and, if the coverings of 1 Corinthians 11 are not veiling at all, is irrelevant. Küchler (p. 106) claims that texts from Qumran offer the best parallels for illumination, but notes an important difference in that '[e]s werden hier zwar nirgends Frauen genannt...gar nicht vorhanden' ('admittedly women are nowhere being mentioned here...not at all present').

35. Contra e.g. Küchler 1986: 95. See also Schreiner (1991: 134-36) who argues e.g.

Given the background outlined in Chapter 9, Section 1, some Corinthians may well have reasoned on the basis of their over-calculated spirituality that in Christ sexuality is negated, that is, woman ought to have authority over her own physical head,[36] gender-based hairstyles no longer appropriate. Angels appear to have been relevant to their claim. Paul (v. 10) agrees that woman, created because man needs her, has her own authority, and that angels are concerned with sexuality.

It has been argued that the man at vv. 7b, c-9 'reflects' the image and glory of God,[37] but evidence at BAGD, s.v. δόξα 1.c is unpersuasive. The man does not *reflect* God's image and glory: he *is* that image and glory (εἰκὼν καὶ δόξα θεοῦ ὑπάρχων). Paul for this reason says he should not be 'covered'.

It has also been argued that (contra Genesis 2) the woman is not viewed here as created in God's image.[38] In fact nothing is said of a difference in creation image; the focus is fixed on differing 'glories'. God's glory is man; the man's glory is the woman (δόξα ἀνδρός ἐστιν); the woman's glory is her dressed, feminine hair (v. 14). It should be noted that the only specifically male glory is the woman herself.

Paul therefore rejects the Corinthian trend towards androgyny. In the Lord, he empasizes (πλὴν v. 11), man and woman have mutually dependant yet distinctive roles.

3. *Conclusion*

Addressing both men and women in a context probably broader than the *ekklesia*, Paul at 1 Cor. 11.3-16 focuses on the glory/honour of God, Christ, and then of both man and woman with respect to hairstyling. He views his argument as normative: men and women are different, and should be seen to be so. Whilst he says nothing of woman having been made in the image of God, he defends the intrinsic created glory of both sexes. The man, who is the woman's 'head', is God's glory, but the woman both supplies the man's glory and presents her own. The created male–female relationship at 1 Cor. 11.3, 7-12 provides an inadequate basis upon which it may be argued that 1 Tim. 2.13-14 reflects Pauline male hierarchical authority.

from Diodorus of Sicily 1.47.5 that three crowns on a statue of Osymandias's mother symbolize her father's, husband's and son's authority. The monolithic form of the statue, however, surely indicates an intention to some extent to honour the woman herself as princess, queen and queen mother. It should be noted in 1 Cor. 11.3-16 that: i. the only explicit 'authority' occurs at v. 10; and ii. the word 'submission' nowhere appears.

36. See e.g. Fee 1988: 519-21.
37. E.g. Conzelmann 1975: 186-88.
38. E.g. Küchler 1986: 84-88.

Appendix 3

ADAM AND EVE IN GENESIS 1–3
(see pp. 212, 249)

Appreciation of the interpretation of the Creation–Fall at 1 Tim. 2.13-14 requires identification not only of what Genesis itself does and does not say but also of the ways in which interpreters in the hellenistic era saw that ancient record. In this way a foundation may be laid upon which to test conclusions about the Author's meaning. Sources for Genesis 1–3 will not here be addressed, because the literary form is one carefully constructed whole which early Christians considered history (cf. Mt. 19.4-5; Lk. 3.23-38; Rom. 5.12-14; 15.22; 1 Cor. 11.21-22, 45-49; 2 Cor. 11.3; Jude 14; *Barn.* 6.9; *1 Clem.* 50).[1] Relevant issues, or those commonly claimed to be relevant, reduce to four.

1. *The Nature of the Pre-Fall Relationship*

Much debate about the pre-Fall Adam–Eve relationship originates in the perceived need to define it as either: i. male dominion with female subordination; or ii. equal in the sense of having interchangeable responsibilities and interests. Neither is appropriate. The relationship is characterized by limited differences which, although clearly envisaging Adam's headship, do not amount to hierarchical dominion requiring Eve's subordination.[2]

Much of the polarization in the literature stems from the introduction of words such as 'authority', 'dominion' and 'hierarchy', all of which, having to do with rule,

---

1. E.g. Driver 1907: iii; Cassuto 1961: 88-94; S.B. Clark 1980: 15; Wenham 1987: 78. For the unity of the intricately structured 2.4b–3.24 see e.g. Walsh 1977: 161-77; Trible 1983: 73.

2. Gritz (1991: 57) first finds neither equality nor hierarchy present, but then claims equality is. Hayter (1987: 102-103, 114) more accurately speaks of 'an equality of nature and status', 'identical humanness, an equal dignity', but for her 'common task' see below. Swartley (1986: 90) correctly writes 'the notion of equality...needs careful scrutiny, both for its empirical meaningfulness and its subtle hijacking of the biblical agenda'. Ortlund (1991: 99, 102, 106) correctly rejects 'undifferentiated sameness', and carefully distinguishes between headship and domination, but in fact envisages dominion–subordination. See further in n. 6.

must be defined by their context.[3] Here, however, such words *do not appear in the context*: they are introduced on the basis of the woman's role as the man's 'helper' and New Testament headship–subordination passages (e.g. 1 Cor. 11.3; Eph. 5.22-24). Much circularity results: Eve is said to be created 'subordinate' to Adam's 'authority', New Testament headship–subordination said to be based upon the 'hierarchy' God created in Adam and Eve. No matter how carefully such words are modified, they carry a great deal of 'baggage': their connotations are various.[4] The principle of first mention[5] is vital here. Is there evidence in Genesis 1–3 that Adam had command-type authority over his helper, Eve?[6]

In Gen. 1.28 the man and woman are given the same mandate, but sexual differences allow for differing priorities and abilities. In ch. 2 role difference is implied in the distinctive foci of the man upon his task in the garden (v. 15) and the woman upon the man as his companion/helper (*'ēzer* v. 18), but these suggest neither degrees of importance nor clear or inherent division of labour (Exod. 18.4; Deut. 33.7; Pss. 121.2; 146.5).[7] Each account is characterized by or allows for some non-hierarchical[8] difference. Some Jews in the hellenistic era appear to have recognized

3. '[T]he precise nature of...rule is as various as the...situations in which the action or state so designated occur. It seems to be the situation in all languages and cultures that words for oversight, rule, government must be defined in relation to the situation out of which the function arises' (*TWOT*, I, 534). See also Appendix 2 n. 15.

4. See e.g. *Macquarie Dictionary*, s.v. authority (ranging from 'right to control' to 'title to respect'); but note less range at s.v. dominion (1. power/right to govern and control; sovereign authority. 2. rule/sway; control/influence).

5. Hartill 1965: 70.

6. Clines (1990: 30-35, 42-45) reduces even God's help to 'inferiority' by calling it assistance to man's own fight (2 Chron. 18.31-32), but he ignores e.g. 2 Chronicles 20 where, Israel having sought help (vv. 4-13), the battle is God's own (vv. 15, 17, 22, 29-30). He also limits Eve's help to procreation (Gen. 1.28; 3.16) but, although at 1.26-28 he maximizes androcentricity, at 3.16-19, by implying that Adam's 'sphere' is work (p. 33), he effectively renders procreation (foremost at 1.28) gynocentric. He furthermore obscures the contextual implication of 2.15 at v. 18. Ortlund (1991: 104) claims that helping by nature entails subordination. Dictionary definitions of 'subordinate' as 'secondary/subservient to', or 'under the authority of' (e.g. *Concise Oxford*; *Macquarie*) preclude this (cf. parents helping their children, teachers their pupils, and medical workers their patients). Submission of self-interest to another's welfare does not require subordination to that other. Introduced 'subordination–dominion' language necessarily evokes a power structure unidentifiable in the pre-Fall relationship. 'Helper' should be neither over- nor under-interpreted.

7. Cassuto 1961: 128; *TWOT*, II, 660-61; Westermann 1984: 227; Wenham 1987: 68. Sarna (1989: 21-23) says that wordplay in *Gen. R.* indicates woman's higher intelligence. Trible (1983: 90) believes that *'ēzer* would connote superiority if *kᵉnegdô* did not specify mutuality, but Gardner (1990: 5-6) points out that *kᵉnegdô* (for which see below) denotes only a creature of the same species. In fact, *'ēzer* denotes neither superiority nor inferiority. Prohl 1957: 37. Freedman (1983: 56-58) argues that the words together speak of 'a power equal to man' and superior to that of the animals. See also Keener 1992: 116.

8. Throughout this discussion 'hierarchy' should be understood to mean 'one having

this: in *Apoc. Mos.* 15–30 Eve depicts herself in charge of half of paradise, her account a separate, unified narrative presenting a version of the Fall which was subsequently absorbed into Adam's (Levison 1989: 135-50).

There is inadequate foundation to claim that the pre-Fall man has commanding authority over,[9] or responsibility to provide for or protect,[10] the woman. 1.26-28 is concerned with increase of the human race and its dominion over the earth and the animal kingdom. Neither is mentioned in ch. 2, where the focus is on the man's role in the garden and his need for companionship.[11] The correct reading at 2.15 appears to be 'The Lord God…put…(the man) in the garden…to serve and guard', tilling (v. 5) being introduced only after the expulsion (3.23).[12] The serving (like the guarding) seems at least to include the garden as object,[13] and implies respect for both the earth and plant life (Trible 1983: 85, 88). Therefore, although 1.28 focuses on the subjugation of the earth, and although ch. 2 does not deny the man's dominion over that earth, the passages view the mankind–earth relationship from different perspectives. Human dominion over the earth, then, involves respecting and serving it. This should serve as a caution when defining an inter-human relationship where dominion is not mentioned. Many claim that the man exercises dominion in naming the animals,[14] and/or that the woman is subordinate to him because she is derived from him,[15] named by him[16] and created for his sake.[17] The order of events implies

a role of command and another having a subordinate role'. I realise that hierarchy is not necessarily characterized simply by command–subordinate relations: the orthodox view is that the Trinity is characterized by both ontological equality and role subordination, and thus both unity and hierarchy. However, relations between human beings upon whose story important practices are established require specific definition, without which 'role subordination' is fraught with practical obscurities, e.g. did Adam give orders and Eve obey? In what did Eve's own adult free will properly consist? In the context of human life 'hierarchy' necessarily connotes concepts of subordination to command (no matter how sinless and benevolent). It is one thing to recognize that God the Son subordinated himself to God the Father, and to cite texts which establish that fact; it is entirely another to claim that pre-Fall Eve was Adam's subordinate if the record establishes no such fact, but New Testament passages, themselves requiring interpretation by Genesis 1–3, must be called in to do so.

9.   As noted by Bruce 1982b: 8; Giles 1985: 11-20; Hayter 1987: 96-102; Bilezikian 1987: 421-22; 1989: 37. Contra e.g. Delitzsch 1888: 166; Dillman 1897.

10.   Contra e.g. S.B. Clark 1980: 28, 31; Woodhouse 1985a: 13; Moo 1991: 190.

11.   Contra Cassuto (1961: 127) who claims that this section emphasizes the ethical (cf. sexual 1.27) aspect of the man–wife relationship, and Sarna (1989: 21) who says the dominant theme is the human condition.

12.   Cassuto 1961: 100-105, 121-23. Contra e.g. Clines 1990: 33.

13.   See also Trible 1983: 77, 85. Contra Sailhamer (1990: 45-46) who claims that Adam was to 'worship and obey' in a priestly capacity.

14.   E.g. Griffith-Thomas 1946: 42; Cassuto 1961: 92; Sakenfeld 1975: 224-25; Vawter 1977: 74; Trible 1983: 92-94, 97; Sarna 1989: 22.

15.   E.g. S.B. Clark 1980: 25-26. See also G. Davies 1986: 90; Barnett 1989: 234.

16.   E.g. Vawter 1977: 75; Hurley 1981: 209-12; Wenham 1987: 70; Blomberg 1988: 407-408; Clines 1990: 38-39; Ortlund 1991: 102-103 with nn. 25-26. Moo (1980: 79-80)

that the purpose in bringing the animals to Adam to see what he will name them is that he will understand that none is suitable as his corresponding ($k^e negd\hat{o}$)[18] companion (v. 20b).[19] This naming appears to be more an exercise in intelligence and discernment than an expression of dominion.[20] Nothing suggests that the man has dominion over the woman. Hebrew name-giving did not express such a relationship (e.g. Ruth 4.17),[21] and the non-personal *'iššāh* (cf. 3.20) is given in a simultaneous self-naming, acknowledging sameness.[22] The woman is certainly created for the man's sake, but he benefits in that his aloneness is remedied, not in the acquisition of a subordinate. As the man is not subordinate to his source, the earth, the woman's derivation implies no subordination to him.[23] His cry[24] (2.23) expresses his joy that

claims that Adam 'predicts determinatively' Eve's character. Apart from the naming, however, only what was already obvious is stated (2.23; 3.20).

17. E.g. G. Davies 1986: 90; Gardner 1990: 9. See also Blomberg 1988: 407; Ortlund 1991: 102.

18. Delitzsch 1888: 140; Driver 1907: 41; Cassuto 1961: 127-28; Leupold 1970: 130; Westermann 1984: 227. Freedman (1983: 58) believes the only philologically defensible meaning is 'equal'. Cf. Walsh (1977: 164, 174 with n. 32) who translates 'matching' but denies mutuality.

19. Leupold 1970: 130, 133; Barth 1970: 291-93; Boice 1982: 107-108; Bilezikian 1989: 31-32. Delitzsch (1888: 141) argues that the purpose is to arouse in the man a desire for a partner. See also Giles 1985: 16; Harris 1987: 28-29. Anderson (1989: 125-29) traces instructive purpose and the idea that *zō'th hapa'am* (v. 23) expresses joy at finding a sexual partner in *ARN* B.8; *b. Yeb.* 63a; *m. ha-Gadol*; *Gen. R.* 17.4; Josephus, *Ant.* 34-35; (probably) *Pseudo-Jonathan* for v. 20; *Jub.* 3.2-5a, 6.

20. See also Ramsey 1988: 34-35.

21. Wives do the naming in 28 out of 46 Old Testament cases: Motyer 1980: 1051; J.G. Baldwin 1984: 165-66. See also Bilezikian 1989: 259-61. Trible (1983: 99-100, 133) and M.J. Evans (1983: 16) claim that '*name*' together with '*call*' (as at 2.19; 3.20 but not 2.23) does indicate the exercise of power. See also Sakenfeld 1975: 225-26; Giles 1985: 17; Hayter 1987: 100; Gritz 1991: 56 and n. 39. However, Gardner (1990: 8) argues that origin of names is in view. Ramsey (1988: 24-35) clearly demonstrates both the fallacy in Trible's claim, and that naming neither connotes control nor determines character, and Clines (1990: 38) that in Genesis 1 all naming is exclusively by 'calling'. S.B. Clark (1980: 26) also rejects Trible here.

22. Cassuto 1961: 136; Bratsiodis 1979: 227; Freedman 1983: 58; Sarna 1989: 23. Blomberg (1988: 408) points out that the individual naming of an animal would not mean that no authority was exercised when that species was named as a whole. Nevertheless, dominion over the animals is not in question (1.28) and, since many Old Testament women bestow names, there is no sure foundation for the claim that 2.23 expresses authority.

23. Trible 1983: 101; Bilezikian 1989: 30-31, 255-58. Gardner (1990: 7, 9) argues that: i. an analogy is suggested in that, as the woman stands in the same relation to the man as he to the earth, as he is to serve/tend the earth she is to serve/tend the man; and ii. 3.16b, featuring already-existing pain, indicates a degree of pre-Fall servitude. Cassuto (1961: 121-22), however, argues that the best reading has the man serving the garden rather than the ground, so, although the earth is part of the garden, Gardner's analogy is somewhat forced. Derivation does not in any case set the pattern of relationships: the man is not designed as a

she is just like him.[25] Both possess free will (2.15-17; 3.6), and tasks appear likely to be organized according to physical ability, talent or interest. A suitable/corresponding helper is most naturally envisaged creatively contributing ideas and abilities. A man whose situation without her has been declared 'not good' is most naturally envisaged as both eager for and stimulated by such contribution.

As mentioned above, relying heavily on New Testament passages discussed elsewhere in this study, some interpret pre-Fall Eve as ontologically equal with (1.27-29), but functionally subordinate to or dependent upon, Adam (2.18, 21-22).[26] It should be very clearly noted that, although the pre-Fall record features discernible differences in the relationship which form the basis of some New Testament teachings, those differences as they appear in Genesis do not amount to functional hierarchy.[27] Dependence is mutual: the man could function without the woman, but he needs her (v. 18); the woman is derived from the man and formed as his companion, but nowhere here is she his subordinate. The introduced words 'hierarchy', 'dominion' and 'rule'[28] inevitably introduce the idea that the man is authorized to direct and the woman required to obey those (sinless) directions. The word 'subordinate'[29] distorts the relationship described in Genesis 1–2.[30] *Precisely because the New Testament supports male headship by Adam's prior creation and racial representation, definitions of the pre-Fall relationship, whilst giving full weight to both, should not confuse them with hierarchical command-subordination-type dominion.*[31]

In the hellenistic era Genesis chs. 1–2 were understood to be complementary versions of the same story. With that in view, Eve is created in the image of God

suitable companion for the earth. Moreover, discomfort in natural bodily functions involves no servitude. S.B. Clark (1980: 25-26) claims that the objection that man is not subordinate to the earth is absurd since woman's creation is closer to generation, the principle upon which subordination by precedence is built. Precedence, however, has to do with inheritance rather than subordination. Contra also Bloesch (1982: 25, 32) who, although defining the hierarchy as partnership, nevertheless envisages its adjustment in light of Christ.

24.   Arguing that the poem is such are e.g. Driver 1907: 43; Walsh 1977: 164, 174; Westermann 1984: 231; Hayter 1987: 99; Ramsey 1988: 35; Sarna 1989: 23.

25.   Vawter (1977: 75) notes the similar Gen. 29.14. See also Delitzsch 1888: 144; Cassuto 1961: 135-36; Bilezikian 1987: 422.

26.   E.g. Foh 1979: 61-63; S.B. Clark 1980: 25-26; Knight 1980: 42-44; Boice 1982: 110.

27.   See again my n. 7 above. Foh (1979: 61) and S.B. Clark (1980: 24) acknowledge the absence of explicit evidence that the pre-Fall woman must obey the man.

28.   E.g. Foh 1979: 62; Knight 1980: 31.

29.   E.g. Foh 1979: 62; Boice 1982: 110.

30.   S.B. Clark (1980: 24-26, 28, 41-42, 44) defines the relationship as voluntary unity-subordination, but, despite his careful discussion, 'subordination' connotes a required response to an established power, and neither requirement nor establishment can be substantiated pre-Fall.

31.   The plea of Harris (1990: 343 n. 27) for accurate terminology conveying defineable concepts deserves serious consideration here.

with the same mandate as Adam, but with a different focus within that mandate. With *Apoc. Mos.* 15–30 (see above) in mind, it should be concluded that this non-hierarchical difference was ignored or distorted by contemporary writers only when there is adequate evidence to that effect.

2. *The Extent of the Sin*

Many claim that the sin occasioning Adam and Eve's examination and judgment in Genesis includes her conversation with the serpent,[32] her version of the prohibition (3.3),[33] her wavering trust in God,[34] her independant action,[35] or Adam's 'listening to' her (v. 17)[36] distinct from his acting upon what she, having already sinned, said. Whatever actions preceding their taking and eating of the forbidden fruit (3.6) may be called, however, they cannot, in context, convincingly be described as or likened to sin. The action forbidden (2.16-17) is the action about which they are questioned (3.11b), to which they confess (vv. 12-13), and for which they are judged.[37]

Adam and Eve both appear as free agents capable of resisting temptation *and* deception.[38] As the story is recorded, if the woman listened to the serpent, admired the fruit, carefully considered its proposed benefits yet, even though deceived, refused to eat, she would remain innocent.[39] At 3.6 *'immāh* and plural address by the serpent may indicate that Adam is present throughout.[40] Although no final

32. E.g. Kline 1967: 84.

33. Claiming that Eve exaggerates are e.g. *Midr. R.* 19.3; *Sanh.* 29a; von Rad 1972a: 88; Kidner 1973: 67-68; Westermann 1984: 239; Wenham 1987: 73. Skinner (1930: 74) says she unconsciously intensifies; Sarna (1989: 24) that she introduces unreasonable strictness. Denying exaggeration are e.g. Delitzsch 1888: 152; Cassuto 1961: 145. Walsh (1977: 165) says that she innocently embellishes, inexplicably paraphrases. Cf. Trible (1983: 110), who says that she interprets and so is intelligent and perceptive.

34. E.g. Leupold 1970: 144, 147-48, 151. See also Roloff 1988: 141; Ortlund 1991: 106 with n. 39. Schaeffer (1972: 85) believes the matter was decided when Eve believed the serpent, not God. That, however, appears virtually simultaneous with the taking of the fruit.

35. E.g. Delitzsch 1888: 165; Simpson 1954: 47; Hendriksen 1955: 110; Prohl 1957: 39-40; Keil and Delitzsch 1968: 103; Olthuis 1976: 143; Woodhouse 1985a: 13; G. Davies 1986: 92.

36. Leupold 1970: 172-73. See also Meinertz 1931: 39. Ortlund (1991: 107, 110 and nn. 50-51) claims that Eve usurped and Adam abandoned headship.

37. Walsh (1977: 166, 171, 177) identifies the focus of the entire narrative in *wayō'kal* (3.6b).

38. It seems unlikely that Adam is not seen as capable of deception: otherwise Eve alone is expected to remain obedient when deceived, making her potentially the stronger character.

39. Bonhoeffer (1959: 69) notes that her answer to the serpent remains on the plane of ignorance.

40. Higgins (1976: 645-46) discusses the possibility of an adverbial interpretation of *'immāh*, and notes that feminine singular address by the serpent would not capture the joint command.

decision may be reached on this point, it may not simply be assumed that he is not. Ancient literary conventions dictate that dialogue may take place only between two speakers,[41] so there may be three players here. If he is absent[42] there is no reason to expect that the woman is required to obtain his permission to act. The man is no-where given dominion over her, and God does not charge her with taking unilateral action. From this record alone the conclusion that her sin consists solely in taking and eating the fruit would be unavoidable if it were not for the 'rule' (*māšal*) of her post-Fall judgment. Possible meanings for this word will be discussed below, but it is important to note that, whatever it means, it involves authority undetectable pre-Fall. The woman is in breach of no command or natural law when she acts inde-pendantly. If the man is present throughout,[43] he makes no apparent attempt to prevent her talking with the serpent or eating the fruit. If he had been set in author-ity he would be responsible either to protect and/or direct her, and so would be in breach of a commandment or natural law by not attempting to do so. Yet God does not charge him with dereliction of duty. The man's judgment (vv. 17-19) concerns his emulation of a *fallen* wife in disobedience to the command at 2.17. He is nowhere commanded not to 'listen to' *pre-Fall* Eve: on the contrary, she is created as his suitable companion. Whether or not he is present during her temptation, even if he were to listen very carefully to a long and persuasive enticement (see below), to reach towards the fruit, yet to decide to obey God rather than eat, he would, according to this record, remain innocent. He too must take and eat to disobey. The only sin here is disobedience to the command of 2.17.

It may be concluded that an author in the hellenistic era interprets Eve's sin as including rebellion against Adam only if that author makes that view sufficiently clear.

3. *Eve's Role in the Fall*

The evidence in Genesis does not support common claims that Eve is more apt to be deceived,[44] more liable to yield to temptation,[45] or in some way more vulnera-ble,[46] than Adam. She is formed in God's image from material taken from the

41. Vawter 1977: 79; Walsh 1977: 167 n. 18; Westermann 1984: 239.

42. As e.g. *Apoc. Mos.* 15.2-3; 7.2; Milton 1667: 8.385-86, 421-24; Leupold 1970: 152-53; S.B. Clark 1980: 30.

43. As e.g. Delitzsch 1888: 155; Cassuto 1961: 148; Sakenfeld 1975: 225; Trible 1983: 112-13; Sarna 1989: 25; Ortlund 1991: 107 with n. 40; C. Kroeger and R. Kroeger 1992: 20, 123.

44. Contra e.g. Liddon 1897: 19; E.F. Brown 1917: 20; Simpson 1954: 47.

45. Westermann 1984: 250. See also Barnett 1989: 234. Contra e.g. Luther 1535–36: 151; Driver 1907: 44; Stibbs 1967: 1171; Leupold 1970: 143; Barnes 1975: 1136.

46. Leupold 1970: 130; Foh 1979: 63. Giles (1985: 18) points out that at 3.2-3 the plural indicates that the woman sees herself directly answerable to God. Contra e.g. Skin-ner 1930: 73; Bonhoeffer 1959: 76; Unger 1981: I, 15. Sarna (1989: 24) and Bilezikian (1987: 422; 1989: 43-45, 50, 180, 262-63, 297-98) argue for vulnerability in that she had

man,[47] as his suitable helper receives the same mandate, and is held responsible for her actions. The serpent's choice of her as his target indicates no characteristic weakness on her part.[48] If the man is present, she is represented as an (not necessarily 'the') acceptable spokesperson for them. If the man is absent, her correspondence to him is sufficient to suggest that the serpent's craft is exercised in the manner of address, not the choice of audience. The record simply does not state why the woman is addressed, but she was not uniformly interpreted as weaker or more vulnerable in the hellenistic era.[49]

The woman is also frequently portrayed as tempting the man to eat by sexual or specifically feminine means.[50] Again evidence is lacking.[51] Although as eager as she to divert blame (3.12, 13b), Adam nowhere pleads sexual vulnerability. Verse 3.17 informs the reader that Eve spoke to him, but Adam himself says only that she gave him some of the fruit (v. 6) and focuses his blame on God. This suggests that, whether or not he is present during her temptation, the woman simply invites him to eat.[52] The Heb. *hiśî 'anî* (v. 13) never means 'seduce' in a sexual sense,[53] so Jewish views that the serpent copulates with Eve (e.g. *4 Macc.* 18.7-8; *b. Yeb.* 103b; *b. 'Abod. Zar.* 22b; *b. Sabb.* 146a), or that marital sex is sinful (*Gen. R.* 9.7), distort the text, differ from other Jewish tradition, and cannot be paralleled in the New Testament (cf. 1 Cor. 7.2-9; Heb. 13.4).[54]

not received the prohibition directly from God. Keener (1992: 114) notes a similar view in rabbinic sources. See also Driver (1907: 44). S.B. Clark (1980: 30) admits there is no explicit statement to support the vulnerability he sees.

47. Bushnell (1919: §§38-39) argues that 'rib' is a poor translation. See also Cassuto 1961: 134; S.B. Clark 1980: 18; Gritz 1991: 56.

48. See also Hayter 1987: 105. Contra e.g. Alford 1862: 320.

49. Levison 1989: 135-50. Interpretations of Eve as deficient compared to Adam, whether ancient or modern, show every indication of reading Genesis through the lens of views traceable from the earliest extant Greek thought. See Lloyd (1984: *passim*).

50. E.g. Milton 1667: 8.856-61, 877-85, 998-99; Barnes 1975: 1136. See also Cassuto 1961: 148.

51. So Vawter 1977: 79; Westermann 1984: 249-50.

52. Trible 1983: 113, 119. See also Küchler 1986: 35. Higgins (1976: 639-47) traces the tradition that the woman did tempt Adam from as early as Jerome and Tertullian (see also Reuther 1974: 156-58), demonstrating the absence of textual foundation. Some see considerably more than invitation here: Ellicott (1864: 37-38) says Eve persuaded; Hendriksen (1955: 110) that she ruled; Spencer (1974: 219; 1985: 91) that she authoritatively taught. Hurley (1981: 221) confuses persuasion and authority.

53. A.T. Hanson 1968: 77; Küchler 1986: 36.

54. Contra Thackeray 1900: 50-55; A.T. Hanson 1968: 76-77. Hanson (pp. 65-69) himself demonstrates: the doubtful dating of the Jewish sources he uses to identify the idea of Eve's seduction by the serpent prior to Paul and the Author of the Pastorals; the dubious nature of claims that the concept is present in all those Jewish sources; and Philo's non-use of it (*Quaest. in Gen.* I.33, 47, 49). He can certainly date only *2 Enoch* early enough, and that is extant only in Slavonic. His reasoning is further flawed. On the grounds of *Vit. Ad.* 9.1 where Satan appears as an angel, but where Hanson himself says that the idea of seduc-

In the hellenistic era the Jewish view of Eve as the cause of the Fall (e.g. *Gen. R.* 17.8) is not by any means unanimous. Sir. 41.3-4 appears to see death as man's natural lot, and Wis. 2.24 blames the devil for its introduction. *4 Ezra* ascribes human sinfulness to the evil heart acquired by Adam and so his descendants. *Ps. Ezra* 7.118 and *2 Bar.* 23.4 see death as a consequence of Adam's sin. 1QS 3.13-4.26 and *Targ. Ps.-J.* on Gen. 2.7 see evil inherent in mankind as created.[55] Paul in Rom. 5.12 places responsibility for the Fall on Adam.

It should not be assumed, therefore, that a contemporary interpretation of the Fall featuring Eve's deception or prior disobedience necessarily views her as weaker, or her sexuality as the prime cause of that Fall.

4. *The 'Curse' on the Woman*

Claims that at 3.16 God authorizes man's already-existing or post-Fall rule over his wife are now often denied by those noting that this is not a decree. I will return to this claim below, but it should be noted here that not everything in 3.14-19 is intended as a 'curse'. *'ārar* appears in relation to the serpent and the ground, but not the woman and the man.[56] It has been argued that judgments here are consequences rather than punishments,[57] but the curse upon the earth is clearly designed to punish the humans (v. 17a). Moreover, it is difficult to see increase of pain in childbirth and painful toil as anything other than punishments or curses. Nevertheless, the curse on the serpent involves acts of grace towards the humans. First, in spite of the penalty prescribed, some comfort is offered: the race will not only survive (note at v. 20 an undertone of thanksgiving),[58] but the woman's offspring will crush the serpent's head.[59] Secondly, the enmity introduced appears to be an act of grace. Although in 3.1 *'ārûm* may be 'prudent' rather than 'crafty' (cf. LXX φρονιμώτατος 'wisest/shrewdest'), Eve's claim that she was deceived is nowhere challenged, and by the hellenistic era the serpent's intentions are interpreted as sinister

tion is 'not necessarily impl[ied]' (pp. 69, 76), he concludes that Paul at 2 Cor. 11.1-3 'knew of' the seduction idea and refers to it. He also slides from admission (p. 73) that παράβασις (1 Tim. 2.14) cannot certainly be demonstrated to imply a sexual state, to the suggestion (pp. 76-77) that it does. Anderson (1989: 121-48) demonstrates the pre-Christian belief that Adam and Eve had sexual relations in the Garden.

55. Vermes 1992: 223-24. See also Malina 1969: 23-27; Hayman 1984: 15-17.

56. Leupold 1970: 161; von Rad 1972a: 93; Wenham 1987: 81; Sarna 1989: 28.

57. E.g. Sakenfeld 1975: 226; Trible 1983: 123 incl. n. 46, 126, 129-30; Giles 1985: 21. Cf. Freedman (1983: 58), who argues that the punishments are temporary, claiming Adam's is removed at Gen. 5.29, and citing Gen. 30.14-16 and Exod. 21.10 for the temporary nature of the man's sexual mastery over woman. However, Gen. 5.29 speaks only of comfort/rest from toil, not its cessation, and see below for the 'sexual mastery'.

58. Bonhoeffer 1959: 90. Cf. 'affirmation of life' (Sarna 1989: 29), 'cry of faith' (Kidner 1973: 74), but 'stubborn determination' (G.H. Davies 1973: 131).

59. Delitzsch 1888: 165; Bonhoeffer 1959: 86. Cf. G.H. Davies (1973: 131) who finds little comfort in the promise, and Walsh (1977: 175 n. 35) who claims that ultimate victory is not promised.

(Wis. 2.24; 2 Cor. 11.3; Rev. 12.9). When Gen. 3.1 is interpreted in this fashion, God's introduction of enmity between the serpent and the woman (v. 15a) does not include enmity directed at her. That is already in evidence. The enmity of the woman and her offspring for the serpent, moreover, from the human point of view is an act of preservation, not a curse (Boice 1982: 162). These two factors would be sufficient to suggest the possibility that the judgments on the woman and man may include something other than punishments.[60] Thirdly, however, in v. 15b *zera'* is flexible enough to denote either the whole line of descendants or that collective 'seed' epitomized in one individual, and v. 15c allows for the translation 'he will crush your head and you will strike his heel' (NIV).[61] Some deny that Jews and/or Christians in the hellenistic era employed messianic interpretation here,[62] but the evidence does not support that claim: see LXX Gen. 3.15 αὐτός;[63] the Palestinian Targums;[64] Justin, *Dial. with Trypho* 103; Irenaeus, *Adv. Haer.* 4.40.3; 5.21.1. See also allusions at for example Rom. 16.20; Heb. 2.14; Revelation 12, and *Apocalypse of Adam*, whose Jewish gnosticism includes a well-developed myth proclaiming a heavenly redeemer.[65]

60. See e.g. Cassuto 1961: 163; Brueggemann 1982: 49-50. Bushnell (1919: §§98-145) argues that the woman is not cursed at all, translating '[a] snare hath increased thy sorrow and thy sighing', and the warning: '[t]hou art turning away [from God] to thy husband, and he will rule over thee'. The evidence would more convincingly suggest that the man turns away from God to his wife, but note the pre-Fall freedom of both partners. Verse 13 in any case implies that the woman is guilty, vv. 14-19 naturally understood as judgments upon three guilty parties. Others arguing that the man is cursed indirectly but the women not at all include Trible 1983: 126; Bilezikian 1989: 54.

61. Delitzsch 1888: 161-65; Kaiser 1979: 78-79; *TWOT*: I, 253. More cautiously: Driver 1907: 48; Wenham 1987: 81.

62. E.g. Vawter 1977: 83; Westermann 1984: 260-61; Fee 1984: 38; Roloff 1988: 140.

63. See esp. R.A. Martin 1965: 427.

64. Delitzsch 1888: 164; Skinner 1930: 80-81; Leupold 1970: 170; Wenham 1987: 80-81; Vermes 1992: 225. Cf. however, the translations for *Targ. Onq.* of Etheridge (1968: 41) 'He will remember…and thou shalt be observant' and Grossfield (1988: 46-47) 'it will remember…and you will sustain (your hatred) for it to the end [of time]' (i.e. the Messianic era). Etheridge (p. 166) renders *Targ. Pal.* 'they shall make a remedy for the heel in the days of King Messiah', and *Targ. Jer.* 'for these there shall be a remedy for the heel in the days of King Meshiha'. Cf. also *The Fragment-Targums of the Pentateuch* 7, 91 Paris-Bibliotèque national Hebr. 110, P Gen. 3.15, Vatican Ebr. 440, folios 198-227, V Gen. 3.15.

65. Wifall (1974: 361-65) sees royal and messianic significance in Gen. 3.15, arguing that it is adapted from the David story and ancient Near Eastern mythology, and taken up in Rom. 1.3; 1 Cor. 15.25; Gal. 4.4 (?); 2 Tim. 2.8; Revelation 12. Some argue that Gen. 4.1b should be translated 'I have brought forth a man, even the deliver/coming one': e.g. Bushnell 1919: §§77-79, 82-83; Unger 1981: I, 22; Boice 1982: 200-201. See also Kaiser 1979: 79. The difficulties are discussed and this translation ignored or rejected in Dillman 1897: 183-84; Skinner 1930: 101-103; Cassuto 1961: 198-202; Speiser 1964: 30; von Rad 1972: 103; Vawter 1977: 91-92; Westermann 1984: 289-92; Sarna 1989: 32.

There is ample indication, therefore, that contemporary interpreters may not believe every part of the judgments on the woman and the man to be curses. Two things require careful consideration:

i.　Verse 16 is descriptive, not a series of imperatives.[66]

ii.　Like other words involving authority, *māšal* may not be harsh, absolute or even general rule.[67] Its type and extent depend upon its context.[68] Although authority is always evident, *māšal* may be anything from oppression (Judg. 14.4; Isa. 19.4) to stewardship of personnel (Gen. 24.2), control of the temper (Prov. 16.32), the powerful but impersonal relationship of sun and moon to day and night (Gen. 1.18), or righteous, God-fearing rule which is like the light at sunrise or life-giving brightness after rain (2 Sam. 23.3-4) (*TWOT*: I, 1259).

In Gen. 3.16, however, the context in which it must be defined is complicated by the difficult *tᵉšûqāh* occurring elsewhere only at Gen. 4.7 and Song 7.10. Derived from the verb 'be abundant/overflow' (Ps. 65.9; Joel 2.24; 3.13: *TWOT*: II, 913), the noun is here generally translated 'desire/longing'. Yet at Gen. 3.16 the LXX translators chose ἀποστροφή.[69] According to Origen, Aquila translated συνάφεια (combination/union), Symmachus either as Aquila or ὁρμή (desire *or* impulse/inclination), and although Theodotion's version is unknown he translated at 4.7 ἀποστροφή.[70] At 3.16 the word is frequently interpreted as sexual desire.[71] Song 7.10 certainly includes this connotation, but the textually difficult Gen. 4.7 does not (Foh 1979: 67). At 3.16 the sexual connotation cannot be excluded, but the differing context to Song 7.10 is noteworthy. In the latter it is one of joy and love in which an overflow of feeling by a groom for his bride naturally includes sexual

---

66.　Bushnell 1919: §127; Trible 1983: 123; J.G. Baldwin 1984: 163. The LXX translators chose instead of the imperative the future indicative which, being the more heavily marked, Porter (1989a: 420) argues is the stronger command. The translators may nevertheless intend only to emphasize the expectation. See below.

67.　Contra e.g. Knox 1558: 14-15, 22; Weisinger 1866: 417; Prohl 1957: 39; J.G. Baldwin 1973: 18; Moo 1980: 69; Bruce 1982b: 9; Hayter 1987: 107; Tucker and Liefeld 1987: 450; Blomberg 1988: 406 n. 8; P.H. Towner 1989: 217. See also Knight 1980: 43; Witherington 1988: 123 and n. 222; Keener 1992: 120. Giles (1985: 21-22) confusingly claims that this is probably the mildest word for 'rule' and does not connote despotism, but that it is an expression of sin, an assumption of power consequential upon distortion.

68.　See again *TWOT*, I, 534 at n 3.

69.　See also Snaith 1959: 35. Bushnell (1919: §§139, 141-44) with additional note cites similarly the Syriac Peshitta, and Samaritan, Old Latin, Sahidic and Bohairic Coptic, and Ethiopic versions.

70.　*Hexapla* Gen. 3.17 (16), 4.7. See also Bushnell 1919: §132.

71.　E.g. Knobel 1852: 44; Dillman 1897: 162; Keil and Delitzsch 1968: 103; Leupold 1970: 172; Clines 1990: 36. See also Driver 1907: 49; Bonhoeffer 1959: 86. Witherington (1988: 123 and n. 223) says this desire is not part of the curse. Sarna (1989: 28) cites Rashi and Ramban but without necessarily agreeing.

desire.[72] At Gen. 3.16 the woman is being judged.[73] Sexual desire is not necessarily the focus of the 'overflowing/reaching out' and, whatever may be the intended meaning of the Hebrew, the Greek translators of antiquity appear to have something broader in mind. It has also been interpreted as natural submission to marital rule.[74] The object of the 'desire', however, is the man himself.[75] Neither 'sexual desire' nor 'submission to marital rule' is therefore convincing. Since *tᵉšûqāh* provides the context for *māšal* the meaning of neither is clear.

Further obscuring the meaning is the common idea that *tᵉšûqāh* and/or *māšal* are consequences of the Fall in the sense that their distortion of pre-Fall normality is brought about by mankind's action rather than God's decree.[76] Those recognizing the descriptive (generally called 'prophetic') rather than imperative nature of the passage adopt this position.[77] Some declare only *tᵉšûqāh* such a consequence, using the similar language of 4.17 to interpret the 'reaching out' as woman's aspiration to control her husband, and so as her distortion of harmonious pre-Fall submission.[78] This strains both 4.17 and 3.16[79] and shares the faulty view that pre-Fall normality

---

72. Busenitz (1986: 211) points out that even here the object is her presence.

73. *TWOT*, II, 913 notes these differences.

74. E.g. Delitzsch 1888: 166; G.H. Davies 1973: 131; Blomberg 1988: 406. When *māšal* is interpreted as harsh rule this claim is not even a general truth. Boice (1982: 179) argues that it reverses the issue, the woman's original 'helper' role suggesting her willingness, so that only after the Fall would she rebel. The alternative he offers, however, is unpersuasive: see below.

75. This was noted as long ago as Nicholas Fuller, 1612, cited by Bushnell (1919: §128). See also Bilezikian 1989: 55.

76. Reuther (1974: 158-59) traces this idea in the patristic period. For the modern era see e.g. Delitzsch 1888: 166; *Pentateuch and Haftorahs* 1929: 30; Skinner 1930: 83; Leupold 1970: 172; von Rad 1972a: 93; Vawter 1977: 84-85; Knight 1980: 43; Bloesch 1982: 25, 32; Bruce 1982b: 8-9; Brueggemann 1982: 51; Scanzoni and Hardesty 1982: 34-35; M.J. Evans 1983: 19; Giles 1985: 15, 21; G. Davies 1986: 90-91; M.M. Thompson 1986: 96; Hayter 1987: 107, 113-15; Blomberg 1988: 406; Sarna 1989: 28; Bilezikian 1989: 54, 265; Keener 1992: 119. See also S.B. Clark 1980: 33-35, but cf. at n. 89 below.

77. See at n. 57. There is not space here fully to discuss this approach to Gen. 3.16. Briefly: it is claimed that Gal. 3.28 reverses its effects. See e.g. Grimke 1838: 7, 85; Prohl 1957: 39; J.G. Baldwin 1973: 18; 1984: 165; Giles 1985: 21. For response see e.g. Osborne 1977: 348-49; Witherington 1981: 598. Cf. Stendahl (1982: 32-37) who notes a linguistic link between Gal. 3.28 and LXX Gen. 1.27. Meeks (1973: 181, 185) says the New Testament passage overcomes *created* difference, pointing in the direction of man created in God's image, and thereby causing tension with other Pauline passages. The third sentence of Gen. 1.27, however, specifies *how* God creates mankind in his image (Wenham 1987: 32-33), and the division is 'very good' in his eyes (v. 31a). The text of Genesis nowhere describes an original androgynous being.

78. Foh 1979: 69. See also Hurley 1981: 219; Boice 1982: 179; M.J. Evans 1983: 19-20; G. Davies 1986: 91; Harris 1987: 29; Wenham 1987: 81-82; Ortlund 1991: 108-109 with n. 45.

79. Bilezikian (1989: 264-66) calls the strain 'unbearable'. Busenitz (1986: 210) points out that 4.7 is figurative, with Cain both the object of desire and the one cursed, but that

includes marital dominion. Moreover, along with any interpretation of part or all of the passage as directly consequential upon action taken by man rather than God, it distorts the context.

Although v. 16 does not command, it is something more than description. It is part of a context (vv. 14-19) in which God makes various things so. Certainly no imperative is given. No sense is conveyed that childbirth with moderate pain and food obtained with relative ease are in trespass. The message is that in a general sense from now on childbirth *can be expected* to be painful and the production of food *can be expected* to require painful labour. These non-imperative judgments are presented as God's doing.[80]

The entire context, although distorting pre-Fall normality by introducing new norms, at no other point does so by the divine establishment of any aspect of fallen human nature. Even the enmity of the woman and her offspring for the serpent is universally understood as the introduction of aversion for, rather than approved cruelty to, the serpent. This context leaves little room for doubt that, whilst *tᵉšûqāh* and/or *māšal* may introduce change, neither is intended to distort pre-Fall normality in any way which would suggest that God recognizes as inevitable, or establishes (even temporarily) as a new norm, some facet of sinful human nature such as domination or desire to dominate.

With this in mind, *tᵉšûqāh* and *māšal* must be defined in the context of the preceding v. 16a. Again there are difficulties. It is unclear whether v. 16a-b speaks

i.   solely of greatly increased pain in childbirth paralleling v. 16c, or
ii. of greatly increased pain
     a) paralleling the man's pain; and
     b) particularly in childbearing, paralleling v. 16c.

A clue offered in v. 15 supports ii.[81] Logical progression from offspring to childbirth suggests that, in spite of the altered address at v. 16, the background of the serpent's relationship with the woman's offspring[82] is not unrelated. Life is not expected to be easy for those offspring, so painful childbirth (v. 16a) appears to particularize the greatly multiplied general pain which the man and woman in their post-Fall condition to some extent already feel. Verse 16b seems to capture the general pain of bearing children in a fallen world. In this context *tᵉšûqāh* suggests that the woman will reach out, or yearn for, the man himself. Although sexual need would obviously be included, the emotional overflow implies much more.[83]

3.16 is literal, and the desire not part of the man's judgment.

80. Schaeffer 1972: 93-94.

81. For which see Cassuto (1961: 165), who cites 2 Sam. 22.1 and Ps. 18.1. See also Knobel 1852: 43; Dillman 1897: 162 and n. 1; Keil and Delitzsch 1968: 102-103; Leupold 1970: 171; Boice 1982: 178. Preferring i. are e.g. Kidner 1973: 71; Westermann 1984: 262; Busenitz 1986: 206 n. 17. Undecided is Trible 1983: 127.

82. Westermann (1984: 258-59) notes the relative independance of v. 15 from v. 14. See also Cassuto 1961: 161; Sailhamer 1990: 56.

83. For other broader-than-sexual interpretations see Kaiser 1979: 78-79; Scanzoni and

Designed as his companion, in her greatly multipled pain she will need him deeply now. Hellenistic translators seem to have understood *tᵉšûqāh* in this broader way, conveying the idea that she will 'turn' to him.[84] One further possible factor should also be considered. As the context progresses from offspring to childbirth, it pictures not only pain: the promise suggests an additional element to the woman's yearning—a longing to bear from her husband the promised seed[85]/Seed which would bruise the serpent's head.

The type and extent of the rule must be defined in the above context. Since the sin committed is the same in both cases, and the increased pain parallels the painful toil, there is no reason to expect the woman to receive additional punishment, that is, to assume that the rule is a curse.[86] Since it is part of her judgment, not the man's, it appears to involve a response from him as natural in the changed circumstances as is her yearning. In fact, it seems to be a rule having directly to do with her need.[87] Finally, although it must involve some sort of authority undetectable in the pre-Fall relationship, it is introduced by God and must be characterized accordingly. Taking all these factors into consideration, *māšal* seems intended not to focus on the man's power, but to be the life-giving type at 2 Sam. 23.3-4.[88] In fact it appears intended to reassure the woman that she would not be required to fend entirely for herself in her now pain-marred life.[89] In other words, whilst she had always been intended as the man's helper, he would now be expected to take certain responsibility for her.

The extent of this rule is rather more difficult to define, but there are some guidelines. The different judgments suggest a more obvious division of labour than may legitimately be discerned pre-Fall. In this changed world the man now has a dependant and some practical authority over her. This new dependence, responsibility and authority, however, appears in a context suggesting that the mutuality of the pre-Fall situation is intended to continue in some form. The judgment on the man does not specify that he remains dependant upon the woman: it does not mention her at

Hardesty 1982: 35; Trible 1983: 128; Busenitz 1986: 207, 212. See also Cassuto 1961: 165-66; Gritz 1991: 58.

84.   For discussion on ἀπο- and ἐπι- with στροφή see Busenitz (1986: 204-205).

85.   '[T]he longing for motherhood will remain the most powerful instinct in woman' (*Pentateuch and Haftorahs* 1929: 30).

86.   Contra e.g. Ortlund 1991: 108.

87.   Walsh (1977: 168) notes the interweaving of the dual punishments for each party: the serpent to crawl and be crushed; intractable earth and man's labour; and (he claims) motherhood the most profound result of the woman's yearning, and her domination. If the artificially connecting 'motherhood etc.' is omitted there yet remains an interweaving of woman's yearning and man's (unspecified) rule.

88.   Cf. the rule of mankind over the animal kingdom (1.26, 28), never to my knowledge now interpreted simply as power.

89.   S.B. Clark (1980: 32, 35, 677 n. 3) finds a version of this view at least possible, although he views the rule as reaffirmation of a pre-Fall subordination/provider relationship. Sarna (1989: 28) points out that the woman must now depend for sustenance on the man's toil, although see re n. 90.

all. Nevertheless, he needs her to carry out the command of 1.28, and she certainly shares in at least part of his judgment, returning at last to the dust from which he was taken. Since Old Testament women are nowhere portrayed as simply bearers of children (Gen. 20.9; Exod. 35.10-29 esp. vv. 25-26; 36.6; Ruth 2.8, 23; 3.2; Prov. 31.10-31; Song 1.6; Neh. 3.12) it should not be assumed that she is not expected to share to some extent in his painful toil.[90] He needs help even more now. Even though he has some authority and will serve to some extent as her provider, the relationship continues to be one of mutual dependence. This suggests that even though the form of the pre-Fall relationship changes to delegate certain authority to the man, its essence continues to be the norm in post-Fall circumstances. The extent of the rule is best defined with that mutuality in mind.

A further guide-line is found in Old Testament laws and customs for men and women. Although they differ in significant respects, nowhere does male domination over a wife's entire life appear to be the norm: cf. Gen. 21.10-12; 31.14 (noting the apparent freedom of choice); 1 Sam. 1.22-23; 25; Prov. 31.10-31. Where there is enough information to form conclusions, Old Testament wives show evidence of independence, marital influence and consciousness of personal responsibility to God. Legislation assumes them responsible and provides certain protections. Nowhere is there a sense that God has delegated to husbands absolute authority over them. On the other hand, male authority *is* closely associated with sexual and paternity rights. This is evidenced in the toleration of polygamy, and in Numbers: at 5.21-31;[91] and in limited right to veto vows at 30.3-15. Although interpretations of *māšal* in Gen. 3.16 invariably focus upon a power element, a proper balance is required between responsibility and such limited/specific authorities as these. Perhaps in Gen. 3.16 *māšal* includes perception that in a post-Fall world a household head would need to feel confident that children born into his family were his, or to be able to overrule certain kinds of decisions. It should clearly be noted, however, that any such limited authority newly introduced into the relationship does not appear designed as an additional curse upon the woman, and does not grant the man absolute or even general authority over her. As the story is recorded, God himself restructures a relationship which from the beginning involved some non-hierarchical difference. In this context *māšal* introduces limited authority involving responsibility for the woman in her childbearing role and certain rights for the man requiring cautious definition.

Particularly in view of extant Greek translations of *tᵉšûqāh* at Gen. 3.16 (see pp. 326-27 above), it should not be concluded that exegetes contemporary with the Author of 1 Timothy understand that verse otherwise unless there is adequate evidence to that effect.

---

90. Cf. Sarna in n. 89. Leupold (1970: 173) argues that the first word in v. 17 should be pointed *l'ādhām*, meaning, 'unto man' rather than 'Adam'.

91. It is probably worth considering Jn 1.13 οὐδὲ ἐκ θελήματος ἀνδρός in this connection, since it indicates a conception in the hellenistic era of husbands exercising authority in the procreation of children.

BIBLIOGRAPHY

Aalen, S.
    1964   'A Rabbinic Formula in 1 Cor. 14,34', in F. Cross (ed.), *Studia Evangel-ica*. II–III. *Papers* (Berlin: Akademie Verlag): 513-25.

Ackroyd, P.R., and C.F. Evans (eds.)
    1970   *The Cambridge History of the Bible,* I (Cambridge: Cambridge University Press).

Alexander, P.S. (ed.)
    1984   *Textual Sources for the Study of Judaism* (Manchester: Manchester University Press).

Alford, H.
    1862   *The Epistles to the Galatians, Ephesians, Philippians, Colossians, Thes-salonians,—to Timotheus, Titus, and Philemon*, III (London: Rivingtons).

Allegro, J.M. (ed.)
    1968   *Qumran Cave 4* (Oxford: Clarendon Press).

Allison, R.W.
    1988   'Let Women be Silent in the Churches (1 Cor. 14:33b-36): What Did Paul Really Say, and What Did it Mean?', *JSNT* 32: 27-60.

Allworthy, T.B.
    1917   *Women in the Apostolic Church* (Cambridge: Heffer & Sons).

Almlie, G.L.
    1982   'Women's Church and Communion Participation: Apostolic Practice or Innovative Twist?', *Christian Brethren Review* 33: 41-55.

Amundsen, D.W., and C.J. Diers
    1970   'The Age of Menopause in Classical Greece and Rome', *Human Biology* 42: 79-86.

Andersen, F.I.
    1985   '2 (Slavonic Apocalypse of) Enoch', in *OTP*, I: 91-100.

Anderson, G.
    1989   'Celibacy or Consummation in the Garden? Reflections on Early Jewish and Christian Interpretations of the Garden of Eden', *HTR* 82.2: 121-48.

Aquinas
    1862   'In Epistolam 1 ad Timotheum', *Opera Omnia* (Parma: Ficcador): XIII.2.

Attridge, H.W.
    1989   *Hebrews* (Philadelphia: Fortress Press).

Aune, D.E.
    1982   'The Odes of Solomon and Early Christian Prophecy', *NTS* 28: 453-60.

1987   *The New Testament in its Literary Environment* (Philadelphia: Westminster Press).

Baasland, E.
1988   'Die περί-Formel und die Argumentation(ssituation) des Paulus', *ST* 42: 69-87.

Bachmann, D.P.
1936   *Der erste Brief des Paulus an die Korinther* (Leipzig: Deichertsche Verlagsbuchhandlung, 4th edn).

Bachmann, G.A., and S.R. Leiblum
1991   'Sexuality in Sexagenarian Women', *Maturitas* 13: 43-50.

Bailey, K.E.
n.d.   'Women in/of the New Testament: a Middle Eastern Cultural View', (Unpublished; Jerusalem: Episcopal Diocese of Cyprus and the Gulf; Nicosia: Ecumenical Institute [Tantur]): 1-23.

Balch, D.L.
1981   *Let Wives Be Submissive: The Domestic Code in 1 Peter* (SBLMS, 26; Chico, CA: Scholars Press).

Baldwin, H.S.
1995   'A Difficult Word: αὐθεντέω in 1 Timothy 2:12', in Köstenberger, Schreiner and Baldwin 1995: 65-80, 269-305.

Baldwin, J.G.
1973   *Women Likewise* (London: Church Pastoral Aid Society).
1984   'Women's Ministry: A New Look at the Biblical Texts', in Lees 1984: 158-76.

Balsdon, J.P.V.D.
1962   *Roman Women* (London: The Bodley Head).

Bammel, E.
1959–60   'Gottes ΔΙΑΘΗΚΗ (Gal. III:15-17) und das jüdische Rechtsdenken', *NTS* 6: 313-19.

Banker, J.
1987   *The Semantic Structure Analysis of Titus* (Dallas: Summer Institute of Linguistics).

Banks, R.
1976   'Paul and Women's Liberation', *Interchange* 18: 81-105.
1981   *Paul's Idea of Community* (NSW: Anzea).
1985a   *Going to Church in the First Century* (NSW: Hexagon).
1985b   *The Tyranny of Time* (NSW: Anzea).

Barclay, W.
1975   *The Letters to Timothy, Titus and Philemon* (Edinburgh: Saint Andrew Press).

Barnes, A.
1975   *Notes on the NT* (rev. I. Cobbin; London; repr. Michigan: Kregel [1868]).

Barnett, P.W.
1989   'Wives and Women's Ministry (1 Timothy 2:11-15)', *EvQ* 61.3: 225-38.

Barrett, C.K.
1956   'The Eschatology of the Epistle to the Hebrews', in W.D. Davies and D. Daube (eds.), *The Background of the New Testament and its*

Eschatology: In Honour of Charles Harold Dodd (Cambridge: Cambridge University Press): 363-93.

1963   *The Pastoral Epistles* (Oxford: Clarendon Press).

1971   *A Commentary on the First Epistle to the Corinthians* (London: A. & C. Black, 2nd edn).

1974   'Pauline Controversies in the Post-Pauline Period', *NTS* 20: 229-45.

1976   'The Allegory of Abraham, Sarah, and Hagar in the Argument of Galatians', in J. Friedrick, W. Pöhlmann and P. Stuhlmacher (eds.), *Rechtfertigung, Festschrift für E. Käsemann* (Tübingen: Mohr Siebeck): 1-16.

1978   *A Commentary on the First Epistle to the Corinthians* (London: A. & C. Black, 2nd edn).

Bartchy, S.S.

1973   *ΜΑΛΛΟΝ ΧΡΗΣΑΙ: First Century Slavery and the Interpretation of 1 Corinthians 7:21* (SBLDS, 11; Missoula, MT: SBL).

Barth, K.

1970   'The Doctrine of Creation I', *Church Dogmatics*, III (ET; Edinburgh: T. & T. Clark).

Barton, S.C.

1986   'Paul's Sense of Place: An Anthropological Approach to Community Formation in Corinth', *NTS* 32: 225-46.

1990   'Widows', *ExpTim* 101.10: 313.

1992   'The Communal Dimensions of Earliest Christianity: A Critical Survey of the Field', *JTS* 43.2: 399-427.

Bartsch, H.-W.

1965   *Die Anfänge urchristlicher Rechtsbildungen* (Hamburg: H. Reich).

Baskett, J.

1980   *The Horse in Art* (London: Weidenfeld & Nicolson).

Bassler, J.M.

1984   'The Widows' Tale: A Fresh Look at 1 Tim. 5:3-16', *JBL* 103.1: 23-41.

Bauer, W.

1937   *Griechisch-Deutsches Wörterbuch zu den Schriften des Neuen Testaments und der übrigen urchristlichen Literatur* (Berlin: Alfred Töpelmann).

1972   *Orthodoxy and Heresy in Earliest Christianity* (London: SCM Press).

Baugh, S.M.

1994   'The Apostle among the Amazons', *WTJ* 56: 153-71.

1995   'A Foreign World: Ephesus in the First century', in Köstenberger, Schreiner and Baldwin 1995: 13-52.

Baumgarten, J.M.

1957   'On the Testimony of Women in 1QS$_A$', *JBL* 76: 266-69.

Beare, F.W.

1958   *The First Epistle of Peter* (Oxford: Basil Blackwell).

Bedale, S.

1954   'The Meaning of kephalé in the Pauline Epistles', *JTS* 5: 211-15.

Beker, J.C.

1991   *Heirs of Paul* (Minneapolis: Fortress Press).

Belkin, S.

1940   *Philo and the Oral Law* (Cambridge, MA: Harvard University Press).

Bernard, J.H.
 1899 *The Pastoral Epistles* (Cambridge: Cambridge University Press; repr. 1980; Grand Rapids: Baker Book House).

Bettenson, H. (ed.)
 1975 *Documents of the Christian Church* (Oxford: Oxford University Press).

Betz, H.D. (ed.)
 1975 *Plutarch's Theological Writings and Early Christian Literature* (Leiden: E.J. Brill).
 1978 *Plutarch's Ethical Writings and Early Christian Literature* (Leiden: E.J. Brill).

Bilezikian, G.
 1987 'Hierarchist and Egalitarian Inculturations', *JETS* 30.4: 421-26.
 1989 *Beyond Sex Roles* (Grand Rapids: Baker Book House).

Binns, L.E.
 1927 *The Book of Numbers* (London: Methuen).

Bisel, S.
 1980 'A Pilot Study in Aspects of Human Nutrition in the Ancient Eastern Mediterranean with Particular Attention to Trace Minerals in Several Populations from Different Time Periods' (Unpublished PhD dissertation, University of Minnesota).
 1986 'The People of Herculaneum AD 79', *Helmantica* 37: 11-23.
 1987 'Human Bones at Herculaneum', *Rivista di studi Pompeiani*: 123-29.

Blaise, A.
 1954 *Dictionnaire Latin-Français des auteurs chrétiens* (Turnhout: Editions Brepols).

Bloch, S.
 1990 'Why Sport Is Good for You—Jewishly', *The Australian Jewish News* (Melbourne, 31 Aug.): 25.

Bloesch, D.G.
 1982 *Is the Bible Sexist? Beyond Feminism and Patriarchalism* (Westchester, IL: Crossway).

Blomberg, C.L.
 1988 'Not beyond What is Written: A Review of Aida Spencer's "Beyond the Curse: Women Called to Ministry" ', *Criswell Theological Review* 2.2: 403-21.

Blum, E.A.
 1981 '1 Peter', in Gaebelein 1976–90: XII, 209-54.

Blum, G.G.
 1965 'Das Amt der Frau im Neuen Testament', *NovT* 7: 142-61.

Boice, J.M.
 1982 *Genesis* (Grand Rapids: Zondervan).

Bonhoeffer, D.
 1959 *Creation and Fall* (London: SCM Press).

Booth, C.
 1859 *Female Ministry; or Women's Right to Preach the Gospel* (Christian Family Print; repr. 1884).

Boucher, M.
    1969   'Some Unexplored Parallels to 1 Cor 11,11-12 and Gal 3,28: The NT on the Role of Women', *CBQ* 31: 50-58.

Boucher, M., R.J. Dillon, J.R. Donahue, E. Schüssler Fiorenza, E.H. Maly, S.M. Schneiders and R.J. Sklba (Task Force of the Executive Board of the Catholic Biblical Association of America)
    1979   'Women and Priestly Ministry: The New Testament Evidence', *CBQ* 41: 608-13.

Bradley, D.G.
    1953   'The *Topos* as a Form in the Pauline Paraenesis', *JBL* 72: 238-46.

Bratsiodis, N.P.
    1979   ' *'īsh*', *TDOT*, I: 227.

Brecht, F.J.
    n.d.   *Motive- und Typengeschichte des griechischen Spottepigramms*, (*Philologus* Supplement, 22) Part 2.

Bremmer, J.N.
    1987   'The Old Women of Ancient Greece', in J. Blok and P. Mason (eds.), *Sexual Asymmetry: Studies in Ancient Society* (Amsterdam: J.C. Gieben): 191-215.

Brewer, D.I.
    1992   *Techniques and Assumptions in Jewish Exegesis Before 70 CE* (Tübingen: Mohr Siebeck).

Bromiley, G.W.
    1979   'The Interpretation of the Bible', in Gaebelein 1976–90: I, 60-80.

Brooten, B.J.
    1982   *Women Leaders in Ancient Synagogues* (Chico, CA: Scholars Press).
    1985   'Early Christian Women and their Cultural Context: Issues of Method in Historical Reconstruction', in A. Yarbro Collins (ed.), *Feminist Perspectives on Biblical Scholarship* (SBL; Chico, CA: Scholars Press): 65-91.

Brown, E.F.
    1917   *The Pastoral Epistles* (London: Methuen).

Brown, H.
    1995   'The New Testament against Itself: 1 Timothy 2:9-15 and the "Breakthrough" of Galatians 3:28', in Köstenberger, Schreiner and Baldwin (eds.) 1995: 197-208.

Brown, W.K.
    1887   *Gynethics, or The Ethical Status of Women* (New York: Funk & Wagnalls).

Brox, N.
    1969   *Die Pastoralbriefe* (Regensburg: F. Pustet).

Bruce, F.F.
    1967   'The Epistles of Paul', in M. Black (ed.), *Peake's Commentary on the Bible* (Melbourne: Nelson): 932-35.
    1968–69   'Recent Contributions to the Understanding of Hebrews', *ExpTim* 80: 260-64.
    1978   ' "All Things to All Men": Diversity in Unity and Other Pauline Tensions', in R.A. Guelich (ed.), *Unity and Diversity in New Testament Theology: Essays in Honour of G.E. Ladd* (Grand Rapids: Eerdmans): 82-99.

1982a   *The Epistle to the Galatians* (Grand Rapids: Eerdmans).
1982b   'Women in the Church: A Biblical Survey', *Christian Brethren Review* 33: 7-14.
1983   *1 and 2 Corinthians* (The New Century Bible Commentary; Grand Rapids: Eerdmans [1971]).

Bruce, M., and G.E. Duffield
n.d.   *Why Not? Priesthood and the Ministry of Women* (rev. R.J. Beckwith, Berks.: Marcham Manor Press).

Brueggemann, W.
1982   *Genesis* (Atlanta: John Knox Press).

Buchsbaum, H.J. (ed.)
1983   *The Menopause* (New York: Springer-Verlag).

Bultmann, R.
1955   *Theology of the New Testament*, II (ET; London: SCM Press).

Burridge, R.A.
1992   *What are the Gospels? A Comparison with Graeco-Roman Biography* (*NTS* Monograph Series; Cambridge: Cambridge University Press).

Burton, E. de W.
1898   *Syntax of the Moods and Tenses of NT Greek* (repr. 1955, Edinburgh: T. & T. Clark).
1920   *Galatians* (ICC; repr. 1980; Edinburgh: T. & T. Clark).

Busenitz, I.A.
1986   'Woman's Desire for Man: Genesis 3:16 Reconsidered', *GTJ* 7.2: 203-12.

Bush, P.G.
1990   'A Note on the Structure of 1 Timothy', *NTS* 36: 152-56.

Bushnell, K.C.
1919   *God's Word to Women* (n.d., but in print by 1919; repr. 1976, St. Paul, MN: Christians for Biblical Equality).

Byrne, B.
1988   *Paul and the Christian Woman* (NSW: St. Paul).

Caird, G.B.
1959   'The Exegetical Method of the Epistle to the Hebrews', *Canadian Journal of Theology* 5: 44-51.

Calvin, J.
1579   *Sermons on the Epistles to Timothy and Titus* (repr. of sixteenth- and seventeenth-century facsimile editions, 1983; Edinburgh: Banner of Truth Trust).

Campbell, R.A.
1990   Review of Prior 1989, in *EvQ* 62.4: 372-74.

Carcopino, J.
1956   *Daily Life in Ancient Rome* (Mitcham, Vic.: Penguin Books).

Carrington, R.C.
1970   'Houses, Italian', in *OCD*: 532-33.

Carroll, K.L.
1953   'The Expansion of the Pauline Corpus', *JBL* 72: 230-37.

Carson, D.A.
1986   *Exegetical Fallacies* (Grand Rapids: Baker Book House).

1988 *Showing the Spirit: A Theological Exposition of 1 Corinthians 12–14* (Grand Rapids: Baker Book House).

1991 ' "Silent in the Churches": On the Role of Women in 1 Corinthians 14:33b-36', in Piper and Grudem (eds.) 1991: 140-53, 487-90.

Carson, D.A., and S.E. Porter (eds.)

1993 *Biblical Greek Language and Linguistics* (JSNTSup, 80; Sheffield: Sheffield Academic Press).

Cassuto, U.

1961 *A Commentary on the Book of Genesis* (ET; Jerusalem: Magnes Press): Part I.

Cervin, R.S

1989 'Does Κεφαλή Mean 'Source' or 'Authority over' in Greek Literature? A Rebuttal', *TrinJ* 10.1: 85-112.

Chadwick, H. (ed.)

1959 *The Sentences of Sextus* (Cambridge: Cambridge University Press).

Charles, R.H. (ed.)

1902 *Jubilees* (London: A. & C. Black).

Clark, E.A.

1983 *Women in the Early Church* (Wilmington, DE: Michael Glazier).

Clark, S.B.

1980 *Man and Woman in Christ* (Ann Arbor: Servant Books).

Clines, D.J.A.

1990 'What Does Eve Do to Help? And Other Irredeemably Androcentric Orientations in Genesis 1–3', in *idem* (ed.), *What does Eve do to Help? And Other Readerly Questions to the Old Testament* (JSOTSup, 94; Sheffield: Sheffield Academic Press): 25-48.

Clouse, B., and R. Clouse (eds.)

1989 *Women in Ministry: Four Views* (Downers Grove, IL: InterVarsity Press).

Coggins, R.J., and J.L. Houlden (eds.)

1990 *A Dictionary of Biblical Interpretation* (London: SCM Press).

Cohen, A.

1949 *Everyman's Talmud* (London: J.M. Dent & Sons [1932]).

Collins, R.F.

1988 *Letters That Paul Did Not Write* (Wilmington, DE: Michael Glazier).

Colson, F.H.

1917–18 ' "Myths and Genealogies": A Note on the Polemic of the Pastoral Epistles', *JTS* 19: 265-71.

Colson, F.H., and G.H. Whitaker (eds.)

1929–62 *Philo* (10 vols. with 2 supplements; LCL; London: Heinemann).

Concise Oxford Dictionary

1951 (Oxford: Oxford University Press, 4th edn [1959]).

Concordance to the Apocrypha/Deuterocanonical Books of the Revised Standard Version

1983 Derived from the Bible Data Bank of the Centre Informatique et Bible, Abbey of Maredsous. Foreword by B.M. Metzger (Grand Rapids: Eerdmans).

Conzelmann, H.

1975 *1 Corinthians* (ET; Philadelphia: Fortress Press).

1987 *Acts of the Apostles* (ET; Philadelphia: Fortress Press).

Cooke, G.A.
 1951   *Ezekiel* (Edinburgh: T. & T. Clark).
Cooper, W.
 1976   *No Change* (London: Arrow).
Countryman, L.W.
 1980   *The Rich Christian in the Church of the Early Empire: Contradictions and Accommodations* (Lewiston, NY: Edwin Mellen Press).
Cowell, F.R.
 1972   *Everyday Life in Ancient Rome* (London: Batsford).
Craigie, P.C.
 1976   *The Book of Deuteronomy* (NSW: Hodder & Stoughton).
Criswell, W.A.
 1976   *The Holy Spirit in Today's World* (Grand Rapids: Zondervan).
Crouch, J.E.
 1972   *The Origin and Intention of the Colossian Haustafel* (Göttingen: Vanden-hoeck & Ruprecht).
Culham, P.
 1986   'Again, What Meaning Lies in Colour!', *ZPE* 64: 235-45.
Dahl, N.A.
 1969   'The Atonement: An Adequate Reward for the Akedah? (Ro 8:32)', in E. Ellis and M. Wilcox (eds.), *Neotestamentica et Semitica: Studies in honour of M. Black* (Edinburgh: T. & T. Clark): 15-29.
Dalais, F.S., G.E. Rice, A.L. Murkies, R.J. Bell and M.L. Wahlqvist
 1996   'Effects of Dietary Phytoestrogens in Postmenopausal Women', in *Abstracts. 8th International Congress on the Menopause*, 3–7 Nov., Sydney: P315.
Daly, R.J.
 1977   'The Soteriological Significance of the Sacrifice of Isaac', *CBQ* 39: 45-75.
Danforth, D.N. (ed.), and W.J. Dignam, C.H. Hendricks and J.V.S. Maeck (assoc. eds.)
 1977   *Obstetrics and Gynecology* (Hagerstown, MD: Harper & Row, 3rd edn).
Datan, N., A. Antonovsky and B. Maoz
 1981   *A Time To Reap: The Middle Age of Women in Five Israeli Subcultures* (Baltimore: Johns Hopkins University Press).
Daube, D.
 1946   'Participle and Imperative in 1 Peter', appended note in Selwyn 1946: 467-88.
 1949   'Rabbinic Methods of Interpretation and Hellenistic Rhetoric', *HUCA* 22: 239-64.
 1956   *The New Testament and Rabbinic Judaism* (London: Athlone Press).
 1972   *Civil Disobedience in Antiquity* (Edinburgh: Edinburgh University Press).
Dautzenberg, G.
 1975   *Urchristliche Prophetie: ihre Erforschung, ihre Voraussetzungen im Judentum und ihre Struktur im ersten Korintherbrief* (Stuttgart: W. Kohl-hammer).
 1989   'Zur Stellung der Frauen in den paulinischen Gemeinden', in Dautzenberg, Merklein and Müller 1989: 182-224

Dautzenberg, G., H. Merklein and K. Müller (eds.)
    1989   *Die Frau im Urchristentum* (Freiburg: Herder).
Davies, G.
    1986   '1 Timothy 2:8-15', in B. Webb (ed.), *Personhood, Sexuality, and Christian Ministry* (Sydney: Moore Theological College): 84-97.
Davies, G.H.
    1973   'Genesis', in C.J. Allen (gen. ed.), *Broadman Bible Commentary*, I (Nashville: Broadman): 101-304.
Davies, S.L.
    1980   *The Revolt of the Widows* (Carbondale, IL: Southern Illinois University Press).
Davies, W.D.
    1965   *Paul and Rabbinic Judaism* (London: SPCK).
    1989   *Torah in the Messianic Age and/or the Age to Come* (*JBL* Monograph Series, 7; Philadelphia: SBL).
Davis, J.J.
    1976   'Some Reflections on Galatians 3:28, Sexual Roles and Biblical Hermeneutics', *ETSJ* 19: 201-208.
Dean-Jones, L.
    1994   *Women's Bodies in Classical Greek Science* (Oxford: Clarendon Press).
De Boer, M.C.
    1980   'Images of Paul in the Post-apostolic Period', *CBQ* 42.3: 359-80.
Delcor, M.
    1971   'Melchizedek from Genesis to the Qumran Texts and the Epistle to the Hebrews', *JSJ* 2: 115-35.
Delitzsch, F.
    1888   *Genesis*, I (ET; Edinburgh: T. & T. Clark).
Delling, G.
    1931   *Paulus' Stellung zu Frau und Ehe* (Stuttgart: W. Kohlhammer).
Denniston, J.D.
    1987   *The Greek Particles* (Oxford: Clarendon Press).
Dewey, J.
    1992   '1 Timothy', in C. Newsom and S. Ringe (eds.), *The Women's Bible Commentary* (London: SPCK): 353-58.
Dibelius, M.
    1953   *An die Kolosser, Epheser, An Philemon* (Tübingen: Mohr Siebeck).
    1961   *Die Formgeschichte des Evangeliums* (Tübingen: Mohr Siebeck, 4th edn).
    1975   *Geschichte der urchristlichen Literatur* (Munich: Chr. Kaiser Verlag).
Dibelius, M., and H. Conzelmann
    1972   *The Pastoral Epistles* (ET; Philadelphia: Fortress Press).
Dibelius, M., and H. Greeven
    1976   *James* (ET; Philadelphia: Fortress Press).
Dillman, D.A.
    1897   *Genesis Critically and Exegetically Expounded*, I (ET; Edinburgh: T. & T. Clark).
Dixon, S.
    1988   *The Roman Mother* (Norman: University of Oklahoma).

1992 *The Roman Family* (Baltimore: Johns Hopkins University Press).
Dodd, C.H.
 1953 *New Testament Studies* (Manchester: Manchester University Press).
 1965 *The Old Testament in the New* (Philadelphia: Fortress Press).
Dods, M.
 1910 *The Expositor's Greek Testament*, IV (London: Hodder & Stoughton).
Donelson, L.R.
 1986 *Pseudepigraphy and Ethical Argument in the Pastoral Epistles* (Tübingen: Mohr Siebeck).
 1988 'The Structure of Ethical Argument in the Pastorals', *BTB* 18: 108-13.
Dowley, T. (ed.)
 1977 *The History of Christianity* (NSW: Anzea).
Driver, S.R.
 1907 *The Book of Genesis* (London: Methuen).
 1951 *The Book of Ezekiel* (ICC; Edinburgh: T. & T. Clark).
Drury, J.
 1973 'The Sower, the Vineyard, and the Place of Allegory in the Interpretation of Mark's Parables', *JTS* 24: 367- 79.
Dumbrell, W.J.
 1977 'The Role of Women: A Reconsideration of the Biblical Evidence', *Interchange* 21: 14-22.
Duncan, G.S.
 1929 *St. Paul's Ephesian Ministry* (London: Hodder & Stoughton).
 1956 'Important Hypotheses Reconsidered VI: Were Paul's Imprisonment Epistles Written from Ephesus?', *ExpTim* March: 163-66.
 1956–57 'Paul's Ministry in Asia: The Last Phase', *NTS* 3: 211-18.
Duncan, J.G.
 1923 'πιστὸς ὁ λόγος', *ExpTim* 35: 141.
Dunn, J.D.G.
 1983 'Discernment of Spirits: A Neglected Gift', in W. Harrington (ed.), *Witness to the Spirit* (Manchester: n.p.): 79-96.
 1988 *Romans 9–16*, XXXVIIIb (Dallas: Word Books).
Easton, B.S.
 1932 'New Testament Ethical Lists', *JBL* 51: 1-12.
 1948 *The Pastoral Epistles* (London: SCM Press).
Eight Translation New Testament
 1974 (Wheaton, IL: Tyndale House).
Ellicott, C.J.
 1864 *The Pastoral Epistles of St. Paul* (London: Longman, Green, Longman, Roberts, & Green, 3rd edn).
Elliott, J.K.
 1992 Review of Fanning 1990, in *NovT* 34.1: 102-104.
Ellis, E.E.
 1957 *Paul's Use of the Old Testament* (Edinburgh: Oliver & Boyd).
 1959 'The Problem of Authorship: First and Second Timothy', *RevExp* 56.4: 343-54.
 1975 'Paul and his Opponents', in J. Neusner (ed.), *Christianity, Judaism and Other Greco-Roman Cults* (Leiden: E.J. Brill): I, 264-98.

1978   *Prophecy and Hermeneutic in Early Christianity* (Grand Rapids: Eerdmans).

1980   'Dating the New Testament', *NTS* 26: 487-502.

1981   'The Silenced Wives of Corinth (1 Cor. 14:34-35)', in E.J. Epp and G.W. Fee (eds.), *New Testament Criticism: Its Significance for Exegesis* (Oxford: Clarendon Press): 213-20.

1986   'Traditions in 1 Corinthians', *NTS* 32: 481-502.

1987   'Traditions in the Pastoral Epistles', in C.A. Evans and W.F. Stinespring (eds.), *Early Jewish and Christian Exegesis* (Atlanta: Scholars Press): 237-53.

Englishman's Hebrew and Chaldee Concordance of the Old Testament

1874   II (London: S. Bagster & Sons, 3rd edn).

Esler, C.C.

1989   'Horace's Old Girls: Evolution of a Topos', in T.M. Falkner and J. de Luce (eds.), *Old Age in Greek and Latin Literature* (Albany: State University of New York Press): 172-82.

Estienne, H. (Stephanus)

1572   *Thesaurus Graecae Lingvae* (Paris).

Etheridge, J. W. (ed.)

1968   *The Targums of Onkelos and Jonathan ben Uzziel on the Pentatueuch with the fragments of the Jerusalem Targum From the Chaldee: Genesis and Exodus* (New York: Ktav).

Evans, M.J.

1983   *Woman in the Bible* (Downers Grove, IL: InterVarsity Press).

Evans, O.E.

1977   'On Revising Dates', *ExpTim* 88: 244-45.

Falconer, R.

1937   *The Pastoral Epistles* (Oxford: Clarendon Press).

1941   '1 Timothy 2:14, 15. Interpretative Notes', *JBL* 60: 375-79.

Fanning, B.M.

1990   *Verbal Aspect in New Testament Greek* (Oxford: Clarendon Press).

Fee, G.W.

1984   *1 and 2 Timothy, Titus* (San Francisco: Harper & Row).

1985   'Reflections on Church Order in the Pastoral Epistles, with Further Reflection on the Hermeneutics of *ad hoc* Documents', *JETS* 28.2: 141-51.

1988   *The First Epistle to the Corinthians* (NICNT; Grand Rapids: Eerdmans).

1994   *God's Empowering Presence: The Holy Spirit in the Letters of Paul* (Peabody, MA: Hendrickson).

Fell, M.

1666   *Womens Speaking Justified and Other 17th Century Writings About Women* (London; repr. 1989, C. Trevett [ed.]; London: Quaker Home Service).

Filson, F.V.

1941   'The Christian Teacher in the First Century', *JBL* 60: 317-28.

Finkelstein, L.

1941   'The Transmission of the Early Rabbinic Traditions', *HUCA* 16: 115-35.

Finley, M.I.
    1962   *The World of Odysseus* (Mitcham, Vic.: Pelican Books).
    1981   'The Elderly in Classical Antiquity', *Greece and Rome* 28: 156-71.
Fiore, B.
    1986   *The Function of Personal Example in the Socratic and Pastoral Epistles* (Rome: Biblical Institute Press).
Fitzer, G.
    1963   *'Das Weib schweige in der Gemeinde'* (Munich: Chr. Kaiser Verlag).
Flanagan, N.M., and E.H. Snyder
    1981   'Did Paul Put Down Women in 1 Cor. 14:34-36?', *BTB* 7: 10-12.
Flint, M.
    1982   'Male and Female Menopause: A Cultural Put On', in A. Voda *et al.* (eds.), *Changing Perspectives on Menopause* (Austin: University of Texas Press): 363-75.
Foakes Jackson, F.J., and K. Lake (eds.)
    1922–42   *The Beginnings of Christianity.* I. *The Acts of the Apostles* (5 vols.; London: Macmillan).
Foerster, W.
    1959   'ΕΥΣΕΒΕΙΑ in den Pastoralbriefen', *NTS* 5: 213-18.
    1977   'νόμος', in *TDNT*, III: 1034-35.
Foh, S.
    1979   *Women and the Word of God* (Phillipsburg, NJ: Presbyterian & Reformed Publishing).
Forbes, C.B.
    1988/89   Unpublished notes from a lecture at Wollongong, NSW.
    1993   'Comments on Dr. John Pryor's Paper'. Summary of unpublished paper, *Society for the Study of Early Christianity Newsletter* 17: 13-14.
    1995   *Prophecy and Inspired Speech in Early Christianity and its Hellenistic Environment* (WUNT; Tübingen: Mohr Siebeck).
Ford, J.M.
    1971   'A Note on Proto-Montanism in the Pastoral Epistles', *NTS* 17: 338-46.
Forestell, J.T.
    1979   *Targumic Traditions and the New Testament.* Annotated bibliography with a New Testament Index (SBL Aramaic Studies, 4; Chico, CA: Scholars Press).
Formanek, R. (ed.).
    1990   *The Meanings of Menopause: Historical, Medical, and Clinical Perspectives* (Hillsdale, NJ: Analytic Press).
Frame, J.E.
    1979   *Epistles of St. Paul to the Thessalonians* (Edinburgh: T. & T. Clark).
France, R.
    1984   'The Church and the Kingdom of God', in D. Carson (ed.), *Biblical Interpretation and the Church* (Nashville: Thomas Nelson): 30-44.
Freedman, R.D.
    1983   'Woman: A Power Equal to Man', *BARev* Jan./Feb.: 56-58.
Friedländer, L.
    1965   *Roman Life and Manners under the Early Empire*, I (ET; London: Routledge & Kegan Paul).

n.d.   *Roman Life and Manners under the Early Empire*, II (ET; London: Rout-
            ledge).

Fung, R.Y.K.
    1987   'Ministry in the New Testament', in D.A. Carson (ed.), *The Church in the
            Bible and the World* (Exeter: Paternoster Press): 180-212.

Furnish, V.P.
    1968   *Theology and Ethics in Paul* (Nashville: Abingdon Press).
    1970   'Development in Paul's Thought', *JAAR* 38: 289-303.

Fussell, G.E.
    1965   *Farming Technique from Prehistoric to Modern Times* (London: Per-
            gamon Press).

Gaebelein, F.E. (ed.)
    1976–90 *The Expositor's Bible Commentary* (12 vols.; Grand Rapids: Zondervan).

Gardner, A.E.
    1990   'Genesis 2:4b-3: A Mythological Paradigm of Sexual Equality or of the
            Religious History of Pre-exilic Israel?', *SJT* 43: 1-18.

Garnsey, P.
    1988   *Famine and Food Supply in the Graeco-Roman World* (Cambridge: Cam-
            bridge University Press).

Giblin, C.H.
    1971   ' "The Things of God" in the Question Concerning Tribute to Caesar (Lk
            20:25; Mk 12:17; Mt 22:21)', *CBQ* 33: 510-27.

Gildersleeve, B.L.
    1908   'Stahl's Syntax of the Greek Verb', *AJP* 29.4: 389-409.

Giles, K.
    1977   *Women and their Ministry* (E. Malvern, Vic.: Dove).
    1983   'New Testament Patterns of Ministry', *Interchange* 31: 43-60.
    1985   *Created Woman* (Canberra: Acorn Press).
    1989   *Patterns of Ministry among the First Christians* (Melbourne: Collins
            Dove).

Goodenough, E.R.
    1953–1968 *Jewish Symbols in the Graeco-Roman Period*, XI (New York: Pantheon).

Goodman, M.
    1990   'The Biomedical Study of Menopause', in Formanek 1990: 135-39.

Goodwin, W.W.
    1879   *A Greek Grammar* (repr. 1974; London: Macmillan).
    1889   *Syntax of the Moods and Tenses of the Greek Verb* (repr. 1965; London:
            Macmillan).

Goppelt, L.
    1972   'Prinzipien neutestamentlicher Sozialethik nach dem 1. Petrusbrief', in
            H. Baltensweiler and B. Reicke (eds.), *Neues Testament und Geschichte:
            Historisches Geschehen und Deutung im Neuen Testament, Oscar Cull-
            man zum 70. Geburtstag* (Tübingen: J.C.B. Mohr): 285-96.
    1973   'Jesus und die "Haustafel" Tradition', in P. Hoffmann, N. Brox and
            W. Pesch (eds.), *Orientierung an Jesus. Für J. Schmid* (Freiburg: Her-
            der): 93-106.
    1982   *Theology of the New Testament*, II (ET; Grand Rapids: Eerdmans).
    1993   *A Commentary on 1 Peter* (ET; Grand Rapids: Eerdmans).

Gordon, A.J.
1894   'The Ministry of Woman', *Missionary Review of the World* 7: 910-21.
Gordon, T.D.
1995   'A Certain Kind of Letter: The Genre of 1 Timothy', in Köstenberger,
            Schreiner and Baldwin 1995: 53-63.
Gore, R.
1984   'The Dead Do Tell Tales at Vesuvius', *National Geographic* 165.5: 557-
            613.
Goulder, M.D.
1992   'Exegesis of Genesis 1-3 in the New Testament', *JJS* 43.2: 226-29.
Graham, H.H., and R.M. Grant (trans. and intro.)
1978   'The Letter of Clement to Corinth (1 Clement)', in Sparks 1978: 15-54.
Grant, M.
1990   *The Visible Past: Greek and Roman History from Archaelogy 1960–90*
            (London: Weidenfeld & Nicolson).
Grant, R.M.
1978   Review of J.A.T. Robinson 1976, in *JBL* 97: 294-96.
Gray, G.B.
1976   *A Critical and Exegetical Commentary on Numbers* (Edinburgh: T. & T.
            Clark).
Greene, J.G.
1984   *The Social and Psychological Origins of the Climacteric Syndrome*
            (England: Gower).
Griffin, J.
1985   *Latin Poets and Roman Life* (London: Gerald Duckworth).
Griffith-Thomas, W.H.
1946   *Genesis* (repr. 1973; Grand Rapids: Eerdmans).
Grimke, S.M.
1838   *Letters on the Equality of the Sexes and the Condition of Woman* (New
            York: Burt Franklin; repr. 1970; New York: Lenox Hill).
Grisbrooke, W.J.
1990   *The Liturgical Portions of the Apostolic Constitutions* (Bramcote, Not-
            tingham: Grove).
Gritz, S.H.
1991   *Paul, Women Teachers, and the Mother Goddess at Ephesus* (Lanham,
            MD: University Press of America).
Grossfeld, B. (ed.)
1988   'Targum Onqelos to Genesis', in *The Aramaic Bible*, VI (Wilmington,
            DE: Michael Glazier).
Grudem, W.
1982   *The Gift of Prophecy in 1 Corinthians* (Lanham, MD: University Press of
            America).
1985   'Does *kephalé* ("head") Mean "Source" or "Authority Over" in Greek
            Literature? A Survey of 2,336 Examples', in Knight 1985: 49-80.
1987   'Prophecy—Yes, But Teaching—No: Paul's Consistent Advocacy of
            Women's Participation without Governing Authority', *JETS* 30.1: 11-23.
1991   'The Meaning of Kephale ("Head"): A Response to Recent Studies', in
            Piper and Grudem (eds.), 1991: 425-68, 534-41.

Guite, H.F.
    1989–90   'Tense, Mood, and Aspect', *ExpTim* 101: 346-47.
Gunther, J.J.
    1973   *St. Paul's Opponents and their Background* (Leiden: E.J. Brill).
Gutbrod, W.
    1967   'νόμος', in *TDNT*, IV: 1059-83.
Guthrie, D.
    1970   *New Testament Introduction* (London: Tyndale Press).
    1990   *The Pastoral Epistles* (Leicester: Inter-Varsity Press, 2nd edn).
Habel, N.
    1985   *The Book of Job* (Philadelphia: Westminster Press).
Haenchen, E.
    1971   *The Acts of the Apostles* (trans. from the 14th [1965] German edn. by B. Noble, G. Shinn and H. Anderson; rev. R. McL. Wilson; Oxford: Basil Blackwell).
Hallowell, A. Davis
    1884   *James and Lucretia Mott: Life and Letters* (Boston: Houghton Mifflin).
Hanson, A.T.
    1966   *The Pastoral Letters* (Cambridge: Cambridge University Press).
    1968   *Studies in the Pastoral Epistles* (London: SPCK).
    1974   *Studies in Paul's Technique and Theology* (London: SPCK).
    1976   'Back to AD 70', *Times Literary Supplement*, 8 Oct.: 1285.
    1981   'The Domestication of Paul: A Study in the Development of Early Christian Theology', *BJRL* 63: 402-18.
    1982   *The Pastoral Epistles* (New Century Bible Commentary; Grand Rapids: Eerdmans).
    1988   'Hebrews', in D.A. Carson and H.G.M. Williamson (eds.), *It is Written: Scripture Citing Scripture. Essays in Honour of B. Lindars* (Cambridge: Cambridge University Press): 292-302.
    1989   'Paul Wrote 2 Timothy!', *ExpTim* 101.1: 30-31.
Hanson, R.P.C.
    1970   'The Bible in the Early Church', in Ackroyd and Evans 1970: I, 412-53.
Hardesty, N.A.
    1984   *Women Called to Witness: Evangelical Feminism in the 19th Century* (Nashville: Abingdon Press).
Hardy, E.R.
    1978   '*Redating the New Testament* by John A.T. Robinson', *CH* 47: 215.
Harris, T.J.
    1987   'The Buck Stops Where? Authority in the Early Church and Current Debate on Women's Ministry', *Interchange* 41: 21-33.
    1990   'Why Did Paul Mention Eve's Deception? A Critique of P.W. Barnett's Interpretation of 1 Timothy 2', *EvQ* 62: 335-52.
Harrison, P.N.
    1921   *The Problem of the Pastoral Epistles* (London: Humphrey Milford, Oxford University Press).
    1948   Review of Spicq 1947, *JTS* 49: 204-10.
    1955   'The Authorship of the Pastoral Epistles', *ExpTim* 67.3: 77-81.

Hart, M.E.
    1975   'Speaking in Tongues and Prophecy as Understood by Paul and at
                Corinth, with Reference to Early Christian Usage' (unpublished PhD dis-
                sertation, University of Durham).
Hartill, J.E.
    1965   *Biblical Hermeneutics* (Grand Rapids: Zondervan).
Hatch, E.
    1898   'Pastoral Epistles', in *Encyclopaedia Britannica*, XVIII (Edinburgh:
                Black): 348-51.
Hatch, E., and H.A. Redpath
    1954   *A Concordance to the Septuagint* and the Other Greek Versions of the
                Old Testament (including the Apocryphal Books) (Graz: Akademie Ver-
                lag; repr. 1964; Oxford: Clarendon Press).
Hauck, F.
    1967   'μαργαρίτης', in *TDNT*, IV: 472-73.
Hay, D.M.
    1973   *Glory at The Right Hand: Ps. 110 in Early Christianity* (Nashville:
                Abingdon Press).
Haykin, M.A.G.
    1985   'The Fading Vision?', *EvQ* 57.4: 291-305.
Hayman, A.P.
    1984   'The Fall, Freewill and Human Responsibility in Rabbinic Judaism', *SJT*
                37: 13-22.
Hays, R.B.
    1988   Review of Koch 1986, *JBL* 107.2: 331-33.
Hayter, M.
    1987   *The New Eve in Christ* (London: SPCK).
Heater, H.
    1982   *A Septuagint Translation Technique in the Book of Job* (CBQMS, 11;
                Washington, DC: the Catholic Biblical Association of America).
Hederich, B.
    1803   *Graecum Lexicon Manuale* (London: Wilks & Taylor).
Heinemann, J.
    1971   'Amidah', in *EncJud*, II: 838-45.
Heiser, C.B.
    1981   *Seed to Civilization* (San Francisco: Freeman).
Hemer, C.J.
    1989   *The Book of Acts in the Setting of Hellenistic History* (Tübingen: Mohr
                Siebeck).
Henderson, J.
    1987   'Older Women in Attic Old Comedy', *TAPA* 117: 105-29.
Hendriksen, W.
    1955   *1 and 2 Thessalonians; 1 and 2 Timothy and Titus* (repr. 1983, Edinburgh:
                Banner of Truth Trust).
    1973   *The Gospel of Matthew* (Edinburgh: Banner of Truth Trust).
    1976   *Ephesians* (Edinburgh: Banner of Truth Trust).
Héring, J.
    1962   *The First Epistle of St. Paul to the Corinthians* (London: Epworth Press).

Higgins, J.M.
    1976   'The Myth of Eve: The Temptress', *JAAR* 44: 639-47.
Hill, C.C.
    1992   *Hellenists and Hebrews* (Minneapolis: Augsburg–Fortress).
Hillard, T.
    1989   'Republican Politics, Women, and the Evidence', *Helios* 16.2: 165-82.
Hinson, G.G.
    1990   Review of Prior 1989, *RevExp* 87: 643-44.
Hitchcock, F.R.M.
    1927–28   'Latinity in the Pastorals', *ExpTim* 39: 347-52.
    1929   'Tests for the Pastorals', *JTS* 30: 272-79.
    1940   'Philo and the Pastoral Epistles', *Hermathena* 56: 113-35.
Hodge, C.
    1857   *An Exposition of the First Epistle to the Corinthians* (London: J. Nisbet).
Holtz, G.
    1965   *Die Pastoralbriefe* (Berlin: Evangelische Verlagsanstalt).
Holtzmann, H.J.
    1892   *Lehrbuch der historisch-kritischen Einleitung in das Neue Testament* (Freiburg: Mohr Siebeck).
Hommes, N.J.
    1969   'Let Women be Silent in the Church: A Message Concerning the Worship Service', *Calvin Theological Journal* 4: 5-22.
Hooker, M.
    1963–64   'Authority on her Head: An Examinaton of 1 Cor.xi,10', *NTS* 10: 410-16.
Horsley, G.H.R.
    1982–89   *New Documents Illustrating Early Christianity* (5 vols.; North Ryde, NSW: Macquarie University Ancient History Documentary Research Centre).
    1992a   'The Inscriptions of Ephesos and the New Testament', *NovT* 34.2: 105-68.
    1992b   'The Mysteries of Artemis Ephesia in Pisidia: A New Inscribed Relief', *Anatolian Studies* 42: 119-50.
Horsley, G.H.R., and John A.L. Lee
    1997   'A Lexicon of the New Testament with Documentary Parallels: Some Interim Entries, 1', *FN* 10: 55-84.
Hort, F.J.A.
    1898   *The First Epistle of Peter I.1–II.17* (New York: Macmillan).
    1909   *The Epistle of St. James* (London: Macmillan).
Houlden, J.L.
    1976   *The Pastoral Epistles* (London: Penguin Books).
    1990a   Review of Prior 1989, *JTS* 41: 206-207.
    1990b   'Christian Existence in the Pastorals', *ExpTim* 101.10: 312-13.
Howard, J.K.
    1983   'Neither Male nor Female: An Examination of the Status of Women in the New Testament', *EvQ* 55: 31-42.
Howe, E.M.
    1979   'The Positive Case for the Ordination of Women', in K. Kantzer and S. Gundry (eds.), *Perspectives on Evangelical Theology: Papers from the*

Thirtieth Annual Meeting of the ETS (Grand Rapids: Baker Book House): 267-76.

Hugenberger, G.P.
1992 'Women in Church Office: Hermeneutics or Exegesis? A Survey of Approaches to 1 Tim. 2:8-15', *JETS* 35: 341-60.

Hull, G.G. (ed.)
1987 *Equal to Serve* (Old Tappan, NJ: Revell).

Hull, S.D.
1987 'Exegetical Difficulties in the "Hard Passages" ', in G.G. Hull 1987: 251-66.

Humphreys, A.E.
1901 *The Epistles to Timothy and Titus* (Cambridge: Cambridge University Press).

Hunter, A.M.
1961 *Paul and his Predecessors* (London: SCM Press).

Hurd, J.C.
1965 *The Origin of 1 Corinthians* (London: SPCK; New York: Seabury).

Hurley, J.B.
1973a 'Man and Woman in 1 Corinthians: Some Exegetical Studies in Pauline Theology and Ethics' (unpublished PhD dissertation, Cambridge University).
1973b 'Did Paul Require Veils or the Silence of Women? A Consideration of 1 Cor. 11:2-16 and 1 Cor. 14:33b-36', *WTJ* 35: 190-220.
1981 *Man and Woman in Biblical Perspective* (Leicester: Inter-Varsity Press).

Huther, J.E.
1866 *Handbuch über die Briefe an Timotheus und Titus* (Göttingen: Vandenhoeck & Ruprecht).

Jacobs, L.
1971 'Women', in *EncJud*, XVI: 623-28.

Jannaris, A.N.
1968 *An Historical Greek Grammar* (Hildersheim: Georg Olms, repr.).

Jebb, S.
1970 'A Suggested Interpretation of 1 Ti. 2:15', *ExpTim* 81: 221-22.

Jenkins, C.
1909 'Origen on 1 Corinthians', *JTS* 10: 42.

Jeremias, J.
1963 *Die Briefe an Timotheus und Titus* (Göttingen: Vandenhoeck & Ruprecht).
1969 *Jerusalem in the Time of Jesus* (trans. F.H. and C.H. Cave; London: SCM Press).
1977 'Μωυσῆς', in *TDNT*, IV: 848-53.

Jervell, J.
1960 *Imago Dei* (Göttingen: Vandenhoeck & Ruprecht).

Jervis, L.A.
1995 '1 Corinthians 14:34-35: A Reconsideration of Paul's Limitation of the Free Speech of Some Corinthian Women', *JSNT* 58: 51-74.

Jewett, R.
1979 'The Sexual Liberation of the Apostle Paul', *JAAR* 47.1: 55-87.

Johnson, A.F.
1986   'Response' (to Liefeld 1986), in Mickelson (ed.) 1986: 154-60.
Johnson, M.D.
1985   'Life of Adam and Eve', in *OTP*, II: 249-56.
Johnston, R.K.
1978   'The Role of Women in the Church and Home: An Evangelical Testcase in Hermeneutics', in W. Ward Gasque and W.S. Lasor (eds.), *Scripture, Tradition, and Interpretation: Essays Presented to E.F. Harrison* (Grand Rapids: Eerdmans): 234-59.
1986   'Biblical Authority and Interpretation: The Test Case of Women's Role in the Church and Home Updated', in Mickelsen 1986: 30-41.
Judge, E.A.
1974   'St. Paul as a Radical Critic of Society', *Interchange* 16: 191-203.
1985   'The Churches and the Teaching of Paul on Women' (unpublished paper presented at Women in the World of the New Testament Seminar, Macquarie University, 15–16 Mar.).
1992   'Reading the New Testament in Late Antiquity'. Summary of unpublished paper in *Society for the Study of Early Christianity Newsletter* 16, 3–5 Oct.
Kähler, E.
1959   'Zur "Unterordnung" der Frau im Neuen Testament', *Zeitschrift für Evangelische Ethik* 3: 1-13.
1960   *Die Frau in den paulinischen Briefen: unter besonderer Berücksichtigung des Begriffes der Unterordnung* (Zürich: Gotthelf).
Kaibel, G.
1965   *Epigrammata Graeca* (repr.; Hildersheim: Georg Olms).
Kaiser, W.C.
1976   'Paul, Women and the Church', *Worldwide Challenge* 3: 9-12.
1979   *Towards an Old Testament Theology* (Grand Rapids: Zondervan).
Kajanto, I.
1968   *On the Problem of the Average Duration of Life in the Roman Empire* (Helsinki: Suomalainen Tiedeakatemia).
Kamlah, E.
1970   '῾ΥΠΟΤΑΣΣΕΣΘΑΙ in den neutestamentlichen "Haustafeln" ', *Verborum Veritas, Festschrift für G. Stählin* (Wuppertal: Brockhaus): 237-43.
Kanjuparambil, P.
1983   'Imperatival Participles in Rom.12:9-21', *JBL* 102: 285-88.
Karris, R.J.
1973   'The Background and Significance of the Polemic of the Pastoral Epistles', *JBL* 92: 549-64.
1977   'Women in the Pauline Assembly: To Prophesy, but Not to Speak?', in L. and A. Swidler (eds.), *Women Priests: A Catholic commentary on the Vatican Declaration* (New York: Paulist Press): 205-208.
Käsemann, E.
1968   *Essays on New Testament Themes* (London: SCM Press).
Kee, H.C.
1995   'Defining the First-century CE Synagogue: Problems and Progress', *NTS* 41.4: 481-500.

Keener, C.S.
1992   *Paul, Women and Wives: Marriage and Women's Ministry in the Letters of Paul* (Peabody, MA: Hendrickson).
Keep, P.A. van
1983   'The Climacteric in Different Cultural Contexts', in H. and B. van Herendael, F.E. Riphagen, L. Goessens and H. van der Pas (eds.), *The Climacteric: An Update*. Proceedings of the fourth Jan Palfijn Symposium, European Conference on the Menopause, Antwerp, Sept. 1–2: 11-18.
Keil, C.F., and F. Delitzsch
1968   *Biblical Commentary on the Old Testament* (trans. J. Martin; Grand Rapids: Eerdmans).
Kelly, J.N.D.
1972   *The Pastoral Epistles* (London: A. & C. Black).
Kenny, A.
1986   *A Stylometric Study of the New Testament* (Oxford: Clarendon Press).
Kepple, R.J.
1976–77   'An Analysis of Antiochene Exegesis of Galatians 4:24-26', *WTJ* 39: 239-49.
Key, D.
1984   'Women in the Church', in Lees 1984: 141-52.
Kidd, R.
1990   *Wealth and Benificence in the Pastoral Epistles* (SBLDS, 122; Atlanta: Scholars Press).
Kidner, D.
1973   *Genesis* (TOTC; London: Tyndale Press).
Klein, M.L. (ed.)
1980   *Fragment-Targums of the Pentateuch*, II (Rome: Biblical Institute).
Klein, W.C.
1962   'The Church and its Prophets', *ATR* 44.1: 1-17.
Kline, M.
1967   'Genesis', in D. Guthrie, J.A. Motyer, A.M. Stibbs and D.J. Wiseman (eds.), *The New Bible Commentary Revised* (London: Inter-Varsity Press): 79-114.
Knight, G.W.
1968   *The Faithful Sayings in the Pastoral Letters* (Kampen: Kok).
1975   'The New Testament Teaching on the Role Relationship of Male and Female with Special Reference to the Teaching/Ruling Functions in the Church', *JTS* 18.2: 81-91.
1980   *The New Testament Teaching on the Role Relationship of Men and Women* (Grand Rapids: Baker Book House).
1984   'ΑΥΘΕΝΤΕΩ in Reference to Women in 1 Tim. 2:12', *NTS* 30: 143-57.
1985   *The Role Relationship of Men and Women: New Testament Teaching* (Chicago: Moody Press).
1992   *The Pastoral Epistles* (Grand Rapids: Eerdmans).
Knobel, A.
1852   *Genesis* (Leipzig: Weidmann).
Knoch, O.
1988   *1. und 2. Timotheusbrief, Titusbriefe* (Würzburg: Echter Verlag).

Knox, J.
    1558   *The First Blast of the Trumpet Against the Monstrous Regiment of Women* (repr. 1972, New York: Da Capo).

Koch, D.-A.
    1986   *Die Schrift als Zeuge des Evangeliums* (Tübingen: Mohr Siebeck).

Koester, H.
    1982   *History and Literature of Early Christianity*, II (Philadelphia: Fortress Press).

Köhler, L.
    1953   *Hebrew Man* (trans. J.C.B. Mohr [Siebeck]; London: SCM Press).

Koivisto, R.A.
    1977   'Stephen's Speech: A Case Study in Rhetoric and Biblical Inerrancy', *JETS* 20: 353-64.

Kono, S., Y. Sunagawa, H. Higa and H. Sunagawa
    1990   'Age of Menopause in Japanese Women: Trends and Recent Changes', *Maturitas* 12: 43-49.

Köstenberger, A.J.
    1994   'Gender Passages in the NT: Hermeneutical Fallacies Critiqued', *WTJ* 56: 259-83.
    1995   'Syntactical Background Studies to 1 Timothy 2:12 in the New Testament and Extrabiblical Greek Literature', in Porter and Carson 1995: 156-79.

Köstenberger A.J., T.R. Schreiner and H.S. Baldwin (eds.)
    1995   *Women in the Church: A Fresh Analysis of 1 Timothy 2:9-15* (Grand Rapids: Baker Book House).

Kraft, R.A. (trans. and intro.)
    1978   'The Didache', in Sparks 1978: 305-19.

Kroeger, C.
    1979   'Ancient Heresies and a Strange Greek Verb', *Reformed Journal* 29: 12-15.
    1986   '1 Timothy 2:12: A Classicist's View', in Mickelsen 1986: 225-44.
    1987a   'The Apostle Paul and the Greco-Roman Cults of Women', *JETS* 30.1: 25-38.
    1987b   'The Classical Concept of Head as "Source" ', in G.G. Hull 1987: 267-83.

Kroeger, C., and R. Kroeger
    1978a   'An Inquiry into Evidence of Maenadism in the Corinthian Congregation' (SBLSP, 2; Missoula, MT: Scholars Press).
    1978b   'Pandemonium and Silence at Corinth', *Reformed Journal* 28: 6-11.
    1992   *I Suffer not a Woman: Rethinking 1 Timothy 2:11-15 in Light of Ancient Evidence* (Grand Rapids: Baker Book House).

Küchler, M.
    1986   *Schweigen, Schmuck und Schleier: Drei neutestamentliche Vorschriften zur Verdrängung der Frauen auf dem Hintergrund einer Frauenfeind-lichen Exegese des Alten Testaments im antiken Judentum* (Göttingen: Vandenhoeck & Ruprecht).

Kugel, J.L., and R.A. Greer
    1986   *Early Biblical Interpretation* (Philadelphia: Westminster Press).

Kümmel, W.G.
    1965   *Introduction to the New Testament* (ET; London: SCM Press).

Küng, H.
 1963   *The Living Church: Reflections on the Second Vatican Council* (ET; London: Sheed & Ward).
Lake, K., and S. Lake
 1938   *Introduction to the New Testament* (London: Christophers).
Lambert, C.
 1995   'Diet Can Cool Flushes', *Sunday Herald Sun*, Melbourne, 3 Sept.
Lampe, P.
 1985   'Iunia/Iunias: Sklavenherkunft im Kreise der vorpaulinischen Apostel (Röm 16:7)', *Zeitschrift für die neutestamentliche Wissenschaft und die Kunde der älteren Kirche* 76: 132-34.
Lane, W.L.
 1964–65   '1 Tim. IV.1-3: An Early Instance of Over-Realised Eschatology?', *NTS* 11: 164-67.
Lane Fox, R.
 1986   *Pagans and Christians* (Ringwood, Vic.: Penguin Books).
Leadbetter, B.
 1992   'Where Did Constantine's Idea of Christ Come From?'. Summary of unpublished paper, *Society for the Study of Early Christianity Newsletter* 15: 10-11.
Leaney, A.R.C.
 1960   *The Epistles to Timothy, Titus and Philemon* (London: SCM Press).
Lee, J.A.L.
 1993   'The Continuing Challenge of New Testament Lexicography' (unpublished paper presented at the Ancient History in a Modern University Conference at Macquarie University, NSW, July).
 1997   'Hebrews 5:14 and ῞ΕΞΙΣ: a History of Misunderstanding', *NovT* 39.2: 151-76.
Lees, S. (ed.)
 1984   *The Role of Women* (Leicester: Inter-Varsity Press).
Lefkowitz, M.R., and M.B. Fant
 1982   *Women's Life in Greece and Rome: A Source Book in Translation* (London: Gerald Duckworth).
Legg, J.D.
 1968   'Our Brother Timothy: A Suggested Solution to the Problem of the Authorship of the Epistle to the Hebrews', *EvQ* 40: 220-23.
Leipoldt, J.
 1953   *Die Frau in der antiken Welt und im Urchristentum* (Gütersloh: Gerd Mohn).
Letham, R.
 1990   'The Man–Woman Debate: Theological Comment', *WTJ* 52: 65-78.
Leupold, H.C.
 1970   *Exposition of Genesis*, I (Grand Rapids: Baker Book House).
Levison, J.R.
 1985   'Is Eve to Blame? A Contextual Analysis of Sirach 25:24', *CBQ* 47: 617-23.
 1988   *Portraits of Adam in Early Judaism: From Sirach To 2 Baruch* (JSPSup, 1; Sheffield: Sheffield Academic Press).

1989 'The Exoneration of Eve in the Apocalypse of Moses 15–20', *Journal for the Study of Judaism* 20.2: 135-50.

Liddon, H.P.
1897 *Explanatory Analysis of St. Paul's First Epistle to Timothy* (London: Longmans, Green).

Liefeld, W.L.
1986 'Women, Submission and Ministry in 1 Corinthians', and 'Response' (to Kroeger 1986), in Mickelsen 1986: 134-54, 244-48.
1987 'Women and the Nature of Ministry', *JETS* 30.1: 49-61.

Lightfoot, D.
1975 *Natural Logic and the Greek Moods: The Nature of the Subjunctive and Optative in Classical Greek* (The Hague: Mouton).

Lightfoot, J.B.
1903 *Saint Paul's Epistle to the Phillipians* (London: Macmillan).
1905 *Saint Paul's Epistle to the Galatians* (London: Macmillan).

Lightfoot, N.R.
1976 'The Role of Women in Religious Services', *ResQ* 19.3: 129-36.

Lightman, M., and W. Zeisel
1977 'Univira: An Example of Continuity and Change in Roman Society', *CH* 46: 19-32.

Lindars, B.
1991 *The Theology of the Letter to the Hebrews* (Cambridge: Cambridge University Press).

Lindboe, I.M.
1990 *Women in the New Testament: A Select Bibliography* (Bibliography Series, 1; Oslo: University of Oslo, Faculty of Theology).

Lindsell, H.
1976 'Egalitarianism and Scriptural Infallibility', *Christianity Today*, March: 45-46.

Lips, H. von
1979 *Glaube-Gemeinde-Amt* (Göttingen: Vandenhoeck & Ruprecht).

Llewelyn, S.R. (with the collaboration of R.A. Kearsley)
1992 *New Documents Illustrating Early Christianity*, VI (North Ryde, NSW: Macquarie University Ancient History Documentary Research Centre).

Lloyd, G.
1984 *The Man of Reason: 'Male' and 'Female' in Western Philosophy* (London: Methuen).

Lock, W.
1924 *The Pastoral Epistles* (repr. 1978, Edinburgh: T. & T. Clark).

Locke, J.
1705–1707 *A Paraphrase and Notes on the Epistles of St. Paul to the Galatians, 1 and 2 Corinthians, Romans, Ephesians*, I (ed. A.W. Wainwright; Oxford: Clarendon Press).

Longenecker, R.
1970 *The Christology of Early Jewish Christianity* (London: SCM Press).
1975a 'Literary Criteria in Life of Jesus Research: An Evaluation and Proposal', in G.F. Hawthorne (ed.), *Current Issues in Biblical and Patristic Interpretation* (Grand Rapids: Eerdmans): 217-29.

1975b   *Biblical Exegesis in the Apostolic Period* (Grand Rapids: Eerdmans).
1978   'The Melchizedek Argument of Hebrews: A Study in the Development and Circumstantial Expression of New Testament Thought', in R.A. Guelich (ed.), *Unity and Diversity in New Testament Theology: Essays in Honor of George E. Ladd* (Grand Rapids: Eerdmans): 161-85.
1981   'The Acts of the Apostles', in Gaebelein 1976–90: IX, 205-573.
1986   'Authority, Hierarchy and Leadership Patterns in the Bible', in Mickelsen (1986: 66-85.

Louw, J.P.
1959   'On Greek Prohibitions', *Acta Classica* 2: 43-57.

Louw, J.P., and E.A. Nida
1988   *Greek–English Lexicon of the New Testament based on Semantic Domains* (New York: United Bible Societies).

Luther, M.
1527–28   *Works*. XXVIII. *Lectures on 1 Timothy* (ed. H.C. Oswald; St. Louis: Concordia).
1535–36   *Works*. I. *Lectures on Genesis chs. 1–5* (ed. J. Pelikan; St. Louis: Concordia).

MacDonald, D.R.
1979   'Virgins, Widows, and Paul in Second Century Asia Minor' (SBLSP, 1; Missoula, MT: Scholars Press): 169-84.
1980   'A Conjectural Emendation of 1 Cor. 15:31-32, or "The Case of the Misplaced Lion Fight" ', *HTR* 93: 266-67.
1983   *The Legend and the Apostle* (Philadelphia: Westminster Press).

MacDonald, M.Y.
1988   *The Pauline Churches* (Cambridge: Cambridge University Press).

Mackay, E.V., N.A. Beischer, L.W. Cox and C. Wood
1983   *Illustrated Textbook of Gynaecology* (Sydney: W.B. Saunders).

MacMullen, R.
1980   'Women in Public in the Roman Empire', *Historia* 29.2: 208-18.

Macquarie Dictionary
1985   (Dee Why, NSW: Macquarie Library).

Malherbe, A.J.
1983   *Social Aspects of Early Christianity* (Philadelphia: Fortress Press).
1984   ' "In Season and out of Season": 2 Timothy 4:2', *JBL* 103.2: 235-43.

Malina, B.J.
1969   'Some Observations On the Origin of Sin in Judaism and St. Paul', *CBQ* 31: 18-34.
1983   *The New Testament World: Insights from Cultural Anthropology* (London: SCM Press).

Mandilaras, B.G.
1972   *Studies in the Greek Language* (Athens: n.p.).
1973   *The Verb in the Greek Non-Literary Papyri* (Athens: Hellenic Ministry of Culture and Sciences).

Maoz, B., N. Dowty, A. Antonovsky and H. Wijsenbeek
1970   'Female Attitudes to Menopause', *Social Psychiatry* 5.1: 35-40.

Mare, W.H.
    1981   '1 Corinthians', in Gaebelein 1976–1990: X, 173-297.

Marshall, I.H.
    1973   'Palestinian and Hellenistic Christianity: Some Critical Comments', *NTS* 19: 271-87.
    1984   'The Role of Women in the Church', in Lees (ed.) 1984: 177-97.
    1991   *1 Peter* (Downers Grove, IL: InterVarsity Press).

Martin, R.A.
    1965   'The Earliest Messianic Interpretation of Genesis 3:15', *JBL* 84: 425-27.

Martin, R.P.
    1984   *The Spirit and the Congregation: Studies in 1 Corinthians 12–15* (Grand Rapids: Eerdmans).

Martin, W.J.
    1970   '1 Cor.11:2-16: An Interpretation', in W.W. Gasque and R.P. Martin (eds.), *Apostolic History and the Gospel, Biblical and Historical Essays Presented to F.F. Bruce on his 60th Birthday* (Grand Rapids: Eerdmans): 231-41.

Matthiae, A.
    1829   *A Copious Greek Grammar*, II (trans. E.V. Blomfield; London: John Murray, 4th edn).

Maurer, C
    1972   'παρατίθημι', in *TDNT*, VIII: 162-64.

McEleney, N.J.
    1974   'The Vice Lists of the Pastoral Epistles', *CBQ* 36: 203-19.

McKay, A.G.
    1975   *Houses, Villas and Palaces in the Roman World* (New York: Cornell University Press).

McKay, K.L.
    1965   'The Use of the Ancient Greek Perfect down to the Second Century A.D.', *Institute of Classical Studies Bulletin* 12: 1-21.
    1972   'Syntax in Exegesis', *TynBul* 23: 39-57.
    1974   'Further Remarks on the "Historical" Present and Other Phenomena', *Foundations of Language* 11: 247-51.
    1977   *Greek Grammar for Students: A Concise Grammar of Classical Attic with Special Reference to Aspect in the Verb* (Canberra: Australian National University Department of Classics).
    1981   'On the Perfect and Other Aspects in New Testament Greek', *NovT* 23.4: 289-329.
    1982   'The Latin Verb: Basic Syntax' (Canberra: unpublished).
    1985   'Aspect in Imperatival Constructions in the New Testament Greek', *NovT* 27.3: 201-26.
    1992   'Time and Aspect in New Testament Greek', *NovT* 34.3: 209-28.
    1994   *A New Syntax of the Verb in New Testament Greek* (New York: Peter Lang).

McRay, J.
    1963   'The Authorship of the Pastoral Epistles: A Consideration of Certain Adverse Arguments to Pauline Authorship', *ResQ* 7: 2-18.

Meade, D.G.

    1987   *Pseudonymity and Canon* (Grand Rapids: Eerdmans).

Mealand, D.L.

    1988   'Computers in New Testament Research: An Interim Report', *JSNT* 33: 97-115.

    1989   'Positional Stylometry Reassessed: Testing a Seven Epistle Theory of Pauline Authorship', *NTS* 35: 266-86.

Meecham, H.G.

    1946-47   'The Use of the Participle for the Imperative in the New Testament', *ExpTim* 58: 207-208.

Meeks, W.A.

    1973   'The Image of the Androgyne: Some Uses of a Symbol in Earliest Christianity', *HR* 13: 165-208.

    1983   *The First Urban Christians* (New Haven: Yale University Press).

Meinertz, M.

    1931   *Die Pastoralbriefe des Heiligen Paulus* (Bonn: Peter Hanstein).

Mercadante, L.A.

    1978   *From Hierarchy to Equality* (Vancouver: GMH Books).

Merkel, H.

    1991   *Die Pastoralbriefe* (Göttingen: Vandenhoeck & Ruprecht).

Metzger, B.M.

    1951   'The Formulas Introducing Quotations of Scripture in the NT and the Mishnah', *JBL* 70: 297-307.

    1958-59   'A Reconsideration of Certain Arguments against the Pauline Authorship of the Pastoral Epistles', *ExpTim* 70: 91-94.

    1968-69   'Recent Contributions to the Understanding of Hebrews', *ExpTim* 80: 260-64.

    1975   *A Textual Commentary on the Greek New Testament* (London: United Bible Societies).

    1981   *The Text of the New Testament: Its Transmission, Corruption and Restoration* (Oxford: Clarendon Press, 2nd edn).

Michaelis, W.

    1930   'Pastoralbriefe und Gefangenschaftsbriefe', in D.O. Schmidt (ed.) *Paulusstudien* (1st Series; Gütersloh: C. Bertelsmann), Part 6: 102-59.

Michaelson, S., and A.Q. Morton

    1971-72   ' "Last Words": A Test of Authorship for Greek Writers', *NTS* 18: 192-208.

Michel, O.

    1966   *Der Brief an die Hebräer* (Göttingen: Vandenhoeck & Ruprecht).

Mickelsen, A. (ed.)

    1986   *Women, Authority and the Bible* (Downers Grove, IL: InterVarsity Press).

    1987   'Does Order of Creation, Redemption, and Climax Demand Female Supremacy? (A Satire)', in G.G. Hull 1987: 245-50.

Mills, H.

    1984   'Greek Clothing Regulations: Sacred and Profane?', *ZPE* 55: 255-65.

Milton, J.

    1667   *Paradise Lost* (repr. 1968, Menston, UK: The Scolar Press).

Mitchell, M.
    1989   'Concerning ΠΕΡΙ ΔΕ in 1 Corinthians', *NovT* 31.3: 229-56.

Moffatt, J.
    1941   *The First Epistle to the Corinthians* (London: Hodder & Stoughton).
    1979   *The Epistle to the Hebrews* (ICC; Edinburgh: T. & T. Clark [1924]).

Mollenkott, V.
    1976   'Women and the Bible: A Challenge to Male Interpretation', *Sojourners* Feb.: 21-25.

Montgomery, H.B.
    1924   *Centenary Translation of the New Testament*, II (Boston: n.p.).

Moo, D.J.
    1980   '1 Timothy 2:11-15: Meaning and Significance', *TrinJ* 1: 62-83.
    1981   'The Interpretation of 1 Timothy 2:11-15: A Rejoinder', *TrinJ* 2: 198-222.
    1991   'What Does it Mean not to Teach or have Authority over Men? 1 Timothy 2:11-15', in Piper and Grudem (eds.) 1991: 179-93.

Moody Smith, D.
    1972   'The Use of the Old Testament in the New', in J.M. Efird (ed.), *The Use of the Old Testament in the New and Other Essays* (Durham, NC: Duke University Press): 3-65.

Moore, B., and H. Kombe
    1991   'Climacteric Symptoms in a Tanzanian Community', *Maturitas* 13: 229-34.

Moore, R.
    1981   'Personification of the Seduction of Evil: "The Wiles of the Wicked Woman" ', *RevQ* 10.4: 505-19.

Morell, T.
    1815   *Lexicon Graeco-Prosodiacum* (repr. 1824, Cambridge: Smith).

Morris, J.
    1973   *The Lady was a Bishop* (New York: Macmillan).

Morris, L.
    1971   *1 Corinthians* (TNTC; London: Tyndale Press).
    1988   *The Epistle to the Romans* (Leicester: Inter-Varsity Press).

Mortley, R.
    1981   *Womanhood: The Feminine in Ancient Hellenism, Gnosticism, Christianity and Islam* (Sydney: Delacroix Press).

Mott, L.
  1849, 1872 'Discourses by Lucretia Mott', in Hallowell 1884, Appendix 4: 487-91, 552-53.

Motyer, J.A.
    1980   'Name', in *IBD*, II: 1050-53.

Moule, C.F.D.
    1962   'Luke and the Pastoral Epistles', in *The Birth of the New Testament* (London: A. & C. Black), Excursus II: 220-22.
    1965   'The Problem of the Pastorals: A Reappraisal', *BJRL* 47: 430-52.
    1968   *An Idiom Book of New Testament Greek* (Cambridge: Cambridge University Press).

Moulton, J.H.
  1906   *A Grammar of New Testament Greek*, I (Edinburgh: T. & T. Clark, 2nd edn).
  1908   *A Grammar of New Testament Greek*, I (repr. 1985; Edinburgh: T. & T. Clark, 3rd edn).
Müller, K.
  1989   'Die Haustafel des Kolosserbriefes und das antike Frauenthema', in Dautzenberg, Merklein and Müller 1989: 263-319.
Müller-Bardorff, J.
  1958   'Zur Exegese von 1 Timotheus 5,3-16', *Gott und die Götter. Festgabe für Erich Fascher zum 60. Geburtstag* (Berlin: Delling): 113-33.
Munro, W.
  1988   'Women, Text and the Canon: The Strange Case of 1 Corinthians 14:33-35', *BTB* 18: 26-31.
Murkies, A.L., C. Lombard, B.J.G. Strauss, G. Wilcox, H.G. Burger and M.S. Morton
  1995   'Dietary Flour Supplementation Decreases Post-menopausal Hot Flushes: Effect of Soy and Wheat', *Maturitas* 21.3: 189-95.
Murkies, A.L., G. Wilcox and S.R. Davis
  1998   'Clinical Review 92: Phytoestrogens', *Journal of Clinical Endocrinology Metabolism* 83.2: 297-303.
Murphy, D.J.
  1977   '*Redating the New Testament* by J.A.T. Robinson', *TS* 38: 563-64.
Murphy-O'Connor, J.
  1973   'Community and Apostolate', *The Bible Today* 11: 1260-66.
  1976   'The Non-Pauline Character of 1 Corinthians 11:2-16?', *JBL* 95: 615-21.
  1978   'Corinthian Slogans in 1 Cor.6:12-20', *CBQ* 40: 391-96.
  1980   'Sex and Logic in 1 Corinthians 11:2-16', *CBQ* 42: 482-500.
  1983   *St. Paul's Corinth, Texts and Archaeology* (Wilmington, DE: Michael Glazier).
  1986   'Interpolations in 1 Corinthians', *CBQ* 48: 81-94.
  1988   '1 Corinthians 11:2-16 Once Again', *CBQ* 50.2: 265-74.
  1991   '2 Timothy Contrasted with 1 Timothy and Titus', *RB* 98.3: 403-18.
Neusner, J. (ed.)
  1985   *Genesis Rabbah*, I (Atlanta: Scholars Press).
Nicole, R.
  1986   'Biblical Authority and Feminist Aspirations', in Mickelsen 1986: 42-50.
Niederwimmer, K.
  1989   *Die Didache* (Göttingen: Vandenhoeck & Ruprecht).
Nock, A.D.
  1972   *Essays on Religion and the Ancient World* (2 vols.; Oxford: Clarendon Press).
North, H.
  1966   *Sophrosyne: Self-Knowledge and Self-Restraint in Greek Literature* (Ithaca, NY: Cornell University Press).
Noth, M.
  1968   *Numbers* (ET; London: SCM Press).

Novak, E.R., G. Seegar Jones and H.W. Jones
    1972   *Novak's Textbook of Gynecology* (Baltimore: Williams & Wilkins, 8th edn).

Oberlinner, L.
    1994   *Die Pastoralbriefe: Auslegung*, I (Freiburg: Herder).

Odeberg, H.
    1977   'Ἰαννῆς, Ἰαμβρῆς', in *TDNT*, III: 191-93.

Odell-Scott, D.W.
    1983   'Let the Women Speak in Church. An Egalitarian Interpretation of 1 Cor. 14:33b-36', *BTB* 13: 90-93.
    1986   'In Defense of an Egalitarian Interpretation of 1 Cor. 14:34-36. A Reply to Murphy-O'Connor's Critique', *BTB* 16: 100-103.

Oden, T.A.
    1989   *First and Second Timothy and Titus* (Louisville: John Knox Press).

Oepke, A.
    1967   'μεσίτης', in *TDNT*, IV: 615-18.

Okin, S.M.
    1979   *Women in Western Political Thought* (Princeton, NJ: Princeton University Press).

Olthuis, J.H.
    1976   *I Pledge You my Troth* (New York: Harper & Row).

Orr, W.F., and J.A. Walther
    1982   *1 Corinthians* (New York: Doubleday).

Ortlund, R.C.
    1991   'Male–Female Equality and Male Headship', in Piper and Grudem (eds.) 1991: 95-112.

Osborne, G.R.
    1977   'Hermeneutics and Women in the Church', *JETS* 20: 337-52.

Osburn, C.D.
    1982   'ΑΥΘΕΝΤΕΩ (1 Timothy 2:12)', *ResQ* 25.1: 1-12.

Oster, R.
    1988   'When Men Wore Veils to Worship: The Historical Context of 1 Corinthians 11.4', *NTS* 34: 481-505.
    1993   Review of C. Kroeger and R. Kroeger 1992, *BA* 56.4: 225-27.

Owen-Ball, D.T.
    1993   'Rabbinic Rhetoric and the Tribute Passage (Mt. 22:15-22; Mk. 12:13-17; Lk. 20:20-26)', *NovT* 35.1: 1-14.

Padgett, A.
    1984   'Paul on Women in the Church: The Contradictions of Coiffure in 1 Corinthians 11:2-16', *JSNT* 20: 69-86.
    1987a   'Wealthy Women at Ephesus. 1 Timothy 2:8-15 in Social Context', *Interpretation* 41: 19-31.
    1987b   'The Pauline Rationale for Submission: Biblical Feminism and the *hina* Clauses of Titus 2:1-12', *EvQ* 59.1: 39-52.

Pagels, E.H.
    1974   'Paul and Women: A Response to Recent Discussion', *JAAR* 42: 538-49.

Panning, A.J.
    1981   'AΥΘΕΝΤΕΙΝ: A Word Study', *Wisconsin Lutheran Quarterly* 78: 185-91.

Pansini, F., P. Albertazzi, G. Bonaccorsi, L. Zanotti, C. Campobasso, C. Negri, D. de Aloysio, G. Mollica and F. Bottiglioni
    1996   'Soy and Hot Flushes', in *Abstracts: 8th International Congress on the Menopause*, 3–7 Nov., Sydney: P312.

Pape, D.R.
    1976   *In Search of God's Ideal Woman* (Downers Grove, IL: InterVarsity Press).

Parry, R. St.J.
    1920   *The Pastoral Epistles* (Cambridge: Cambridge University Press).

Parvey, C.F.
    1974   'The Theology and Leadership of Women in the NT', in Reuther 1974: 117-49.

Patte, D.
    1975   *Early Jewish Hermeneutic in Palestine* (SBL and Scholars Press Dissertation Series, 22, repr. 1990, Atlanta: Scholars Press).

Patzia, A.G.
    1980   'The Deutero-Pauline Hypothesis: An Attempt at Clarification', *EvQ* 52: 27-42.

Payne, P.B.
    1981   'Libertarian Women in Ephesus: A Response to Douglas J. Moo's Article "1 Timothy 2:11-15: Meaning and Significance" ', *TrinJ* 2: 169-97.
    1986   'The Interpretaton of 1 Timothy 2:11-15; A Surrejoinder', (Minneapolis: unpublished study commissioned by the Committee on Ministerial Standing, Evangelical Free Church of America): 96-115.
    1995   'Fuldensis, Sigla for Variants in Vaticanus, and 1 Cor.14.34-5', *NTS* 41.2: 240-62.

Penn-Lewis, J.
    1919   *The Magna Charta of Woman* (Bournemouth: Overcomer Book Room; repr. 1975; Minneapolis: Bethany Fellowship).

Pentateuch and Haftorahs
    1929   Chief Rabbi (ed.) (Oxford: Oxford University Press).

Perkins, P.
    1987   'Marriage in the New Testament and its World', in W. Roberts (ed.), *Commitment to Partnership* (New York: Paulist Press): 5-33.
    1988   'Women in the Bible and its World', *Interpretation* Jan.: 33-44.

Perriman, A.C.
    1993   'What Eve Did, What Women Shouldn't Do: The Meaning of AΥΘΕΝΤΕΩ in 1 Timothy 2:12', *TynBul* 44: 129-42.

Pfeiffer, R.
    1968   *History of Classical Scholarship* (Oxford: Clarendon Press).

Phipps, W.E.
    1982   'Is Paul's Attitude toward Sexual Relations Contained in 1 Cor.7:1?', *NTS* 28: 125-31.

Pierce, R.W.
    1987   'Male/female Leadership and Korah's Revolt: An Analogy?', *JETS* 30.1: 3-10.

Piper, J., and W. Grudem
    1991   'An overview of central concerns: questions and answers', in Piper and Grudem (eds.) 1991.

Piper, J., and W. Grudem (eds.)
    1991   *Recovering Biblical Manhood and Womanhood: A Response to Evangelical Feminism* (IL: Crossway).

Plummer, A.
    1888   'The Pastoral Epistles', in W.R. Nicoll (ed.), *The Expositor's Bible* (London: Hodder & Stoughton).

Pomeroy, S.B.
    1975   *Goddesses, Whores, Wives, and Slaves: Women in Classical Antiquity* (New York: Shocken Books).

Porter, S.E.
    1989a   *Verbal Aspect in the Greek of the New Testament, with Reference to Tense and Mood: Studies in Biblical Greek*, I (New York: Peter Lang).
    1989b   'The Language of the Apocalypse in Recent Discussion', *NTS* 35.4: 582-603.
    1989c   'Wittgenstein's Classes of Utterances and Pauline Ethical Texts', *JETS* 32.1: 85-97.
    1989d   'Studying Ancient Languages from a Modern Linguistic Perspective: Essential Terms and Terminology', *FN* 2: 147-72.
    1990a   'The Pauline Concept of Original Sin, in Light of Rabbinic Background', *TynBul* 41.1: 3-30.
    1990b   'Romans 13:1-7 as Pauline Political Rhetoric', *FN* 3: 115-39.
    1992   *Idioms of the Greek New Testament* (Sheffield: Sheffield Academic Press).
    1993   'What Does it Mean to be "Saved by Childbirth" (1 Timothy 2.15)?', *JSNT* 49: 87-102.

Porter, S.E., and D.A. Carson (eds.)
    1995   *Discourse Analysis and Other Topics in Biblical Greek* (JSNTSup, 113; Sheffield: Sheffield Academic Press).

Powers, B.W.
    1975   'Women in the Church: The Application of 1 Timothy 2:8-15', *Interchange* 17: 55-59.

Pratt, J.
    n.d.   *The Head, the Headship, the Head-Covering* (Hong Kong: Christian Reading Room).

Prior, M.
    1989   *Paul the Letter-Writer, and the Second Letter to Timothy* (JSNTSup, 23; Sheffield: Sheffield Academic Press).

Procksch, O.
    1977   'ἁγιασμός', in *TDNT*, I: 113.

Prohl, R.C.
    1957   *Women in the Church* (Grand Rapids: Eerdmans).

Pryor, J.
  1993   'Jesus and Women: A Second Look at the Issue'. Summary of unpublished paper, *Society for the Study of Early Christianity Newsletter* 17: 4-13.
Quinn, J.D.
  1981   'Parenesis and the Pastoral Epistles', in M. Carrez, J. Doré, and P. Grelot (eds.), *De la Torah au Messie: Etudes d'exégèse et d'herméneutique bibliques offertes à Henri Cazelles pour ses 25 années d'enseignement à l'Institut* (Paris: Desclée): 495-501.
  1990   *The Letter to Titus* (AB; Sydney: Doubleday).
Rad, G. von
  1972a   *Genesis* (rev.; Philadelphia: Westminster Press).
  1972b   *Wisdom In Israel* (London: SCM Press).
Radice, R., and D.T. Runia (in collaboration with R.A. Bitter, N.G. Cohen, M. Mach, A.P. Runia, D. Satran and D.R. Schwartz)
  1988   *Philo of Alexandria: An Annotated Bibliography 1937–86* (Leiden: E.J. Brill).
Ramm, B.
  1970   *Protestant Biblical Interpretation* (Grand Rapids: Baker Book House).
Ramsay, W.M.
  1913   *The Teaching of Paul in Terms of the Present Day* (London: Hodder & Stoughton).
Ramsey, G.W.
  1988   'Is Name-giving an Act of Domination in Genesis 2:23 and Elsewhere?', *CBQ* 50.1: 24-35.
Rawson, B.
  1986a   'The Roman Family', in Rawson 1986: 1-57.
  1986b   'The Expansion of Rome', in J. Boardman, J. Griffin and O. Murray (eds.), *The Oxford History of the Classical World* (Oxford: Oxford University Press): 417-37.
Rawson, B. (ed.)
  1986   *The Family in Ancient Rome* (Sydney: Croom Helm).
Reed, J.T.
  1992   'Cohesive Ties in 1 Timothy: In Defense of the Epistle's Unity', *Neot* 26.1: 131-47.
  1993   'To Timothy or not? A Discourse Analysis of 1 Timothy', in Carson and Porter 1993: 90-119.
  1995   'Identifying Themes in the New Testament: Insight from Discourse Analysis', in Porter and Carson 1995: 75-101.
Reicke, B.
  1957   'Die Gnosis der Männer nach 1 Petr.3[7]', in W. Eltester (ed.), *Neutestamentliche Studien für Rudolf Bultmann: zu seinem siebzigsten Geburtstag am 20. August 1954* (Berlin: Alfred Töpelmann, 2nd corrected edn): 296-304.
Reid, R.
  1964   'The Use of the Old Testament in the Epistle to the Hebrews' (unpublished PhD dissertation, Union Theological Seminary, New York).

Rendall, F.
 1910 *The Expositor's Greek Testament*, III (London: Hodder & Stoughton).
Rengstorf, K.H.
 1953 'Die neutestamentlichen Mahnungen an die Frau, sich dem Manne unter-
     zuordnen', in W. Foerster (ed.), *Verbum dei manet. Festschrift für D.O.
     Schmitz* (Witten: Luther): 131-45.
 1954 *Mann und Frau im Urchristentum* (Köln: Westdeutscher).
 1964 'διδάσκω', in *TDNT*, II: 135-48.
 1967 'μανθάνω', in *TDNT*, IV: 406-13.
Rengstorf, K.H. (ed.)
 1973–83 *Complete Concordance to Flavius Josephus* (4 vols.; Leiden: E.J. Brill).
Reuther, R.R.
 1974 'Misogynism and Virginal Feminism in the Fathers of the Church', in
     Reuther 1974: 150-83.
Reuther, R.R. (ed.)
 1974 *Religion and Sexism* (New York: Simon & Schuster).
Revised Version Apocrypha
 1905 (Oxford: Oxford University Press).
Ridderbos, H.
 1977 *Paul: An Outline of his Theology* (ET; London: SPCK).
Robeck, C.M.
 1975a 'The Gift of Prophecy in Acts and Paul, Part 1', *Studia Biblica et
     Theologica* 5.1: 15-36.
 1975b 'The Gift of Prophecy in Acts and Paul, Part 2', *Studia Biblica et Theo-
     logica* 5.2: 37-54.
Robert, L.
 1965 'Qualités familiales', *Hellenika* 13: 39.
Roberts, M.D.
 1983 'Woman Shall be Saved: A Closer Look at 1 Timothy 2:15', *Reformed
     Journal* 33.4: 18-22.
Robertson, A.T.
 1923 *A Grammar of the Greek New Testament in the Light of Historical
     Research* (New York: Doran, 4th edn).
 1934 *A Grammar of the Greek New Testament in the Light of Historical
     Research* (Nashville: Broadman, 4th edn).
Robertson, A.T., and A. Plummer
 1911 *First Epistle of St. Paul to the Corinthians* (ICC; repr. 1983, Edinburgh:
     T. & T. Clark).
Robins, R.H.
 1951 *Ancient and Mediaeval Grammatical Theory in Europe, with Particular
     Reference to Modern Linguistic Doctrine* (London: Bell).
 1968 *A Short History of Linguistics* (London: Indiana University Press).
Robinson, D.W.B.
 1977 Review of J.A.T. Robinson 1976, *RTR* 36: 23-25.
Robinson, J.A.T.
 1976 *Redating the New Testament* (Philadelphia: Westminster Press).
Roloff, J.
 1988 *Der erste Brief an Timotheus* (Zürich: Benzinger Verlag).

Ross, J.M.
  1992   'Floating Words: Their Significance for Textual Criticism', *NTS* 38: 153-56.
Rouselle, A.
  1988   *Porneia: On Desire and the Body in Antiquity* (ET; Oxford: Basil Blackwell).
Rowley, H.H. (ed.)
  1970   *The Century Bible* (Melbourne: Nelson).
Ryrie, C.C.
  1958   *The Place of Women in the Church* (New York: Macmillan).
Safrai, S.
  1976   'The Synagogue', in S. Safrai and M. Stern in cooperation with D. Flusser and W.C. van Unnik (eds.), *The Jewish People in the First Century*, II (Assen: Van Gorcum): 908-44.
  1987   *The Literature of the Sages* (Philadelphia: Fortress Press), Part 1.
Sailhamer, J.H.
  1990   'Genesis', in Gaebelein 1976–1990: II, 1-284.
Sakenfeld, K.D.
  1975   'The Bible and Women: Bane or Blessing?', *TTod* 32: 222-33.
Salmon, G.
  1886   *A Historical Introduction to the Study of the Books of the New Testament* (London: J. Murray).
Salom, A.P.
  1963   'The Imperatival Use of the Participle in the New Testament', *AusBR* 11: 41-49.
Sanders, E.P.
  1977   *Paul and Palestinian Judaism* (Philadelphia: Fortress Press).
Sandys, J.E.
  1964   *The History of Classical Scholarship*, I (New York: Hafner).
Sarna, N.M.
  1989   *Genesis* (Jerusalem: Jewish Publication Society).
Saucy, R.L.
  1974   'The Husband of One Wife', *BSac* 131: 229-40.
  1994   'Women's Prohibition to Teach Men: An Investigation into its Meaning and Contemporary Application', *JETS* 37.1: 79-97.
Sauer, J.D.
  1994   *Historical Geography of Crop Plants: A Select Roster* (London: CRC Press).
Scanzoni, L., and M. Hardesty
  1982   *All We're Meant to Be* (Waco, TX: Word Books).
Schaeffer, F.A.
  1972   *Genesis in Time and Space* (Downers Grove, IL: InterVarsity Press).
Schenke, H.-M.
  1975   'Das Weiterwirken des Paulus und die Pflege seines Erbes durch die Paulus-Schule', *NTS* 21: 505-18.
Schippers, R.
  1966   'The Pre-synoptic Tradition in 1 Thessalonians II 13-16', *NovT* 8: 223-34.

Schmidt, D.D.
    1993   Verbal Aspect in Greek: Two Approaches', in Carson and Porter 1993: 63-73.

Schmithals, W., and W. Werbeck
    1961   'Pastoralbriefe', in K. Galling (ed.), *Die Religion in Geschichte und Gegenwart, Handwörterbuch für Theologie und Religionswissenschaft*, V (Tübingen: Mohr Siebeck, 3rd edn): 144-48.

Schofield, C.I. (ed.)
    1967   *New Schofield Reference Bible* (New York: Oxford University Press).

Scholer, D.M.
    1975   'Exegesis: 1 Tim.2:8-15', *Daughters of Sarah* 1.4: 7-8.
    1980   'Women's Adornment: Some Historical and Hermeneutical Observations on the New Testament Passages', *Daughters of Sarah* 6.1: 3-6.
    1983   'Hermeneutical Gerrymandering: Hurley on Women and Authority', *TSF Bulletin* May–June: 11-13.
    1986   '1 Timothy 2:9-15 and the Place of Women in the Church's Ministry', in Mickelsen 1986: 193-219.

Schrage, W.
    1974   'Zur Ethik der neutestamentlichen Haustafeln', *NTS* 21.1: 1-22.

Schreiner, T.R.
    1991   'Head Coverings, Prophecies and the Trinity', in Piper and Grudem (eds.) 1991: 124-39.
    1995   'An Interpretaton of 1 Timothy 2.9-15: A Dialogue with Scholarship', in Köstenberger, Schreiner and Baldwin 1995: 105-54.

Schrevel, C.
    1823   *Cornelii Schrevellii Lexicon Manuale Graeco-Latinum and Latino-Graecum* (Edinburgh: Bell & Bradfute).
    1826   *Schrevelius Greek Lexicon* (ET; London: Craddock & Joy).

Schroeder, D.
    1959   'Die Haustafeln des Neuen Testaments (Ihre Herkunft und ihr theologischer Sinn)' (unpublished PhD dissertation; Hamburg University).

Schröger, F.
    1968   *Der Verfasser des Hebräerbriefes als Schriftausleger*, Biblische Untersuchungen, IV (Regensburg: F. Pustet).

Schürer, E.
    1979   *The History of the Jewish People in the Age of Jesus Christ (175BC–AD135)*, II (ed. G. Vermes, F. Millar and M. Black; rev. edn, Edinburgh: T. & T. Clark).

Schüssler Fiorenza, E.
    1983   *In Memory of Her* (New York: Crossroad).
    1987   'Rhetorical Situation and Historical Reconstruction in 1 Corinthians', *NTS* 33: 386-403.

Schwyzer, E.
    1988   *Syntax und syntaktische Stilistik*. II. *Griechische Grammatik: auf der Grundlage von Karl Brugmanns Griechischer Grammatik* (ed. A. Debrunner; Munich: C.H. Beck, 5th, unaltered, edn).

Scott, E.F.
    1936   *The Pastoral Epistles* (London: Hodder & Stoughton).

Scroggs, R.
1972   'Paul and the Eschatological Woman', *JAAR* 40: 283-303.
1974   'Paul and the Eschatological Woman Revisited', *JAAR* 42: 532-37.
Segal, A.F.
1977   *Two Powers in Heaven: Early Rabbinic Reports about Christianity and Gnosticism* (Leiden: E.J. Brill).
1984   ' "He Who did not Spare his own Son...": Jesus, Paul, and the Akedah', in P. Richardson and J.C. Hurd (eds.), *From Jesus to Paul: Studies in Honour of Francis Wright Beare* (Waterloo, Ontario: Wilfred Laurier University Press): 169-84.
Selwyn, E.G.
1946   *The First Epistle of St. Peter* (London: Macmillan).
Semmens, J.P.
1983   'Sexuality', in Buchsbaum 1983: 173-80.
Seyffert, G.
1957   *A Dictionary of Classical Antiquities: Mythology, Religion, Literature, Art* (rev. and ed. H. Nettleship and J.E. Sandys; London: George Allen & Unwin, 3rd edn).
Shipp, G.P.
1979   *Modern Greek Evidence for the Ancient Greek Vocabulary* (Sydney: Sydney University Press).
Sidlow Baxter, J.
1973   *Explore the Book* (repr. 6 vols. in one, Grand Rapids: Zondervan).
Sigountos, J.G., and M. Shank
1983   'Public Roles for Women in the Pauline Church: A Reappraisal of the Evidence', *JETS* 26.3: 283-95.
Silva, M.
1993   'A Response to Fanning and Porter on Verbal Aspect', in Carson and Porter 1993: 74-82.
1995   'Discourse Analysis and Philippians', in Porter and Carson 1995: 102-106.
Simpson, E.K.
1954   *The Pastoral Epistles* (London: Tyndale Press).
Skeat, T.C.
1979   ' "Especially the Parchments": A Note on 2 Timothy IV.13', *JTS* 30: 173-77.
Skinner, J.
1930   *Genesis* (ICC; Edinburgh: T. & T. Clark).
Sloyan, G.S.
1978   '*Redating the New Testament* by John A.T. Robinson', *Horizons* 5: 96-99.
Smith, W. (ed.)
1873   *Dictionary of Greek and Roman Biography and Mythology*, II (London: John Murray).
Smyth, H.W.
1963   *Greek Grammar* (rev. G. Messing; Cambridge, MA: Harvard University Press).
Snaith, N.H.
1959   *Notes on the Hebrew Text of Genesis I–VIII* (London: Epworth Press).

Snodgrass, K.R.
    1986   'Galatians 3:28: Conundrum or Solution?', in Mickelsen 1986: 161-81.
Snyder, G.F.
    1978   'John A.T. Robinson: *Redating the New Testament*', *CBQ* 40: 134-36.
Soden, H. von
    1893   *Die Briefe an die Kolosser, Epheser, Philemon, die Pastoralbriefe*, III
                (Leipzig: Mohr Siebeck, 2nd edn): Section 1.
Souter, A.
    1960   *A Pocket Lexicon to the Greek New Testament* (Oxford: Clarendon Press).
Sparks, J. (ed.)
    1978   *The Apostolic Fathers* (ET; Nashville: T. Nelson).
Speiser, E.A.
    1964   *Genesis* (AB; New York: Doubleday).
Spencer, A.D.B.
    1974   'Eve at Ephesus', *JETS* 17: 215-22.
    1985   *Beyond the Curse: Women Called to Ministry* (Nashville: T. Nelson).
Spicq, C.
    1947   *Les épitres pastorales* (Paris: Librairie Lecoffre).
Squires, J.
    1992   'Patristic Views of the Evangelists' Purposes'. Summary of unpublished
                paper, *Society for the Study of Early Christianity Newsletter* 16: 6-7.
Stagg, F.
    1972   'The Abused Aorist', *JBL* 91: 222-31.
Stagg, F., and E. Stagg
    1978   *Woman in the World of Jesus* (Philadelphia: Westminster Press).
Stählin, G.
    1974   'χήρα', in *TDNT*, IX: 453-58.
Stanley, C.D.
    1990   'Paul and Homer: Greco-Roman Citation Practice in the First Century
                CE', *NovT* 32.1: 48-78.
Steiner, M.
    1983   'Psychobiologic Aspects of the Menopausal Syndrome', in Buchsbaum
                1983: 151-60.
Stendahl, K.
    1982   *The Bible and the Ordination of Women* (ET; Philadelphia: Fortress Press).
Stenger, W.
    1974   'Timotheus und Titus als literarische Gestalter', *Kairos* 16: 252-67.
Stibbs, A.M.
    1967   'The Pastoral Epistles', in D. Guthrie, J.A. Motyer, A.M. Stibbs and D.J.
                Wiseman (eds.), *The New Bible Commentary Revised* (London: Inter-
                Varsity Press): 1166-86.
Stiefel, J.H.
    1995   'Women Deacons in 1 Timothy: A Linguistic and Literary Look at
                "Women Likewise…" (1 Tim 3.11)', *NTS* 41.3: 442-57.
Stone, M.E.
    1992   *A History of the Literature of Adam and Eve* (Atlanta: SBL, Scholars
                Press).

Stouffer, A.H.
    1981   'The Ordination of Women: Yes', *Christianity Today* 25: 256-59.
Strong, J.
    n.d.   *The Exhaustive Concordance of the Bible* (Iowa Falls: Riverside).
Sturdy, J.
    1976   *Numbers* (Cambridge: Cambridge University Press).
    1979   '*Redating the New Testament* by John A.T. Robinson', *JTS* 30: 255-62.
Sukwatana, P., J. Meekhangvan, T. Tamrongterakul, Y. Tanapat, S. Asavarait and
P. Boonjitrpimon
    1991   'Menopausal Symptoms among Thai Women in Bangkok', *Maturitas* 13:
              217-28.
Swartley, W.M.
    1986   'Response' (to Longenecker 1986), in Mickelsen 1986: 85-91.
Sweet, J.P.M.
    1966–67   'A Sign for Unbelievers: Paul's Attitude to Glossalalia', *NTS* 13: 240-57.
Swete, H.B.
    1916   'The Faithful Sayings', *JTS* 18: 1-7.
Swetnam, J.
    1981   *Jesus and Isaac. A Study of the Epistle to the Hebrews in the Light of the*
              Aqedah (Rome: Biblical Institute Press).
Swidler, L.
    1976   *Women in Judaism* (Metuchen, NJ: Scarecrow).
    1979   *Biblical Affirmations of Women* (Philadelphia: Westminster Press).
Talbert, C.H.
    1984   'Paul's Understanding of the Holy Spirit: The Evidence of 1 Corinthians
              12–14', *Perspectives in Religious Studies* 11: 95-108.
Thackeray, H. St.J.
    1900   *The Relation of St. Paul to Contemporary Jewish Thought* (London:
              Macmillan).
Thayer, J.H.
    1961   *A Greek–English Lexicon of the New Testament* (Edinburgh: T. & T.
              Clark, 4th edn).
Theissen, G.
    1982   'Social Integration and Sacramental Activity: An Analysis of 1 Cor.
              11:17-34', in J.H. Schütz (ed.), *The Social Setting of Pauline Christianity*
              (ET; Philadelphia: Fortress Press): 154-74.
Thiede, C.P.
    1992   *The Earliest Gospel Manuscript? The Qumran Papyrus 7Q5 and its*
              Significance for New Testament Studies (Exeter: Paternoster Press).
Thompson, J.W.
    1979   'The Conceptual Background and Purpose of the Midrash in Hebrews
              11', *NovT* 19.3: 209-23.
Thompson, M.M.
    1986   'Response' (to Longenecker 1986), in Mickelsen 1986: 91-96.
Thompson, W.E.
    1972   'Athenian Marriage Patterns: Remarriage', *California Studies in Classical*
              Antiquity 5: 211-25.

Thorley, J.

1988   'Subjunctive Aktionsart in New Testament Greek: A Reassessment', *NovT* 30: 193-211.

1989   'Aktionsart in New Testament Greek: Infinitive and Imperative', *NovT* 31: 290-315.

Thrall, M.E.

1965   *1 and 2 Corinthians* (Cambridge: Cambridge University Press).

Thurston, B.B.

1989   *The Widows* (Minneapolis: Fortress Press).

Tolbert, M.A.

1983   'Defining the Problem: The Bible and Feminist Hermeneutics', *Semeia* 28: 113-26.

Towner, P.H.

1986   'The Present Age in the Eschatology of the Pastoral Epistles', *NTS* 32: 427-48.

1989   *The Goal of our Instruction* (JSNTSup, 34; Sheffield: Sheffield Academic Press).

Towner, W.S.

1982   'Hermeneutical Systems of Hillel and the Tannaim: A Fresh look', *HUCA* S3: 101-35.

Trible, P.

1982   'Feminist hermeneutics and Biblical Studies', *The Christian Century* 3–10 Feb.: 116-18.

1983   *God and the Rhetoric of Sexuality* (Philadelphia: Fortress Press).

1985   *Texts of Terror* (Philadelphia: Fortress Press).

Trudinger, L.P.

1966   'Some Observations Concerning the Text of the Old Testament in the Book of Revelation', *JTS* 16: 82-88.

Trummer, P.

1978   *Die Paulustradition der Pastoralbriefe* (Frankfurt am Main: Peter Lang).

Tucker, R.A., and W. Liefeld

1987   *Daughters of the Church* (Grand Rapids: Zondervan).

Turner, N.

1963   *Syntax*, in J.H. Moulton (ed.), *A Grammar of New Testament Greek*, III (repr. 1980, Edinburgh: T. & T. Clark).

Unger, M.F.

1981   *Unger's Commentary on the Old Testament* (2 vols.; Chicago: Moody Press).

Urbach, E.E.

1975   *The Sages*, I (ET; Jerusalem: Magnes Press).

Van der Horst, P.W.

1990   'Sarah's Seminal Emission: Hebrews 11:11 in the Light of Ancient Embryology', in D.L. Balch, E. Furguson and W.A. Meeks (eds.), *Essays in Honor of Abraham J. Malherbe* (Minneapolis: Fortress Press): 287-302.

1991   *Ancient Jewish Epitaphs* (Kampen: Kok Pharos).

Vawter, B.

1977   *On Genesis: A New Reading* (New York: Doubleday).

Vermes, G.
1975   *Post-biblical Jewish Studies* (Leiden: E.J. Brill).
1983   *Scripture and Tradition in Judaism* (Leiden: E.J. Brill).
1987   *The Dead Sea Scrolls* (Ringwood, Vic.: Penguin Books, 3rd edn).
1992   'Genesis 1–3 in Post-biblical Hebrew and Aramaic Literature before the
            Mishnah', *JJS* 43.2: 221-25.
Verner, D.C.
1983   *The Household of God* (SBLDS, 71; Chico, CA: Scholars Press).
Vine, W.E.
1975   *Expository Dictionary* (London: Oliphants).
Wagner, G. (ed.)
1979   *Bibliographical Aids* 12. *An Exegetical Bibliography on the Letters to the
            Thessalonians, to Timothy and to Titus* (Rüschlikon-Zurich: Baptist Theo-
            logical Seminary).
Walker, W.O.
1975   '1 Corinthians 11:2-16 and Paul's Views Regarding Women', *JBL* 94:
            94-110.
1983   'The "Theology of Woman's Place" and the "Paulinist" Tradition',
            Semeia 28: 101-12.
Wallace-Hadrill, A.
1991   'Houses and Households: Sampling Pompeii and Herculaneum', in B.
            Rawson (ed.), *Marriage, Divorce and Children in Ancient Rome* (Oxford:
            Clarendon Press): 191-227.
Walsh, J.T.
1977   'Genesis 2:4b–3:24: A Synchronic Approach', *JBL* 96.2: 161-77.
Waltke, B.K.
1978   '1 Corinthians 11:2-16: An Interpretation', *BSac* 135: 46-57.
1992   '1 Timothy 2:8-15: Unique or Normative?', *Crux* 28.1: 22-27.
Ward-Perkins, J., and A. Claridge
1980   *Pompeii AD 79* (Sydney: Australian Gallery Directors Council).
Wedderburn, A.J.M.
1978   'Adam in Paul's Letter to the Romans', *Studia Biblia* 3: 413-30.
Weeks, N.
1972   'Of Silence and Head Coverings', *WTJ* 35.1: 21-27.
Weidinger, K.
1928   *Die Haustafeln. Ein Stück urchristlicher Paränese* (Leipzig: J.C. Hin-
            richs).
Weisinger, A.
1866   *Biblical Commentary on St. Paul's Epistles to the Philippians, to Titus,
            and the First to Timothy*, (ET; Edinburgh: T. & T. Clark, 3rd edn).
Weiss, B.
1885   *Briefe an Timotheus und Titus* (Göttingen: Vandenhoeck & Ruprecht).
Weiss, J.
1910   *Der Erste Korintherbrief* (Göttingen: Vandenhoeck & Ruprecht).
Wells, L.S.A.
1979   'The Books of Adam and Eve', in *APOT* (repr.), II: 123-33.
Wendland, H.-D.
1970   *Ethik des Neuen Testaments* (Göttingen: Vandenhoeck & Ruprecht).

Wenham, G.J.
    1979   *The Book of Leviticus* (Grand Rapids: Eerdmans).
    1987   *Genesis 1–15*, I (Waco, TX: Word Books).
Westcott, B.F.
    1892   *The Epistle to the Hebrews* (Grand Rapids: Eerdmans, 2nd edn).
Westcott, B.F., and F.J. Hort
    1882   *Introduction to the New Testament in the Original Greek, with Notes on Selected Readings* (New York: Harper & Brothers; repr. 1988, Peabody, MA: Hendrickson).
Westermann, C.
    1984   *Genesis 1–11* (trans. J.J. Scullion; London: SPCK).
Weymouth, R.F.
    1890   *The Rendering into English of the Greek Aorist and Perfect* (repr., London: J. Clarke, 4th edn).
Whitaker, R.E. (director)
    1988   *Eerdmans Analytical Concordance to the RSV* (Grand Rapids: Eerdmans).
Whitbourne, S.K.
    1985   *The Aging Body* (New York: Springer-Verlag).
White, N.J.D. (ed.)
    1910   *The Pastorals*, IV (London: Hodder & Stoughton).
WHO
    1981   *Research on the Menopause* (World Health Organization Technical Report Series, 670; Geneva: WHO).
Wiebe, B.
    1994   'Two Texts on Women (1 Tim. 2:11-15; Gal. 3:26-29). A Test of Interpretation', *HBT* 16: 54-85.
Wifall, W.
    1974   'Gen. 3:15: A Protevangelium?', *CBQ* 36: 361-65.
Wilcox, M.
    1965   *The Semitisms of Acts* (Oxford: Clarendon Press).
    1979   'The Promise of the "Seed" in the New Testament and the Targumim', *JSNT* 5: 2-20.
    1991   'Jesus, Women and Judaism'. Summary of unpublished paper in *Society for the Study of Early Christianity Newsletter* 13: 9-10.
Wiles, G.P.
    1974   *Paul's Intercessory Prayers* (Cambridge: Cambridge University Press).
Williams, D.
    1977   *The Apostle Paul and Women in the Church* (California: Regal).
Wilshire, L.E.
    1988   'The TLG Computer and Further Reference to ΑΥΘΕΝΤΕΩ in 1 Timothy 2:12', *NTS* 34: 120-34.
    1993   '1 Timothy 2:12 Revisited: A Reply to Paul W. Barnett and Timothy J. Harris', *EvQ* 65.1: 43-55.
Wilson, D.R.
    1978   *Science and Archaeology* (Harmondsworth: Penguin Books).
Wilson, E.
    1849   *A Scriptural View of Woman's Rights and Duties, in all the Important Relations of Life* (Philadelphia: W.S. Young).

Wilson, S.G.
    1976   'The Portrait of Paul in Acts and the Pastorals', in G. MacRae (ed.), *SBL Seminar Papers* (2 vols; Missoula, MT: Scholars Press): 397-411.

Windisch, H.
    1930   'Sinn und Geltung des apostolischen Mulier taceat in ecclesia', *Christliche Welt* 44: 411-25.

Winter, B.W.
    1978   'The Lord's Supper at Corinth: An Alternative Reconstruction', *RTR* 37: 73-82.
    1988a   'Providentia for the Widows of 1 Timothy 5:3-16', *TynBul* 39: 83-99.
    1988b   'The Public Honouring of Christian Benefactors', *JSNT* 34: 87-103.
    1994   *Seek the Welfare of the City: Christians as Benefactors and Citizens* (Grand Rapids: Eerdmans).

Wire, A.C.
    1990   *The Corinthian Women Prophets* (Minneapolis: Fortress Press).

Witherington, B.W.
    1981   'Rite and Rights for Women: Galatians 3:28', *NTS* 27: 593-604.
    1988   *Women in the Earliest Churches* (SNTSMS, 59; Cambridge: Cambridge University Press).

Wolfson, H.A.
    1962   *Philo*, I (Cambridge, MA: Harvard University Press).

Wolter, M.
    1988   *Die Pastoralbriefe als Paulustradition* (Göttingen: Vandenhoeck & Ruprecht).

Wolters, A.
    1993   Review of C. Kroeger and R. Kroeger 1992, *Calvin Theological Journal* 28: 208-13.

Woodhouse, J.
    1985a   'The Ordination of Women: Are the Barriers Biblical?', *Southern Cross* June: 12-13.
    1985b   'The Ordination of Women: Are the Barriers Biblical?', *Southern Cross* July: 16-18.

Wycherley, R.E.
    1970   'Houses, Greek', in *OCD*: 531-32.

Yadin, Y.
    1958   'The Dead Sea Scrolls and the Epistle to the Hebrews', in C. Rabin and Y. Yadin (eds.), *Scripta Hierosolymitana: Aspects of the Dead Sea Scrolls,* IV (Jerusalem: Hebrew University): 36-55.

Yamauchi, E.
    1973   *Pre-Christian Gnosticism* (London: Tyndale Press): Part 2.

Yarbrough, R.
    1992   'I Suffer not a Woman', *Presbyterion* 18: 25-33.

Ydit, M.
    1971   'Women', in *EncJud*, VIII: 6.

Yoder, J.H.
    1982   *The Politics of Jesus* (Grand Rapids: Eerdmans).

Yule, G.U.
    1944   *The Statistical Study of Literary Vocabulary* (Cambridge: Cambridge University Press).
Zerwick, M.
    1987   *Biblical Greek* (ET; Rome: Scripta Pontificii Instituti Biblici).
Zerwick, M., and M. Grosvenor
    1981   *A Grammatical Analysis of the Greek New Testament* (Rome: Biblical Institute Press).

INDEXES

INDEX OF REFERENCES

OLD TESTAMENT

NEW TESTAMENT

CLASSICAL AUTHORS

OTHER ANCIENT SOURCES

INDEX OF AUTHORS